Judith S. Beck, Ph.D.

Continued on back

IMAGERY

Imagery

Current Theory, Research, and Application

Edited by

Anees A. Sheikh
Department of Psychology
Marquette University
Milwaukee, Wisconsin

A WILEY-INTERSCIENCE PUBLICATION

JOHN WILEY & SONS

New York ● Chichester ● Brisbane ● Toronto ● Singapore

Library of Congress Cataloging in Publication Data:

Main entry under title:

Imagery: current theory, research, and application.

  (Wiley series on personality processes)
  "A Wiley-Interscience publication."
  Includes indexes.
  1. Imagery (Psychology) I. Sheikh, Anees A. II. Series.
[DNLM: 1. Imagination. BF 367 I3092]

BF367.I462. 1983   153.3′2   82-20191
ISBN 0-471-09225-8

Printed in the United States of America

10 9 8 7 6 5 4 3 2 1

To my beloved children

NADEEM, SONIA, AND IMRAN

Contributors

Kathryn Lutz Alesandrini, College of Education, The University of Iowa, Iowa City, Iowa

R. Ashton, Department of Psychology, University of Queensland, St. Lucia, Brisbane, Australia

Theodore X. Barber, Cushing Hospital, Framingham, Massachusetts

Ian Begg, Department of Psychology, McMaster University, Hamilton, Ontario

B. Richard Bugelski, Department of Psychology, State University of New York at Buffalo, Buffalo, New York

Donn Byrne, Department of Psychology, State University of New York at Albany, Albany, New York

Barbara L. Forisha, Department of Psychology, The University of Michigan–Dearborn, Dearborn, Michigan

Charles S. Jordan, Department of Psychiatry and Behavioral Sciences, Medical University of South Carolina, Charleston, South Carolina

Kathryn Kelley, Department of Psychology, State University of New York at Albany, Albany, New York

Donald L. King, Department of Psychology, Howard University, Washington, D.C.

Stephen M. Kosslyn, Department of Psychology, Brandeis University, Waltham, Massachusetts

Robert G. Ley, Department of Psychology, Simon Fraser University, Burnaby, British Columbia, Canada

Martin S. Lindauer, Department of Psychology, State University College at Brockport, Brockport, New York

David F. Marks, Department of Psychology, University of Otago, Dunedin, New Zealand

Marc Marschark, Department of Psychology, The University of North Carolina at Greensboro, Greensboro, North Carolina

Steven Pinker, Department of Psychology, Massachusetts Institute of Technology, Cambridge, Massachusetts

D.P.J. Przybyla, Department of Psychology, State University of New York at Albany, Albany, New York

Alan Richardson, Department of Psychology, University of Western Australia, Nedlands, Western Australia

Peter W. Sheehan, Department of Psychology, University of Queensland, St. Lucia, Brisbane, Australia

Anees A. Sheikh, Department of Psychology, Marquette University, Milwaukee, Wisconsin

Richard M. Suinn, Department of Psychology, Colorado State University, Fort Collins, Colorado

Roni B. Tower, Department of Psychology, Yale University, New Haven, Connecticut

K. White, Department of Psychology, University of Queensland, St. Lucia, Brisbane, Australia

Sheryl C. Wilson, Cushing Hospital, Framingham, Massachusetts

John C. Yuille, Department of Psychology, University of British Columbia, Vancouver, British Columbia, Canada

Series Preface

This series of books is addressed to behavioral scientists interested in the nature of human personality. Its scope should prove pertinent to personality theorists and researchers as well as to clinicians concerned with applying an understanding of personality processes to the amelioration of emotional difficulties in living. To this end, the series provides a scholarly integration of theoretical formulations, empirical data, and practical recommendations.

Six major aspects of studying and learning about human personality can be designated: personality theory, personality structure and dynamics, personality development, personality assessment, personality change, and personality adjustment. In exploring these aspects of personality, the books in the series discuss a number of distinct but related subject areas: the nature and implications of various theories of personality; personality characteristics that account for consistencies and variations in human behavior; the emergence of personality processes in children and adolescents; the use of interviewing and testing procedures to evaluate individual differences in personality; efforts to modify personality styles through psychotherapy, counseling, behavior therapy, and other methods of influence; and patterns of abnormal personality functioning that impair individual competence.

IRVING B. WEINER

University of Denver
Denver, Colorado

ix

Preface

It seems that every other major book or article on the subject of imagery includes the lament that the behaviorist John B. Watson, who labeled the arguments in favor of the significance of imagery as "bunk," succeeded in banishing images from the domain of scientific psychology. But why continue to bewail an error that has already been righted? Surely the time has come to stop cursing Watson, to cease lamenting, and to rejoice over the robust "return of the ostracized" (Robert Holt, Imagery: The Return Of The Ostracized, *American Psychologist*, 1964, **19**, 254–264).

From a position of near disgrace, imagery has risen to be "one of the hottest topics in cognitive science" (Ned Block, *Imagery*, MIT Press, 1981, p. 1). In recent years, the significance of imagery in the areas of memory, learning, thinking, perception, motivation, emotion, psychophysiology, and numerous other aspects of human behavior has been established convincingly. Research also has revealed the functional characteristics that distinguish imagery from verbal symbolic processes.

During the last decade alone, hundreds of important journal articles and dozens of books on imagery have appeared. Three major journals almost exclusively devoted to imagery have been launched. Two professional imagery associations which organize annual conferences have been formed. In addition, several major conferences and symposia on imagery have been staged across the country and attendance at these meetings has been growing steadily.

In spite of this enthusiasm about imagery, no one book that reflects the current state of knowledge in a comprehensive manner appeared. This book represents an attempt to fill the need, although it would be vain to expect to do complete justice to this rapidly expanding field in one volume.

This book consists of 17 chapters. All are written by experts: the majority of the contributors are nationally and internationally esteemed for their work on imagery, and others are unequivocally in the process of establishing themselves as authorities in their areas. The book is divided into three major sections: theory, research, and application. Chapters are assigned to the various sections according to their major thrust, but a considerable emphasis on research is evident in almost all chapters. In a book of this type, it is not feasible to totally avoid overlapping between chapters. Considerable care has been taken to keep it to a minimum; where it does occur, it does not constitute repetition, for the point is always illuminated from a different perspective.

Section 1 furnishes a historical introduction to the topic, a possible definition, and a discussion of the various types of imagery (Chapter 1), and it introduces the reader to a wide range of theoretical viewpoints of imagery, including the views of those who do not look kindly upon the role of imagery in cognition. The chapter by Steven Pinker and Stephen Kosslyn (Chapter 2) is particularly extensive in its coverage. The theories discussed include Paivio and Bower's Dual Codes; Neisser's Percept Analogy; Hebbs's Cell Assemblies; Moran's Propositional Model; Kosslyn, Schwartz, and Pinker's Array Theory; Trehub's Neural Networks; Finke's Levels of Equivalence; Shepard's Psychophysiological Complementarity; Pylyshyn's Tacit Knowledge Account; and Hinton's Structural Descriptions.

In Section 2 detailed reviews of research in six major fields are presented: assessment of imagery; role of imagery in development; imagery and language; cerebral laterality and imagery; imagery and creativity; and the fantasy-prone personality. In three of the chapters in this section (Chapters 9, 11, and 12), the authors not only review research, but present heretofore unpublished findings of their recent work. Even though this section is an excellent review of some of the most exciting developments, it of course does not cover everything of significance that has occurred in this area. Those looking for ideas for further research on imagery will find this section, and in fact the whole book, to be a storehouse of intriguing issues that invite scientific scrutiny.

The last section acquaints the reader with the practical uses of imagery in five significant areas including therapy and diagnosis, sexual behavior, arts, sports, and advertising.

This book, I believe, will prove invaluable to students, researchers, and practitioners in the fields of psychology, psychiatry, education, and sociology—in fact, to all interested in understanding the nature and function of imagery and in applying it to various real-life situations.

To conclude, I would like to thank all the contributors of chapters and the staff of John Wiley and Sons for their cooperation and encouragement at various stages of the book's preparation. I am particularly indebted to Herb Reich and Richard Bugelski for their generous assistance and advice. I also wish to express my sincere appreciation to my wife, Katharina, for her valuable assistance and support throughout the preparation of this volume.

ANEES A. SHEIKH

Milwaukee, Wisconsin
March 1983

Contents

PART ONE

Theory

CHAPTER 1

Imagery:
Definition and Types

ALAN RICHARDSON

To what do we refer when we employ terms such as "imagery," "images," or "imaging"? Do we refer to events, processes, or both? Is imagery an explanatory construct or is it a phenomenon to be explained? If different types of imagery can be identified, what are their theoretical and practical functions?

Answers to these and related questions vary greatly, and it is often unclear whether this variation is due to any genuine differences in the facts and their interpretation or whether some more fundamental conceptual confusions exist. The purpose of this chapter is to sharpen some important conceptual distinctions prior to settling on a particular definition of the term "imagery" and providing provisional criteria by which its various types might be identified.

It is hoped that this approach will serve to clarify an area of research and theorizing that has become unnecessarily muddled. Part of the value of such an attempt comes from the research implications that clarification of issues can produce.

HISTORICAL BACKGROUND

As might be expected from an examination of the theory, research, and applications in other areas of psychology, conceptual chaos often results from a failure to recognize differences in the questions asked. When psychologists were first interested in the study of consciously experienced events, they were obliged to distinguish between the contents of experiences that originated in the immediate stimulation of a sensory surface (percepts) and the contents of experiences that, although similar in many ways, occurred in the absence of such stimulation (images).

Thus the resulting study of mental images sought answers to a particular set of questions. Could an imaginal experience always be distinguished from

3

a perceptual experience (Perky, 1910)? Could an imaginal experience ever be as intense as the perceptual experience on which it was based (Schaub, 1911)? Could an imaged representation (a memory image) carry the same amount of information as its perceptual counterpart (Fernald, 1912)? Under what conditions does an image spontaneously emerge into awareness (Fox, 1914)?

These questions have a clear basis in the need to clarify the *nature* of imagery by contrasting and comparing it with perception and to understand the *function* of imagery by inquiring into the conditions of its arousal and the information that it can make available. Imagery, as a phenomenon in its own right, took over from perception all the relevant analytic terms. Imagery came in all sensory modalities, and its contents had the same variable attributes of intensity, duration, stability, and so on. It also had unique attributes in its visual form such as location within the head or within the external environment, and in all its forms it varied in the extent to which its content could be voluntarily controlled.

For some psychologists (structuralists), the image was also a basic theoretical element that could combine with sensory and affective elements to produce every variety of complex experience. For others of a more functionalist persuasion, imagery was freed from this narrow theoretical role to become an individual difference variable of great potential importance (Betts, 1909). Can those whose imagery has certain characteristics, such as vividness, perform certain tasks with greater accuracy or speed compared with those whose imagery lacks these characteristics?

All these questions assume a fundamental interest in consciously experienced events. A new orientation toward many psychological problems is established when the importance of such events is questioned, and after a brief transition period a new use is found for terms such as "imagery," "images," and "imaging." Perhaps the turning point came when the Würzburg psychologists demonstrated that thought processes could take place without the mediation of any consciously experienced imagery. Woodworth (1906, p. 703) describes the general procedure that produced evidence in support of imageless thought: "The experimenter sets some problem, which the subject is to solve promptly. As soon as the solution is reached—or even before—the experimenter interrupts the further course of the subject's thought, and calls for a description of the process of seeking and finding the solution." If the question is an easy one, "the answer may come automatically, and consciousness seem blank, save for the words employed." This imageless thought phenomenon was a topic of much debate between those who accepted these findings and those who denied them (Humphrey, 1951). By the time that everyone had come to accept the fact of imageless thought, functionalist psychologists drew the weak conclusion that imagery played no part in some thought processes. It was left to the behaviorists to make the stronger claim that imagery, of an experiential kind, was irrelevant to all thought processes—an epiphenomenon without scientific interest.

Perhaps the full transition to a new use for the term "image" originated with the testing movement and the factor analytic study of cognitive abilities in the 1920s and 1930s. The work of Griffiths (1927) and El Koussy (1935) was influential in linking visual imagery with visualization and spatial manipulation ability. By the time of Michael (1949) and Barratt (1953) confusion of the two had been brought to the point where McBain (1954) could employ a memory for designs test as a measure of visual imagery. At least in relation to the term "visual imagery," its referent appears no longer to be a visual experience occurring in the absence of a visual stimulus from the outside world, but a performance (behavioral) referent. Alongside its older experiential meaning, then, a newer behavioral meaning had emerged as the referent for terms such as "imagery," "images," and "imaging."

CONTEMPORARY BACKGROUND

One of the major sources of confusion that came to dominate the contemporary interest in imagery studies can be seen from this brief account. If imagery, regardless of its conceptual and operational definitions, had remained a theoretical and research backwater, it would have mattered little that a few psychologists became muddled in their thinking about the issues involved. But with the shift of interest from the problems and concepts of stimulus and response (S–R) learning theory to the problems and concepts of cognition, imagery studies have burgeoned. From the late 1950s onward, the output of research has increased exponentially. Psychologists were drawn into this new imagery movement for different reasons, and it will help to understand what has taken place since by giving a brief account of them.

For myself, it arose from a general dissatisfaction with the prevailing views on what counted as an acceptable problem for psychological investigation and what counted as acceptable evidence. Problems, it seemed, must be couched in behavioral and/or physiological language, and data collection procedures should, in principle if not always in practice, be based on behavioral and/or physiological events.

I could find no logical reasons and, later, no empirical (procedural) reasons for neglecting problems and data that developed from a serious and systematic concern for experiential events (Richardson, 1965, 1980). The problems to be studied in human psychology admitted of three kinds of data, not merely two, and mental imagery in its traditional sense, as a percept like experience, provided a way into the general theoretical and methodological questions that interested me.

Some of the other concerns that led other psychologists toward the field of imagery studies may be divided into those based on experiential and those based on behavioral considerations.

Experiential

Widespread concern over the misleadingly termed "brainwashing" of prisoners of war (POWs) in Korea resulted in the availability of money for studies on the psychological effects of perceptual isolation. Beginning with the work of Donald Hebb and his colleagues at McGill University, a huge literature accumulated during the 1960s, much of which related to reports of spontaneously occurring non-object-bound experiences (images) of an impressive vividness and variety. Interest in hallucinations reemerged as an active research area, and a milestone book on this topic appeared (West, 1962).

While these developments were taking place the drug movement became a major social problem, and subjective experiences of an imaginal kind were regularly reported as one of the significant consequences of lysergic acid diethylamide (LSD) and mescaline intoxication. Further interest in the occurrence of vivid perceptlike experiences was expressed by engineering psychologists faced with radar operators, high-flying solitary fighter pilots, and snow cat drivers in Antarctica, all of whom endangered their lives and their equipment by "seeing" things that were not physically present.

Images, as experiential events to be explained, became a serious practical problem. Even more important in the long run became the need to characterize these images more precisely. Not only were there modality differences, but differences in vividness, complexity, and location. A revival of interest in many old questions took place. Under what conditions are vivid complex visual images located externally or internally? If located externally, some people believe in them (hallucination), whereas others recognize the source as within themselves. Why?

Even at this time, imagery as a quasi-perceptual experience was of interest as an explanatory construct. In the early 1960s Peter Sheehan was investigating the part played by imagery vividness in the manifestation of different hypnotic phenomena, and Brian Start and I were interested in the relationship of imagery vividness and controllability to the effectiveness of mental practice (Richardson, 1967, 1967a; Start & Richardson, 1964).

Behavioral

Chiefly as a result of developments in computer engineering, many mainstream psychologists took over the concepts of information processing and used the computer and its programming procedures as a potent analogy. The new cognitive psychology that was being born at this time began to use imagery as a major theoretical construct. Bugelski (1977, pp. 39–40) states:

> For some (Miller et al., 1960), the image is some kind of global cognitive map, "all the accumulated, organized knowledge that the organism has about itself and its world." For others (Paivio, 1971) it is, in at least some respects, the equivalent of meaning. For Mowrer (1960) it is an internal model which controls approach and avoidance behavior. Some investigators cautiously view imagery

as a helpful, if unexplained, mnemonic device (Atkinson & Raugh, 1975). Others (Anderson & Bower, 1973) have used it as a stepping stone to more "powerful" forms of representation, namely propositions, as cognitive mechanisms. Still others (Brewer, 1974; Pylyshyn, 1973) regard imagery as lacking in utility as a proper mechanism for accounting for cognitive behavior (Pylyshyn) or the higher mental processes, including the explanation of meaning (Brewer). . . . The revival of interest in imagery occurred in the context of a revolution in verbal learning. This revolution brought about the rejection of nonsense syllables and the substitution of ordinary words, sometimes in sentences or paragraphs and a new concern over what the learner had to contribute to the learning and/or retrieval process.

Perhaps the first thing to notice about the behavioral approach is its use of imagery as an explanatory construct, that is, an independent variable. By comparison, the examples of experiential concerns are mostly with imagery as something to be explained, that is, a dependent variable. This is a major difference but not an absolute one. In discussing imagery as an experienced event later in this chapter, the way in which differences in the vividness of voluntarily produced thought imagery produce different effects on a variety of psychological activities is exemplified further.

CURRENT CONCEPTUAL CONFUSIONS

Of those workers interested in imagery as an explanatory construct three different positions may be noted. Some, like Evans (1980), adopt the behavioral approach as the only one acceptable and discuss the experiential only for purposes of dismissal. Others, like Paivio (1971), Kosslyn (1973), and Shepard (1978), adopt the behavioral approach for empirical research purposes but seem to allow some role for experienced images in their interpretations. Little has been done to show that the explanatory functions of imagery, differently conceived and measured, may serve different purposes.

The aim of what follows in this section is threefold: (1) to describe some of the ambiguities in the use of imagery concepts for an understanding of how knowledge is represented (coded); (2) to consider some confusions in the use of imagery when interpreting mental rotation and scanning phenomena; and (3) to show that spatial abilities and mental imagery abilities are psychometrically independent of each other.

The Representation of Knowledge

What Paivio (1971) has been attempting to demonstrate is the way in which imagery can affect the acquisition, transformation, or retrieval of different classes of information. Defined conceptually, imagery (typically visual imagery) is one of two types of cognitive code (the other is a verbal code). Operationally, this code is presumed to be activated either in individuals who have a preference for using this code (to be discussed later), in anyone when instructed to image, or when the stimulus can be assumed to require visual imagery processing. In paired associate learning, for example, performance is affected by the stimulus properties of the words employed. When concrete nouns are to be associated, they are learned more readily than when abstract nouns, of equal familiarity and meaningfulness, are to be associated. The explanation of this finding is said to be the greater ease with which images can be formed to concrete nouns than to abstract nouns. Thus concrete nouns benefit from being encoded imaginally as well as verbally, whereas abstract nouns are restricted much more to encoding in the verbal mode alone.

Although reports of imagery vividness do not form any part of these operational procedures, all three imply that awareness of quasi-perceptual events is involved at some time or in some way. The instruction to image makes the assumption that all subjects have had the experience of forming an image and will do so when asked. Merely to show that certain effects follow when this instruction is given is not enough to justify the theoretical argument unless one has independent evidence that the subject has indeed formed a visual image. What the nature of this visual image is becomes the next question but it is not asked. The characteristics of noun stimuli are established by asking for imagery vividness ratings. In this way concrete nouns are found to be better mediators than abstract nouns; they are rated as arousing more vivid imagery. Again, the question is raised as to what this thing called "imagery" is that can be more or less vivid. It is not the noun itself, but something aroused by the noun. Finally, the Individual Differences Questionnaire seeks information on preferred ways of thinking and learning. All questions converge to give scores on a verbal scale and on a separate imagery scale. To what extent is the individual aware of having an habitual preference for thinking and learning by means of labeling and "talking to himself or herself" and to what extent is he or she aware of having an habitual preference for thinking and learning by means of imaging and "picturing to himself or herself"? The nature (definition and attributes) of verbal and imaginal experiences remains, as before, unknown and unexamined.

There may be many reasons for the failure to explore this problem of definition more carefully, but the following quotations suggest that the twin spectres of E. B. Titchener and J. B. Watson are still unlaid. The first is a formal definition of imagery that denies the relevance of conscious experience. The term "image" or "imagery" is ". . . used to refer to a memory code or associative mediator that provides spatially parallel information that can mediate overt responses without necessarily being consciously experienced as a visual image" (Paivio, 1971, pp. 135–136).

We return to this problem of conscious and unconscious imagery in a moment. Now for the second quotation: "the charge of mentalism, or subjectivity, has little force because implicit verbal responses are every bit as inferential as mental images—they are *mental words* which like images must be inferred from overt behavior and the stimulus situation in which it occurs'' (Paivio, 1970, p. 386). Experiential events, and the testimony provided by individuals concerning them, have many conceptual and methodological problems, but they are not insoluble in principle and frequently not insoluble in practice (Richardson, 1980). This area of human psychology can be opened up to serious and systematic examination without people fearing the old charge of mentalism.

Concern for the way in which information (knowledge) is represented in the brain or in the unaware part of the psyche is essential. No apologies are required of the psychologist who makes mutually supporting and confirmed inferences from different behaviors and then proceeds to draw theoretical conclusions that two codes must be postulated to account for the results. This is part of the psychologist's job.

The two questions that must always be asked on such occasions however, are whether the psychologist's conclusion is correct and, if so, whether the characteristics of the explanatory mechanism (physiological, experiential, or convenient fiction, inferred from behavior) are clearly and unambiguously described. Something has been said concerning this latter question—more later—but what of the former?

Some, like Pylyshyn (1973, 1979) have argued that all knowledge must be represented in a single propositional (abstract) code. The necessity of having two codes is denied. How might this debate be reconciled, or is one view absolutely right and the other absolutely wrong? As we know from previous debates in the history of psychology [e.g., the Baldwin–Titchener controversy (Krantz, 1969)], the facts are seldom in dispute; rather, it is their selection and interpretation that causes so much of the rumpus. The same correlation matrix of cognitive test scores can be used to support the view that one major underlying mental ability exists (the *g* factor) or that a number of different independent abilities provide a better description of the intellect (the group factors). Whether some form of associationism (S–R theory) or some form of relationism (Gestalt theory) is adopted depends on the set of facts selected for interpretation. Organisms can learn to make absolute discriminations between two stimuli or relative discriminations.

To require a choice to be made between the propositional view of how knowledge is represented and the dual-coding view may be to misconceive the problem. Perhaps a reconciliation of the two views is possible. In discussing this possibility, Yuille and Catchpole (1977) cite the approach of Piaget, who attempts to incorporate both the representational (e.g., figurative) and the process (e.g., operational) planes of thought within his theoretical scheme. Images are one form of figurative element that may be used in the service of more abstract logical processes. Thus reconciliation of the opposing views might provide a better solution than attempts to annihilate one or the other.

Mental Rotation and Mental Scanning

Another group of psychologists have converged on the field of imagery studies through their interest in visual information processing. What occurs psychologically when we attempt to solve visual spatial problems? Attempts to answer this general question have resulted in the development of two related lines of investigation. Roger Shepard and his colleagues (Shepard, 1978; Shepard & Metzler, 1971) have concentrated on the problem of mental rotation, whereas Stephen Kosslyn and his colleagues (Kosslyn et al., 1979) have been more interested in the nature of mental scanning.

The chronometric studies of this group have produced performance data (behavior) on spatial tasks that are of considerable interest and importance, but they often write as if the act of mentally rotating an object or of mentally scanning an object involved, required, or implied the presence of visual images in awareness.

As with the earlier students of visualization and spatial manipulation, who were interested primarily in individual differences, these more recent students of visual information processing have become entangled in conceptual problems. Visual imagery of a quasi-perceptual nature is not necessary to the performance of these spatial tasks, and confusion results when it is introduced. Two examples will help to illustrate the nature of this confusion. How long does it take to identify whether a line drawing of a hand is that of the right or left hand when it is presented in each of six orientations (0°, 60°, 120°, 180°, 240°, and 300°) and with either the palm or back of the hand showing? Cooper and Shepard (1975, p. 56) investigated this problem and concluded that the subject's decision, and consequently the time necessary to make it, was the result of "first imagining one of their own hands moved into the position of the presented hand, and then testing for a match or mismatch." What is to be understood by the term "imagining" as used in this context? It certainly suggests that the subject is, in some sense, looking at a hand that is not physically present—but in what sense? Might it not be that the subject "just knows" what it would be like if that hand were in the same position as the presented hand? No sensory or perceptlike content need be in awareness to have this particular feeling of knowing. The conceptual problem now becomes difficult. What is the nature of this feeling of knowing? How does it arise? Why does it take longer to emerge in some tasks than in others? By allowing the term "imagining" to suggest visual imagery, as most of us experience it in awareness, a commonsense interpretation is assumed but is not justified.

Again, in the research reported by Kosslyn et al. (1979) constant reference is made to what seems to be the phenomenal experience of visual content. For example, it is asserted that the results of one group of studies "support the claim that the images we experience are spatial entities" (Kosslyn et al., p. 537). But how, if at all, are "the images we experience" involved in, or relevant to the process of mental scanning? To decide whether the top of a horse's tail is higher off the ground than its knees does not *require* the emergence into consciousness of a pictured horse. Richardson (1979, p. 563) states:

First, the subject may know the answer and simply give it. This is the imageless thought phenomenon and, of course, begs the question as to the kind of non-conscious cognitive process involved. Second, the subject may report that the solution process is accompanied by a vague awareness of a tactile–kinaesthetic spatial layout from which appropriate inferences are drawn. Third, a reasoning process may be reported, that seems to the subject, to involve an internal monologue in which the known relations of a horse's knees to its shoulders and hindquarters, and hence to the top of its tail are considered and an answer is given. Mixtures of these last two strategies and of visual imagery may be reported by some subjects who wish to check their answer more thoroughly before giving it.

Spatial Abilities and Mental Imagery Abilities

The beginnings of the confusion described in the last section were referred to in an earlier section. There is a long-standing assumption that spatial and imagery abilities must have something in common, and it probably derives from two main sources. One is the commonsense belief that *visualization* of something, such as the arrangement of furniture in a room for instance, is synonymous with *imaging* this scene. The other is the need to find an objective performance measure, such as a spatial manipulation test, that can replace or at least provide added support for subjective self-ratings.

The facts do not necessarily justify the assumption, for instance, Barratt's (1953) conclusion that "imagery is an important component in the solution of those tasks that involve the 'mental' manipulation of spatial relations" was misleading. When subjects are asked to rate the vividness of their imagery *after* having completed a spatial task, the quality of their performance is likely to influence the magnitude of their ratings (Danaher & Thoresen, 1972; Sheehan & Neisser, 1969). Thus subjects who have performed well may attribute their success to their "visualizing" ability, which then leads to higher ratings on a visual imagery scale, whereas subjects who have performed poorly may produce correspondingly lower ratings.

In almost all studies that have included spatial ability measures and vividness of imagery measures, the correlations have been small and insignificant. Factor analysis shows that visual and other imagery tests load a factor that is orthogonal to the one on which tests of spatial ability are loaded (Di Vesta et al., 1971; Richardson, 1977).

Studies that attempt to measure imagery ability by combining scores on a spatial task such as the Minnesota Paper Form Board and a self-report imagery measure such as the imagery section of the Individual Difference Questionnaire (Ernest & Paivio, 1971) compound the conceptual and operational confusion. The writer has himself been guilty of this offense (Richardson, 1969, p. 85) and understands the temptation, but from now on it must be resisted.

One must insist not only on the difference between spatial and imaginal abilities, but also on the difference between both of these and the cognitive style dimension of verbalizer–visualizer (Richardson, 1977a). Regardless of their operational definition, the term "abilities" refers to a level of performance (high or low) that is achieved. A "cognitive style," on the other hand, refers to a habitual preference for performing perceptual, learning, recall, or problem-solving tasks in one way rather than another.

A preference for a verbalizing style is a preference for linguistic encoding (labeling or naming) for reading the instructions on how to do something rather than having someone demonstrate the task. A preference for a visualizing style is a preference for literal encoding (i.e., the spatial layout of physical features) and attention to the sensory properties of the stimuli (e.g., color). The conscious accompaniment of thought for the verbalizer is the experience of inner speech; for the visualizer, it is the experience of inner pictures. Each extreme on this dimension is also associated with a different respiration pattern (Richardson, 1977a).

To have a strong preference for one or other style can have no more than an indirect association with its counterpart in the ability domain. As a result, it is likely, but not necessary, that a preference for the verbalizer style will emerge on the basis of having learned that one has a greater ability to perform well on verbal tasks. Similarly, a preference for the visualizing style is likely to result from having discovered that one has superior spatial abilities.

In the Richardson (1977a) study it was found that a sample of verbalizers had a higher mean score than did the visualizers on Part A of the Mill Hill vocabulary scale. Other unpublished studies by the writer have not found a significant difference of this kind. Again, from Table 1.1, it can be seen that

TABLE 1.1.   Factor Loadings of Nine Tests on Imagery Abilities, Spatial Abilities, and Cognitive Style (Principal Components Analysis with Varimax Rotation)

Factors Tests	I Imagery Abilities	II Spatial Abilities	III Cognitive Style
5. Absorption	.85	.05	−.07
1. Imagination inventory	.80	−.03	.14
3. QMI visual	.60	−.03	.28
6. Hypnagogic imagery	.56	−.05	.03
10. MPFB	−.01	.95	.31
11. Picture memory	.00	.32	−.08
12. S & M	−.18	.27	.45
2. Style of thinking	.23	−.08	.77
9. VVQ	.15	−.02	.63

scores on the verbalizer–visualizer questionnaire (VVQ) and on a newly created measure of this same cognitive style each load on the same factor as two different measures of spatial ability. However, other unpublished studies have not always shown this pattern of results.

All the tests shown in Tables 1.1 and 1.3 were part of a larger battery administered over a 3-week period. The independence of spatial abilities and imagery abilities is demonstrated once again.

Tests numbered 1, 2, 3, 5, 6 and 9 in Table 1.1 are the same as those appearing in Table 1.3 and described later; those numbered 10, 11, and 12 are as follows:

10.   Revised Minnesota Paper Form Board (MPFB); Form DB of this test was used with a 20-minute time limit (administered in the first week of testing).

11.   Picture Memory Test: This test was used by Lumsden (1965). It requires a subject to look at a picture for 3 minutes. At the end of this time it is removed and a second picture presented that is in some ways similar to and in some ways different from the first. Five minutes are allowed in which to use the second picture as a basis for judging the truth or falsity of 30 statements comparing features of the first and second pictures. The score is the number of statements judged correctly.

12.   S & M Test: This is a 2-minute test requiring judgments of similar or different to 20 pairs of three-dimensional objects. It is based on the mental rotation task described by Shepard and Metzler (1971) and was constructed by Phillips and Rawles (1979) (administered in the third week of testing).

The Essential Distinction Reiterated

On the basis of all that has been said thus far, one essential distinction has emerged. The term "mental imagery" may refer to an inferred construct or process of an essentially nonphenomenal kind *or* to an experienced event of a quasi-sensory or quasi-perceptual (phenomenal) kind. Nothing that we yet know about these two usages can justify the assumption that their conceptual and operational meanings overlap in any way.

Ideally, this essential distinction should be preserved by giving each a different name. But as nomenclature debates seldom achieve general agreement, the least we can expect is that workers in the field of mental imagery will find ways of making their own usage clear and never assume or imply that the other usage is involved in any way.

As matters stand at the moment, the nonphenomenological usage appears to include three groups of psychologists: (1) those such as Allan Paivio (1972), Ulric Neisser (1972), and Theodore Sarbin (1972), who explicitly state that the experience of having a mental image is not an essential part of its nature or function; (2) those such as Roger Shepard (1971) and Stephen Kosslyn (1973), who are interested primarily in processes associated with visual information processing; and (3) those who have used one or another test of spatial ability for the investigation of individual differences in imaging ability as these latter supposedly relate to such other cognitive activities as verbal learning (Hollenberg, 1970), memory (J. Richardson, 1976), and problem solving (Shaver et al., 1974).

The remainder of this chapter is concerned with imagery defined as a phenomenally present quasi-perceptual event or an event of this kind that is capable of becoming phenomenally present. Unless the context indicates otherwise, the terms ''mental image,'' ''imagery,'' or ''imaging'' refer exclusively to this definition.

A GENERAL DEFINITION AND CLASSIFICATION OF MENTAL IMAGERY

Before a general definition of mental imagery is presented, a seeming paradox must be resolved. It is necessary to distinguish between conscious and nonconscious imagery. The nonconscious imagery has nothing to do with the nonconscious inferred construct notion discussed earlier. The latter is *unnoticeable,* but the former is merely *unnoticed.* The unnoticeable events comprise all the inferred abilities and processes plus the biochemical and bioelectrical events that are the physiological concomitants of consciously experienced images or trains of images.

However, unnoticed quasi-perceptual contents (images) are always potentially noticeable. The evidence, such as it is (Pope & Singer, 1978), suggests that human adults have a continual, night-and-day stream of imaginal events going on within them. Given the appropriate conditions, each of us can tune in and watch. One function of training programs designed to improve the vividness of voluntarily produced images is to make us more aware of what is continually taking place within us. Just as an art teacher may bring the usually unnoticed effect of light and shade on the trunk of a tree to the students' attention, so the imagery trainer may help the weak imager to relax and pay attention to the sensory details of similar internally represented events. For example, the imagery trainer might say, ''Imagine a flower in all its detail. (Pause.) Notice its colour and texture; the exact shape of its petals; its scent, if it has one. (Pause.) Now just look at it and notice any changes that take place in its appearance.''

This guided imagery procedure can help to draw attention to what might be called the *imagery channel.* If we switch to this channel (attend to it), we find ourselves in touch with a motivationally influenced source of information about ourselves. When this information is discussed with a therapist, it is claimed to have strong integrative influences on the personality (Leuner, 1977; Sheikh & Panagiotou, 1975).

The potentiality for experiencing mental images appears to be a species-wide characteristic. The fact that imagery goes unnoticed by some people almost all the time may be attributed to a variety of causes, but its potential for being noticed by anyone under appropriate conditions is unquestionable. What is now needed is a more precise definition of mental imagery and a careful description of criteria that can help to distinguish its various types.

Some years ago, I (Richardson, 1969) gave a working definition that was intended to cover all types of phenomenally experienced imagery. With the exception of the fourth characteristic, it still seems to embody the essense of what is to be understood by this concept in the present context. Thus "Mental imagery refers to (1) all those quasi-sensory or quasi-perceptual experiences of which (2) we are self consciously aware and which (3) exist for us in the absence of those stimulus conditions that are known to produce their genuine sensory or perceptual counterparts, and which (4) may be expected to have different consequences from their sensory or perceptual counterparts" (Richardson, 1969, pp. 2–3).

The reason for denying the adequacy of the fourth characteristic is the increasing evidence that self-initiated thought imagery of a concrete sensorylike kind (i.e., not verbal imagery embodied in inner speech) can have consequences that appear to be indistinguishable from their genuine sensory counterparts. As this is a matter of great importance to any discussion concerned with the nature and functions of voluntarily produced thought imagery, it is discussed at greater length later. For the present it suffices to remind the reader of what every schoolboy knows. Clear and unmistakeable physiological consequences follow from voluntary absorption in a favorite sexual fantasy.

In the publication from which this definition of mental imagery is taken, four classes or types of imagery were distinguished: after imagery; eidetic imagery; memory (now called "thought") imagery; and imagination imagery. The arbitrariness of this classification is recognized; the classification serves mainly as an expository convenience. "It is convenient because it (makes) it possible to focus on some characteristics of imagery that would not otherwise stand out so clearly in discussion. It is arbitrary because so much of the phenomenal experience is similar for each class, though no one knows to what extent imagery of one class is related to imagery of another" (Richardson, 1969, p. 127).

This fourfold classification of mental imagery is used once again later, but before it is introduced, some data are presented to qualify the assertion that it is an arbitrary classification. Differences in mental imagery can be established most easily by reference to differences in the conditions that arouse it and/or differences in its phenomenal characteristics.

The first major study to investigate this problem was carried out by Robert Holt (1972) and his associates at the Research Center for Mental Health at New York University. In the second of the two studies reported by them, afterimagery was assessed in terms of how convincing the description had been, following fixation of a black-and-white design. Measures of eidetic imagery were based on childhood recollections. Thought imagery differences were obtained from ratings on the presence of movement, color, sound, and other sensory qualities in answers to a series of relevant questions. For example, "Imagine an automobile; when you have a mental image, describe it to me." Various measures of imagination imagery were obtained, including ratings of hypnagogic and hypnopompic imagery based on interview data, ratings of imagery based on the effects of 8 hours of perceptual isolation, and ratings on other interview data concerning day-and-night dream imagery and on dream frequency.

From the descriptions provided, it is not possible to estimate the quality of the information obtained in this study. A total of 28 male college students participated, and when scores on the 13 imagery variables were intercorrelated, only 10 of the 78 correlations were found to be statistically significant at the 10% level or better. "It is noteworthy that six of these involve either the reported frequency of dreaming or the reported vividness and amount of sensory qualities in dreams: Subjects who report dreaming most often have the richest thought imagery and tend to describe their daydreams as containing visual or auditory images (or both) and to describe their dreams as vivid with sensory imagery." An association between dream recall frequency and vividness of visual imagery has since been reported by Hiscock and Cohen (1973) and Richardson (1979a).

Reports of eidetic or eideticlike imagery in childhood showed a significant correlation of 0.39 with adult experiences of entoptic phenomena (phosphenes), 0.35 with the after-image measure, and 0.34 with rated vividness of a memory image based on this afterimage. The overall finding that 62 of the 78 correlations were positive is interpreted by Holt (1972, p. 21) as indicating "a kind of introspectiveness or awareness of subjective phenomena in general. . . . There may be a tendency for people to direct attention inward or outward which might be expected to introduce a degree of positive correlation. . . ." This observation has been made by others (e.g., Richardson, 1972), but more detailed and carefully considered checks on the implications of this interpretation are required. In one attempt to examine whether reports of imagery vividness were more likely to occur in association with reports of more familiarity with internal events, some differences were found between men and women. Richardson (1977, p. 40) states that "Though females do not differ significantly from males in their familiarity with internal events it is possible that they are more biased in the direction of rating their images as vivid when they have greater familiarity with other classes of subjective experiences than when they have not. For men, overall familiarity with internal events is unconnected with ratings of imagery vividness."

Having said this, what impressed Holt (1972) overall was the degree of "demonstrated and replicated independence of the various forms of mental imagery" (p. 21). Perhaps this can be seen most clearly in Table 1.2, where correlations between the relevant measures of each imagery type are given.

With the exception of afterimagery, which has a significant (p = .10) correlation with childhood recollections of eidetic imagery, all the other forms of imagery as operationally defined here appear to be independent of one another. Even the two examples of imagination imagery appear to be uncorrelated. However, Freedman et al. (1962) did find a statistically significant association between reports of naturally occurring hypnagogic imagery and reports of imagery under perceptual isolation conditions. A similar result was obtained by Freedman and Marks (1965) in a study of photic stimulation imagery.

Some further data relevant to the independence of these four types of imagery were obtained by the writer as part of a larger study referred to earlier. The tests shown in Table 1.3 are described below and comprise 9 of 20 that were administered over a 3-week period to 50 third-year psychology undergraduates. The three testing sessions and the large number of tests and other tasks were intended to reduce the probability of forming strong test-taking sets.

The description of each variable (test) is as follows:

1. *Imagination inventory: first week*. This test is reported by Barber and Wilson (1979) and consists of eight items found to correlate significantly with the Creative Imagination Scale reported in the same article. It appears to measure various aspects of imagery, including vividness; the similarity of imagined consequences to real consequences (e.g., placing one's foot in iced water); enjoyment of make-believe play when young; and reading for the

TABLE 1.2. Correlation Matrix of Imagery Measures from Holt's (1972) Study[a]

Imagery Measures	After-imagery	Eidetic Imagery	Thought Imagery	Imagination Imagery Hypnagogic– Hypnopompic	Imagination Imagery Isolation Vividness
Afterimagery	—	.35*	−.26	.02	.05
Eidetic Imagery		—	.01	−.27	.21
Thought Imagery			—	.14	.19
Imagination Imagery					
Hypnagogic– Hypnopompic				—	.01

[a]This table is derived from Table 3 in Holt (1972, p. 20).
*p = .10.

TABLE 1.3. Matrix of Correlations for Males and Females on Nine Different Measures of Imagery and Image-Related Phenomena

Males n = 14 / Females n = 36	1 Imagination Inventory	2 Style of Thinking	3 QMI Visual	4 QMI Total	5 Absorption	6 Frequency Hypnagogic Image	7 Frequency Dream Recall	8 Dream in Color	9 VVQ
1 Imagination Inventory	—	.37	.36	.36	.53*	.46	.14	.45	.17
2 Style of Thinking	.44**	—	.43	.19	-.29	.05	.01	-.03	.64**
3 QMI Visual	.61***	.44**	—	.91**	.41	.15	-.01	.43	.44
4 QMI Total	.69***	.48**	.79***	—	.52*	.06	-.12	.34	.37
5 Absorption	.71***	.39**	.58***	.55***	—	.53*	.26	.77***	-.28
6 Frequency Hypnagogic	.53***	.18	.29*	.17	.55***	—	.66**	.69**	-.18
7 Frequency Dream Recall	.26	.12	.03	.04	.31	.46**	—	.35	-.30
8 Dream in Color	.24	-.11	.43**	.22	.22	.19	.16	—	-.15
9 VVQ	.23	.45**	.21	.11	.25	.39**	.11	.13	—

***p < .001.
**p < .01.
*p < .05.

purpose of stimulating one's imagination rather than assisting one's intellectual interests.

2. *Style of thinking: second week.* This is a 10-item test constructed by the writer and including some of the items presented in a paper by Torrance et al. (1977). In two independent studies conducted prior to the one under discussion it had been found that each item correlated with total scores on this test and with total scores on the VVQ (see below). Like the VVQ, it aims to measure the verbalizer–visualizer cognitive style.

3. *QMI—visual: second week.* This is the five-item vividness of visual imagery subscale from the revised Betts test constructed by Sheehan (1967) and published as an appendix in Richardson (1969).

4. *QMI—total score: second week.* This is the full 35-item scale mentioned in paragraph 3 above.

5. *Absorption: second week.* This is a 28-item version of the scale reported by Tellegen and Atkinson (1974). This version aimed to eliminate items that appeared to have an obvious content overlap with imagery vividness items from other scales. As its name suggests, this scale attempts to measure the extent to which an individual can become immersed (absorbed) in any ongoing activity, so as to become oblivious to all distractions as when "deep" into a film or novel.

6. *Frequency with which hypnagogic imagery is reported under natural conditions: third week.* Subjects were asked to circle the appropriate answer on a seven-point scale (ranging from "never" to "every day") in response to the question: "How frequently do you experience 'suddenly appearing' images, thoughts, or sensations when you become drowsy, but before falling asleep?" This was part of a more complete questionnaire on hypnagogic imagery included in the battery of tests and based on a similar one used by Schachter and Crovitz (1977).

7. *Frequency of dream recall: third week.* This is the scale used originally by David Cohen and fully described in Richardson (1979a). It has a range of eight points.

8. *Dream in color: third week.* This is scored zero (False) and one (True) according to the response given to the statement, "Some of my dreams have been in color (as opposed to black and white)."

9. *VVQ: third week.* This is the verbalizer–visualizer scale described in Richardson (1977a). It has a range of 15 points and measures, the extent to which an individual has a habitual preference for imaginal (visual) or verbal modes of consciously experienced thought.

Substantial correlations are observable for both sexes between absorption scores and scores on the following: imagination inventory; total vividness of imagery scores on the QMI; and frequency of experiencing hypnagogic imagery. Both the absorption scale and the imagination inventory appear to measure more than one kind of imagery variable, such as imagery vividness as well as involvement in imaged content. Correlations for both sexes are low and nonsignificant between the vividness of voluntarily produced thought imagery (total QMI scores) and the frequency of spontaneously occurring imagination imagery (reported hypnagogic imagery).

These illustrative findings are quoted to show the difficulties that exist in studying the extent to which awareness or complexity of, or absorption in, one type of imagery is associated with awareness of some other type of imagery. There is no logical reason why those who can voluntarily produce vivid thought images should also spend more time attending to spontaneously occurring imagination images (i.e., hypnagogic images). Given the different conditions under which these images are being aroused (voluntary versus spontaneous) and the clear difference between the concepts of vividness and frequency, it is hardly surprising that no significant correlations are found.

Any serious attempt to discover an imagery typology by correlation and factor analytic procedures must employ measures that require comparable ratings on all the dimensions of imagery that can be identified phenomenally (e.g., vividness, controllability, complexity, color). The conditions for arousing different types of imagery must also be comparable. Either spontaneous or voluntary imagery should be studied, but preferably not both together. Thus the picture stimulus method might be used to arouse eidetic imagery (Haber & Haber, 1964); the blocked problem solution or confusion method to arouse thought imagery (Sheehan & Lewis, 1974) and the photic stimulation method (Freedman & Marks, 1965) or the perceptual isolation method (Zubek, 1969) to arouse imagination imagery. Individuals subjected to all these arousing conditions could be asked to rate all relevant dimensions of any imagery that resulted, and both quantitative and qualitative similarities and differences could be established from these results.

When spontaneously occuring imagery has been examined in this way, it might be possible to explore voluntarily produced imagery in a comparable way. But what would it mean to ask for the voluntary production of an eidetic or an imagination image? Not many people obtain spontaneous eidetic images, but as Haber (1979, p. 619) has observed, "It is an empirical question, yet to be tested, as to whether subjects classified as eidetic by the picture induction procedure also give responses classified as eidetic when these responses are elicited by other procedures." Again, it may be found possible for some people, under some conditions, to gain some degree of voluntary control over their imagination images. At the moment such control is extremely rare and limited in extent (McKellar, 1979).

Until a more rational theoretical and/or empirical basis is established, the fourfold typology described earlier in this section will have to serve. Let us examine the nature of each type and the provisional criteria by which it may be identified.

Afterimagery

Prolonged and/or intense stimulation in at least four sensory modalities have well-established sensorylike consequences when the stimulation ceases. After being exposed to a lightning flash, we continue to have a visual sensation of light in the darkness that follows. After rocking for several hours in a small boat, a rocking sensation persists after coming ashore; and after wearing a hat for some time, the pressure of its rim seems to continue after its removal. According to Boring (1942), comparable aftereffects of temperature also occur. Details of the conditions that affect the quality of peripherally stimulated afterimages in the visual mode are provided by Brown (1965), and a discussion of some research on afterimages obtained from vividly experienced thought images (centrally stimulated afterimages) is provided by Richardson (1969).

As with all types of mental imagery, the vast bulk of research on the afterimage has been concerned with the visual modality. Experientially, the primary defining characteristics of the visual afterimage are its content, which appears as if located externally, and its movement, which corresponds to movements of the eyes.

Some related, and perhaps more interesting, visual phenomena have been classified as subtypes of afterimage. One of these is *recurrent imagery* (Hanawalt, 1954), and a brief mention of its characteristics is repeated here in the hope that it may stimulate some experimentally based research. Reports of its natural occurrence are common, but so far I have found no studies that have attempted to investigate the necessary and sufficient conditions of its emergence into awareness.

Like ordinary visual afterimagery, the conditions for arousing recurrent imagery seem to involve prolonged and intense stimulation, but the similarity ceases here. The stimulus object must not be stationary, as for the formation of an ordinary afterimage, but must be in the form of constantly repeated examples of a similar but not identical kind. Thus the criteria of prolonged and intense stimulation refer to several hours of exposure to the stimulus examples, such as an afternoon spent berry picking or weeding in bright sunlight. However, the consequences of this exposure are often delayed, as in the following example from Hanawalt (1954, pp. 170–171). "After a family excursion into a blackberry patch, my wife reported to me as she closed her eyes after retiring that she could see beautiful blackberries, just perfect for picking, hanging in great profusion. Upon closing my eyes I discovered that I too saw them." He then goes on to comment on this experience, "The images greatly impressed me for they were neither after-images in the usual sense, nor were they memory images. The images were positive and appeared to be located in the eyes rather than projected. They were very vivid; they could be *seen* not just imagined as in the case of memory images. In this respect they were like the usual after-image. Introspectively they appeared to be a retinal phenomenon." He goes on to note one other characteristic that has been commented on by others and that, indeed, anyone can verify, "My wife and I both saw idealized images; the berries were large, purple tinged, luscious and profuse. . . . During the excursion we had seen many small berries, green berries and bird pecked berries, but in our images not an imperfect berry appeared."

In a paper on hypnagogic imagery (classified as a form of imagination imagery in this chapter) Peter McKellar (1979) suggests that one kind, "perseverative," is in fact the same as recurrent imagery. He writes, "Many people who have done fruit picking are familiar with it. After a day of berry picking, one imager reported seeing 'raspberries, endless raspberries'" (p. 192). Here we have a conflict between the criteria employed in classifying imagery types. I attempted to use the characteristics of prolonged, intense stimulation by varied examples of relatively similar objects; Peter McKellar, on the other hand, has used the conditions that exist immediately prior to experiencing these images. However, it should be noted that drowsiness between waking and sleeping, that is, the hypnagogic state, is not necessary for the appearance of recurrent (perseverative) images. Merely closing the eyes while standing fully awake in a darkened room is often sufficient for them to appear.

Eidetic Imagery

Confusion in the use of the adjective "eidetic" can be attributed to two sources, one of them ancient and the other modern. The ancient source derives from the belief that "eidetic imagery" is another name for the popular concept of photographic memory. An example of this belief, that visual memory of exceptional accuracy is a defining property of this type of imagery, is given by Kagan and Havemann (1972). They describe eideticism as "the ability possessed by a minority of people to 'see' an image that is an exact copy of the original sensory experience." However, no contemporary researchers on eidetic imagery employ exceptional accuracy as one of its defining properties.

The modern source of confusion arises from the use of the adjective "eidetic" to describe an imagery experience voluntarily created by a client at the behest of a clinical psychologist for purposes of diagnosis and treatment. This usage is particularly associated with the clinical work of Akhter Ahsen (1977, 1979). He defines an eidetic image as, "a normal subjective visual image which is experienced with pronounced vividness: although not necessarily evoked at the time of the experience by an external object, and not necessarily, dependent on a previous experience of an actual situation it is 'seen' inside the mind or outside in the literal sense of the word, and this 'seeing' is accompanied by certain somatic events as well as a feeling of meaning" (1977, p. 6).

To distinguish this definition and the clinical concerns associated with it from the more common contemporary definition to be described and discussed shortly, Ahsen has called his usage a "structural" definition and contrasted it with the more common "typographic" definition.

The Structural School

Ahsen (1977, p. 21) says of the structural school that it "studies the eidetic in its dynamic structuring form under various conditions. These eidetic structural experiences have been extensively reported by individuals who are not necessarily eidetikers, and can be studied in their many forms under controlled conditions to provide information on their nature and function.''

To elicit these structural eidetic images a typical procedure is to ask, ''Picture your parents in the house where you lived most of the time with them, the house which gives you the feeling of a home. Where do you see them? What are they doing? How do you feel when you see the images?''

This procedure and the vivid spontaneously changing (imagination) images that usually result seems to have more in common with such other diagnostic and therapeutic uses of imagination imagery as have been developed by Robert Desoille, Roberto Assagioli, and Hanscarl Leuner (See Jordan, 1979). For example, Leuner requires his clients to imagine situations that are believed to elicit a variety of basic conflicts and current concerns. In the first of these imagined situations the relaxed client is instructed to, ''Picture yourself in a meadow. Look about and notice what you can see. What time of year is it? What are you wearing?, etc.''

In partial justification for his use of the term ''eidetic,'' Ahsen (1977) refers to some of the early writers who sometimes employed it in a similar fashion. For example, Allport (1924, p. 100), in discussing what might count as eidetic imagery includes, ''those spontaneous images of phantasy which, though possessed of perceptual character, cannot be said to be literally revivals or restorations of any specific previous perception.''

Clearly, no law precludes calling ''spontaneous images of phantasy'' by the name ''eidetic.'' What one would like to preclude is confusing two empirically different phenomena.

The Typographic School

Since the general reawakening of interest in all types of mental imagery (Holt, 1964), Ralph Norman Haber and his associates have done the most to establish research into eidetic imagery on a sound experimental footing. In attempting to distinguish eidetic imagery from all other types of mental imagery, Haber (1979, p. 619) writes:

> I would like to restrict the term ''eidetic imagery'' to those cases the respondent reports as modality specific, and for which some converging operations are available to support the specificity of the modality. An image differs from a percept in that the latter occurs in the presence of stimulation whereas the former occurs when there is no stimulus present. Eidetic images differ from other images, or from memory more generally, in that the former are represented in a specific sensory modality, such as vision, audition, touch, and so on. . . . What is critical is that the subject says (and acts as if) he is currently seeing (or hearing, etc.) something that is not presently stimulating him. If the report is not explicitly anchored in a specific modality, it should not be included as eidetic imagery, but treated more generally as nondescript imagery, or thinking, or fantasy, as the case may be.

To obtain a modality specific experience of seeing "something that is not presently stimulating him," a picture stimulus is presented to the eidetiker, who looks at it—as any other picture—for a 30-second period. On its removal the picture continues to be seen.

Which criteria, however, might reassure the skeptical psychologist concerning the truth of the claim that someone continues to see, at least some of the picture content, after the picture stimulus has been removed? The following criteria are those most commonly employed in contemporary research. When the picture stimulus is removed:

1.   A visual experience must be reported which has the qualities of (a) being *seen* as a real object (or picture) is seen; (b) being *located* in front of the eyes on the plane of the original stimulus picture; and (c) having a *duration* of at least 40 seconds.

2.   Eye movements are made while the imaged picture is being examined. Unlike an afterimage, the eidetic image of the picture stimulus remains still while the eyes move from feature to feature.

3.   A description of the imaged picture is requested. In general, this description must be given in the present tense. A shift to the past tense should occur when the eidetic image has faded and an account of the picture content is given from memory.

Criteria 1a, b, and c depend on the subject's reports. They are phenomenological reports and serve to distinguish eidetic images from afterimages and memory (thought) images. Although afterimages cannot be formed by scanning the original stimulus, they will always move with the eyes once they have been formed and the stimulus removed. It is also unusual for afterimages when formed on the basis of comparable, poorly illuminated stimuli, to persist for periods in excess of 40 seconds. As far as is known, no memory (thought) image is "seen" in the way that an eidetic image is seen.

Criteria 2 and 3 are in the nature of converging operations designed to substantiate that subjects are not merely using visual metaphors to describe their memory of the picture. With children as young as 5 or 6 years among one's subjects, the need to have confidence in the truth of any testimony that they give is especially important. All these criteria need to be satisfied on four different pictures before one is classed as an eidetiker and one's images as genuine eidetic images.

Are these criteria good enough or is there still room for doubt concerning the "reality" of the eidetic image? Are those who fulfill all these criteria merely those who are highly suggestible or extremely sensitive to the expectations of the tester? The need to reject these nagging possibilities has led to a search for fakeproof objective tests, as in the case of Stromeyer and Psotka (1970); but so far the particular test devised by them has been found so stringent that most subjects, otherwise classifiable as eidetikers, have not been able to fulfill its requirements.

Must the skeptical psychologist withhold recognition until knockdown evidence of a fakeproof kind is provided? Clearly, the skeptical psychologist must independently judge this matter, but even now there are two other sources of evidence that he should know about before any negative conclusions are drawn. The first is internal evidence based on the subject's report, and the second is external evidence based on video records of that subject's expressive behavior.

The following extract is taken from a verbatim interchange with a 7-year-old boy in our own sample of eidetic children. The picture that he has just seen was based on the "policeman and pig" silhouette reproduced by Morsh and Abbott (1945).

E: (Turns off the projector). Here we go. Keep on looking. Can you see anything there now?

S: Yes.

E: What can you see?

S: Just the same picture as there was on the screen.

E: O.K. Can you point to the things and tell me what you can see?

S: I can see a pig with a policeman.

E: Can you point to that for me?

S: A pig with police hat, it was (points) just down there.

E: Is it there now?

S: Yes.

E: O.K. What else can you see? Tell me what you can see right now and point to it.

S: Now I can see a big policeman that's a bulldog. . . .

E: Yes.

S: (Points) . . . standing up.

E: Yes.

S: And I can see a brick wall. And that's all.

E: Can you point to the brick wall for me?

S: It's just up there (points) going up like that.

E: O.K. How many stripes does the policeman have on each arm? Can you see that?

S: About six.

E: Lots of stripes?

S: Yes.

   . . . the inquiry continues and E goes on to ask for details of the castle which, in the stimulus picture, is at the extreme left center. It has a flag on top. . . .

E: *Can you point to the flag on the castle? Can you see a castle there?*

S: *No, I can't.*

E: You see where the wall is?

S: (Acknowledges.)

E: *Just to the left of that there might be a castle there.*

S: *I can't see any castle.*

E: O.K. All right. What else can you see?

S: I can see (pauses) a lady coming round the corner.

E: Can you point to her?

S: Just up there (points).

E: (Acknowledges.)

S: And a man coming round the other side (points), just over there.

E: Are the policeman and the pig still there?

S: Yes.

The importation of new visual occurrences into an eidetic image has been reported in previous studies (Klüver, 1926), but the point of special interest in this interchange concerns the child's refusal to accept the suggestion that the castle is present in his image (see italicized section). If the child sees something, it is reported; if he sees nothing, then nothing is reported. However, when the image has faded, the child is able to report details of the castle and its flag when asked what he remembers from the original picture stimulus. It is invariably the case that the child makes a clear distinction between what the child "sees" in the image and what he or she "knows" was in the picture.

Witnessing an eidetic child in action provides a most compelling kind of additional evidence. Haber (1979, p. 560) notes the effect on skeptical colleagues when they are taken to observe an eidetic child. It "never fails to convert them into accepting the report as a genuine description of the visual imagery the child can see before his eyes even though the easel is blank." In our own research we have taken video sound recordings of both eidetic and noneidetic children and have constructed a 15-minute film for demonstration purposes. When shown to our own skeptical colleagues, its effect has been to convince them that something is going on that cannot be explained in terms of suggestibility or expectancy effects.

One final piece of evidence on the distinctiveness of eidetic imagery as a phenomenon that is unrelated to spatial and verbal abilities and, aparently, unconnected with the ability to voluntarily produce thought images, is provided by Paivio and Cohen (1979), who tested 219 male and female children and found 15 who fulfilled at least some of the Haber and Haber (1964) criteria. Scores on a modified version of the Betts QMI (Sheehan, 1967) and on some spatial and verbal ability tests were also included in the analysis. Four factors emerged: spatial ability; eidetic ability; ability to produce vivid thought imagery; and verbal ability.

Eidetic ability exists. It is alive and well in the minds of about 5% of our primary school children. How it comes into existence and what function(s) it serves, if any, are unknown. A major attack on these problems requires large numbers of eidetic children. Individual testing is very expensive in time and money; thus a simple screening procedure to find those most likely to have eidetic abilities is highly desirable. Part of our research effort has been devoted to this problem, and preliminary results suggest that the solution may be easier than was once thought.

Thought Imagery

In discussing afterimagery and eidetic imagery, it has been possible to specify both the sufficient conditions for their arousal and the major phenomenal characteristics of the resulting images. We know little of the subject characteristics that mediate these two events. Even afterimages are not guaranteed by the nature of the stimulus. Some people immediately see their visual afterimages; others do not. Woodworth (1938, p. 557) noted that "Many students require some practice before seeing the afterimage, because it is one of those subjective phenomena which our whole practical life leads us to disregard." Practice appears to reduce the time, in seconds, that it takes to become aware of afterimages (Reinhold, 1957). Knowing what to attend to and learning to attend to it, when it is present, may be the critical subject conditions that intervene between the stimulus picture and the experiential response of seeing an afterimage. No comparable information is available on eidetikers.

If all the criteria necessary for the clear identification and differentiation of eidetic images and afterimages are difficult to establish, the task of distinguishing thought imagery from these, and later from imagination imagery, is even more so. Certainly, thought imagery can be defined negatively; it is not the type of imagery that can be experienced after fixating a black square or scanning a high contrast picture for 30 seconds, but can we do better than that?

In 1969 I attempted a rather lame description of this type of imagery as "the common and relatively familiar imagery of everyday life. It may accompany the recall of events from the past, the ongoing thought processes of the present or the anticipatory actions and events of the future. Though it may occur as a spontaneous accompaniment to much everyday thought of this kind it is far more amenable to voluntary control than all other forms of imagery" (Richardson, 1969, p. 43).

Because this description embraces more than images of remembered events, the term "thought imagery" (Holt, 1972) is now considered a more apt name than "memory imagery." This type of imagery varies considerably in vividness and controllability, both from person to person and perhaps within the same person from day to day. Although test–retest correlations on measures of voluntarily produced thought imagery are adequate (White et al., 1977), they are not so high that genuine fluctuations might not exist in addition to random errors introduced by the relative elasticity of some items.

Although some people can apparently project their thought images onto an external surface, most spontaneously occurring thought imagery appears to be indefinitely localized. A few people claim to have exceptional vividness and clarity of thought images, but for the great majority of people the contents of this type lack the compelling "thereness" of perceptual contents or of the contents observable in afterimagery and eidetic imagery. Thought images are more often like hazy etchings, often incomplete and easily dissolved if attention is fixed on them for very long.

Spontaneous thought imagery emerges into awareness under statable conditions, and it is with these conditions that we begin. This description is followed by a consideration of voluntary thought imagery and the functions that it may serve.

Spontaneous Thought Imagery

Among the first psychologists to provide a detailed discussion of conditions associated with the emergence of spontaneous thought images was Fox (1914). His analysis suggested that, whenever goal-directed thought is blocked or becomes confused and uncertain, imagery will be aroused that may facilitate a solution.

Sheehan and Lewis (1974) attempted to demonstrate the truth of this analysis by means of an experiment. As it is the only one of its kind, it is described in detail. The basic task required a set of 50 short sentences to be rated for familiarity. Each sentence contained either two abstract or two concrete nouns. Noun pairs had been selected beforehand so that each member of the pair could be equated, as far as possible, on vividness (25 abstract noun pairs and 25 concrete noun pairs), meaningfulness, and frequency of occurrence in written English. The second word in each pair was an obvious one in relation to the first, for example, admiral—ship, butterfly—insect, ability—aptitude. However, in constructing the short sentences to be rated for familiarity, it was so arranged that the two nouns that matched on vividness (i.e., both were concrete or both were abstract) were always nonobvious in relation to each other, for instance, admiral—meat, butterfly—tool, ability—hostility.

Three groups of subjects rated the sentences for "familiarity" without this attribute receiving any more detailed definition. Members of the first group (minimum expectation) were told, in addition, that the purpose of the experiment was to study individual differences in the ratings. Those in the second group (medium expectation) were told that learning was of interest to the investigators, but no other details were given. Finally, the members of the third group (maximum expectancy) were told, specifically, to remember each sentence. The purpose of these different instructional sets was to achieve different degrees of confusion or uncertainty in the minds of those taking part. As it turned out, this manipulation was unsuccessful.

After all 50 sentences had been rated for familiarity, the members of each group were given the first recall task. This consisted of the presentation of 14 nouns, with the request that its "obvious" response partner (noun) should be recalled and announced within the 8 seconds allowed. As all nouns from the original matched lists had appeared in one or other of the sentences, the request to recall the "obvious" noun match provided a hint that these previously seen words were to be used as the pool from which to draw.

An example will help to clarify the nature of this recall task. During the first stage of the experiment a participant might have seen sentences like the following: "There is the butterfly, here is the tool" and "There is the chair, here is the insect." If the noun "butterfly" were now given during the recall task, the "obvious" response expected was the noun "insect." However, the task is left deliberately vague to enhance the feeling of confusion and uncertainty.

After each response on the first recall test, ratings on a 7-point confusion scale were requested, in which "1" represented a feeling of extreme confusion and uncertainty while attempting recall, and "7" represented a feeling of extreme certainty. At the completion of all 14 items of this recall test, participants were asked whether they had been aware of any imagery while attempting to recall any of the "obvious" noun responses and, if so, to rate its average level of vividness on a 7-point scale. A second recall test followed this rating; it contained the same set of stimulus nouns as before. Again, the participants were asked about the presence of imagery and required to rate its vividness.

Because the second recall test was identical with the first, its familiarity should have made it less confusing. As a result, there should have been fewer reports of imagery and lower ratings on vividness. These two recall tasks were intended as a second, and as it turned out, successful, attempt to manipulate the amount of uncertainty or confusion experienced.

Instructions during the initial "learning" part of the experiment had no effect on the results, but in the recall part, confusion was significantly greater on trial one than on trial two for both abstract and concrete nouns. Again, significantly more imagery that was reported to be significantly more vivid was aroused on the first more confusing trial than on the second, less confusing trial.

As predicted on the basis of Fox's (1914) results this study confirmed that the greater confusion (sense of uncertainly, bafflement, or frustration) that is produced in the course of a thought or action sequence, the more likely it is that imagery will be aroused and the more vivid it will be. That this study did not demonstrate the adaptive utility of the imagery evoked is probably a product of the experimental design. No attempt was made to sample the imagery content, and even if it had been attempted, the difficulty of classifying it as either relevant (potentially or actually adaptive) or irrelevant in relation to the extremely vague problem (i.e., finding the "obvious" response nouns) would have been very great.

Little research on the adaptive value of spontaneously occurring thought imagery has been undertaken, but one line of inquiry is worth pursuing. Studies by Sheehan (1972) have shown that the uncertainty and confusion produced for the person who is unexpectedly asked to recall something that he or she has not learned thoroughly may produce images of the learning situation that facilitates the reconstruction of at least some of the material required. The capacity to form vivid images gives greater benefit to the individual in the incidental learning situation and aids recovery of this material if unexpected recall is requested.

Voluntary Thought Imagery

Instructions from oneself or from another to form an image of something constitutes the basis of most self-report measures of imagery vividness (White et al., 1977) and of many behavioral treatment methods (Cautela, 1977). However, attempts to examine the functional value of this ability in relation to such cognitive processes as learning, recall, and problem solving have resulted in a somewhat confused research literature (Ernest, 1977). In contrast to this confusion is the general agreement of researchers who have examined the role of voluntary thought imagery in relation to affective processes. Its effectiveness is well documented.

To the extent that one can construct *vivid* imagery and *absorb* oneself into its content, consequences are likely to result that are remarkably similar to those that result from the actual stimulus situation. This belief has existed from antiquity (McMahon, 1976) but was not demonstrated experimentally until recent times. The first study to be described is one undertaken in our own laboratory (Richardson & Taylor, 1982).

A large sample of first-year undergraduates completed the Profile of Mood States (McNair et al., 1971) and the Imagination Inventory described earlier in this chapter. On the basis of their scores, four groups of subjects were formed. Two groups comprised subjects with vivid imagery but differing in mood (i.e., on the depression scale); the other two comprised subjects with weak imagery but differing in mood. When attending individually for the treatment stage, each subject was tested once again on the Profile of Mood States and was, in addition, timed while counting from 1 to 10 (Teasdale et al., 1980). Following the treatment in which those in the low mood groups were asked to imagine a series of self-selected "happy" events and those in the high mood group were asked to imagine a series of "sad" events, the original experiential and behavioral measures of mood were readministered. The results showed changes in mood in the predicted direction, but these changes were significantly greater for those subjects who had vivid imagery available to them.

The second study, by Ken White of Queensland University, serves to illustrate the subtlety of the effects that can be produced by utilizing vivid, voluntarily produced thought imagery. A preliminary experiment was conducted to establish whether men and women who believed they could control their autonomic responses could in fact control their salivation. Seven males and seven females were selected, all of whom had been practicing transcendental meditation for at least 9 months. The experimenter began by saying, "I am interested in seeing how much you can increase and decrease salivation at will." There followed a standard procedure used in all the subsequent experiments. Each person was asked to swallow, open the mouth for insertion of a preweighed dental swab under the tongue, and then to keep the mouth and jaws as still as possible. Instructions were then given according to a preestablished sequence to either increase or decrease the amount of saliva present in the mouth. Each trial lasted 30 seconds after which the swab was removed and placed in a sealed container for later weighing. The results were clear; a significant difference was obtained between the amount of saliva secreted under the "increase" and under the "decrease" instructions. A postexperimental inquiry showed that those who had personally relevant imagery (i.e., the strategy of imaging specific stimulus events) may have been successful in achieving differences in the amount salivated.

In the last and most important of the experiments reported, three groups of imagers (10 in each) were selected from a total of 289 university students who had completed the revised Betts test (QMI) of imagery vividness: 10 were vivid imagers; 10 were moderate; and 10 were weak. Each subject was presented with a list of 10 food substances and asked to rank them in order of preference from most liked to least liked. Each subject's first, fourth, seventh, and tenth food preference was used in that subject's particular series of imaging trials. The question of interest was whether Pavlov's law of strength (Luria, 1973) would be found to hold for the salivation responses produced to the images of each food substance. This law states that "strong, significant stimuli elicit strong responses and weak or insignificant stimuli elicit weak responses" (Luria, 1975, p. 75).

The results were highly significant for the vivid imagers who showed a progressively reduced amount of saliva in response to the four substances imaged. Thus for the vivid imagers, who could produce imaged situations most nearly like perceived situations, the law of strength was clearly confirmed. The results for the moderate imagers were significant, although the slope of the line relating imaged stimuli and responses was less steep; for the weak imagers, the slope was almost flat and not statistically significant.

If voluntarily produced vivid thought imagery can mediate reactions of this kind, its potential for understanding and treating psychosomatic complaints needs to be more fully explored. Regardless of the purpose for which imagery is used, however, the evidence suggests that *vividness* is one of its essential attributes. What happens to those whose imagery is weak? Are they to be denied the possibility of benefitting from this form of treatment?

The implication of these questions is another question. Is it possible to train a weak imager to become a vivid imager and then demonstrate that he functions like a vivid imager? Within the early behavior therapy tradition this question was theoretically crucial (Lazarus, 1964), and some untested but interesting suggestions were advanced by Laura Phillips (1971) to improve both the vividness and controllability of a client's imagery. Other procedures emphasizing deep relaxation and concentration exercises have been suggested from the more humanistic side of psychology by Samuels and Samuels (1975), but again, no evidence of improvement is provided.

The first attempt to check on the effectiveness of a training program is provided in an unpublished study by the Queensland researchers Walsh et al. (1978). Three groups of six vivid and six weak imagers were formed on the basis of total scores on the revised Betts test. Each group met for a period of 20 minutes on four successive days. One group did nothing between the pretests (Betts test and salivation test) and the posttests (Betts test and salivation test). Another group focused its attention on the topic of imagery by discussing its therapeutic uses, but no training was attempted. Neither group changed significantly between the pre and the posttests.

On each occasion when the 12 members of the experimental group met, stimuli appropriate to one or other modality were described, and practice in imaging all the details that could be observed was undertaken. Visual, kinaesthetic, and auditory imaging was practiced on the first day, gustatory and olfactory on the second, tactile and organic on the third, and a composite imagery exercise involving all seven modalities on the fourth day. Homework exercises were given between meetings.

As might be expected, no change was found in the six vivid imagers. They had nowhere to go but down and in fact remained at the same level. The six weak imagers had nowhere to go but up, and this they did with surprising alacrity. Not only did they rate their imagery as significantly more vivid, which might mean no more than a response to the demand characteristics of the situation, but when asked to image their favorite food and the situation that provoked their greatest anxiety, they salivated in a way that was indistinguishable from those who were untrained (natural) vivid imagers. Much saliva was produced after imaging their favorite food, whereas very little saliva was produced after imaging an anxiety-creating situation.

Imagination Imagery

Spontaneously occurring thought imagery is usually a continually changing phenomenon. As we become aware of it under conditions of puzzlement or uncertainty, concrete sensorylike information is forced into the focus of our attention and provides us with the material from which deliberate choices can be made. It may be relatively vivid or weak, but it seldom seriously distracts us from the goings-on in our physical and social environment.

However, if the adaptive demands of the external world are reduced so that attention can be safely withdrawn from it, the characteristics of spontaneous thought imagery *may* change into the characteristics of imagination imagery. The phenomenal qualities of *novelty, substantiality,* and *color,* which have sometimes been used to discriminate imagination imagery from thought imagery (Richardson, 1969), may represent qualitative changes at some point in a series of quantitative changes.

As attention is further withdrawn from the external world of perceptual events, it may become increasingly attached to events in the inner imaginal world. If this dissociative shift is prolonged, we can become absorbed in the quasi-perceptual content that we find there. As we become increasingly resistant to external distractions and our absorption in imaginal events intensifies, the experience may take on new qualities.

The content of these more intense image experiences may be unexpected and apparently unconnected with any identifiable memories from one's personal past (i.e., novel); it may have the appearance of being physically present (i.e., substantiality); and it may be very detailed in texture and vividly colored.

The ease with which individuals become increasingly absorbed in their imaged content varies from person to person. It is likely that those who find it easiest are those who can become absorbed most easily in the events suggested to them by another (e.g., a hypnotist) or by themselves. Considerable evidence has accumulated to show that individual differences in the ability to become absorbed in imaginal content (fantasy) is closely associated with the ability to manifest phenomena, such as analgesia and hallucinations, which are traditionally connected with the concept of hypnosis (Barber & Wilson, 1979; Hilgard, 1970; Spanos & McPeake, 1975; Tellegen & Atkinson, 1974).

From Table 1.3 it can be seen that the scores obtained from people who most and least frequently experience naturally occurring hypnagogic images (a form of imagination imagery) are more highly correlated with measures of absorption in imaged events than with the ability to construct thought images voluntarily as measured by the revised Betts test. Thus frequency of hypnagogic experiences is correlated with the Tellegen and Atkinson (1974) measure of absorption (males, $r = .53$; females, $r = .55$) and with the Barber and Wilson (1979) imagination inventory measure of absorption (males, $r = .46$; females, $r = .53$). By contrast, the frequency of hypnagogic experiences correlates only poorly with the vividness of voluntarily produced thought imagery as measured by the revised Betts test. For the males, the highest correlation is 0.15; for females, it is 0.29. These latter correlations are both in relation to the visual modality. When total scores on the Betts test are used, the correlation drops to 0.06 for males and 0.17 for females.

The tentative conclusion to be drawn from these theoretical and empirical considerations is that spontaneous thought imagery and imagination imagery may be on a phenomenological continuum. As one becomes increasingly absorbed into one's inner world, quantitative (e.g., vividness) and qualitative (e.g., novelty) changes may occur in the contents of the imagery that arises.

As is suggested in a moment, absorption into one's inner world with its increased probability of becoming aware of imagination imagery can occur in the waking state as well as in the hypnagogic state and the dream state. Each of these three states can be indexed by its characteristic EEG trace (Foulkes et al., 1966), but the arousal of imagination images, as they have been defined here, has been in need of empirical demonstration for subjects placed in the waking state.

This demonstration has been provided by Foulkes and Fleisher (1975). In this EEG study employing 20 relaxed waking subjects lying on a bed for 45–60 minutes in a moderately illuminated room, 11 of them experienced spontaneous images of hallucinatory vividness, often with novel content and typically in color.

Attention must now be given to the stated condition of relaxation. Relaxation appears to facilitate the emergence of images into awareness. Although relaxation was not part of their theoretical explanation, Morgan and Bakan (1965), in a perceptual deprivation study, found that 11 of 18 subjects reported images when placed in a reclining position, compared with only three out of 18 when in the sitting position. Experiential and physiological evidence supports the commonsense expectation that lying down is more relaxing than sitting up (Segal & Glicksman, 1967).

We relax when we feel safe and secure, but perhaps the psychological importance of this is that attention is withdrawn from the external world and the quantity and quality of sensory input is reduced. However, as relaxation deepens, sleep is likely to intervene and at some time dream images will occur, but often without any conscious awareness that we are having them. In the hypnagogic and waking state a high level of cognitive arousal maintains an alert awareness of the I/Me distinction. One can be aware that one is experiencing an image.

Many superficially different stimulus conditions can create these two fundamental conditions of alertness and attention to inner events. Although they are not sufficient for an awareness of imagination images to take place, they appear to facilitate the process of becoming aware. These superficially different stimulus conditions include the normal hypnagogic state that exists between waking and sleeping (Schachter, 1976), perceptual isolation (Zubek, 1969), hallucinogenic drugs (Masters & Houston, 1967), photic stimulation (Freedman & Marks, 1965), pulse current stimulation (Knoll & Kugler, 1964), sleep deprivation (Bliss & Clark, 1962), meditation (Pinard, 1957), and crystal gazing (McKellar, 1977). All these conditions reduce the amount of varied sensory input yet allow, or in some instances promote, a high level of cognitive arousal. Hallucinogenic drugs, for example, are said to be both "sensory poisons and diencephalic stimulants" (West, 1962).

The range of sensory and perceptlike content evoked by these stimulus conditions extends from meaningless patches and flashes of colored light through geometric shapes, to faces, objects, and integrated scenes. When integrated scenes occur singly or in the continuous form of fantasy, the content is most likely to depend on current motivational–affective states. As Klinger (1971, p. 356) has suggested, "the content of fantasy reflects current concerns . . . fantasy processes constitute a continuous cycling of . . . elements that are most likely to be relevant to the individual's life situation. In the course of fantasy, a person works over, recombines and sometimes reorganizes the information creatively. Fantasy thus serves as a channel for performing preparatory work fortuitously between emergencies."

This view of the function of fantasy may be appled to night dreams (Faraday, 1972) as well as daydreams and also to those, typically briefer, hypnagogic and hypnopompic states between waking and sleeping. These latter states are often associated with a personally relevant type of image called *autosymbolic* by Herbert Silberer (1909). In one of my own experiences of this kind I saw a vividly colored rocket (like a firework). It appeared ready for take off but almost immediately I saw that it was carved out of solid wood and had no hope of going anywhere. The personal meaning of this vision was instantly apparent. It was emblematic of an idea that had been in my thoughts for some time. In that moment I knew, without any doubts, that the idea was not going to work—it was not going to get off the ground.

Imagination images often seem to serve as the vehicle by which understanding occurs. Sometimes this understanding is a genuine creative insight following a long period of preparation and incubation. Indeed, this insight corresponds to the illumination stage of problem solving described by Graham Wallis (1926). In other real-life situations imagination images may emerge into awareness with rather less useful consequences. Holt (1964, p. 257) gives the following examples, "Radar operators who have to monitor a scope for long periods, long distance truck drivers in night runs over turnpikes . . . jet pilots flying straight and level at high altitudes; operators of snow cats and other such vehicles of polar exploration, when surrounded by snow storms—all of these persons have been troubled by the emergence into consciousness of vivid imagery, largely visual but often kinaesthetic or auditory, which they may take momentarily for reality."

These imagery experiences occurring in real-life situations might be explained, once again, by reference to the reduction in varied sensory input (producing monotony) while in a general state of cognitive arousal (alertness). As might be expected, the same set of stimulus conditions affect different people in different ways. For example, it has been shown that some people will experience vivid imagination images after only 10 minutes of sensory isolation (Ziskind & Augsburg, 1962), whereas others fail to experience any images after isolation periods as long as 2 weeks (Zubek et al., 1963).

Those who fail to experience imagination images under the facilitating conditions just described may be employing defensive strategies that inhibit awareness (Foulkes et al., 1966), whereas those who do experience them may be more interested in and attentive to internal happenings. For example, Holt and Goldberger (1959), replicated by Goldberger and Holt (1961), describe those who experienced imagination imagery in their perceptual isolation experiments as having more "intellectual flexibility and emotional freedom." Again, in a photic stimulation study by Freedman and Marks (1965) those who experienced most imagery were described as having "an artistic, sensitive and creative self concept."

As noted earlier in this chapter, it is probable that a stream of noticeable events is always present. Whether these events are actually noticed depends on the presence of appropriate facilitating conditions and a disposition to attend to them when their salience is increased.

CONCLUSIONS

During the history of psychology, questions about cognitive states and processes have changed, sometimes in dramatic and sometimes in more subtle ways, but the term "imagery" has persisted throughout. On some occasions this ubiquitous term has been used for purposes of description; on others, for purposes of explanation; and on others again, for both purposes. More specifically, imagery has referred to either a class of inferred cognitive constructs and processes or a class of more or less perceptlike experience.

Perhaps the first conclusion to be drawn from these historical facts is that they must become more salient in the minds of all those engaged in the field of imagery studies. Conceptually and operationally, these two broad groups of meanings must be clearly separated in our theorizing and research. It must never be assumed that the two usages of the word "imagery" have any overlap of any kind. If a relationship between imagery defined in these two ways can ever be justified theoretically, it must be confirmed empirically. Only confusion can result from a failure to recognize this distinction.

A second conclusion might be that no group of psychologists can claim an exclusive right to use of the term "imagery." It is not a registered brand name or a copyrighted trademark. It can be insisted only that users impose on themselves an obligation to make their own usages clear and not allow other usages to become unwittingly fused or confused with them. It has been the main aim of this chapter to assist in this process of clarification.

REFERENCES

Ahsen, A. Eidetics: An overview. *Journal of Mental Imagery*, 1977, **1**, 5–38.

Ahsen, A. Eidetics: Redefinition of the ghost and its clinical application. *Behavioral and Brain Sciences*, 1979, **2**, 594–596.

Allport, G. W. Eidetic imagery. *British Journal of Psychology*, 1924, **15**, 99–120.

Anderson, J. R., & Bower, G. H. *Human associative memory*. Washington, D.C.: Winston, 1973.

Atkinson, R. C., & Raugh, M. R. An application of the mnemonic keyword method to the acquisition of a Russian vocabulary. *Journal of Experimental Psychology: Human Learning and Memory,* 1975, **104,** 126–133.

Barber, T. X., & Wilson, S. C. Guided imagining and hypnosis: Theoretical and empirical overlap and convergence in a new creative imagination scale. In A. A. Sheikh and J. T. Shaffer (Eds.), *The potential of fantasy and imagination.* New York: Brandon House, 1979.

Barratt, P. E. Imagery and thinking. *Australian Journal of Psychology,* 1953, **5,** 154–164.

Betts, G. H. *The distribution and functions of mental imagery.* New York: Teachers College, Columbia University, 1909.

Bliss, E. L., & Clark, L. D. Visual hallucinations. In L. J. West (Ed.), *Hallucinations.* New York: Grune and Stratton, 1962.

Boring, E. G. *Sensation and perception in the history of experimental psychology.* New York: Appleton, 1942.

Brewer, W. F. The problem of meaning and the interrelations of the higher mental processes. In W. B. Weimer and D. S. Palermo (Eds.), *Cognition and the symbolic processes.* New York: Wiley, 1974.

Brown, J. L. After images. In C. H. Graham (Ed.), *Vision and visual perception.* New York: Wiley, 1965.

Bugelski, B. R. Imagery and verbal behavior. *Journal of Mental Imagery,* 1977, **1,** 39–52.

Cautela, J. R. Covert conditioning: Assumptions and procedures. *Journal of Mental Imagery,* 1977, **1,** 53–64.

Cooper, L. A., & Shepard, R. N. Mental transformation in the identification of left and right hands. *Journal of Experimental Psychology: Human Perception and Performance,* 1975, **104,** 48–56.

Danaher, B. G., & Thoresen, C. E. Imagery assessment by self-report and behavioral measures. *Behavior Research and Therapy,* 1972, **10,** 131–138.

Di Vesta, F. I., Ingersoll, G., & Sunshine, P. A factor analysis of imagery tests. *Journal of Verbal Learning and Verbal Behavior,* 1971, **10,** 471–479.

El Koussy, A. A. II. An investigation into the factors in tests involving the visual perception of space. *British Journal of Psychology Monograph Supplement,* 1935, No. 20.

Ernest, C. H. Imagery ability and cognition: A critical review. *Journal of Mental Imagery,* 1977, **1,** 181–216.

Ernest, C. H., & Paivio, A. Imagery and verbal associative latencies as a function of imagery ability. *Canadian Journal of Psychology,* 1971, **25,** 83–90.

Evans, J. St. B. T. Thinking: Experiential and information approaches. In G. Claxton (Ed.), *Cognitive psychology: New directions.* London: Routledge and Kegan Paul, 1980.

Faraday, A. *Dream power.* London: Pan, 1972.

Fernald, M. R. The diagnosis of mental imagery. *Psychological Review Monograph Supplement,* 1912, **14,** No. 58.

Foulkes, D., & Fleisher, S. Mental activity in relaxed wakefulness. *Journal of Abnormal Psychology,* 1975, **84,** 66–75.

Foulkes, D., Spear, P. S., & Symonds, J. D. Individual differences in mental activity at sleep onset. *Journal of Abnormal Psychology,* 1976, **71,** 280–286.

Fox, C. The conditions which arouse mental images in thought. *British Journal of Psychology,* 1914, **6,** 420–431.

Freedman, S. J., & Marks, P. A. Visual imagery produced by rhythmic photic stimulation: Personality correlates and phenomenology. *British Journal of Psychology,* 1965, **56,** 95–112.

Freedman, S. J., Grunebaum, H. V., Stare, F. A., & Greenblatt, M. Imagery in sensory deprivation. In L. J. West (Ed.), *Hallucinations.* New York: Grune and Stratton, 1962.

Goldberger, L., & Holt, R. R. *A comparison of isolation effects and their personality correlates in two divergent samples.* A.S.D. Technical Report 61-417. Wright-Patterson Air Force Base, Ohio.

Griffiths, C. H. Individual differences in imagery. *Psychological Monographs,* 1927, **37,** Whole No. 172.

Haber, R. N. Twenty years of haunting eidetic imagery: Where's the ghost? *Behavioral and Brain Sciences,* 1979, **2,** 583–629.

Haber, R. N., & Haber, R. B. Eidetic imagery: I. Frequency. *Perceptual and Motor Skills,* 1964, **19,** 131–138.

Hanawalt, N. G. Recurrent images: New instances and a summary of the older ones. *American Journal of Psychology,* 1954, **67,** 170–174.

Hilgard, J. R. *Personality and hypnosis.* Chicago: University of Chicago Press, 1970.

Hiscock, M., & Cohen, D. B. Visual imagery and dream recall. *Journal of Research in Personality,* 1973, **7,** 179–188.

Hollenberg, C. K. Functions of visual imagery in the learning and concept formation of children. *Child Development,* 1970, **41,** 1003–1015.

Holt, R. R. Imagery: The return of the ostracized. *American Psychologist,* 1964, **19,** 254–264.

Holt, R. R. On the nature and generality of mental imagery. In P. W. Sheehan (Ed.), *The function and nature of imagery.* New York: Academic Press, 1972.

Holt, R. R., & Goldberger, L. *Personological correlates of reactions to perceptual isolation.* WADC Technical Report 59-753. Wright-Patterson Air Force Base, Ohio, 1959.

Humphrey, G. *Thinking: An introduction to its experimental psychology.* London: Methuen, 1951.

Jordan, C. S. Mental imagery and psychotherapy: European Approaches. In A. A. Sheikh and J. T. Shaffer (Eds.), *The potential of fantasy and imagination.* New York: Brandon House, 1979.

Kagan, J., & Havemann, E. *Psychology: An introduction* (2nd ed.). New York: Harcourt, 1972.

Klinger, E. *Structure and functions of fantasy.* New York: Wiley, 1971.

Klüver, H. An experimental study of the eidetic type. *Genetic Psychology Monographs,* 1926, **1,** 70–230.

Knoll, M., & Kugler, J. Pulse current analysis of elementary visual hallucinations by coincidence circuits in the brain. *International Conference on Microwaves,*

Circuit Theory, Information Theory, Part 2, Tokyo, Japan, 1964.

Kosslyn, S. M. Scanning visual images: Some structural implications. *Perception and Psychophysics*, 1973, **14**, 90–94.

Kosslyn, S. M., Pinker, S., Smith, G. E., & Shwartz, S. P. On the demystification of mental imagery. *Behavioral and Brain Sciences*, 1979, **2**, 535–581.

Krantz, D. L. The Baldwin-Titchener controversy: A case study in the functioning and malfunctioning of schools. In D. L. Krantz (Ed.), *Schools of psychology*. New York: Appleton, 1969.

Lazarus, A. A. Crucial procedural factors in desensitization therapy. *Behavior Research and Therapy*, 1964, **2**, 65–70.

Leuner, H. Guided affective imagery: An account of its development. *Journal of Mental Imagery*, 1977, **1**, 73–92.

Lumsden, J. *The structure of immediate memory*. Unpublished Ph.D. thesis, University of Western Australia, 1965.

Luria, A. R. The qualitative assessment of levels of wakefulness. *Soviet Psychology*, 1973, **11**, 73–84.

Masters, R. E. L., & Houston, J. *The varieties of psychedelic experience*. London: Anthony Blond, 1967.

McBain, W. N. Imagery and suggestibility: A test of the Arnold hypothesis. *Journal of Abnormal and Social Psychology*, 1954, **49**, 36–44.

McKellar, P. Autonomy, imagery and dissociation. *Journal of Mental Imagery*, 1977, **1**, 93–108.

McKellar, P. Between wakefulness and sleep: Hypnagogic fantasy. In A. A. Sheikh and J. T. Shaffer (Eds.), *The potential of fantasy and imagination*. New York: Brandon House, 1979.

McMahon, C. E. The role of imagination in the disease process: Pre-Cartesian history. *Psychological Medicine*, 1976, **6**, 179–184.

McNair, D. M., Lorr, M., & Droppleman, L. F. Profile of mood states (manual). *Educational and Industrial Testing Service*. San Diego, Cal., 1971.

Michael, W. B. The nature of space and visualization abilities: Some recent findings based on factor analysis studies. *Transactions of the New York Academy of Sciences*, 1949, Series 2, **11**, 275–281.

Miller, G. A., Galanter, E., & Pribram, K. *Plans and the structure of behavior*. New York: Holt, 1960.

Morgan, R. F., & Bakan, P. Sensory deprivation hallucinations and other sleep behavior as a function of position, method of report, and anxiety. *Perceptual and Motor Skills*, 1965, **20**, 19–25.

Morsh, J. E., & Abbott, H. D. An investigation of after-images. *Journal of Comparative Psychology*, 1945, **38**, 47–63.

Mowrer, O. H. *Learning and the symbolic processes*. New York: Wiley, 1960.

Neisser, U. Changing conceptions of imagery. In P. W. Sheehan (Ed.), *The function and nature of imagery*. New York: Academic Press, 1972.

Paivio, A. On the functional significance of imagery. *Psychological Bulletin*, 1970, **73**, 385–392.

Paivio, A. *Imagery and verbal processes*. New York: Holt, 1971.

Paivio, A. A theoretical analysis of the role of imagery in learning and memory. In P. W. Sheehan (Ed.), *The function and nature of imagery*. New York: Academic Press, 1972.

Paivio, A., & Cohen, M. Eidetic imagery and cognitive abilities. *Journal of Mental Imagery*, 1979, **3**, 53–64.

Perky, C. W. An experimental study of imagination. *American Journal of Psychology*, 1910, **21**, 422–452.

Phillips, L. W. Training of sensory and imaginal responses in behavior therapy. In R. D. Rubin, H. Fensterheim, A. A. Lazarus, & C. M. Franks (Eds.), *Advances in behavior therapy*. New York: Academic Press, 1971.

Phillips, R. J., & Rawles, R. E. Recognition of upright and inverted faces: A correlational study. *Perception*, 1979, **8**, 577–583.

Pinard, W. J. Spontaneous imagery: Its nature, therapeutic value and effect on personality structure. *Boston University Graduate Journal*, 1957, **5**, 150–153.

Pope, K. S., & Singer, J. L. (Eds.) *The stream of consciousness; Scientific investigations into the flow of human experience*. New York: Plenum, 1978.

Pylyshyn, Z. W. What the mind's eye tells the mind's brain: A critique of mental imagery. *Psychological Bulletin*, 1973, **80**, 1–24.

Pylyshyn, Z. W. Imagery theory: Not mysterious—just wrong. *Behavioral and Brain Sciences*, 1979, **2**, 535–581.

Reinhold, D. B. Effect of training on perception of after-images. *Perceptual and Motor Skills*, 1957, **7**, 198.

Richardson, A. Has mental practice any relevance to physiotherapy? *Physiotherapy*, 1964, **50**, 148–151.

Richardson, A. The place of subjective experience in contemporary psychology. *British Journal of Psychology*, 1965, **56**, 223–232.

Richardson, A. Mental practice: A review and discussion. (1) *Research Quarterly*, 1967, **38**, 95–107.

Richardson, A. Mental practice: A review and discussion. (2) *Research Quarterly*, 1967a, **38**, 263–273.

Richardson, A. *Mental imagery*. London: Routledge and Kegal Paul, 1969.

Richardson, A. Voluntary control of the memory image. In P. W. Sheehan (Ed.), *The function and nature of imagery*. New York: Academic Press, 1972.

Richardson, A. The meaning and measurement of memory imagery. *British Journal of Psychology*, 1977, **68**, 29–43.

Richardson, A. Verbalizer–visualizer: A cognitive style dimension. *Journal of Mental Imagery*, 1977a, **1**, 109–126.

Richardson, A. Conscious and non-conscious imagery. *Behavioral and Brain Sciences*, 1979, **2**, 563–564.

Richardson, A. Dream recall frequency and vividness of visual imagery. *Journal of Mental Imagery*, 1979a, **3**, 65–72.

Richardson, A. *The experiential dimension of psychology*. Unpublished book manuscript, 1980.

Richardson, A., & Taylor, C. Vividness of mental imagery and self-induced mood change. *British Journal of Clinical Psychology*, 1982, 21, 111-117

Richardson, J. T. E. Procedures for investigating imagery and the distinction between primary and secondary memory. *British Journal of Psychology*, 1976, **67**, 487–500.

Samuels, M., & Samuels, N. *Seeing with the mind's eye*. New York: Random House, 1975.

Sarbin, T. R. Imagining as muted role-taking: A historical–linguistic analysis. In P. W. Sheehan (Ed.), *The function and nature of imagery*. New York: Academic Press, 1972.

Schacter, D. L. The hypnagogic state: A critical review of the literature. *Psychological Bulletin*, 1976, **83**, 452–481.

Schachter, D. L., & Crovitz, H. F. "Falling" while falling asleep: Sex differences. *Perceptual and Motor Skills*, 1977, **44**, 656.

Schaub, A. de Vries On the intensity of images. *American Journal of Psychology*, 1911, **22**, 346–368.

Segal, S. J., & Glicksman, M. Relaxation and the Perky effect: The influence of body position on judgments of imagery. *American Journal of Psychology*, 1967, **80**, 257–262.

Shaver, P., Pierson, L., & Lang, S. Converging evidence for the functional significance of imagery in problem solving. *Cognition*, 1974, **3**, 359–375.

Sheehan, P. W. A shortened form of Betts' questionnaire upon mental imagery. *Journal of Clinical Psychology*, 1967, **23**, 386–389.

Sheehan, P. W. A functional analysis of the role of visual imagery in unexpected recall. In P. W. Sheehan (Ed.), *The function and nature of imagery*. New York: Academic Press, 1972.

Sheehan, P. W., & Lewis, S. E. Subjects' reports of confusion in consciousness and the arousal of imagery. *Perceptual and Motor Skills*, 1974, **38**, 731–734.

Sheehan, P. W., & Neisser, U. Some variables affecting the vividness of imagery in recall. *British Journal of Psychology*, 1969, **60**, 71–80.

Sheikh, A. A., & Panagiotou, N. Use of mental imagery in psychotherapy: A critical review. *Perceptual and Motor Skills*, 1975, **41**, 555–585.

Shepard, R. N. The mental image. *American Psychologist*, 1978, **33**, 125–137.

Shepard, R. N., & Metzler, J. Mental rotation of three-dimensional objects. *Science*, 1971, **171**, 701–703.

Silberer, H. (1909). Report on a method of eliciting and observing certain symbolic hallucination phenomena. In D. Rapaport (Ed.), *Organization and pathology of thought*. New York: Columbia University Press, 1951.

Spanos, N. P., & McPeake, J. D. The effects of involvement in everyday imaginative activities and attitudes toward hypnosis on hypnotic suggestibility. *Journal of Personality and Social Psychology*, 1975, **31**, 594–598.

Start, K. B., & Richardson, A. Imagery and mental practice. *British Journal of Educational Psychology*, 1964, **34**, 280–284.

Stromeyer, C. F., & Psotka, J. The detailed texture of eidetic images. *Nature*, 1970, **225**, 347–349.

Teasdale, J. D., Fogarty, S. J., & Williams, J. M. G. Speech rate as a measure of short-term variation in depression. *British Journal of Social and Clinical Psychology*, 1980, **19**, 271–278.

Tellegen, A., & Atkinson, G. Openness to absorbing and self-altering experiences ("absorption"), a trait related to hypnotic susceptibility. *Journal of Abnormal Psychology,* 1979, **83,** 268–277.

Torrance, E. P., Reynolds, C. R., Riegel, T., & Ball, O. Your style of learning and thinking: Preliminary norms, abbreviated technical notes, scoring keys, and selected references. *Gifted Child Quarterly,* 1977, **21,** 563–573.

Wallis, G. *The art of thought.* New York: Harcourt, 1926.

Walsh, F. J., White, K. D., & Ashton, R. *Imagery training: Development of a procedure and its evaluation.* Unpublished research report, Department of Psychology, University of Queensland, 1978.

West, L. J. A general theory of hallucinations and dreams. In L. J. West (Ed.), *Hallucinations.* New York: Grune and Stratton, 1962.

White, K., Sheehan, P. W., & Ashton, R. Imagery assessment: A survey of self-report measures. *Journal of Mental Imagery,* 1977, **1,** 145–170.

Woodworth, R. S. Imageless thought. *Journal of Philosophy, Psychology and Scientific Methods,* 1906, **3,** 701–708.

Woodworth, R. S. *Experimental psychology.* New York: Macmillan, 1938.

Yuille, J. C., & Catchpole, M. J. The role of imagery in models of cognition. *Journal of Mental Imagery,* 1977, **1,** 171–180.

Ziskind, E., & Augsburg, T. Hallucinations in sensory deprivation—method or madness. *Science,* 1962, **137,** 992–993.

Zubek, J. P. *Sensory deprivation: Fifteen years of research.* New York: Appleton, 1969.

Zubek, J. P., Welch, G., & Saunders, M. G. Electroencephalographic changes during and after 14 days of perceptual deprivation. *Science,* 1963, **139,** 490–492.

CHAPTER 2

Theories of Mental Imagery

STEVEN PINKER AND STEPHEN M. KOSSLYN

The notion of a "theory of mental imagery" strikes many people as peculiar. To some, it is obvious that images are simply pictures in the head. To others, it is obvious that the term really does not refer to anything—talk of images is like talk of Pete in the expression "For Pete's sake"; it is just a figure of speech. But images clearly cannot be actual pictures in the head. Who would look at them? And it seems perverse to claim that the vast majority of people who report pictorial images are in fact either mistaken or lying. If images are not actual pictures, however, what can they be? Given the difficulty of studying imagery scientifically and the differences in preconceptions held by different researchers, it is no surprise that there are many distinct answers to this question. It is the purpose of this chapter to outline the general conceptions of imagery that have been developed to date. It is of considerable interest that many of these theories—those explaining thought processes as formal symbol-manipulating operations—are the first of their kind, ever. A genuinely new idea is a rare event in the history of thought, and thus we spend proportionally more time on these newest developments. Although it is beyond the scope of this chapter to review the large empirical literature that bears on the theories, occasionally we point out the outstanding strengths or weaknesses of a particular view with respect to specific findings.

Our review is organized into two sections: (1) discussion of approaches outlined before 1975 and (2) presentation of approaches outlined after that date. This division also corresponds roughly with an expository difference. Since the older theories are reviewed in some detail elsewhere (Kosslyn, 1980; Paivio, 1971), they are presented here only in bare outline [this also applies to the newer array and artifact theories; see Kosslyn, (1981) and Kosslyn et al. (1979)]. On the other hand, most of the newer theories (Shepard, Finke, Trehub, and Hinton) have not yet been discussed in print at length; they will receive a more generous treatment but, due to limitations

---

The preparation of this chapter was supported by NSF grants BNS 80-24337 and 82-16546 to Steven Pinker and BNS 79-12418 to Stephen Kosslyn. We thank Jeannette Hanlon for her assistance.

of space, a briefer one than they deserve. Within each section the reader may also discern a division between theorists that we may call, following Dennet (1980), *iconophiles* (those attributing special properties to mental imagery representations and giving the reported spatial nature of images some important theoretical status) and the *iconophobes* (those who believe that images are mentally represented in the same way as other forms of thought, with no special status accorded to some intrinsic "spatial" or "pictorial" nature).

THEORIES AND MODELS

All cognitive theories purport to describe the way the brain functions when tasks in a given domain are carried out. The reason a theory is "cognitive" rather than "physiological" hinges on the level of abstraction of this description: cognitive theories describe function roughly on the level one would use to describe a computer algorithm, which, of course, one can do even in total ignorance of the physical makeup of the computer. Physiological theories, on the other hand, describe the actual operation of brain cells. In both cases, however, data are explained by reference to a hypothetical sequence of events in the brain.

It is important to begin by distinguishing between theories and models. A *theory* is an unambiguous statement of (1) the entities in a system and (2) the lawlike relations among them. In cognitive theories, the entities are information structures and rules, which can be combined in processing sequences determined by a set of principles describing the putative "architecture" of the "mental computer." In physiological theories the entities are cells, or populations of cells, which are combined in accordance with principles of synaptic transmission and plasticity. In either case a *specific* theory is intended only to account for a particular task or experimental preparation, whereas a *general* theory is intended to account for performance in all tasks in a given domain (such as language, reasoning, or in our case, imagery).

There often is more than one way of stating a theory, using different kinds of logical or mathematical notation, which makes it more or less easy for the theorist to perform particular computations of the theory's consequences. This last point is important insofar as the different expressions of a theory do not constitute different theories: as long as the same entities are being described and the same laws of combination are being considered, the theory itself is the same. In cases in which two statements are not empirically distinguishable by any conceivable test under any circumstances, we thus have, ipso facto, two notational variants of the same theory.

In contrast to a theory, a *model,* such as a running computer simulation, set of equations, or physical analogue, is not unambiguous. Models contain three kinds of properties (Hesse, 1963): theory-relevant ones are in fact specified by the theory; theory-irrelevant ones are there simply to flesh out the model to a sufficient degree that it can actually generate simulations of behavior and are not meant to be taken seriously in their own right; and theory-neutral properties are not clearly in either of the other two categories. For example, in a computer model the functions carried out by particular subroutines may be theory relevant but the details of how procedures within the subroutines work may be theory irrelevant (being a consequence of properties of the particular programming language and the hardware available to the theorist); and the fact that the program is executed serially may be theory neutral (if one has no reason to expect serial or parallel processing in the brain when it performs tasks in the domain of the theory). It is useful to distinguish between two kinds of model: specific and general. Specific models are designed to account for data in one particular task or experimental paradigm. Sternberg's (1966) model of how people verify whether a probe digit is in a previously memorized list is a good example. General models are meant to account for data in an entire domain of tasks. Anderson and Bower's (1973) model of human associative memory is a good example of this sort of model. Importantly, general models embody the entire set of entities and lawlike principles posited by a general theory.

It is important to be as clear as possible about what sort of theoretical statement one is dealing with—general theory, specific theory, general model, or specific model. One reason for this is that one cannot use the same criteria of evaluation for the different kinds of statement. That is, what counts as a fair test of a theory (e.g., its ability to generate numerically precise predictions) is not necessarily fair for a general model (perhaps the number-generating parts are not meant to be theory relevant) or for a specific model (which may not even deal with the task at hand). In the ensuing discussion of conceptions of imagery, therefore, we attempt first to identify the kind of statement being made and end the discussion with an evaluation of its adequacy. But how should we evaluate the relative adequacies of different theories and models? Is this not in some ways like evaluating apples and oranges? Yes, it is—but apples and oranges can in fact be evaluated with respect to specific dimensions, such as their size, weight, and reflectance. Thus our next task must be to lay out some criteria that will cut across the different kinds of proposals.

Evaluation of Theories and Models

The problem of how to evaluate theories and models is not new, and we have gained considerable inspiration from Chomsky's (1965, 1967) concepts of alternative forms of adequacy for theories of syntax. These notions were used to develop ways of evaluating theories and models of on-line processing by Kosslyn (1980), and we are developing our current concepts from this beginning. It is useful to distinguish three kinds of adequacy: behavioral, process, and explanatory adequacy. The measure of each sort of adequacy varies according to whether one is dealing with a specific model, specific theory, general model, or general theory. Let us consider each in turn.

A *specific model* is designed to account for performance in a particular task, and it achieves behavioral adequacy if in fact it accounts for the input–output relationships and quantitative data patterns in that task. A specific model achieves process adequacy if it can account for patterns in the data by reference to a sequence of underlying processes. For example, Sternberg (1966) accounts for the additive effects of stimulus clarity and set size in a short-term recognition task by positing independent encoding and comparison stages. A specific model gains explanatory adequacy only by virtue of either a specific theory, general model, or general theory. That is, the explanatory adequacy hinges on an independent motivation for positing *those* operations in *that* order as opposed to logically possible alternatives. Inasmuch as the way one accounts for data using the specific model hinges on the model's theory-relevant properties, and those properties are clearly motivated by general principles posited by a theory or general model, the specific model can be said to have some degree of explanatory adequacy.

A *specific theory* attains behavioral and process adequacy in the same way as does a specific model. In this case, however, there is no question of which properties of the account are doing the work, given that there are no theory-irrelevant or theory-neutral properties to worry about. A specific theory gains explanatory adequacy only by virtue of a general theory. In a cognitive theory, the general theory specifies the kinds of structures and processes that can be invoked in processing data under given conditions, and it specifies the principles according to which such processing will proceed. These general constraints—in the ideal case—fully dictate the domain-relevant components of the specific theory of performance in a particular task. But it is rare that one has a complete general theory and, hence, all the principles necessary to dictate all the details of specific theories. Thus a specific theory will often include details that are filled in for that special case (and only when these details are taken seriously at the level of theory will one have a specific theory rather than a specific model). Hence the explanatory adequacy of a specific theory again rests on the independent motivation for its details, which are inherited from the claims inherent in the general theory.

Now let us consider *general models*. A general model is a particular instantiation, or embodiment, of a general theory. When given a particular input configuration, a general model will process that input in a determinate way. A description of the sequence of processing invoked by a particular stimulus is exactly equivalent to a description of a specific model for the task in which that stimulus is input. Thus one can regard general models as devices that generate specific models for the tasks within a given domain. A general model is behaviorally adequate if it can produce specific models for all the tasks in a domain and if these specific models are themselves behaviorally adequate. A general model attains process adequacy if the specific models it generates are themselves process adequate *and* if the relationships among the data patterns from different tasks can be understood by reference to shared components posited by the general model. That is, some tasks will recruit common structures and processes, and to the extent that these particular shared components have fixed properties (say, if a matching process always compared two digits more rapidly than two random forms), these properties should be apparent in each task. The explanatory adequacy of a general model is again determined by the degree to which its features are motivated by the claims of a general theory. To the extent that the theory-relevant properties really are motivated by general principles of a theory, the general model attains explanatory adequacy. It is worth noting that a major advantage of trying to develop general models is that one is forced to be consistent in explaining data from individual tasks. Thus, given that theories are often developed by first exploring models, if one attempts to develop *general* models, one will be forced to formulate principles of some generality within the theory, principles that will in fact extend over the entire domain of phenenomena at hand.

Finally, let us consider a general cognitive theory. The *general theory* attains behavioral and process adequacy just as does a general model, but it does so by producing specific theories (not specific models) for each task in the domain. A general cognitive theory attains explanatory adequacy from three possible sources. First, some of the structures and processes may be necessary in order to perform the requisite computations. Some kind of conditional branching process, for example, seems absolutely required for any kind of complex information processing. Second, some of the components may be a result of the physical organization of the brain. The organization of the brain could be a consequence of evolutionary pressures and/or structural principles that dictate how neurons can be interconnected. It is worth noting that even if evolutionary principles are responsible for the organization of some components of the brain, the computations that the brain is now performing are not necessarily those that were selected: the properties of the brain that allow it to do certain things at present could have been merely incidental concomitants of other properties that were in fact selected. The third source of explanatory adequacy is the impact of the environment. The environment can affect the brain, either directly (through drugs or induced hormonal reactions in the body) or by setting the stage for higher-order "chunking" when sets of processes are used in conjunction often. That is, if a given sequence of operations is used frequently, it is possible that that sequence can be "compiled" into a new, higher-order unit. Each of these properties is discussed at greater length in Chapter 5 of Kosslyn (1980).

In the remainder of this chapter we consider a number of classes of theories and models of imagery. We first classify each conception as to the type of formulation it is and after describing it, attempt to measure the adequacy of the formulation. The attempt to assess the adequacy of each conception serves two purposes: (1) it should serve to dispel any illusions that there is a theory that is "correct" at this point in time; and (2) more importantly, it should underline the respects in which current conceptions are in need of further development.

OLDER THEORIES

Paivio's and Bower's Dual-Code Theories

It has long been held that images are like "pictures in the head." No recent theorist has maintained the strong "first-order isomorphism" claim that images are literally pictures, but many have treated images metaphorically as if they were pictures. The foremost theorist in this vein today is Allan Paivio (1971). Paivio emphasizes that we have two kinds of codes in which to store information; pictorial and verbal. Paivio's operational definitions of imagery hinge in large part on contrasts with *verbal* representations, that is, memory traces for actual words in a particular language.

Images are thought to be concrete (i.e., they represent specific instances and are modality specific) and parallel, in contrast to verbal representations, which are abstract (can represent classes directly and are amodal) and sequential. Paivio's theory is very closely tied to the data, which bear primarily on the role of different materials in enhancing memory for lists of words and word pairs. Paivio has found that concrete words are remembered better than abstract words and that pictures are remembered better than either kind of word. These sorts of results are the main focus of his theory, and his invoking of image and verbal codes allows him to explain the results: concrete words and pictures are redundantly stored in image codes in addition to verbal ones, whereas abstract words can be stored only in the verbal code. Paivio clearly intends his views to be a general theory, but they do not cover a well-defined domain. That is, the views fail to address the bulk of work on the format, generation, inspection, and transformation of images (Kosslyn, 1980). Paivio cannot be faulted for this since most of this work came after his theory was formulated. But nevertheless, in terms of the data now available [see Kosslyn et al. (1981) for a brief overview], the theory falls woefully short of even attaining behavioral adequacy. Even for the tasks that are addressed by the theory, there is no attempt to specify the way they are actually performed. Thus the theory cannot attain process adequacy, let alone explanatory adequacy.

One other major theorist who falls into this camp is Bower (1972). Bower emphasizes that we can distinguish between *how* something looked and *what* it looked like. In the former case we have a quasi-pictorial representation, whereas in the latter we have something more akin to a verbal (or "propositional") representation. Memory images provide a kind of "direct contact'' with the appearance of a thing by essentially recreating the experience of seeing it; verbal or propositional representations do not evoke a perceptlike experience but convey information only about a thing's properties. The two sorts of information are stored in qualitatively different kinds of codes, which follow Paivio's distinction fairly closely. According to Bower, an image is evoked when ''central mechanisms are generating a (probably sequential) pattern of information which corresponds more or less to the structural information in the original perception.'' Further, there is ''structural isomorphism between the information presently available to us [in the image] and the information picked up from the stimulus event we are remembering'' [while it was occurring] (Bower, 1979, p. 58). These general ideas seem on the level of a theory proper. Unfortunately, most of our reservations about Paivio's views can also be applied here. However, Bower does attempt to build some measure of process adequacy into his theory. He hypothesizes that a ''common generative grammar'' may underlie production of images and verbal strings, and he describes how such a grammar might operate. These claims, however, are so sketchy that one cannot generate specific theories or models for any particular tasks solely on the basis of the theory.

Neisser's Percent-Analogy Theory

The traditional view of mental imagery that appears repeatedly over centuries of philosophy and psychology [see Chapter 11 in Kosslyn (1980)] is that images are percepts that arise from memory rather than from sensory input. The picture-in-the-head theories can be regarded as one particular species of this general view, but they are by no means the only ones. The theory of imagery one has, in this view, depends on one's theory of perception; and not all theories of perception posit picturelike perceptual representation. A good example of a nonpictorial percept-analogy theory is that given by Neisser (1976, 1978, 1979; Neisser & Kerr, 1973). Neisser adopts Gibson's (1966) view of perception: He regards it as ''automatic'' and ''direct.'' In this view, there is no picturelike representation. Rather, images—like percepts—are of spatial layouts. A layout is a stable arrangement of objects with intrinsic three-dimensional shapes occupying fixed positions along a stationary surface. This layout is in contrast to the fluctuating shapes and locations of light patterns that fall on the two-dimensional retinal surfaces as we move our eyes and heads. Neisser rejects Gibson's strong position that no processing takes place during perception; he claims instead that the brain *is* a processing device but one that does not use distinct representations. That is, Neisser rejects the structure–process distinction that permeates theorizing in the rest of cognitive psychology and artificial intelligence. Rather, the brain just ''picks up'' invariant information from the environment, partly in accordance with what one anticipates seeing in a given context. Critically, this kind of ''picking up'' activity can be invoked solely on the basis of anticipating a stimulus, even in its absence. This kind of ''perceptual anticipation'' results in a mental image, in a spatial layout being perceived in the absence of the appropriate sensory input. This view has the regrettable consequence of leading one to predict that being able to "see" the visible surfaces in an image is irrelevant; only the intrinsic viewer-independent spatial relationships among objects are included in the layout. This claim would, at first glance, seem to have been disproved by Keenan and Moore (1979), and Kosslyn and Alper (1977). Furthermore, Pinker (1980b) and Pinker and Finke (1980) have shown that people are quite good at perceiving viewer-specific perspective properties in images, even in images of views of scenes that they had not witnessed perceptually. Even if the theory could be said to have some measure of behavioral adequacy, it clearly does not have process adequacy or explanatory adequacy. It is important to note, however, that Neisser seems to reject the presuppositions on which our analysis of process adequacy is based. That is, he claims that there *is* no distinct set of cognitive operations underlying task performance. If he was correct, his task would be to specify the neurological operations that underlie performance in this task—and our criteria apply as much to these sorts of theories and models as to the more abstract cognitive ones (which are couched at the level of description of an algorithm or computation, not of the underlying hardware). In addition, there is some question about the logical coherence of Neisser's view, as is discussed by Hampson and Morris (1978). For example, if image formation is identical to anticipating an object that does not appear, why, when we form images, are we not surprised or disappointed?

Hebb's Cell Assemblies

At least since the time of David Hartley, the British associationist, theorists have speculated about the neurophysiological mechanisms underlying imagery. Hebb (1968) presented a now classic theory of this sort. In his view, an image is formed when some of the same neurological structures in the brain that are activated during perception are activated in the absence of the appropriate sensory input. Hardly anyone would deny this claim, of course, but what makes Hebb's views interesting is that he adds some details. *Cell assemblies,* or groups of neurons forming a recurrent synaptic path, are organized hierarchically: The lowest-order assemblies respond to specific visual contours, in particular retinal locations, and higher-order assemblies are triggered by any one of a set of lower-order ones, thereby corresponding to a disjunction of the lower-order contours. As a consequence, the activation of higher-order assemblies produces fuzzy or generic images, and the activation of lower-order ones produces sharp, detailed images. Furthermore, cell assemblies at a given level are connected by the neural assemblies triggering particular eye movements and, thus, are activated in the same sequence as would occur when one visually examined an object. The order of sequencing produces an organization in the image that constrains the way one can scan it and access it in general. Hebb's views are clearly intended as a general theory, but unfortunately they are too vague to produce specific theories or specific models for most imagery tasks. Furthermore, Hebb's claim that images are accessed according to the eye movement sequence performed when the scene was encoded loses points for the theory in behavioral adequacy. It seems that a scene, once encoded, can be imagined and then scanned in virtually any direction in three-dimensional space (Pinker, 1980b). Furthermore, image scanning differs, both in its rate and in its sensitivity to the relative depths of objects, from physical eye movements (Pinker, 1980b).

Propositional Theories

According to these theories, also called "structural-description" theories, image representations are no different in kind from the representations underlying conceptual knowledge and abstract thought. The quasi-pictorial aspect of images that is apparent to introspection is treated as an epiphenomenon, and all mental representations consist of logical propositions containing symbolic variables and constants (e.g., "SIZE[k,100]," "LOCATION [K,X,Y]"). Kosslyn (1980, Chapter 5) reviews these theories in some detail (Baylor, 1971; Farley, 1974), and we do not duplicate his efforts here. Instead, we provide one early example; later we turn to a recent propositional theory that was not reviewed earlier.

Moran's (1973) theory posits that all mental representations, including those underlying images, are "symbolic," and furthermore that there are no special image operations. In his view, memory consists of a collection of "productions" (Newell & Simon, 1972). Each of these consists of two parts: the "condition" specifies what information must be in active memory or incoming from the senses for the "action" to be produced. The action usually results in an alteration of the contents of short-term memory. In Moran's theory there is a single short-term store for information from all modalities, and this store has a limited capacity. The contents of short-term memory are constantly in flux as new information either arrives from the senses or is activated from long-term memory.

Moran's theory was designed to account for performance in a particular task. Subjects in this task were asked to image a path described by a sequence of directions (e.g., "north, west, northwest . . ."). For each direction, the subject was to image a line segment of a standard length connected onto the end of the previous segment. The subjects "thought aloud" while performing the task, and the theory was devised to provide an account for these verbal reports.

Although Moran claims to have a general theory, he in fact has a specific model. The mechanisms he describes are tailor-made to provide accounts for one task, and they are embodied in a running computer simulation model, not all of whose properties are necessarily relevant to human psychology.

The theory is inconsistent with the basic facts of modality-specific interference (Segal, 1971) and with many of the data on image processing reviewed by Kosslyn et al. (1981); thus it lacks behavioral adequacy. For the one task for which it was designed, it may have process adequacy as an account of how the *verbal reports* are generated, although this need not be equivalent to an account of image processing itself, of course. The model also has some degree of explanatory adequacy insofar as some of its properties—the limited capacity short-term store and use of productions—were motivated by a more general theory (Newell & Simon, 1972). Ultimately, even this modicum of explanatory adequacy will stand or fall depending on the explanatory adequacy of the general theory itself.

NEWER THEORIES

Kosslyn, Shwartz, and Pinker's Array Theory

These theories posit different kinds of representation in active visual memory and long-term memory. In active memory there is an arraylike medium, also subserving visual perception, that mimics a coordinate space. Objects are depicted by selectively activating cells in this array, just as a matrix in a computer memory can be filled with elements whose distribution in the matrix defines the shape of some object or scene. These active-memory representations underlie the experience of imagery, and it is claimed that the quasi-pictorial properties that people report when they use imagery in fact arise from structural properties of this underlying representation. For example, the array seems to have a grain, making smaller images more difficult to examine, and a determinate size and shape, making peripheral and behind-the-head objects difficult to imagine and recall (Kosslyn, 1980; Kosslyn et al., 1979). In contrast, long-term memory stores not just quantitative information, from which the depictive representation in active memory is displayed, but also lists of facts in a "symbolic" or "propositional" format. The propositional information allows one to image parts or objects in novel combinations in the array, creating detailed images of objects or scenes. Furthermore, because a single image may be composed by activating a number of distinct encodings that fade and are refreshed at different times, the image in active memory may itself be organized into parts according to their relative fadedness.

Array theories posit at least three kinds of processes. First, there must be a means of interpreting the patterns depicted in the array. A "mind's eye" process, identical to pattern recognition processes in visual perception, acts to associate given patterns with symbolic descriptions. Second, there must be processes that fill the array with the contents of long-term memory files. From what we know about mental-image generation, we can state that these processes must be sufficiently powerful to form image patterns at novel

sizes and locations and in novel combinations. Third, the data require processes that shift points from cell to cell in various ways, accounting for the
ability to execute mental rotations, size scalings, translations, and so on
(Kosslyn et al., 1981).

These theories are intended to be general over the domain of how information is represented in, and accessed from, visual mental images. As such,
they fare reasonably well on the criterion of behavioral adequacy; they are
able to produce specific theories and models that account for the data in
specific tasks. Furthermore, the array theory, described by Kosslyn (1980)
and further developed by Pinker (1980a, 1981) and Shwartz (1979), fares well
on the criterion of process adequacy, providing explicit accounts of the
internal processes that allow one to accomplish tasks in the domain. For
example, people's relative success at imagining the details of objects at
particular sizes, locations, and orientations is explained in terms of fixed
properties of the array structure, specifically its size, homogeneity, isotropy,
and grain (Finke & Kosslyn, 1980; Kosslyn, 1980). Similarly, the fact that
judgments of the shape or presence of parts in images are systematically
affected by the parts' sizes, locations, and orientations (Cooper & Shepard,
1973; Kosslyn, 1980) is accounted for by pattern recognition processes operating on array patterns (as they do in perception) that conflate size, shape,
and orientation into a single arrangement of activated cells (rather than list-
searching processes that could access a shape parameter in a proposition
without showing effects of the contents of other propositions asserting the
objects' orientations or locations).

It is too early to tell how well these theories fare on the third criterion,
explanatory adequacy. There are no ironclad principles outside the domain
of data for positing the putative structures and processes. (Nor are there
principles arguing against these components, we might add.) However, recently there have been some gropings in that direction. Waltz (1979), Hayes-
Roth (1979), Funt (1976), and Pinker (1980a) offer some suggestions as to
why it may be computationally advantageous for a visual-information processing system to be able to access and transform internally generated array
patterns. And as we see later, some recent conjectures have appeared in the
work of Shepard, Finke, and Trehub concerning the neurophysiological constraints and evolutionary causes of structures and processes of the sort
posited by array theories.

Trehub's Neural Networks

Arnold Trehub (1977) has outlined a seldom-cited but remarkably comprehensive neural model of pattern recognition and visual imagery, similar in
substance to the array theory. In very brief outline, the model has the
following properties:

1. Contour extractors of an unspecified nature transform the two-di-

mensional retinal intensity array into a two-dimensional neural array in which every neuron corresponds to a retinal locus, signaling the presence of an edge at that locus when "on" and the absence of an edge at that locus when "off." These cells are called "mosaic cells" and correspond to the "surface array" in the array theory.

2.   A large number of neurons have dendrites, each of which synapses with every mosaic cell. These "filter cells" are spontaneously active, and when one fires concurrently with some subset of active mosaic cells, depicting some shape, the synapses joining the active mosaic cells to that filter cell become stronger. When that subset of mosaic cells fires again (i.e., when that retinal pattern recurs), that filter cell will be more active than any other filter cell (thanks to a set of assumptions about inhibitory connections and properties of synapse strengthening that are too complex to outline here). That filter cell thus now serves as a "template" or "detector" for that shape.

3.   Another large set of neurons have *axons,* each of which synapses with every mosaic cell. By a process similar to that in paragraph 2, an originally uncommitted cell of this sort develops stronger synapses with an active subset of the mosaic cells. Subsequently, when such a "class" cell is activated externally, it will recreate the original pattern of stimulation in the mosaic. This corresponds to generation of a visual image of a pattern from memory, analogous to the array theory's "PICTURE" subroutine.

4.   Another set of cells serve to link each mosaic cell with some other mosaic cell. The two linked cells can represent (a) a retinal locus and another retinal locus differing from the first by a small clockwise rotation about the fovea, (b) same, but related by a counterclockwise rotation, (c) same, but related by a small amount of dilation centered on the fovea, and (d) same, but related by a contraction. A "command" cell synapses with every linking cell in a, another one synapses with all the linking cells in b, and so on. When activated, a command cell activates mosaic cells related to the currently active ones by a small rotation or size scaling, depending on which command cell was activated, and suppresses the original pattern of activation. Constant repetition of this procedure corresponds to a mental rotation or size scaling on the array pattern, which can be used to normalize a familiar stimulus in an unfamiliar orientation so that it can be "recognized by" (i.e., it can fire) a filter cell. Alternatively, when a pattern is first seen, each of its rotated or size-scaled transforms can be assigned its own filter cell to detect transformed patterns directly on future occasions. Transformations must be incremental because the hardwired connections only link cells with their neighbors; larger transformations thus require repeated commands to the transformation network.

5.   Yet another set of cells form synapses with concentric subsets of mosaic cells; so when one such cell is activated, it "primes" some focal region of the visual field of a given size centered on the retina. This corresponds to focal attention.

6.   Several other arrays, called *retinoids,* containing cells that can remain

active for brief periods of time are also available. The cells of each retinoid have inputs and outputs in one-to-one fashion with mosaic cells, and also they are interconnected with one another in specific ways; the interconnections themselves are excitable by particular command neurons. One retinoid executes translations in each of four directions; another assembles information from successive glances into a composite two-dimensional pattern; a third represents the "straight-ahead" direction of the viewer's body relative to the scene by a single activated point, whose position is updated by taking eye, head, and body movements into account; and a fourth assembles information from several content cells in memory into a single spatial arrangement, corresponding to a hypothetical or imagined scene.

Trehub's proposals constitute a general model since they refer to particular neural constructs some of whose properties are theory relevant (e.g., strengthening of synapses whose two neurons fire simultaneously) and others of which are theory irrelevant (e.g., the precise nature of the equation describing the course of strengthening). The model is behaviorally and process adequate in some respects (e.g., it is consistent with all the experimental results that motivate the array structure of the array theory) and inadequate in others. For example, Trehub incorrectly conjectures that in a Shepard and Metzler task, mental rotation will be carried out over a full 360° regardless of the original angular discrepancy between the two stimuli; that it will take longer to compare objects differing greatly in size than two objects differing only slightly; and also that mental translations of a constant Euclidean distance will take longer in a diagonal direction than in vertical and horizontal directions. However, many of the incorrect behavioral predictions, with the possible exception of the anisotropy of scanning rates, are not based on crucial theory-relevant properties of the model (e.g., rotation could be made self-terminating in the model by allowing a high-threshold neuron fed by all the filter cells to inhibit the rotation command neuron when one filter cell fired strongly, signaling a shape match).

Of greater concern are several problems related to process adequacy. First, it appears highly likely that shape recognition is defined over representations of an object's three-dimensional shape, whereas Trehub's normalize-then-template-match model works over two-dimensional representations. Addition of three-dimensional normalization networks would be extremely difficult since the normalization would have to compute the effects of foreshortening, occlusion, and other perspective effects in comparing the current mosaic pattern to stored patterns [however, see Pinker (1981) for one suggestion based on the array theory that might be adaptable here]. Second, there must exist a distinct neuron for every shape that a person could learn over a lifetime, and each of these neurons must synapse with *all* 700,000 neurons in the mosaic array. This crucial assumption is of dubious neurophysiological plausibility. Third, by accomplishing mental transformation by use of hardwired networks linking each mosaic cell to some other mosaic cell, Trehub is committed to the view that *every* mental image transformation (including shearing, bending, melting, compression, and other deformations) is computed by its own, innate interconnecting network. Although it seems likely that there *are* innate constraints on possible mental transformations [see Kubovy (1979) for one proposal], the mechanisms required by Trehub's position would seem overly specific. Finally, when Trehub offers an extremely simple solution to one of the most difficult problems in cognitive science, shape recognition, we worry. Historically, template-plus-normalization schemes have been found to be overly sensitive to minor perturbations in the scale and surface details of patterns. Although Trehub tries to lick these problems with inhibitory connections of various sorts, we would feel far more comfortable about his proposals if he could simulate his model on a computer and get it to correctly classify complex, realistic, visual scenes, even ones whose contours and edges are extracted beforehand (presumably by other mechanisms).

Although Trehub cannot make strong claims of explanatory adequacy for his model (since there are many other ways to wire 60 million neurons together), he can at least argue that his proposals are by and large not incompatible with what we know about the anatomy and physiology of the nervous system. For example, he estimates the number of neurons needed by his model and finds that the human visual system can accommodate that number several times over. In general, we feel that the model's explanatory adequacy might best emerge from a symbiotic relationship with the more computational array theory, which it resembles so closely. The array theory can provide an explanation for the arraylike structures of Trehub's model in terms of the computational efficiency it provides in solving certain tasks; Trehub's model can confirm that the array theory does not implicate any mechanisms that cannot be instantiated in a simple way in the neurophysiological substrate.

Finke's "Levels of Equivalence"

Ronald Finke (1980) has reviewed a large number of experimental findings of imagery, many of them his own, and has suggested a framework in which to interpret imagery phenomena in general. If we consider the visual system to be composed of a hierarchy of levels of processing, starting with the retinal intensity/wavelength arrays and culminating in conceptual knowledge of the objects seen, we may ask, "At which of these levels can mental images occur?" We may do so by (1) choosing some telltale experimental phenomenon specific to visual processing at some level in the hierarchy; (2) having subjects form an image of the visual pattern that normally elicits the phenomenon and testing whether the phenomenon still obtains; and (3) informing subjects about the eliciting visual pattern, without asking them to form an image of that pattern, and testing whether the phenomenon still obtains. If the effect obtains in case 2, but not case 3, we have evidence that images can occur at levels of visual processing other than abstract conceptual thought, specifically, at the level that the study of perception suggests is the substrate of that effect. Because these effects motivate a distinction between mental imagery and abstract thought, Finke calls attention to the fair number of them that have been discovered, including orientation-contingent color aftereffects following the imagination of bar patterns on colored fields, and the falloff of acuity in mental images of dots formed at increasing distances from the center of the visual field.

Like Shepard's complementarity theory, Finke's levels theory is far too heuristic and imprecise to allow one to generate behaviorally and process-adequate models of entire imagery tasks. However, by tying mental images to visual processing stages that perhaps are neurally identifiable, Finke is making progress toward explanatory adequacy. That is, following his strategy, we should eventually be able to say that images have property x because they occur in neural structure s from whose physiology x is a necessary consequence. In some cases this might even resolve current debates about whether the computational format of images is an array or a structural description. If we had reason to believe that images occur in the peripheral layers of area 17 of the visual cortex, for example, we could rule out most structural-description theories. That is because we know that neurons in area 17 are sensitive only to extremely local properties of retinal stimuli, such as the type of edge present at a small circumscribed location, whereas structural descriptions almost invariably contain more global predicates like an object's or part's overall shape, orientation, or size.

There is one shortcoming in Finke's presentation, however. Finke rejects as ill advised any attempt to specify the format or nature of images themselves, suggesting instead that images be characterized by comparing their effects on the visual system with those of physical objects. Our objection runs as follows. Given the doctrine of materialism and the existence of perceptual illusions, we are forced to say that objects do not themselves have effects on the visual system; rather, their effects are mediated by reflected light energy transduced by the photoreceptors into patterns of neural activity. In modern cognitive psychology, we describe these neural patterns and subsequent neural patterns triggered by them in a vocabulary more abstract than actual neural firings, namely, in the vocabulary of mental representations and the computational processes that act on them. We then identify mental entities, such as percepts or images, with particular representations (factoring out of the problem the nature of the qualia, or subjective experiences, associated with visual processes, since they are as intractable as a scientific problem can be). Thus if similar effects obtain when people see an object and when they imagine it, it must mean that the representations normally activated by the retinal intensity array also can be activated by neural processes originating from higher levels of the nervous sytem. Characterization of the nature of an image is then identical to characterization of the functional properties of those representations (and Finke's data are of considerable help in this task). This implies that the correct comparison is between the representations triggered by retinal patterns (percepts) and the representations triggered from long-term memory (images), specifically, whether the two are identical, overlapping, disjoint, and so on. The external object itself plays no immediate role, nor does any notion of an unanalyzed "image" itself, since the image is identical to particular representations (minus qualia). When Finke proposes that "the mental images themselves, once formed, cause these visual mechanisms to become activated. That is, . . . images are the source of this activation, not the product of it," he seems to be committing himself to a form of psychophysical dualism—mental images cause but never correspond to neural events. This violates the principles of modern functionalist cognitive psychology (Fodor, 1981), not to mention materialist philosophy of science in general, and thus must count against the explanatory adequacy of Finke's scheme.

Nonetheless, we feel that these programmatic comments of Finke's are detachable from his synthesis of the imagery data and his recommendations for designing and interpreting imagery experiments. Thus we applaud his efforts as an important contribution to the eventual specification of process-adequate and explanatorily adequate theories of visual imagery.

Shepard's "Psychophysical Complementarity"

Roger Shepard's elegant findings on the process of mental rotation (Cooper & Shepard, 1973; Shephard & Metzler, 1971) have served as an acid test for all recent theories and models of imagery (Anderson, 1978; Hinton, 1979a,b; Kosslyn, 1980; Pinker, 1980a). However, until very recently, Shepard himself has been reluctant to propose a model detailing the cognitive capacities recruited during mental transformations and how these capacities interact to accomplish the transformation. In a recent paper entitled "Psychophysical Complementarity," Shepard (1981) integrates data from mental transformations, shape recognition, and apparent motion and uses them to motivate some highly preliminary hypotheses about the mental structures and processes involved in imagined transformations. He also attempts to justify these hypotheses in light of evolutionary theory. In this section, we summarize briefly the data that Shepard addresses and the theory he constructs in response, and we examine the theory according to our usual criteria. Because Shepard's theoretical proposals have not yet been discussed in the imagery literature, we devote considerable space to them.

Shepard considers the following findings:

1.   In comparing the shapes of two three-dimensional bodies, people claim to mentally rotate one into the orientation of the other before making the comparison and, in fact, take proportionally more time to do the task for object pairs with greater angular disparity. Furthermore, the degree of linearity and the rate of rotation are quite similar for rotations in the frontal

plane and rotations in depth [see Pinker, (1980a) for a summary of the rate comparisons from different experiments].

2. When two three-dimensional bodies differing in orientation are alternately presented to a subject, the alternation is perceived as a rocking motion of a single rigid object. The greater the angular disparity between the alternate views, the greater must be the minimum interval between them that allows the perception of a rigid rotation. The linear relation between time and angular disparity is identical regardless of whether the successive views differ in the frontal plane or in depth. Furthermore, the perceptual system seems to "find" the shortest rotation that will appear to bring one view into correspondence with the other, so that shapes with rotational symmetry or near-symmetry will not need as long an interstimulus interval for the perception of rigid rotation for certain angular disparities as asymmetrical shapes would need.

3. When examining two-dimensional line drawings (which, of course, could be the projections of an infinite number of distinct three-dimensional shapes), people involuntarily perceive them as the three-dimensional solid object (a) that has the most symmetry and simplicity, (b) whose two-dimensional projection would display the fewest topological changes when the object is rotated slightly in depth, and (c) (for moving patterns) that remains rigid throughout the motion.

Shepard proposes the following theory to account for these findings. An imagined or perceived shape is represented as a set of points, with each point embedded in a multidimensional "space" with its own non-Euclidean geometry. These spaces do not literally correspond to isolatable spatial regions of the brain, but they presumably reside in neural networks whose interconnections mimic the hypothesized geometry of the space (i.e., the strength of the connections between neurons, or perhaps neural assemblies, is proportional to the distance between corresponding points in the abstract "space" posited by the theory). The different spaces are organized into a hierarchy that weights them according to their relative importance in the organism's visual processing. When a point in a space representing the object's shape and orientation is activated, the activation spreads as a wave with decreasing amplitude through the space, activating the surrounding points in proportion to their "distance" according to the metric implicit in the geometry of that space. Each of these surrounding points represents the results of a possible transformation of the object, so the proximity of two points in a space can be interpreted as representing the ease of mentally transforming one object into another, or, equivalently, their perceptual similarity. The more heavily a particular space is weighted, the stronger will be the wave of excitation emanating from an activated point.

Shepard's substantive claim is that the most highly weighted space will have a geometry such that the set of points with the strongest interconnections will correspond to the set of possible orientations of a single rigid object in three-dimensional space. Thus a linear path along the surface of such a spherical subspace will represent a continuous rigid rotation of an object about a particular fixed axis. Since this distance metric will allow activation to spread most strongly from an activated point to points representing the same object following a rigid rotation in three-dimensional space, we have the beginnings of an account for the three sets of findings mentioned earlier. Mental rotations are continuous because intermediate points in the spherical space must be traversed when activation spreads from one point to another. The maximum rotation rate is determined by the rate of propagation of neural activation through the spatial medium, and it is linear presumably because the distance metric in the subspace is homogeneous (corresponding to the isotropy of the physical space in which the organism evolved). Apparent motion along the shortest angular trajectory is the result of two successively activated points in the space maximally activating the shortest linear path connecting them within that space. And the interpretation of three-dimensional shape can be highly sensitive to the results of possible rotations of a hypothesized shape because when that shape is hypothesized by activating a point in the space, the points representing small transformations of that shape are activated as well. Our perceptual systems give a high weight to interpretations of moving points as rotating rigid three-dimensional bodies because the distances (strength of connections) between points representing rigidity-preserving transformations are shorter than those representing non-rigidity-preserving transformations. Finally, our perceptual systems give a high weight to interpretations of two-dimensional line drawings as regular, symmetrical three-dimensional objects because the space representing their set of rigid rotations is completely folded back onto itself (within a higher-dimensional space); nearly symmetrical objects are represented in spaces partially folded back onto themselves. Such convolutions cause the spreading activation of a point representing a symmetrical object to return to itself, augmenting its own activation and thus favoring the interpretation of the external object as symmetrical.

Shepard's highly original ideas are difficult to classify in our scheme, but it seems that they come closest to constituting a general theory. The hypotheses are not instantiated in an explicit computer or mathematical model with theory-relevant and theory-irrelevant properties, so they are not a model; nor are they narrowly addressed to a small number of laboratory tasks, so they are not specific. What makes Shepard's theory especially difficult to compare with the other theories is that its domain is not imagery in general (e.g., the storage, generation, and inspection of images), but transformational processes that cut across imagery, pattern recognition, and spatial reasoning. Thus estimates of the theory's generality, so important to our evaluation criteria, cannot easily be compared with those for other theories. Furthermore, Shepard is careful to point out that his proposals are extremely tentative and preliminary, with many details remaining to be specified. Still it is possible to assess how well it covers the phenomena it addresses and, as we shall see, its process and explanatory adequacy, notwithstanding its current lack of specificity.

Shepard's theory is behaviorally adequate inasmuch as it correctly accounts for the empirical data on image transformations and perceptual biases that he cites. However, Shepard's theory fails the behavioral-adequacy criterion inasmuch as it does not specify a sufficient number of processing components to generate specific models accounting for the data on imagery tasks collected over the past decade, or even to specify all the mental processes intervening between stimulus and response in a single task. That is so because Shepard is describing only a part of the imagery faculty, the transformational component. Furthermore, Shepard has not specified the precise geometry needed for his spatial media, nor their form of instantiation in neural tissue in sufficient detail to generate even a behaviorally adequate specific model of image transformations. This is probably too much to ask of a proposal as preliminary as Shepard's. However, it is still possible to evaluate the process adequacy of the proposals, even in their tentative form. We do this by judging whether the description of the transformational component has process adequacy in itself (which it does, given that it uses common mechanisms to account for data patterns in related tasks), and, more importantly, whether it is compatible with process-adequate theories of other imagery subcomponents (i.e., the other subcomponents can provisionally serve as black boxes with inputs from and outputs to Shepard's mechanisms). Problems would arise only if it were not clear how Shepard's mechanisms could be interfaced with the other perceptual and imagery subcomponents.

Unfortunately, these potential problems may be real ones for Shepard. Models of cognitive subcomponents couched in more traditional information-processing terms usually have well-defined inputs and outputs. However, Shepard's "analogue" model is described as a self-contained sytem into which a single object has somehow found its way to be subject to transformations defined by the intrinsic geometry of the space. Left unspecified are three interactions between the representational spaces and other cognitive subcomponents: recognition processes; generation processes; and executive processes.

First, it is unclear what sort of processes locate points in their appropriate positions in the various spaces on the basis of the retinal intensity arrays. Indeed, it is unclear how one could define a set of innate "spaces" sufficiently rich and differentiated so that every recognizable shape (faces, cars, furniture, tools, etc) can be represented by a unique subspace, let alone how recognition processes could activate just the right points in the right subspace, given a specific retinal pattern. Recent computational treatments of pattern recognition (Marr & Nishihara, 1978) have shown how the shape recognition problem can be made more tractable by representing the geometrically cohesive parts of an object separately, linked by coordinate vectors specifying the positions of the parts relative to each other. That way there need not be an innate specification of every potential complex shape, like a particular car or giraffe. Of course, in an attempt to reduce the dimensionality of his spaces in the face of the vast numbers of shapes humans can recognize, Shepard could adopt this hierarchical decomposition scheme into his theory. Thus there would be one set of spaces for spherical objects, one set for cylindrical ones, one for parallelepipeds, and so on, interconnected by vectors specifying spatial adjunct relations. But then the tendency to imagine or perceive the smooth rigid transformations of an object cannot easily be captured by the geometry of some single space—one of the key attractions of Shepard's hypotheses. There would have to be some other process coordinating several transformations in several spaces in a way that preserves overall object rigidity.

The problem of how the correct subspaces are activated at the correct time reappears when image generation is considered. Both introspective and experimental evidence show that images are generated out of parts, sometimes in novel combinations, and that the amalgams or newly defined parts thereof can then be subject to inspection and transformation processes (Kosslyn, 1980). This, too, requires either an innate space with sufficient dimensions to represent uniquely every imaginable object or combination of objects, or else a nonspatial process activating and coordinating the activation in various subspaces depending on what the person wishes to imagine. As before, the former option seems at first glance implausibly complex, and the latter option puts a greater emphasis on the conceptually driven or nonanalogue processes than is in keeping with the flavor of Shepard's hypotheses.

Finally, it appears that image transformation processes are to a certain extent under executive or voluntary control, rather than inevitably triggered by a pattern of activation in a space of neural connections. For example, it seems that we can choose at will which object in an image will be altered by which transformation, in which direction, to which extent, and at which rate (Kosslyn, 1980, 1981; Pinker, 1980b), although to be sure there are also constraints on each of these sets of options. Accomplishment of this flexibility would require an executive process, possibly capable of "priming" selected paths to selected extents in selected subspaces, which would require a fairly complex accessing network permeating the spaces. This network presumably would be controlled by the executive "passing" it the name of the desired transformation and a parameter list (specifying extent, rate, etc.) Again, it is not clear to what extent such a symbol-manipulating transformational network would be compatible with Shepard's analogue system, whose behavior is an inevitable consequence of its intrinsic structure and current pattern of activation.

In sum, the fact that image transformations can be fed by richly diverse sorts of information from the retinas during perception and from combinations of long-term memory files during imagination, all under the flexible control of the executive, shows that a process-adequate theory must allow the image transformation system to be interfaceable with other cognitive processes, some of which will be more symbolic than analogic. This flexi-bility, of course, is a major motivation for propositional approaches to im-agery (Pylyshyn, in press), but as Shepard argues, the severe constraints on transformation processes show that a universal computational system is not a process-adequate model of imagery, either. The array theory we discuss elsewhere contains a single, Euclidean analogue space interfaced to symbolic list-manipulating routines, and we feel that a hybrid model of this sort is needed to account for the particular combination of constraint and flexibility found in the imagery system. It is, of course, possible that Shepard's set of analogue non-Euclidean spaces could also form part of a process-adequate hybrid model of visual representation; our comments do not imply that this cannot be done, only that we see no straightforward way to do it. But Shepard's proposals are still tentative, and we hope that these points will be addressed as the proposals are elaborated in the future.

Perhaps Shepard's most intriguing proposals are those that attempt to justify his model by evolutionary considerations and, hence, attempt to meet the explanatory adequacy criterion head-on. Shepard argues that eons of commerce with a three-dimensional, homogeneous, isotropic, continuous, and locally Euclidean space of animate rigid and semirigid objects caused the mammalian brain to mirror in its connectivity structure the properties of that space and the possible trajectories of objects in it. Like most evolu-tionary arguments, Shepard's appeals both to the principle of natural selec-tion (analogous to an argument that early hominids' erect posture enabled them to carry food or use tools, which conferred on them a reproductive advantage) and to a principle of "new use of old parts" (analogous to an argument that humans' S-shaped spine is the consequence of evolution to an erect posture of a spine originally belonging to quadrupeds). Shepard's hypothesis that the neural medium underlying visual transformations makes rigid continuous three-dimensional motion easy to compute is an example of the former sort of argument. Surely it pays an organism in this world to compare unfamiliar patterns to well-learned ones by applying just those transformations (e.g., orientation, translation, and scaling of apparent size) that invert physically possible transformations conserving intrinsic shape. Similarly, an organism predicting or keeping track of the visual appearance of semivisible objects moving relative to it would be most vigilant if it sim-ulated internally a continuous motion of those objects rather than arbitrary moment-to-moment position changes, or for that matter, changes of intrinsic shape or number. And a perceptual bias toward seeing ambiguous patterns as solid rigid objects in non-singular orientations is also a good ecological bet in a natural terrestrial environment.

Other proposals—that mental transformations are rate limited or that other mental faculties, such as music and language, have a spatial organi-zation—fall into the second class of evolutionary accounts, those appealing to the nature of the existing biological "building blocks" from which natural selection must choose the best arrangement. For example, in many circumstances it might hurt an organism to have to compute transformations incrementally—to adapt one of Shepard's examples, a pursued animal carrying a long bone in its mouth and approaching a narrow vertical opening would do better to compute the necessary 90° rotation of its head instantly than to mentally run through the entire rotation degree by degree. If the organism is constrained to do so despite a selection pressure to the contrary, a "new use of old parts" argument is called for. In this case the argument may be that voluntary mental transformations are computed in a spatial medium subserving the perception of moving objects and that the rate of continuous rotation computed therein is limited by the rate of propogation of neural activation. Unfortunately, since we do not understand the principles of neural organization and processing relevant to cognition nor the phylogenetic sequence for visuocognitive abilities in mammals, such arguments usually fail to show conclusively why human cognitive abilities *must* have evolved the way they did and show only that they *did* evolve that way. That is, we know of no evolutionary or neural principle that dictates that organisms could not have evolved a mental rotation operator, independent of the perceptual structures recording physical motion, that computed rotations swiftly and independent of the amount of rotation computed. Thus we are left more with an evolutionary conjecture than an evolutionary argument (and Shepard himself would be the first to agree with this assessment). Evolutionary accounts of the second sort do not really attain explanatory adequacy given our current state of knowledge, therefore, unless the precise neural constraints they appeal to are needed independently for accounts of other, unrelated cognitive phenomena. Still, it is only by offering conjectures in the way Shepard does that imagery theories can aspire to explanatory adequacy. One recurring criticism of analogue and array-type theories (Anderson, 1978; Pylyshyn, 1981) is that the incremental nature of mental transformations is not strongly motivated by the nature of the mechanisms intrinsic to the theory (Kosslyn, 1980, 1981, Kosslyn, et al., 1979). Shepard's conjectures on the evolutionary bases of visual transformation mechanisms are a welcome step in the direction of explanatory adequacy, even in their highly preliminary state.

In summary, Shepard's psychophysical–complementarity hypotheses, because of the vagueness of the details of the proposed mechanisms and their relation to other cognitive subcomponents, have only moderate behavioral and process adequacy. However, by considering visual transformations in the context of evolution in a three-dimensional world, Shepard has made greater strides toward explanatory adequacy than one usually finds in discussions of imagery.

Artifact Theories

These theories are not properly theories of imagery per se, but rather of how the data collected in imagery experiments were produced. On these views the data collected in imagery experiments in fact tell one nothing about images per se but rather are a consequence of either task demands or demand characteristics.

Pylyshyn (1981) is the most recent proponent of the view that the data reflect task demands. According to Pylyshyn, the data on image scanning and related phenomena [see Kosslyn (1980) for a review] are to be explained by reference to four ideas:

1. In order to follow the instructions used in an image task (e.g., to rotate an imagined pattern), the subjects must try to anticipate what would happen in the corresponding actual situation.

2. Subjects have the requisite tacit knowledge to know how objects would behave in the analogous physical situation and how their visual systems would record these events.

3. Subjects have the requisite psychophysical skills to time their button pushes and other responses appropriately, mimicking the responses they would have made were they actually viewing the to-be-imaged stimulus as described.

4. None of the computations involved in understanding the instructions, acessing and using stored tacit knowledge or making responses involves actual manipulation of a quasi-pictorial image.

For example, when subjects are asked to "scan" mentally from one imagined object to another, they interpret the task as a challenge to mentally simulate some physical event, such as the act of moving one's eyes or the perception or a moving object. Since they know that moving objects take longer to traverse greater distances, perhaps they retrieve a mental quantity corresponding to the distance they have to "scan" and set a mental clock to tick away for a duration proportional to that quantity before responding. They thereby appear to be scanning an image (which was Kosslyn's interpretation of such results) without doing anything of the sort.

In this view, then, everything one knows about the world, physics, and one's own perceptual and cognitive abilities could enter into production of data in imagery tasks. The same argument, however, can be made about *any* cognitive task. For example, Sternberg's (1966) finding that subjects require more time to verify the presence of probes in larger memorized sets could be a consequence of subjects simulating the act of searching through longer lists of items on a page.

Pylyshyn (1981) treats his view as a general theory. This view has behavioral adequacy inasmuch as the imagery data resemble those from some analogous perceptual tasks. But this is not always the case, as is pointed out by Finke (1980), Kosslyn (1981), and Kosslyn, et al. (1979). In addition, the view fails to attain even a fragment of process adequacy, given that it does not specify the cognitive processing that does underlie production of the data (except to say that quasi-pictorial images are not involved). And there are no arguments for the explanatory evidence for this view—in fact, inasmuch as the tacit knowledge theory explicitly holds that any sequence of mental computations of any sort could underly so-called image processing, it also must hold that theories of mental imagery per se *cannot* attain explanatory adequacy even in principle—that explanatorily adequate theories will probably refer to computational atoms or general processing constraints that hold across all domains of thought (Pylyshyn, in press).

The demand characteristic view is similar to the task demands one insofar as the experimental data are explained without positing the processing of a mental image. In this case, however, the data purportedly are produced not because of implicit task demands built into the instructions, but rather because subjects somehow discern the predictions of the experiment and attempt to "help out." Thus, according to this view, it is not following the instructions per se that elicits the behavior, but other cues (possibly in conjunction with active attempts by the subjects to guess the hypothesis). Richman et al. (1979) present one version of this theory—which is clearly intended to be at the level of a specific theory—applying only to particular tasks. They show that when subjects are asked to guess the hypothesis in an image-scanning experiment, they often can do so and can predict general trends in the data (the precise predictions are off by a factor of 5, however). Thus, this theory has some degree of behavioral adequacy [however, see Kosslyn et al. (1979) for some problems for specific versions of these accounts]. The theory does not specify what sorts of cognitive processing go on, however, and thus falls short on our other measures of adequacy.

Hinton's Structural Descriptions

Geoffrey Hinton (1979a,b) described a variant of the structural description or propositional theory of visual representation, which represents scenes as graph structures whose nodes correspond to objects and their parts and whose edges are labeled with the spatial relationship that is true of pairs of parts. Hinton's own variant is motivated by a set of demonstrations showing that people are unable to perceive spatial relations holding among parts of an image or to rotate one part of an image relative to the rest, unless they conceive of the object in such a way that the part to be processed forms an integral unit in the conceptualization. When the conceptualization is changed with the object held constant (such as when a cube resting on one corner is described as two tripods linked by a zigzag ring), the perceivable relationships and transformable parts change with it. In general, the preferred conceptualization will be the one that described parts of objects relative to a reference frame coinciding with the object's axes of symmetry.

Three features differentiate Hinton's theory from other structural description theories (Baylor, 1971; Palmer, 1975). First, each part has an intrinsic set of "significant directions," or an originless cartesian coordinate system, aligned with it. Parts are interrelated by specifying the angles between their intrinsic sets of significant directions. Second, there is a second set of labels relating the significant directions of each part to a single set of directions aligned with the organism's retinal axes. Third, every piece of quantitative information (e.g., an angle relating one set of directions to one another) is specified by an activated point on a continuous analogue scale, and changing the value of a parameter involves shifting the activated point along the scale to a new position. The first feature is to account for the effect of descriptions of the intrinsic shape of an object on image processing (Hinton, 1979a); the second feature accounts for images having an implicit "vantage point" with respect to which perspective properties can be detected (Pinker, 1980a,b; Pinker and Finke, 1980); the third feature accounts for the well-known gradualness of mental rotation (Shepard & Metzler, 1971).

Hinton's theory is computationally powerful and precise enough to generate specific models for many of the empirical results on imagery reported in recent years, and thus it attains a high degree of behavioral adequacy. However, we feel that by excluding processes that fill and transform a visual array (presumably he would posit the array itself as a representational medium necessary for bottom-up shape recognition), Hinton fails to provide motivated accounts for a large set of empirical phenomena that can be expressed fairly naturally by processes operating on an array during imagination. For example, the incremental nature of rotation in Hinton's system flows from his stipulation that quantities are represented by a unidimensional analogue scale, which has no independent motivation. Representation of shape by an array pattern, on the other hand, provides several reasons why incremental rotations are more computationally desirable (Kosslyn, 1980; et al., 1979) and, furthermore, why rotation rates should be sensitive to pattern size (Shwartz, 1981) and relatively insensitive to pattern complexity [Schwartz (1981); see Kosslyn (1980) for a review]. Second, it is unclear why objects imagined to be concealed, tiny, or out of view (Fiske et al., 1979; Keenan & Moore, 1979; Kosslyn & Alper, 1978) are difficult to remember. Third, it is puzzling that subjects cannot imagine patterns with small details at locations in the visual field as eccentric as those at which they can imagine patterns with larger details [Finke & Kosslyn (1980); see Finke (1980) for related findings] or why the shape of the imagery field should be elliptical rather than rectangular (which would be the case if maximum size were constrained by the lengths of two unidimensional scales representing orthogonal directions). Fourth, like Trehub's, Hinton's theory incorrectly predicts that mental comparisons of perceived or remembered magnitudes (e.g., numbers or animals' sizes) should take longer when the to-be-compared items differ by a large amount than when they differ by a small amount [in fact, the opposite occurs; see Kosslyn (1980) for a review]. Finally, Hinton's demonstrations of the difficulty of reparsing images, his most important source of empirical evidence, can be explained quite naturally by independently motivated array properties (Kosslyn, 1980).

It is possible that Hinton could account for these findings and others with a similar message reviewed in Kosslyn (1980) and Finke (1980), but in many cases it appears that in so doing Hinton would have to simulate an increasing number of properties of an array in his structural description (e.g., specifying separately the locations of very tiny, local regions of objects to motivate the gradualness and size sensitivity of rotation; computing the parts that are currently visible and deleting those that are not to account for the memory results; positing a single nonhomogeneous, two-dimensional analogue scale instead of separate one-dimensional scales to account for the imagery acuity findings). But then, we predict, it would be more economical to allow imagery processes to access the visual array directly, rather than to have the array sealed off from memory-driven processes while those processes simulate each of its properties. If so, Hinton's structural description theory would not be process adequate, since it would do the right things for the wrong reasons.

Nonetheless, by addressing the viewer-centeredness of images, the incremental nature of image transformations, and the relative ease of examining and transforming different image subpatterns, Hinton has outlined the most psychologically motivated structural description theory we have seen. If a theory in this class turns out to be correct, it will probably resemble Hinton's; if not, it will probably be because of experiments designed with Hinton's theory and data in mind.

CONCLUSIONS

As we move from older to newer theories of mental imagery, two trends become apparent, both of them salubrious to the scientific study of imagery. One is the increasing precision and generality of theorizing. Early theories were either extremely vague, such as Paivio's and Hebb's (leading Pylyshyn, in his early critique of imagery theories, to claim prematurely that computational explicitness and precision alone favored propositional accounts of imagery), or extremely task specific, such as Moran's. Recently, however, there have been theories that are simultaneously broad in scope and precise in detail, such as the array theory and Hinton's structural description theory. This trend largely has been made possible by the increasing use of the computer as a modeling medium for complex mental phenomena and (logically, but not chronologically indepedently) by the increasing use of computational processes and structures as the theory-relevant elements of hypotheses about human cognition. The second trend, seen in the work of Shepard, Trehub, and Finke, is to tie imagery more closely to biological considerations, such as the architecture and evolution of the visual systems of higher mammals. We welcome both these trends since they herald the day when imagery debates will hinge not on semantic quibbles or ideological loyalties, but on which theory fares best in empirical accuracy, parsimony, and elegance.

REFERENCES

Anderson, J. R. Arguments concerning representations for mental imagery. *Psychological Review*, 1978, **85**, 249–277.

Anderson, J. R., and Bower G. H. *Human associative memory*. New York: Winston, 1973.

Baylor, G. W. A Treatise on Mind's Eye. Ph.D. dissertation, Carnegie-Mellon University, 1971.

Bower, G. H. Mental imagery and associative learning. In L. Gregg (Ed.), *Cognition in learning and memory*. New York: Wiley, 1972.

Chomsky, N. *Aspects of the theory of syntax*. Cambridge MIT Press, 1965.

Chomsky, N. *Current issues in linguistics*. The Hague: Mouton, 1967.

Cooper, L. A., & Shepard, R. N. Chronometric studies of the rotation of mental images. In W. G. Chase (Ed.), *Visual information processing*. New York: Academic Press, 1973.

Dennett, D. C. *Brainstorms*. Montgomery, Vt.: Bradford Books, 1980.

Farley, A. M.VIPS: A visual imagery and perception system; the result of protocol analysis. Ph.D. dissertation, Carnegie-Mellon University, 1974.

Finke, R. A. Levels of equivalence in imagery and perception. *Psychological Review*, 1980, **87**, 113–132.

Finke, R. A., & Kosslyn, S. M. Mental imagery acuity in the peripheral visual field. *Journal of Experimental Psychology: Human Perception and Performance*, 1980, **6**, 126–139.

Fiske, S. T., Taylor, S. E., Etcoff, N. L., & Laufer, J. K. Imaging, empathy, and causal attribution. *Journal of Experimental Social Psychology*, 1979, **15**, 356–377.

Fodor, J. A. The mind–body problem. *Scientific American*, 1981, **244**, 114–123.

Funt, B. V. WHISPER: A computer implementation using analogues in reasoning. Ph.D. thesis, University of British Columbia, 1976.

Gibson, J. J. *The senses considered as perceptual systems*. Boston: Houghton Mifflin, 1966.

Hampson, P. J., & Morris, P. E. Unfulfilled expectations: A criticism of Neisser's theory of imagery. *Cognition*, 1978, **6**, 79–85.

Hayes-Roth, F. Distinguishing theories of representation: A critique of Anderson's "Arguments concerning mental imagery." *Psychological Review*, 1979, **86**, 376–392.

Hebb, D. O. Concerning imagery. *Psychological Review*, 1968, **75**, 466–477.

Hesse, M. B. *Models and analogies in science*. London: Sheed and Ward, 1963.

Hinton, G. E. Some demonstrations of the effects of structural descriptions in mental imagery. *Cognitive Science*, 1979a, **3**, 231–250.

Hinton, G. E. Imagery without arrays. *The Behavioral and Brain Sciences*, 1979b, **2**, 555–556.

Keenan, J. M., & Moore, R. E. Memory for images of concealed objects: A reexamination of Neisser and Kerr. *Journal of Experimental Psychology: Human Learning and Memory*, 1979, **5**, 374–385.

Kosslyn, S. M. *Image and mind*. Cambridge, Mass.: Harvard University Press, 1980.

Kosslyn, S. M. The medium and the message in mental imagery: A theory. *Psychological Review,* 1981, **88,** 46–66.

Kosslyn, S. M., & Alper, S. N. On the pictorial properties of visual images: Effects of image size on memory for words. *Canadian Journal of Psychology,* 1977, **31,** 32–40.

Kosslyn, S. M., Pinker, S., Smith, G. E., & Schwartz, S. P. On the demystification of mental imagery. *The Behavioral and Brain Sciences,* 1979, **2,** 535–581.

Kosslyn, S. M., & Schwartz, S. P. Empirical constraints on mental imagery. In (J. Long and A. Boddely (Eds.), *Attention and performance* Hillsdale, N.J.: Lawrence Erlbaum Associates, 1981.

Kubovy, M. Two hypotheses concerning the interrelation of perceptual spaces. In (L. D. Harmon (Ed.), *Interrelations of the communicative senses.* Cleveland, Ohio: Case Western Reserve, 1979.

Marr, D., & Nishihara, H. K. Visual information processing: Artificial intelligence and the sensorium of sight. *Technological Review,* 1978, **81,** 2–23.

Moran, T. P. The symbolic imagery hypothesis: a production system model. Ph.D. dissertation, Carnegie-Mellon University, 1973.

Neisser, U. *Cognition and reality.* San Francisco: Freeman, 1976.

Neisser, U. Anticipations, images, and introspections. *Cognition,* 1978, **6,** 169–174.

Neisser, U. Images, models, and human nature. *The Behavioral and Brain Sciences,* 1979, **2,** 561.

Neisser, U., & Kerr, N. Spatial and mnemonic properties of visual images. *Cognitive Psychology,* 1973, **5,** 138–150.

Newell, A., Simon, H. A. *Human problem solving.* Englewood Cliffs, N.J.: Prentice-Hall, 1972.

Paivio, A. Imagery and verbal processes. New York: Holt, 1971.

Palmer, S. E. Visual perception and world knowledge: Notes on a model of sensory-cognitive interaction. In D. A. Norman and D. E. Rumelhart (Eds.), *Explorations in cognition.* San Francisco: Freeman, 1975.

Pinker, S. Mental imagery and the visual world. MIT Center for Cognitive Science Occasional Paper, #4, 1980a.

Pinker, S. Mental imagery and the third dimension. *Journal of Experimental Psychology,* 1980b, **109,** 354–371.

Pinker, S. *The mental representation of 3-D space.* Unpublished manuscript, 1981.

Pinker, S. & Finke, R. A. Emergent two-dimensional patterns in images rotated in depth. *Journal of Experimental Psychology: Human Perception and Performance,* 1980, **6,** 244–264.

Pylyshyn, Z. The imagery debate: Analogue media versus tacit knowledge. *Psychological Review,* 1981, **88,** 16–45.

Pylyshyn, Z. *Foundations of Cognitive Science.* Montgomery, Vt.: Bradford Books, in press.

Richman, C. L., Mitchell, D. B., & Reznick, J. S. Mental travel: Some reservations. *Journal of Experimental Psychology: Human Perception and Performance,* 1979, **5,** 13–18.

Segal, S. J. Processing of the stimulus in imagery and perception. In S. J. Segal (Ed.), *Imagery: Current cognitive approaches*. New York: Academic Press, 1971.

Shepard, R. N., & Metzler, J. Mental rotation of three-dimensional objects. *Science, 1971*, **171**, 701–703.

Shepard, R. N. Psychophysical complementarity. In M. Kubovy and J. R. Pomerantz (Eds.), *Perceptual organization*. Hillsdale, N.J.: Lawrence Erlbaum Associates, 1981, pp. 279–341.

Shwartz, S. P. Studies of mental image rotation: Implications for a computer simulation of visual imagery. Ph.D. dissertation, The Johns Hopkins University, 1979.

Shwartz, S. P. *Mental image size and rotation speed: Evidence for Quasi-pictorial visual images*. Unpublished paper, 1979.

Sternberg, S. High-speed scanning in human memory. *Science, 1966*, **153**, 652–654.

Trehub, A. Neuronal models for cognitive processes: Networks for learning, perception and imagination. *Journal of Theoretical Biology, 1977*, **65**, 141–169.

Waltz, D. L. On the function of mental imagery. *Behavioral and Brain Sciences, 1979*, **2**, 569.

CHAPTER 3

Imagery and the Thought Processes

B. RICHARD BUGELSKI

There is no way one can begin to discuss the role of imagery in thinking without coming up against the mind–body problem. Fodor (1981) has recently described an approach that cognitive psychologists might endorse that circumvents the problem. He suggests a "functionalist" orientation that rests on what he calls a *central state identity theory*. Such a theory assumes an identity between mental states and neurophysiological events in the brain. Specifically, he identifies certain mental particulars, for example, a reported headache, with some corresponding physical state. He calls this a doctrine of "mental particulars." Such a doctrine is held to rest on a base of "token physicalism"; that is, not all possible mental states are assumed to be neurophysiological—only those that we currently know about. There might be some other, as yet unknown, mental states that might not be neurophysiological. A thorough going neurophysiological base would be "type physicalism." Fodor sees no need for such commitment. (How we know about our currently known mental states is not explained.)

On the assumption of token physicalism, then, mental states, events, and processes are the same as their physical activities in the brain that occur when such states are "experienced." As physical events, mental states participate in causal relationships; that is, one mental state can cause another. There need be no necessarily observable behavior to set limits on what a cognitive psychologist might consider worthy of study. As Fodor points out, a behavioristic approach is severely limited to observations of overt activity.

The advantage of the central state identity theory, argues Fodor, is that one can take a variety of explanatory constructs of psychology, such as fears, feelings, and beliefs, at face value. At the same time, because different kinds of physical systems can process the same kinds of "information," one can deal with the software, or programs, of a system without concerning oneself with the physical processing system. Psychology can be free of physiology.

What Fodor believes that the central identity theory accomplishes is to license the use of mentalistic terms as long as one can accumulate useful data at some level of observation, with the quiet understanding that there is a particular physical or neurophysiological state underlying, and, in fact, identical with the mental one. With this license one can even attribute, as Fodor does, mental states to a soda-dispensing machine.

The Fodor approach is in sharp contrast to the traditional behaviorist orientation, which he characterizes as avoiding reference to any nonbehavioral (overt) events. Yet post-Watsonian behaviorists were not averse to introducing internal motoric, glandular, visceral, and even inner-speech, events to aid their efforts toward accounting for stimulus–response relationships. Fodor does not consider the heavy emphasis of neobehaviorists on mediation in sequential behavior. The proposals of Hull (1943), about r_g values, the r_m values of Osgood (1953), the cell assemblies of Hebb (1949), and the movement-produced stimuli described by Guthrie (1935) were all calculated to account for alleged mental states, expectancies, goal direction, and even thoughts. Hull specifically nominated the r_g as the "surrogate of thought." Nor should Skinner (1953) be omitted from the list of behaviorists concerned with inner behavior. Skinner describes visual imagery, for example, as "inner-seeing" behavior. More recently, King (1978) has identified images as neural events without departing from a behaviorist position into a world of subjectivity.

Fodor gives encouragement to modern cognitive psychologists to pursue their work with programs or software, and this is, of course, most proper. The only danger is that the programs will include assumed processes and structures that go beyond any foreseeable kind of neurophysiology, placing impossible demands on the physiologist and finding fault, not with their own inventions, but with the physiologist who cannot find sensations, percepts, deep structure, schemas, learnings, representations, propositions, memory, or concepts in the nervous system. The fact that there may be no such things is apparently given short consideration. There is the additional danger that there will be a return to the nativistic rationalism such as Fodor (1976) advocates.

The preceding comments are not meant to impose any restrictions on theorizing or speculating or on any research operations in which anyone cares to indulge. Rather, it is hoped that such ventures would pay more than lip service attention to conceivable neurophysiology and not insert black boxes into larger black boxes. A research program where people are asked to "image" a previously presented stimulus while viewing a present stimulus to combine the two, that is, image and percept, into a now more complete percept might (Stromeyer & Psotka, 1970) be tempered by an awareness of the Segal-Fusella (1970) studies that demonstrated the difficulty of visual imagery while actually looking at something else. We note that the Segal–Fusella work was not physiological per se. It merely pointed out the role of the presumed visual structures in the brain. Similarly, 100 years of study of eidetic imagery (Haber, 1979) might have profitted from some appreciation of what an image might actually be beyond a hasty identification of imagery with recalled perceptions.

IMAGERY AND THOUGHT

With the above introduction we can consider two kinds of "inner" activity, thinking and imagery, both long considered "mental." We can attempt to determine something about them and to determine whether they are related in any way. The subject of thinking really has not received much attention from psychologists compared with their other prolific activities. From the very beginning of scientific psychology under Wundt, thinking was considered a "higher mental process," a complex product of more elementary activities including imagery, and not something to be studied in itself, because of its complexities. The findings of the Würzburg school were of no great positive help, although they set a trend by denying the role of imagery in thinking. The fact that the Würzburgians were not studying thinking but rather time measured in thousandths of a second apparently did not disturb them. The finding that subjects were not aware of imagery during the intervals observed was dismissed by Wundt himself as irrelevant to the argument. The later efforts of Watson (1914) to exile imagery and to treat thinking as only verbal behavior, implicit or overt, proved too sterile to enlist researchers, and the subject of thinking was pretty much ignored except by those concerned with concepts and ideas. Vigotsky, Piaget, and Kohler acquired prominence and enthusiastic followers despite the vagueness of their observations. Their strong conclusions were enough to encourage those who find behavioral methods and assumptions distasteful. Despite years of study of "concepts" such as "conservation" and "insight" and of "concepts" themselves, we are not much further ahead today than if their work had never been reported. It may behoove us to take another look at what the behaviorists have been saying all along; perhaps something has been overlooked both by some behaviorists and their critics. Instead of taking the Fodor approach and his software, perhaps more can be gained if we reexamine the hardware. The results may not be much more satisfying, but they might point the way to a beginning of a solution of the thinking problem.

Imagery, Language, and Cognition

The three words in the heading are the title of a recent book by Kaufmann (1980) that is a welcome and challenging effort to deal with thinking wherein imagery and language are taken to be the only meaningful operations in thinking. Kaufmann roundly and soundly criticizes the conclusions of Piaget, Furth, Bruner, Köhler, Neisser, and Fodor, among others and, in general,

clears away much of the confusion that prevails and prevents a more pro-
ductive approach to an analysis of thinking. We do not repeat the criticisms
here, and the reader is urged to peruse Kaufmann's work. Kaufmann has
the courage to denounce the common acceptance of "concepts" and other
"structures" masquerading as entities. Concepts for Kaufmann are merely
capacities to respond appropriately to some situations. Such capacities are
acquired and limited in relation to opportunities to learn. Concepts are not
mental entities enjoying some kind of life in an ethereal space, held as
"possessions," as implied in such statements: he now has the concept of
conservation. Concepts are, in fact, only a disguise for "ideas" that psychologists are as yet still too embarrassed to introduce in their writings,
although some come very close with their schemas, propositions, and deep
structures. When Kaufmann presents his own solutions to the problem of
thinking, he takes the stand that imagery and verbalization are the only tools
of thought. With this position there is no dispute as far as the present writer
is concerned. Kaufmann's interest in "creative" thinking and problem solving, however, is not the present concern and his failure to consider the basic
issues of how imagery should be defined and how verbalizations operate in
other than problem-solving situations require a more basic approach, which
is amplified below.

Thinking as a Routine Bodily Process

As living creatures we all undergo considerable internal activity, most of
which goes along more or less continuously and is not easily observed,
discussed, or understood. Our breathing, digestion, circulation, glandular
secretions, and so on, along with their neural innervations and accompaniments, are routine activities. Some of these, over the centuries, have been
probed by skilled observers who described some of their observations—
these descriptions we now refer to with the words "knowledge" or "information." For the present purpose, "knowledge" and "information" are,
like concepts, only capacities to respond in a descriptive pattern of verbal
reactions and not possessions of some mentalistic stores. Other activities,
often involving small muscular systems or small adjustments in muscular
systems including the vocal apparatus, have also been described from time
to time, but not quite so completely. The neural accompaniments of such
activities are less subject to observation, and our "information" about these
is rather limited. Some of this reduced muscular and neural activity goes on
when we are not actively engaged in some easily observable behavior like
running—this is not to say, however, that it does not go on when we are
running, for example, but the running activity is much more obvious and
readily observable. When we are sitting or lying down, "doing nothing"
(i.e., an observer does not find anything of interest—the subject is quiet,
not conversing, not engaged in any overt activity), we are also engaged in
small muscle and neural activity that we normally disregard. When asked

"What are you doing?" we might respond with "I'm thinking." Such a response is of no great help to the observer as he or she does not and cannot know what we are actually doing. We might not be thinking at all—although the probability is that we are; we probably are always thinking, just as we are always breathing, and, as in the case of breathing, more or less effectively. Our breathing is not always smooth and regular—it changes in pace, depth, and duration and is interrupted by sneezes, coughs, and other disturbances.

The point is that there is no point in singling out *thinking* as some special, unique function of humans as Descartes did. *Cogito ergo sum* was not any more or less valid a syllogism than *I breathe, therefore I am*. Descartes would have existed regardless of whether he thought. His circulation was just as necessary to his existence as were his thoughts, perhaps more so. By distinguishing thought from other physical activities, Descartes created the fiction of the mind and its postulated activities so that thoughts were now free to circulate in a nonspatial arena, freed from a physical body. The Descartian legacy lives on in modern cognitive psychology, which more and more freely and frequently speaks of mental phenomena and mental activities and persists in the folly of trying to discover how the mind works. The efforts of Watson and his followers, the neobehaviorists, to create a scientific psychology based on a monistic materialism have been forgotten.

The fact is that Descartes is alive and well and living in "cognition land." If we are to make some progress in the attempt to describe thinking, we must reject that legacy and the very concept of cognition and its associate, information processing. To begin with, we can admit that we can acquire data and that we can "process" data, but there is no such *thing* as "information" and, consequently, no way to process it. There can be no science dealing with nonexistent "stuff." We must return to an appreciation of the animal organism as a material structure with various kinds of materialistic operation occurring inside the skin and push along in our observations as best we can, however long it takes. What needs to be done is to clear away the obstacles to our progress. The major obstacle is the failure to define our problem in realistic terms. The first requirement is to define the issues, problems, and terms. The terms in most immediate need of definition are "thinking" and "imagery."

THE DEFINITION OF THINKING

Thinking has been characterized above as a more or less constant activity of small muscles or small contractions of large muscles along with neural activity, unspecified, and presently unspecifiable. We talk about thinking when we do not observe the thinker in large-scale muscle activity, even such activity as talking. When people are talking, we tend to say that they are talking, not thinking, although we do make some exceptions when we refer to people "thinking on their feet" (as if that were an inappropriate position). Sometimes lecturers are said to be thinking faster than they are talking or thinking about what they will say next or later while they are still saying what we are hearing. Freudians differentiate between speech and thought as when someone has a speech accident and says something that presumably was not "meant" to be said but *thought* it, unconsciously, so they say. Whatever fault we may find with Freud, we might consider the notion that thinking does not have to be conscious, anymore than breathing.

Thinking is commonly considered to be "covert" activity, that is, occurring inside the skin and therefore difficult to observe or identify. As such an activity, there is no basis for hypothesizing that the activity consists of generating thoughts, ideas, hypotheses, or other mystical products. Thinking is an activity. In some instances we can identify some parts of that activity as in the classical studies of Jacobsen (1932) and in current electroencephalographic (EEG) studies. Other current studies of split-brain patients contribute some additional light on the activities of the two hemispheres of the brain where patients solve certain kinds of problems with the right brain and left hand while other problems are solved with the left brain and right hand. In the latter case speech can be employed to report the solution or answer to a question; in the former it cannot. We cannot identify thinking solely with the use of speech, as that would disqualify the split-brain patient who solves problems of certain kinds with the right hemisphere; it would also eliminate deaf-mutes, preverbal children, and animals. There is no reason to disqualify these cases. To argue that Köhler's apes were not thinking would be to engage in human chauvinism.

The above comments are not designed to deny that speech and small vocal apparatus actions do not participate in thinking. On the contrary, with adult humans, it is highly probable that little thinking goes on without such activity. The question really pertains to what part of thinking involves speech and language and what kinds of thinking can proceed without speech. In short, what is the role of speech in thinking? The answer to this question can be delayed until more immediate matters are considered.

We can start best by asking "When do we think?" It is implied above that we are always thinking, but psychologists have generally chosen to believe that we think only when we have a problem. The implication is that problems are solved by thinking when they most commonly are solved by surrender, somebody else, the passage of time, and manifest behavior (so-called trial and error), and when they are solved by thinking, it may not be because the thinker followed some laws of logic or thought well. We always think as well as we can. It does no good to tell someone to think right or straight or to be logical. The solutions commonly come by chance; the answer, if it comes, just comes. The notion that we think only when we have problems probably comes from John Dewey (1910), who published his influential *How We Think* a long time ago. According to Dewey, we think when we have no habit to handle a given stimulus situation. Actually all that

that says is that we think when we are not engaged in overt behavior. It is true, to be sure, that if we are not engaged in overt behavior, our behavior (except for our posture—sitting or lying down) will be covert. But frequently we may have no problem in the sense of some pressing need to take some course of action. We may have nothing to do except sit idly, or, on the other hand, we may be engaged in even strenuous or quite obvious overt behavior (routine mass production factory work, eating, reading, and bathing) that does not prevent or interfere with some of covert neural activity that can occur along with some verbal activity. Who does not think at the dinner table? Is eating so demanding a task that it engages us completely? It may be if we are famished, but not normally. We can think while eating, taking a shower, typing, and even while sleeping. Our dreams are a kind of thinking— they are covert, but they are certainly marked by various overt activities and particular kinds of brain wave patterns and eye movements. The thinking in dreaming may be very vivid although most often quite disorganized and uncontrolled by the reality situation. Daydreams are similarly uncontrolled with the difference that one generally can state that he is daydreaming, if asked, whereas no one can do the same about night or sleep dreams until they are over.

There is one aspect of thinking behavior that is of special importance. The allusion to daydreams just given suggests that thinking, whatever else it may be, involves our past histories, what is too loosely called "memory." It is doubtful that anyone could think in the absence of a history, of past experiences, that is, without having been programmed. The program is probably not neatly organized and systematic, but then neither is our thinking. We think what we have to think, not what we might want to think. We are victims of our past history. The point is quite simply made if we ask a child to think about atomic energy and the child has never heard of either atoms or energy. Most of our thinking in unfamiliar areas will be rather ill suited to the situation. So-called interdisciplinary scholars are not famous for success at problem solving. Even within a single discipline the specialization among members is so striking that one cannot do much thinking about a colleague's problems.

So far it has been emphasized that thinking is not some special kind of activity that occurs in the absence of other activity or only on special occasions. The kind of activity that goes on when we are thinking is going on more or less continuously. The social importance of the activity may be nil, and its practical value may be negligible. No problems need be either involved or solved—in reality, most of our problems are not solved by our thinking but by other circumstances or the thinking of others who direct us or propose solutions that we can accept. To refer to thinking as a "higher mental process" is narcissistic whimsy. Thinking is neither higher nor lower than any other physiological activity. Some people spend more time in "covert" activity than others, and some of these achieve great reputations as scholars, teachers, inventors, philosophers, and so on than do others, some of whom spend equal or greater amounts of time in the same kinds of activity. The difference between a "great" thinker and the common person is that the great thinker has had a different history and has thinking that involves different reactions, some of which prove useful.

The Thinking Process

What actually goes on when we think? The answer depends on the circumstances and conditions under which we raise the question. A woman trying on a new dress or hair style might ask a husband or friend "What do you think?" The respondent may not have thought anything but under these circumstances says something like "It's nice" or "It's *you*." What has occurred hardly deserves the label of "thinking." It is a social convention and the verbal responses might well be lies. The respondent may not have described his thinking at all—a point to be remembered when we consider the role of language in thinking. It is unlikely that one could simultaneously think contradictory "thoughts." When we ask someone for an opinion on a novel, a film, or a television show we may again obtain social conventions, polite evasions, or brief responses such as "It's great—you must read it." In such cases it might be better not to ask what someone thinks or thought but what was the emotional reaction to—or how that person felt about a certain thing. If we pursue the matter and force someone to actually discuss a book, question, issue, or problem, we find that the respondent now pauses and, at least for a while, "reflects." Reflection amounts to going through some kind of recall exercise that is too loosely called a "memory search." The "memory" is not an object, a storehouse, or a bin to be searched, and there is no one to search it as a separate internal observer of inner contents. The memory is the person, reacting to stimuli, both the external (in the form of the initial question) and internal stimuli, as one process arouses another. The processes aroused are accompanied by emotional reactions and are not necessarily orderly or systematic. Try recalling the contents of any novel read recently. Will you start with word 1 on page 1 and recall the words? That would take about as much time as the original reading. What will actually happen is that the episodes, events, scenes, characters, and so on in the novel will appear to occur to you in varied and scrambled order. Some exciting or provocative event will be recalled from the middle or the end, and jumps will occur back and forth as one continues the recall process. In talking about the ongoing recall, the respondent will try to impose some kind of order on the reports so as not to appear stupid or disorganized and will suppress statements about the conclusion until the beginning has been described, and so on. The respondent will omit reporting events of a trivial nature that come to mind and may omit incidental characters or incidents and come through with a synopsis, precis, more or less of a "framework," but this is what the respondent reported—not recalled. No one remembers in the form of a plot, schema, theme, plan, or any other such structure. The nervous system has no way to store schemata. Any seriation that occurs will be in the report, not necessarily in the recall. Schemata are *products* of a report.

If the circumstances are more material, for example, a car will not start in cold weather, the owner of the car also thinks. It occurs to the car owner (who has learned that cold weather lowers battery efficiency) that the car battery is weak. The gas line might be frozen—the owner has heard about that, too; maybe the "points" are corroded—and so on through a trouble-shooting list, the length of which depends on the background in automotive repairs the owner has acquired. Most of the thinking in such cases is inef-fective and the owner calls the garage, another "thought." Experienced mechanics solve the problem, usually without much thought as they have a routine of replacing everything they "think of" until the car starts.

We can turn now to an area that is commonly recognized as calling for real thinking, the area of mathematics. If John can dig 2 feet of trench per hour and Henry can dig 3 feet per hour, how long will it take the two boys to dig 8 feet? Here we have a mathematical problem, and we admire the young algebra student who can solve it. We do not especially admire anyone who answers "4" to the question of "how much are 2 and 2?" Yet the admiration of the algebra problem solver is no more warranted as far as the processes engaged in than of the simple addition expert. Nothing any more mysterious goes on in the one than in the other. Each has learned to talk to himself or herself, that is, subvocally, and has acquired certain verbal habits that function in the given cases. What is interesting about the two cases is that when someone says "2 and 2 make 4," we find the answer coming quickly (from the 10-year old) whereas the answer to the ditch problem takes a little longer—it obviously involves more steps and more verbal habits. The young algebraist says "Let John's output be X and Henry's be $X + 1$," and so on. The qualitative nature of the activity has not changed; it is still verbal behavior. There is an additional step that is commonly overlooked. In "2 and 2 make 4," the response is strictly verbal. It can be acquired by a 2-year old who does not know what "2" means. Most youngsters can count to 20 or 100 without the slightest "notion" of what numbers amount to. Many people can multiply 9 times 8 without the additional verbal habit that amounts to knowing that 9 has been added to itself 7 additional times. The reactions are verbal habits and unworthy of special distinction. In the algebra problem, however, the young student probably first "thinks" of a ditch, of two boys, and the boys must be distinct in some way. At this point some new internal activity takes place. The solver enjoys some imagery. But the imagery is immediately translated into verbal statements. The boys' rates are given different names, and X and $X + 1$ come into the situation because algebra calls for verbal habits that deal with letters and not people or ditches or any concrete objects. The boy who has "learned" algebra can solve the problem; those unfortunates who have not learned it cannot solve it as directly. They will take much longer, dealing with John and Henry and ditches, shovels, and dirt. They might start with, "Well, it will take John 4 hours alone, and Henry will take, let's see, 8 divided by 3 is $2\frac{2}{3}$, and together it ought to take less than either. Now, if John digs 2 feet and Henry digs 3 feet in the first hour, that's five feet, or 5 feet per hour together; then, they can finish the 8 feet in, uh, 5 goes into 8, $1\frac{3}{5}$, and a fifth is 12 minutes, so $\frac{3}{5}$ is 36 minutes, and the 1 hour makes 1 hour and 36 minutes." In both cases numbers as verbal responses have entered the picture. We have become used to thinking of numbers as symbols, because they are "abstract," that is, they can stand for anything—apples, horses, books, and so on. The fact that they are such symbols, however, does not change the inner activity through which they operate; they remain verbal habits.

Consider a different kind of thinking, that involving relationships. Henry is older than Mary and Mary is younger than Sue. Is Henry older or younger than Sue? The problem has no solution, but that only makes it better for our purpose. How does one attack such a problem? Here it does not help to translate into *X, Y,* and *Z.* The thinker pondering the problem will, in most cases, report that he "pictures" Henry, Mary, and Sue in some order. But "older" is a category that cannot be "pictured" directly. It is translated or transformed into something that can be pictured. Henry becomes *bigger,* taller, heavier, perhaps almost an adult—one does tend to "picture" children in such problems when first names are used. Henry stands forth as taller than Mary. We also "picture" Mary shorter than Sue, but Sue we cannot picture effectively with Henry. We report that the problem cannot be solved; that is, no satisfying answer can be provided. But this kind of problem and many related kinds of problems force us to think about pictures and picturing, in short, imagery. We found our nonalgebraist picturing John and Henry but saw that the algebraist did not need pictures except in the initial reactions. For Henry, Mary, and Sue, everyone needs pictures or uses them despite some denials. We need to inquire into imagery.

THE NATURE OF IMAGERY

Modern cognitive psychology is quite comfortable with imagery. Comfort does not include assigning any importance to the role of imagery for some psychologists. For them imagery may be an epiphenomenon—they prefer to talk about "representations," a term that is assumed to be free of the subjectivism associated with imagery and its implications of introspection, its connotation of "pictures" somewhere in the head, and its long history of banishment from scientific approaches. The fact that representations have no specified physiological base does not deter anyone from talking about them. In any event, it is now considered perfectly proper to talk about imagery in the sense that it is no longer a dirty word. In 1914 Watson rejected imagery as a meaningless term, a "ghost" of sensation, with "sensation" an equally meaningless term for Watson. In writing about thinking, Watson turned to "inner speech," subvocal, "implicit" responses, and identified thinking with talking to oneself. He did not consider the awkward notion of who was doing the talking or who was the self. Paivio (1971) has pointed out that the basis for assuming implicit speech has no more solid a foundation than the assumption of imagery. Both are implicit, inner, internal, unobservable. (Watson did try to demonstrate movements of the larynx and of the tongue in thinking but his findings were never accepted as proof of anything). Although Watson was willing to accept a whole variety of inner responses, including kinesthetic stimuli, he found it unnecessary or undesirable to deal with images that he could easily have translated into "inner neural responses." Even if sensations were omitted from the theory, it was possible for Watson to deal with "sensory responses," and there was no reason to prevent Watson from accepting the conditioning of such responses and calling them images. Leuba (1940) approached the proper position by defining images as conditioned sensations. He was only a step away from where he should have moved, namely, to defining images as conditioned sensory responses. Nothing further is required to accept imagery into the structure of psychology if one accepts the undeniable notion that we do respond to stimulation of our sense organs, in one way or another, and that such responses can be conditioned. For the latter we ask no more than to assume that something like conditioning does occur. Without the assumption of conditioning, psychology should surrender to nativists and forget about its ambitions.

Characteristics of Imagery

The assumption that the image is a conditioned response opens a much wider door than traditionally allowed for those inclined to include imagery in their speculations. It calls for the recognition that imagery is at least a neural activity that like other neural activity involving sense organs may well be accompanied by motor reactions to some degree just as ordinary seeing and hearing may be accompanied by eye movements and ear adjustments. Pupillary and lens reactions as well as eye movement are routinely involved in seeing and may be minimally present in visual imagery. Like other neural reactions, we can assume that imagery will not be static but, rather, an activity that follows other activity and precedes still other activity. To restrict ourselves to visual imagery for the moment, there will be no static or any other kinds of "pictures in the mind" for some "mind's eye" to observe. Watson was eminently correct in proposing the banishment of such terminology, which presently is enjoying a revival, being quietly introduced in the disguise of quotation marks. We can presume that there can be no such things as eidetic images in the form of "pictures" "out there." Haber's (1979) extensive studies of alleged "eidetikers" boiled down to the finding that so-called eidetic children were different from other children only in the fact that they used the present tense in reporting about previously shown pictures. They were in no way superior in their descriptions or different in any other characteristics. At best we might consider *recurring* images or "instant replays," but the notion of a static image somehow just sitting there for inspection is contradictory to everything we know about neural action and must be dismissed.

Incidentally, Paivio's (1971) suggestion that there is a distinction between imagery and verbal activity on the dimension of sequentiality appears to be unallowable. Images are every bit as dynamic as language and flow along in sequences, one leading to another (Bugelski, 1974). It can be routinely shown that people can "tie" one image to another almost indefinitely under suitable instructions. In his studies the present author has asked people to "think" about some item, for example, a soldier, then a sofa, then soldier and sofa, then wine, and then sofa and wine, trying to form images of the pairs of items in such sequences. They generally are quite successful with lists of 20 or 25 words, even though the words have no association frequency of any moment. A bizarre story commonly evolves with many irrelevant features that succeeding editing could remove. How many authors operate in this fashion? Or do they think first of "plots" and "schema"? It is not suggested here that some writers do not use "formulas" to start some story. Certainly one can *verbalize* a formula about "boy meets girl," and so forth to get started.

The basic operational function of imagery has been alluded to above. Images are responses. As such, they generate stimuli, just as any other responses do. Such image-produced stimulation can lead to other imagery or overt responses. They are similar in function to Guthrie's (1935) movement-produced stimuli, Osgood's (1953) r_m and Hull's (1943) r_g values. Because of their heavy neural loading, they are probably most easily described as Hebb's (1949) cell assemblies.

Traditionally images have been described as vague, fleeting, and lacking the intensity of the responses to the original stimulation. Such descriptions are entirely appropriate, and one could hardly expect anything else of a conditioned response which by definition lacks the original stimulus and is rarely a precise reproduction of the original response to the unconditioned stimulus. But an even more important consideration has been suggested by Hebb (1949). Most common objects to which we are exposed are encountered on numerous occasions in various settings, positions, angles of regard, and so on. We see our mothers in the kitchen, the living room, at picnics, dressed in various garbs, sitting, standing, lying down, and so on. The visual responses have some commonality, and the corresponding imagery will also be so endowed. The word "mother," then, will evoke not only one image or cell assembly, but perhaps dozens simultaneously with no single, clear-cut, or even immediate reaction. It will be what Hebb called a "t" or *total* kind of integrated response consisting of parts of many cell assemblies. Subjectively, it will be vague and fleeting, as it well should be. Hypothetically one may have stronger, richer imagery of something seen rarely or even once, such as the image of Greenland seen from an airplane for a few seconds. The failure of a satisfactory image to occur may be due to the additional fact that frequent verbalization may lead to a simple verbal response to a stimulus that might previously have aroused imagery. It may no longer do so because a verbal reaction short-circuits it. Images can get in the way of problems calling for verbal solutions.

The Subjective Quality of Imagery

Some people claim they have no imagery. Such a claim is absurd as it would imply that these people had never learned anything. They would not know what an alarm clock was when they awakened to its ring and might just as well spend the rest of the day in bed as they could not find their way out of it. The point is that learning and retention amount to the acquisition of imagery as conditioned responses and its stimulation. As a simple example, we consider the acquisition or learning of the *meaning* of an apple. We can for the moment ignore the connotative meanings, the emotional aspects of a reaction, to the stimulus of an apple. A child first exposed to an apple cannot know what it is (we can ignore some probable reactions to something that is round and colored). The parent shows the child an apple and calls it by that name. The child hears "apple" while looking at it. Later on, perhaps after several occasions, the child hears the word "apple" and something happens inside her that is different from whatever happens when she hears "baby" or "shoe." The something that happens is a neural event corresponding in some respects to the neural events that occurred when she was looking at it. Skinner calls this "inner seeing." That helps, but not much, as we do not know what "outer" seeing might be. We do see, to be sure, but no psychologist has yet described the act of seeing other than that when we see, we make appropriate responses to some visual stimulus. The responses may be gross, overt, or minimal, like saying "apple" when one is asked to identify a particular fruit. If the apple is a realistic wax copy, one might be wrong. In any case the inner response is all that an image can be. It is, presumably, always a response to some stimulation, external or internal and, most importantly, conditionable. The response will commonly be extremely brief, giving way to or being replaced by other inner responses that it, in turn, generates. It can be restored and "held" for some short periods by re-presenting the conditioned stimulus, just as seeing can be prolonged by focusing on some external object; even the latter kind of continuous seeing is interrupted by periods of nonseeing (Hebb, 1949). The inner response may also be retained for some short intervals by recurrent stimulation of an internal variety that Hebb called "phase sequences."

Thus far nothing has been said about the alleged subjectivity of images, of their arrival into "consciousness," or of any other mental factor. Most images are probably "unconscious" in that the response occurs and terminates without the imager talking about it or "knowing" that it had occurred. When one does talk about one's imagery, the description will be no better, as a communication to others, than a report of a bellyache, headache, some pain, or other internal activity such as a grumbling in the stomach. There will be reference to external world objects, to be sure, but one might as well try to describe one's heartbeat as to describe an image. Many words might be used, but the correspondence of the words to the event might be minimal and indirect. Skinner has addressed this problem of describing internal events (1953) and points out how the social community can come to agree about descriptions of bruises or other external damage to the body, but the degree of agreement about a headache report obviously suffers. When someone reports, "My head is splitting," we can sympathize in part from appreciation of logs being split, but noticing that the head involved is quite intact, we can hardly agree with the report and may say "Take an aspirin." To some extent we can learn to describe some images, and, if not in words, we can identify scenes, objects, and even pictures of people previously seen. We can help a police artist construct a sketch of a criminal, although the sketches do not usually resemble the individuals with any precision. To the extent that we can describe someone previously observed, we are describing an image as there is no other basis for the description than some internal event that is being restimulated into occurring by verbal cues or by other internal events, as when the victim of a robbery says, "Oh, yes, he was wearing a cap, and, uh, dark glasses." Descriptions solicited from several people can result in varying identifications of a person as tall, short, medium, and so on. Such descriptions should not be denigrated as they can only be poor because of the usually brief periods of original observation. Apples have been seen thousands of times, but bank robbers have been observed only momentarily and under disturbed conditions.

One further aspect of imagery should be noted. Images are not some kinds of bare, simple, lonely, abstract concretisms. One does not just image a chair, for example, as some distillation of chairdom. It is always a specific chair, in a specific locale, perhaps of a specific time of one's life. It has size, color, texture, and location; it is somebody's chair, and so forth. One does not image a horse "as such"—it is a living, active creature, of a color and size normally seen in some real world. What is more, the image does not just "sit" there but becomes integrated into more and more complex response patterns that can change in a multitude of ways as different stimuli come to bear. Thus, as Bower (1970) pointed out, an image of a whale can be adorned with a hat, a cigar, and anything else that might be suggested or occur to the imager. An image of "John" can be, contrary to Fodor (1976), both tall and fat, lying down or standing, as called for by suitable stimulation. If John is ordinarily regarded as both fat and tall, an image of John will not deny either feature. How one comes to *describe* the image might vary with the questions that might be asked. In any case the image will not repose quietly for detailed inspection but will vary with all sorts of instructions or situational demands. The image can correspond to a view at a distance or close up as in Kosslyn et a.l's (1979) experiments. The veridicality of an image will be a function of one's experience. One who has not seen the Eiffel Tower except in photographs cannot have a "good" image of that structure. On the other hand, a dog can be imaged as huge or tiny depending on the stimulus situation. To repeat, images are responses to stimuli and their characteristics will be functions of our experience to a range of stimulus features.

A special point should be made that illustrates the relation of language to imagery. If people who no longer use a childhood language are asked to respond to words in that language, they will react with imagery related to childhood. When the same words are employed in translation to their present language, their imagery, as reported, will be to current experience (Bugelski, 1977).

There is no compelling reason for concern about the reportability of images. We can accept them as internal, mediating responses and proceed to study their role in whatever activities people engage in. In the present instance, our concern is with thinking. We can now look at the image in the thinking activity.

IMAGERY AND THOUGHT

We have already described thinking as an activity that is more or less continuous although perhaps minimal when we are engaged in gross motor activity. Even in such instances, as in splitting logs, for example, the splitter thinks about how to strike the wedge with the maul or where to aim the axe. In driving a car along the road the driver is constantly observing the road, traffic, intersections, and so on and making preliminary adjustments. He is, in short, expecting certain events to occur in a proper sequence. Such expectancies have been described by Hebb as the antedating firing of cell assemblies that would shortly be fired by impending stimuli. The behaviorist's description of mediating stimuli and responses to such stimuli all refer to the same thing, some internal process that runs off as a consequence of appropriate stimulation and that generates the next response in a series.

This is not to say that all imagery in "anticipatory" as Neisser (1967) argues. Some images are anticipatory; most are more likely to be operative when nothing is expected to happen. In a daydream we do not anticipate any realistic manipulations of wistful fancies.

The accounts of internal responses presented by Hebb and Hull seem at least promising. We can now add the "image" to these internal events or responses and recognize that thinking is a serial activity where one response is replaced by another until some stimulus situation is removed or changed. Thinking, however, often occurs in the absence of immediate situational stimuli that require some adjustment. We can think about situations that are far afield, where quite literally we can do nothing ourselves and where the situation will not be changed as a result of our thinking. Thus we can think about possible American MIAs (soldiers missing in action) in Viet Nam all day long, and nothing of consequence would be accomplished. We can think about a problem such as what to do about a herd of deer on a small island where the population of deer has exceeded the food supply and some deer might starve. The situation is remote, and the probability of any action on our part is small. How do we think about such a problem? First, why do we think of it? A report is heard on the radio or seen in a newspaper. Some people (those with conditioned emotional reactions to starving animals) become concerned. They start to "think" about the deer. Only humans can think about such a problem as only humans have the language possibilities that are required to state the problem or initiate it. Thus the words "deer," "starving," "island," and so on will arouse the appropriate internal events, that is, imagery, and these in turn will arouse additional associated events. One will have "images" of deer alone, together, jumping, nibbling on tree bark, and so forth. "Food" or "starvation," as words, will arouse other imagery of what animals eat; the imagery will probably be restricted to vegetarian animals; and imagery of islands will arouse additional imagery of boats, helicopters, and so on to bring food to the animals. Hunters will have imagery of shooting down the herd from helicopters, and so on. Some of the imagery will be named or verbalized, leading to more imagery. One will recall some of the verbal messages of the newscast that described the problem as difficult of solution for various "reasons." Eventually the thinking process about that area of event, that is, the sequence of imagery, will cease because of other external events; for example, the telephone rings, and we are off thinking about something else, meaning that new trains of imagery and verbalisms are initiated.

Note that the images occur to the thinker, who does not choose or initiate any of them. One cannot help what one is thinking about and thinks only what one does think. There is nothing "creative" about the process. The content is determined by past experience. The immediate imagery may have many situational determinants related to the past experience as has been suggested by students of the "laws of association." One can ordinarily dismiss or interrupt some imagery by verbal self-stimulation and have a new train start. On the other hand, some imagery will persist and keep recurring as when one has "a song running through" one's head. A tune whistled in the morning can keep up a sporadic existence for several hours.

THE ROLE OF LANGUAGE IN THINKING

We have already indicated that the human being capable of language will use it. We repeat the caveat that the deaf-mute or child will not be able to think as efficiently in some situations where language is a help. What is the nature of this help? The verbal human can react to situations with verbal responses. In the "2 times 2" situation the verbal human merely responds verbally—no imagery is required, or, for that matter, useful. As problems increase in scope, difficulty, number of variables, and so on, the verbal human will make an increasing number of such verbal responses. Some of these will arouse imagery, appropriate or not, to the solution. There is not much else that can go on. The nervous system is incapable of operating with anything other than neural responses. There are no "stored" ideas, concepts, abstractions, propositions, or other "representations." There are only neurons firing or not firing. When one has learned something, it is not that anything has been stored within that person. It is only a matter of changes in the neural firing patterns. One does not search a memory or conjure up any nonphysical operations. There is no point to talking about a "memory" as there can be no such *thing*.

Estes (1980) comes close to an appropriate appreciation of memory when he states that memory amounts to changes in the organism that make one different from what he was before. After some experience (learning) one is able to do things, for example, make verbal responses, that could not be made before. Nothing has been stored, but a change in the person has occurred. The change itself can change or disappear or be difficult to stimulate into action, especially if the stimulus or stimulus pattern in not quite the same. We then say "I forgot."

Our thinking is controlled by whatever stimulation taps our past experience. On the adult human level such stimulation is largely verbal and much of our behavior is verbal regardless of whether there is anything worthy of being distinguished as thinking going on. Some of the verbalization will generate imagery, but quite often it will not. Sometimes the imagery will be helpful in the sense of being adjustive and eliminating problems; sometimes it will only create problems.

Language is full of buzz words that generate emotions and imagery. In the political arena we face problems because different people use the same words and "mean" different things, that is, have different, personal, individual imagery underlying the words. Words such as democracy, human rights, quality education, inner city, civil rights, The International Year of the Handicapped, and so on all mean a variety of things to a variety of people. These words initiate different imagery in different people. Although language is the basic means of communication, there is little real communication among people. We do the best we can. As psychologists we would do better if we avoided the buzz words of our field: sensation, minds, storage, coding, and so on.

The Problem of Concepts

Much of the difficulty in appreciating the nature of thinking arises from the fictions we have invented in trying to elevate thinking from the "lower" processes. Fodor (1976) has invented a "language of thought" that does not rest on verbalizations or imagery and that apparently goes on by way of some other mechanisms. Such mechanisms are familiar to us under the labels of "concepts" and "abstractions" that can now be considered. A favorite concept of psychologists is the "category," and we can start there.

We should recognize that words such as "concept" and "category" do not refer to anything an individual possesses. "Category," like "concept," is a basket word that a variety of different objects might be called on different occasions. If we say the word "animal," we do not necessarily communicate anything except to arouse the image of a dog in most people (Bugelski, 1970), a horse in someone else, or perhaps a cat in another. When we have some occasion to talk about a group of living creatures that includes cats, dogs, and horses, we can speak of animals, but we should remember that we are simply speaking of more than one living creature and not much more than that. We do not think in categories or concepts. As Kaufmann (1980) has emphasized, there are no such entities as concepts. They are verbal skills. The Vigotsky (1962) experiments prove only that given a puzzle, deliberately contrived to be difficult, people will venture guesses, that is, try to please the experimenter, by mouthing one noise or another. When they find they are correct on one occasion, they will use the same noise later only to be told that they are now incorrect. They now must remember that more than one feature of an object must be examined and must learn another verbal rule. Eventually, depending on the experimenter's needs, they are able to make some one noise in the presence of some object that has a number of characteristics, each of which had to be learned independently. They are now said to have a concept. Actually all they have is a collection of noises, a verbal rule, that meets an experimenter's stipulations. The situation is no different in mathematics and so-called logical or symbolic thinking. People are able, on suitable instruction, to work with Venn diagrams, formulas, various symbols, to follow verbal instructions (rules) and to solve all kinds of problems. This does not mean that they have "concepts" of identity, exclusion, or of any other nature. Children learn to "take" square roots and may become quite skillful about it. They can be told what a square root is, that is, how one writes down a certain number, but what is a concept of a square root? Does such a concept exist in anyone? Or is it one or several statements that mathematicians can make in a given situation?

Abstractions

In the realm of mathematics we are told that numbers are abstractions, that is, concepts of some sort. It is true that numbers can be verbalized to a variety of objects, for example, sheep, blades of grass, stars, people, and so on. Clearly, they are not things in themselves but must be somehow independent of the objects that are counted or enumerated. Primitive people are reported to be unable to count beyond 2 or the number of fingers, perhaps fingers and toes. They are said to have no or a limited "concept of number."

They might be more properly described as having a limited number of numbers to apply in counting situations, quite possibly with a limited number of counting situations to deal with. Does anyone, even the most astute mathematician, have a concept of 21? A different concept of 22? Or does he "see," that is, image, either the numerals involved or a collection of objects, perhaps dots or an ace and a king of playing cards, or merely a collection of items that do not appear to provoke some number utterance such as 1, 2, or 3, which could be readily made to a small collection of items? In tachistoscopic tests we do fairly well up to 7 or 9 by way of uttering a correct response. Beyond that our "concepts" get into difficulty and become mixed up with each other. We see a "lot" or a mess, a pile (all words for other "concepts"?). Just because the word "pile" is used when one is faced with a heap of rubbish, shoes, hay, money, or anything else, must we have a concept of a pile, or does not Pavlovian generalization serve to provoke a common word response when similar stimulation occurs? We learn to call any collection of objects "a pile." No "concepts" need be involved.

The alleged difference between abstract and concrete is only that. Any word is already abstract whether it applies to a brick or to some conceptual term such as "number," "happiness," or "liberty." No one has successfully refuted Bishop Berkeley's contention that one thinks in specific images, even in the most elevated cerebral realms. Words themselves are concrete noises or concrete smudges on paper. They are "symbols" in the sense of substitutes; in Pavlov's language they belong to a "second signal system." They are not thereby anymore abstract than any other symbols like flags, medals, or cups or bells and lights. When we think, the images and words we use are concrete, material, physiologically produced events. They are not abstractions in some ethereal world. Numbers or words, whether written or spoken, are symbols only in the sense of second signal systems. The word "dollar" and the dollar sign $ do not differ in levels of abstraction. They are equivalents and differ only in that the sign $ cannot be spoken but only be written or read. When read, however, the same verbal response will be uttered as when the word "dollar" is read. Both are merely items in second signal system. Calling them "abstractions" or "concepts" does not help as we cannot work with concepts or abstractions. We come down to the basic human limitation that we can only think in images and that the images are sometimes conditioned reactions to words. We can also manipulate words themselves as we do in mathematical exercises, logical operations, and normal attempts at communication. Recitation of a string of noises such as $a^2 + b^2 = c^2$ does not differ in essence from a string such as $2 + 2 = 4$. In each case a "problem" might be solved by the utterance. Admirers of problem solvers will say that the reciter has engaged in "thinking." The comment is not only gratuitous and superfluous, it is redundant. Mathematical rules or any other rules are learned as vocal–verbal responses and occur when appropriate stimuli impinge on those who have learned. Not all vocalizations need be considered as tools of thinking. Many of our verbal patterns are

just vocal habits, as when one says "As it were . . ." or "So to say . . . ."
They fill in gaps while we think of what to say next, that is, permit new
images to occur.

Creative Thinking

An important caveat must be introduced in recognizing the preoccupation
of many with "creative thinking." As suggested earlier, thinking is not
something that one engages in or not at whim. It goes on continuously and
cannot be any better than it happens to be. One might as well tell someone
else to be more intelligent than one is as to say "Use your head . . . ."
Creative thinking is no different from any other kind. Thinking, although
not a passive process, is not subject to initiation or direction on command
from any source. Thinking just occurs, and what the thinking amounts to is
what imagery happens to occur to someone. One cannot bid nor forbid
certain images to appear. They occur to appropriate stimuli if the appropriate
background is there to begin with. Ignoring the problems of criteria for
effective or creative thinking, we can recognize that everyone thinks as well
as that person can. It is possible to provide hints, prevent anticipated errors,
and so on in attempting to direct someone's thinking, but the imagery that
will occur to the thinker will be strictly his or her own, arising from the
thinker's past experience. One cannot control thought or improve it, although
it is possible to control situations and circumstances that might channel some
relevant imagery in certain directions.

Imagery and Action: Ideomotor Action

A most significant paper by Greenwald (1970) has received less than deserved
attention. In this paper Greenwald revived the old Jamesian notion of ideomotor action and restated it in conditioning terms. According to Greenwald,
any action or response will generate feedback stimuli; such stimuli will tend
to antedate the response if the response is made with some frequency.
Eventually, because of antedating, the kinesthetic or movement-produced
stimuli, like Hebb's cell assemblies, will be occurring more or less simultaneously with the response and even slightly before it. They can then come
to serve as conditioned stimuli for the response and substitute for the original
stimulus. Such stimuli will, of course, not occur in an environmental vacuum
and can be conditioned to other external stimuli. Thus any stimulus that can
become associated with the feedback stimulus can give rise to the response.
Assuming that the kinesthetic stimulus operates in the same way as an image,
we then have the situation where an image can lead to an action, either
through association with the kinesthetic stimulus, or subsequently, through
its own conditioning with the response. The image can, therefore, directly
elicit the action. We arrive at the conclusion that overt behavior can be the
consequence of one or of a chain of images with the "thought being father

to the act." Because James preceded the Pavlovian efforts, he had to leave his own statement of ideomotor action somewhat vague, and it was not widely viewed with favor. The Greenwald suggestions open the door to an account of the initiation of instrumental behavior (Bugelski, 1979).

Imagery and Emotion

No account of the role of imagery in thinking would be complete without mention of Mowrer's (1960) analysis of the role of language, imagery, and emotion in what passes for thinking and meaning. According to Mowrer, we must distinguish between denotative and connotative meanings. Osgood (1953) had, with his semantic differential, provided a reasonable account of connotative meanings with his finding of the heavy loading of the emotional (pleasant–unpleasant) factor in his ratings. Mowrer accepted such an emphasis and held that most of the meaning of any word was probably a positive or negative emotional reaction. In his famous sentence "Tom is a thief," both Tom and thief would arouse emotional reactions that made up the heart of the meaning. There was a problem, however, in that the emotional factor did not appear to be sufficient to account for all of the meaning. There was still the problem of which Tom and what kind of thief, or in what situations Tom was a thief—some specific source of *denotative adjectives* was missing. Mowrer suggested boldy, for the times, that the denotative specifics were to be found in the associated imagery. Thus "Tom" aroused not only the emotional response associated with him in our backgrounds, but also the images of Tom; "thief" similarly aroused appropriate imagery. With the imagery and emotion, the thought of Tom as a thief could be accounted for, as could the meanings of other verbal expressions of words that were not especially emotional on the Osgood scales. One can be quite indifferent and unemotional about a kumquat and still know what a kumquat is by having an image of a kumquat. To Mowrer's credit, he did not hesitate to introduce imagery to account for denotative meaning, and, as an extension of meaning, to account for the operation of "symbolic processes" or thinking.

CONCLUSIONS

The account of imagery and its role of a mediator in thinking may not satisfy many readers because it does not immediately lead to easily implemented research hypotheses. Hebb's account of his cell assemblies was generally praised but also found somewhat barren of experimental handholds. The purpose of a theory, however, is not only and necessarily to be heuristic and provide research prospects for supporters. One function of a theory is to make sense of a number of previously unrelated findings. It is presumed that the account of imagery provided above has done so. The test of a theory, however, is in its susceptibility to experimental support or disproof. In the present case, because the theory is based on neural reactions, the tests will necessarily be outside the scope of skills of most psychologists who are not physiologically trained. Fortunately, there are such experts available, however, and one supporting research has been reported by John (1959). How positively the support will be accepted will depend on the general skepticism of most psychologists, and it might be argued that the support is largely imaginary. But John reported that he had conditioned cats to respond positively and negatively to high and low tones, respectively. Brain wave patterns of responses to the two tones were identifiably different. One could predict from the brain wave pattern what the animals would do. We have here an instance of where a particular physiological response precedes (causes) a particular response. Now when an intermediate tone was sounded, the brain wave patterns, presumably by stimulus generalization, prior to additional differentiation, tended to resemble either the pattern to the high tone or to the low tone. It could again be predicted what the animal would do. We have then the situation called for by the account of imagery as a neural process leading, in this case, to overt action. An external stimulus that arouses a particular neural response (which we have identified with the image) will on some occasion be aroused by some other stimulus and lead to the appropriate action. Such a demonstration is in keeping with the description of imagery presented here. On the heuristic side, there are some, perhaps more feeble, kinds of support from the recognition that imagery is not a static process in the findings (Bugelski, 1974) of indefinitely long chaining of imagery and the incidental learning of such chains.

To those who decry reductionism and argue against physiological orientations for psychologists, I recall the arguments of Fodor mentioned in the introduction.

The mind–body problem is not going to be solved by ignoring the body, whereas it might well be solved by ignoring the mind. Fodor (1981) chooses the path of dealing with software, and that is perfectly acceptable as much can be learned without constant reference to the nervous system. It is, however, important to recognize that the software must be spun out of material that is real and palpable, and not out of "hole" cloth. The characteristics of imagery must be appreciated before imagery is employed as an explanatory variable. In this chapter imagery has been described as a dynamic, changing, neural event. There is no requirement that imagery be "conscious" or describable. For those who prefer, it can be a "hypothetical construct" like any other conditioned response and with the additional feature of serving as a mediator over extensive periods of time through restimulation. With the help of verbal stimulation, images can become complex and novel patterns that can serve the requirements of the most unusual thinkers of whatever degree of normality. The voices and visions of hallucinating psychotics are equally well accounted for. They, like the rest of us, are always thinking, and like the rest of us, frequently to no avail. Thinking must be regarded as a routine, continuous operation, not a special operation that comes into being only when we encounter problems. Perhaps that is what James (1890) meant by his "stream of consciousness."

REFERENCES

Bower, G. Imagery as a relational organizer in associative learning. *Journal of Verbal Learning and Verbal Behavior,* 1970, **9,** 529–537.

Bugelski, B. R. Words and things and images. *American Psychologist,* 1970, **25,** 1002–1012.

Bugelski, B. R. Images as mediators in one-trial paired-associate learning. III. Sequential functions in social lists. *Journal of Experimental Psychology,* 1974, **103,** 298–303.

Bugelski, B. R. Imagery and verbal behavior. *Journal of Mental Imagery,* 1977, **1,** 39–52.

Bugelski, B. R. *Principles of learning and memory.* New York: Praeger, 1979.

Dewey, J. *How we think.* Boston: Heath, 1910.

Estes, W. Is human memory obsolete? *American Scientist,* 1980, **68,** 62–69.

Fodor, J. A. *The language of thought.* Hassocks, Sussex: Harvester Press, 1976.

Fodor, J. A. The mind–body problem. *Scientific American,* 1981, **244,** 114–124.

Greenwald, A. G. Sensory feedback mechanisms in performance control. *Psychological Review,* 1970, **77,** 73–99.

Guthrie, E. R. *The psychology of learning.* New York: Harper, 1935.

Haber, R. N. Twenty years of haunting eidetic imagery: Where is the ghost? *The Behavioral and Brain Sciences,* 1979, **2,** 583–629.

Hebb, D. O. *The organization of behavior.* New York: Wiley, 1949.

Hull, C. L. *The principles of behavior.* New York: Appleton, 1943.

Jacobsen, E. Electrophysiology of mental activities. *American Journal of Psychology,* 1932, **44,** 677–694.

James, W. *Principles of psychology.* New York: Holt, 1890.

John, E. R. Comments on papers in *The central nervous system and behavior.* In M. A. Brazier (Ed.), New York: Josiah Macy Jr. Foundation, 1959.

Kaufmann, G. *Imagery language and cognition.* Bergen: Universititsforlaget, 1980.

King, D. L. Image theory of conditioning, memory, forgetting, functional similarity, fusion, and dominance. *Journal of Mental Imagery,* 1978, **2,** 47–62.

Kosslyn, S., Panker, S., Smith, G. E. and Schwartz, S. On the demystification of mental imagery. *The Behavioral and Brain Sciences,* 1979, **2,** 535–582.

Leuba, C. Images as conditioned sensations. *Journal of Experimental Psychology,* 1940, **26,** 345–351.

Mowrer, D. H. *Learning theory and the symbolic processes.* New York: Wiley, 1960.

Neisser, U. *Cognitive psychology.* New York: Appleton, 1967.

Osgood, C. E. *Method and theory of experimental psychology.* New York: Oxford University Press, 1953.

Paivio, A. *Imagery and verbal processes.* New York: Holt, 1971.

Segal, S., & Frisella, V. Influence of imaged pictures and sounds on detection of visual and auditory signals. *Journal of Experimental Psychology,* 1970, **83,** 458–464.

Skinner, B. F. *Science and human behavior.* New York: Macmillan, 1953.

Stromeyer, C. F., III, & Psotka, J. The detailed texture of eidetic images. *Nature,* 1970, **225,** 347–349.

Vigotsky, L. S. *Thought and language.* Cambridge: MIT Press, 1962.

Watson, J. B. *Behavior.* New York: Holt, 1914.

CHAPTER 4

Mental Imagery
and Consciousness:
A Theoretical Review

DAVID F. MARKS

Conceptualizations of imagery in cognitive psychology have generally deemphasized one of its most blatant and essential features: images are events in consciousness. The view that imagery is an abstract memory code denuded of any consciousness fails to provide an adequate analysis of all the common observations and facts. This chapter is based on the traditional concept of imagery as a quasi-perceptual phenomenon occurring in the absence of a sensory stimulus. There is a large data-base congenial to this conception, including the steadily mounting evidence that imagery is functionally equivalent and complementary to perception (Finke, 1980; Shepard & Podgorny, 1978). This data base also confirms the notion—contrary to a common superstition—that verbal reports provide useful, reliable data on imagery functioning. Verbal reports of imagery experience can be as predictive of performance as any of the so-called objective measures.

Mental imagery has not received the same degree of theoretical analysis applied to other cognitive functions such as attention, perception, and memory. The historical reasons for this are well known. The chief objection raised to the idea of consciously experienced mental imagery is that consciousness and conscious states can be known only through introspection and verbal reports. Many disparaging words have been written along these lines over the years, and the alleged unreliability of verbal reports has become the bête noire of imagery research. In my view this criticism of imagery reports is pure dogma having little to do with the facts. Imagery reports are

I would like to thank Gill Pow and Ian Hodgson for their able assistance in collecting experimental data and Geoffrey Loftus of the University of Washington for providing research facilities. I also thank Ray Hyman and other members of the Cognitive Laboratory at the University of Oregon who provided a stimulating environment in which the main ideas for this research program could be developed while I was on sabbatical leave; Carol Hunter, Barry Dingwall; Branko Coebergh, Carol Bell, Lonny Carey, and Margaret Stanley-Hunt, students who provided invaluable help during the preparation of this chapter.

no more introspective or inward-looking than perceptual reports and in fact are based on the activation of the same neural networks and mechanisms. Hebb (1968, pp. 467–468) put it this way: "with regard to a report of imagery, . . . one is not describing the image but the apparent object. This becomes clear if one observes the apparent locus of what one is describing. One does not perceive one's perceptions, nor describe them; one describes the *object* that is perceived . . . the mechanism of imagery is an aberrant mechanism of exteroception, not a form of looking inward to observe the operations of the mind."

The principal issue at stake in evaluating verbal reports is whether one variable can reliably predict some other variable. Where the predictor variable comes from is not important, provided it does the job of predicting reliably and well. If verbal reports can provide successful predictors of performance, they are as good a data source as any other producing the same level of prediction. When a certain level of lawfulness is found in the relationships between different variables, it becomes possible to construct theories and models of the processes involved. Verbal reports themselves are becoming an important data base for cognitive theory (Ericsson & Simon, 1980).

IMAGERY, CONSCIOUSNESS, AND COGNITION

Consciousness and Attention

As Mandler (1975) has pointed out, the concepts of *consciousness* and *focal attention* have much in common. In fact, it is difficult to make operational distinctions between the two concepts. When we attend to sights, sounds, tastes, smells, and other stimuli from our sensory world, we are certainly involved in the process of being conscious of these stimuli. It is also true that conscious awareness is filled not only by sensory stimuli, but by thoughts, images, and feelings. Fantasy, imagery, daydreaming, and other mental activities in our stream of consciousness have been termed *stimulus-independent thought* (Antrobus, 1968; Singer, 1978).

Since George Miller's (1956) historical paper entitled "Magical number seven plus or minus two," a considerable number of theories have been constructed on the notion of attention as a limited capacity information channel (Broadbent, 1971; Deutsch & Deutsch, 1963; Kahneman, 1973, Moray, 1970; Norman, 1976; Treisman, 1969). Somehow imagery was by-passed in this theorizing, and yet does it not have a call on the process of attention? Given that our span of conscious awareness is strictly limited, there is an important set of questions concerned with the problem of how entry into conscious awareness is determined. What determines the particular object of our attention at any given moment, and how rapidly can our attention be switched from one object to another? How much automatic processing occurs prior to the decision to select or focus on a particular item? Many such issues have provided the impetus for a large amount of research over the last quarter century. Given that imagery is functionally equivalent to perception at certain levels of the nervous system (Finke, 1980; Hebb, 1968), how can we best characterize the selective process that operates on perceptual input while images and thoughts may be simultaneously activated in the same system?

In a previous article (Marks, 1977) I proposed a simple flowchart model of the relationship between consciousness, perception, and imagery. The essential features of this model are depicted in Figure 4.1, together with channels for nonconscious or automatic processing and for the execution and coordination of responses.

One of the main features of this model has often been overlooked in models of attention: *information activated in memory* (thoughts, ideas, and images) *and perceptual stimuli share a single stage of information processing.* Whatever else it might involve, this shared stage contains a lot of what we mean when we speak of "focal attention," "consciousness," and "awareness."

This idea certainly is not new, and a relatively small group of theorists have bravely attempted to encompass the subjective experience of consciousness in their models of cognition (Mandler, 1975; Posner & Keele, 1970; Shallice, 1972; Singer, 1966). Many of the major cognitive texts appear to shy away from any discussion of consciousness, even to the point of not including the word as an entry in their subject index (Anderson, 1980; Neisser, 1967). Yet with no consciousness, we have no perception, no imagery, no thought, and no feeling—nothing but S and R and an empty organism.

If we take the logical step of defining consciousness as attention, there should be no particular problem in including it in cognitive theory. Also, a large number of key findings on mental imagery can be sensibly integrated with the much larger literature on human cognition.

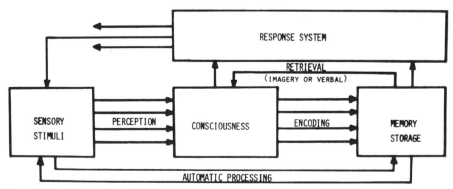

Figure 4.1.   A general model of consciousness and cognition (adapted from Marks, 1977).

Imagery, Perception, and Memory

Recent cognitive theory has placed considerable weight on the notion that the coding of ideas and thoughts in memory can be represented as an associative network of "nodes" that become activated or primed under appropriate conditions (Anderson & Bower, 1973; Colling & Loftus, 1975; Quillian, 1969; Quillian, 1968; Rumelhart, et al., 1972; Wickelgren, 1979). Learning is seen as the strengthening of associations between nodes and forgetting as a weakening of associations through decay or interference from competing associations with other nodes. Retrieval in the form of recognition involves mapping the incoming stimulus onto the existing node network. Recall entails the activation of some portion of the node structure on the basis of a supplied question or cue in the test situation (Wickelgren, 1979). Although most cognitive theory has been concerned primarily with verbal and semantic memory, basically the same analyses can be applied to visual imagery and memory. There has been very little research on imagery in other modalities; thus most of what follows is concerned with the visual modality only.

Hebb (1949, 1968) has indicated how the mechanics of inspecting visual stimuli and of generating memory images share a similar sequentially organized pattern of activity. Saccadic eye movements generated in perceiving a visual pattern alternate with fixations that activate what Hebb terms *cell assemblies*. Hebb's cell assemblies are the physiological substrate of the cognitive theorist's "nodes." Successive fixations and their associated cell assemblies are activated in central (foveal) vision; therefore, the various part-perceptions obtained with each fixation are anatomically superimposed. For this reason, Hebb (1968) concluded that the eye movements themselves must have an important organizing function in visual perception as they separate the various part perceptions obtained by each fixation.

In Hebb's (1968) view, imagery is a reinstatement of perception in which cell assemblies are reactivated in the absence of the stimulus pattern on which they were originally based. Vivid imagery results from the reactivation of first-order cell assemblies that encode specific sensory features such as colors, shapes, and angles, whereas "higher-order assemblies are the basis of less specific imagery and nonrepresentational conceptual processes" (Hebb, 1968, p. 466).

Thinking along lines similar to those of Hebb, Noton and Stark (1971) proposed that the internal representation of a pattern is a *feature ring* consisting of a set of features alternating with motor traces of the eye movements made while scanning these features. A scanpath consisting of a repeated cycle of fixations over a given scene would later be repeated during the recognition of the scene. Noton and Stark (1971) were able to identify such scanpaths in 25% of the total viewing time during learning trials and on 65% of recognition trials, especially in the initial eye movements early in the recognition process. Some higher-order process than the feature ring must also have a controlling influence on subjects' fixations, as only a limited proportion of eye movements fall into any specific scanpath cycle. Noton and Stark were aware of the fact that patterns and scenes are normally recognized very quickly with few or no saccadic eye movements. This also implies some higher-level representation of imagery beyond a feature ring consisting of a series of sensory–motor traces. Just as we may shift our attention over a scene while keeping our eyes perfectly still, so can we "scan" an image without making eye movements. Therefore, I would not agree with Hebb's (1968) conclusion that eye movements are necessary for the generation of visual images, although they may be useful under certain conditions.

The issue concerning the representation of imagery in memory is currently a controversial matter. Paivio (1971) has argued for a dual-coding theory in which two systems of representation, one verbal and one pictorial, provide separate but interrelated memory codes. Whereas Pylyshyn (1973) has argued for a single propositional system and Potter (1980) for a third, higher-level conceptual code in which concepts are represented amodally in addition to Paivio's dual system, Anderson (1978) has concluded that there is a "fundamental indeterminancy in deciding issues of representations." The debate continues (Anderson, 1979; Hayes-Roth, 1979; Pylyshyn, 1979), and there is no point in elaborating on it here (Pinker & Kosslyn, Chapter 2 in this volume). Following Hebb (1968), I shall simply make the assumption that *imagery is encoded on a number of different levels. Activation of the lowest level produces vivid quasi-perceptual imagery experience, while activation of higher levels corresponds to conceptual, abstract meaning.* Higher levels have superordinate control over lower levels. In perception this would imply coordination of the sensory–motor adjustments such as eye movements and orienting responses. Individual differences in imagery reflect varying abilities to activate lower levels of encoding consisting of sensory features such as colors, textures, and shapes at a sufficiently concrete level to produce a conscious mental image.

Interference Effects

One of the consequences of a limited capacity system is that the amount of space or effort available for any particular activity is dependent on that already used up by other tasks. One approach to the measurement of attentional demands of a given task is to assess the change in performance that follows the addition of a second task (Keele, 1973). If perception and imagery share the same information channel, interference will result when both processes are activated at the same time.

Interference between signal detection and various kinds of daydreaming, fantasy, and imagery has been demonstrated in an impressive series of experiments conducted by John Antrobus and Jerome Singer [reviewed by

Singer (1978)]. In these studies stimulus-independent mentation was monitored by way of simple verbal or manual responses based on generally accepted criteria.

In one study Antrobus (1968) obtained a linear regression of reported stimulus-independent thought on information handling rate that accounted for 83% of the between-cell variance. Singer's group concluded from their studies that "cognitive events resulting from either sensory inputs or memory inputs are produced by a common, limited-capacity cognitive system" (Singer, et al., 1971).

Other researches on the tradeoff between "internal" and "external" information processing have concentrated specifically on imagery per se. Some elegant research by the late Sydney Joelson Segal, together with Vincent Fusella (Segal & Fusella, 1970, 1971), followed up the Perky effect originally discovered in 1910. Perky found that when subjects were asked to image common objects (e.g., a banana or a leaf) while dim facsimiles were presented to them on a screen, they tended to report an image rather than a perceptual experience. Segal and Fusella (1970) showed that the generation of irrelevant visual images impaired visual signal detections more than irrelevant auditory images (see Table 4.1). Auditory images, on the other hand, produced more interference in an auditory detection task than did visual images. Segal and Fusella (1971) demonstrated similar modality-specific interference in a total of six different sensory modalities (vision, audition, touch, smell, taste, and kinesthesis). A further important finding was that unfamiliar images produced more interference in signal detection than familiar or repeated images.

The fact that images interfere with perception suggests channel space is taken up by images in competition with perceptual signals. Also, less familiar images require more focal attention than do familiar images. The modality-specific effects indicate that at some level of the sensory pathway, imagery and perception activate the same neuronal structures. This can lead to confusion in conscious experience between the two types of activation, although confusions would be rare under normal conditions.

Similar conclusions can be drawn from a well-known series of experiments by Brooks (1968) in which various methods of issuing responses were combined with differing kinds of stimulus input, diagrams, or sentences. Brooks

TABLE 4.1.   Frequency of Hits and False Alarms (FAs), d', and Likelihood Ratios (Lx) for Visual and Auditory Imagery (Segal & Fusella, 1970, Experiment II)

Task	Visual Signal			Auditory Signal		
	Hits/FA	d'	LX	Hits/FA	d'	Lx
Visual imagery	0.61/0.078	1.70	2.63	0.67/0.037	2.23	4.48
Auditory imagery	0.63/0.036	2.13	4.78	0.61/0.067	1.78	2.96

found that recall of diagrams suffers from interference when spatial movements used in recall were required in a different pattern from the diagram to be recalled. The interference was much stronger when the movements in recall had to be visually or tactually monitored. The same spatial or tactual movements concurrent with the recall of sentences did not produce interference. Similar interference effects have been replicated many times (Atwood, 1971; Byrne, 1974; Janssen, 1976). Brooks (1968, p. 367) concluded that "By requiring two different tasks within the same modality, one is forcing a split of attention that is not required if the recall and signalling were done in different modalities."

Substitution Effects

If imagery is functionally equivalent to perception, it should be possible under certain conditions to use imagery as a substitute for perception. Hallucinations, dreams, hypnagogic fantasy, and other vivid forms of imagery may be mistaken for reality, and many imagery techniques in therapy rely on the principle of substitution (Cautela & Baron, 1977; Kazdin & Smith, 1979; Sheikh & Panagiotou, 1975). The main hazard in this type of research is the avoidance of various artifacts created by the subject's willingness to anticipate and follow the experimenter's assumptions and hypotheses. Many experiments on the comparison of imagery with perception are fairly transparent from the subject's viewpoint, and the findings are clouded by the real possibility of subject compliance (Kosslyn et al., 1979; Mitchell & Richman, 1980; Orne, 1962; Richman et al., 1979).

An ideal situation for preventing "demand characteristics" and other such artifacts is one where the subjects are unable to determine the expected results. A recent study by Finke and Schmidt (1977) capitalized on the surprising (to a naive subject) McCollough effect in which complementary-color aftereffects can be induced by specific bar gratings presented against colored backgrounds (McCollough, 1965). Finke and Schmidt compared the normal McCollough effect adaptation procedure in which the horizontal and vertical bars and two associated colors are presented together with an imagination condition in which the subjects were shown the colors and imagined the bars or were shown the bars and imagined the colors. Finke and Schmidt used a forced-choice test procedure in which eight pairs of achromatic test patterns were presented, each consisting of horizontal and vertical bar patterns on opposite sides of the slide. Subjects selected which half of the test slide appeared most red, or if a greenish tint was present, the half that appeared least green.

To detect the use of confounding strategies (e.g., deliberate matching of color responses to the adaptation condition), subjects were asked to report on the strategies they used. Of 144 subjects, 55 were eliminated on this basis, and 49 of these reported using the association strategy; that is, if red was associated with horizontal bars during adaptation, the horizontal bars were chosen as the more red in the test even though the subject apparently experienced no genuine color aftereffect.

Finke and Schmidt analyzed the results for the remainder of subjects who had not been excluded, and a weak McCollough effect was obtained for the bar imagination condition when the colors used were complementary (red and green). For noncomplementary colors (red and yellow) and when the colors were imagined instead of actually presented, a weak reversed McCollough effect was obtained (MacKay & MacKay, 1973). Although the effects obtained were weaker than the standard McCollough effect, the results clearly show that feature-contingent color aftereffects may be obtained when imagery of the bar patterns is substituted for their actual perception.

A recent experiment conducted in my own laboratory has confirmed and extended the result obtained by Finke and Schmidt (1977). Twenty female subjects, aged 16 and 17, were individually adapted and tested. The subjects were initially shown two achromatic slides, one containing horizontal bar gratings, and the other containing vertical bar gratings, projected on a screen subtending an area of 28° by 42° approximately 1.5 m from the subject. The spatial frequency of the gratings was 2.2 cycles per degree. Following presentation of the two gratings for 30 seconds each, each subject was shown two colored slides, in Wratten gelatin filters, red (#25) and green (#58), in alternating 10-second intervals for a total adaptation period of 5 minutes. When a particular color appeared on the screen, each subject was instructed to image a specific bar grating, and combinations of color with orientation were counterbalanced across subjects. A series of 20 forced-choice test trials followed immediately after adaptation by use of procedure identical to Finke and Schmidt's, except that my test patterns had a higher spatial frequency of 4.2 cycles per degree. Also, my subjects were asked to make their choices purely on the basis of the appearance of color. In addition, I asked subjects to tilt their heads to a 90° angle in the last 10 test trials to determine whether the predicted reversal occurred in the color aftereffects observed.

The results seemed to fall into three groups, as indicated in Table 4.2:

TABLE 4.2.   Mean Forced-Choice Discrimination Scores for Three Groups of Subjects Following Imagination of Bar Gratings

		Mean Response Rate	
Group	n	Head Upright	Head Tilt of 90°
Positive McCollough effect	10	15.6/20	7.7/10
No color aftereffect	4	10.0/20	3.2/10
Reversed McCollough effect	6	2.0/20	3.0/10

one group of McCollough-effect responders (n = 10) who reported 13 or more McCollough effect responses, a group who responded at around chance level (n = 4), and a group who reported a reversed McCollough effect (n = 6). Perhaps the most interesting result was the high rate of color reversal (average = 7.7 in 10 trials) in the group of McCollough-effect responders accompanying the 90° head tilt. It was obviously not easy for these subjects to believe their eyes when the colors on the screen gradually reversed sides as they tilted over their heads to the horizontal plane! This effect genuinely surprised the subjects and couldn't possibly be attributed to demand characteristics. Note that in the other two groups, colors tended *not* to reverse with head tilt, suggesting that some process other than the true McCollough effect was in operation.

Even when the expected phenomenon is a surprising one, not known or expected by the subjects, these results confirm the hypothesis that imagery is functionally equivalent to, and can substitute for, perception. Individual differences in the results obtained are discussed later in this chapter.

Imagery in Altered States of Consciousness

It is not possible in this brief review to give anything like a complete analysis of the many ways that imagery enters into various altered states of consciousness. All that can be done is to give an overly simple indication of the degree to which the available data are congruent with the flowchart model in Figure 4.1.

Sensory Deprivation

Generally speaking, it can be seen that in the awake state reductions or restrictions in patterned stimulus input will release attentional capacity for internally derived, stimulus-independent processes. This general principle is supported empirically by one of the more dramatic aspects of sensory deprivation experience in which consciousness is flooded by imagery and fantasy. This flood of fantasy may approach hypnagogic or hallucinatory levels of vividness at times (Bexton et al., 1954; Lilly, 1956; Shurley, 1962).

Meditation and Relaxation

Another less dramatic means for stopping or slowing down the rate of processing of information is provided by various methods of meditation or relaxation. By closing the eyes and using a simple repetitious image or thought (the *mantra*), or with eyes open, by concentrating on a specific visual, auditory, or tactile stimulus, the limited attention span can be used to shut off or limit extraneous thought and its associated anxieties (Ornstein, 1972).

Drowsiness and Sleep

The most vivid forms of imagery that many people possibly ever experience are those which accompany drowsiness and sleep. Again, the key feature would appear to be the closing of the "doors of perception" that drowsiness and sleep entail. The hypnagogic, hypnopompic, and dream states are recognized by a particularly vivid and autonomous form of imagery that sometimes incorporates themes or perseverations from mundane experience (McKellar, 1979).

Emotions, Feelings, and Heightened Arousal

Many of the classic emotions and feelings such as happiness, love, fear, anger, sadness, hope, and sexual arousal are accompanied by imagined scenes and situations in our fantasy world. Deliberate attempts to control or heighten these emotions are becoming an important part of modern cognitive behavior modification in which imagery plays a central role. To the extent that imagery techniques such as covert conditioning bring about generalized changes in overt behavior, we have further evidence of functional equivalence between imagery and perception.

Drugs

Drugs such as cannabis and the hallucinogens that affect the quantity and vividness of imagery and fantasy on a fairly major scale are also noted for their detrimental effects on tasks involving careful monitoring of the environment (Casswell and Marks, 1973; LeDain, 1973; MacAvoy & Marks, 1976). Whereas functions other than imagery and fantasy are obviously changed by these drugs, an alteration in the relationship between an awareness of "reality" (veridical, mundane perception) and of private fantasy seems to be a key feature of, and perhaps the motivation for, their consumption.

Remote Viewing

Two physicists at Stanford Research Institute claim to have discovered a highly accurate, psychic type of remote imaging ability that they claim may be widely distributed in the population (Targ & Puthoff, 1974). In their experiments various subjects are reported to have accurately imaged and described remote locations by use of nonsensory (psychic) means. Close scrutiny of Targ and Puthoff's protocols, however, reveals that the results are based on the availability of sensory cues and other methodological flaws (Marks, 1981e; Marks & Kammann, 1978). Similar objections have been raised concerning many other researches on paranormal imagery and perception (Hansel, 1980). The black box labeled "Consciousness" in Figure 4.1 thus contains no input that is not derived from either ordinary sensory perceptual processes or memory retrieval. A major factor in the widespread belief in extrasensory perception may be the tendency to subjectively validate (i.e., to force match) imagery from dreams, memory, or the imagination with real-world events on a selective basis (Marks & Kammann, 1980).

Further Implications of the General Model

On the assumption that consciousness is invaded by stimuli from two major sources, it is necessary to be able to distinguish one source (perception) from the other (memory). This ability is intriguing and crucial, and in the waking state it is remarkable how rarely it breaks down unless drugs, pathology, or some profound alterations in consciousness are involved. More research is needed on how the ability to distinguish percepts from vivid images develops. Longitudinal research would be of great value in addressing this issue.

Another implication of the general model is that higher-order operations conducted on the contents of consciousness, such as judgments, choices, and comparisons, should have outcomes that are entirely independent of the contents' origins, perceptual or memorial. Shepard (1978) refers to this property as *second-order isomorphism*. Hence the mental rotation of a pattern (Shepard & Metzler, 1971) and comparative reaction times for imaged or symbolic stimuli (Marks, 1972b) have properties similar to those applying to the processing of stimuli physically present. An excellent review on cognitive processes that resemble perceptual processes can be found in Shepard and Podgorny (1978).

A further aspect of the general model is an acknowledgment of two major forms of memory retrieval that are a function of two types of coding, the imagery system and the verbal system (Paivio, 1971). The debate (see above) concerning the issue of how many levels of representation there are will no doubt continue for some time, but it is widely acknowledged that we are normally aware of two modalities in conscious thought, the verbal system and the imagery system. There is no need to enter into the debate on the number of types of mental representation as this chapter is concerned primarily with imagery as a conscious experience, not as an abstract code in the brain.

Finally, one of the most striking features of conscious imagery is the wide range of individual differences reported. It is necessary to assume that individual differences are bound to occur in the mechanisms that govern the flow of information into and out of consciousness. The processes of perception, encoding, and retrieval all display a large range of individual variation and the relationship of these variations to consciously experienced mental imagery are the major concern of the rest of this chapter. But first it is necessary to review the methodology of using verbal reports.

VERBAL REPORTS OF IMAGERY

Many imagery phenomena such as dreams; daydreams; hallucinations; eidetic imagery; and hypnagogic, hypnopompic, and hypnotic states have been reported and described in the literature at a qualitative level down through the ages. A challenging problem is to develop methodologies yielding reliable measures of conscious imagery experience and then study how imagery and other functions interact in the performance of specific tasks and activities. In this context, verbal reports of imagery provide a fertile data source.

Perhaps the most stubborn, noncontroversial observation about the mental image is the enormous variation to be found in the quality reported by different individuals. Individual differences are often seen as a nuisance factor by the researcher who usually does everything possible to minimize what is generally regarded as a major source of "error." The traditional Fisherian analysis-of-variance approach to hypothesis testing is viewed almost as a battle against the pervasive enemy of within-group variance that, by contributing to the denominator of the F value, only helps to reduce any significance there may otherwise have been in the results. In my view this approach to psychology is a limited one and, in the long run, unlikely to succeed. Individual variation is not only fascinating and deserving of study in its own right, but provides the key to some interesting and possibly important cognitive mechanisms.

Most theories in psychology are tested nomothetically by manipulating an independent variable across experimental conditions and measuring the effects on some dependent variable. It remains perfectly possible to test theories by allowing the independent variable(s) to vary not only across conditions, but also across people. Underwood (1975) cites an example of a theory in which recognition memory is a function of frequency discriminations. After 50 studies, Underwood confesses that he belatedly appreciated the individual differences approach to the testing of his theory: people with fine or precise frequency discriminations must show good recognition memory, whereas people with poor or imprecise frequency discriminations must show poor recognition memory. Underwood (1975, pp. 129–130) concluded: "The point is that, had we been so wise as to perceive it, the fiftieth study should have been the first study. If the data from this first study did not approve of the individual differences relationship inherent in the theory, there would have been no theory, no 50 studies." I believe the same argument could be applied in almost any theoretical context.

Our definition of imagery as conscious, quasi-perceptual experience necessitates the use of verbal report measures of individual differences. As Neisser (1972, 1976) has pointed out, what we report of our private experience may depend on the demand characteristics of the situation. For example, to some extent a subject may report his or her imagery to be relatively vivid if that is what he or she perceives the experimenter wants (Sheehan & Neisser, 1969). However, *comparisons between subjects who characteristically report radically different imagery when tested under identical conditions would not be confounded by different demand characteristics.* Hence between-subject comparisons are potentially more interesting than comparisons of performance at supposedly different imagery levels within subjects, although the latter may also have predictive value.

A recent attack on verbal reports as a data source by Nisbett and Wilson (1977) is based on their observations of failure among subjects to make accurate retrospective reports on the stimuli controlling their responses. However, Nisbett and Wilson's evidence was obtained from a highly selected range of situations especially contrived to test the hypothesis that verbal reports could not always be relied on. No attempt was made to appraise the evidence as a whole, and consequently their conclusions concerning verbal reports were seriously overgeneralized beyond the nonrepresentative situations that they constructed. It would seem more useful to construct a taxonomy of situations and methods where verbal reports are useful and reliable as predictors in contrast to others where verbal reports are not useful, as Ericsson and Simon (1980) have done. For critiques of Nisbett and Wilson's (1977) arguments, including statistical errors, see Smith and Miller (1978) and White (1980). The results to be presented in the next two sections strongly confirm Ericsson and Simon's (1980, p. 247) conclusion that "verbal reports, elicited with care and interpreted with full understanding of the circumstances under which they were obtained, are a valuable and thoroughly reliable source of information about cognitive processes."

Attempts at correlating verbal reports of imagery with cognitive and other types of performance can fail for many different reasons. For reviews of this research, see Marks (1972a), Sheehan (1972), White et al. (1977), and Ernest (1977). As noted above, testing procedures must be carefully controlled to avoid demand characteristics and other artifacts that may hinder one's ability to obtain accurate repeatable results. Many of the findings reported below have been replicated, in some cases many times.

The research to be reviewed utilized a scale developed by the author and called the *Vividness of Visual Imagery Questionnaire* (VVIQ). The VVIQ contains 16 items, 5 of which are derived from the original Betts *Questionnaire upon Mental Imagery*, and each item is imaged and rated twice, once with the eyes open and once with the eyes closed. It can be administered in a few minutes to individuals or groups who are required to rate the imagery evoked by each item along a 5-point rating scale. The VVIQ has a high reliability and a simple, unitary factor pattern (Marks, 1973a; White et al., 1977).[1]

For research purposes, it is recommended that the VVIQ be administered twice to each subject, with a few days or weeks between the two administrations. This enables a check to be made for subject error in utilizing the rating scale. Experience has shown that a small number of subjects mistakenly reverse the polarity of their ratings. This error may be detected if the difference in the total score obtained on the two occasions is far in excess of the standard error of measurement. Administration on a third occasion can be used as the deciding score. This precaution saves correlations from plummeting towards zero artifactually as a result of one or two careless subjects.

The scale used in the VVIQ is given in Table 4.3. Note that a low total

TABLE 4.3.   Rating Scale Used in the VVIQ

Image Description	Rating
"Perfectly clear and as vivid as normal vision"	1
"Clear and reasonably vivid"	2
"Moderately clear and vivid"	3
"Vague and dim"	4
"No image at all, you only 'know' that you are thinking of the object"	5

score implies high-quality visual imagery, that is, imagery that is clear and vivid, whereas a high score implies poor-quality imagery, that is, imagery that is vague and dim or nonexistent.

IMAGERY DIFFERENCES AND MEMORY

The evidence reviewed thus far provides good confirmation of the general model of imagery and consciousness proposed in Figure 4.1. Strong tests of the model are provided by making predictions about how individual differences in the quality of conscious imagery can be expected to affect cognitive functioning. Do individuals who experience and reliably report clear and vivid, high-quality mental imagery perform tasks differently from individuals reporting poor quality imagery? More specifically, does imagery aid memory? Is the good imager's performance superior to that of the poor imager in tasks where imagery is necessarily involved? If so, what processes and mechanisms can be found to explain the differences in the quality of imagery available to individuals while performing these kinds of tasks? Are imagery differences fixed, or do they depend on the context? Is imagery quality amenable to training, enabling higher achievements and improvements in task performance? The remainder of the chapter is concerned with these issues.

Picture Recall

Prediction 1

Good visualizers are able to recall pictures more accurately than are poor visualizers. Recall involves the activation of portions of the neural network or feature ring in which a picture is encoded to permit retrieval of the information at a conscious level. Good visualizers should be able to do this more easily and accurately. This prediction was tested in a series of experiments in which color slides consisting of real life scenes and montages were projected for 20 seconds. A typical stimulus is shown in Figure 4.2.

Figure 4.2.   One of the illustrations used in experiments on picture recall.

Following each slide, a delay of 40 seconds occurred, and then a series of multiple choice questions was presented. To illustrate the type of questions, those employed for the stimulus of Figure 4.2 were as follows:

1. How many people were holding a glass: one, two, or three?
2. What color was the hairband of the girl in the middle: yellow, green, or orange?
3. Which of the two men had a beard: man on the left, man on the right, or neither man?
4. Was the girl on the left drinking: through a straw, directly from a glass, or not at all?
5. How many people could be seen wearing bathing suits: two, three, or four?
6. What shape was the buckle of the girl on the right: square, rectangular, or circular?
7. What color was the wall of the room: white, green, or yellow?

Subjects chose one answer from the three alternatives provided. In some studies, only five questions per slide were used, and other minor variations in procedure have occurred in different studies.

An important procedural point is that in many of these studies subjects were asked to count backward in 3 prior to the slide presentation, or immediately following the slide presentation, to prevent verbal labeling and encoding of the slide material (Peterson and Peterson, 1959). Although it is recognized that counting leads to a general decrement in memory performance (Freund, 1971), it is a useful precaution against verbal processes swamping the imagery differences that might otherwise occur. More details of the picture recall studies can be found in Marks (1972a, 1973a).

The results of these studies consistently show that good visualizers, assessed by vividness ratings on the 5-point VVIQ scale, are more accurate in picture recall than are poor visualizers. A reciprocal transformation of the VVIQ scores is usually taken before calculating the correlation coefficient as the reciprocal is more linear with recall. Correlation between the transformed VVIQ score (1/V) and recall accuracy are typically in the range +0.50 to +0.65. The highest correlation to date is +0.73 ($df = 28$; $p < .001$) obtained in my laboratory by Hodgson (1977) with a group of 30 unselected students.

McKelvie and Demers (1979) tested good and poor visualizers' ability to recall pictures and also abstract words and concrete words. In this experiment 70 male students completed the VVIQ, and the 16 lowest scorers and the 16 highest scorers were chosen to form two experimental groups. Two months after the VVIQ had been administered, memory tests were presented. Eighteen lists of stimuli were presented with 10 items per list. Short-term recall occurred immediately after each list, and long-term recall at the end of all the lists. Good visualizers produced a significantly higher short-term recall for all types of material, but they did particularly well with concrete words. The results for long-term recall were extremely interesting as the good visualizers produced a significantly higher recall for both concrete words and pictures ($p < .01$ in both cases) but *not* for abstract words. McKelvie and Demers' (1979) results are an important confirmation of the greater accuracy of good visualizers in the recall of pictures. In addition, this study extends the finding to concrete words, but not to abstract words. The possession of imagery is obviously useful only in recalling vivid items that can in principle be imaged. Prediction 1 is confirmed, therefore, and the predicted imagery advantage can be extended to concrete words.

Picture Comparison

Prediction 2

Good visualizers are able to detect a difference between a picture stored in memory and a new picture more quickly than are poor visualizers. This prediction was tested by Gur and Hilgard (1975), who used 30 pairs of pictures from the Meier Art Judgment Test (Meier, 1940). Each pair consisted of one black and white copy of an original art work and a slightly modified version of that work in the same style. The 30 pairs were divided into two sets, with 15 pairs in each, and 20 adult volunteers were each tested individually after completing the VVIQ. Two procedures were used: simultaneous presentation in which the subject looked at a pair of pictures and then pointed as quickly as possible at the part of the picture in which the two art words differed; successive presentation in which the subject first saw one picture for 30 seconds, then closed her eyes for 20 seconds, and then saw the second picture. Again, she had to point as quickly as possible to the part in which the picture was different from the previously presented picture.

The correlation between the mean response time for the total of 30 test items and the VVIQ was -0.74 ($p < $ .001), indicating that the more vivid the imagery, the more quickly the subject could detect the difference between the pictures. A comparison between the means indicated that the poor imagers reacted significantly more slowly in the successive mode of presentation than in the simultaneous mode, whereas the good imagers were not affected by presentation mode. Gur and Hilgard (1975) concluded: "Presumably those who have vivid imagery can make a 'matrix' comparison by overlaying the presented picture with the imaged one, and in that way promptly detect the difference."

Berger and Gaunitz (1977) studied a task similar to Gur and Hilgard's but measured the accuracy of detections instead of speed. They gave the subjects exposures of 7 and 5 seconds instead of 20 or 30 seconds as Gur and Hilgard and I had done. The results showed a trend in the expected direction for the 5-second condition, but the imagery group differences were not significant. Berger and Gaunitz concluded that the VVIQ was inefficient as a measure of imagery ability and suggested that demand characteristics caused the earlier reported effects. However, nobody would wish to claim that the VVIQ (or any other variable!) can reliably predict performance differences between good and poor imagery in *any* parameter of any memory task. On the contrary, the specific nature of the conditions and performance measures that good imagers do better (or worse) on can illuminate the processes involved.

Despite their initial loss of faith in the VVIQ, Berger and Gaunitz (1979) persevered in their experiments and proved this very point. In their second study, Berger and Gaunitz homed in on the coding strategies subjects use to detect picture differences. Subjects were required to examine 10 pairs of pictures in which only one picture in the pair was exposed at a time. The 24 subjects were compelled to vacillate between the two pictures until a difference was spotted. Subjects were instructed to do this as quickly as possible, and the dependent variable in this study, as in Gur and Hilgard's, was not accuracy but speed. Following the 10 trials the subjects completed a form in which they reported on coding strategies utilized in the discrimination task. Twelve subjects reported using the "detail strategy" in which details are selected from a picture for comparison with the other picture, and 12 reported using the "image strategy" in which the picture is imaged and then compared as a whole.

Although Berger and Gaunitz (1979) concluded that the VVIQ could not discriminate between good and poor imagers' performance on the task, their own results indicated otherwise. Although the detail strategy was overall the faster and yielded no imagery differences, the image strategy produced a mean response time of 18.5 seconds for good imagers and 32.9 seconds for poor imagers ($p < $ .01). This result thus strongly confirmed the findings in Gur and Hilgard's (1975) experiment in which the detail strategy would not have been useful. The earlier study by Berger and Gaunitz (1977), which had relatively brief exposure times, would have favored the detail strategy that is primarily a matter of *verbal,* rather than imagery, coding. Also it should be noted that in the earlier studies on recall (Marks, 1973b), verbal coding strategies were deliberately blocked by including the backward-counting procedure, a point that Berger and Gaunitz (1977, 1979) had apparently overlooked. When imagery is used, and not verbal strategies, Prediction 2 is clearly confirmed.

Picture Recognition

Prediction 3

Good visualizers are able to recognize pictures more accurately than are poor visualizers. The process of recognizing a picture involves the reactivation of a neural network (or feature ring) as the stimulus is mapped onto the existing node structure in memory. As we have seen, good visualizers are able to detect small differences between two successively presented pictures more rapidly than are poor visualizers, and Prediction 3 is thus a natural expectancy. This has been tested in a series of three experiments (Marks, 1982b), and the results provide unambiguous confirmation of the prediction. In all three experiments a signal detection measure d' was used to evaluate subjects' performance.

The first set of recognition data was collected in the context of an investigation of cannabis effects on memory. Forty subjects studied sets of 128 pictures (in color) and 128 words following the administration of placebo or marijuana (7 mg Δ9-THC). Each stimulus was exposed for 5 seconds. One week later the subjects returned to the laboratory and were given a yes/no recognition test in the same or the opposite state of consciousness. The results were consistent across all experimental conditions in producing better recognition performance for pictures among the good visualizers ($r = -.38$, $p < .02$) and poorer recognition performance for words ($r = .31, p < .05$).

The finding of poorer word recognition among the good visualizers is interesting in the light of Paivio's (1971) dual-coding model of memory and indicates that subjects with a high ability for visualization may be less efficient at processing verbal material, at least at the level of recognition. However, I did not obtain this result in the second experiment in the series in which the recognition test immediately followed the study trials and drug-altered states of consciousness were not involved.

The second experiment involved the presentation of 100 pictures, half of which were natural scenes and half abstract works of art; and 100 words, half of which were concrete nouns and half were abstract nouns. Each slide was exposed for 5 seconds, and in this study the subjects were 42 males aged 16 or 17 years. The only type of stimulus that produced a significant correlation between d' and the VVIQ was the natural scenes ($r = -.45$, $p < .01$). The correlations for the abstract pictures, concrete nouns, and abstract nouns were $-.09$, $+11$, and $-.14$, respectively.

In the third experiment, conducted in Geoffrey Loftus's laboratory at the University of Washington, 27 female subjects viewed a series of 60 natural scenes divided into three sets for exposure times of 100, 500, and 2000 milliseconds. The subjects were also tested on a short series of 16 black-and-white drawings with an exposure of 500 milliseconds. A forced-choice recognition test immediately followed the study phase of each block of slides. As the number of slides in each block was rather small, an average value of d' was calculated for each subject to increase the reliability of the scores. The mean d' values correlated $-.49$ ($p < .01$) with the subjects' VVIQ scores. Taken together, the series of three experiments provides strong confirmation of Prediction 3.

IMAGERY DIFFERENCES AND PERCEPTION

Having established a reliable and significant relationship between imaging ability and the accuracy of recognition and recall, a number of studies were conducted to determine where these individual differences come into play in the chain of events between registration and retrieval. An important stage in determining memory performance is the initial perception of the stimulus to be remembered. In this section we present a number of predictions related to the general notion that good visualizers produce a higher level of picture memory performance because they encode more efficiently during the presentation of the stimulus.

Eye Movements

Prediction 4

Good visualizers scan pictures more rapidly than do poor visualizers, thereby encoding more information per unit time. This prediction emerged from some interesting data published by Geoffrey Loftus (1972) of the University of Washington in which recognition performance for pictures was found to be a monotonically increasing function of the number of eye fixations during study. Loftus plotted his data as a set of group means, d' as a function of the number of fixations. A reanalysis of Loftus's raw data was conducted in which I correlated d' with the mean number of fixations over subjects. The correlation was $+.52$ ($p < .02$).

To test the prediction that good visualizers could be rapid scanners, the electrooculogram (EOG) of 30 subjects was recorded while they examined a number of pictures with an exposure time of 20 seconds (Marks, 1982a).

Their recall was tested using a multiple-choice question technique as described above.

Imagery vividness ratings obtained in the experiment correlated $-.50$ ($p < .01$) with subjects' mean fixation rates during exposure of the pictures; therefore, Prediction 4 is confirmed.

Prediction 5

In scanning pictures, good visualizers are able to make larger saccades than are poor visualizers, thereby encoding more information from the picture. Large individual differences occur in the extent of saccadic movements during picture perception. It has been established that the extent of saccades varies over the time course of picture viewing. Initially, over the first four or five eye movements, the mean saccadic distance steadily increases (Marks, 1982c) and then decreases as viewing time progresses (Antes, 1974). However, values of the maximum saccadic distance (SD_{max}) can vary by as much as 3:1 across subjects. It must be assumed that the eyes can move only to a point already seen in peripheral vision. Therefore, SD_{max} would appear to be a measure of how far into the picture a subject can see while fixating. According to Prediction 5, good visualizers would be expected to have larger values of SD_{max}. The EOG study mentioned above (Marks, 1982a) found a correlation between SD_{max} and imagery ability of $-.53$ ($p < .01$); therefore, Prediction 5 is confirmed.

Prediction 6

Good visualizers have more consistent scanpaths than poor visualizers. The recognition of pictures is accompanied by the repetition of scanpaths originating during perception of the to-be-remembered picture (Noton & Stark, 1971). The scanpath itself is encoded in the neural network representing a picture in memory; therefore, the more consistently a subject repeats the scanpath during perception, the more strongly encoded the picture will become in memory. It thus seems probable that good visualizers will have more consistent scanpaths than poor visualizers.

Preliminary confirmation of this prediction was reported by Lai (1975). A more exacting test of this prediction has recently been conducted on scanpaths obtained from six good visualizers and six poor visualizers who had participated in a picture recognition experiment. Each subject saw six pictures for either 2 or 5 seconds each. Immediately following each exposure of a picture, the same picture was then reexposed for the same duration. The subjects' expectancy was that a recognition test would take place after studying the slides on the two occasions. Subjects' scanpaths were obtained by use of a Mackworth eye-movement recorder and a video tape recorder [see Marks (1982d) for more details].

To evaluate the consistency of each subject's scanpaths, the 12 scanpaths belonging to each subject were drawn in black ink on separate sheets of paper and were placed in two sets corresponding to the first and second viewings of the set of six pictures. Judges who were blind to the correct pairings were asked to try to match set 1 against set 2 on the basis of the general shape and pattern of the scanpaths in each set. A ranking procedure was used in which all six scanpaths from set 1 were ranked in order of their similarity to each scanpath in set 2. This procedure enables a precise quantitative estimate to be placed on the consistency of any given set of scanpaths because the more consistent the scanpaths, the more easily they can be matched.

The results for the four judges are presented in Table 4.4 and the scanpaths for two typical subjects are displayed in Figure 4.3. Ideally for perfectly similar scanpaths, the sum of ranks would be 6 (i.e., six rank values of 1), whereas highly inconsistent scanpaths would give a sum of ranks of 21. The results showed that none of the poor visualizers' scanpaths were sufficiently consistent to be matched. However, the scanpaths for five of the six good visualizers were matched at a highly significant level.

Figure 4.3 gives the complete set of scanpaths for two subjects. The rows labeled A through F give scanpaths for the six pictures. The good visualizer is clearly more consistent than the poor visualizer. These results strongly confirm Lai's (1975) data and Prediction 6.

Prediction 7

Good visualizers extract more information per fixation than do poor visualizers. When people examine a picture for the purpose of later recognition, there appear to be two types of information available: specific detail information and general visual information (Loftus & Bell, 1975). Familiarity with

TABLE 4.4.   **Sums of Ranks and Probability Values for Judges' Matchings of Each Subject's Scanpaths**

Subject	VVIQ Score	d'	Sums of Ranks				p Value
			1	2	3	4	
CH	53	2.81	11	12	13	13	<.001
MT	51	2.57	14	13	10	16	<.001
EP	53	3.07	17	11	14	16	<.025
JB	44	2.40	20	21	17	13	NS*
JP	58	3.22	13	10	8	9	<.001
FJ	58	3.15	11	12	5	16	<.001
TH	79	2.15	21	27	19	20	NS
LL	66	3.04	14	17	16	15	NS
CN	95	2.39	28	12	30	15	NS
CW	68	1.81	17	15	26	24	NS
VL	87	2.07	14	16	19	16	NS
CM	85	2.38	21	21	25	24	NS

*Not significant.

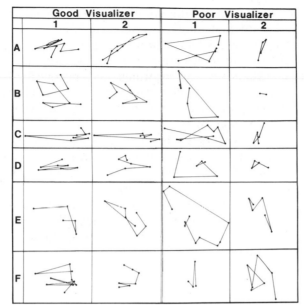

Figure 4.3. Scanpaths obtained for a good visualizer and a poor visualizer who examined six pictures (A–F) for 2 seconds on two separate occasions.

the target picture steadily increases over time; however, the gist of a picture is usually acquired quite rapidly, during the first fixation (Biederman, 1972; Potter, 1975).

Information is extracted not only in foveal vision where acuity is highest, but also in peripheral vision. My own data on saccadic distances in picture perception indicate that information as far as 17° away from the fixation point can be processed sufficiently well to program eye movements (Marks, 1982c). Researches conducted by Geoffrey Loftus have demonstrated that the encoding of a detail provides a quantum jump in the familiarity of a picture (Loftus & Bell, 1975; Loftus & Kallman, 1979). Informative details are fixated earlier, more often, and for longer durations than are noninformative details (Loftus & Mackworth, 1978). Good visualizers might thus be expected to encode details from pictures at a faster rate.

Preliminary data on encoding rates were obtained in a study in which subjects were shown a series of 60 color slides of various natural scenes. Twenty slides were shown at each of three exposure times (100, 500, and 2000 milliseconds), and a yes/no recognition test occurred at the end of each study period in which the 20 previously viewed slides were shown with 20 new slides in random order. A total of 27 subjects were tested, and on the basis of their VVIQ scores, the best seven visualizers were compared with the worst seven. There were insufficient observations at each exposure time to calculate d'; hence the results are presented in Table 4.5 in terms of a performance measure that takes into account both correct and incorrect recognitions, hit rate minus false-alarm rate. The results indicate that good visualizers encode more information than do poor visualizers ($p < .05$) at the 100-millisecond exposure, during which time only one fixation is possible. The performance of the good visualizers at the 500-millisecond exposure matches that of the poor visualizers in the 2-second exposure condition. Hence Prediction 7 is confirmed.

Experiments by Ernest (1979) also confirm Prediction 7. Ernest's criterion for selection of subjects was based on a composite measure of both objective (spatial ability) and verbal report measures of imagery ability. Ernest found that good visualizers have lower recognition thresholds in perceiving unfamiliar pictures and lower recognition latencies for both familiar and unfamiliar pictures. Ernest showed that performance differences between good and poor visualizers do not extend to word recognition or to the perception of environmental sounds.

Eye Movements in Imagery

In the light of the theory that imagery is the reactivation of neural networks laid down in perception (Hebb, 1968), it would not be surprising if vivid memory imagery included the eye movements in the original scanpath. As we have already seen, good visualizers produce more consistent scanpaths and thus have more strongly encoded imagery networks. This leads to the notion that good visualizers would be expected to repeat the scanpath eye movements as part of the image recall (Hebb, 1968). Although this hypothesis turned out to be wrong, we shall list it as Prediction 8.

Prediction 8

Good visualizers make more eye movements during the recall of images than poor visualizers. This prediction was tested in two studies, in which subjects' eye movements were recorded during the perception, imagery, and recall of pictures (Hodgson, 1977; Marks, 1973a). The good visualizers, who

TABLE 4.5.   Average Correct Recognition Rates Minus Average Incorrect Recognition Rates for Good and Poor Visualizers

Group	Exposure Time (milliseconds)		
	100	500	2000
Good visualizers	.47	.83	.83
Poor visualizers	.29	.73	.83
Means	.39	.78	.83

were more accurate in recall, actually made *fewer* eye movements in imagery than the poor visualizers. In the Hodgson study, the correlation between imagery vividness and eye-movement rate across 30 subjects was $-.50$ ($p < .01$). Only prior to incorrect recall, or if positional cues were provided in questioning the subject, did eye movements occur appropriate to the location of the required information in the original scene.

This result, contrary to the prediction as stated, suggests that eye movements do *not* occur in cases where a vivid image can be easily activated. I agree with Wickelgren's (1979, p. 76) proposal that "good imagers can generate more complex images in a single focus than can poor imagers." Anybody can image what is behind his head in a familiar room or shift attention across a familiar scene without making eye movements. *Any visual image can be activated without the necessity for eye movement providing it is strongly encoded in memory.* Eye movements are generated only when specific features and details are difficult to recall such as when the image is highly complex or unfamiliar. When an image has been reactivated in consciousness, eye movements would actually be disruptive as any new sensory–motor activity would produce interference.

Mental images can obviously never be "scanned" with the eyes in any literal sense. And quite obviously there is no "mind's eye" at work "inside the conscious mind." Nor does the mind even have an "inside." These metaphors have long outlived their usefulness and ought to be quickly dropped from the scientific literature.

Prediction of Imagery Vividness

In the light of the moderately high correlations that have been found between imagery vividness reports and various objective parameters, it is possible to combine the predictive power of several of these parameters using multiple linear regression. A regression analysis was performed on the picture recall data collected by Hodgson (1977) in which the following measures were available for one group of 30 subjects: picture recall (*PR*), maximum saccadic distance in perception (SDP_{max}), fixation rate during perception (*FRP*), fixation rate during imagery (*FRI*), and the mean image vividness rating for the pictures prior to recall (*VR*). In addition, average blink rate (*BR*) over the test period provided a measure of the subject's arousal, another variable relevant to the generation of vivid imagery. High arousal and a high blink rate is associated with low imagery vividness ($r = +.50$; $p < .01$).

A summary of the intercorrelations obtained in this study is given in Table 4.6. The multiple correlation coefficient R of image vividness with the variables SDP_{max}, *FRP*, *FRI*, *BR*, and *PR* was $+.80$, giving a coefficient of determination R^2 of .64 ($p = 1.78 \times 10^{-4}$). Hence 64% of the variance in the subjects' image vividness reports was explained on the basis of the five predictor variables. This result, in combination with the other evidence contained in this chapter, indicates the futility of arguments concerning the

TABLE 4.6. Intercorrelations of Experimental Variables and Imagery Vividness Across Subjects (Hodgson, 1977)

	SDP_{max}	FRP	FRI	BR	PR
Image vividness VR^a	.51	.38	.56	.50	.75
Saccadic distance SDP_{max}	—	.43	.39	.44	.63
Fixation rate in perception FRP		—	.00	−.04	.37
Fixation rate in imagery FRI^a			—	.54	.65
Blink rate BR^a				—	.41

[a]Note that reciprocal transformations were taken of these variables to improve linearity, thus reversing the sign of the correlations.

unreliability of verbal reports. *Imagery reports clearly show lawful relationships to objective variables over which the subjects can have no conscious awareness or ability to control.* Explanations in terms of "demand characteristics" as postulated by Berger and Gaunitz (1977) and echoed by J. Richardson (1978) would have to be stretched very far indeed to encompass these results.

Central Processes and Imagery

Many of the studies described thus far have been concerned primarily with peripheral measures of perceptual functioning, although evidence has also been presented that good visualizers are capable of faster, stronger encoding of the visual features in pictures. However, there is obviously scope for more research on the central mechanisms of imagery functioning.

An important series of experiments conducted by Ronald Finke at the Massachusetts Institute of Technology has made some interesting discoveries. As Finke (1980) recently reviewed his work, I shall present only a brief summary. Finke's research strategy has been to determine levels of equivalence between imagery, perception, and thought. At level 1, forming a mental image, thinking of an object and perception of the object result in equivalent effects. At level 2, perception of an object results in different effects from those that occur when the same object is imaged or thought about. At level 3, imaging of an object results in effects similar to those obtained with perception of the object, but effects different from those that occur in thinking about the object without imagery present.

Prediction 9

Good visualizers experience a stronger McCollough effect than do poor visualizers using their imagery to produce the bar gratings in the adaptation period. I have already discussed Finke and Schmidt's (1977) data showing that weak McCollough effects can be obtained in the situation where subjects imagine bar gratings on colored backgrounds. Finke and Schmidt (1978) took this research one step further by determining whether the resulting after-effects depended on subjects' imagery vividness with use of the VVIQ. As in the previous experiment subjects who reported deliberately using association strategies were eliminated from the data analysis. The results for the subjects who reported that they always based their judgments on the color of the test pattern showed that only the vivid imagers made a significant number of McCollough effect responses, confirming Prediction 9. As noted above, these results cannot be explained in terms of the subjects' knowledge or expectancies as they simply do not know what to expect in this situation.

Prediction 10

Good visualizers will have larger fields of resolution in imagery than will poor visualizers. Finke and Kosslyn (1980) tested this prediction by using a measure of peripheral acuity in which subjects were asked to form mental images of two small dots and to judge their discriminability as the dots' imaginary location was moved further along the horizontal and vertical meridians. The peripheral acuity of imaged dots was directly compared to that of perceived dots. Fields of resolution in imagery were found to increase as the separation between the dots was raised, as is the case for perceptual acuity. Vivid imagers, assessed using the VVIQ, showed fields of resolution in imagery equal to those obtained in perception. Nonvivid imagers, however, showed fields of resolution that were considerably smaller, confirming Prediction 10.

Prediction 11

Mental images of movements will produce larger aftereffects in good visualizers than in poor visualizers. This experiment, reported by Finke (1979), provides another example of how subjects' expectancies are opposite to the results obtained and thus provides a strong test of the imagery prediction. When people point at a target viewed through optically displacing prisms, systematic errors occur to one side, but with practice the movements become more accurate, provided feedback is given. When the prisms are removed errors are now made by pointing to the target's opposite side. Finke (1979) observed that vivid imagers manifested larger aftereffects when they imagined they saw the adaptation errors than poor visualizers, confirming Prediction 11.

An earlier confirmation of this prediction was conducted in my own laboratory (Marks, 1977). In a study of mental practice of a physical skill (rotary pursuit tracking) it was found that mental practice, using imagery rehearsal, produced a much larger improvement in the physical skill in a group of good visualizers.

IMAGERY DIFFERENCES AND STATES OF CONSCIOUSNESS

A neatly parsimonious assumption would be along the lines, "once a good imager, always a good imager." Our model has proposed one system of neural coding for images shared by, and based on, the neural coding of perceptual inputs. Therefore, it would be expected that a good, vivid imager in one state of consciousness might be a good imager in any other state of consciousness. Holt (1972) reviewed the evidence on this hypothesis and, generally speaking, reached a negative conclusion. However, Holt's own data were based on the Sheehan (1967) revision of the original Betts scale, which is multimodel and thus potentially insensitive to experiences that are primarily visual in nature. We briefly present results on imagery in three states of consciousness (dreams, hypnagogic state, and hypnosis), all of which seem to produce moderate but significant correlations with imagery vividness reports from the normal waking state.

Dream Recall Frequency

Prediction 12

Good visualizers in the waking state will have a higher dream recall frequency than will poor visualizers. If dreams are experienced more vividly, we could speculate that they will be more memorable and recalled more frequently (Hiscock & Cohen, 1973). Alan Richardson (1979) confirmed this prediction in a survey of unselected samples of 42 female and 42 male subjects. Richardson gave his subjects the VVIQ, the Crowne and Marlowe (1964), the social desirability scale and a dream recall frequency questionnaire used originally by Hiscock and Cohen (1973). The social desirability scale was found to correlate slightly with the VVIQ; thus partial correlation coefficients were calculated to partial out the effect of social desirability on dream recall frequency reports. In confirmation of Prediction 12, significant correlations with dream recall frequency occurred for females (.36, $p < .01$) for the VVIQ with eyes-open and for males with eyes-open and eyes-closed VVIQ scores (.26, $p < .05$). Further research could be directed at obtaining vividness ratings directly following awakening from the REM state and to correlate these ratings with VVIQ ratings from the waking state.

Hypnagogic and Hypnopompic Imagery

Prediction 13

Good visualizers in the waking state will report more occurrences of hypnagogic imagery than will poor visualizers. A preliminary test of this prediction was recently conducted by two students at the University of Otago, Ann Power and Joanne Hawley. Thirty-two naive student volunteers completed the VVIQ and also a special questionnaire designed to elicit reports on the hypnagogic state. One of the questions on the Power/Hawley Questionnaire simply asked: "Have you ever experienced visual imagery (i.e., mentally 'seen' things) just before falling asleep?" The 22 students who replied affirmatively to this question reported significantly more vivid imagery on the VVIQ than did the 10 students who reported never having experienced the hypnagogic state (Mann–Whitney $U = 49$, $p = .007$). Although more detailed research is warranted, this preliminary result provides confirmation of Prediction 13 and supports similar data on dream recall frequency.

Hypnotic Susceptibility

Prediction 14

Good visualizers in the waking state will be more susceptible to hypnotic induction than will poor visualizers. Research on the relationship between imagery ability and hypnotic susceptibility is well developed, and there has been good confirmation of this prediction, particularly with female subjects. Research using the VVIQ (Crawford, 1978; McKenley & Gur, 1975; 't Hoen, 1978) and the Betts QMI (Sheehan et al., 1978; Sutcliffe et al., 1970) has yielded a positive relationship between waking imagery vividness and the capacity to be hypnotized.

The Generality of Imagery Differences

Although the correlations obtained between waking imagery vividness for scale items and imagery reports from altered states of consciousness are statistically significant, they are only moderate in size (around .2 to .3). The amount of unexplained variance in predicting imagery from one state to another thus runs at around 90–95%. Holt's (1972, p. 21) conclusion hence appears to be valid, that is, that when potential suggestibility and acquiescence factors are taken into account: "the remarkable fact that remains is the demonstrated and replicated independence of the various forms of visual imagery."

In a study previously reported [by McKellar, Marks & Barron, cited in Marks (1972b)], we found no differences in the capacity for good and poor visualizers to form and use interactive imagery in a mnemonic technique, the method of loci. Both groups of subjects were able to make significant improvements in their recall by use of an imagery strategy. Also, there is no direct evidence that dream imagery, or hypnagogic imagery, is actually any less vivid among poor imagers as defined by imagery reports in the waking state. All we have are data indicating lower frequencies of *recalling* imagery after these states are over. This leads to the exciting prospect that · the awareness of imagery, and our ability to use it for any specific goal or purpose, is learnable and could be acquired with appropriate experience and training. There is very little information on imagery training, and this area provides much scope for future investigation.

SUMMARY AND CONCLUSIONS

(1) Imagery is functionally equivalent and complementary to perception. The evidence suggests that the two processes share conscious awareness and are represented by the same neuronal networks in the brain.

(2) Visual imagery and visual perception are based on the encoding of features extracted from the environment using scanpaths that vary in the degree of consistency across subjects.

(3) The encoding of visual imagery occurs on different levels: at level 1, as a neural network of features from which conscious images may be formed; and at a higher, nonconscious level, as an "executive" system of abstract–conceptual representation that controls the activity of the lower level.

(4) Verbal reports of imagery provide highly reliable predictors of cognitive functioning. Imagery reports proper can be predicted from variables such as fixation rate, saccadic distance, and scanpath consistency of which the subjects have no awareness or ability to control.

(5) Demand characteristics cannot possibly explain these results because even if the subjects could be influenced in this way under well-controlled conditions, the subjects are not able to predict the results that actually occur.

(6) Visualization is a set of specific skills that enter into a wide range of activities on a highly predictable basis. However, the capacity for experiencing high-quality imagery is, to some degree, context- and state-specific, indicating the importance of learning and biological factors.

(7) The prospect of training and improving imagery skills, in the light of their wide potential for application, is a truly exciting one.

REFERENCE NOTE

1. A copy of the VVIQ, together with instructions for administration, may be obtained from the author.

REFERENCES

Anderson, J. R. Arguments concerning representations for mental imagery. *Psychological Review,* 1978, **85,** 249–277.

Anderson, J. R. Further arguments concerning representations for mental imagery: A response to Hayes-Roth and Pylyshyn. *Psychological Review,* 1979, **86,** 395–406.

Anderson, J. R. *Cognitive psychology and its implications*. San Francisco: Freeman, 1980.

Anderson, J. R., & Bower, G. H. *Human associative memory*. Washington, DC: Winston, 1973.

Antes, J. R. The time course of picture viewing. *Journal of Experimental Psychology*, 1974, **103**, 62–70.

Antrobus, J. S. Information theory and stimulus-independent thought. *British Journal of Psychology*, 1968, **59**, 423–430.

Atwood, G. E. An experimental study of visual imagination and memory. *Cognitive Psychology*, 1971, **2**, 290–299.

Berger, G. H., & Gaunitz, S. C. B. Self-rated imagery and vividness of task pictures in relation to visual memory. *British Journal of Psychology*, 1977, **68**, 283–288.

Berger, G. H. & Gaunitz, S. C. B. Self-rated imagery and encoding strategies in visual memory. *British Journal of Psychology*, 1979, **70**, 21–24.

Bexton, W. H., Heron, W., & Scott, T. H. Effects of decreased variation in the sensory environment. *Canadian Journal of Psychology*, 1954, **8**, 70–76.

Biederman, I. Perceiving real world scenes. *Science*, 1972, **177**, 77–80.

Broadbent, D. E. *Decision and Stress*. New York: Academic, 1971.

Brooks, L. R. Spatial and verbal components of the act of recall. *Canadian Journal of Psychology*, 1968, **22**, 349–368.

Byrne, B. Item concreteness vs spatial organization as predictors of visual imagery. *Memory and Cognition*, 1974, **2**, 53–59.

Casswell, S., & Marks, D. F. Cannabis induced impairment of a divided attention task. *Nature*, 1973, **241**, 90–91.

Cautela, J. R., & Baron, M. G. Covert conditioning: A theoretical analysis. *Behavior Modification*, 1977, **1**, 351–368.

Collins, A. M., & Loftus, E. F. A spreading-activation theory of semantic processing. *Psychological Review*, 1975, **82**, 407–428.

Collins, A. M., & Quillian, M. R. Retrieval time from semantic memory. *Journal of Verbal Learning and Verbal Behavior*, 1969, **8**, 240–247.

Crawford, H. J. Relationship of hypnotic susceptibility to imagery vividness, absorption, and daydreaming styles. Paper presented at the Western Psychological Association Annual Meeting, 1978.

Crowne, D. P., & Marlowe, D. *The approval motive: Studies in evaluative dependence*. New York: Wiley, 1964.

Deutsch, J. A., & Deutsch, D. Attention: Some theoretical considerations. *Psychological Review*, 1963, **70**, 80–90.

Ericsson, K. A., & Simon, H. A. Verbal reports as data. *Psychological Review*, 1980, **87**, 215–251.

Ernest, C. H. Mental imagery and cognition: A critical review. *Journal of Mental Imagery*, 1977, **1**, 181–216.

Ernest, C. H. Visual imagery ability and the recognition of verbal and nonverbal stimuli. *Acta Psychologica*, 1979, **43**, 253–269.

Finke, R. A. The functional equivalence of mental images and errors of movement. *Cognitive Psychology*, 1979, **11**, 235–264.

Finke, R. A. Levels of equivalence in imagery and perception. *Psychological Review,* 1980, **87,** 113–132.

Finke, R. A., & Kosslyn, S. M. Mental imagery acuity in the peripheral visual field. *Journal of Experimental Psychology: Human Perception and Performance,* 1980, **6,** 126–139.

Finke, R. A., & Schmidt, M. J. Orientation-specific color aftereffects following imagination. *Journal of Experimental Psychology: Human Perception and Performance,* 1977, **3,** 599–606.

Finke, R. A., & Schmidt, M. J. The quantitative measure of pattern representation in images using orientation-specific color aftereffects. *Perception and Psychophysics,* 1978, **23,** 515–520.

Freund, R. D. Verbal and non-verbal processes in picture recognition. Unpublished doctoral dissertation, Stanford University, 1971.

Gur, R. C., & Hilgard, E. R. Visual imagery and the discrimination of differences between altered pictures simultaneously and successively presented. *British Journal of Psychology,* 1975, **66,** 341–345.

Haber, R. N. Twenty years of haunting eidetic imagery: Where's the ghost? *The Behavioral and Brain Sciences,* 1979, **2,** 583–629.

Hansel, C. E. M. *ESP and parapsychology: A critical re-evaluation.* Buffalo, N.Y.: Prometheus Books, 1980.

Hayes-Roth, F. Distinguishing theories of representation: A critique of Anderson's "Arguments concerning mental imagery." *Psychological Review,* 1979, **86,** 376–382.

Hebb, D. O. *The Organization of behavior.* New York: Wiley, 1949.

Hebb, D. O. Concerning imagery. *Psychological Review,* 1968, **75,** 466–477.

Hiscock, M., & Cohen, D. B. Visual imagery and dream recall. *Journal of Research in Personality,* 1973, **7,** 179–188.

Hodgson, I. Visual imagery and eye movements. Unpublished honors dissertation, University of Otago, 1977.

Holt, R. R. On the nature and generality of mental imagery. In P. W. Sheehan (Ed.), *The function and nature of imagery,* New York: Academic Press, 1972.

Janssen, W. *On the nature of the mental image.* Soesterberg, the Netherlands: Institute for Perception, 1976.

Kahneman, D. *Attention and effort.* Englewood Cliffs, N.J.: Prentice-Hall, 1973.

Kazdin, A. E., & Smith, G. A. Covert conditioning: A review and evaluation. *Advances in Behaviour Research and Therapy,* 1979, **2,** 57–96.

Keele, S. W. *Attention and human performance.* Pacific Palisades, Cal.: Goodyear, 1973.

Kosslyn, S. M., Ball, T. M., & Reiser, B. J. Visual images preserve metric spatial information: Evidence from studies of image scanning. *Journal of Experimental Psychology: Human Perception and Performance,* 1979, **4,** 47–60.

Lai, D. C. *Biocybernetic factors in human perception and memory* (Technical Reports 6741–6745). Stanford, Cal.: Information Systems Laboratory, Stanford University, 1975.

Le Dain, G. *Final Report of the commission of inquiry into the non-medical use of drugs.* Ottawa: Information Canada, 1973.

Lilly, J. C. Mental effects of reduction of ordinary levels of physical stimuli on intact healthy persons. *Psychiatric Research Reports of the American Psychiatric Association,* 1956, **5,** 1–28.

Loftus, G. R. Eye fixations and recognition memory for pictures. *Cognitive Psychology,* 1972, **3,** 525–551.

Loftus, G. R., & Bell, S. Two types of information in picture memory. *Journal of Experimental Psychology: Human Learning and Memory,* 1975, **104,** 103–113.

Loftus, G. R., & Kallman, H. J. Encoding and use of detail information in picture recognition. *Journal of Experimental Psychology: Human Learning and Memory,* 1979, **5,** 197–211.

Loftus, G. R., & Mackworth, N. H. Cognitive determinants of fixation location during picture viewing. *Journal of Experimental Psychology: Human Perception and Performance,* 1978, **4,** 565–572.

MacAvoy, M. G., & Marks, D. F. Divided attention performance of cannabis users and non-users following cannabis and alcohol. *Psychopharmacologia,* 1976, **44,** 147–152.

MacKay, D. M., & MacKay, V. Orientation-sensitive aftereffects of dichoptically presented color and form. *Nature,* 1973, **242,** 477–479.

Mandler, G. Consciousness: Respectable, useful, and probably necessary. In R. Solso (Ed.), *Information processing and cognition: The Loyola symposium.* Hillsdale, N.J.: Lawrence Erlbaum Associates, 1975.

Marks, D. F. Individual differences in the vividness of visual imagery and their effect on function. In P. W. Sheehan (Ed.), *The function and nature of imagery,* New York: Academic Press, 1972a, pp. 83–108.

Marks, D. F. Relative judgment: A phenomenon and a theory. *Perception and Psychophysics,* 1972b, **11,** 156–160.

Marks, D. F. Visual imagery differences in the recall of pictures. *British Journal of Psychology,* 1973a, **64,** 17–24.

Marks, D. F. Visual imagery differences and eye movements in the recall of pictures. *Perception and Psychophysics,* 1973b, **14,** 407–412.

Marks, D. F. Imagery and consciousness: A theoretical review from an individual differences perspective. *Journal of Mental Imagery,* 1977, **2,** 275–290.

Marks, D. F. Sensory cues invalidate remote viewing experiments. *Nature,* 1982e, 292, 177.

Marks, D. F. Individual differences in visual imagery and their relationship to perception and memory. In preparation, 1982a.

Marks, D. F. Imagery differences and recognition memory for pictures and words. In preparation, 1982b.

Marks, D. F. Saccadic distance as a predictor of visual memory. In preparation, 1982c.

Marks, D. F. Scanpath analysis and picture recognition. In preparation, 1982d.

Marks, D. F., & Kammann, R. Information transmission in remote viewing experiments. *Nature,* 1978, **274,** 680–681.

Marks, D. F., & Kammann, R. *The psychology of the psychic.* Buffalo, N.Y.: Prometheus Books, 1980.

McCollough, C. Color adaptation of edge-detectors in the human visual system. *Science,* 1965, **149,** 1115–1116.

McKellar, P. Between wakefulness and sleep: Hypnagogic fantasy. In A. A. Sheikh and J. T. Shaffer (Eds.), *The potential of fantasy and imagination,* New York: Brandon House, 1979, pp. 189–197.

McKelvie, S. J., & Demers, E. G. Individual differences in reported visual imagery and memory performance. *British Journal of Psychology,* 1979, **70,** 51–57.

McKenley, P. & Gur, R. R. Imagery, absorption, meditation, and drug use on correlates of hypnotic susceptibility. Paper presented at the annual meeting of Society for Clinical and Experimental Hypnosis, Chicago, October 10, 1975.

Meier, N. C. *The Meier art tests: I. Art judgment.* Iowa City, Iowa: Bureau of Educational Research and Service, 1940.

Miller, G. A. The magical number seven plus or minus two: Some limits on our capacity for processing information. *Psychological Review,* 1956, **63,** 81–97.

Mitchell, D. B., & Richman, C. L. Confirmed reservations: Mental travel. *Journal of Experimental Psychology: Human Perception and Performance,* 1980, **6,** 58–66.

Moray, N. *Attention: Selective processes in vision and hearing.* New York: Academic Press, 1970.

Neisser, U. *Cognitive psychology.* Englewood Cliffs, N.J.: Prentice-Hall, 1967.

Neisser, U. Changing conceptions of imagery. In P. W. Sheehan (Ed.), *The function and nature of imagery,* New York: Academic Press, 1972, pp. 234–252.

Neisser, U. *Cognition and reality.* San Francisco: Freeman, 1976.

Nisbett, R. E., & Wilson, T. D. Telling more than we can know: Verbal reports on mental processes. *Psychological Review,* 1977, **84,** 231–259.

Norman, D. *Memory and attention.* New York: Wiley, 1976.

Noton, D., & Stark, L. Scanpaths in saccadic eye movements while viewing and recognizing patterns. *Vision Research,* 1971, **11,** 929–942.

Orne, M. T. On the social psychology of the psychological experiment: With particular reference to demand characteristics and their implications. *American Psychologist,* 1972, **17,** 776–783.

Ornstein, R. *The psychology of consciousness.* San Francisco: Freeman, 1972.

Paivio, A. *Imagery and verbal processes.* New York: Holt, 1971.

Perky, C. W. An experimental study of imagination. *American Journal of Psychology,* 1910, **21,** 422–425.

Peterson, L. R., & Peterson, M. J. Short-term retention of individual verbal items. *Journal of Experimental Psychology,* 1959, **58,** 193–198.

Posner, M. I., & Keele, S. W. Time and space as measures of mental operations. Paper presented at the Annual Meeting of the American Psychological Association, 1970.

Potter, M. Meaning in visual search. *Science,* 1975, **187,** 965–966.

Potter, M. C. Mundane symbolism: The relations among objects, names, and ideas. In N. R. Smith and M. B. Franklin (Eds.), *Symbolic functioning in childhood.* Hillsdale, N.J.: Lawrence Erlbaum Associates, 1980.

Pylyshyn, Z. W. What the mind's eye tells the mind's brain: A critique of mental imagery. *Psychological Bulletin,* 1973, **80,** 1–24.

Pylyshyn, Z. W. Validating computational models: A critique of Anderson's indeterminacy of representation claim. *Psychological Review,* 1979, **86,** 383–394.

Quillian, M. R. Semantic memory. In M. Minsky (Ed.), *Semantic information processing,* Cambridge: MIT Press, 1968.

Richardson, A. Dream recall frequency and vividness of visual imagery. *Journal of Mental Imagery,* 1979, **3,** 65–72.

Richardson, J. T. E. Mental imagery and memory: Coding ability or coding preference. *Journal of Mental Imagery,* 1978, **2,** 101–116.

Richman, C. L., Mitchell, D. B., & Reznick, J. S. Mental travel: Some reservations. *Journal of Experimental Psychology: Human Perception and Performance,* 1979, **5,** 13–18.

Rumelhart, D. N., Lindsay, P. H., & Norman, D. A. A process model for long-term memory. In E. Tulving and W. Donaldson (Eds.), *Organization of memory.* New York: Academic Press, 1972.

Segal, S. J., & Fusella, V. Influence of imaged pictures and sounds on detection of visual and auditory signals. *Journal of Experimental Psychology,* 1970, **83,** 458–464.

Segal, S. J., & Fusella, V. Effects of images in six sense modalities on detection of visual signal from noise. *Psychonomic Science,* 1971, **24,** 55–56.

Shallice, T. Dual functions of consciousness. *Psychological Review,* 1972, **79,** 383–393.

Sheehan, P. W. A shortened form of Betts' Questionnaire upon Mental Imagery. *Journal of Clinical Psychology,* 1967, **23,** 386–389.

Sheehan, P. W. A functional analysis of the role of visual imagery in unexpected recall. In P. W. Sheehan (Ed.), *The function and nature of imagery.* New York: Academic, 1972, pp. 149–174.

Sheehan, P. W., McConkey, K. M., & Law, H. G. Imagery facilitation and performance on the creative imagination scale. *Journal of Mental Imagery,* 1978, **2,** 265–274.

Sheehan, P. W., & Neisser, U. Some variables affecting the vividness of imagery in recall. *British Journal of Psychology,* 1969, **60,** 71–80.

Sheikh, A.A., & Panagiotou, N., Use of mental imagery in psychotherapy: A critical review. Perceptual and Motor Skills, 1975, 41, 555-585.

Shepard, R. N. The mental image. *American Psychologist,* 1978, **33,** 125–137.

Shepard, R. N., & Metzler, J. Mental rotation of three dimensional objects. *Science,* 1971, **171,** 701–703.

Shepard, R. N., & Podgorny, P. Cognitive processes that resemble perceptual processes. In W. K. Estes (Ed.), *Handbook of learning and cognitive processes.* Hillsdale, N.J.: Lawrence Erlbaum Associates, 1978.

Shurley, J. T. Hallucinations in sensory deprivation and sleep deprivation. In D. J. West (Ed.), *Hallucinations,* London: Grune & Stratton, 1962.

Singer, J. L. *Daydreaming.* New York: Random House, 1966.

Singer, J. L. Experimental studies of daydreaming and the stream of thought. In K.

S. Pope and J. L. Singer (Eds.), *The stream of consciousness: Scientific investigations into the flow of human experience*. New York: Plenum, 1978.

Singer, J. L., Greenberg, S., & Antrobus, J. S. Looking with the mind's eye: Experimental studies of ocular motility during daydreaming and mental arithmetic. *Transactions of the New York Academy of Sciences*, 1971, **33**, 694–709.

Smith, E. R., & Miller, F. D. Limits on perception of cognitive processes: A reply to Nisbett and Wilson. *Psychological Review*, 1978, **85**, 355–362.

Sutcliffe, J. P., Perry, C. W., & Sheehan, P. W. Relation of some aspects of imagery and fantasy to hypnotic susceptibility. *Journal of Abnormal Psychology*, 1970, **76**, 279–287.

Targ, R., & Puthoff, H. Information transfer under conditions of sensory shielding. *Nature*, 1974, **251**, 602–607.

't Hoen, P. Effects of hypnotizability and visualizing ability on imagery-mediated learning. *International Journal of Clinical and Experimental Hypnosis*, 1978, **26**, 119–127.

Treisman, A. M. Strategies and models of selective attention. *Psychological Review*, 1969, **76**, 282–299.

Underwood, B. Individual differences as a crucible in theory construction. *American Psychologist*, 1975, **30**, 128–134.

White, K., Sheehan, P. W., & Ashton, R. Imagery assessment: A survey of self-report measures. *Journal of Mental Imagery*, 1977, **1**, 145–170.

White, P. Limitations on verbal reports of internal events: A refutation of Nisbett and Wilson and of Bem. *Psychological Review*, 1980, **87**, 105–112.

Wicklegren, W. *Cognitive psychology*. Englewood Cliffs, N.Y.: Prentice-Hall, 1979.

CHAPTER 5

Imagery Effects on Memory: Theoretical Interpretations

JOHN C. YUILLE AND MARC MARSCHARK

AN IMAGERY PARABLE

Once upon a time, there was a scarecrow. In the course of his long life, he was treated with both kindness and disdain. At times, the people and wizards of the valley paid him homage for the fashion in which he handled the bothersome crows. At other times, however, he was treated as an outcast; the inhabitants of the valley would point to his straw nature and say that he was not worthy of their company.

After a particularly long period of rejection, during which others would not even mention his name (which was Icon), the scarecrow came to be championed by several wizards from the North. Under the leadership of the wise Finn, these wizards convinced the people that this scarecrow was able to manage even the most troublesome crows. It was proclaimed that ignoring the crows was foolish and shortsighted, and since only the strawman was able to deal with them, the wizards of the North suggested that the scarecrow should be accepted by all the people. For a number of years the strawman was adopted by all in the valley, and his fame grew.

But dark words came from some wizards of the East and far West, who thought the people were coming to believe in the scarecrow as a true man. They said that the wizards of the North placed too much faith in this man of straw. In both the East and the far West they declared that the scarecrow was no man at all, but a clever machine that could be built from the basic elements of all being—mathematical formulae. These wizards loudly declared that they could build such a machine, although they did not. In reaction, the wizards of the North vowed that the strawman was no machine, but they seemed unable to describe his essence. However, they were no longer content to stress only that he could scare the crows, and they tried to give the scarecrow even more responsibilities. Clearly, the scarecrow became the center of controversy for the two groups of wizards.

One day a young wizard from the Northeast (who looked very much like one from the far West) announced to all the wizards: "Look ye, you can never know whether the scarecrow is man or machine, for I can build a machine that looks and acts like a man, and I can find a man that can do all that a machine can do. The wizards of the North say that the scarecrow is not a man, but they truly think him to be one. The wizards of the East and the far West claim that the strawman is a machine but they cannot build a machine that manages all of the crows. Therefore, let us cease this wizardry and make beautiful sculptures instead. The sculptures will scare the crows, we can display them to our colleagues, and no one will claim that they are true men."

A loud cry arose from all the other wizards. In the North they said, "The scarecrow is best for our needs—make your sculptures if you like, but they will not replace our strawman. He is strong and good, and a sculpture would be but an image of the scarecrow." The wizards of the East and the far West cried: "How can you say that our formulae serve no purpose? They are the source of all life, and our machines can do the work of gods. Make sculptures as you may, for it is a fair proposition, but they have naught to do with the nature of our work. Our formulae are elegant and yet simple, and sculptures would be but machines of a different sort."

So the wizards of the North returned to the scarecrow and once again vowed to champion his fame. In the East and the far West, the wizards turned to their machines and vowed to make a strawman of their own. At the same time, two wizards from someplace else smiled, and shook their heads in disbelief that their peers would find such serious disagreement concerning the scaring of crows.

In 1972 a text edited by Peter Sheehan (Sheehan, 1972) appeared that reviewed empirical and theoretical issues relevant to imagery. Included was a chapter by Allan Paivio entitled "Analysis of the role of imagery in learning and memory." Paivio described the stimulus and individual difference factors that appeared to affect the use of imagery. He also outlined his dual-coding model of the role of visual and verbal processes in memory, a model that remains one of the major theoretical interpretations of imagery proposed to date. The purpose of the present chapter is to review and evaluate theoretical developments related to the role of imagery in memory that have occurred since the publication of Paivio's (1972) review. One of our concerns is the modification of the dual-coding model during the past decade. This model persists as the major statement assigning a principal role to imagery in memory. However, other models of imagery have appeared recently, and although the memory aspects of them have not been explicated, we examine the form that these other models have taken. The most striking recent events have been the negative reactions to imagery theories. The computer has moved from metaphor to testing ground of some psychological models. One consequence of this has been the appearance of computational models of cognition, and the proponents of these models have been critical of all the imagery based interpretations. This has resulted in an analogue (i.e., imagery)–computational debate. After examining this debate and the type of data referred to by the antagonists, we offer some thoughts about the like-lihood of resolving the arguments and our prognosis for imagery models of memory.

THE DUAL-CODING MODEL

For almost two decades, Paivio has been a leading researcher and theore-tician in relating memorial processes to imagery. A large body of empirical work (a synopsis of which is found below) has led him to conclude that "imagery variables are among the most potent memory factors ever dis-covered" (Paivio, 1972, p. 253). His interpretation of these variables has been in terms of his dual-coding model (Paivio, 1971). The primary hypoth-esis of this model is that the two major modes of coding experience are verbal and imaginal. Verbal processes are seen to involve "a functional symbolic system (and) are assumed to be auditory–motor in nature" (Paivio, 1971, p. 12). Imagery is the representational mode for nonverbal thought, involving dynamic processes similar to active perception (Paivio, 1976). Verbal codes are assumed to be sequentially organized; that is, the units of verbal thinking (words) are believed to be linked in associative chains. Im-agery, in contrast, can integrate information into a single, simultaneous representation. These two systems, although separate, are hypothesized to be richly interconnected.

There are three basic psychological assumptions either implicit or explicit to Paivio's model. First, the image is considered to have perceptual-like qualities (i.e., the model adopts a sensationalistic epistemology). Images are memory traces of percepts, and the perceptual nature of the image is pre-sumed to make it a valuable tool in aiding certain types of problem solving. For example, "scanning" mental images of objects can yield information about their relative sizes or positions; because such information was in the original percept, it can be retained in the image. This quality facilitates memory because the image can be integrated into a single representation. Once the integrated image is formed, it can be stored and, with an appropriate cue, retrieved later.

The cue-assisted retrieval of images illustrates the second basic assump-tion in Paivio's model: human memory involves the storage of images (in contrast to a reconstructive view of memory). Images are stored or filed away and can be later retrieved by either verbal or visual cues. It should be noted, however, that the structure of memory has not been specified by Paivio. That is, the problems of how images are organized in memory, how cues access specific images, have not been addressed. The final assumption of Paivio's model is that learning fundamentally involves the formation of associations. In the verbal mode, associations result in a chain of words, whereas imaginal associations lead to an integrated image.

The reader may note that these assumptions of dual-coding theory have a familiar ring. In fact, the associative mental chemistry of John Stuart Mill presented almost the same view of imagery. Mill, working in the tradition of British empiricism, but adding novel ideas that gave associationism more flexibility, made imagery central in his philosophy of mind. He believed the image to be quasi-perceptual, inferior in intensity but otherwise similar to the original percept. He claimed that learning involves the formation of links, governed by the laws of association. Finally, he asserted that a complex idea (image) could be formed by blending together single images in a process analogous to chemical combination. The purpose of noting this historical parallel is not to question more recent theoretical contributions, but to emphasize the persistence of this view of imagery. Western philosophy has almost constantly assumed that images are mental elements and that they form the basis of memory. Why has this interpretation proved so viable?

SOME HISTORICAL NOTES

The assignment of a central theoretical role to imagery in memory appears to have originated in the classical era in Greece. For example, in *De Anima*, Aristotle wrote "the soul never thinks without a mental picture" [quoted in Yates (1966), p. 32]. Rejecting Plato's rationalism, Artistotle assumed that knowledge comes from experience. The sensations interpreted by the common sense are permanently recorded like the impression of a seal in wax (a continuation of Plato's metaphor). The impressions are in the form of images, which are pale copies of the original percept. The images are related to one another on the basis of the laws of association.

The image was revived by Aquinas in the thirteenth century in his attempt to reconcile Aristotle's philosophy with Christian dogma. Empiricism also made a recovery and became essential to British philosophy. From Hartley to Mill, the successive versions of British philosophy always incorporated the image as an element of mind. For example, David Hume insisted that all mental events could be understood in terms of the association of mental images (which were pale copies of sensations). Perhaps the persistence of this view of imagery, in association with an empirical epistemology, reflects the introspective character of much of Western philosophy. The concern of the empiricists was focused on the nature and contents of consciousness. Apparently, the phenomenology of their experience always included images, encouraging them to readily equate thought and imagery.

An important occurrence in the history of imagery was the weakening of the long-established relationship between the concepts of imagery and association. When psychology attempted to become an empirical science in the late nineteenth century, it retained most of the concepts of British empiricism. Thus the building blocks of Wundt's mental structure were images, feelings, and sensations. Memory was not, however, a central concern of either Wundt or his many critics. Ebbinghaus, the one person during this period to emphasize memory, took the unusual step of trying to remove meaning from learning materials. Hoping to study memory and association in its purest form, Ebbinghaus tried to exclude the effects of past learning by inventing the nonsense syllable. With this invention, he assured that most of the learning he studied would occur by rote repetition. The opportunity to use images or any semantic code was thus restricted, and a tradition was established that the formation of associations could be studied in isolation.

The impression should not be created that there were no attempts to relate imagery and memory during this early period of psychological research. However, the studies that were done seemed to generate more questions than answers. For example, Juddand Cowling (1907) asked subjects to commit a picture to memory after successive presentations of parts of the picture. To their surprise, they found that subjects could not "see" the whole, integrated mental image all at once. This did not fit with the intuitive assumption about the integrative capacity of the imagery system. Fernald (1912) required his subjects to memorize a set of letters forming the border of a square (the Binet letter square). When required to "read" letters from their memory image in a backward order, the subjects became confused and made a number of errors. This seemed to clash with the assumed quasi-perceptual nature of the image.

These results were typical of the difficulties encountered in early research on imagery. In fact, whether imagery was essential to thought was a major point of both theoretical and empirical disagreement in German psychology at the turn of the century. The dependency of researchers on trained introspection as their principal method of study assured that the results reflected more about the training the subjects received than about the basic nature of mental processes. The frustration resulting from the confused pattern of results helped to bring about the American behaviorist revolution, which not only rejected trained introspection as a valid method of studying memory, but also banished imagery as a legitimate concern of psychology.

From approximately 1915 until 1960, imagery was ostracized from the discipline (Holt, 1964). Throughout this hiatus in imagery research, the study of memory was a central concern of academic psychologists. Continuing the tradition begun by Ebbinghaus, North American researchers assumed that learning involved the formation of associative bonds (now described in S–S and S–R terms). Imagery and association, so long wed in Western philosophy, remained divorced in the developing discipline of psychology. It is intriguing that once imagery reappeared in the 1960s [see Holt (1964) for a review of the reasons for the resurrection of imagery], it immediately was reunited with association. The major force behind the renewed interest in the role of imagery in memory was Paivio. In fact, S–R associationism persisted in theories of memory in the 1960s, with images becoming an acceptable vehicle for association. Some of the empirical reasons for this are elaborated in the next section of this chapter. In any event, Paivio (1971) argued that words and images are "elicited" as associative reactions to external stimuli.

Thus, in spite of periods of low popularity, the image again vied for a central place in models of cognition. As Paivio has noted, "One of the most striking facts concerning the history of the concept (imagery) is that it has been repeatedly criticized and opposed and yet the critics never quite succeeded in burying the image" (Paivio, 1976, p. 47). The persistence of this view of imagery is, at the very least, a testimonial to its intuitive appeal.

REAPPEARANCE OF IMAGERY IN MODELS OF MEMORY

We now examine the data base that aided the reappearance of imagery in models of memory in the 1960s, with an emphasis on the evidence supporting the dual coding model. Beginning with the work of Bugelski (1962), a variety of studies established the importance of mediation as a strong predictor of performance in verbal learning tasks (Keiss & Montague, 1965; Paivio et al., 1966). For some, mediation involved implicit verbalization and conditioned bodily response in the throat, limbs, and retina. To several researchers, however, internalized language held no more logical or empirical appeal than did imagery. Both had to be inferred on the basis of memory performance, and although some nonverbal (but associative) mediation seemed an essential component of meaning (Osgood, 1966; Paivio, 1963), this was not captured by the notion of implicit muscular or visceral reactions. In retrospect, it appears that perhaps the strongest argument against the imagery position in the 1960s was its strong intuitive appeal. The more likely a subject was to report conscious awareness of memorial processes, the less likely were those processes to be considered functional.

The general acceptance of a central role for mediators in memorial processes led to a number of investigations of mediation and its relationship to characteristics of to-be-learned material. Many researchers (Bower, 1967, 1970; Bugelski et al., 1968; Paivio, 1965, 1969; Paivio & Madigan, 1968; Paivio & Yuille, 1967) found imagery to be both a generative heuristic and a consistent predictor of recall performance. The majority of these studies involved the manipulation of stimulus attributes or instructional sets. Consideration of stimulus attributes centered on the relationship between the image-evoking quality of concrete stimuli relative to abstract stimuli and the observed differences in the recall of those materials. Stimulus concreteness was found to facilitate recall performance in a variety of tasks, including paired-associative learning, serial learning, discrimination learning, free recall, cued recall, and recognition [see Paivio (1971), for a review]. Furthermore, instructions for subjects to use images as mediators (Bower, 1970, Bugelski et al., 1968) generally produced strong facilitation of learning and recall performance relative to instructions for verbal mediation. When imagery instructions failed to produce increments in performance, the results could usually be accounted for in terms of ceiling effects caused by the spontaneous use of imagery with concrete materials, even when instructions called for subjects to refrain from mediation or to use some other method (Paivio, 1971).

The image-evoking character of concrete materials was generally acknowledged during this period, but the casual link between imagery and recall was less well defined. In particular, it was unclear whether imagery effects could be more parsimoniously attributed to other variables such as the specificity–generality dimension (Paivio, 1963), lexical complexity (Kintsch, 1972), or meaningfulness (Paivio & O'Neill, 1970) and several others. Meaningfulness proved the most stubborn of these alternatives, insofar as it was shown to be empirically related to learning in virtually all tasks where imagery was facilitative. Furthermore, concrete nouns generally exceeded abstract nouns on rated meaningfulness (Paivio et al., 1968b), and it proved extremely difficult to separate the two variables in manipulative studies. Meaningfulness defined as Noble's (1952) m, continued to be evaluated as a viable if inconsistent, predictor of recall in a number of studies [see Paivio (1971, pp. 256–259) for a summary] until passing away quietly, unable to compete with the consistently robust effects of imagery. Nonetheless, many researchers continued to seek alternative explanations for the apparent functional effects of imagery in terms of attributes related to meaningfulness such as relational organization (Bower, 1970) and distinctiveness (Paivio et al., 1968a).

Paivio's (1969, 1971) elaboration of a dual-coding model of memory provided a theoretical framework for the interpretation of imagery effects consistent with virtually all relevant empirical findings in the memory literature. The theory combined a conceptual peg mnemonic system with a two-process theory of meaning. The conceptual peg hypothesis was based on classical mnemonic systems that emphasized the associative nature of recall. As with the classical systems, the conceptual peg hypothesis assumed that the ease of association, and thus memory, was a function of the concreteness of to-be-recalled events and, in particular, the sense ability of those items that served as cues for others. The conceptual peg hypothesis thus led to the prediction that whereas the imagery values of both stimulus and response items should affect performance in paired-associate tasks, the imageability of the stimulus should be relatively more important than that of the response. Paivio (1965) had evaluated the relative importance of stimulus and response imagery by using the four combinations of concrete and abstract stimulus and response nouns. Consistent with the conceptual peg prediction, the effect of concreteness on the stimulus side of the pairs accounted for far more variance than that on the response side (Paivio, 1963; Paivio & Yarmey, 1966). Findings of this sort were in no way predictable on the basis of meaningfulness as the effective variable.

Dual-coding theory's two-process theory of meaning (Paivio, 1969) generated far more research than did the conceptual peg hypothesis and served a more important role in the interpretation of diverse findings concerning the functional validity of imagery. Generally, this interpretation of concreteness and imagery effects assumed that nonverbal imagery was associatively aroused as an essential, if not dominant, part of the meaning for some stimuli such as pictures and concrete words. Associative arousal of meaning to abstract words, in contrast, was assumed to be primarily intraverbal in nature. The theory thus explicitly indicated that whereas memory for concrete materials is likely to involve both verbal and nonverbal codes, abstract material typically is coded only verbally. The effect of concreteness on memory was thus hypothesized to be a function of the activation of verbal or nonverbal codes or both, depending on individual differences, the particular task involved, and the functional utility of the codes within that task. All other things being equal, recall of concrete materials should be better than that of abstract materials both because there are two different routes available to obtain the information and because dually coded items should prove more resistant to forgetting than singly coded items.

The two-process model was supported by several kinds of evidence including the findings that the labeling of picture stimuli and imaging to word stimuli facilitated their recall relative to "within-modality" coding alone (Bahrick & Boucher, 1968). Perhaps the strongest support for the hypothesis came from a study by Paivio and Csapo (1969). They found that when stimuli were presented at a very fast rate, one assumed to preclude picture naming and imaging to words, and differences in recall between pictures and words were eliminated. At a slower rate, however, both recall and recognition increased from abstract words to concrete words to pictures. According to Paivio and Csapo, this reflected the relative ease with which subjects were able to generate and store labels for the pictures and images for concrete and abstract words during the interstimulus intervals.

Numerous other studies in the 1960s demonstrated a functional difference between verbal and imaginal memory processes. Among these were the findings that simply instructing subjects to use imagery as a mnemonic facilitated performance in free recall and serial learning (Jensen & Rowher, 1965); Brook's (1967, 1968) demonstrations of modality-specific interference of verbal and spatial processing systems during concurrent verbal and spatial tasks; and Bower's (1967, 1970) finding that subjects using interactive images in paired–associate learning tasks were able to remember significantly more than were subjects under either normal instructions or instructions to image the two items separately. The above studies, however, should suffice as a general overview of the way in which imagery was investigated by use of verbal learning paradigms.

As cognitive psychology entered the 1970s, the traditional emphasis on the learning and memory of word lists disappeared and the investigation of imagery focused on its organizational function in the comprehension of and memory for language. Many of the studies that created this interest were based on Bartlett's (1932) findings concerning memory for prose. Pompi and Lachman (1967), for example, reported one investigation in which subjects received the words to a relatively concrete story either in prose form or in a random order. Those who read the connected form later tended to think that they had seen new words that were consistent with the theme of the passage. Errors of this kind, however, were not made with the random presentation, thus effectively ruling out any simple verbal associative explanation of those effects. They concluded that the meaning of connected discourse may be abstracted and then stored in the form of integrated "surrogate structures" such as images or themes [see also Dooling & Lachman (1971) and Sulin & Dooling (1974)]. Yuille and Paivio (1967) explored the possibility that the mental representation of verbal materials in studies of this sort might be in the form of visual images. Subjects in their study were given learning and recall trials for lists of words in either syntactically well-formed or random orders; the paragraphs from which the lists were drawn varied in rated concreteness. Yuille and Paivio reasoned that if thematic content were stored as images, the facilitative effects of organization should be directly related to the concreteness of the passage. Since abstract material could only be stored in a verbal, sequential manner, it would not be expected to benefit from holistic organization. As predicted, the results were in agreement with the findings of Pompi and Lachman insofar as concrete materials were concerned: recall was higher with syntactic as compared to random organization. Abstract materials, in contrast, showed no effect of thematicity, indicating reduced utilization of integrative encoding (Just & Brownell, 1974).

Begg (1972) reported a study that further seemed to indicate the integrative, organizational importance of imagery in memory for concrete language as compared to the verbal sequential nature of memory for more abstract language. He hypothesized that concrete phrases such as "white horse" could be represented in memory as unitary images whereas abstract phrases such as "absolute truth" had to be represented as verbal strings corresponding to the organization of the input. Subjects learned lists of either concrete or abstract, two-word phrases and then were tested for free and cued recall. In free recall of concrete material, Begg found that the proportion of words recalled did not differ as a function of whether the lists were presented as phrases or single words. That is, the number of phrases recalled was about the same as the number of words recalled, despite the fact that there were twice as many words in the former. In free recall of the abstract material, however, the proportion of words recalled from single word lists was twice the proportion of words recalled after presentation of phrases. Presumably, concrete materials were able to be stored in the form of integrated mental images that could contain either one or two word concepts. Abstract materials, in contrast, were assumed to have been encoded sequentially, and thus abstract phrases took twice the memory capacity of single words. Both of these findings appeared to provide support for the assumption that concrete language materials can be represented in the form of holistic, integrated representations (i.e., images), whereas abstract materials are tied to the sequential organization of the linguistic input.

Subsequent to Begg's (1972) study, and contrary to both the interpretation of his results and the dual-coding theory, several studies indicated that abstract prose materials could be integrated to the same extent as concrete materials. Franks and Bransford (1972), for example, found that subjects could integrate series of nonconsecutive but semantically related abstract sentences into apparently holistic representations. Similar conclusions were indicated in the findings of Brewer(1975). He had subjects memorize lists of concrete and abstract sentences, each of which contained a word with a relatively frequently used synonym. Substitution of synonyms in recall, a frequent finding with concrete materials (Begg & Paivio, 1969), varied from 6 to almost 78%. Most importantly, substitutions were equally frequent for concrete and abstract sentences. These results, as with the Franks and Bransford (1972) findings, appear inconsistent with image theories of sentence memory since abstract materials would not be expected to benefit from the integrative encoding presumed characteristic only of an imagery format (Begg & Paivio, 1969; Paivio, 1971). Brewer interpreted his results, in fact, as indicating that information from both concrete and abstract sentences is stored in memory in the form of nonlinguistic, but nonimage, abstract representations.

Marschark and Paivio (1977) further investigated the integrative processing of concrete and abstract sentences. In two of their experiments subjects learned lists of either concrete or abstract sentences and then were given cued recall tasks in which the cues were words that did not appear in the input but that were judged to represent salient characteristics of the situations described (Pompi & Lachman, 1967). Contrary to predictions from dual-coding theory, Marschark and Paivio's findings indicated that abstract as well as concrete prose materials can be stored in memory in some integrated, holistic form. Despite the commonality with regard to integration effects, however, concrete and abstract conditions also differed in ways consistent with dual coding. Among other findings, overall levels of recall were higher for concrete sentences in all experiments, and subjects memorizing concrete materials reported the use of imaginal strategies whereas those receiving abstract materials preferred verbal processes. The results of this study thus presented a theoretical puzzle comparable to that indicated by conflicting findings obtained by other researchers. On one hand, concrete sentences were clearly recalled better than were abstract sentences, but when recall did occur, both types were able to be recalled in an integrated manner.

Insofar as the inconsistencies in their data could not be resolved on the basis of either dual- or single-code theories, Marschark and Paivio suggested the possibility that some abstract, semantic code might underlie memory for both concrete and abstract language materials at a level different from the one that yields evidence indicating functionally distinct processing systems. Separate verbal and imaginal systems thus might account for the robust quantitative differences found in the recall of concrete and abstract materials, whereas the common coding system could provide a means of preserving integrated memory representation of meaning. This suggestion represented a substantial change in dual-coding theory, one that is discussed in the conclusion section below.

Findings of the sort described by Marschark and Paivio, Brewer, and Franks and Bransford, detracted somewhat from the earlier comprehensiveness ascribed to imagery as a memory construct. At the same time, however, numerous studies, including most of those described in this section, appeared to indicate the functional involvement of imagelike representations in a variety of memory phenomena. Although some findings have indicated that processing of verbal material may not be constrained by the rigid, sequential organization of the input string, the diversity of studies indicating the operation of some parallel or synchronous processing modality has, to date, resisted all comprehensive explanations other than that based on imagery.

Insofar as imagery has been a consistent and reliable predictor of recall, very few investigators have argued that, at least at the level of subject strategies, something like imagery is not a factor in memory tasks. However, the data base for dual-coding theory has weakened in the past decade, with many findings challenging the model. We appear to be left with the intuitive appeal, in the tradition of Simonides (Yates, 1966) that imagery is functional in memory, without an adequate model of the nature of the image. In fact, those who have been most willing to speculate about the nature of imagery have been interested in perception and problem solving rather than memory.

THE STRUCTURAL PERSPECTIVE ON IMAGERY

An alternative to the functional approach to imagery is based on attempts to define the relationship between imagery and perception. The concern with the structure of the image was essentially a question concerning the role of visual memory in perception. It was evident to early researchers that visual information from successive eye fixations had to be extracted and remain available for some amount of time in order to allow for object identification. The accumulating "residue" could not simply be a series of copies or iconic images of previous patterns since continuous masking would prevent synthesis of the percept (Neisser, 1967). Neisser's analysis-by-synthesis approach to cognition typified this view in the assumption that visual perception is a constructive act. Neisser referred to such synthesis in the case of visual processing, however, only as "visual memory," its form remaining unspecified beyond noting its similarity to "resurrected vision" in the form of images. Other investigators, however, were less timid in their suggestions that imagery and perception both activated the same neural substrate (Bruner, 1957; Hebb, 1949). Empirical evidence for this position goes back as far as Perky's (1910) classic study in which subjects were shown to be unable to distinguish faintly projected stimuli from their own images.

There is an extremely diverse body of more recent literature relevant to this structural approach to imagery research, and much of it is reminiscent of the Perky phenomenon. A number of researchers, for example, have made use of same–different judgment tasks in a variety of perceptual matching studies, such as the mental rotation experiments of Shepard, Cooper, and their colleagues (Cooper & Shepard, 1973; Shepard & Metzler, 1971) and the letter-matching studies of Posner and his colleagues (Posner, 1969; Posner & Keele, 1967; Posner & Mitchell, 1967). The results of this research consistently appeared to confirm the functional role of imagelike representations in matching tasks [see Shepard & Podgorny, (1978) for a review].

Shepard and Chipman (1970) first used the perceptual matching task in a memory experiment that required subjects to judge the similarity in shape of several U.S. states. Subjects in one condition compared visually presented, maplike outlines of pairs of states. Subjects in the other condition compared shapes of the same states on the basis of representations generated internally to the names of the states. On the basis of similarities in the patterns of data obtained for the two conditions, as well as subjects' introspective reports, Shepard and Chipman concluded that in the nonperceptual condition subjects based their judgments on imagelike internal representations that preserved the structural features of the familiar map shapes. Evidence from Shepard's (1975) mental rotation experiments indicated that empirical similarities of this sort were stronger for subjects who reported greater use of imagery strategies.

Podgorny and Shepard (1978) presented further evidence concerning the spatial structure of internally generated images. They used a task in which subjects were presented with a visual grid (e.g., 5×5 matrix) within which they were to image various familiar patters of filled in squares. The fidelity with which subjects were able to represent particular patterns was tested by presenting probe dots in randomly determined spatial locations. Subjects simply decided, as quickly as possible, whether the probes were on or off the imaged figure. Among other findings, Podgorny and Shepard found that "on-stimulus" probes were responded to faster than were "off-stimulus" probes, that reaction times increased with the number of squares in a stimulus pattern, and that reaction times to probes varied relative to the imaged pattern but not to the absolute location of the location of the squares. These data were almost identical to data obtained when subjects actually saw the figures superimposed on the grids. Thus subjects were able to generate and make use of visual images that preserved spatial locations in a manner analogous to the way in which perceptual stimuli are interpreted.

Most of Podgorny and Shepard's stimulus patterns were familiar letters (e.g., T, L, E) that were presented to subjects prior to the imagery task. They obtained comparable results, however, when they used nonmeaningful patterns imaged on a smaller grid. These findings seemed to implicate spatial imagery in matching tasks involving short-term memory. Several recent experiments, however, have questioned Shepard's conclusions. In the so-called mental rotation task, for example, subjects see a pair of block figures;

one may be the mirror image of the other, or it may be a rotated version. The latency to correctly identify a rotated pair is a direct function of the angular rotation separating the two figures. Shepard (1978) concluded that the internal image is rotated holistically, taking real time to manipulate; however, both Pylyshyn (1979a) and Yuille and Steiger (1979) have reported evidence that appears to contradict this assertion. The latter two reports concluded that figural complexity affects "mental rotation" task performance, contrary to Shepard's assertion. Steiger and Yuille (1979) reported a memory analogue of the mental rotation task. Subjects committed a block figure to memory and then examined comparison figures (mirror or rotated versions of the memorized figure) one at a time. Reaction times were barely affected by the rotational separation of the memory and comparison figures. The pattern of results suggested that a holistic image did not mediate performance, and the authors proposed that nonimaginal problem solving abilities might be involved in "mental rotation."

The possibility of imagelike representations in long-term memory has been extensively studied by use of the symbolic comparison paradigm introduced by Moyer and Landauer (1967) with number stimuli. In that and several other studies (Buckley & Gillman, 1974; Parkman, 1971; Restle, 1970) subjects compared magnitudes of numbers given their numeric representations as stimuli [but see Buckley & Gillman (1974)]. The primary finding from all these studies was that the farther apart were the magnitudes of two numbers, the shorter was the reaction time to identify one as the larger or smaller. Moyer and Landauer (1967) suggested that this finding indicated that numbers might be symbolically stored as internal "analogues," whereas other researchers suggested alternative formats.

Given the nonconcrete nature of number stimuli and the fact that subjects do not report anything like mental finger counting in the number comparison task, this symbolic distance effect was not originally interpreted in terms of imagery. The situation changed, however, when Moyer (1973) obtained similar findings when subjects compared real-world sizes of animals, after being presented with their names as stimuli. Moyer's findings were consistent with both the structural tradition of rearoused perceptions (Neisser, 1967) and the functional tradition of the nonverbal retention of relational information (Paivio, 1971). The focus of imagery research thus quickly came to bear on subjects' abilities to compare, manipulate, and scan images in the same way that they can perceptual stimuli.

Paivio (1975) used the symbolic comparison task to evaluate the role of the imagery system in processing information from memory. He presented subjects with pairs of pictures or printed names of animals and objects differing in rated, real-life size. In the experiments of interest, subjects chose either the conceptually larger member of each pair or the one that appeared to be farther away. Consistent with predictions from the imagery position, reaction time to choose the larger pair members decreased as differences in memory size increased, and, overall, latencies to picture stimuli were faster than to word stimuli, indicating the former's greater ease of access to the analogue information. Furthermore, Paivio found that with picture stimuli but not words the speed of size comparisons was significantly decreased when real-life (memory) size relations conflicted with those depicted. This effect reversed when subjects judged the relative distance of the same pairs. Paivio interpreted his results in terms of the mediating effects of internal analogue representations (i.e., images) that contain relative size information among other physical attributes of the objects. Paivio pointed out, however, that analogue information could be functional in tasks of this nature without any conscious experience of imagery.

A number of other studies, in fact, indicated similar advantages for picture stimuli over word stimuli in comparisons of more abstract dimensions such as time, quality, and temperature (Holyoak & Walker, 1976); animal ferocity and intelligence [Banks & Flora (1977); Kerst & Howard, (1977); but see Paivio & Marschark (1980)]; and pleasantness (Paivio, 1978). Some researchers (Banks & Flora, 1977; Kerst & Howard, 1977) suggested that such findings should be embarrassing to imagery theorists who would have to argue that such abstract attributes are represented in verbal rather than imaginal codes. Proponents of the imagery position, however, have argued that although dimensions such as pleasantness and ferocity are conceptually abstract, they remain attributes of things rather than of words and accordingly may be memorially represented in some analogue form (Paivio, 1978). At present, this controversy remains unresolved. Although much of the difficulty for image theories can be avoided by the preceding argument, the original demonstrations of distance effects with numbers as stimuli still create problems (Holyoak & Walker, 1976; Moyer & Landauer, 1967; Parkman, 1971; Restle, 1970). It does not appear that imagery provides a satisfactory account of those findings, and yet some analogue representational system appears to be required. In answer to this requirement, some alternative imagery theories have appeared in the last few years that differ from the dual-code theory.

CONTEMPORARY IMAGERY ALTERNATIVES TO DUAL CODING

It is interesting to note that Paivio's dual-coding model remains the only major theoretical model employing imagery as a central concept in the interpretation of memory phenomena. Other imagery models that have been proposed have only tangential application to the study of memory (Bruner, 1964; Kaufman, 1980; Shepard, 1978). For example, one of the most prolific writers on the topic of imagery in the last few years has been Stephen Kosslyn. In a recent theoretical paper (Kosslyn et al., 1979) and a text entitled *Image and Mind* (1980), Kosslyn has assumed the role of champion for the centrality of imagery in models of cognition. Basing his theorizing on research concerning the role of imagery in problem-solving tasks, Kosslyn et al. (1979, p. 536) defined images as "temporary spatial displays in active memory that are generated from more abstract represenations in long-term memory. Interpretive mechanisms (a 'mind's eye') work over ('look at') these internal displays and classify them in terms of semantic categories." The differences from the dual-coding model are obvious. Images, here, are generated from long-term memory rather than retrieved, as Paivio has proposed. Thus images are not the memorial units in Kosslyn's model (although he apparently believes that some basic images are stored, to be used as components in generating complex images). The approaches of Kosslyn and Paivio are similar in assuming a "mind's eye" that can extract information from images, and only from images, and both agree that there is no need for this process to be conscious. That is, at least certain types of knowledge (e.g., relating to size and to distance information) can best be represented imaginally.

As noted earlier, one problem with dual-coding theory is the lack of specification of the nature of the image. Paivio has been careful to define the stimulus factors that he believes should elicit or encourage imaginal processes; generally, the image has been described in contrasting or negative terms. Imaginal processing is parallel, in contrast to the serial verbal process, or images are "nonverbal processes." Kosslyn has been more specific about what the term "image" means to him, and as a result, has provided the most detailed theory of imaginal processes to date (Kosslyn, 1980). Calling it a *CRT protomodel*, Kosslyn has described a computer simulation of the imagery generation processes, with the CRT display serving as the analogue of the image. Long-term memory is assumed to consist of two types of knowledge. The first contains the "perceptual literal memory" of the appearance of an object, and this seems to be similar to Paivio's assumption that images are stored in memory. However, the second aspect of memory proposed by Kosslyn differs from Paivio's model, since it assumes the nonverbal, nonimaginal storage of the facts about an object, in a propositional format. Using both types of memorial information, the computer program can generate a CRT display of an object, or combination of objects. The dot matrix, CRT display reflects the presumed interobject distance information, size information, and resolution qualities of an image.

Kosslyn's explicit view of the purpose of imagery has been echoed by Shepard (1978). As noted earlier, Shepard and his colleagues have reported a series of studies concerned with the "mental rotation" of geometric forms and letters. Although memory has not been a concern of Shepard, except for short-term memory in one study (Shepard & Podgorny, 1978), his assumptions appear to be similar to Kosslyn's. That is, Shepard proposes that mental images can be generated from memory information (the form of the latter is not specified) and used to aid in the solution of spatial problems. The image allows "scanning" of information not easily accessed in any other form. Although Shepard has elaborated a variety of scientific and creative endeavors that he believes to be mediated by imagery (Shepard, 1978), he has not provided any more detail than outlined above about the nature of imagery processes.

NEGATIVE REACTIONS TO IMAGERY MODELS

Paivio, Kosslyn, and Shepard represent what might be called the proimagery position in cognitive psychology. Although they differ concerning the nature of the memory processes underlying imagery, they are uniform in providing the image an essential place in models of cognition. Their critics, however, have been many, and they have been strong in their attack on imagery-based theories. These negative reactions reflect a general change that has occurred in the study of cognitive processes in the past few years. Neisser (1967) led the change in psychology in the late 1960s when the last vestiges of S–R mediational theory were discarded in favor of the use of cognitive descriptions. Mental processes again became a respectable domain of concern to psychologists.

The renewed interest in mentalistic concepts was, in part, a reflection of substantial developments in computer science. As software complexity increased, computers began to be discussed as "intelligent." If the storage, retrieval, and organization of information are appropriate descriptors for the intelligent activities of the computer, why not use the same language to describe mental processes? Indeed, computer metaphors quickly appeared in descriptions of human memory (Atkinson & Shiffrin, 1968). More recently, rather than serving simply as an analogue, the computer has become the arena of testing some psychological theories. For example, Anderson and Bower (1973) presented a computer program called HAM (for human associative memory) and argued that the program represented a theory of psychological functions involved in memory and language (Norman & Rumelhart, 1975). The basic assumption of this type of modeling is that memory involves an abstract or symbolic code. All knowledge may be represented, for example, as a propositional network composed of nodes (representing concepts) connected by links (which represent the relationships between concepts). Memory is thus amodal, and imagery effects are interpreted in terms of the amodal codes. Images themselves are assumed either not to exist or to be epiphenomenal.

Some proponents of the propositional perspective have presented direct attacks on imagery-based models of memory. For example, Kieras (1978) proposed a propositional interpretation of imagery effects in verbal learning studies. Like Paivio, Kieras assumed that perceptual and semantic information differ, but the difference for Kieras was to be found in the nature of the propositional code, and not the modality (i.e., imaginal vs. verbal) of storage. Kieras asserted that his version of the propositional model was superior to dual-coding theory in accounting for so-called imagery effects.

Dual-coding theory has also been attacked from a combined empirical and physiological perspective. Das et al. (1975) suggested that Paivio's distinction between simultaneous and successive processes is correct, but that this was the only distinction needed to deal with cognitive abilities. The imagery–verbal distinction was assumed to be redundant (Kirby & Das, 1976; Paivio, 1976). Das et al. argued that paired-associate memory for concrete nouns correlates with a variety of reasoning tasks that require simultaneous processing. They also argued that an imagery system cannot have any neurophysiological reality.

A major defender of the propositional position, and the chief critic of imagery models (although we are certain that this is not a role to which he aspires) is Zenon Pylyshyn. In a series of articles (1973, 1980, 1981) he has sought to reify the computational approach to cognition. He argues that there exist basic similarities between cognitive operations and computational procedures. Cognitive processes can be adequately modeled by formal operations operating on symbolic structures (e.g., computer data structures). The computer program thus becomes the tool for the evaluation of the cognitive theory because the program can represent the proposed computational procedures. Pylyshyn has explicitly rejected the need to postulate images because "there is nothing about the representation itself that requires one class of transformation rather than another" (Pylyshyn, 1980, p. 115).

Thus in the past decade, whereas the number of proponents of models of imagery has expanded, the criticisms of imagery theories have become stronger and more varied. We now turn to an evaluation of the likelihood that this debate can be solved and a consideration of the appropriateness of imagery theories of models of cognition.

FUTURE OF THE IMAGERY DEBATE

The popularity of imagery has a volatile history, and it has varied from total rejection to complete acceptance. Perhaps more than any other factor, its intuitive appeal has allowed the concept to persist. The imagery concept has made a strong recovery from its period of exclusion in North American psychology, but there are serious problems with theories advocating a central role for imagery in memory. The most prominent of such models, the dual-coding hypothesis due to Paivio, has several shortcomings. The primary one is that the nature of memory is not specified. Whereas Paivio (1976) is content to say that such specification is an empirical question, some theoretical guide must be provided for research; the nature of memory is not going to reveal itself in some inductive fashion from research. More to the point, Paivio seems to implicitly assume a trace theory of memory. That is, when he discusses the storage and retrieval of images, he seems to believe that there are imagery traces. There are a number of difficulties with the trace position [see Loftus and Loftus (1980) for a summary], and much of contemporary research supports a reconstructive view of memory. Although Paivio (1976) has implied that his model is compatible with a reconstructive view, he has not specified how this is so. Thus, there is no description in dual-coding theory of the structure or organization of memory. What are the relationships between different types of image (e.g., specific vs. general concepts)? How do retrieval cues access the appropriate images? This type of question remains unanswered.

There appear to be problems with the verbal half of dual-coding theory as well. It is beyond the scope of this chapter to deal with these difficultues, but it should be noted that Paivio's ideas about language (Paivio & Begg, 1981) do not interface well with recent developments in linguistics. A principal problem here is specification of the nature of the nonverbal meaning that underlies language (Chomsky, 1980). In fact, the idea of some amodal code as the basis of meaning, and memory has become widely accepted in psychology. Not only research related to language, but much of the memory work (Bransford, 1979) seems consistent with amodal, semantic coding. Although Paivio (Marschark & Paivio, 1977) has noted the possibility of such codes, their role in dual-coding theory has not been elaborated. It seems likely that the inclusion of basic amodal coding in the model would require a major revision.

In summary, if dual-coding theory is to remain a viable concern of researchers of memory, it must be substantially elaborated. The required developments in the model include the specification of the nature and structure of memory and the relationship of language and meaning to imagery. If such modifications are not attempted, dual-coding theory will remain a functional interpretation of imagery. That is, it will be only an assertion that imagery is of functional importance in human memory, a conclusion that has a long history.

The imagery model due to Shepard fares less well than Paivio's on critical examination. The theoretical outline is vague, again mostly describing what Shepard believes images can do. The assumptions that Shepard does specify, for example, that images are quasi-perceptual, are manipulated holistically, and take real time to manipulate are being challenged on empirical grounds. Unless future research provides some insight into the reasons for the empirical inconsistencies, the prognosis for Shepard's approach is not good. Of course, Shepard may make major changes in his model to accommodate the empirical results, but the resulting model would clearly have to be very different from the limited one he has presented to date.

Kosslyn stands on firmer ground than the other theorists relative to the criticisms raised to this point. That is, he has been willing to explicate his imagery theory. Although the memory implications of the model have not been detailed, as this has not been a central concern, there is every hope that this will be offered in future versions of Kosslyn's model. However, there seems to exist a fundamental flaw in Kosslyn's approach to imagery modeling. In his CRT protomodel, the program contains all the information necessary to generate the CRT display. From the point of view of the computer, there is no need to generate the visual display, as size and distance information could be extracted from the computer data base. The CRT display is simply one of an infinite variety of representations of this base and is of value only to a human observer. If what Kosslyn means by "imagery" is to be found in the form of the data base, the distinction between imagery and other forms of representation of knowledge becomes blurred. Thus, in generating this computer simulation of the imagery process, it appears that Kosslyn has confirmed the suspicions of those who hold a computational approach to cognition: imagery is a redundant concept.

The controversy between the computational and imagery models is the most important development for cognitive psychology in the past 10 years. Although this debate has raged and apparently become more heated in the past couple of years, one author has provided a pessimistic view of its outcome. Anderson (1978, 1979) has suggested that there is no possibility of resolution of the differences between the computational and imagery positions. Basically, he has argued that modifications can be made in each position to account for any empirical outcome. Thus he believes that it is impossible to find a research situation whose outcome will resolve the issue in favor of one or the other perspective. Anderson suggests that since computational and imagery models are functionally equivalent, there may be advantages to retaining both views, much as the wave and particle theories of light are employed in physics. However, he argues, we should remain aware that the two alternatives are only working models, and not representations of the actual processes mediating performance. He asserts that what we produce can only be models, and the debate about the validity of equivalent representational systems (i.e., the computational and the imaginal) is a waste of time. Although Anderson's position has been attacked (Hayes-Roth, 1979; Pylyshyn, 1979b), Anderson (1979) has claimed that the attacks have missed the point. In any event, it seems that the antagonists have elected to ignore Anderson and continue the debate, apparently believing that their differences are real, and very much worthy of defense (Kosslyn, 1981; Pylyshyn, 1981).

In spite of Anderson's remarks, the computational approach remains the most serious challenge that imagery models have faced. Pylyshyn (1980) has implied that a computational perspective is the only viable one for cognitive psychology. Fodor (1980) has been more explicit in offering arguments that no other approach is possible if psychology desires to be a science. These authors are providing strong arguments for adopting a position that would once again remove imagery from psychology. In our view, the computer is not an adequate metaphor for mental processes. If the computational option is selected, psychology will become a narrow, restricted discipline, relegated to the modeling of the selected range of processes that can be simulated in a computer program. In his critique of a recent Pylyshyn article, Grossberg (1980) claimed that there is a fundamental difference between humans and computers. Human cognition involves nonlinear interactions which "cannot be embedded into the binary and serial structure of computer computations without tearing apart the metric and topological interrelations of the internal representations" (Grossberg, 1980, p. 136).

If imagery is to be a viable component in theories of memory, there must be some substantial redevelopments of imagery models. The converging influences of linguistics, the reconstructive nature of memory, and the flexibility of human problem-solving abilities appear to demand that any model of memory include some nonverbal, nonimaginal memory code. A model of memory that includes images thus must provide a description of the interface between amodal coding and imagery processes. For example, images may be viewed as a particular form of representation generated from information contained in amodal codes. The sticky problem here is that the theorist must demonstrate what advantage there is for the system to translate amodal to imaginal codes. It would seem more efficient to work at the level of the amodal code. It is easy to fall into the homunculus trap, as Kosslyn has, and have a "mind's eye" that scans the internal image. This does not, however, appear to portend a satisfactory solution to the problem.

One model of cognition has included both an amodal and imagery code. Piaget [in particular, Piaget & Inhelder (1973)] proposed that memory ("in the broad sense") consists of the mental structures, schemata, that the individual uses to assimilate experience. Images are not elements in these structures, but they are tools that the system can employ to aid problem solving. Piaget asserts that children can imitate some aspects of the environment or anticipate the consequences of their actions by utilizing images. Apparently, Piaget did not believe that such anticipation could occur without the aid of images. The Piagetian approach may be a possible resolution to the computational–imagery debate [see Yuille & Catchpole (1977) for an elaboration of this idea]. However, before such an alternative becomes viable, the meaning of the concept "scheme" and the nature of the mental structure must be elaborated. Although this constitutes a major task, it might be a more worthwhile expenditure of effort than the continuation of the current debate.

REFERENCES

Anderson, J. R. Arguments concerning representations for mental imagery. *Psychological Review*, 1978, **85**, 249–277.

Anderson, J. R. Further arguments concerning representations for mental imagery: A response to Hayes-Roth and Pylyshyn. *Psychological Review*, 1979, **86**, 395–406.

Anderson, J. R., & Bower, G. H. *Human associative memory*. New York: Winston, 1973.

Atkinson, R. C., & Shiffrin, R. M. Human memory: A proposed system and its control processes. In K. W. Spence & J. T. Spence (Eds.), *The psychology of learning and motivation*, Vol. 2. New York: Academic Press, 1968.

Bahrick, H. P. & Boucher, B. Retention of visual and verbal codes of the same stimuli. *Journal of Experimental Psychology*, 1968, **78,** 417–422.

Banks, W. P., & Flora, J. Semantic and perceptual processes in symbolic comparisons. *Journal of Experimental Psychology: Human Perception and Psychophysics*, 1977, **3,** 278–290.

Bartlett, F. C. *Remembering: A study in experimental and social psychology.* London: Cambridge University Press, 1932.

Begg, I. Recall of meaningful phrases. *Journal of Verbal Learning and Verbal Behavior*, 1972, **4,** 431–439.

Begg, I., & Paivo, A. Concreteness and imagery in sentence meaning. *Journal of Verbal Learning and Verbal Behavior*, 1969, **8,** 821–827.

Bower, G. A multicomponent theory of the memory trace. In K. W. Spence & J. T. Spence (Eds.), *The psychology of learning and motivation*, Vol. 1. New York: Academic Press, 1967.

Bower, G. Imagery as a relational organizer in associative learning. *Journal of Verbal Learning and Verbal Behavior*, 1970, **9,** 529–533.

Bower, G. Mental imagery and associative learning. In L. Gregg (Ed.), *Cognition in learning and memory.* New York: Wiley, 1972.

Bransford, J. D. *Human cognition,* Belmont, CA: Wadsworth, 1979.

Brewer, W. F. Memory for ideas: Synonym substitution. *Memory and Cognition*, 1975, **3,** 458–464.

Brooks, L. R. The suppression of visualization in reading. *Quarterly Journal of Experimental Psychology*, 1967, **19,** 289–299.

Brooks, L. R. Spatial and verbal components of the act of recall. *Canadian Journal of Psychology*, 1968, **22,** 349–368.

Bruner, J. S. Neural mechanisms in perception. *Psychological Review*, 1957, **64,** 340–358.

Bruner, J. S. The course of cognitive growth. *American Psychologist*, 1964, **19,** 1–15.

Buckley, P. B., & Gillman, C. G. Comparisons of digits and dot patterns. *Journal of Experimental Psychology*, 1974, **63,** 409–412.

Bugelski, B. R. Presentation time, total time, and mediation in paired-associate learning. *Journal of Experimental Psychology*, 1962, **63,** 409–412.

Bugelski, B. R., Kidd, E., & Segman, J. Image as a mediation as a mediator in one-trial paired associate learning. *Journal of Experimental Psychology*, 1968, **76,** 69–73.

Chomsky, N. Rule and representation. *The Behavioral and Brain Sciences*, 1980, **3,** 1–61.

Cooper, L., & Shepard, R. N. Chronometric studies of the rotation of mental images. In W. G. Chasse (Ed.), *Visual information processing.* New York: Academic Press, 1973.

Das, J. P., Kirby, J., & Jarman, R. F. Simultaneous and successive synthesis: An alternative model for cognitive abilities. *Psychological Bulletin*, 1975, **82**, 87–103.

Dooling, D. J., & Lachman, R. Effects of comprehension on the retention of prose. *Journal of Experimental Psychology*, 1971, **88**, 216–222.

Fernald, M. R. The diagnosis of mental imagery. *Psychological Monographs*, 1912, **19**, 299–317.

Fodor, J. A. Methodological solipsism considered as a research strategy in cognitive psychology. *The Behavioral and Brain Sciences*, 1980, 3, 63–109.

Franks, J. J., & Bransford, J. D. The acquisition of abstract ideas. *Journal of Verbal Learning and Verbal Behavior*, 1972, **3**, 311–315.

Grossberg, S. Human and computer rules and representations are not equivalent. *The Behavioral and Brain Sciences*, 1980, **3**, 136–138.

Hayes-Roth, F. Distinguishing theories of representation: A critique of Anderson's "Arguments concerning mental imagery." *Psychological Review*, 1979, **86**, 376–382.

Hebb, D. O. *The organization of behavior*. New York: Wiley, 1949.

Holt, R. R. Imagery: The return of the ostracized. *American Psychologist*, 1964, **19**, 154–164.

Holyoak, K. J., & Walker, J. H. Subjective magnitude information in semantic orderings. *Journal of Verbal Learning and Verbal Behavior*, 1976, **15**, 287–299.

Jensen, A. R., & Rowher, W. D. Syntactical mediation of serial and paired–associate learning as a function of age. *Child Development*, 1965, **36**, 601–608.

Judd, C. H., & Cowling, D. J. Studies in perceptual development. *Psychological Review, Monograph Supplement No. 34*, 1907, 349–369.

Just, M. A., & Brownell, H. H. Retrieval of concrete and abstract prose descriptions from memory. *Canadian Journal of Psychology*, 1974, **28**, 339–350.

Kaufmann, G. *Imagery, language, and cognition: Toward a theory of symbolic activity in human problem-solving*. Bergen: Universitetsforlaget, 1980.

Keiss, H. O., & Montague, W. E. Natural language mediators in paired-associate learning. *Psychonomic Science*, 1965, **3**, 549–550.

Kerst, S., & Howard, J. Mental comparisons for ordered information on abstract and concrete dimensions. *Memory and Cognition*, 1977, **5**, 227–234.

Kieras, D. Beyond pictures and words: Alternative information processing models for imagery effects in verbal memory. *Psychological Bulletin*, 1978, **85**, 532–554.

Kintsch, W. Abstract nouns: Imagery versus lexical complexity. *Journal of Verbal Learning and Verbal Behavior*, 1972, **11**, 59–65.

Kirby, J. R., & Das, J. P. Comments on Paivio's imagery theory. *Canadian Psychological Review*, 1976, **17**, 66–68.

Kosslyn, S. *Image and mind*. Cambridge, Mass.: Harvard University Press, 1980.

Kosslyn, S. The medium and the message in mental imagery: A theory. *Psychological Review*, 1981, **88**, 46–66.

Kosslyn, S., Pinker, S., Smith, G., & Shwartz, S. On the demystification of mental imagery. *The Behavioral and Brain Sciences*, 1979, **2**, 535–581.

Loftus, E. F., & Loftus, G. R. On the permanence of stored information in the human brain. *American Psychologist*, 1980, **5**, 409–420.

Marschark, M. & Paivio, A. Integrative processing of concrete and abstract sentences. *Journal of Verbal Learning and Verbal Behavior*, 1977, **16**, 217–231.

Moyer, R. S. Comparing objects in memory: Evidence suggesting an internal psychophysics. *Perception and Psychophysics*, 1973, **13**, 180–184.

Moyer, R., & Landauer, T. The time required for judgements of numerical inequality. *Nature*, 1967, **215**, 1519–1520.

Neisser, V. *Cognitive psychology*. New York: Appleton, 1967.

Noble, C.E. The role of stimulus meaning (*m*) in serial verbal learning. *Journal of Experimental Psychology*, 1952, 437–446.

Norman, D. A., & Rumelhart, D. E. *Explorations in cognition*. San Francisco: Freeman, 1975.

Osgood, C. E. Meaning cannot be *r(m)*? *Journal of Verbal Learning and Verbal Behavior*, 1966, **5**, 402–407.

Paivio, A. Learning of adjective–noun paired associates as a function of word order and noun abstractness. *Canadian Journal of Psychology*, 1963, **18**, 146–155.

Paivio, A. Abstractness, imagery, and meaningfulness in paired-associate learning. *Journal of Verbal Learning and Verbal Behavior*, 1965, **4**, 32–38.

Paivio, A. Mental imagery in associative learning and memory. *Psychological Review*, 1969, **76**, 241–263.

Paivio, A. *Imagery and verbal processes*. Hillsdale, N.J.: Lawrence Erlbaum Associates, 1971.

Paivio, A. A theoretical analysis of the role of imagery in learning and memory. In P. W. Sheehan (Ed.), *The function and nature of imagery*. New York: Academic Press, 1972.

Paivio, A. Perceptual comparisions through the mind's eye. *Memory and Cognition*, 1975, **3**, 635–647.

Paivio, A. Images, propositions, and knowledge. In J. M. Nicholas (Ed.), *Images, perception, and knowledge*. Dordrecht: Reidel, 1976.

Paivio, A. Mental comparisons involving abstract attributes. *Memory and Cognition*, 1978, **6**, 199–208.

Paivio, A., & Begg, I. *The psychology of language*. Englewood Cliffs, N.J.: Prentice-Hall, 1981.

Paivio, A. & Csapo, K. Concrete-image and verbal memory codes. *Journal of Experimental Psychology*, 1969, **80**, 279–285.

Paivio, A., & Madigan, S. A. Imagery and association value in paired-associate learning. *Journal of Experimental Psychology*, 1968, **76**, 35–39.

Paivio, A., & Marschark, M. Comparative judgments of animal intelligence and pleasantness. *Memory and Cognition*, 1980, **8**, 39–48.

Paivio, A., & O'Neill, B. J. Visual recognition thresholds and dimensions of word meaning. *Perception & Psychophysics*, 1970, **8**, 273–275.

Paivio, A., & Yarmey, D. Pictures versus words as stimuli and responses in paired-associate learning. *Psychonomic Science*, 1966, **5**, 1235–1236.

Paivio, A., & Yuille, J. Mediation instructions and word attributes in paired-associate learning. *Psychonomic Science*, 1967, **8**, 65–66.

Paivio, A., Yuille, J., & Smythe, P. C. Stimulus and response abstractness, imagery, and meaningfulness, and reported mediators in paired-associate learning. *Canadian Journal of Psychology*, 1966, **20**, 362–377.

Paivio, A., Rogers, T. B., & Smythe, P. C. Why are pictures easier to recall than words? *Psychonomic Science*, 1968a, **11**, 137–138.

Paivio, A., Yuille, J., & Madigan, S. A. Concreteness, imagery, and meaningfulness values for 925 nouns. *Journal of Experimental Psychology Monograph Supplement*, 1968b, **76**, (p. 1, Part 2).

Parkman, J. M. Temporal aspects of digit and letter inequality judgments. *Journal of Experimental Psychology*, 1971, **91**, 191–205.

Perky, C. W. An experimental investigation of imagination. *American Journal of Psychology*, 1910, **21**, 422–452.

Piaget, J., & Inhelder, B. *Memory and intelligence*. New York: Basic Books, 1973.

Podgorny, P., & Shepard, R. N. Functional representations common to visual-perception and imagination. *Journal of Experimental Psychology: Human Perception and Performance*, 1978, **4**, 21–35.

Pompi, K. F., & Lachman, R. Surrogate processes in the short-term retention of connected discourse. *Journal of Experimental Psychology*, 1967, **75**, 143–150.

Posner, M. I. Abstraction and the process of recognition. In G. Bower & J. T. Spence (Eds.), *The Psychology of Learning and Motivation*, Vol. 3. New York: Academic Press, 1969.

Posner, M. I., & Keele, S. W. Delay of visual information from a single letter. *Science*, 1967, **158**, 137–139.

Posner, M. I., & Mitchell, R. F. Chronometric analysis of classification. *Psychological Review*, 1967, **74**, 392–409.

Pylyshyn, Z. W. What the mind's eye tells the mind's brain: A critique of mental imagery. *Psychological Bulletin*, 1973, **80**, 1–24.

Pylyshyn, Z. W. The rate of "mental rotation" of images: A test of a holistic analogue hypothesis. *Memory and Cognition*, **7**, 19–28, 1979a.

Pylyshyn, Z. W. Validating computational models: A critique of Anderson's indeterminacy of representation claim. *Psychological Review*, 1979b, **86**, 383–394.

Pylyshyn, Z. W. Computation and cognition: Issues in the foundations of cognitive science. *The Behavioral and Brain Sciences*, 1980, **3**, 111–169.

Pylyshyn, Z. W. The imagery debate: Analogue media versus trait knowledge. *Psychological Review*, 1981, **88**, 16–45.

Restle, F. Speed of adding and comparing numbers. *Journal of Experimental Psychology*, 1970, **83**, 274–278.

Sheehan, P. W. (Ed.), *The function and nature of imagery*. Englewood Cliffs, N.J.: Prentice-Hall, 1972.

Shepard, R. N. Form, formation and transformation of internal representations. In R. Solso (Ed.), *Information processing and cognition: The Loyola Symposium*. Hillsdale N.J.: Lawrence Erlbaum Associates, 1975.

Shepard, R. N. The mental image. *American Psychologist*, 1978, **33**, 125–137.

Shepard, R. N., & Chipman, S. Second-order isomorphism of internal representations: Shaper of states. *Cognitive Psychology*, 1970, **1,** 1–17.

Shepard, R. N., & Metzler, J. Mental rotation of three-dimensional objects. *Science*, 1971, **171,** 701–703.

Shepard, R. N., & Podgorny, P. Cognitive processes that resemble perceptual processes. In W. K. Ester (Ed.), *Handbook of learning and cognitive processes*, Vol. 5, Hillsdale, N.J.: Lawrence Erlbaum Associates, 1978.

Steiger, J. H., & Yuille, J. C. *Long-term memory and mental rotation.* Paper presented at the annual meeting of the Psychonomic Society, Phoenix, 1979.

Sulin, R.A. , & Dooling, D. J. Intrusion of a thematic idea in retention of prose. *Journal of Experimental Psychology*, 1974, **103,** 255–262.

Yates, F. A. *The art of memory.* London: Routledge and Kegan Paul, 1966.

Yuille, J. C., & Catchpole, M. J. The role of imagery in models of cognition. *Journal of Mental Imagery*, 1977, **1,** 171–180.

Yuille, J. C., & Paivio, A. Abstraction and recall of connected discourse. *Journal of Experimental Psychology*, 1967, **82,** 467–471.

Yuille, J. C., & Steiger, J. H. *Nonholistic processing in mental rotation.* Paper presented at the annual meeting of the Canadian Psychological Association, Quebec City, 1979.

CHAPTER 6

Image Theory of Conditioning

DONALD L. KING

At least superficially, mental imagery resides at the crossroads between perception and memory. The experience of a stimulus in its absence is perceptual in nature, sometimes almost completely so (Perky, 1910; Segal, 1972), but the source of this experience is memory. Moreover, by now there are many indications that the effects of perceiving and imagining stimuli on behavior are similar (Segal & Fusella, 1970). These results support the proposal that stimulus-produced and memorial representations affect the nervous system similarly. With this proposition as a starting point, it is possible to construct a theory of classical and instrumental conditioning.

I will review my image theory of conditioning (King, 1979). However, the present treatment more strongly emphasizes the position that perceptual processes underlie conditioning. The chapter closes with a brief discussion of ways in which human memory may also be related to perception.

CLASSICAL CONDITIONING

A stimulus S_1 is assumed to result in a temporary neural representation T_1, and the behavioral and experiential effects of S_1 are believed to be mediated by this T_1. That is, T_1 permits S_1 to be described, results in the experience of S_1, enables decisions about S_1 to be accurately made, and is the immediate cause of the nonverbal responses that S_1 elicits. In addition, T_1 leads to a permanent representation P_1 that corresponds to S_1. It is assumed that under certain conditions P_1 is activated, that is, transformed back into T_1. Moreover, the S_1- and P_1-produced T_1s are sufficiently similar that they often have related behavioral and experiential outcomes. Thus, in the absence of S_1, the P_1-to-T_1 transformation may permit the description of S_1, result in the experience (image) of S_1, enable decisions about S_1, and produce nonverbal responses similar to those elicited by S_1.

The preceding statements imply that an indication of an image of S_1 (e.g., a person's apparently complying with a request to imagine S_1) is likely to be accompanied by consequences similar to those produced by S_1 itself.

This is because the S_1- and P_1-produced T_1s are similar—T_1 and T_1'. And, in fact, many studies do suggest that real stimuli and imagining the same stimuli affect behavior similarly. Of most relevance to classical conditioning is the evidence indicating that stimulus-produced and image-related non-verbal responses are similar. For example, thinking about food is accompanied by salivation (Wooley & Wooley, 1973), imagining that tap water is sour also increases salivation (Barber et al., 1964), imagining that one's arm is immersed in cold water when it is actually in water at room temperature increases heart rate and muscle tension (Barber & Hahn, 1964), and imagining lifting a weight with the right arm raises electromyographic activity in that arm (Jacobsen, 1930). In each of these instances the corresponding real stimulus produces a qualitatively similar response. This similarity between stimulus-produced and image-related nonverbal responses is analogous to the similarity between the conditioned response (CR) and unconditioned response (UCR).

How the CR Occurs

Pairings between the conditioned stimulus (CS) and unconditioned stimulus (UCS) result in the permanent representations (Ps) for these stimuli being connected or grouped; P_{CS}–P_{UCS} is formed. This is the well-known stimulus–stimulus learning assumption. However, it is most likely more accurate to view this CS–UCS association in terms of the way stimuli interact to function holistically in perception (below). When the CS occurs again, it contacts the P_{CS}–P_{UCS}. The CS-produced T_{CS} "finds" the P_{CS}–P_{UCS} by way of its P_{CS} component. The hypothesized consequence of this contact is the transformation of P_{UCS} into T_{UCS}. The activation of P_{UCS} in this manner is a core assumption. The P-produced T_{UCS} should result in much the same response as the S-produced one, because S- and P-produced Ts are assumed to function similarly. As was stated earlier, this assumption is based on evidence indicating that stimulus-produced and image-related effects on behavior are similar, and it is relied on repeatedly. The P-produced T_{UCS} is thus directly responsible for the traditional CR (i.e., a CR similar to a UCR). Consider, for example, a P_{CS}–P_{food} connection. The CS activates the P_{food} component, and the resulting P-produced T_{food} results in salivation (the CR), much as the S-produced T_{food} does.

This theory is consistent with verbal reports suggesting that an occurrence of the CS results in an expectation of the UCS, thinking about it, and on occasion a vivid image of it (Leuba, 1940). These reports may derive from the occurrence of a P-produced T_{UCS}, the same event that is assumed to be responsible for the CR. This is because temporary brain events (Ts) have been assumed to permit descriptions and experiences of stimuli. The theory also handles the immediate reversal of galvanic skin response (GSR) discrimination learning that occurs when the experimenter indicates that the UCS will no longer follow the CS + but will, instead, follow the CS − (Grings et al., 1973; Wilson, 1968). Theoretically, a P-produced T_{UCS} stemming from the instructions may be responsible for the newly occurring CR to the original $CS-$. Similarly, the P-produced T_{UCS} that has occurred because of the $CS+-$ UCS pairings is, as a result of the instructions, replaced by a P-produced T for the absence of the UCS (nothing). Most importantly, the theory dovetails with the evidence indicating that stimulus-produced and image-related non-verbal responses (e.g., salivation) are similar. This is because the traditional CR is similar to the UCR and because the CR is assumed to result from a P-produced T_{UCS}, thereby implicating imagery.

S, T, and P: Additional Comments

The posited relationships among S, T, P, and behavior are further discussed here.

T_1 does not necessarily enable descriptions and experiences of S_1, decisions about S_1, and nonverbal responses of S_1. Clearly, there is imageless thought. Nevertheless, P-produced Ts may underlie this thought. Consider, for example, our ability to select a red object from a group of 10 objects, each of a different color. It is difficult to understand how this task is successfully completed without assuming that the word "red" results in some kind of representation of the color red. This seems to be true regardless of whether this color is experienced while performing the task. Research on short-term memory suggests that distractor stimuli impair retention. They probably inhibit images of stimuli as well, which presumably has much to do with why images are more frequent during relaxation and sleep. The CS itself probably functions as a distractor stimulus, thereby reducing the vividness of the image of the UCS. The effects of real stimuli are also suppressed, and completely so, for example, in binocular fusion, apparent movement, and metacontrast. But extensive suppression also occurs when two conversations or two typical visual inputs are taking place simultaneously. For example, Neisser and Becklen (1975) showed that simultaneously monitoring ballgame and handgame videotape presentations noticeably impairs detection of events in both tapes. In addition, we are able to apprehend the meaning of words without being able to perceive their visual presence (Allport, 1977). In summary, both image-related and stimulus-produced influences are suppressed, and, moreover, there is stimulusless perception as well as imageless thought.

S_1- and P_1-produced T_1s are typically not identical since they usually only affect behavior similarly. The primary difference between these two Ts appears to be quantitative; the amount of P_1-produced T_1 is less. This accords with the descriptions of images being less detailed (vivid) than the descriptions of real stimuli, and with the amplitude of image-related nonverbal responses (e.g., salivation) being less than the amplitude of stimulus-produced ones.

Because T_1 is assumed to mediate descriptions of, decisions about, and the nonverbal responses of S_1, these behaviors should covary as the amount of P-produced T_1 changes. There are indications that the vividness of images, extent of retention, and the strength of image-related nonverbal responses are positively correlated (Sheehan, 1972; Shor, 1966). Despite this, it may be that the CR is more likely to occur than an image of the UCS. Also, image-related nonverbal responses frequently occur during thought when it is problematical that the relevant stimuli are being imagined (McGuigan, 1978). Perhaps the threshold for the experience of a previously occurring stimulus is generally higher than the threshold for its nonverbal responses.

The distinction between Ts and Ps is derived logically. Previously occurring stimuli may continue to be processed in various including more elaborate ways (Craik & Tulving, 1975); they are not viewed as passing through a fixed sequence of stages. However, at some point the processing of a stimulus terminates, and yet it is often remembered. Hence its representation must be permanently stored.

Retention in general is assumed to occur through the activation of Ps. However, there may be no representation P_1 that corresponds precisely to the individually presented S_1. This is because the representations for individual stimuli may interact to form groups. For example, an incomplete picture (S_1) is initially not identified as representing a specific object. Subsequently, the complete picture (S_1 and S_2) is shown and is recognized as the object. Theoretically, T_{S_1} and T_{S_2} interact to form T_{S_1}–T_{S_2}. Moreover, when the original S_1 is re-presented, it is readily identified as the specific object and is no longer described as it was originally. Similarly, the simultaneous presentation of two words affects the subsequent recognition of one of these words when it is re-presented individually (Light & Carter-Sobell, 1970). So a memorial group (P_{S_1}–P_{S_2}) is established that affects perception of the individually presented stimuli that contributed to the group.

The basic fact of perceptual learning also means that the assumption that S_1 results in T_1 requires elaboration. The developing (not completed) S_1-produced T_1 may contact the Ps for other stimuli. This T_1 and these Ps (or their activated Ts) may then interact to yield an outcome that corresponds to the described or recognized S_1. Considering the above example, the incomplete picture is subsequently recognized as representing a specific object because the developing S_1-produced T_1 interacts with the P_{S_1}–P_{S_2} group. Perception of the CS changes as a consequence of CS–UCS pairings (below). Therefore, classical conditioning entails the occurrence of perceptual learning. This suggests that the CS (presented alone) interacts with P_{CS}–P_{UCS} (the memorial group), as in other instances of perceptual learning. Note, moreover, that the explanation of the similarity between the CR and UCR is based, in part, on the same assumption.

Additional Parallels between Conditioning and Imagining

The CR resembles the UCR, and image-related nonverbal responses are similar to stimulus-produced ones. This analogy between conditioning and imagining derives, theoretically, from both the CR and UCR and stimulus-produced and image-related responses resulting from much the same T, whether it is S- or P- produced. Similar interpretations apply to other analogues between conditioning and imagining. The amplitude of the CR is usually less than that of the UCR. Likewise, the amplitude of image-related nonverbal responses is typically less than that of stimulus-produced responses. Some responses, for instance, overt leg and finger movements, are relatively difficult to classically condition, whereas others, such as salivation and the GSR, condition readily. Much the same ordering of response strengths seems to occur when stimuli are imagined. For example, the effect of imagining shock to a limb on limb movement probably must frequently be detected electromyographically, whereas imagining food noticeably increases salivation. Varying the amount or intensity of the UCS and the extent of deprivation produces correlated changes in CR and UCR strength (DeBold et al., 1965; Sheafor & Gormezano, 1972). Similarly, imagining larger amounts or intensities of UCSs and imagining food and water when more deprived probably result in stronger image-related responses, although I know of only indirect evidence (Shaw, 1940; Staats & Hammond, 1972). Nevertheless, a strong UCR is not always accompanied by a strong CR (Mackintosh, 1974, p. 92), and this is discussed briefly later.

The effects of imagining also bear on the problem of the qualitative similarity between the CR and UCR. There is little overt classical conditioning of mouth movements when food is delivered to a receptacle, but when milk is injected into the mouth, the CS produces vigorous mouth movements [Soltysik, Kierylowicz, & Divac, as described by Konorski (1967, p. 270)]. I suspect that mouth movements would similarly be greater when food is imagined inside the mouth rather than in a receptacle. The CR of an increase in motor activity is frequently reported when a food UCS is employed. Animals probably tend to be similarly excited when exposed to real but unavailable food. Humans may also frequently become motorically excited when they perceive unavailable attractive stimuli and imagine stimuli that they would approach if actually present.

Pairings between Neutral Stimuli

Image theory maintains that pairing two neutral stimuli, S_1 and S_2, results in a learned association involving these stimuli through the same process that is responsible for classical conditioning. That is, the conditioning process is operative even though there is no CR, UCR, or drive. Thus the S_1-produced T_{S_1} is assumed to contact P_{S_1}–P_{S_2}, with a P-produced T_{S_2} resulting. If S_2 itself does not elicit a response, it follows that the P-produced T_{S_2} should also fail to. Of course, this tallies with the frequently observed failure of S_1–S_2 pairings to yield a CR. Nonetheless, it is clear that paired neutral stimuli affect the CR. For example, sensory preconditioning occurs, and it is now considered to be a robust outcome. A second reason for maintaining that paired neutral stimuli are associated through conditioning is that when a neutral stimulus does elicit a response, the CR may occur. In one study (Fink, 1954), S_2 was a tone and it elicited a key press through instructions. The S_1 came to produce a similar although covert response. A third reason is that extinction becomes essentially a case of pairings between two neutral stimuli, the CS and the absence of the UCS, for example, the conditioning chamber without the reinforcer. The claim that the absence of the UCS functions as a stimulus seems legitimate, since the absence of a stimulus does control responding (Kamin, 1965).

Because pairing neutral stimuli may result in classical conditioning, this learning probably frequently occurs in everyday life, such as when an opening door is followed by a person in the doorway. Words and their referents are frequently paired, and words result in representations of their referents (Paivio, 1971), even in a chimpanzee (Premack, 1971b). Image theory is thus consistent with a classical conditioning approach to language learning. The neutral stimuli need not be successive (Rescorla, 1980). Learned associations occur among simultaneously present stimuli in imitation and observation learning (Kohn & Dennis, 1972; Menzel, 1973). Moreover, classical conditioning and perceptual recognition may be viewed as lying on a continuum. Recognition frequently involves exposure to simultaneously present neutral component stimuli appearing in similar spatial locations, and Rescorla and Cunningham (1979) found that superior conditioning occurs when paired neutral stimuli are spatially contiguous.

CS–UCS Similarity and Altered Perception of CS

Classical conditioning improves as the paired stimuli become more similar (e.g., Rescorla & Furrow, 1977; Testa, 1975; the above spatial contiguity result). Time durations can be discriminated between, so it is appropriate to postulate the existence of time-correlated stimuli. Two paired stimuli always contain quite similar time elements (as long as they are relatively brief). Indeed, time similarity may frequently provide almost the only basis for an acquired CS–UCS connection since the CS and UCS are typically quite different in most respects.

The effect of a relatively long CS–UCS interval on delayed conditioning poses a problem. The CS as a whole cannot be assumed to be increasingly forgotten as the CS–UCS interval increases since it is still present at the moment of UCS onset. Perhaps the functional (effective) time-correlated stimulus for the CS corresponds to roughly the midpoint of its duration. Granted this, an increase in the length of the CS–UCS interval will decrease the psychological similarity between the CS and UCS, and this should decrement conditioning. This averaging possibility implicates the operation of an abstractive process in an elemental conditioning situation.

CS Perceived as UCS

The influence of CS–UCS similarity on conditioning relates to interpreting the CS–UCS connection in terms of the formation of a perception-like group. This is because in perception stimuli are more likely to interact to function as a composite as their similarity increases. An early report (Breland & Breland, 1961) suggests that CSs may be manipulated with paws, rooted, or swallowed by raccoons, pigs, and porpoises and whales, respectively. The stimuli included coins for raccoons and pigs and balls and inner tubes for porpoises and whales and were thus presumably somewhat similar to the food reinforcers that were employed. The auto-shaping (sign tracking) phenomenon is related. Animals frequently direct responses at the CS that are similar to the UCR. For example, Brown and Jenkins (1968) found that pigeons peck an illuminated key when it is paired with response-independent food. The extent of auto-shaping increases as CS–UCS similarity increases (Hearst, 1978, p. 70). Breland and Breland's response-oriented "instinctive drift" explanation of their results does not address the influence of CS–UCS similarity. Consequently, it seems reasonable to suggest that when the CS and UCS are sufficiently similar, the perceived similarity of the CS to the UCS is increased, sufficiently so that, for instance, raccoons and pigeons manipulate and peck the CS because it resembles real food.

Image theory is consistent with the possibility that the CS comes to be recognized as relatively similar to the UCS. In perception, simultaneously present stimuli frequently interact to form groups (wholes). That is, S_1 and S_2 may form a group (T_{S_1}–T_{S_2}) that is permanently stored (as P_{S_1}–P_{S_2}). A group or blob may underlie the perception of most stimuli, including everyday stimuli such as a large red square (Lockhead, 1972). The group would frequently correspond to a stimulus that is a smoothly integrated composite of the simultaneously present stimuli that contribute to it. This entails a modification in the perception of the contributing component stimuli. They may frequently tend to be perceived as more similar to each other than when they do not contribute to the same group. In addition, P-produced Ts may also contribute to the group and hence alter the corresponding percept. Group formation seems to be more likely as the similarity of the simultaneously present stimuli increases. According to image theory, after conditioning has occurred, the CS results in the simultaneous occurrence of an S-produced T_{CS} and a P-produced T_{UCS}. These two Ts may form a group through a perceptual process, just as the S-produced Ts for S_1 and S_2 frequently do (King, 1974). This follows from the position that S- and P-produced Ts affect the nervous system similarly. In addition, the tendency for the S-produced T_{CS} and the P-produced T_{UCS} to form a group may increase as the similarity between the CS and UCS increases. This is because the S-produced Ts for S_1 and S_2 may, in general, be more likely to group as S_1–S_2 similarity increases. Finally, the outcome of the combination between the S-produced T_{CS} and the P-produced T_{UCS} may be that the CS is perceived as more similar to the UCS than it is prior to conditioning.

That recognition of the CS is altered as a consequence of conditioning would be a perceptual learning outcome. The effect of set on recognition (Epstein & Rock, 1960; Wallach, et al., 1953) is a traditional perceptual learning outcome, and it can be similarly interpreted. In this type of result, exposure to a S_1–S_2 stimulus results in a S_1–S_x stimulus being subsequently recognized as more similar to the S_1–S_2 stimulus than it was initially. Considering the Epstein and Rock and Wallach et al. reports, the ambiguous picture of an old/young woman and a stationary shadow, respectively, correspond to S_1–S_x. The stimulus establishing the learning is an unambiguous stimulus of an old (or young) woman and a transforming shadow (which results in the perception of a rotating three-dimensional object), and they can be regarded as S_1–S_2. Thus S_1 represents the communality between S_1–S_2 and S_1–S_x. The result of interest is that when S_1–S_x follows exposure to S_1–S_2, it tends to be recognized as S_1–S_2; the ambiguous face is perceived as the unambiguous one, and the stationary shadow is perceived as a three-dimensional object rather than as a two-dimensional shape. Note that S_1–S_x and S_1–S_2 are initially somewhat similar, that learning occurs, and that when S_1–S_x is subsequently presented it is recognized as being more similar to S_1–S_2 than initially. These three considerations also apply to the possibility that the CS is recognized as fairly similar to the UCS as a consequence of conditioning. Theoretically, S_1–S_2 or CS–UCS pairings result in a P_{S_1}–P_{S_2} or P_{CS}–P_{UCS} connection. The subsequent presentation of S_1–S_x or the CS results in T_{S_1}–T_{S_x} or T_{CS}, but also in a P-produced T_{S_2} or T_{UCS}. These S- and P-produced Ts interact to form perceptual groups, and as a consequence S_1–S_x or the CS resembles S_1–S_2 or the UCS more than it did initially. (In addition, perception of the S_x component of S_1–S_x is probably suppressed.)

Typical apparent movement in which S_1, then a blank period, and then S_2 all briefly occur can be similarly analyzed. S_1 and S_2 are considered functionally similar stimuli, even though they may correspond to fairly different forms at longer durations. This is because the brief durations may not provide the nervous system with sufficient time to analyze the figural detail of S_1 and S_2. Wertheimer (1912/1961) reports that with sufficient trials, apparent movement continues to be perceived when only S_1 is presented. He describes other set effects as well. Kolers (1972, Chapter 10) reviews these and additional findings that suggest a strong role for perceptual learning in apparent movement. Therefore, one aspect of apparent movement may involve the almost complete perceptual integration of S_1 and the memorial representation of S_2. And classical conditioning may similarly involve perceptual integration, successively paired stimuli, and the functional similarity of these stimuli. Nevertheless, understanding of apparent movement is at best complicated by the failure of perceptual integration to occur when S_1 and S_2 are simultaneous.

Attention to the CS

Several considerations suggest that the CS is more strongly attended to as a consequence of conditioning. For conditioning to occur, the CS probably must be discriminated from background stimuli. In support, the CR does occur in the presence of background stimuli, and its strength decreases as conditioning continues (Mackintosh, 1974, p. 15). In addition, stimulus generalization gradients along a dimension of the CS become steeper as conditioning continues (Mackintosh, 1974, p. 518). The effects of discrimination learning on stimulus generalization (Jenkins & Harrison, 1960) and subsequent discrimination learning (Lawrence, 1949) suggest that it increases attention to discriminative stimuli. This is relevant since the CS presumably must be discriminated from background stimuli. Moreover, the delay of inhibition result and the increasing tendency for the strongest portion of the CR to occur directly before the onset of the UCS (Mackintosh, 1974, p. 62) suggest that animals discriminate between the earlier and later parts of the CS. The very fact that a part of the CS acquires control over responding suggests that the CS is attended to. Classical conditioning of the GSR and muscle tension components of the orienting response is well known. Animals frequently look in the direction of the CS (Zener, 1937). The rear and startle responses that rats make to lights and sounds prior to conditioning reappear as a consequence of conditioning (Holland, 1980), perhaps because conditioning once again increases attention to these stimuli. The orientation response may index attention to a stimulus (King, 1979, pp. 251–252). Granted this, the fact that the CS produces the orienting response suggests that conditioning increases attention to it.

The cause of the assumed greater attention to the CS would seem to be related to the ability of the UCS to elicit a strong orienting response, that is, attention to the UCS. Thus the CS may be perceived as similar to the UCS in terms of attention. Moreover, the increase in attention to the CS would be a perceptual learning outcome. Consequently, this increase is related to the earlier discussed possibility that the CS comes to be recognized as fairly similar to the UCS. That is, through conditioning the CS may be perceived as more similar to the UCS in terms of both object quality and attention. Image theory handles these perceptual learning possibilities as well as the fact of CR–UCR similarity: the P-produced T_{UCS} combines with the T_{CS} through a perceptual process as well as being responsible for the CR.

Positive-Feedback Mechanism

There is evidence for the position that a more strongly attended to CS results in better conditioning. More intense CSs generally lead to superior conditioning. However, when the CS is a reduction in the intensity of a background noise, a larger decrease in its intensity yields a stronger CR (Kamin, 1965). Thus it is the extent of the difference between the CS and background stimuli that predicts performance. A stimulus that differs markedly from the background stimulus should produce a strong orienting response. Repeated exposure to a CS generally impairs subsequent conditioning with this CS, a result referred to as *latent inhibition*. Preexposure to the CS is an habituation procedure, and presumably it results in the CS producing a progressively weaker orienting response. Thus both this latent inhibition result and the effect of the difference between the CS and background stimulus suggest that greater attention to a CS results in better conditioning. Contrary evidence is that negative rather than positive transfer occurs when the same CS is subsequently employed with a second, more intense UCS (Hall & Pearce, 1979). However, integration between the two shock intensities may have occurred for the group receiving the identical CSs, and contrast may have occurred for the second.

A positive-feedback mechanism may contribute to classical conditioning, particularly when the CS initially differs little from background stimuli. A CS–UCS pairing probably increases attention to the CS (see the previous section). A subsequent pairing with this perceptually altered CS may thus result in improved conditioning (see the immediately preceding paragraph). And improved conditioning should result in a further increase in attention to the CS, with the consequence that the next pairing will facilitate conditioning once again, and so on. This simple feedback process may be partly responsible for the increase in CR strength that occurs with training. It also follows that CR strength will be relatively low when the UCS does not elicit attention. Some failures of CR strength to follow UCR strength (Mackintosh, 1974, p. 92) might thereby be understood.

Integration and Suppression

It is thought that the CS–UCS connection will eventually be viewed in terms of the suppressive as well as the integrational influences that abound in perception. Both Pavlov (1927) and Kamin (1969) discovered that when two CSs occur in compound, the amount of conditioning produced by one of the CSs is less than when it is presented individually. The well-known Rescorla and Wagner (1972) theory accounts for these over-shadowing and blocking outcomes and successfully predicts other surprising results. This theory ascribes a limiting role to the UCS rather than maintaining that an increase in attention to one CS often decreases attention to a second. In my estimation, there is too much empirical evidence against this theory (Dickinson & Mackintosh, 1979), and there are too many considerations supporting a role for learned attention to the CS for the theory to be helpful in the long run. Moreover, conditioning to one CS can be facilitated by the simultaneous occurrence of a second CS. I suspect that compound CSs result in facilitation when the components are relatively similar, for instance, by virtue of appearing in the same solution (Rusiniak et al., 1979), and otherwise suppression tends to occur. A perception-like integration between the CS and UCS was discussed earlier, and it appears to increase with an increase in CS–UCS similarity. It may also turn out that suppression between the CS and UCS occurs. The UCS may tend to suppress elements of the CS that differ from it.

Of course, there are a number of puzzling problems that have not been considered. Several postconditioning manipulations involving the original UCS, the first-order CS, and the deprivation level fail to affect second-order conditioning (Rescorla, 1978), and some of this work is mentioned later. Conditioning is critically affected by the relation between the CS and UCS, perhaps because survival pressures result in the ready acquisition of certain CS–UCS associations (Garcia & Koelling, 1966). The result that omission of the reinforcer reduces blocking (Dickinson & Mackintosh, 1979) has not been dealt with.

Other Theories Assuming Activation of P

The theories of Hebb (1949, 1968) and Konorski (1967) also assume that P becomes activated, that is, transformed back into the temporary form. The cell assembly (Hebb) and gnostic unit (Konorski) correspond to P. Phase sequences (Hebb) are connected Ps, and gnostic units can become associated. Activation of cell assemblies permits the description and experience of a stimulus. For example, activation of the three cell assemblies comprising the phase sequence for a triangle through focusing on one corner of the triangle permits the description of the triangle as a whole (Hebb, 1949, Chapter 5). In other words, S- and P-produced Ts enable the description of their corresponding stimuli. For Konorski, activated gnostic units are responsible for both perceptions and nonverbal responses. Consequently, connected gnostic units mediate set and recognition perceptual learning outcomes (pp. 185–190). Moreover, activation of the UCS gnostic unit through the CS and the CS–UCS connection is responsible for CR–UCR similarity (pp. 265–267). The assumption that the P-produced T is quantitatively less than the S-produced one is made when Hebb (1968) assumes that a memory image is not accompanied by the firing of first-order assemblies. Konorski also essentially makes this assumption (p. 172).

Konorski (1967) also maintains that the traditional CR results from an image of the UCS, and evidence that stimulus-produced and image-related nonverbal responses are similar is mentioned. However, this evidence is considered infrequently and anecdotally (Konorski, 1967, pp. 233, 303). In addition, it is mentioned only at the end of the first chapter on classical conditioning and in the context of the role of classical conditioning in human behavior. Konorski introduces a large number of ideas, and some of them are not consistent with the present approach. Drives are necessary for the formation of associations (p. 271), and there are hunger (p. 271) and fear (p. 281) drives that are integral to the conditioning process. He (p. 271) maintains that the food drive mediates the increase in CR strength that occurs with deprivation. He (p. 289) discusses the effect of the amount and intensity of the UCS in terms of the strength of the CS–UCS connection (neither drive nor the UCR are implicated). Drives related to various biological needs or classes of stimuli are not part of the current system. A different kind of comment is that Konorski almost entirely fails to consider changes in the

perception of the CS in the two classical conditioning chapters. These presumed changes help to relate classical conditioning, perception, and P-ac-
tivation theory.

Recent treatments of classical conditioning from a cognitive perspective
(Hearst, 1978; Rescorla, 1978) are not closely concerned with the assumption
of a P-to-T transformation. Moreover, there is no definite attempt to account
for the similarity between the CR and UCR. Estes (1973, p. 272) relies on
stimulus–response theory to explain the occurrence of the CR, although his
theory is cognitive in other respects. Somewhat similarly, Hearst (1978)
suggests that both stimulus–stimulus and stimulus–response learning occurs
in classical conditioning.

INSTRUMENTAL CONDITIONING

A cognitive theory of instrumental conditioning is described that does not
leave the animal "lost buried in thought" (Guthrie, 1952, p. 143). In brief,
it is maintained that the nervous system functions so as to increase the
amount of S-produced T for a positive reinforcer, that it should thus operate
to increase the amount of P-produced T for the same stimulus, and that it
does so by approximating the stimulus correlated with performing the instrumental response (S_{IR}), thereby executing the instrumental response (IR).
That S- and P-produced Ts affect the nervous system similarly is also central
to the theory of classical conditioning. For example, this assumption leads
directly to an explanation of CR–UCR similarity. Support for the similar
influence of S- and P-produced Ts includes the related effect of perceiving
and imagining on behavior.

The Basic Theory

The S_{IR} is the stimulus that occurs when the IR takes place. It usually
includes kinesthetic stimuli and may include other stimuli (e.g., the sight of
an extending arm). For reward learning, the background (e.g., conditioning
chamber) stimulus is paired with the S_{IR}, and the S_{IR} predicts the positive
reinforcer. Because of the first pairing, classical conditioning between the
background stimulus and S_{IR} occurs. (Neutral stimuli are assumed to become
associated through the classical conditioning process.) The second pairing
results in classical conditioning between the S_{IR} and the reinforcer. Subsequently, while the animal is in the learning situation, the background stimulus
should (according to the theory of classical conditioning) result in a P-produced
$T_{S_{IR}}$ through contacting the connected Ps for the background stimulus and
S_{IR}. This T is similar to the S-produced $T_{S_{IR}}$. Therefore, it should interact
with the connected Ps for the S_{IR} and the reinforcer to yield a P-produced
T for the reinforcer. The amount of this T for the reinforcer is probably
relatively small, however, since the actual S_{IR} has not yet occurred ($T_{S_{IR}}$

was P-produced). That is, the amount of P-produced T for the reinforcer should increase as the actual S_{IR} (and hence the IR) occurs.

When an animal approaches or consumes a positive reinforcer, this probably means that it behaves so as to increase or maintain the amount of the S-produced T for this reinforcer. What is being assumed is that the stimuli occurring in the approach and consumption sequence affect the amount of the same temporary brain event, T for the reinforcer, and that the amount of this T increases up until some event in the sequence. Otherwise, the position that the nervous system functions so as to increase the amount of an S-produced T for a positive reinforcer is tautological. (When a stimulus is consistently approached, the nervous system must be behaving so as to produce some brain event through exposure to this stimulus.)

It was indicated above that while an animal is in the learning situation, a relatively small amount of P-produced T for the positive reinforcer should occur. In addition, it was just proposed that when an animal obtains a positive reinforcer, it (its nervous system) behaves so as to increase the amount of S-produced T for this reinforcer. The S- and P-produced Ts affect behavior similarly—this is the critical assumption for both classical and instrumental conditioning. It follows that the nervous system should function so as to increase the amount of P-produced T for the reinforcer. It was also indicated above that if the animal makes the S_{IR} occur, the amount of P-produced T for the reinforcer would increase. (Recall that classical conditioning between the S_{IR} and the reinforcer is the basis for this increase.) Thus the nervous system should function so as to bring about (produce) the S_{IR} (because doing so increases the amount of P-produced T for the reinforcer). And it is assumed that the nervous system is successful in this attempt (see also the next section). Bringing about the S_{IR} means that the IR is executed, the outcome to be explained.

The probability of the IR also decreases as a consequence of conditioning, and the explanation of this is essentially identical. Considering punishment learning, the classically conditioned associations are between the learning situation stimulus and S_{IR} and between the S_{IR} and negative reinforcer. This means that while the animal remains in the learning situation, a relatively small amount of P-produced T for the negative reinforcer occurs. The animal then roughly approximates the IR (because it does so either naturally or through training). Equivalently, the stimulus correlated with the response of the moment becomes more similar to the S_{IR}. Therefore, an increase in the amount of P-produced T for the negative reinforcer should occur (as a result of the classical conditioning between the S_{IR} and this reinforcer). Animals ordinarily behave so as to decrease the amount of S-produced T for a negative reinforcer. This resembles the earlier assumption for a positive reinforcer and is again almost tautological. For example, as an animal escapes from shock, the S-produced T for shock is being terminated. Furthermore, the shock itself cannot directly result in escape—it must be some neural event that is causal (presumably the amount of the S-produced T). The nervous system should also behave so as to reduce the amount of P-produced T for a negative reinforcer. This is because S- and P-produced Ts function similarly. Moreover, the amount of P-produced T for the negative reinforcer can be reduced by reducing the similarity between the current response-correlated stimulus and S_{IR}. If this occurs, it means that the IR is not closely approximated; that is, its probability decreases.

The inference that animals behave so as to both increase and decrease the amount of a P-produced T for a reinforcer is consistent with indications that humans tend to bring about images of positive reinforcers and terminate images of negative reinforcers. When we are deprived of food, we are apparently more likely to imagine food (Atkinson & McClelland, 1948; Sanford, 1937). Also, the probability of responses is changed when imagining positive or negative stimuli is contingent on making these responses (Upper & Cautela, 1979). For instance, high imagers overestimate the sizes of circles more than low imagers, provided the overestimations are followed by the opportunity to imagine pleasant scenes (Tondo & Cautela, 1974). In addition, food-deprived subjects are more likely to make a button-press response that delivers names of food than are satiated subjects (Harms & Staats, 1978). Perhaps the names were effective because of the P-produced Ts for food that they presumably produced.

Closed-Loop Theory

Wiener (1967) proposed that responses such as an arm extension for a cigar and driving a car in the middle of a lane are made through a closed-loop (feedback) process rather than in an inflexible manner. The closed-loop process entails detection of a discrepancy between a current state (e.g., the spatial position of an extending arm at one moment in time) and a target state (e.g., the spatial position of the cigar). In addition, detections of discrepancies are followed by response adjustments (error corrections). Moreover, the size of the discrepancies are reduced as a result of the response adjustments providing feedback (response-correlated information) about their current size. The discrepancy is eventually eliminated; that is, the response is executed. Closed-loop theory predicts novel appropriate responding. For example, if an arm is in a strange position, discrepancy is detected, and the following response adjustments and additional detections of discrepancies eventuate in obtaining the cigar. The room thermostat operates by a closed-loop process, as do many electronic systems.

Closed-loop theory aids in understanding how the nervous system brings about the S_{IR}. For reward learning, roughly speaking, the discrepancy between the stimulus correlated with the response of the moment and S_{IR} is reduced. However, unlike the cigar and car examples, the target is not perceived. That is, it is not the S_{IR} itself but the P-produced T for the S_{IR} that is involved in discrepancy reduction. Recall that this T derives from the previous classical conditioning between the background stimulus and

S_{IR}. Thus the nervous system functions (successfully) to reduce the discrepancy between the S-produced T of the current response and the P-produced T for the S_{IR}. Equivalently, the nervous system behaves so as to match an S-produced T with the P-produced T for the S_{IR}. Hence the S_{IR} is increasingly approximated. (Also, the S-produced T for the current response may combine in a perception-like manner with the P-produced $T_{S_{IR}}$ since these two Ts correspond to relatively similar stimuli. Hence the outcome of this perceptual integration process may be causal, with the size of the discrepancy being correlated with the quantitative variation in this outcome.) The factor driving the reduction in discrepancy is the increase in the amount of P-produced T for the positive reinforcer that occurs as the reduction continues. That is, closer approximations to the S_{IR} are progressively more likely because each one increases the amount of the P-produced T for the reinforcer. This increase in amount occurs because of the previous classical conditioning between the S_{IR} and the reinforcer. And when the S-produced T for the current response is sufficiently close to the P-produced T for the S_{IR}, the IR has occurred.

For punishment learning, animals tend to approximate the previously occurring IR. Thus the discrepancy between the S-produced T for the current response and the P-produced T for the S_{IR} tends to be reduced. However, concurrently the amount of P-produced T for the negative reinforcer increases. Consequently, the nervous system should function so as to increase the discrepancy between the S-produced T for the current response and the P-produced T for the S_{IR}.

Execution of a sequence of responses can be very rapid, ballistic (short-duration) movements can be made, and the initiation of a response necessarily occurs without peripheral feedback. Also, the response adjustments called for by closed-loop theory are seldom overt. Moreover, instrumentally conditioned responses and skilled movements occur with little or no peripheral contribution (Kelso, 1977; Taub et al., 1965). Therefore, the locus of the closed-loop process must frequently be within the central nervous system.

Results with fixed-ratio (FR) and related schedules accord with the position that the discrepancy between the current response-correlated stimulus and the P-produced $T_{S_{IR}}$ affects the IR. For FR schedules, the IR is the number of responses required for a reinforcer since this number causes the reinforcer to occur. The S_{IR} is the stimulus correlated with making the required number of responses. An approximation to this stimulus can be postulated since animals discriminate between similar numbers of responses in the absence of experimenter-provided cues (Hobson, 1975). One observation is that rats tend to approach the food tray just prior to completing the number of responses delivering food (Platt & Johnson, 1971). Another is that pigeons frequently temporarily pause after executing runs of 9 to 18 responses on the FR 100 component of a mixed FR 10 FR 100 schedule (Alferink & Crossman, 1975). There were no experimenter-provided stimuli to cue the approach and pausing responses. For the first study, perhaps the food tray was approached when the discrepancy between the T for the current response-correlated stimulus and the P-produced $T_{S_{IR}}$ became relatively small and hence difficult to detect. And pausing may have resulted when the T for the current response-correlated stimulus became too dissimilar to the P-produced $T_{S_{IR}}$ for the performance of 10 responses. So, by arranging for the IR to consist of observable (in these instances, numbers of) components, the consequences of the S_{IR} being both increasingly and decreasingly approximated can seemingly be determined.

Other Types of Instrumental Conditioning, Approach and Escape, and Contrast

This theory of instrumental conditioning requires that the stimulus the IR delivers (e.g., food) tends, when perceived, to be either approached or escaped from. Without this tendency to approach or escape, the nervous system should not function so as to increase or decrease the amount of the P-produced T for the stimulus the IR delivers, and thus instrumental conditioning should not occur. Therefore, this approach and escape are critical. Consequently, it is maintained that, in general, IRs that increase in probability deliver stimuli that are more likely to be approached than the stimuli present prior to the performance of the IR. Likewise, IRs that decrease in probability deliver stimuli that are more likely to be escaped from than the stimuli present prior to the execution of the IR. For some types of conditioning (e.g., avoidance learning), these statements are appended to refer to the stimulus that would occur if the IR were not made.

In avoidance, escape, and omission learning, the IR omits or terminates the reinforcer, that is, causes nothing in particular—for example, the conditioning chamber alone—to occur. Therefore, the theory of instrumental conditioning requires that a normally relatively neutral stimulus complex such as a conditioning chamber tends to be approached or escaped from when a reinforcer occurs at other times. There is reasonably strong evidence supporting this position. One finding is that rats escape from an area in which they previously received food (Adelman & Maatsch, 1956). This outcome can also be viewed as a contrast effect; the escape is opposite in direction to the approach response to food. Moreover, approach and escape from a neutral stimulus occurring in the absence of a reinforcer may, in general, be interpreted in terms of contrast.

Contrast effects in instrumental conditioning are well known. For instance, they may involve two positive reinforcers (Mellgren, et al., 1972) and two negative reinforcers (Nation, et al., 1974). The contrast effect in this type of study is the displacement of the strength of the IR in a direction opposite to the relative value of the reinforcer in the second learning situation. Contrast effects on learned responses are believed to be accompanied by contrast effects on the responses to the perceived reinforcers. (This is consistent with the assumption, discussed below, that IR strength is related to the strength of the response to the perceived stimulus that the IR delivers.) Both Flaherty and Largen (1975) and Tinklepaugh (1928) report contrast effects on the responses to perceived reinforcers. The former observed that the rate of intake of a 32% sucrose solution was increased when rats drank a 4% solution just previously; also, exposure to the 32% solution decreased consumption of the 4% one. The latter observed that monkeys respond aggressively and temporarily escape from lettuce when it occurs in the absence of a banana. Perhaps two simultaneously present reinforcers also result in a contrast outcome. For example, a monkey might accept lettuce with considerable reluctance if a banana were adjacent to it but under an immovable glass cover. Thus two memorial representations of reinforcers (Mellgren et al., 1972), a perceived reinforcer and a memorial representation of another reinforcer (Flaherty & Largen, 1975; Tinklepaugh, 1928), and two simultaneously perceived reinforcers may all yield contrast outcomes. This possibility is consistent with the position that S- and P-produced Ts affect behavior similarly.

Of most relevance to avoidance, escape, and omission learning are contrast effects on the responses to perceived neutral stimuli that occur in the absence of the reinforcer. The Adelman and Maatsch (1956) report was mentioned previously. In addition, pigeons respond aggressively when they remain in a chamber in the temporary absence of food (Azrin et al., 1966). This emotional response contrasts with the positive one that food produces. The S- of a go/no-go successive discrimination is also a neutral stimulus that occurs in the temporary absence of a positive reinforcer. Since it establishes escape learning (Rilling et al., 1973), it presumably tends to be escaped from, which opposes the approach response to the positive reinforcer. Moreover, responding to the S- of both simultaneous and successive reward learning discriminations is actively inhibited (the well-known inhibitory stimulus generalization result; the evidence that animals do not approach S- when it is presented alone and similar findings reviewed by Mackintosh, 1974, p. 548). There is also evidence from classical conditioning. A CS paired with the temporary absence of food is escaped from (Wasserman et al., 1974), again a contrast effect. A CS paired with the absence of shock establishes reward learning (Weisman & Litner, 1969) and thus presumably tends to be approached. CSs paired with termination of UCSs may also be approached or escaped from in a contrast manner (King, 1979, pp. 77–78).

In avoidance, escape, and omission learning, the IR causes the background stimulus to occur in the absence of the reinforcer. The reviewed evidence indicates that the background stimulus and also specific neutral stimuli (e.g., typical CSs) are approached or escaped from and produce complementary emotional behavior in the direction of contrast when they occur in the absence of the reinforcer. Moreover, contrast effects also occur between two positive or negative reinforcers. Taken as a whole, this evidence supports the contention that the stimulus that the IR causes to occur in avoidance, escape, and omission learning, that is, the background stimulus in the absence of the reinforcer, tends to be approached or escaped from. Granted this, the explanations of reward and punishment learning, which are based on the occurrence of approach or escape from the perceived reinforcer, also apply to these other types of instrumental conditioning. Avoidance learning will be considered in particular. The IR causes the background stimulus to occur in the absence of shock. Presumably, this background stimulus tends to be approached because of a contrast effect that stems from the P-produced T for shock. Thus the IR probably causes a stimulus to occur that tends to be approached, as is assumed to hold for all types of instrumental conditioning in which the probability of the IR increases.

The present emphasis on approach and escape is supported by work in which the strength of approach to stimuli that the IR delivers is measured. One measure is the base rate of manipulating an operandum (Premack, 1963a). Another is the time spent perceiving a stimulus (Premack, 1963b, 1971a). He (1963a) found that reward learning occurs only when the IR delivers a stimulus (operandum) that is more likely to be approached (manipulated) than the stimulus (another operandum) present before the IR is made. In another study (Premack, 1971a), rats were deprived of water, and drinking caused wheel rotation and hence forced running to occur. The rate of drinking decreased; that is, punishment learning occurred, and it was predicted by the greater time spent drinking than running prior to conditioning. However, the same contingency resulted in reward learning of drinking when the rats were not deprived of water. Correspondingly, with satiation, the base level running response was stronger than the base level drinking response. Other research (Premack, 1963b) showed that the strength of an IR is quantitatively related to the strength of approach to the perceived reinforcer.

These last two findings lead directly to an explanation of the effects of amount and deprivation of reinforcement on IR strength since both perceived food and water are probably more strongly approached when larger in amount and when animals are deprived. Effects of amount and deprivation on CR strength were also explained in terms of responses to perceived reinforcers (i.e., UCRs). Motivational concepts need not be introduced, although attention to the reinforcer may play a role, as previously mentioned. The quantitative relationship between IR strength and the strength of the approach to the perceived reinforcer is also handled by image theory. This stronger approach suggests that the amount of the S-produced T for the reinforcer is increased more quickly. The nervous system should thus function so as to increase the amount of the P-produced T for the reinforcer more quickly, and this can be accomplished by executing the IR more quickly.

There are reports that after instrumental conditioning has been established, satiation or changes in the value of the reinforcer affect performance relatively weakly even though they noticeably influence the response to the perceived reinforcer (Holman, 1975; Morgan, 1974). Moreover, Holland and

Rescorla (1975) found that satiation and a change in the value of the UCS do not affect second-order conditioning. Perhaps the values for the S_{IR} and the first-order CS are relatively permanently altered as a consequence of their association with the reinforcer, much as one stimulus can permanently alter the identification of a second stimulus in perception. This possibility implies that extinction much more than some other procedures is capable of once again altering the values for the S_{IR} and first-order CS.

Novel Appropriate Instrumental Responding

Closed-loop theory and hence the present approach predict that novel appropriate responding may occur while the IR is being executed. There is scattered supporting evidence. A surgical treatment greatly modifies response topography on a maze task but has little effect on error performance (Lashley & Ball, 1929). Humans can accurately execute a simple movement from a new starting position (Adams & Goetz, 1973). MacNeilage (1970) comments on the variability and novelty of speech production.

The paucity of evidence for the occurrence of novel appropriate modifications of the IR is thought to be due to a lack of trying. This evidence could, I believe, be obtained by either deflecting an IR as it is being made or by altering the effect of the IR on an experimenter-provided "artificial" response-correlated stimulus. Consider, for example, the following catch-up prediction. An animal would be reward trained to move either a slider in a groove or a dot on a screen from a start to a finish position in almost exactly 2 seconds. Then, on a single test trial, the force or rate of responding on the operandum required to move the slider or dot at the same speed as in training would be altered—for example, made greater. This means that at the start of the test trial the slider or dot would be moving at a slower speed than at the end of training. The prediction is that the force or rate of responding on the operandum would be greater during the latter portion of the test trial than during the latter portion of the training trails; that is, the animal would respond in a new way and thereby catch up.

Some situations in which novel appropriate responding occurs will be discussed. This is because they are consistent with both the possibility that the IR can be suitably modified in new ways and the theoretical approach to instrumental conditioning.

Novel responding occurs when a new response is imitated. Delayed imitation of a new response occurs in rats (Kohn & Dennis, 1972) and also in a chimpanzee (Hayes & Hayes, 1952). Using a learning set procedure, Hayes and Hayes also trained the chimpanzee to immediately imitate a series of highly improbable responses.

What will be called *construction learning* occurs when an animal duplicates a presented or remembered stimulus. Examples are completing a puzzle with the help of a picture of it and terminating nail banging when a nail is flush to the wall (discussed in Miller et al., 1960, Chapter 2). Premack (1975) reports the occurrence of novel appropriate delayed construction learning in a chimpanzee. On the initial trial and without preliminary training, one chimpanzee placed photographs of a chimpanzee's two eyes, nose, and mouth (each on a hard backing) in approximately the correct positions of a photographed outline of a chimpanzee's face.

There are other types of novel appropriate responding of an instrumental nature. New responses occur that have response-correlated consequences that approximately match an abstract representation (Schmidt, 1975). For example, the letter "A" can be written in an entirely new way. Premack (1971b) describes more complex examples involving knowledge of language in a chimpanzee. In one instance the plastic word for "cherry" was paired with an actual cherry but not involved in concept learning with the plastic words for "color of" and "red." Nevertheless, the chimpanzee exhibited transfer, matching "color of cherry" with "red." Another type of novel response occurs when people make new responses on the basis of their description by someone else, such as a tennis instructor. In addition, we ourselves can be the source of a memorial representation for the stimulus correlated with a novel response, such as when we tell ourselves to "aim higher" after a first attempt in a new situation.

Instrumental conditioning, delayed imitation, delayed construction learning, and the other indicated types of novel appropriate responding may be fundamentally related. In each case the novel response may be executed through the nervous system matching response-correlated stimuli with memorial representations. The memorial representation corresponds to the S_{IR} for instrumental conditioning, the stimulus provided by the demonstrator's prior response for delayed imitation, and the previously occurring to-be-duplicated stimulus for delayed construction learning. Moreover, in each case, the matching may be accomplished through a closed-loop process. Detection of discrepancy between the current response-correlated stimulus and the memorial representation initiates further responding with discrepancy reduction resulting. Also, it seems clear that overt response adjustments (error corrections) frequently occur for at least some of the indicated types.

Parallels Between CS and S_{IR}

The S_{IR} and the following stimulus (the one that the IR delivers) have been assumed to become associated through classical conditioning. The numerous similarities between classical and instrumental conditioning are viewed as derived from this classical conditioning within instrumental conditioning.

Some similarities will be quickly mentioned. Lengthening both the CS–UCS and the delay of reinforcement interval impairs conditioning. Salient CSs facilitate conditioning, and so do S_{IR}s that differ greatly from background stimuli (i.e., IRs that provide a large amount of feedback). Discrimination learning between similar CSs is relatively difficult, as it is between similar

IRs and hence $S_{IR}s$. The S_{IR} as well as a second CS is overshadowed by CS, and the S_{IR} results in a CR-like response (Mackintosh & Dickinson, 1979).

Because the S_{IR} is analogous to the CS, responses to the CS bear on the theory of instrumental conditioning. It is well known that CSs are approached and escaped from. Approach to or escape from a CS means that the amount of the S-produced T for the CS is increased or decreased. Since an S_{IR} is analogous to a CS, animals should also tend to increase or decrease the amount of an S-produced $T_{S_{IR}}$. And image theory takes this position when it assumes that an animal behaves so as to bring about or avoid bringing about the S_{IR}. For example, in omission learning the S_{IR} (and IR) are paired with the absence of a positive reinforcer. Because animals avoid the corresponding CS (Wasserman et al., 1974), they should also attempt to avoid bringing about the S_{IR}. Image theory goes on to assume that this attempt is successful. The position that an animal behaves so as to bring about or avoid bringing about the S_{IR} is also supported by the basic conditioned reinforcement result that CSs establish instrumental conditioning. When this conditioning occurs, an animal literally either brings about or avoids bringing about a CS. Since a S_{IR} is analogous to a CS, an animal may bring about or avoid bringing about the S_{IR}. The following is illustrative. The establishment of reward learning by a CS paired with the absence of shock (Weisman & Litner, 1969) means that the subjects behaved so as to bring about this CS. The S_{IR} in avoidance learning is also paired with the absence of shock. This suggests that animals also behave so as to bring about this S_{IR}, thereby performing the IR.

Consider that the experimenter arranges for a CS that is paired with a positive UCS to move around in space. Animals would probably tend to follow the moving CS. Consequently, when the CS would move in a new direction, the animals would be making novel responses. Animals might also be deflected from the CS (or, for a negative CS, have their escape route blocked), and novel responding would possibly ensue. Image theory assumes that an animal brings about (approaches) or avoids bringing about (correlated with escapes from) the S_{IR}, including in new ways. This position accords with the described novel approach and escape responses to the analogous CS.

Other Theories of Instrumental Conditioning

Ideomotor theory (Greenwald, 1970; James, 1890; Konorski, 1967, pp. 190–194, Chapter 10) assumes that activation of the P for the S_{IR} results in the IR directly. Konorski (Chapter 10) also assumes that drive and drive reduction are required for instrumental conditioning. Ideomotor theory cannot straightforwardly account for IRs that decrease in probability. This is because activation of the $P_{S_{IR}}$ results in the occurrence rather than in the elimination of the corresponding response. A second problem is that it cannot explain novel appropriate responding. The response must have previously occurred for its $P_{S_{IR}}$ to be activated.

The present approach to instrumental conditioning closely resembles Mowrer's (1960a, 1960b) theory. Considering reward learning, Mowrer indicates that the S_{IR} functions as a positive secondary reinforcer, that the animal thus tries to obtain the S_{IR}, and that the way it does so is "to make or accentuate the *response* that has previously produced" it (1960b, p. 9). Also, classical conditioning between the S_{IR} and the reinforcer is assumed. The important aspect of the reinforcer is emotional—hope and fear are conditioned. However, the idea of a representation of a stimulus is accepted; for instance, he refers (sometimes) to hope of food. He (1960b, Chapter 7) relates his theory to closed-loop theory and believes that it requires the assumption of a representation or image. Human motor learning is analyzed as involving a comparison between "the feedback from actual performance of an activity and a *standard* of performance" (1960b, p. 277) or reference signal. He also states (1960b, p. 112) that the processes underlying instrumental conditioning and delayed imitation are essentially identical. Sheffield's (1965) approach to instrumental conditioning is fairly similar, but he probably errs in designating the CR as the source of feedback.

Mowrer devotes little attention to classical conditioning, and he fails to treat representations of stimuli systematically. His reference to the expectancy of the UCS (1960a, p. 59) is vague. He seems to offer no account of CR–UCR similarity. That stimulus-produced and image-related nonverbal responses are similar is not considered in either the summary (Chapter 1) or image (Chapter 7) chapters of the second volume. He (1960b, Chapter 7, p. 166) writes several times to the effect that an "image is a conditioned sensation." Similarly, Staats and Lohr (1979, p. 86) imply that images derive from conditioning (e.g., "the basic conditioning principles involved in the acquisition of images" and "learning theory accounts of images"). The present position is essentially the reverse—the CR derives from an image, or, more correctly, a P-produced T. In respect to instrumental conditioning, Mowrer does indicate that hope and approach and fear and escape are correlated. However, it seems that approach and escape are not discussed in relation to changes in the amount of the P-produced T for the reinforcer. Also, the relevance of the possibility that we tend to imagine those stimuli that we approach is apparently missed. His position that response-correlated stimuli are not central to avoidance learning (1960a, p. 32) is a mistake.

Adams (1971) employs closed-loop theory in accounting for the acquisition and maintenance of relatively slow simple movements in the human motor learning area. According to Adams, the stimulus correlated with the performance of the current response is matched to a memorial representation of the stimulus correlated with a previous response, as in the present theory. He relies on a stimulus–response mechanism called the *memory trace* to initiate the response. The memory trace is also responsible for the response adjustments (error corrections) that follow detections of discrepancies (p.

143). This brings closed-loop theory dangerously close to traditional stimulus–response theory. Greenwald (1970, p. 80) does, in fact, interpret closed-loop theory in stimulus–response terms. Adams (p. 144) rejects this position, however, pointing out that response corrections are probably possible when new errors occur (i.e., novel appropriate responding may take place) and went on to provide such a demonstration (Adams & Goetz, 1973).

In principle, at least, response initiation, ballistic responses, and error corrections, including very rapid novel ones, can all be mediated by a central closed-loop process. A large number of central responses may be simultaneously initiated. The one providing the least discrepancy with a previously activated representation may then continue to be excited (or excited more strongly), thereby producing an overt response. Since a large number of central responses occur, some of them could be new. Because these responses are not peripheral, error corrections could be very rapid. Empirical support for a central closed-loop process exists (Wallace & McGhee, 1979; Zelaznik et al., 1978). The latter found that humans accurately perform a 130-millisecond timing response with prior training being limited to only exposure to approximations of the auditory response-correlated stimuli for this response. These stimuli were provided by a demonstrator's responses, so the study indicates that auditory imitation of a very rapid response can occur on the first trial. Since a novel response was made, there could have been no stimulus–response connection for it. Since it was ballistic, presumably there was no time for peripheral feedback to guide it. In addition, it is not clear how a motor program for this response would be prepared (Schmidt, 1975).

SUMMARY AND IMPLICATIONS FOR MEMORY

The core assumption is that S- and P-produced Ts affect the nervous system similarly. The related effects of real and imagined stimuli on behavior are consistent with this assumption. Regarding classical conditioning, the resemblance between the CR and UCR is viewed as due to the occurrence of similar Ts, one P and the other S produced. Supporting evidence is that image-related and stimulus-produced nonverbal responses are similar. In addition, T_{CS} and T_{UCS} are viewed as forming a perception-like group much as S-produced Ts do in general. This perspective accords with both the influence of CS–UCS similarity on conditioning and the effect of conditioning on the perception of the CS.

For instrumental conditioning, it is assumed that the nervous system functions so as to increase or decrease the amount of both S- and P-produced Ts that correspond to stimuli that are approached and escaped from, respectively. Support for this includes suggestions that humans tend to imagine those stimuli that they are likely to approach. Considering reward learning, the S_{IR} and the positive reinforcer are assumed to become associated through classical conditioning. Consequently, progressively closer approximations of the S_{IR} should result in progressively larger amounts of the P-produced T for the reinforcer. It follows that the nervous system should attempt to bring about the S_{IR} and hence the IR. And it is assumed that a closed-loop process enables the nervous system to be successful in this attempt.

Memory as Perception

P-produced Ts have been assumed to affect the nervous system much like S-produced Ts do, and P-produced Ts stem from memory by definition. Therefore, memory may be governed by perceptual processes (King, 1978).

The existence of perception-like groups over a retention interval might be inferred from the result that pairing stimuli affects the later recognition of individually presented members of these pairs (Light & Carter-Sobell, 1970). Another indication of a relationship between perception and memory is that physically and semantically distinctive stimuli facilitate both perceptual search (Jonides & Gleitman, 1972) and retention (Restorff, 1933).

Memory may be more a matter of a perception-like suppression process than a limited capacity one. The evidence that addition of information can aid retention appears to be too pervasive for the limited capacity notion to prevail. The addition of context can improve retention (Rohwer, 1966). Addition of dissimilar information to stimuli makes them more memorable (Nelson et al., 1976). There are many indications that perceptual suppression increases as a second stimulus becomes more similar to the one to be perceived. Likewise, more similar distractor stimuli reduce retention more (Reitman, 1974). Unfortunately, it is difficult to predict when an increase in similarity results in grouping and when it leads to suppression, but this seems to be true for both perception and memory.

Paradoxically, the occurrence of perception-like groups in memory may both aid and hinder retention. Perceptual groups entail the suppression of relatively similar percepts—for example, the two monocular percepts in binocular fusion, alternative percepts in Gestalt figures, two stationary stimuli in apparent movement, and so on. Consider memorial groups formed between paired associates or among two or more items of a list. The remaining items are similar to the ones that group in location, time of occurrence, and so on. Much as perceptual groups suppress related percepts, the indicated memorial groups may suppress the remaining similar items. Functional set size may therefore be reduced, with retention thereby being facilitated.

Nevertheless, the formation of memorial groups may contribute importantly to forgetting. The functional similarity of the temporal information possessed by different stimuli probably increases with the passage of time (Yntema & Trask, 1963), probably relatively automatically (Hasher & Zacks, 1979). Perhaps this increase in similarity between stimuli over time increases their tendency to group. The result may be a representation that corresponds to an abstract property of the stimuli contributing to the group, such as words as a general category. As discussed above, the group that is formed should suppress related stimulus information that does not contribute to it. In this way the distinctive information possessed by the individual stimuli contributing to the group may be suppressed. Thus the loss in detail with the passage of time that is certainly a basic characteristic of forgetting (Bahrick et al., 1967) may result from an increase in functional similarity and group formation.

Perceptual grouping probably occurs more strongly as the number of similar individual stimuli that are present increases (Palmer & Bucher, 1981; Restle, 1979). Perhaps stimulus number often similarly affects memorial grouping. This possibility has some support. Training with a larger number of exemplars of a concept aids concept learning (Homa & Chambliss, 1975). With the passage of time, a progressively larger number of stimuli may possess functionally similar temporal information (Yntema & Trask, 1963). This increase in number may promote grouping and thus result in greater suppression of the distinctive information possessed by individual stimuli.

REFERENCES

Adams, J. A. A closed-loop theory of motor learning. *Journal of Motor Behavior,* 1971, **3,** 111–149.

Adams, J. A., & Goetz, E. T. Feedback and practice as variables in error detection and correction. *Journal of Motor Behavior,* 1973, **5,** 217–224.

Adelman, H. M., & Maatsch, J. L. Learning and extinction based upon frustration, food reward, and exploratory tendency. *Journal of Experimental Psychology,* 1956, **52,** 311–315.

Alferink, L. A., & Crossman, E. K. Mixed fixed-ratio schedules: Priming and the pre-ratio pause. *Psychological Record,* 1975, **25,** 123–130.

Allport, D. A. On knowing the meaning of words we are unable to report: The effects of visual masking. In S. Dornic (Ed.), *Atention and performance VI.* Hillsdale, N.J.: Lawrence Erlbaum Associates, 1977, pp. 505–533.

Atkinson, J. W., & McClelland, D. C. The projective expression of needs: II. The effect of different intensities of the hunger drive on thematic apperception. *Journal of Experimental Psychology,* 1948, **38,** 643–658.

Azrin, N. H., Hutchinson, R. R., & Hake, D. F. Extinction-induced aggression. *Journal of the Experimental Analysis of Behavior,* 1966, **9,** 191–204.

Bahrick, H. P., Clark, S., & Bahrick, P. Generalization gradients as indicants of learning and retention of a recognition task. *Journal of Experimental Psychology,* 1967, **75,** 464–471.

Barber, T. X., Chauncey, H. H., & Winer, R. A. Effect of hypnotic and nonhypnotic suggestions on parotid gland response to gustatory stimuli. *Psychosomatic Medicine,* 1964, **26,** 374–380.

Barber, T. X., & Hahn, K. W., Jr. Experimental studies in "hypnotic" behavior:

Physiologic and subjective effects of imagined pain. *Journal of Nervous and Mental Disease,* 1964, **139**, 416–425.

Breland, K., & Breland, M. The misbehavior of organisms. *American Psychologist,* 1961, **16**, 681–684.

Brown, P. L., & Jenkins, H. M. Auto-shaping of the pigeon's key-peck. *Journal of the Experimental Analysis of Behavior,* 1968, **11**, 1–8.

Craik, F. I. M., & Tulving, E. Depth of processing and the retention of words in episodic memory. *Journal of Experimental Psychology: General,* 1975, **104**, 268–294.

DeBold, R. C., Miller, N. E., & Jensen, D. D. Effect of strength of drive determined by a new technique for appetitive classical conditioning of rats. *Journal of Comparative and Physiological Psychology,* 1965, **59**, 102–108.

Dickinson, A., & Mackintosh, N. J. Reinforcer specificity in the enhancement of conditioning by posttrial surprise. *Journal of Experimental Psychology: Animal Behavior Processes,* 1979, **5**, 162–177.

Epstein, W., & Rock, I. Perceptual set as an artifact of recency. *American Journal of Psychology,* 1960, **73**, 214–228.

Estes, W. K. Memory and conditioning. In F. J. McGuigan and D. B. Lumsden (Eds.), *Contemporary approaches to conditioning and learning.* Washington, DC: Winston, 1973, pp. 265–286.

Fink, J. G. Conditioning of muscle action potential increments accompanying an instructed movement. *Journal of Experimental Psychology,* 1954, **47**, 61–68.

Flaherty, C. F., & Largen, J. Within-subjects positive and negative contrast effects in rats. *Journal of Comparative and Physiological Psychology,* 1975, **88**, 653–664.

Garcia, J., & Koelling, P. A. Relation of cue to consequence in avoidance learning. *Psychonomic Science,* 1966, **4**, 123–124.

Greenwald, A. G. Sensory feedback mechanisms in performance control: With special reference to the ideo-motor mechanism. *Psychological Review,* 1970, **77**, 73–99.

Grings, W. W., Schell, A. M., & Carey, C. A. Verbal control of an autonomic response in a cue reversal situation. *Journal of Experimental Psychology,* 1973, **99**, 215–221.

Guthrie, E. R. *The psychology of learning* (rev. ed.). New York: Harper, 1952.

Hall, G., & Pearce, J. M. Latent inhibition of a CS during CS–US pairings. *Journal of Experimental Psychology: Animal Behavior Processes,* 1979, **5**, 31–42.

Harms, J. Y., & Staats, A. W. Food deprivation and conditioned reinforcing value of food words: Interaction of Pavlovian and instrumental conditioning. *Bulletin of the Psychonomic Society,* 1978, **12**, 294–296.

Hasher, L., & Zacks, R. T. Automatic and effortful processes in memory. *Journal of Experimental Psychology: General,* 1979, **109**, 356–388.

Hayes, K. J., & Hayes, C. Imitation in a home-raised chimpanzee. *Journal of Comparative and Physiological Psychology,* 1952, **45**, 450–459.

Hearst, E. Stimulus relationships and feature selection in learning and behavior. In S. H. Hulse, H. Fowler, and W. K. Honig (Eds.), *Cognitive processes in animal learning.* Hillsdale, N.J.: Lawrence Erlbaum Associates, 1978, pp. 51–88.

Hebb, D. O. *Organization of behavior.* New York: Wiley, 1949.

Hebb, D. O. Concerning imagery. *Psychological Review,* 1968, **75,** 466–477.

Hobson, S. L. Discriminability of fixed-ratio schedules for pigeons: Effects of absolute ratio size. *Journal of the Experimental Analysis of Behavior,* 1975, **23,** 25–35.

Holland, P. C. CS–US interval as a determinant of the form of Pavlovian appetitive conditioned responses. *Journal of Experimental Psychology: Animal Behavior Processes,* 1980, **6,** 155–174.

Holland, P. C., & Rescorla, R. A. The effect of two ways of devaluing the unconditioned stimulus after first- and second-order appetitive conditioning. *Journal of Experimental Psychology: Animal Behavior Processes,* 1975, **1,** 355–363.

Holman, E. W. Some conditions for the dissociation of consummatory and instrumental behavior in rats. *Learning and Motivation,* 1975, **6,** 358–366.

Homa, D., & Chambliss, D. The relative contributions of common and distinctive information on the abstraction from ill-defined categories. *Journal of Experimental Psychology: Human Learning and Memory,* 1975, **1,** 351–359.

Jacobsen, E. Electrical measurements of neuromuscular states during mental activities: II. Imagination and recollection of various muscular acts. *American Journal of Physiology,* 1930, **94,** 22–34.

James, W. *Principles of psychology,* Vol. 2. New York: Holt, 1890.

Jenkins, H. M., & Harrison, R. H. Effect of discrimination training on auditory generalization. *Journal of Experimental Psychology,* 1960, **59,** 246–253.

Jonides, J., & Gleitman, H. A conceptual category effect in visual search: O as letter or as digit. *Perception & Psychophysics,* 1972, **12,** 457–460.

Kamin, L. J. Temporal and intensity characteristics of the conditioned stimulus. In W. F. Prokasy (Ed.), *Classical conditioning: A symposium.* New York: Appleton, 1965, pp. 118–147.

Kamin, L. J. Predictability, surprise, attention and conditioning. In B. A. Campbell and R. M. Church (Eds.), *Punishment and aversive behavior.* New York: Appleton, 1969, pp. 279–296.

Kelso, J. A. S. Motor control mechanisms underlying human movement reproduction. *Journal of Experimental Psychology: Human Perception and Performance,* 1977, **3,** 529–543.

King, D. L. Perception, binocular fusion, and an image theory of classical conditioning. *Perceptual and Motor Skills,* 1974, **39,** 531–537.

King, D. L. Image theory of conditioning, memory, forgetting, functional similarity, fusion, and dominance. *Journal of Mental Imagery,* 1978, **2,** 47–62.

King, D. L. *Conditioning: An image approach.* New York: Gardner, 1979.

Kohn, B., & Dennis, M. Observation and discrimination learning in the rat: Specific and nonspecific effects. *Journal of Comparative and Physiological Psychology,* 1972, **78,** 292–296.

Kolers, P. A. *Aspects of motion perception.* Elmsford, N.Y.: Pergamon, 1972.

Konorski, J. *Integrative activity of the brain.* Chicago: University of Chicago Press, 1967.

Lashley, K. S., & Ball, J. Spinal conduction and kinesthetic sensitivity in the maze habit. *Journal of Comparative Psychology,* 1929, **9,** 71–105.

Lawrence, D. H. Acquired distinctiveness of cues: I. Transfer between discriminations on the basis of familiarity with the stimulus. *Journal of Experimental Psychology,* 1949, **39,** 770–784.

Leuba, C. Images as conditioned sensations. *Journal of Experimental Psychology,* 1940, **26,** 345–351.

Light, L. L., & Carter-Sobell, L. Effects of changed semantic context on recognition memory. *Journal of Verbal Learning and Verbal Behavior,* 1970, **9,** 1–11.

Lockhead, G. R. Processing dimensional stimuli: A note. *Psychological Review,* 1972, **79,** 410-419.

Mackintosh, N. J. *The psychology of animal learning.* New York: Academic, 1974.

Mackintosh, N. J., & Dickinson, A. Instrumental (type II) conditioning. In A. Dickinson and R. A. Boakes (Eds.), *Mechanisms of learning and motivation: A memorial volume to Jerzy Konorski.* Hillsdale, N.J.: Lawrence Erlbaum Associates, 1979, pp. 143–169.

MacNeilage, P. F. Motor control of serial ordering of speech. *Psychological Review,* 1970, **77,** 182–196.

McGuigan, F. J. Imagery and thinking: Covert functioning of the motor system. In G. E. Schwartz and D. Shapiro (Eds.), *Consciousness and self-regulation: Advances in research and theory,* Vol. 2. New York: Plenum, 1978.

Mellgren, R. L., Wrather, D. M., & Dyck, D. G. Differential conditioning and contrast effects in rats. *Journal of Comparative and Physiological Psychology,* 1972, **80,** 478–483.

Menzel, E. W. Chimpanzee spatial memory organization. *Science,* 1973, **182,** 943–945.

Miller, G. A., Galanter, E., & Pribram, K. H. *Plans and the structure of behavior.* New York: Holt, 1960.

Morgan, M. J. Resistance to satiation. *Animal Behaviour,* 1974, **22,** 449–466.

Mowrer, O. H. *Learning theory and behavior.* New York: Wiley, 1960a.

Mowrer, O. H. *Learning theory and the symbolic processes.* New York: Wiley, 1960b.

Nation, J. R., Wrather, D. M., & Mellgren, R. L. Contrast effects in escape conditioning of rats. *Journal of Comparative and Physiological Psychology,* 1974, **86,** 69–73.

Neisser, U., & Becklen, R. Selective looking: Attending to visually specified events. *Cognitive Psychology,* 1975, **7,** 480–494.

Nelson, D. L., Reed, V. S., & Walling, J. R. Pictorial superiority effect. *Journal of Experimental Psychology: Human Learning and Memory,* 1976, **2,** 523–528.

Paivio, A. *Imagery and verbal processes.* New York: Holt, 1971.

Palmer, S. E., & Bucher, N. M. Configural effects in perceived pointing of ambiguous triangles. *Journal of Experimental Psychology: Human Perception and Performance,* 1981, **7,** 88–114.

Pavlov, I. P. *Conditioned reflexes* (G. V. Anrep, transl.). Oxford: Oxford University Press, 1927.

Perky, C. W. An experimental study of imagination. *American Journal of Psychology,* 1910, **21,** 422–452.

Platt, J. R., & Johnson, D. M. Localization of position within a homogeneous behavior chain: Effects of error contingencies. *Learning and Motivation*, 1971, **2**, 386–414.

Premack, D. Prediction of the comparative reinforcement values of running and drinking. *Science*, 1963a, **139**, 1062–1063.

Premack, D. Rate differential reinforcement in monkey manipulation. *Journal of the Experimental Analysis of Behavior*, 1963b, **6**, 81–89.

Premack, D. Catching up with common sense or two sides of a generalization: Reinforcement and punishment. In R. Glaser (Ed.), *The nature of reinforcement*. New York: Academic Press, 1971a, pp. 121–150.

Premack, D. Language in chimpanzee? *Science*, 1971b, **172**, 808–822.

Premack, D. Putting a face together. *Science*, 1975, **188**, 228–236.

Reitman, J. S. Without surreptitious rehearsal, information in short-term memory decays. *Journal of Verbal Learning and Verbal Behavior*, 1974, **13**, 365–377.

Rescorla, R. A. Some implications of a cognitive perspective on Pavlovian conditioning. In S. H. Hulse, H. Fowler, and W. K. Honig (Eds.), *Cognitive processes in animal learning*. Hillsdale, N.J.: Lawrence Erlbaum Associates, 1978.

Rescorla, R. A. Simultaneous and successive associations in sensory preconditioning. *Journal of Experimental Psychology: Animal Behavior Processes*, 1980, **6**, 207–216.

Rescorla, R. A., & Cunningham, C. L. Spatial contiguity facilitates Pavlovian second-order conditioning. *Journal of Experimental Psychology: Animal Behavior Processes*, 1979, **4**, 267–275.

Rescorla, R. A., & Furrow, D. R. Stimulus similarity as a determinant of Pavlovian conditioning. *Journal of Experimental Psychology: Animal Behavior Processes*, 1977, **3**, 203–215.

Rescorla, R. A., & Wagner, A. R. A theory of Pavlovian conditioning: Variations in the effectiveness of reinforcement and nonreinforcement. In A. H. Black and W. F. Prokasy (Eds.), *Classical conditioning II: Current research and theory*. New York: Appleton, 1972, pp. 64–99.

Restle, F. Coding theory of the perception of motion configurations. *Psychological Review*, 1979, **86**, 1–24.

Restorff, H. von. Über die Wirkung von Bereichsbildungen im Spurenfeld (Analyse von Vorgangen in Spurenfeld). *Psychologie Forschung*, 1933, **18**, 299–342.

Rilling, M., Kramer, T. J., & Richards, R. W. Aversive properties of the negative stimulus during learning with and without errors. *Learning and Motivation*, 1973, **4**, 1–10.

Rohwer, W. D., Jr. Constraint, syntax and meaning in paired–associate learning. *Journal of Verbal Learning and Verbal Behavior*, 1966, **5**, 541–547.

Rusiniak, K. W., Hankins, W. G., Garcia, J., & Brett, L. P. Flavor–illness aversions: Potentiation of odor by taste in rats. *Behavioral and Neural Biology*, 1979, **25**, 1–17.

Sanford, R. N. The effects of abstinence from food upon imaginal processes: A further experiment. *Journal of Psychology*, 1937, **3**, 145–159.

Schmidt, R. A. A schema theory of discrete motor skill learning. *Psychological Review*, 1975, **82**, 225–260.

Segal, S. J. Assimilation of a stimulus in the construction of an image: The Perky effect revisited. In P. W. Sheehan (Ed.), *The function and nature of imagery*. New York: Academic, 1972, pp. 203–230.

Segal, S. J., & Fusella, V. Influence of imaged pictures and sounds on detection of auditory and visual signals. *Journal of Experimental Psychology*, 1970, **83**, 458–464.

Shaw, W. A. The relation of muscular action potentials to imaginal weight lifting. *Archives of Psychology*, 1940, 247, 1–50.

Sheafor, P. J., & Gormezano, I. Conditioning the rabbit's (Oryctolagus cuniculus) jaw-movement response: US magnitude effects on URs, CRs, and pseudo-CRs. *Journal of Comparative and Physiological Psychology*, 1972, **81**, 449–456.

Sheehan, P. W. A functional analysis of the role of visual imagery in unexpected recall. In P. W. Sheehan (Ed.), *The function and nature of imagery*, New York: Academic, 1972, pp. 149–174.

Sheffield, F. D. Relation between classical conditioning and instrumental learning. In W. F. Prokasy (Ed.), *Classical conditioning: A symposium*. New York: Appleton, 1965, pp. 302–339.

Shor, R. E., Orne, M. T., & O'Connell, D. N. Psychological correlates of plateau hypnotizability in a special volunteer sample. *Journal of Personality and Social Psychology*, 1966, **3**, 80–95.

Staats, A. W., & Hammond, O. W. Natural words as physiological conditioned stimuli: Food-word-elicited salivation and deprivation effects. *Journal of Experimental Psychology*, 1972, **96**, 206–208.

Staats, A. W., & Lohr, J. M. Images, language, emotions, and personality: Social behaviorism's theory. *Journal of Mental Imagery*, 1979, **3**, 85–106.

Taub, E., Bacon, R. C., & Berman, A. J. The acquisition of a trace-conditioned avoidance response after deafferentiation of the responding limb. *Journal of Comparative and Physiological Psychology*, 1965, **59**, 275–279.

Testa, T. J. Effects of similarity of location and temporal intensity pattern of conditioned and unconditioned stimuli on the acquisition of conditioned suppression in rats. *Journal of Experimental Psychology: Animal Behavior Processes*, 1975, **1**, 114–121.

Tinklepaugh, O. L. An experimental study of representative factors in monkeys. *Journal of Comparative Psychology*, 1928, **8**, 197–236.

Tondo, R. R., & Cautela, J. R. Assessment of imagery in covert reinforcement. *Psychological Reports*, 1974, **34**, 1271–1280.

Upper, D., & Cautela, J. R. *Covert conditioning*. Elmsford, N.Y.: Pergamon, 1979.

Wallace, S. A., & McGhee, R. C. The independence of recall and recognition in motor learning. *Journal of Motor Behavior*, 1979, **11**, 141–151.

Wallach, H., O'Connell, D. N., & Neisser, U. The memory effect of visual perception of three-dimensional form. *Journal of Experimental Psychology*, 1953, **45**, 360–368.

Wasserman, E. A., Franklin, S. R., & Hearst, E. Pavlovian appetitive contingencies and approach versus withdrawal to conditioned stimuli in pigeons. *Journal of Comparative and Physiological Psychology*, 1974, **86**, 616–627.

Weisman, R. G., & Litner, J. S. Positive conditioned reinforcement of Sidman avoidance behavior in rats. *Journal of Comparative and Physiological Psychology,* 1969, **68,** 597–603.

Wertheimer, M. Experimentelle Studien über das Sehen von Bewegung. *Zeitschrift für Psychologie,* 1912, **61,** 161–265 [transl. in part in T. Shipley (Ed.), *Classics in psychology.* New York: Philosophical Library, 1961, pp. 1032–1089.]

Wiener, N. *The human use of human beings: Cybernetics and society.* New York: Avon Books, 1967 (originally published in 1950).

Wilson, G. D. Reversal of differential GSR conditioning by instructions. *Journal of Experimental Psychology,* 1968, **76,** 491–493.

Wooley, S. C., & Wooley, O. W. Salivation to the sight and thought of food: A new measure of appetite. *Psychosomatic Medicine,* 1973, **35,** 136–141.

Yntema, D. B., & Trask, F. P. Recall as a search process. *Journal of Verbal Learning and Verbal Behavior,* 1963, **2,** 65–74.

Zelaznik, H. N., Shapiro, D. C., & Newell, K. M. On the structure of motor recognition memory. *Journal of Motor Behavior,* 1978, **10,** 313–323.

Zener, K. The significance of behavior accompanying conditioned salivary secretion for theories of the conditioned response. *American Journal of Psychology,* 1937, **50,** 384–403.

PART TWO

Research

CHAPTER 7

Assessment of Mental Imagery

PETER W. SHEEHAN, R. ASHTON, AND K. WHITE

In 1977 we reported (White et al., 1977) that research on self-report inventories of imagery was strong and viable, and the data firmly emphasized the function of imagery rather than its nature. Self-report measures of imagery relied exclusively on subjects' verbal reports of their experiences that were then interpreted by investigators for what they revealed about imagery. Although there is no sure criterion for distinguishing "objective" and "subjective" measures of imagery, by the turn of the century it was clear that some measures could lay considerable claim to the term "objective" in the way that they approached the assessment of imagery.

Historically, the early emphasis on objective tests was established by Titchener (1909), Angell (1912), Davis (1932), and Woodworth (1938), whose tests were designed, for the most part, so that behavior on them could be associated with typical imagery, emphasizing the notion of "type" rather than heterogeneity of function. In a test planned for auditory imagery, for instance, the investigator was seldom interested in a predominance of other types of imagery. Much of the reasoning behind Davis's work, for example, was based on the assumption that visual work requires visual imagery and auditory work requires auditory imagery. The objection that can be specif ically raised against this assumption, however, is that a person could recall an object being a "sounding" object without any image of the sound at all. Woodworth (1938) himself drew attention to the different interpretations that could be placed on data supplied by objective tests. He clearly recognized, for instance, that the modality in which the words are presented is no sure criterion of the imagery used by the subject in recall. For the most part, early objective tests of imagery seemed to have too little to offer to justify their use by researchers. It was difficult to locate indices of behavior that did not require recourse of some kind to introspection to define the task's meaning, and authors were too extreme (Fernald, 1912) when they argued that the distinction between objective and subjective assessment of imagery was unequivocal. They served a major purpose, however, in forcing researchers to recognize that sheer reliance on the veracity of introspection can be discriminated from the correlation of an introspective report with objective or publicly observable behavior. If the correlation is a consistent one, the behavior may automatically indicate that imaging has taken place, although for the most part the introspection is needed to establish the correlation in the first instance.

The impact of questionnaire measures of imagery moved the field of psychology away from the notion of imagery type, and this is well illustrated by Betts's (1909) data on his "Questionnaire Upon Mental Imagery." Betts's most significant findings were that there are strong individual differences in ability to image voluntarily and that vivid imagery is distributed fairly evenly amongst the different modalities (contrary to the beliefs of others such as Galton and Titchener). Few subjects lacked the ability to evoke images when required, but marked individual differences were found in the degree of clearness and vividness of the imagery. Armstrong (Galton, 1883), using Galton's questionnaire, claimed that visual imagery predominated. Titchener, too, emphasized the predominance of visual imagery, but French (1902), using the latter questionnaire, failed to confirm this result. Betts's (1909) data revealed an intermodality consistency in the ratings of vividness of imagery that had hitherto been unrecognized. For all seven modalities between 50 and 68% of ratings were associated with points 1, 2, and 3 of the 7-point rating scale, indicating a wide occurrence of vivid imagery. Betts's evidence stressed subjects' general ability to image, even though subjects may select certain forms of imaging and use them somewhat more often than other types. Contemporary research in mental imagery now assumes a general capacity to image, and although current research emphasizes or focuses on the visual modality, investigators no longer really challenge the notion that subjects have the ability to summon up (at request, or spontaneously) images in other modalities as well.

It took some time for the notion of individual differences in imagery capacity to be integrated into research on imagery process, and until the 1970s studies that correlated memory or perception performance with individual differences either in reported imagery at the time of the experiment or individual differences in response to imagery questionnaire items were the exception rather than the rule. At the present stage of the current research scene, however, appeal to differences in reported imagery is well entrenched in the literature. Finke and Kosslyn [1980]; see also Finke [1980], for example, analyzed the variation in performance of good and poor imagers and drew the conclusion that particular processing mechanisms are implicated in the visual system from the fact that vivid imagers show more extensive effects when forming images than do nonvivid imagers. In their study subjects were tested for vividness of imagery prior to the experiment, and the design crossed imagery and perception conditions with separate groups of vivid and nonvivid imagers. Results revealed that vivid imagers showed fields of resolution (defined as regions of the visual field within which two observed or imagined dots could be resolved) in imagery that were comparable in size to fields of resolution in perception. Nonvivid imagers showed fields of resolution that were smaller than those found in perception.

There appear to be a number of factors that are relevant to this growth in interest about individual differences in imagery. Four major ones can be outlined. First, there has been an increased acceptance of verbal reports as data that can reveal important aspects of process. That movement is captured forcibly by Ericsson and Simon (1980), who emphasize that verbal reports have been too frequently dismissed in the past as variants of the discredited process of introspection as, according to contemporary argument, their status is really such that they can stand as important data in their own right. Second, relevant to psychology's reassessment of the significance of verbal data there has been a concomitant growth in its recognition of the complexities of cognitive functioning; the idiosyncracies of subjects' responses are now open to detection by new and novel procedures of assessment. The third factor in this resurgence of interest in imagery ability assessment is the added sensitivity of researchers in the issue of demand characteristics as an alternative means of explaining experimental effects. Investigators have come to rely, for example, on what subjects say about an experiment and what they think about its purpose in order to discount alternative explanations of the data in terms of subjects' expectations or perceptions about the appropriateness of their response. Kosslyn et al. (1978), for instance, showed that images may have spatial properties and demonstrated that response latencies associated with imagery are positively associated with actual physical distances on a map. In this instance the results suggest that subjects deal with their mental image scanning in a way similar to that in which they deal with actual visual scanning of pictures. Richman et al. (1979) countered by arguing that Kosslyn's results could be due to demand characteristics associated with his test procedures and suggested that subjects' knowledge of moving objects and their characteristics influenced their response latencies in the mental travel test situation. The debate is continuing (Mitchell & Richman, 1980), and although this example is outside the scope of this chapter, we use it to illustrate the argument that the status of subjects' reports as providing prime emphasis on the source of potential artifact (threatening the validity of the investigators' data) has served implicitly to enhance the status of subjects' reports about other aspects of their experience—namely, the subjective features or characteristics (e.g., vividness and clarity) of their mental imagery.

The final factor associated with this resurgence of interest in the assessment of individual differences is the movement of imagery research away from the analysis of function to the investigation of process. We digress briefly to emphasize this point . Broadly speaking (Sheehan, in press), several distinct eras in the history of imaginative consciousness can be outlined. The first derives from psychology's initial philosophical concerns about introspection and its status. This issue surfaces frequently in the discipline (Ericsson & Simon, 1980). The second era stems from behaviorism's rejection of the study of imagery in principle where imagery came not only to be discussed as something without functional significance, but as a phenomenon that didn't really exist. The genuineness of mental phenomena reasserted itself, however, and psychology moved away from the strictures of behaviorism to argue vigorously for the reality and relevance of imagery. This is the era that was heralded by advances in brain research, dreaming, and analyses of thought processes. The movement reached its highpoint in the early 1970s. During this stage there was renewed interest in self-report scales of imagery functioning and ability differences as they related to both memory and perceptual performance, and also with imagery as an important component of thought in the subject's stream of consciousness. This last facet, in particular, led to the development of new procedures of assessment that aimed to recognize more sensitively than others that came before, the complexities and intricacies of human consciousness. Imagery research is now in a fourth (and obviously not final) period characterized by theoretical sophistication. Questions about how imagery function have come to be replaced by questions about why it operates in the way that it does. This is the era of debate about mental imagery as involving pictorial or propositional representations (Anderson, 1978) and of the concept of imagery as analogous to displays generated on a cathode ray tube (CRT) by a computer program (Kosslyn et al., 1979). As a result of this emphasis on process, new and innovative procedures of testing have been developed to explore implications for process, and verbal testimony has come to be accepted as just one more tool in the investigator's armentarium for analysis of mechanism.

This brief look at the history of imagery and the development of its procedures of assessment serves to prepare us for discussing a variety of modes of assessment that, for the most part, stress the relevance of verbal testimony. There are instances where investigators have attempted to develop strictly objective measures of assessment, and we discuss these later in relation to eidetic imagery, which is the imagery phenomenon that has generated the most excitement in this respect. We move first, however, to outline some of the general issues that are current in the field of assessment and to classify the various tests that has been developed. We then, in turn, examine objective tests of (eidetic) imagery, review self-report questionnaires and the data bearing upon their utility, and consider the development of new procedures of assessment that attempt to focus more on the idiosyncracies of subjects' experiences. The latter type of measure illustrates most forcibly the need to consider the behavior *and* experience of subjects in relation to the test situations in which they are placed. Finally, we conclude the chapter by drawing out some issues for future research that have been relatively untapped and require attention.

SOME GENERAL ISSUES

It is important to recognize the part method plays in the emergence (and ensuing understanding) of imagery phenomena. The interleaving of function, process, and method represents a major issue for consideration in the field (Sheehan, in press), and a range of methodologies exists for investigating imagery [see Richardson (1969) and Sheehan (1978) for review], each conveying different implications for measurement. They range from relying heavily to not at all on subjects' testimonies about their imagery experience. The more objective paradigms relate to the analysis of selective interference effects involving modality conflict (Brooks, 1967), reaction times to similar and dissimilar stimuli (Kosslyn, 1980; Posner, 1973), and the analysis of mental transformations (Cooper & Shepard, 1973). The more subjective and experience-based methodologies (that are heavily dependent on verbal testimony) relate to ongoing features of the stream of consciousness (Pope & Singer, 1978) and retrospective accounts of events as previously experienced (Sheehan & McConkey, 1982.) Independent of this classification of models or strategies of research, investigators may treat subjects' testimonies about their imagery as primary data for analysis, either by collecting evidence on subjects' abilities beforehand or incorporating individual differences in subjects' capacities formally into the design of the experiment (Finke & Kosslyn, 1980). Attempts may also be made to statistically illustrate underlying dimensions or processes that account for individual variation in subjects' reported experience (Singer & Antrobus, 1963, 1972).

Considering the range of methodologies and modes of measurement that exist, it is important to recognize that approaches to cognitive assessment clearly vary in the ease of access they gain to relevant cognitive information (Kendall & Korgeski, 1979), and it is not at all clear how we can relate aptitude for imagery as measured by the tests that we employ in one situation to the manifestation of imagery skills in other situations. In addition, we need to differentiate what makes imagery different from thinking, remembering, and seeing (Finke, 1980) and how well imagery measured by one set of tasks correlates with the imagery evoked by other procedures of assessment, both in and across different situations. The fact that imagery as measured by self-ratings may not be the same as the process underlying other (e.g., objectives) tests of imagery raises the question of the convergent or discriminant validity of the measures. The data need to define for us not only the relationship among the various measures, but how the measures converge (or diverge) with respect to the underlying process that is being assumed.

Kendall and Korgeski (1979, p. 18) capture well the challenge that faces the researcher when they define some of the issues that they consider are relevant to understanding imagery. An "image . . . of short duration and sometimes minimal salience must be translated (inexactly) into language, edited (probably) for social acceptability or to fit demand characteristics, and finally spoken to the clinician or researcher. He or she must then try to understand this communication, translate it into something that has meaning . . . and compare it on a variety of characteristics with similar data from other individuals." Here Kendall and Korgeski raise the many problems of validity that threaten imagery assessment (e.g., those that illustrate artifact as an alternative explanation of subjects' reports) and the difficulties of measuring the process in question at the time when it occurs. This last problem is illustrated, in particular, by the problems of assessing eidetic imagery. Here, the procedures of measurement themselves may interfere with the phenomena being investigated, and one can anticipate some of the advantages of experience-based procedures of assessment that are more specifically designed to tap the immediacy of subjects' experience.

With these general issues in mind, we move now to broadly classify the tests of imagery that are discussed in the literature. We then sample the different types of test and review evidence available on their reliability and validity.

CLASSIFICATION OF MEASURES

For the most part, the measurement of imagery function has focused on the assessment of imagery *ability*. The first category relates to the performance measures where imagery ability is inferred from behavioral performance on samples of test items or selected cognitive tasks. These tests are classifiable as "objective" and derive in nature from the early objective tests of Woodworth, Fernald, and Angell that we have already discussed in our opening remarks. The performance tests that are most interesting, however, are those that have been rather uniquely developed in association with the assessment of eidetic imagery; we review these in more detail later in the chapter since the field of eidetic imagery has generated a great deal of excitement and debate about the appropriateness of specific test procedures and perhaps can lay best claim to generating the "most objective" tests of all.

Related to this category of ability tests are those defined as being spatial in character. Although these are often explicitly aimed at arousing imagery when they are administered, imagery on the tests is generally associated with the mental manipulation of spatial relationships. Examples of tests that probe this dimension of cognitive functioning are the spatial relations subtest of Thurstone's (1938) test of Primary Mental Abilities, the Minnesota Paper Form Board (Likert & Quasha, 1970), Thurstone and Jeffrey's (1956) Flags test, and Bennett et al. (1947) Space Relations test.

By far the largest number of tests of imagery ability fall into our second category, the questionnaire or self-report inventories, where subjects are asked to report on characteristics of their imagery such as its vividness or the ease with which it can be controlled. Examples of self-rating measures of this kind that we reviewed in our previous article (White et al., 1977) are Galton's (1883) breakfast table questionnaire, the shortened form of the Betts Questionnaire Upon Mental Imagery [QMI; Sheehan (1967), Gordon's (1949) Test of Visual Imagery Control, Marks's (1973) Vividness of Visual Imagery Questionnaire (VVIQ), Singer and Antrobus's Imaginal Processes Inventory (Singer & Antrobus, 1963, 1972), Paivio's (1971) Individual Differences

Questionnaire (IDQ), and Richardson's (1977a) shortened version of Paivio's scale, which focuses on a particular subset of 15 items selected from the original test.

Our third major category of measures deals with the assessment of aspects of subjects' consciousness that more directly reflect experience. Examples of such techniques are the thought-sampling method of assessment developed by Klinger (1978), which attempts to assess subjects' "current concerns." The essential difference between this kind of assessment and questionnaire modes of measurements is that self-report inventories of the kind illustrated by the QMI, VVIQ, and IDQ for the most part involve retrospective comment by the subject on past experiences. It can be argued that tests tapping the ongoing stream of experience may be more valid for measuring those aspects of cognition that characterize current everyday thinking. There are several variations in method that fall within this category. Subjects, for instance, may be asked to think out loud, speaking continuously while thinking. There are problems with this technique, as Klinger (1978) indicates, and a more sensitive mode of assessment is for the investigator to stop the subject in the middle of what he or she is doing and request narrative descriptions of what has been occurring in consciousness just before the interruption. Although this procedure is flexible and unobtrusive, it has the disadvantage of engaging the subject in retrospective report, but it exploits recent memory and contrasts with questionnaire measures where items are relevant to memory of events that rarely have taken place in the immediate past. Procedures tapping the immediate experience of subjects can lend themselves also to the application of specific rating procedures. A major advantage of tests of this kind is the sensitivity with which they address the idiosyncratic aspects of subjects' experience, and that goal is best pursued by facilitating subjects' participation in the measurement process in an active, involving fashion.

A number of techniques have applied particular procedures to facilitate the active involvement of subjects, and one test that we discuss in some detail is the Experiential Analysis Technique (EAT) (Sheehan et al., 1978). Here, the investigator typically probes in a relatively unstructured fashion to solicit information about imagery, cognitions, and feelings, and rating scales are then systematically applied to the data. The general thrust of in vivo thought sampling, the EAT, and other tests in this category, is that they are suited to detecting qualitative characteristics of subjects' thought processes and are appropriate for the assessment of cognitive styles or characteristic modes of cognition that subjects may bring to bear on their attempts to solve the tasks set for them by the investigator.

We turn now to consider examples of these three major categories of imagery assessment: (1) the assessment of eidetic imagery, discussion of which we use to focus on the development of specific objective tests; (2) data available on the utility of self-report measures of imagery function, particularly as the data bear on those tests in a way that was not discussed in our 1977 review; and (3) the EAT and the data that bear on this test which we discuss as an example of a mode of measuring imagery function that samples the complexities of consciousness that questionnaire measures and other modes of assessment frequently exclude or fail to consider. We don't consider in detail specific modes of assessment that are designed for particular purposes, such as Wilson and Barber's (1978) Creative Imagination Scale (CIS), which specifically uses suggestibility test tasks in its assessment of subjects' abilities, and Hollon and Kendall's Automatic Thought Questionnaire, which has been designed to study negative cognitions associated with clinical depression (Kendall and Korgeski, 1979).

OBJECTIVE MEASURES AND EIDETIC IMAGERY ASSESSMENT

Eidetic imagery is essentially defined by the presence of an externally projected image of an object that is distinguished from a negative afterimage with respect to its duration (it is long), its properties of color (it is positive in color rather than complementary or negative in character), and the fact that it can be scanned with ease without any apparent lessening of its intensity or clarity. Definition of the phenomenon has been extensively discussed by Haber and Haber (1964), who outlined multiple criteria for specifying its presence. Aside from those just outlined, the eidetic subject typically describes his or her other image in the present tense and recalls the details with relative (although not complete) accuracy. Somewhat more relentlessly than for other forms of imagery, investigators of eidetic imagery have pursued objective modes of assessment that have attempted to move away from essential reliance or trust on what the experiencing subject testifies. And more so than other forms of imagery (e.g., memory imagery), investigators continue to quarrel about the criteria for defining its occurrence.

As Haber (1979) indicates, there are essentially two main choices regarding procedure that are available to the researcher. The investigator may present a stimulus object or picture to the subject and test subsequently for the presence or absence of eidetic imagery or instruct subjects directly to imagine a stimulus or set of stimulus events. The picture-induction method is easily adaptable to the laboratory and avoids the problems of instructing subjects to image, thereby losing control of the defining characteristics of the stimulus to be imaged. The predominant procedure of testing is the easel procedure, which presents a picture to subjects on an easel and subjects are asked to focus on the same location when the picture is removed. On removal, the subject is then asked what he or she can see. The demand to report a picture that is "out there" (on the easel) is strong and clear in this instance, but it is argued that the enormous variability in the facility with which eidetic imagery is reported chracterizes the genuineness of the subject's response; eidetic imagery is reported relatively rarely, and it seems hardly plausible to assert that the obvious demand character of the procedures operates effectively on only a very small number of persons. The protocols for the easel procedure (Haber & Haber, 1964; Leask et al., 1969) suggest that other difficulties are more likely to affect our interpretation of the data, however; Jaynes (1979), for instance, comments that the naming of objects by the subject during testing can facilitate the fading of the image and thus argues that a nonverbal technique for testing of the image is to be preferred. Jaynes's concern here is supported by the data collected by Haber showing that eidetic children can and frequently do prevent an image from forming by naming or labeling the objects in a picture while seeing it.

The vigorous search for nonverbal techniques of assessment can be explained on other grounds as well, and the reasons for the developments in technique are historical as well as methodological. The easel procedure was initially devised by Jaensch to explore his theory about afterimages, and the technique was adapted directly by Haber and developed. Afterimages have particular properties that lend themselves to nonverbal testing (e.g., procedures can be applied to nonverbally test the image's predictable color features; and objective testing can be made of the afterimage's spatial properties, following Emmert's Law). One suspects, however, that a more plausible reason for the search for objectivity lies in the multiplicity of subjective criteria that have been adopted through time by investigators who claim they have defined the presence of eidetic imagery (Doob, 1965, Haber & Haber, 1964, Sheehan, 1973, Siipola & Hayden, 1965). The phenomenon of eidetic imagery is rare but compelling when it does occur, and investigators have had to appeal to several, not just one, indices of verbal report to try to establish its validity. If the response is so compelling for so few, it would indeed be desirable to have just one objective procedure that captures its presence. And the search for that procedure has been intense.

The random-dot stereograms test of eidetic imagery aims to achieve this goal and is largely accepted as an "unfakable" test of eidetic imagery. Following this procedure, the subject views a computer-generated random-dot pattern until an appropriate image is built up, and on viewing another matrix of random dots, fusion of the first with the second reveals a stimulus form that cannot be identified by inspection of either figure alone. The technique was used with remarkable success by Stromeyer and Psotka (1970), who produced a subject who could identify the hidden forms reliably and correctly. Although their exact findings have not been replicated, if one accepts that the forms are impossible to deduce from the stimulus procedure (as seems reasonable), this single case provides clear and objective evidence for the presence of eidetic imagery. The basic principle of the random-dot stereogram test (the fusing of stimuli to indicate a hidden stimulus form) is captured in Haber's own adaptation of the technique, which relies on the fusing of two concrete pictures. Following this version, a meaningful picture is separated into separate pictures by assigning the different contours of the single version to one or the other of two divided pictures. Either decomposed version is presented for a brief period of time sufficient to facilitate an eidetic image and is then removed. The other version is then presented after a brief delay. The alignment of an eidetic image of the first picture with the second produces a coherent and meaningful whole that is easily reported by the subject (e.g., the emergence of a human face).

Haber claims that there are difficulties with the stereogram test that are overcome by his composite picture test, but the debate about the suitability of the two sets of procedures is not easily resolved by the data at hand. It appears that the incidence of eidetic imagery that occurs when the random-dot stereogram method is adopted is far smaller than when eidetic imagery is measured using Haber's composite picture method. Stromeyer and Psotka (1970) demonstrated success with only one subject, and Merritt (1979), using a self-test modification of the random-dot stereogram, found not a single person in a million subjects who was able to demonstrate eidetic imagery when asked to perform in the presence of the experimenter; even one of Haber's subjects who was tested for such imagery could not perform the task successfully. Merritt (1979, p. 612) concluded that eidetic imagery must for most eidetikers "be a very delicate mental achievement." The most successful study to use the stereogram method is one conducted by Wallace (1978), who found four subjects in his research program who reported eidetic imagery. Wallace focused on highly hypnotizable subjects who were asked to age regress and who had memories of eidetic abilities in childhood. Spanos et al. (1979), however, using the same type of subject found no one who was successful on the stereogram task, and they could not replicate Wallace's findings.

Looking at the data collectively, the extent of infrequency of occurrence of eidetic imagery by use of the most stringent objective test available seems to challenge the notion that a small subset of the population (mostly children) will demonstrate eidetic imagery when appropriately tested. Haber (1979) makes the point, however, that the random-dot stereogram procedure is too difficult for subjects and that the picture composite test was developed precisely because it provided meaningful stimuli with which the child could work. Failure on either test (random-dot stereogram or composite picture) could also indicate that the child is unable to satisfy the demands of testing; those who fail the tests, for instance, may still be quite eidetic (by other criteria) but may not have sufficiently complete, persistent, or movable images to enable them to perform the test task (Haber, 1979). Certainly, the data collected indicate that not all subjects who satisfy the other criteria for the presence of eidetic imagery (e.g., report of positive image color and present tense in description) pass the composite picture test, and it remains unclear whether this expresses the fact that the procedures of testing are inadequate or highlights a limitation in the proficiency with which subjects can image in this particular fashion (eidetically).

There are other variants of the fusion technique. Julesz (1971), for instance, describes random-dot correlograms as an alternative method that can be adopted. Correlograms are similar to stereograms, except that the shapes that are indicated are not the result of binocular disparities; instead, the right and left random-dot arrays are identical except for uncorrelated or negatively correlated areas. Under conditions of binocular viewing, the identical areas create binocular fusion, whereas binocular rivalry is created by the uncorrelated or negatively correlated areas. The subject's task is then to report which quadrant of the stimulus figure contains the rivalry inducing patch. The technique would still be termed too difficult by Haber but is an interesting variant of the fusion technique that yet remains to be researched in detail.

A major problem that we have discussed in relation to the easel procedure is that the verbalizations of the eidetic subject during the inspection of an inducing picture may hinder or interfere with the completeness or accuracy of the eidetic image. A specific procedure that overcomes this difficulty and is relatively easy for the subject to execute is that of tracing. The technique has been suggested by Jaynes (1979) and independently applied by Dirks (1978) for a subject located by Dirks and Neisser (1977), to provide a further way of indexing eidetic imagery in an objective fashion. Essentially, the technique involves tracing an eidetic image for the purpose of comparison with a tracing of the actual object or a memory drawing of the same picture (which can be by the same subject or by other eidetic or noneidetic children). Jaynes suggests that comparison of tracings by eidetic children with memory drawings of the same stimulus by noneidetic children is likely to reinforce the claims that are traditionally made for the relative accuracy of eidetic imagery as compared with the other forms of imagery. The technique, however, has not been widely researched and remains to be generally adopted by workers in the field. Data that are in hand [cited by Neisser (1979)] suggest that tracings by eidetiker subjects who are tested do not faithfully reproduce outlines previously produced by superimposing the tracing paper on the actual object. Results indicate that the tracing of an eidetic image is something the subject makes up rather than sees and that eidetic imagery represents a construct rather than a copy of the actual object.

Currently the data suggest that tests that probe the subjective aspects of people's eidetic experience are more likely to demonstrate differences between eidetic and other forms of imagery. Marks (1979), for example, found differences between eidetikers and control subjects by use of an "Open Circle" test that was borrowed from Hatakeyama (1975). Following this technique, a small circle is placed in front of the subject who is instructed to gaze at its center and told that the investigator will name a color. The subject then tries to image the color that was named inside the circle and reports what is observed. Data reveal the presence of strong color reports for eidetikers as compared with control subjects and qualitative and quantitative differences between the two groups of subjects in other respects as well. Coming to a similar conclusion to that offered by Neisser, Marks asserts that the basic nature of eidetic imagery is not reproductive, but flexible and constructive. Haber theorizes about eidetic imagery, however, in a way that allows for relative (not absolute) accuracy and recognizes that eidetic images are built up on the basis of the experiencing subject's cognitive state at the moment and are unlikely to be completely or faithfully accurate.

In summary, the data that are available present eidetic imagery as a puzzling phenomenon that continues to challenge researchers' ingenuity for developing new and innovative procedures of testing. Reports of its presence are highly compelling in a small sample of the population, and tests that are subjective (viz., those that use verbal report criteria) seem more likely to yield evidence of its presence than tests that are objective or attempt to rely exclusively on behavioral indices of performance. No other form of imagery, though, highlights quite so acutely the contributions to the understanding of imagery and how it functions that can be made by *both* subjective and objective assessment, and we hope in this respect that the detail of our discussion is instructive.

We turn now to focus on questionnaire measures of imagery. We aim to assess the contribution that such verbal report tests make to the understanding of imagery and to summarily review recent evidence relating to their correlates.

QUESTIONNAIRE MEASURES OF IMAGERY

In our 1977 article we extensively reviewed verbal report measures of imagery functioning and reported on data associated with their reliability and validity. Concurrent with our review, Ernest (1977) published a comprehensive survey of the literature on individual differences in imagery ability in the areas of memory, learning, and conceptual processes. In her review she contrasted the relative merits of self-ratings and objective measures in detail and drew conclusions that were in relative harmony with our own and that concur with those made in more recent surveys of techniques of imagery assessment (Kendall & Korgeski, 1979). We concluded earlier that the data generally fail to indicate the actual processes or dimensions that the various tests aim to measure, although the utility of many of the tests has been amply demonstrated. We now consider recent evidence on the correlates of function in relation to self-report measures of imagery; only the major tests of imagery function are reviewed.

Correlates of Function

Betts QMI

This shortened, 35-item, version of Betts's (1909) original Questionnaire Upon Mental Imagery measures imagery vividness in seven modalities (Sheehan, 1967). Imagery vividness as measured by the test has been positively related to: creativity in men but not in women (Forisha, 1978); improvement in a physical skill with the use of mental practice (White et al., 1979); increase, but not decrease, in heart rate (Carroll et al., 1979); field independence in women (Sousa-Poza et al., 1979); extraversion–introversion (if level of neurosis is controlled) (Stricklin & Penk, 1980); higher sexual arousability (Harris et al., 1980); and psychadelic drug flashbacks (Matefy, 1980).

Gordon's Test of Imagery Control

This test was designed to differentiate autonomous from controlled visual imagery (Gordon, 1949), and scores on the 12-item test have been positively related to performance on a divergent thinking task (Durndell & Wetherick, 1976b), production of verbal images (Khatena, 1976); vocabulary and IQ scores (Tedford & Penk, 1977); and hypnotic insusceptiblity in females but not males (Spanos et al., 1976b).

Vividness of Visual Imagery Questionnaire (VVIQ)

Marks' (1973) VVIQ is an extended (16-item) version of the QMI visual imagery subscale. As assessed by this test, visual imagery has been related positively to cross-modal matching (Cairns & Coll, 1977), paired associate recall (Rossi & Fingeret, 1977), hypnotizability (Bowers, 1978, Coe et al., 1980; Hoen, 1978), larger McCullough aftereffects (Finke & Schmidt, 1978), frequency of dream recall (Richardson, 1979), extent of acceleratory cardiac control (Carrol, et al., 1979), memory performance (McKelvie & Demers, 1979), performance in a visual memory task among those using an image coding strategy (Berger & Gaunitz, 1979), the functional equivalence between imagery and perception (Finke, 1979, 1980; Finke & Kosslyn, 1980), and right lateral eye movements (Otteson, 1980).

Individual Differences Questionnaire (IDQ)

This test as devised by Paivio (1971), and its abbreviated (15-item) form (the Verbalizer–Visualizer Questionnaire (VVQ), defined by Richardson, 1977a), assesses two habitual thinking modes: imaginal and verbal. Visualizers have been shown to be better than verbalizers in the recall of high-imagery material (Hiscock, 1976), have more regular breathing patterns (Richardson, 1977a), have produced less uniform eye movement responses (Richardson, 1978), and report more spontaneous visual extrasensory experiences (Irwin, 1979).

Imaginal Processes Inventory (IPI)

As developed by Singer and Antrobus (1972), the IPI contains among its 28 scales two that have special relevance in the imagery area: Visual Imagery in Daydreams and Auditory Imagery in Daydreams. Although these scales have not received wide individual attention, Huba et al. (1977) report that both have high loadings on the same second-order factor they labeled Positive–Constructive Daydreaming. Cundiff and Gold (1979) also report that the Visual Imagery in Daydream scale is significantly correlated with Gordon's test of imagery control.

New Self-Report Tests

Since our last review a number of new self-report imagery tests that cover a variety of topics have been developed. Some of these tests are purely experimental—yielding scores, for example, that define group membership (Ikeda & Hirai, 1976; Owens & Richardson, 1979); others are based on specific theoretical considerations [e.g., relating to suggestibility; see Barber & Wilson (1979) and Wilson & Barber (1978)]; but by far the largest group consists of tests designed to overcome apparent deficiencies in existing self-report questionnaires. Guy (Guy & McCarter, 1978), for instance, developed a scale specifically to measure the vividness of emotive images; Lane (1977) saw the need for a new, longer, and more diverse measure of imagery control, whereas Switras (1978) produced an alternate test instrument that assessed both vividness and control, and Reing (1978) developed a multisensory imagery (MSI) scale to evaluate teacher competency.

We now examine a sample of the factors affecting imagery test scores on self-report measures of the kind we have reviewed. Specifically, we consider evidence relating to sex differences, social desirability, and the role of suggestion.

Factors Affecting Test Data

Sex Differences

Data reported in Table 7.1 strongly support the position that sex differences in self-reported imagery are nonsignificant. These unanimous findings are in direct contrast to those in our earlier review (White et al., 1977), where we

TABLE 7.1. Sex Differences in Self-Reported Imagery

Investigator	Sample	Tests	Findings
Lane (1977)	Undergraduate	Own test	No significant differences
Beech & Leslie (1978)	Undergraduate	QMI	No significant differences
Guy & McCarter (1978)	Undergraduate & administrators	QMI; Guy emotive imagery scale	No significant differences
Reing (1978)	Teacher trainees	MIS	No significant differences
Ashton & White (1980)	Undergraduate	QMI	No significant differences

reported a tendency for females to report more imagery than males. Previous reports of sex differences may be due in part to an artifact of the tests that were used (Ashton & White, 1980); however, the fact that a variety of tests were used in the studies (Table 7.1) suggests that the absence of sex differences is a valid finding.

Social Desirability and Test Responses

The issue of how much questionnaire measures of imagery are influenced by demand-type characteristics persists as a vexing unsolved problem. Further evidence, summarized in Table 7.2, supports our previous conclusion that "subjects' expectancies about responses do affect test scores at least to some extent" (White et al., 1977, p. 156), and general findings on factors affecting the interpretation of verbal report findings (Ericsson & Simon, 1980) serve to reinforce the same conclusion.

Relevance of Suggestion

Many of the studies that reveal a relationship between imagery ability and speed of processing point to suggestion as an important variable. Ashton et al. (1978), for example, found that good imagers (as assessed by the visual items of Betts's original test) recognized whether a projected thumbless image of a hand was that of the right or left hand significantly faster than did poorer imagers only if the experimenter suggested that evoking an image may help to solve the problem. Similarly, Berger and Gaunitz (1977), using a picture discrimination test, found that good imagers were faster than poor ones [as assessed by Marks's (1973) VVIQ test], but only if an image strategy was used by the subject. Finally, Ernest (1978) showed that high imagers

TABLE 7.2.   Social Desirability and Performance Outcomes on Self-Report Tests of Imagery

Investigator	Subjects	Test Situations	Results
McLemore (1976)	U/G	A factor analytic study of imagery, response bias, and social desirability	Betts's QMI and Gordon's test scores unaffected by response bias but susceptible to social desirability
Hiscock (1978)	U/G	MC;[a] QMI (visual and auditory scales); IDQ & Gordon's test of imagery control	No significant correlations of any test with MC
McKelvie and Demers (1979)	High School & U/G	E instructions & VVIQ	Instructions, but not format, significantly effected subjects' responses
Richardson (1979)	U/G	MC & VVIQ	Social desirability positively related to scores on VVIQ

[a]MC represents social desirability scale (Crowne & Marlowe, 1964).

were faster at picture recognition than were poor ones [here the individual questionnaire of Ernest and Paivio (1971) was used to categorize the subjects]. Again, however, the effect was found only if the use of a nonverbal (imagery) strategy was suggested to the subjects.

Some Summary Observations

For the most part, in contrast to performance tests of imagery, self-report ratings of imagery tend to correlate together only moderately at best. Self-report measures of imagery also correlate hardly at all with spatial ability tests, and studies continue to confirm that there are multiple dimensions within single test domains; McGee (1979), for instance, concludes that there are two factors responsible for subjects' scores in the spatial domain alone.

Close analysis of the content of the different self-report measures, however, reveals features of the tests that may help explain the absence of uniformity in the data and the relative paucity of evidence that supports the discriminant validity of the measures. As Ernest (1977) indicates, for example, the VVIQ and IDQ are exclusively visual in the emphasis of their items, whereas the Betts QMI spreads its items over seven different sensory modalities and has less of an element of imagery control associated with its items than does the VVIQ. Use of thinking also separately characterizes the IDQ. These and other differences may help to index the multidimensional character of the various self-report inventories that are available and that prevents us, as Ernest argues, from making global statements about the construct validity of the tests in question. Some surprising discrepancies nevertheless highlight the measures involved. The data tell us, for instance (Ernest, 1977), that self-ratings of imagery control are more obviously related to objective measures of spatial imagery than to self-ratings of imagery vividness. Yet, analysis of the content of Gordon's test of imagery control would suggest there ought to be a strong association with vividness of imagery—if imagery ability is a common dimension underlying performance across tests (Ashton & White, 1974; White & Ashton, 1977).

Results from studies that investigate the correlations among the various measures continue to be inconsistent. Rimm and Bottrell (1969), for instance, examined the pattern of relationships among a sample of measures of imagery vividness (including self-ratings of vividness, test of paired associate learning, a picture memory task, and changes in behavior associated with the imagining of emotionally arousing and neutral scenes). Self-ratings of imagery correlated obviously only with the response change ratings, and not with the other measures that were expected to tap imagery ability; and comparable inconsistencies were found by Rehm (1973) and Hiscock (1978). Studies on the reliability of the imagery ability measures, however, continue to reveal that self-report inventories are reliable and stable in the scores they yield within subjects and over time on the same subjects who are retested. The accuracy of what the tests measure is far more at issue, it seems, than

TABLE 7.3.   Internal Reliabilities of Self-Report Questionnaires

Investigator	N	Sample	Estimate	Test	Results
Westcott & Rosenstock (1976)	147	U/G	Alpha	QMI Gordon	.90–.94 .53–.74
Rossi (1977)	119	U/G	Alpha	VVIQ	.91 session 1 .94 session 2
Cartwright et al. (1978)	118	U/G	Alpha	Modified QMI Figural Mimetic Symbolic	 .75 .80 .80
Guy & McCarter (1978)	67	U/G and administrators	Alpha	Guy emotive imagery scale	.86
Reing (1978)	63	U/G and teacher trainees	Kendall's W	MIS	.81
Switras (1978)	350	U/G	Alpha		Own test

					Form A	Form B
				Vividness	.78–.97	.79–.97
				Control	.68–.95	.71–.95
Barber & Wilson (1979)	22	—	Split half	CIS	.89	
Taylor & Falcomer (1979)	166	Students 14–17	Split half	IPI .64–.91	16 scales	

is the consistency of the scores that the tests produce. Tables 7.3 and 7.4 present the relevant data in this respect, and demonstrate the general stability of self report test scores. Table 7.3 shows that internal reliabilities are generally high for both older and more recent tests; and with the exception of the VVQ, the test–retest reliability of the imagery measures is also high.

We move now to consider our third and final category of assessment and

TABLE 7.4.   Test–Retest Reliability Data

Investigator	N	Sample	Interval, Weeks	Estimate	Test	Results
Westcott & Rosenstock (1976)	147	U/G	2	r	QMI Gordon	.72–.75 .81–.86
Rossi (1977)	119	U/G	7	r	VVIQ	.73
Reing (1978)	63	Teacher trainees	15	r	MIS	.84
Barber & Wilson (1979)	22	Students	—	r	CIS	.82
Cundiff & Gold (1979)	39	Female students	6–8	r	IPI (7 scales)	.55–.86
Warren & Good (1979)	53	Junior high-school students	3	r	VVQ M F	.49 .29
					Total	.48

to sample the type of assessment that more directly taps the experiential aspects of subjects' imagery performance.

EXPERIENCE-BASED MEASURES OF IMAGERY

A major goal of most imagery assessment instruments is the measurement of nonverbal consciousness in as accurate and sensitive a manner as possible. Tests may approach that objective in many different ways, and some are more successful in realizing it than others. Behavioral tests attempt to index nonverbal consciousness in an objective and quantifiable way and rely essentially on observations of actual behavior to produce test scores that are then frequently related to subjective report. Self-report tests have the disadvantage that they involve the subject in making judgments about their experiences while they are imaging, thus raising the question of whether the process of making that judgment interferes with the nature of the cognizing that is being assessed. Traditional self-report scales of imagery also focus on limited aspects of imagery functioning and review only a portion of the experiences of the imaging subject. The methods that most conspicuously attempt to overcome this last difficulty and that aim to avoid the limitations that can result from encouraging inferences by subjects about their cognitions are the phenomenologically based modes of measurement that we reviewed early in the chapter. These tests include in vivo thought sampling, thinking out aloud, and event recording where subjects are requested to indicate whenever a particular kind of cognitive event occurs in their consciousness (Klinger, 1978). The techniques incorporated by this approach are deliberately broad ranging in the aspects of subjects' experiences that they address, and they seem particularly appropriate to analyzing the complexity of consciousness. Such techniques make certain assumptions, as do other tests, however. Subjects, for instance, are assumed to be articulate about their experiences, and this seems far less likely if subjects are hindered in any way in their efforts to remember. Conscious events involving imagery are subtle and variable, and the complexity they entail may well be difficult, if not impossible, to capture if the subject is not assisted in some way to retrieve the events that have happened in exactly the way that they occurred. The point should also be made, however, that an independent person who has no knowledge of the events that took place is best equipped to inquire into a subject's experiences; such an investigator is likely to be less biased about what is expected.

One technique that is phenomenologically based and has been developed to measure aspects of cognitive experience through the aided recall of immediately past occurring events is the experiential analysis technique (EAT), which was originally developed for analyzing the characteristic modes of cognition of susceptible subjects in the hypnotic context (Sheehan et al., 1978). The method, however, has applications beyond the field of hypnosis.

It aims to focus primarily on the experience of the subject just past and to sample multiple dimensions of cognitive functioning. Its distinctive methodological features are that it aids recall in a way that attempts to facilitate the access of relevant cognitive information and explicitly taps the idiosyncratic features of subjects' cognitive experience, including imagery, fantasy, and other processes of imagination. Procedurally, the technique employs videotape playback of a preceding test session in the presence of an independent investigator who inquires in a relatively unstructured fashion into subjects' experiences as they are stimulated and recalled while viewing the videotape playback of the previous testing. The test itself is an adaptation of the method of interpersonal process recall (IPR) (Kagan et al., 1963), a method originally developed for use in the counseling context.

The videotape playback of testing (offering subjects a concrete display of events associated, for instance, with the arousal of imagery) offers subjects an immediate and literal record of past experience that facilitates spontaneous comment about its cognitive accompaniments. The method dictates that subjects themselves direct the discussion of their experience by stopping the playback and describing the nature of their feelings, imagery, and cognitions that occurred at the time. The inquirer uses a number of different probes to elicit data, each focusing on potentially relevant aspects of the subject's experience. Inquiry questions are described in detail elsewhere (Sheehan and McConkey, 1982), but are intended to minimize the cues available to subjects as to what are "appropriate" responses to give.

Specific modes of cognition have been isolated that reflect much (though not all) of the variability of subjects' reactions. These categories reflect discrete styles of cognition in subjects' recall of the immediately preceding events, and a number of the styles clearly implicate imagery function. Since the styles are designed to tap responsiveness in the hypnotic situation, they are geared essentially to the different ways in which subjects process suggestions that they receive. The two modes of cognition that have emerged as most relevant to imagery assessment are the "independent" and "constructive" styles. Subjects illustrating an independent style are those who display a tendency to reinterpret the communications they receive in terms of their personal views and experiences. The constructive style, on the other hand, expresses more the tendency of subjects to process the information they receive in a schematic way so as to structure events in an active and effortful fashion. Subjects demonstrating this second style do not necessarily interpret events personally, but rather cognitively respond by actively seeking out ways to synthesize the experience being suggested.

Data on the reliability of these two styles and other imagery-related variables have been provided by Sheehan and McConkey (1982). Judgments were made by two independent raters on EAT records collected following the testing of 44 subjects on three separate (hypnotic) test tasks. The data were rated in terms of the dimensions of independent cognitive style, constructive cognitive style, the presence of individuation (the tendency to accept the communications of the hypnotist in an idiosyncratic way), imagery vividness, imaginative absorption, and the tendency for involuntary response. For the variables, each dimension was rated on a 5-point scale where 0 represented absence of the dimension and 4 indicated the variable was markedly present; both raters scored all subjects on each test item for the different dimensions, and rater 1 scored 10 subjects in order to index intrarater reliability. Table 7.5 presents the data obtained and indicates high intra- and interreliability across the separate cognitive dimensions considered.

Results were further analyzed for the 44 responsive subjects to assess the correlations among the various measures used. Specifically, data were examined for response to a hypnotic dream and hypnotic hallucination task, both of which represent items on standard hypnotic test scales that are said to tap imagery or fantasy ability. Tables 7.6 and 7.7 present the data for the sets of correlations in relation to each task and show considerable intertask differences in the nature of the associations that were observed. Findings for the hallucination task indicated that independent cognizing was less closely associated with this task than it was with subjects' experience of the dream, and the relationship between independent cognizing and individuation was not as strong as that observed for the data relating to subjects' dream experience (although the association was appreciable for both tasks).

Looking across both tasks, we see that differences in the patterns of associations observed suggest the relevance of considering task-style interactions when formulating the processes that underlie imaginative involvment. The most impressive feature of the data [a feature discussed in more detail elsewhere; see Sheehan & McConkey (1982)] is the heterogeneity of responses. Subtle but meaningful patterns of differences and similarities in process features of experience were indicated in relation to the two test tasks, and data suggested that explanation of the variation in objective response and subjective experience is most appropriately made in terms of the various cognitive skills and strategies that subjects brought to bear on their response to the information on the separate tasks that they received. The differences observed pointed, for the most part, to the fact that task constraints frequently defined the type of cognitive style that subjects employed. Data suggest, for instance, that constructive cognizing was altogether unrelated to successful response on the dream task but was more relevant to successful response on the hallucination task. The validity of the method of assessment overall, however, is reinforced by the essential pattern of high correlations that were found among the variables of imagery, absorption and feeling of involuntariness—variables that the literature would suggest ought to be associated if they tap common underlying dimensions of imaginative involvement.

The essential limitation of the method that has just been reviewed, and one shared in common with questionnaire measures of imagery is that it relies exclusively on the verbal reports of subjects about their experience. The weakness also characterizes objective tests that ultimately derive their

TABLE 7.5.   Inter- and Intrarater Reliability Coefficients for a Sample of Cognitive
Dimensions on Three Hypnotic Test Tasks[a]

	Interrater			Intrarater		
Dimensions	Task 1	Task 2	Task 3	Task 1	Task 2	Task 3
Independent style	.67	.00	.95	1.00	.00	.00
Constructive style	.01	.73	.83	.00	.80	.64
Individuation	.88	.68	.71	.96	.97	.95
Imagery ability	.92	.85	.84	1.00	.87	.95
Absorption	.83	.69	.61	.90	.85	.95
Involuntariness	.81	.44	.70	1.00	.85	.93

Source: Data are taken from results to be published in Sheehan and McConkey (1982).
[a]Task 1 was a dream task, task 2 was a finger-lock test, and task 3 was a hallucination task.

meaning from correlation of behavioral data with subjective testimony. The
variables that can affect or influence verbal reports are many and varied,
but it is important to isolate the factors that affect them so as to determine
the conditions that optimize their accuracy and validity. The EAT situation,
for instance, is vulnerable to incompleteness of memory, as are other forms
of retrospective assessment, but adopts specific conditions of testing so as
to reduce the possibility that subjects will simply fill in gaps in their experience because of their failure to remember the events that actually occurred.
Major issues for research consideration are obviously the directness of prob-
ing, the time between events as experienced and events replayed for recall,
and the expectations that inquirer and subject might have about the kinds
of response that are appropriate. The fact that such methods do yield reliable
data and show a strong degree of association between diverse rating measures
of imagery functioning, however, is encouraging.

    A theme that emerges in our analysis of experience-based assessment of

TABLE 7.6.   Intercorrelation Matrix for Six Cognitive Dimensions for Subjects Responding on
the Dream Task

	Dimensions					
Dimensions	1	2	3	4	5	6
1. Independent cognizing		−.15	.77*	.55*	.54*	−.01
2. Constructive cognizing			.15	.23	.14	−.19
3. Individuation				.86*	.77*	.29
4. Imagery ability					.89*	.51*
5. Absorption						.57*
6. Involuntariness						

Source: data are taken from results to be published in Sheehan and McConkey (1982).
*p < .05.

TABLE 7.7. Intercorrelation Matrix for Six Cognitive Dimensions for Subjects Responding on the Hallucination Task

Dimensions	Dimensions					
	1	2	3	4	5	6
1. Independent cognizing		−.11	.46*	.20	.32	−.14
2. Constructive cognizing			.59*	.23	.42	.07
3. Individuation				.67*	.76*	.36
4. Imagery ability					.82*	.71*
5. Absorption						.54*
6. Involuntariness						

Source: data are taken from results to be published in Sheehan and McConkey (1982).
*$p < .05$.

imagery is one that stresses that test situations are relevant to the nature of the data that imagery procedures yield. The problem raises directly the issue of the degree to which test situations access cognitive information in different ways, thus revealing variable facets of imagery process and function. We turn now to consider this issue in more detail.

RELEVANCE OF TEST SITUATIONS

The growth in ingenuity of methods and procedures that has propelled imagery research into its current era of theoretical sophistication (Sheehan, 1978) has largely ignored the contribution that specific test situations make to the associations that are observed between subjects' reports of imagery and their performance in imagery test settings. Analysis of experience-based assessment by means of the EAT showed, for instance, differences in the pattern of relationships among imagery-related variables depending on the nature of the task being performed. Person–treatment interactions are widely acknowledged as critical to theorizing in the field of personality, but in the field of imagery assessment they remain elusive. In research concerned primarily with the mechanisms of perception (Kosslyn et al., 1979), for example, method dominates in the search for process and researchers' frameworks of explanation rarely reflect the complex combinations that may well be occurring between individual differences in imaginative capacity and stimulus features of the test situations in which the subjects are placed. The lack of correlation between self-report measures of imagery may well be, in part, due to the situational specificity of the items such scales present to subjects. Each questionnaire item on tests such as the QMI, VVIQ, and Gordon's test of imagery control, for example, presents subjects with a given situation with which they are asked to identify in terms of their imagery. The value of such stimulus specificity, as Kendall and Korgeski (1979) note, is that subjects can be presented with stimulus situations that are as close as possible to an investigator's chosen criterion. The contribution of the situation per se, however, is especially difficult to partial out from the data.

A program of research that has recently emphasized the relevance of accounting for situational influences in determining the nature of imagery process and function is a series of studies conducted on individual differences in imaginative assorption (Qualls & Sheehan, 1979, 1981a,b). The research measured subjects' capacities on Tellegen and Atkinson's (1974) self-report scale of absorption and related individual differences in absorption to relaxation performance during electromyograph biofeedback and no-biofeedback conditions of testing. In the first of a series of studies in an integrated program of research, high and low absorption subjects were tested under biofeedback and no-feedback conditions and results analyzed in terms of subjects' average percentage decrease in frontal electromyograph (EMG) activity. Data demonstrated an overall equivalence between the two absorption groups in the two test conditions, but an interaction effect between level of absorption and degree of relaxation. More appreciable EMG reductions occurred during no-biofeedback conditions of testing (as compared with feedback conditions) for the high absorption group. Contrary to what one might expect, high absorption subjects relative to low absorption subjects were disadvantaged in the degree of relaxation that they could attain in the biofeedback situation. The presence of the biofeedback signal hindered the use of imaginal strategies by the high absorption group, and verbal reports taken during a postexperimental interview confirmed this interpretation of the data. A second study in the program manipulated instructions to high- and low-absorption subjects in an attempt to encourage them to use imagery in the test setting (Qualls & Sheehan, 1981b). In this experiment subjects in the biofeedback condition were asked to relax as deeply as they could and were told additionally that they might like to think or image pleasant and relaxing things occurring and to persevere in any way that they thought might be helpful to them in their task. Examples were given to demonstrate how imagery might aid them. The data showed that encouragement to image had a substantial effect on subjects; instructions that encouraged the use of imagery yielded appreciably greater relaxation performance than that attained during biofeedback testing when no such imagery encouragement was given. Analysis of verbal reports taken after the testing was completed again confirmed this interpretation of the data.

Results of the kind we have just discussed indicate a delicate interplay between test conditions and imagery capacity. It appears, for example, that standard biofeedback stimulus conditions hinder rather than aid the relaxation performance of high absorption subjects, but this interference can be reduced or minimized by giving instructions to subjects to facilitate or encourage their spontaneous use of imagery. Appeal to imaginative capacity seems necessary to account for the data, but aptitude for imaginative absorption is clearly more relevant to some test situations than to others, and the definition of those factors that foster the demonstration of imaginative capacity obviously requires a detailed and precise definition of stimulus test conditions. Tellegen (1981) argues that perhaps the most important factor in accounting for subject variation in performance in situations of the kind we have just considered is the cognitive set under which subjects respond. He asserts that an *experiential set* (defined in terms of a state of receptivity or openness to experiencing that characterizes events that are naturally occurring) and an *instrument set* (defined as a state of readiness to engage or participate in voluntary and effortful cognitive activity) will lead to different consequences of response, depending on the level of subjects' capacity for imaginative involvement in the first instance. Tellegen's (1981) notion of mental set serves to highlight the fact that imagery ability should be viewed in terms of a demonstrable capacity on the part of subjects to respond in a particular way in a given *class of circumstances*. The range of explanatory power of this distinction between mental sets has yet to be resolved empirically [see Qualls & Sheehan (1981c) for discussion], but debate regarding the issue raises the question of how best to isolate conditions of testing that optimize subjects' capacities for imagery. The literature has long drawn a distinction between voluntary (requested) and spontaneous (unsolicited) imagery, but recent research would appear to suggest that the distinction fails to indicate the degree to which test conditions may affect subjects' imagery responses.

The problem researchers face in defining the person–treatment interactions that involve imagery response brings us finally to consider some of the major issues that present themselves for future research. Research needs to confront the problem of situational influence by analyzing more closely than it has done to date the exact nature of the impact assessment procedures have on the imagery data that emerge. There are other issues, though, that also need to be researched, and we conclude by commenting briefly on these.

DIRECTIONS FOR FUTURE RESEARCH

The Measures

In their review of studies dealing with individual differences in cognitive abilities, Carroll and Maxwell (1979) argued that the significance of aptitude needs to be examined at a particular point of time for particular groups of people. We would argue that their basic point firmly isolates specific directions for future imagery research in the ways that we have just been discussing. In pursuit of that aim, however, it seems likely that analysis of the combinations between ability and test conditions will index the relevance of other processes that may also be important—processes that have been relatively neglected in imagery research. These relate to the display of motivation and emotion; one would expect that perhaps experience-based modes of assessment are better equipped to attest their relevance than are the more constrained measures of imagery function (such as the objective tests and self-report scales that we have reviewed).

Research, of course, will continue to examine the pattern of dependence between the various measures that exist and will persist in its attempt to answer the basic question of whether one underlying process accounts for subjects' performance when artifacts associated with subjects' test behavior are removed. It seems likely, however, that only part of the common variance of subjects' test scores will ever be accounted for in terms of imagery processing, since existing tests differ markedly in the degree to which they access cognitive information. This seems especially so when one contrasts the complexity of process indicated by experience-based instruments of assessment relative to the data produced by standard self-report scales and objective measures of imagery functioning. It could well be that clinical research will take up the gauntlet in this regard, however; factors such as anxiety and depression, for example, are firmly recognized as affecting subjects' self-statements and thoughts about their cognitive functioning (Kendall & Korgeski, 1979).

Finally, in this context, we would argue that research needs to apply different procedures of assessment so as to examine more closely the convergent (as opposed to the discriminative) validity of the various tests that may be employed. Kendall and Korgeski (1979) make this same point when they argue that in vivo thought sampling could well be useful to adopt in association with laboratory assessment methods to enable us to obtain more detailed information about the thoughts of subjects that occur during the experimental procedures. The sampling of cognitive data in a variety of ways will help both to discount alternative explanations of results, such as the view that subjects respond in terms of the judged appropriateness of their behavior, and to assist in sustaining the hope that most researchers in the field prefer to hold—that the various modes of assessment and tests of imagery sample processes in common, at least.

Correlates of Function

An increasing amount of work is being undertaken to relate imagery to physiological functioning. Although self-report measures have not occupied center stage, there is growing evidence that images affect a wide variety of physiological responses. For example, John and Schwartz (1978) have reviewed evidence showing that there are differential changes in EEG patterns between the two cerebral hemispheres as a result of subjects employing different cognitive modes (images or words). Similarly, Ornstein and Galin (1977) have reported hemispheric differences in the amount of alpha shown when a subject tries to solve spatial or verbal–arithmetic tasks. If such results are replicable, the influence of the individual difference parameter on the degree of such differences in activity would be a fruitful issue to pursue.

This brings us finally to the question of cerebral lateralization and its effects. Paivio (1971) made a major and influential statement that the right cerebral hemisphere is specialized for the processing of images and the left, for semantic material. There are some direct tests of this notion with the use of nonverbal or verbal stimulus material (McFarland & Ashton, 1978; Nebes, 1976). An issue of more immediate concern, however, is the effect of individual differences in imagery ability on the extent of lateralization of cerebral function. As is the case with the EEG studies, there is, unfortunately, little extant data. It seems plausible to argue that good imagers will process imaginal material faster and more accurately than will poor imagers. This difference in capacity should be reflected in faster reaction times among the good imagers and, possibly, in a greater interference with left-hand motor performance than would be the case for those with lesser imagery ability. Similarly, the interaction of concrete or high-imagery-rated words with motor or other cognitive performance should be greater in those subjects possessing more intense or vivid imagery [see McFarland et al. (1978) for further elaboration of this position].

Our brief account of cerebral function correlates aims to demonstrate that psychophysical studies can be a fruitful source of data on imagery ability and its function, and a study by Drummond et al. (1978) helps to illustrate the same point in another way. Although images have been shown to influence, or even cause, bodily reactions (Lang, 1979; Weerts & Roberts, 1976), there are few studies that demonstrate that individual differences in imagery ability influence the magnitude of such effects. In a rather complex analysis of the rate of habituation of the skin conductance response to an imaged electric shock evoked by a tone, Drummond et al. (1978) demonstrated that vivid imagers took significantly longer to habituate to the tone than did subjects with less vivid imagery.

These and other studies sample only a limited number of the issues that remain to be researched. The field of imagery is sufficiently fertile that new phenomena are still being unearthed; and, sophisticated though it may be, current theorizing about imagery has not yet explained these phenomena in their full complexity. Until that goal is achieved, assessment procedures will always be required that measure imagery events as accurately and reliably as possible. Hopefully, our review has demonstrated that the options facing the researcher in this crucial task of assessment are rich, varied, and useful.

REFERENCES

Anderson, J. R. Arguments concerning representations for mental imagery. *Psychological Review*, 1978, **85,** 249–277.

Angell, J. R. Methods for the determination of mental imagery. *Psychological Monographs,* 1912, **13,** 61–107.

Ashton, R., & White, K. Factor analysis of the Gordon Test of visual imagery control. *Perceptual and Motor Skill,* 1974, **38,** 945–946.

Ashton, R., & White, K. D. Sex differences in imagery vividness: An artifact of the test. *British Journal of Psychology,* 1980, **71,** 35–38.

Ashton, R., McFarland, K., Walsh, F., & White, K. Imagery ability and the identification of hands: A chronometric analysis. *Acta Psychologica,* 1978, **42,** 253–262.

Barber, T. X., & Wilson, S. C. The Barber susceptibility scale and the creative imagination scale: Experimental and clinical applications. *The American Journal of Clinical Hypnosis,* 1979, **21,** 84–96.

Beech, J. R., & Leslie, J. C. Monitoring the effects of increasing resource demands on the clarity of visual images. *British Journal of Psychology,* 1978, **69,** 323–333.

Bennett, G. K., Seashore, M. G., & Wesman, A. G. *Differential Aptitude Tests.* New York: The Psychological Corporation, 1947.

Berger, G. H., & Gaunitz, S. C. B. Self-rated imagery and vividness of task pictures in relation to visual memory. *British Journal of Psychology,* 1977, **68,** 283–288.

Berger, G. H., & Gaunitz, S. C. B. Self-rated imagery and encoding strategies in visual memory. *British Journal of Psychology,* 1979, **70,** 21–24.

Betts, G. H. *The distribution and functions of mental imagery.* New York: Teachers College, Columbia University, 1909.

Bowers, P. Hypnotizability, creativity and the role of effortless experiencing. *The International Journal of Clinical and Experimental Hypnosis,* 1978, **25,** 184–202.

Brooks, L. R. The suppression of visualization in reading. *Quarterly Journal of Experimental Psychology,* 1967, **19,** 288–299.

Cairns, E., & Coll, P. The role of visual imagery in visual tactual and cross-modal matching. *British Journal of Psychology,* 1977, **68,** 213–214.

Carrol, D., Baker, J., & Preston, M. Individual differences in visual imaging and the voluntary control of heart rate. *British Journal of Psychology,* 1979, **70,** 39–49.

Carroll, J. B., & Maxwell, S. B. Individual differences in cognitive abilities. *Annual Review of Psychology,* 1979, **30,** 603–640.

Cartwright, D. S., Marks, M. E., & Durrett, J. H. Definition and measurement of three processes of imagery representation: Exploratory studies of verbally stimulated imagery. *Multivariate Behavioral Research,* 1978, **13,** 449–473.

Coe, W. C., St. Jean, R. L., & Burger, J. M. Hypnosis and the enhancement of visual imagery. *The International Journal of Clinical and Experimental Hypnosis,* 1980, **28,** 225–243.

Cooper, L. A., & Shephard, R. N. Chronometric studies of the rotation of mental images. In W. G. Chase (Ed.), *Visual information processing.* New York: Academic Press, 1973.

Crowne, D. P., & Marlowe, D. *The approval motive.* New York: Wiley, 1964.

Cundiff, G., & Gold, S. R. Daydreaming: A measurable concept. *Perceptual and Motor Skills,* 1979, **49,** 347–353.

Davis, F. C. Functional significance of imagery differences. *Journal of Experimental Psychology*, 1932, **15**, 630–661.

Dirks, J. Spatial memory of two eidetic subjects. Paper presented to American Psychological Association, Toronto, 1978.

Dirks, J., & Neisser, U. Memory for objects in real scenes: The development of recognition and recall. *Journal of Experimental Child Psychology*, 1977, **23**, 315–328.

Doob, L. W. Exploring eidetic imagery among the Kamba of central Kenya. *Journal of Social Psychology*, 1965, **67**, 3–22.

Drummond, P., White, K., & Ashton, R. Imagery vividness affects habituation rate. *Psychophysiology*, 1978, **15**, 193–195.

Durndell, A. J., & Wetherick, N. E. Reported imagery and two spatial tests. *Perceptual and Motor Skills*, 1976a, **43**, 1050.

Durndell, A. J., & Wetherick, N. E. The relation of reported imagery to cognitive performance. *British Journal of Psychology*, 1976b, **67**, 501–506.

Ericsson, K. A., & Simon, H. A. Verbal reports as data. *Psychological Review*, 1980, **87**, 215–251.

Ernest, C. H. Mental imagery and cognition: A critical review. *Journal of Mental Imagery*, 1977, **1**, 181–216.

Ernest, C. H. Visual imagery ability and the recognition of verbal and non verbal stimuli. *Acta Psychologica*, 1978, **43**, 253–269.

Ernest, C. H., & Paivio, A. Imagery and associative latencies as a function of imagery ability. *Canadian Journal of Psychology*, 1971, **25**, 83–90.

Fernald, M. R. The diagnosis of mental imagery. *Psychological Monographs*, 1912, **14**, 1–169.

Finke, R. A. The functional equivalence of mental images and errors of movement. *Cognitive Psychology*, 1979, **11**, 235–264.

Finke, R. A. Levels of equivalence in imagery and perception. *Psychological Review*, 1980, **87**, 113–132.

Finke, R. A., & Kosslyn, S. M. Mental imagery acuity in the peripheral visual field. *Journal of Experimental Psychology: Human Perception and Performance*, 1980, **6**, 126–139.

Finke, R. A., & Schmidt, M. J. The quantitative measure and pattern representation in imagery using orientation-specific color aftereffects. *Perception and Psychophysics*, 1978, **23**, 515–520.

Forisha, B. L. Creativity and imagery in men and women. *Perceptual and Motor Skills*, 1978, **47**, 1255–1264.

French, P. C. The mental imagery of students. *Psychological Review*, 1902, **9**, 40–56.

Galton, F. *Inquiries into human faculty and its development*. London: Macmillan, 1883.

Gordon, R. An investigation into some of the factors that favour the formation of stereotyped images. *British Journal of Psychology*, 1949, **39**, 156–167.

Guy, M. E., & McCarter, R. E. A scale to measure emotive imagery. *Perceptual and Motor Skills*, 1978, **46**, 1267–1274.

Haber, R. N. Twenty years of haunting eidetic imagery: Where's the ghost? *Behavioral and Brain Sciences,* 1979, **2,** 583–629.

Haber, R. N., & Haber, R. B. Eidetic imagery: I. Frequency. *Perceptual and Motor Skills,* 1964, **19,** 131–138.

Harris, R., Yulis, S., & LaCoste, D. Relationships among sexual arousability imagery ability, and introversion–extraversion. *The Journal of Sex Research,* 1980, **16,** 72–86.

Hatakeyama, T. The constructive character of eidetic imagery. *Tohoku Psycholgica Folia,* 1975, **34, 38–51.**

Hiscock, M. Effects of adjective imagery on recall from prose. *Journal of General Psychology,* 1976, **94,** 295–299.

Hiscock, M. Imagery assessment through self-report: What do imagery questionnaires measure? *Journal of Consulting and Clinical Psychology,* 1978, **46,** 223–230.

Hoen, P. T. Effects of hypnotizability and visualizing ability on imagery mediated learning. *The International Journal of Clinical and Experimental Hypnosis,* 1978, **26,** 45–54.

Huba, G. J., Segal, B., & Singer, J. L. Consistency of daydreaming styles across sample, of college male and female drug and alcohol users. *Journal of Abnormal Psychology,* 1977, **86, 99–102.**

Ikeda, Y., & Hirai, H. Voluntary control of electrodermal activity in relation to imagery and internal perception scores. *Psychophysiology,* 1976, **13,** 330–333.

Irwin, H. J. Coding preferences and the form of spontaneous, extrasensory experiences. *Journal of Parapsychology,* 1979, **43,** 205–220.

Jaynes, J. Palaeolithic cave paintings as eidetic images. *Behavioral and Brain Sciences* (Commentary), 1979, **2,** 605–607.

John, E. R., & Schwartz, E. L. The neuropsychology of information processing and cognition. *Annual Review of Psychology,* 1978, **29,** 1–29.

Julesz, B. *Foundations of cyclopean perception.* Chicago: University of Chicago Press, 1971.

Kagan, N., Krathwohl, D. R., & Miller, R. Stimulated recall in therapy using videotape—A case study. *Journal of Counselling Psychology,* 1963, **10,** 237–243.

Kendall, P. C., & Korgeski, G. P. Assessment and cognitive–behavioral interventions. *Cognitive Therapy and Research,* 1979, **3,** 1–21.

Khatena, J. Autonomy of imagery and production of original verbal imagery. *Perceptual and Motor Skills,* 1976, **43,** 245–246.

Klinger, E. Modes of normal conscious flow. In K. S. Pope and J. L. Singer (Eds.), *The stream of consciousness: Scientific investigations into the flow of human experience.* New York: Plenum, 1978.

Kosslyn, S. M. *Image and mind.* Cambridge, Mass.: Harvard University Press, 1980.

Kosslyn, S. M., Ball, T. M., & Reiser, B. J. Visual images preserve metric spatial information: Evidence from studies of image scanning. *Journal of Experimental Psychology: Human Perception and Performance,* 1978, **4,** 47–60.

Kosslyn, S. M., Pinker, S., Smith, G. E., & Schwartz, S. P. On the demystification of mental imagery. *Behavioral and Brain Sciences,* 1979, **2,** 535–581.

Lane, J. B. Problems in assessment of vividness and control of imagery. *Perceptual and Motor Skills,* 1977, **45,** 363–368.

Lang, P. J. A bio-informational theory of emotional imagery. *Psychophysiology,* 1979, **16,** 495–512.

Leask, J., Haber, R. N., & Haber, R. B. Eidetic imagery in children: II. Longitudinal and experimental results. *Psychonomic Monograph Supplements,* 1969, **3,** 25–48.

Likert, R., & Quasha, W. H. *Revised Minnesota Paper Form Board Test.* New York: The Psychological Corporation, 1970.

Marks, D. F. Visual imagery differences in the recall of pictures. *British Journal of Psychology,* 1973, **64,** 17–24.

Marks, D. Eidetic imagery: Haber's ghost and Hatakeyama's ghoul (commentary). *Behavioral and Brain Sciences,* 1979, **2,** 610–612.

Matefy, R. E. Role-play theory of psychedelic drug flashbacks. *Journal of Consulting and Clinical Psychology,* 1980, **48,** 551–553.

McFarland, K., & Ashton, R. The influence of brain lateralization of function on a manual skill. *Cortex,* 1978, **14,** 102–111.

McFarland, K., McFarland, M. L., Bain, J. D., & Ashton, R. Ear differences of abstract and concrete word recognition. *Neuropsychologia,* 1978, **16,** 555–561.

McGee, M. G. Human spatial abilities: Psychometric studies and environmental, genetic, hormonal, and neurological influences. *Psychological Bulletin,* 1979, **86,** 889–918.

McKelvie, S. J., & Demers, E. G. Individual differences in reported visual imagery and memory performance. *British Journal of Psychology,* 1979, **70,** 51–57.

McLemore, C. W. Factorial validity of imagery measures. *Behaviour Research and Therapy,* 1976, **14,** 399–408.

Merritt, J. O. None in a million: Results of mass screening for eidetic ability using objective tests published in newspapers and magazines (commentary). *Behavioral and Brain Sciences,* 1979, **2,** 612.

Mitchell, D. B., & Richman, C. L. Confirmed reservations: Mental travel. *Journal of Experimental Psychology: Human Perception and Performance,* 1980, **6,** 58–66.

Nebes, R. D. The use of imagery in memory by right and left handers. *Neuropsychologia,* 1976, **14,** 505–508.

Neisser, U. Tracing eidetic imagery. *Behavioral and Brain Sciences,* 1979, **2,** 612–613.

Ornstein, R. E., & Galin, D. Physiological studies of consciousness. In P. R. Lee, R. E. Ornstein, D. Galin, A. Deikman, and C. T. Tart (Eds.), *Symposium on consciousness.* Harmondsworth: Penguin (reprint from The Viking Press edition of 1976), 1977.

Otteson, J. R. Stylistic and personality correlates of lateral eye movements: A factor analytic study. *Perceptual and Motor Skills,* 1980, **50,** 995–1010.

Owens, A. C., & Richardson, J. T. E. Mental imagery and pictorial memory. *British Journal of Psychology,* 1979, **70,** 497–505.

Paivio, A. *Imagery and verbal processes.* New York: Holt, 1971.

Pope, K. S., & Singer, J. L. (Eds.). *The stream of consciousness: Scientific investigations into the flow of human experience*. New York: Plenum, 1978.

Posner, M. I. Co-ordination of internal codes. In W. G. Chase (Ed.), *Visual information processing*. New York: Academic Press, 1973.

Qualls, P. J., & Sheehan, P. W. Capacity for absorption and relaxation during electromyograph biofeedback and no-feedback conditions. *Journal of Abnormal Psychology*, 1979, **88**, 652–662.

Qualls, P. J., & Sheehan, P. W. The role of the feedback signal in electromyograph biofeedback: The relevance of attention. *Journal of Experimental Psychology: General*, 1981a, **110**, 204–216.

Qualls, P. J., & Sheehan, P. W. Imagery encouragement, absorption capacity, and relaxation during electromyograph biofeedback. *Journal of Personality and Social Psychology*, 1981b, **41**, 370–379.

Qualls, P. J., & Sheehan, P. W. Trait-treatment interactions: A reply to Tellegen. *Journal of Experimental Psychology: General*, 1981c, **110**, 227–231.

Rehm, L. Relationships among measures of visual imagery. *Behavior Research and Therapy*, 1973, **11**, 265–270.

Reing, A. B. Imaginal behavioral analysis: A multisensory imagery scale for evaluating a specific teacher competency. *The Journal of Special Education*, 1978, **12**, 153–170.

Richardson, A. *Mental imagery*. London: Routledge and Kegan Paul, 1969.

Richardson, A. Verbalizer–visualizer: A cognitive style dimension. *Journal of Mental Imagery*, 1977a, **1**, 109–126.

Richardson, A. The meaning and measurement of memory imagery. *British Journal of Psychology*, 1977b, **68**, 29–43.

Richardson, A. Subject, task, and tester variables associated with initial eye movement responses. *Journal of Mental Imagery*, 1978, **2**, 85–100.

Richardson, A. Dream recall frequency and vividness of visual imagery. *Journal of Mental Imagery*, 1979, **3**, 65–72.

Richman, C. L., Mitchell, D. B., & Reznich, J. S. Mental travel: Some reservations. *Journal of Experimental Psychology: Human Perception and Performance*, 1979, **5**, 13–18.

Rimm, D., & Bottrell, J. Four measures of visual imagination. *Behaviour Research and Therapy*, 1969, **7**, 63–69.

Rossi, J. S. Reliability of a measure of visual imagery. *Perceptual and Motor Skills*, 1977, **45**, 694.

Rossi, J. S., & Fingeret, A. L. Individual differences in verbal and imagery abilities: Paired associate recall as a function of stimulus and response concreteness. *Perceptual and Motor Skills*, 1977, **44**, 1043–1049.

Sheehan, P. W. A shortened form of Betts questionnaire upon mental imagery. *Journal of Clinical Psychology*, 1967, **23**, 386–389.

Sheehan, P. W. The variability of eidetic imagery among Australian Aboriginal children. *Journal of Social Psychology*, 1973, **91**, 29–36.

Sheehan, P. W. Mental imagery. In B. M. Foss (Ed.), *Psychology survey: No. 1*. London: Allen & Unwin, 1978, Pp. 58–70.

Sheehan, P. W. Imaginative consciousness—function, process, and method. *Imagination, Cognition and Personality,* in press.

Sheehan, P. W., & McConkey, K. M. *Hypnosis and experience: The exploration of phenomena and process.* Hillsdale, N.J.: Lawrence Erlbaum Associates, 1982.

Sheehan, P. W., McConkey, K. M., & Cross, D. G. The experiential analysis technique: Some new observations on hypnotic phenomena. *Journal of Abnormal Psychology,* 1978, **87,** 570–573.

Siipola, E. M., & Hayden, S. D. Exploring eidetic imagery among the retarded. *Perceptual and Motor Skills,* 1965, **21,** 275–286.

Singer, J. L., & Antrobus, J. S. A factor-analytic study of daydreaming and conceptually-related cognitive and personality variables. *Perceptual and Motor Skills,* 1963, Monograph Supplement 3-V17.

Singer, J. L., & Antrobus, J. S. Daydreaming, imaginal processes, and personality: A normative study. In P. W. Sheehan (Ed.), *The function and nature of imagery.* New York: Academic Press, 1972.

Sousa-Poza, J. F., Rohrberg, R., & Merwre, A. Effects of type of information (abstract–concrete) and field dependence on assymetry of hand movements during speech. *Perceptual and Motor Skills,* 1979, **48,** 1323–1330.

Spanos, N. P., Churchill, N., & McPeake, J. D. Experiential response to auditory and visual hallucination suggestions in hypnotic subjects. *Journal of Consulting and Clinical Psychology,* 1976a, **44,** 729–738.

Spanos, N. P., McPeake, J. D., & Churchill, N. Relationships between imaginative ability variables and the Barber suggestibility scale. *The American Journal of Clinical Hypnosis,* 1976b, **19,** 39–46.

Spanos, N. P., Ansari, F., & Stam, H. J. Hypnotic age regression and eidetic imagery: A failure to replicate. *Journal of Abnormal Psychology,* 1979, **88,** 88–91.

Stricklin, A. B., & Penk, M. L. Levels of imagery and personality dimensions in a female prison population. *Journal of Personality Assessment,* 1980, **44,** 390–395.

Stromeyer, C. F. III, & Psotka, J. The detailed texture of eidetic images. *Nature,* 1970, **225,** 347–349.

Switras, J. E. An alternate form instrument to assess vididness and controlability of mental imagery in seven modalities. *Perceptual and Motor Skills,* 1978, **46,** 379–384.

Taylor, P. L., & Falcomer, M. Adolescent daydreaming: The I.Q. effect. *Journal of Mental Imagery,* 1979, **3,** 107–122.

Tedford, W. H., & Penk, M. L. Intelligence and imagery in personality. *Journal of Personality Assessment,* 1979, **41,** 405–413.

Tellegen, A. Practicing the two disciplines for relaxation and enlightenment. *Journal of Experimental Psychology: General,* 1981, **110,** 217–226.

Tellegen, A., & Atkinson, G. Openness to absorbing and self-altering experiences ("absorption"), a trait related to hypnotic susceptibility. *Journal of Abnormal Psychology,* 1974, **83,** 268–277.

Thurstone, L. L. Primary mental abilities. *Psychometrika Monographs,* 1938, No. 1.

Thurstone, L. L., & Jeffrey, T. E. *Flags: A test of space thinking*. Chicago: Industrial Relations Centre, 1956.

Titchener, E. B. *Psychology of the thought process*. New York: Macmillan, 1909.

Wallace, B. Restoration of eidetic imagery via hypnotic age regression: More evidence. *Journal of Abnormal Psychology*, 1978, **87**, 673–675.

Warren, R., & Good, G. The verbalizer–visualizer questionnaire: Further normative data. *Perceptual and Motor Skills*, 1979, **48**, 372.

Weerts, T. C., & Roberts, R. The physiological effects of imagining anger-provoking and fear-provoking scenes. *Psychophysiology*, 1976, **13**, 174 (abstract).

Westcott, T. B., & Rosenstock, E. Reliability of two measures of imagery. *Perceptual and Motor Skills*, 1976, **42**, 1037–1038.

White, K. D., & Ashton, R. Visual imagery control: One dimension or four? *Journal of Mental Imagery*, 1977, **2**, 245–252.

White, K., Sheehan, P. W., & Ashton, R. Imagery assessment: A survey of self-report measures. *Journal of Mental Imagery*, 1977, **1**, 145–170.

White, K. D., Ashton, R., & Lewis, S. Learning a complex skill: Effects of mental practice, physical practice and imagery ability. *International Journal of Sport Psychology*, 1979, **10**, 71–78.

Wilson, S. C., & Barber, T. X. The creative imagination scale as a measure of hypnotic responsiveness: Applications to experimental and clinical hypnosis. *American Journal of Clinical Hypnosis*, 1978, **20**, 235–249.

Woodworth, R. R. *Experimental psychology*. London: Methuen, 1938.

CHAPTER 8

Imagery:
Its Role in Development

RONI BETH TOWER

INTRODUCTION

"Hey, lady—wanna buy a cake?" I heard the little girls almost before I saw them. My dog and I had just rounded the bend on the afternoon's ritual walk. And as the high-pitched voices reached me, the sight of four girls between 2 and 4 years of age came into focus. The toddlers were perched along the curb at the end of a driveway, industriously involved with an elaborate set of miniature pots and pans. As I was somewhat preoccupied with my own daydreams, my initial conclusion was that the girls had set up an adaptation of the timeless lemonade stand and had probably baked (or convinced a mother to bake) cupcakes as an added marketing ploy. So, rather absent-mindedly, I searched my jeans' pockets and then replied, "I'm sorry—but I have no money with me right now." The faces of the girls lit up and they chorused, "But you don't need any money. And here's some cake for your dog." By now I was within comprehension range and had grasped the "game": both Taffy and I then eagerly "sampled" the sand cakes, while I discussed with the girls such weighty matters as the flavors of the icings, the ingredients and procedures in the recipes, the amount of pretend money to be paid, and the possibility of obtaining "a piece of pizza" on the return trip. After being "paid," the smallest girl shyly held out her hand and boldly smiled and announced, "Tip."

The images involved in our transactions were many. Clearly the girls held notions of cakes and of cooking, of selling and of buying, of pretending and of reality. My adult images were perhaps more complex, fueled by memories of my own roadside stands, from the experience of being the consumer of countless commercial transactions, and from years of working with pre-school children. Perhaps only the dog found the experience completely novel, as he is not used to being fed sand in the guise of food.

Thus, cognitively, the experience had many meanings to the children and to me, as we exercised and developed memory and imagination images, rehearsed information concerning appropriate role transactions, identified transformations of information—and censored those that did not meet the rules we had tacitly agreed on, and used elaborations of perceptions and cognitions to extend attention and concentration. We organized, planned, and integrated new sequences; discriminated central from peripheral features of the event; exercised skills in abstracting and generalizing; made distinctions between reality and fantasy (and probed parameters of the latter); and searched for language to use in communicating private experiences. Mutual associations were triggered and cultured, fostering ideational fluency and richness. Above all, we transformed the idiosyncratic and autistic, those most private notions from our own imaginations, into the communicable and shared. Cognitive mechanisms for dealing with ambiguity were explored. Although the girls might have also been amenable to selling me "jewelry," such an extension of the play at my suggestion surely would have violated their control over a central ingredient: they had begun the play and organized it around "cooking" with sand. Shifting the focus to an imaginary train ride would have been still more disconnected and, although a delightful opportunity at another time, an assault on the hierarchy of imagery currently in the girls' heads.

The experience had affective meaning also. The girls found opportunities to control an interpersonal interaction, thus gaining a sense of self-efficacy through influence over others. This mastery and the self-concepts possible only through seeing the concrete impact that one can have on the environment foster the "autonomy" and "initiative" that Erikson (1963) considers the critical developmental tasks of the preschool years. Similarly, it forms the emotional underpinnings for White's "competence" (1959) or for the "ego resiliency" described by Block and Block, (1973, 1976).

Furthermore, the cognitive richness of the interaction fueled both interest and joy, those positive affects aroused as slightly novel information (e.g., the responses of the strange lady and her dog) appears at a tolerable rate (interest). Then expectations of outcome become predictable through matching with the familiar [joy—see Izard (1977); Piaget (1981); Singer (1973); Tomkins (1962, 1963); and Tower & Singer (1980)]. The experience also encouraged spontaneity of responses and breadth of openness in emotional responsiveness. Indeed, enthusiasm was welcomed and rewarded with returned positive affect; pretend hurt and anger at being forgotten in the tipping procedures were recognized as legitimate within the play sequence. Furthermore, the positive affect of the play also reinforced behavior that had been intrinsically motivated—and the elevated sense of security bred by confidence in the positive consequences of internally determined experiences. Finally, the play fostered decreased fear of both a stranger and of the impact of one's internal productions on others—and perhaps a concomitant higher tolerance for ambiguity with its attendant lowering of anxiety. Facial and postural sensitivity were encouraged in the experience, as both real and imagined emotions demanded recognition—and cues for play and nonplay behaviors were thus identified and practiced (Bateson, 1955; Sutton-Smith, 1971).

Third, the transaction was meaningful socially—in terms of both feedback about the self in social situations and in the quality of interpersonal relationships. Individually, the children practiced the waiting behaviors facilitated by imaginal mediation as they patiently "cooked" new cakes, took turns, and awaited my return trip. In the pretend play, they were using a nearly limitless world, that of the imagination, and they were using it not only in the service of their own amusement or understanding, but also in the service of communication. With peers, the imagery was being transformed into make-believe games, thus the gap between the autistic and the socially accepted was bridged. A shared frame of reference thus emerged, yielding far richer and more collaborative play than the individual exploratory play of making sand formations in plastic pots and pans. In addition, the event provided a symbol for group identity, as the girls could now think of themselves collectively as "the bake shop." A medium for positive interaction with adults and peers had been established and poise in social situations nurtured. Leadership and cooperation among the girls emerged as they sought ways to surrender pieces of individual dominance in the service of continuing the group experience. And, most obviously, acculturation was abetted, as the children used their play to assume roles common to their social experience (Stone, 1971).

The above is just a partial catalog of the myriad influences a child's imaginal life has on his or her cognitive, affective, and social development. Clearly, the impact is vast—and, as documented elsewhere, extends throughout the lifespan [for excellent reviews and collections of research summaries, see Pope & Singer (1978); Sheikh & Shaffer (1979); Shorr et al. (1980); and Singer (1974)].

Therefore, the role of imagery in a child's development is well deserving of attention. The current chapter (1) describes the structure of imagery as it appears in early childhood; (2) reviews the natural sequence of development of imagery; (3) considers conditions necessary for the emergence of the natural sequence and those that regulate it; (4) elaborates on the functions of imagery—cognitive, affective, and social correlates or consequences of imaginal processes in children; (5) suggests ways of facilitating the development of imagery in children; and (6) explores the maladaptive extremes of imagination in the child—those cases in which a child's imaginal life is impoverished or becomes more compelling than external reality.

STRUCTURE OF IMAGERY IN CHILDHOOD

To describe the structure of imagery is to suggest a definition of an entity. To describe is not to posit mechanisms by which the entity comes into existence or changes; these are the imaginal processes. Nor does description mean to ascribe motivation or motivating power to the existent entities; these are the meanings of the processes of imaging as well as their content. Rather, it is to conceptualize—or to attempt to use language that has common meanings to create a shared construct—an ephemeral but universal aspect of human experience.

Why are the words in the above paragraph so big? Why is imagery so elusive and its definition so problematic? The issues have been described elsewhere (Horowitz, 1970; Sheehan, 1972; Tower & Singer, 1981) and, for purposes of the discussion that follows, may be temporarily deferred. Indeed, regardless of whether an image is a direct encoding of a distinctly sensory experience (Kosslyn, 1980; Shepard, 1978) or an abstract collection of associated propositions (Lang 1978; Pylyshin, 1973), or most profitably defined by its functions (Paivio, 1971), *phenomenologically* people can and do experience mental representations of objects or experiences, such as a friend's face or the sound of a child's laughter, in the absence of the stimulus. This *representation* serves as the referent of the word "image" in this chapter. It may vary in form—particularly in such characteristics as vividness, controllability, complexity, the specific sensory modality initially represented, the unitary or multiple nature of the modality or modalities, and stability. And it can vary also in content—particularly along continua of perception to fantasy; affectively laden to impersonal subject matter; of source of content; of isolation to complexity; and in sequencing and integration. As has been well documented [see Tower & Singer (1981) for a review], subjective and objective imagery may be quite distinct. Forisha (1975) has replicated this assertion in her studies of children. Nonetheless, regardless of specific form and content, the image is a mental representation of past experience.

Does this suggest that "imagery" is another word for "memory"? Such an identity would be both too broad and too narrow. On the one hand, an image *can be* a memory image, a rather careful replication of an originally experienced smell, taste, movement, touch, or sight. But one would wish to exclude such memories as those concerning appropriate logical operations for solving multiplication problems or rules for remembering the order of the kings and queens of England. The original sensory nature of the experience is here the distinguishing feature. At the same time, the identity would be too narrow—imagination imagery ranges far beyond original experience: it breaks down stored memories; transforms their components; and reintegrates past masteries, much as Picasso did in his art.

To the child, an image is quite simply that which happens internally as an externally absent object or experience is recalled—or as a new experience evokes representations of other ones and demands its own encoding. The imagery of the child can be studied through the projection of such internal notions onto external objects or, eventually, onto their *imagined* existence. In other words, the elaborate imagery of an adolescent's private consciousness is vividly available for all to see in the imaginative productions of the young child (Klinger, 1971; Singer, 1973, 1975). In the current chapter such expressions are considered the indicators of the imagery of the child: pretend play in preschoolers is the "royal route" to internal life. As Weisler and McCall (1976) and Vandenberg (1978) have pointed out, the child's interest–exploration–play behaviors have much to tell us about his or her development. As they note, however, the sequences are not always easy to sort out. In focusing on the *imaginative* play of the child, therefore, we can hope to target those expressions that are most closely tied to the child's representational life.

DEVELOPMENT OF IMAGERY

Major issues in the development of imagery center around (1) the place of imaginal representations in the ongoing cognitive and affective development of the child and (2) the identification and predictability of a sequence to imaginal development.

Relation of Imagery to Cognition and Affect

Piaget believed that the emergence of imagery and its subsequent central role in the evolution of intelligence are hallmarks of the preoperational period in child development (Piaget, 1952, 1962; Piaget & Inhelder, 1969, 1971). Around 18 months of age, when the toddler lifts a shell to his or her lips as though it were a teacup or shakes a scolding finger at an errant teddybear, he or she shows that representations of experiences have formed at a higher level. No longer is the child restricted to active motoric interaction with the environment, but now experiences can be remembered and *symbolized* by other objects, events, and experiences. These internal representations, or images, form the bases of *schemata,* those cognitions on which future understandings are built, expectations established, and to which new inputs are matched.

Initially the schemata are quite simple, a rather direct sensory representation of concrete experience, similar to Bruner's *ikonic* imagery. But as the child *accommodates* to social reality, he or she matches new objects, events, and experiences to the old. When the match fails, the child creates a new image, imitating reality, although understanding is still not complete. For example, I vividly remember overhearing a child announce to a friend of her mother's, in her most adult voice, "You know, Mrs. Smithers, you shouldn't smoke." When asked, "Why not?," the child thought for a moment, then authoritatively replied, "You could burn up." She had accommodated well the televised commercial messages and could behave in socially appropriate ways—although her grasp of the situation was far from mature.

Clearly, encoding a new image (or message or idea) is not the same as understanding it. The affect of interest, aroused by the discrepancy between what one expects and what one receives [called "exploration in play" by Weisler & McCall (1976) and Vandenberg (1978)] is one major energizer of the cognitive process of accommodation or new image formation (Izard, 1977; Piaget, 1952, 1981; Tomkins, 1962, 1963; Tower & Singer, 1980). But the other side of the process is digestion, or *assimilation,* in which the newly encoded image is integrated into existing schemata. As the image is replayed and associated to other images, it becomes familiar—and this recognition of the familiar results in the affect of joy. On one hand the affect of interest fuels differentiation; on the other, joy motivates integration. And thus growth takes place in a predictable dialectical fashion.

Sequencing of Development

Piaget proposed the genetics of intelligence decades ago (Piaget, 1952). In more recent years, empirical work has been able to demonstrate the (1) existence of the cycle [see Herron & Sutton-Smith (1971), Vandenberg (1978), and Weisler & McCall (1976) for fine reviews of the exploration–play relationship, which is even trackable with heart rate variability (Hughes & Hutt, 1979)], (2) the predictable progression to more symbolic and fantasy behavior with age and cognitive development (Fein, 1975; Hurlock, 1971; Nicholich, 1977; Rubin & et al., 1976, Rubin, 1978), (3) the independence of verbal and imaginal processes in young children (Forisha, 1975; Mowbray & Luria, 1973), (4) the ability of children to increasingly differentiate the real and imaginary with age (Morison & Gardner, 1978; Prentice, et al., 1978), and (5) increasing use of pretending and references to imaginative productions with age (Chaille Chaille, 1978; Golumb, 1977). At first, one object stands for another quite similar object; then a part of the body represents an object or idea; then the entire body represents something else. Finally, the very identity of a child may be set aside and sociodramatic play or role taking becomes possible. Whereas the *rate* of the progression may be heavily influenced by mediating factors (to be discussed below), the *sequence* is stable and rather invariant.

CONDITIONS NECESSARY FOR EMERGENCE OF IMAGERY AND IMAGINAL PLAY

Although imagery appears to be wired into the human organism in much the same way that potentials for language or motor behavior are, certain conditions appear to be necessary for it to emerge. Still others help it flourish. In other words, the biological potentials are necessary but not sufficient— they interact with interpersonal and environmental stimuli and events and thus determine imaginal development in complicated, mediated ways.

Internal Mediators

The internal conditions necessary for imaginal growth are neural maturation, affective organization, and affect's concomitant cognitive structuring.

Neural Maturation

The cells of the brain are not well differentiated for specific functions at birth (Rose, 1976). However, as the organism develops, perceptual abilities improve in acuity, and integration of perception and cognition becomes possible. Until a certain level of neurological differentiation has taken place, imagining is impossible and experience can be represented only through direct action (Piaget & Inhelder, 1969). This appears to be primarily a *maturational* constraint—indeed, studies of blind and deaf children show some impoverishment in imaging in the *specific modality* of deficit and in the rate of development (Sarlin & Altshuler, 1978; Silver, 1977; Singer & Lenahan, 1976) but little overall deficiency. So imaginal abilities are not strictly dependent on perception, although they *are* dependent on a level of sophistication in the *organization* of brain functions.

A related concern is hemispheric specialization. As the brain becomes more developed and the hemispheres lateralize more clearly into the specialized functions of the left hemisphere (processing verbal and sequential information) and of the right hemisphere (imaginal–pattern processing), imaginal development is fostered as it improves (1) directly through the increased potentials of the right hemisphere and (2) indirectly through the improvement in the *organization* of thinking. In other words, as language is used increasingly to represent objects and experiences, symbol formation is being practiced and perfected. This *process* of symbol formation and, later, transformation, can be adapted to the information processed in the right hemisphere as well. It is an *organizational* capacity. At this level expertise in one area can be used to eventually abet expertise in another. It is important to note that the emergence of this reciprocity is slow. Studies have demonstrated that in young children, the imaginal and verbal systems develop somewhat independently of each other and become well integrated only in middle childhood, around a mental age of 7 years (Forisha, 1975). At this time the child shows a basic reorganization of thought processes into what Piaget has called "concrete operational thinking": the specific perceptual qualities of an event and associational logic no longer exclusively govern understanding. But *before* this integration takes place, imaginal representations can and do occur and often dominate thought, determine affect, and govern behavior. Indeed, one might argue that encouragement of such right-hemispheric functions strengthens the bases of important later cognitive development, as is discussed below.

Affective Organization

Not only must the brain mature sufficiently to make differentiated perception and the integration of information possible, but the child's affective organization must mature. Indeed, it can be argued that affect is the "energizer" (Piaget, 1981) of cognition and that the two are inseparable (Izard, 1977; Singer, 1973, 1974; Tomkins, 1962, 1963). Piaget (Piaget, 1952, 1981; Piaget & Inhelder, 1969) has stressed the essential motivating power of affect, determining both direction and intensity of cognition and thus its basic role in fueling the accommodation–assimilation cycle. He disagrees with both a Freudian approach, which would have affect the determinant of cognitions, and with the conditioned-learning-theory approach, which would have stimuli themselves be the determinants of understanding. Rather, Piaget claims that the affect of "interest in the world" leads to accommodation with its exploratory power and changing of schemata to allow for novel inputs, whereas "interest in the self" leads to assimilation, with its matching of inputs to schemata already present.

Tomkins (1962, 1963), too, stresses the inseparability of affect and cognition, and he also calls the first of these positive affects "interest," whose arousal is triggered by a moderate rate of novelty and complexity in information. But Tomkins relabels the second "joy"—that affect aroused when a match between a perception or idea and an internal schemata is made and the unknown is reduced. Thus images, the templates against which new information is matched, can be powerful indeed; the discrepancy determines affect.

According to Tomkins (1962, 1963) and as later elaborated by others (Ekman, et al., 1972; Izard, 1977), the external hallmark of joy is the smile. It is this smile that is also the harbinger of new levels of affective organization in the infant (Sroufe & Waters, 1976). And this affective organization, which according to the developmentalists is inseparable but distinct from cognitive organization, arises in an interpersonal context (Sroufe, 1978, 1979; Sroufe & Waters, 1977). The predictability of a caretaker's stability and responsiveness permit both affective differentiation (as joy, or a decrease in arousal because of familiarity of situation, becomes separated from fear, or a high level of novelty and complexity) and a secure emotional base from which future explorations may take place (Ainsworth, 1979; Harrington, et al., 1978). Indeed, it is the "securely attached" child who, at all levels of development, can engage in age-appropriate play. For the preoperational child, the bulk of this play ought to be imaginative: the child imitates his or her perceptions of the external world in attempts to accommodate to it and then assimilates information to the new schemata. Thus some sophistication of affective organization, the "energizer" of cognitive behavior, is essential for growth to occur. If affect is stunted, stereotypy and sterility ensue.

Cognitive Organization

Finally, the schemata that allow for representation must be available. The notion of object constancy—learned usually through experience with a predictable caretaker—must precede the notion of allowing one object to stand for another and eventually an image to stand for an object and then an experience. As imagery becomes more elaborate and the *process* of imaging more utile in a child's life, the schemata also flourish. What was originally the projection of symbols onto new objects (as a child used a block for a truck or a cardboard tube for a horn) becomes part- and then whole-body representation of an image. Hands might become windshield wipers; people might become trees or chickens. Finally, the child can create an alternative temporary self. The sociodramatic play or role playing is the height of imaging, before the entire process becomes internalized in daydreaming (Klinger, 1971; 1975).

Interpersonal Conditions

Security of Attachment

The relationship of a person's response to the physical environment and to the social environment may well be different, but it is likely that behavior in the interpersonal world primes expectations that generalize to all reality (Blatt & Wild, 1976; Piaget, 1981; Singer, 1973; Tower & Singer, 1980). Quite simply, the child who cannot form an image of an important person and maintain its stability is likely to have more difficulty mastering the imaging *process*. Similarly, the child who finds his or her caretaker predictable but evocative of negative emotions (the child who has hostile or rejecting parents) is likely to be *able* to image but to prefer to avoid it, since arousing the schemata recreates the negative affective experience originally associated with them. Although both of these children may well learn to image, their positive involvement in the process is likely to be low, and they could become, as adults, the impoverished daydreamer with a lot of fleeting mind-wandering or the guilt-ridden daydreamer. These two cognitive styles are consistently identified in factor analytic studies of Singer's Imaginal Processes Inventory (Giambra, 1977; Huba, 1979; Singer, 1975; Singer & Antrobus, 1963, 1972). Thus positive interpersonal experience early in life is valuable in fostering *adaptive* imaging.

Modeling

A second way in which a child's interpersonal field vitally affects his or her imaginative capacity and rate concerns the examples that the child has available for imitating imaginative behavior. Empirical work has shown the enormous efficacy of a model in enhancing a child's imaginative play (Dansky, 1980; Feitelson & Ross, 1973; Freyberg, 1973; Marshall & Hahn, 1967; Nahme-Huang et al. 1977; Saltz & Johnson, 1974; Singer & Singer, 1976; Smilansky, 1968; Smith & Sydal, 1978; Wehman & Marchant, 1978). This modeling effect probably has an age "window," however; that is, a range within which it is effective. It appears that this period is between the onset of preoperational thinking and that of formal operational thought (Fein, 1973; Fouts & Liikanen, 1975; Gottlieb, 1973).

Availability of models can be expected to affect imaginativeness not only at the level of individual differences, but also at the level of an entire culture; several empirical studies show that children from lower socioeconomic groups are also cognitively impoverished. Indeed, they are found deficient in imaginativeness in their play (Rubin, 1976; Smilansky, 1968; Smith & Dodsworth, 1978; Tizard & Philips, 1976) irrespective of race (Griffing, 1980). It is likely that a lack of models for pretending in lower socioeconomic class cultures (for a multitude of reasons) inhibits the emergence of this type of play. Furthermore, negative sanctions from disapproving others could well force any intrinsic motivation (and play is by definition intrinsically motivated) into other channels of expression. Data by Farran and Haskins (1980) showed that middle-income mothers spent twice as much time in play with their children as did lower-class mothers. Lamb's data (1976, 1978) underscore the importance of playful interactions in parent–child affective bonding; Freyberg's (1973) study shows the role of playful interactions in imaginative development; and Bishop & Chace's research (1971) demonstrates the relevance of playful interactions to creativity. When this shared positive experience is missing, culturally deprived children are yet more deprived; some of their richest coping resources are left unsanctioned and unnurtured.

Environmental Conditions

In addition to internal and interpersonal influences on imaginal development, the environment itself can be a powerful mediator. Most salient among its influences are those of time and space, freedom from severe deprivation, and the structure in a setting.

Time and Space

Non-goal-directed behavior is unlikely to flourish amid heavy schedules and high levels of communal living. To develop and express his or her private symbolism, a child needs a certain amount of time away from external demands and a certain amount of space that is free from interference by others. Whereas sociodramatic play, an advanced form of imaginative play, by definition requires other children, its roots are laid in the "soldiers" a child moves along his or her blanket or the sequences developed in intimate moments alone with his or her dolls. Perhaps this simple need for privacy and tacit approval of idiosyncratic play behavior explains why children in larger families are less likely to be imaginative (Freyberg, 1973) and why partitioned space facilitates fantasy play (Field, 1980).

Freedom from Severe Deprivation

Although children have been known to continue playing despite countless negative consequences, the child who is always in a state of extreme deprivation is unlikely to develop the abilities that might stand him or her in good stead through a state of severe need (Maslow, 1969). Curiosity and the assimilation of the novel that it abets do not flourish when a child is chronically hungry, tired, sick, or unloved [see White (1959) on competence or Berlyne (1965) on curiosity]. Increasing arousal to an optimal level (Hebb, 1949) simply is not feasible if the level of *negative* arousal is high and persistent.

Structure in the Setting

Although many aspects of the child's behavior appear to be situationally specific (Fein & Apfel, 1979; Johnson, 1978; Rose, et al., 1975), structural components of imaginativeness are more stable over time (Fein & Apfel, 1979; Tower, 1980, Appendix I). Nonetheless, high levels of direction in a setting and much adult-determined activity can have a dulling effect on imaginative play (Carpenter & Huston-Stein, 1980 ; Huston-Stein, et al., 1977). On the other hand, a setting without clear boundaries at all—that is, one in which the child is expected to learn totally through discovery—also has been shown to dampen imaginative play (Johnson, et al., 1980). Perhaps the resolution to this apparent paradox lies in the intrusiveness of the structure and the type of imaginativeness being measured. Elsewhere I have shown that, as suggested by Smilansky (1968), clear differences between expressive and constructive imaginativeness exist (Tower, 1980, Appendix I). Indeed, their correlates are quite dissimilar. The data suggest that it is *constructive* imaginativeness, that which takes place within constraints of play materials and follows rules for creating a product that can be communicated, which leads to all the good things in life, whereas expressive imaginativeness is just that—an expression with little long-range or whole-organism impact. Therefore, a setting that provides clear guidelines for acceptable behavior and a few rules would probably be optimal in fostering imaginative development, whereas one that is totally adult directed would leave the child little room to develop inner resources; and a setting that is extremely laissez-faire would be too independent of goals. Just what are the correlates of imaginative development in childhood? Perhaps this internal resource is of more than passing educational interest and warrants consideration when determining the structure as well as the content of our educational programs.

RELATIONSHIPS BETWEEN IMAGERY AND A CHILD'S SOCIAL, EMOTIONAL AND COGNITIVE DEVELOPMENT

The child's imagery—form, content, and the very process of imaging—has functional aspects in addition to the structural and genetic ones already reviewed. As seen in the introduction to this chapter, these aspects span all facets of a child's life, both internally, the way the child thinks and feels, and externally, the way he or she relates to others or even organizes an environment, to the extent such organizing is within his or her control. Several of these social, emotional, and cognitive correlates of imaginativeness in children have been examined; a few have been subject to experimental investigation.

Relationships *between* cognitions, affects, and behaviors are complex and not necessarily reciprocal [see Emmerich et al. (1979), for empirial validation of the Piagetian point]. Nonetheless, there are frequent overlaps as social experience moderates affect and as affect energizes cognition (Piaget, 1981; Tomkins, 1962, 1963; Tower & Singer, 1980). Similarly, one's cognitive abilities—both in the *processing* of information and in the availability of formed schemata—regulate the input of information and thus affect and the behaviors thereby motivated. Specific facets of all three domains of functioning are considered below. Although they are treated as separate for conceptual clarity, they are functionally interdependent.

Cognitive Benefits of Imagery

By the time a child is 2 years old, he or she has begun to store images in his or her head of how things are or should be. This inner life includes notions of what the child actually is, is not, does do, does not do, can do, and cannot do. This inner life contributes substantially to the small child's world view. And, indeed, the young child finds it difficult to go beyond this egocentrism in perception, concept formation, or empathy for others. Nonetheless, imaginal skills have numerous benefits within this limitation: they facilitate attention and concentration, memory, organization of thinking, divergent cognitive abilities, and language development.

Attention and Concentration

Imaginal skills foster the development of attention and concentration through their impact on (1) conditioned staying power—the pleasurable activities of make-believe play are self-reinforcing and lead to a greater ability to stay with an activity (Singer, 1961, 1973); (2) the *quicker* processing of visual information stemming from faster scanning (Singer, 1974; Weiner, 1975)—this facilitates comfort with a more *reflective* cognitive tempo (Freyberg, 1973; Marshall & Hahn, 1967; Nahme-Huang et al., 1977; Saltz et al., 1977); and (3) development of absorption skills (Csikszentmihalyi, 1975; Qualls & Sheehan, 1980; Tower & Singer, 1980, 1981)—this results in a dramatic ability to focus attention.

Memory

Imagery facilitates the development of memory skills not only through fostering the attention and concentration that permit encoding in the first place, but also through its effects on (1) rehearsal of information, (2) strategies for encoding information, and (3) motivation for retention. First, imaginal processes *require* the rehearsal of information, as internal schemata are matched to external inputs. Practice in such rehearsal appears to improve at least recognition memory (Tower, et al., 1979), and anecdotal data suggest an even broader effect. How often has one observed the small child remembering minute details of the placement of every soldier in a mock battlefield, if the game was interrupted when the dog ran through the playroom? Not only are new inputs likely to be rehearsed more by the imaginative child, but long-term memory is likely to be exercised more frequently, as it is scanned for ideas for new games and activities.

The strategies the high-imagery child uses for encoding are also likely to be broader, as seen in his or her higher rate of recall for information as diverse as picture content (Wilgosh, 1975), story element sequences (Saltz & Johnson, 1974), and themes of stories (Tucker, 1975). Indeed, a great deal of data supports the independence of visual and verbal learning strategies in the young child (Forisha, 1975; Levin & Pressley, 1978; Mowbray & Luria, 1973; Reese, 1975; Tversky, 1973), and it also suggests the value of *both* in aiding memory (Kulhavy & Swenson, 1975; Levin & Divine-Hawkins, 1974; Millar, 1972; Perlmutter & Myers, 1975; Wilgosh, 1975). However, visual strategies appear to be superior to verbal ones for the young child (Reese, 1975; Rohwer, 1970; Wilgosh, 1975). Because of the facilitative effect that imaginative abilities can have on language development, to be discussed shortly, the child who develops and expresses imagery through play is doubly blessed.

Third, the imaginative child is likely to be more motivated to remember information in the first place. Because he or she has learned to transform and recombine experiences—in other words, to use them as inputs for pleasurable play—such activity is likely to become intrinsically motivated.

Organization in Thinking

The imaginative child develops several skills in the organization of information. He or she becomes adept at discriminating information—central from peripheral themes (Garvey, 1974), fantasy from reality (Matthews, 1977; Saltz et al., 1977), and even the self from others (Gilbert & Finell, 1978), and internally from externally generated information (Singer, 1973). In addition, this discrimination leads to improved organizational rules (Garvey, 1974) and an increased ability to abstract (Griffing, 1980; Rubin & Maioni, 1975). The child may even show conservation at an earlier age (Golumb & Cornelius, 1977) and an increased number of cognitive constructs (Ghiaci & Richardson, 1980). Vivid displays of the improved organizational skills of the imaginative child are his or her ability to tell more organized and elaborate stories (Pulaski, 1973; Tucker, 1975) and to integrate new information more effectively (Lieberman, 1965; Sutton-Smith, 1975). A third organizational skill is the imaginative child's improved ability to identify and use transition cues in moving from one type of information to another (Bateson, 1955; Sutton-Smith, 1975).

Divergent-Thinking Skills

A fourth cluster of cognitive benefits of imaginal development concerns its relationship to divergent-thinking skills. It has been shown to improve (1) originality in thinking (Lieberman, 1965; Marshall & Hahn, 1967), (2) associative fluency (Dansky, 1980; Li, 1978; Dansky & Silverman, 1973, 1975; Lieberman, 1965), and (3) cognitive flexibility (Lieberman, 1965; Pulaski, 1973; Sutton-Smith, 1975), often accompanied by reflectivity (Weiner, 1975) and creativity in general (Griffing, 1974). The great facility that the imaginative child develops in having one object stand for another object primes an increased use of the surrounding environment and a variety of cues; these creative abilities have their social correlates, which are discussed shortly.

Language Development

Finally, whereas imaginal and verbal processes are separate in the small child, without full interaction as symbolic functions until middle childhood (Forisha, 1975), the *exercise* of imagery through imaginative play has been shown to facilitate language development. Indeed, experimental studies in which dramatic play of preschoolers and kindergarten children was increased have demonstrated a concomitant increase in (1) vocabulary (Griffing, 1974; Lovinger, 1974), (2) verbalization of stories (Saltz & Johnson, 1974); (3) complexity of sentence structure (Marshall & Hahn, 1967); (4) scores on the verbal expression scale of the Illinois Test of Psycholinguistic Abilities (ITPA) (Jurkovic, 1978; Lovinger, 1974), (5) and amount and adequacy of verbal communication (Jurkovic, 1978; Lovinger, 1974; Marshall & Hahn, 1967). Presumably imaginativeness leads a child to seek more information for his or her games and transformations, experiment across types of information, and express the results in any form available.

Affective Benefits of Imagery

Unless the imaginative child carries the use of imagery to extremes, he or she is heir to rich benefits; gaining self-confidence and security from (1) a differentiated sense of identity; (2) high levels of self-control, (3) generally more positive affective experience, and (4) augmented resources for dealing with stress.

A Differentiated Sense of Identity and Self-Awareness

An imaginative child has a well-elaborated sense of himself or herself. Practice in all the cognitive skills previously discussed has affective implications:

1. The increased discrimination between self and others gained in comfort with role playing fosters an (a) openness to new emotional and cognitive experiences and (b) a concomitant spontaneity (Marshall & Hahn, 1967)—which has been shown to extend even across settings (Lieberman, 1965).
2. The role playing skills (a) augment the child's sense of his or her own

complexity and (b) broaden the world of emotional and social possibilities.

3. Willingness to risk trying on novel identities leads to both greater choice among them and commitment to those that are comfortable.

4. In addition, the child skilled in make-believe play shows increased sensitivity to facial and sensory cues (Singer, 1973), including (a) awareness of his or her own affect (Gilbert & Finell, 1978) and (b) a complementary articulated body concept (Gilbert & Finell, 1978).

5. Furthermore, avenues available for the expression of emotion are broadened—and, indeed, the actual expression of feelings increases with sociodramatic play (Marshall & Hahn, 1967).

6. Finally, the high levels of self-control, positive affect, and effective coping strategies experienced by the imaginative child, all discussed below, further amplify his or her sense of confidence and security.

Improved Self-Control

Imaginative skills also are associated with improved (1) emotional regulation, (2) access to the "flow" experience, (3) behavioral control, and (4) intrinsic motivation.

Emotional Regulation

The accommodation–assimilation cycle is, as Piaget (1981) and others suggest (Izard, 1977; Singer, 1973; Tower & Singer, 1980), fueled by the affects of interest and joy. The child learns to identify his or her optimal level of arousal—which, as Hebb (1949) pointed out, could be an increase as well as a decrease—and to select informational fields that will contribute to maintaining that state. In the face of boredom, novelty is sought; the tension of prolonged exploration is broken by a return to the familiar and fully controlled. Because of this skill at using information to regulate his or her emotions, (Biblow, 1973), the imaginative child shows more control over them—decreased fear (Burstein & Meichenbaum, 1979; Lazarus, 1971; Singer & Singer, 1976; Tower, 1980) and anger when frustrated (Biblow, 1973; Singer & Singer, 1976; Tower, 1980).

A Special State: Flow

The high level of absorption experienced by the imaginative child also primes him or her for the "flow" experience (Csikszentmihalyi, 1976), an intense state in which sufficient trust in the process enables the child to give his or her entire attention over to the matters at hand. The internalized sense of "rightness" in the activity leads to "an almost godlike sense of control" (Furlong, 1976, p. 36).

Behavioral Control

The ability to manage one's affective and attentional states facilitates control over behavior. Three areas in which the imaginative child has been shown to excel over his or her more stimulus- and situation-bound peers are in waiting tolerance (Singer, 1961), in the ability to delay gratification (Moore, 1976; Saltz, et al., 1977), and in managing fearful avoidance behaviors (Burstein & Meichenbaum, 1979; Lazarus, 1971).

Intrinsic Motivation

Finally, access to the internal values of pretending fosters respect for intrinsically motivated behavior in general. As has been noted, that comfort with internal reference points frees a child from the bondage of others' expectations.

Positive Affect

The body of literature documenting the increase in positive affect that accompanies imaginative play is substantial. Several studies (including those by & Freyberg, 1973; Griffing, 1974; Marshall & Hahn, 1967; Nahme-Huang et al., 1977; Singer & Singer, 1976; Singer & Singer, 1977; Tower et al., 1979; Tower, 1980) have shown positive affect to be significantly related to imaginativeness, and Manosevitz, et al. (1973) even found that mothers of children with imaginary playmates report the children's play with their pretend friends to be "happy and in high spirits." Since Underwood, et al. (1973) have shown that instructions to "think happy" can generate positive mood changes (and even result in more generous treatment of the self), the leap from acting-out play to internal thought is reduced.

Emotional Resources for Dealing with Stress

Erikson suggested that dramatic play was "an infantile way of thinking over difficult experiences" (Erikson, 1940, p. 130). Fantasy play certainly does serve as a valuable "adaptive defence" (Gould, 1972). As Singer (1973) has observed, it can help in organizing experiences to give behavior direction. More recently, Burstein and Meichenbaum (1979) studied elementary school children before, during, and after minor surgery that required hospitalization; they included a 7-month follow-up study of recall for events and coping style. Indeed, those children who coped the best with the event and had the lowest levels of residual anxiety were those children who freely used stress-related toys in imaginative play prior to the surgery. They were using the opportunity to do the "work of worrying," expressing their concerns directly through play. Indeed, Gunner-vonGrechten (1978) found that even infants who could master the movements of a frightening toy lost their fear. Lazarus (1971, pp. 211–212) reports one particularly vivid demonstration of imagery's value in reducing fear:

> I recently combined emotive imagery with fantasy imitation in treating an eight-year old boy who was too afraid to visit the dentist. The sequence consisted of having the child picture himself accompanying Batman and Robin on various adventures and then imagining his heroes visiting the dentist while he observed

them receiving dental attention. He was asked to picture this scene at least five times daily for one week. Next, he was to imagine himself in the dentist's chair while Batman and Robin stood by and observed him. He also practiced this image several times a day for one week. He visited the dentist the following week, and according to his mother he sat through four fillings without flinching.

Imagination and fantasy have been used in many forms to shore up the coping skills of children. Whether one supports Lazarus's desensitization approach or relabels it "covert modeling" (Cautela & McCullough, 1978; Kazdin, 1978), behaviorally oriented techniques are effective. Identifying and then modifying a child's internalized fantasies also has been enormously valuable therapeutically, as the work of Gardner (1971) has shown.

Finally, Peller (1971) has provided a long list of ways in which imaginative play can be a valuable coping resource for the child. These ways include (1) imitating someone the child loves or admires, (2) assigning roles to inanimate objects and having them act out the child's wishes and desires without assuming responsibility for the feelings, (3) assuming the role of someone or something that is feared and thus, through mastery by identification, overcoming the fear, (4) taking the role of the "loser" and thus gaining mastery over experiences in which he or she fails, (5) "incognito indulgence" in which "the child lends his motor apparatus to one part of his self and hold his superego in abeyance by declaring: 'That's not really me. You don't have to interfere'" (Peller, 1971, p. 115), (6) clowning, which serves to prevent embarrassment by exaggerating a very real mistake a child has made or imagines it might make, (7) deflected vengeance—using a symbolic object or role for revenge, (8) anticipatory retaliation, (9) furnishing a happy ending to a traumatic experience, (10) creating magic—or a guaranteed happy ending without risk, and (11) manipulation and playful repetition. In other words, Peller summarizes well the multiple benefits of imaginative play in helping a child deal with the negative and stressful sides of life.

Social Correlates of Imaginativeness

Just as the cognitive aspects of imaginal processes and content are rooted in affective life and, in turn, affect it, so they have implications for social behavior. Again, as Emmerich et al. (1979) have shown, they are not *reciprocal*—cognitions are necessary for social behaviors, but the relationships are not as strongly reversible. But they are important to the child's way of living and learning alongside of peers and adults.

Attractiveness to Others

Imaginative children tend to be more sought-after by other children (Rubin & Maioni, 1975; Tower, 1980). Perhaps this correlation reflects recognition of value of the good ideas the imaginative child has. For example, he or she often elaborates on the actual—a stick can become a flag for a march, the bar of a lion's cage, or the baton of the drum major—and transforms the ordinary into the extraordinary. Because of the imaginative child's ability to organize and integrate diverse stimuli, he or she is similarly more likely to turn a wad of cotton into bandages, a wagon into an ambulance and playmates into attendants. When frustrated by not having money to buy peanuts for monkeys at the zoo, the child who frequently uses objects for multiple purposes might think of retrieving a stick to scoop up those that had not quite made it to the cage. Similarly, skill in using the environment to create props has value. It primes a child to see the possibilities of raw materials in creating what he or she needs for play—stones can be cookies for a tea party, money can be made from paper, blocks can form a fire station.

Not only may imaginative children be sought after for their good ideas, but their lower level of aggression (Bankart & Anderson, 1979; Biblow, 1973; Feshbach, 1976; Singer, 1971); and higher level of frustration tolerance (Biblow, 1973; Tower, 1980) make them more pleasant company. Furthermore, tension is decreased by their ability to extend play when frustrated (a child thwarted as an auto mechanic may spot a rag and transform the role to car washer).

Finally, the imaginative child cooperates better (Nahme-Huang et al., 1977; Smilansky, 1968; Tower, 1980). Indeed, he or she is quick to see that cooperation furthers intrinsically rewarding play: "store" becomes easier when there are customers; pirates need a crew and other ships to commandeer; a farmer needs animals or ranch hands. Role taking skills pay off in an appreciation of reciprocity.

Attitudes toward Others

In addition to being more sought after because he or she is better company, the imaginative child may be valued for his or her attitudes toward others. The imaginative child derives pleasure from his or her internal productions and is open to experiences that might be useful input. In addition, by valuing his or her own productions, the child extends respect to the internal experiences of others. Surely, respect is one ingredient of attractiveness.

In addition, the child who is skilled at role playing is more flexible and more empathetic (Rubin, 1976; Rubin & Maioni, 1975). The child who can put him or herself in another's place, by pretending to be a teacher, a baby, or a big brother or a child who is about to move to a new neighborhood is better able to understand another's plight or point of view and can recognize that others behave differently according to context. This child is less egocentric. Interestingly, one study of delinquents found the confined boys developmentally inferior to a comparison group but found that recidivism decreased after training in sociodramatic play (Chandler, 1973). Ambron and Irwin (1975) have found a similar relationship between role-taking skills and moral judgment.

Finally, the imaginative child develops an intrinsic set of standards. His or her willingness to pretend reflects an ability to use the ideas that come from within. Since the generation, expression, and elaboration of such ideas yields positive affects of interest and joy, the child tends to be more willing to rely on his or her own judgment. In addition, the imaginative child's increased respect and tolerance for others' individuality, just mentioned, furthers his or her tolerance of his or her own. This internal security girds the child against pressures to conform and, even better, in the presence of such pressures, leads him or her to offer alternative possibilities to the standard that feels uncomfortable.

Benefits in Learning Situations

The imaginative child is at an advantage when he or she needs to learn from others. First, the child is more receptive to vicarious learning. The habit of drawing content from stories, television, and observations of others as input for his or her own fantasies, has rendered the imaginative child more likely to pay attention to and learn from an intriguing event. Indeed, Jane Tucker's work (1975) has demonstrated the superior recall of stories of imaginative children; an openness to hearing them brings gains.

The imaginative child learns better not only from others' experiences, but also from others' behaviors. His or her well-groomed imagery facilitates storage of actions he or she has witnessed, rehearsal of them in imagination, and generation of situations in which he or she can test out various ways of acting that have been modeled. Thus the teacher who handles an argument between two children by saying, "Jimmy, you had it first. Tell Bobby to give it back" may suggest to the child skilled in pretend play that this is a good way to handle similar situations in the future.

Third, it is easier for the imaginative child to change his or her behavior. By learning appropriate roles and reactions through testing them out in play, the child can develop an inventory of which responses yield which consequences. Alternatives are available, and strategies for evaluating them are developed. Playing "store" can teach one that lines must be tolerated and goods paid for; playing "house" can teach one that others in a family have wants and needs that can have merit; playing "doctor" may lead one to be brave during the quite temporary agony of an allergy shot.

Fourth, this "self-discipline within a role context", mentioned so long ago by Smilansky (1968), can lead to improved self-discipline (Singer, 1973). The child playing Superman is highly unlikely to cry if he or she should fall and scrape a knee: Superman would never respond in such a manner. The privileges of being 3 years old may dawn with brilliant clarity when the child who is playing "baby" realizes he or she cannot swing on a swing, pour his or her own milk, or be read a story. Such knowledge may have transfer value into the child's own life when he or she is required to act more maturely or stick with a difficult interaction or follow another's dictates yet a short while longer.

Fifth, the imaginative child's skill at "organizing and integrating diverse stimuli" also may lead him or her to be more comfortable in new situations and thus to learn more easily from them. The child who can easily play "policeman" and "prisoner" may benefit more from a field trip to the police station than would the child who had not considered trying on either hat. The strangeness of the county jail is mitigated by familiarity with circumstances drawn from imagination. A first flight on a plane may leave the imaginative child free to observe the aerial landscape, if playacting has already prepared him or her for the noise and activity of the jet. Rather than fear, curiosity is aroused. Again, the mechanism for lessening arousal by superior manipulation and matching of information has value.

Finally, the five characteristics just listed converge to form an adaptability, an ease of learning from a range of teaching techniques. Pictures; demonstrations; films; books; lectures; and people, people, people, and more people are regarded as useful in learning about the world and about the self.

Relationships with Adults

Imaginativeness is an asset not only in dealing with peers and in social learning, but also in regard to the relationships a child has with adults.

First, a rich imaginative life facilitates behavior that is intrinsically appealing to adults: a high level of self-control with less aggression and anger, greater frustration tolerance, and a longer attention span that enables the child to wait longer and be happier alone. The child who can amuse himself or herself is simply easier to handle, as one stands in a gas-station line, sees other children off to school, or takes a deep breath over a cup of tea.

Second, this ability to handle imaginatively the difficult situation of being alone, waiting for extended periods, and withstanding frustration is in stark contrast to the alternatives: active exploration, which often leads to interruptions at best and destructiveness at worst, or a glassy-eyed pseudoamnesiac state as a child is drawn from reality demands altogether by the anesthetic pull of the television set. This avoidance of the negative further fosters quality adult–child relationships.

Third, the value of imaginativeness to adults may lead them to sanction and encourage it and thus further enrich relationships. Merely by paying attention to a child's spontaneous play an adult offers tacit approval of it. The positive attention from an adult, who gives a child playing "veterinarian" a napkin as a blanket for a sick horse, is not lost.

Finally, such relationships are likely to be marked by an absence of destructive teasing. The adult who can understand a child's literal way of viewing the world and limited capacities for transformations is more likely to respect the child's need for clarity and difficulty with symbolism. One mother who innocently announced to her son "Daddy will be late tonight. He got tied up" was somewhat taken aback when the child then asked her "Did the Indians get him?"

Management of Social Interaction

Finally, imaginative play can facilitate the child's learning about the place of the self in a social world. As Wolfgang (1974) has noted, dramatic play teaches about "dependency, social awareness, hostility, aggression, possession, power, rivalry, and anxiety." This intensely personal side to socialization is complemented by more cultural levels, as the child learns the strategies for entering and leaving social situations (Lieberman, 1965; Sutton-Smith, 1971), the mythology and rules with which a culture structures reality (Denzin, 1975), and the shared symbolism to which he or she is entitled by heritage (Stone, 1971). The latter is vividly appropriated as the child uses play to form his or her own symbols of group identity; for example, the girls who offered me cakes became the "bake shop ladies."

In summary, a child's imagery capacities, originally arising out of social interactions and flourishing within them, can lead to a host of social benefits. These extend throughout relationships with both peers and adults and have a particularly vivid impact on learning situations.

FACILITATING IMAGINAL DEVELOPMENT

If imaginal development in the child yields all the preceding benefits, then its encouragement is warranted. As has been noted, experimental studies have shown that such development can be encouraged. In addition to (1) letting the internal rewards be their own energizers, (2) providing modeling input and implicit sanction of imaginative behavior, and (3) organizing the reward structure in the culture to permit non-goal-oriented behavior time and space to flourish, specific roles can be helpful and particular strategies effective.

Roles of Adults

To facilitate imaginal development, an adult can (1) be a model to imitate, (2) provide a safe place for imaginative behavior to take place—in a word, permission for such behavior, (3) act as an advocate for imaginative behavior, defending the child to others—other children, parents, grandparents, and teachers—who might be far more goal oriented, (4) help the child understand and appreciate his or her uniqueness and the importance of perceptions, thoughts, and feelings, (5) help the child to reflect on experience better, thus sanctioning assimilation of it rather than a sensation-seeking focus on novelty, and (5) create and maintain a climate that encourages such elaboration on and extending of prior experiences or knowledge rather than analyzing, criticizing, or ignoring it.

Strategies of Value

Not only can roles be suggested, but strategies that transcend roles may be of value. They include (1) encouraging practice without evaluation of products; (2) treating the child and his or her ideas with respect; (3) treating experiences and attitudes toward those experiences with respect; (4) drawing analogies that help to demonstrate the application of a novel idea to new areas or to relate a new experience to a prior one; (5) when evaluation is necessary, (a) evaluating the product and not the child and (b) making sure that the child is clear about both the strengths and weaknesses in the product and not just the weaknesses; (6) encouraging the use of verbs instead of nouns and thinking in terms of function or process rather than in a formal or structural terms; (7) modeling and encouraging the use of many different ways of thinking about something or approaching a task; (8) placing value on individual differences and heterogeneity; and (9) appreciating the child's needs to belong—and helping him or her develop his or her own group norms that value individual differences.

A NOTE ON MALADAPTIVE EXTREMES

As mentioned earlier, the benefits of imaginativeness take place along a continuum. At one extreme are children with impoverished imaginative skills like Chandler's delinquents (1973) or Gould's (1972) anxious children, too threatened by their own imaginal productions to make them. At the other extreme, are children who withdraw into their imaginal lives at cost of solid contact with reality. These dangers have been pointed out elsewhere (Singer, 1973, 1975; Tower & Singer, 1980) and recently have been studied empirically (Tower, 1980). In the current chapter it suffices to say that it is imaginativeness within a solid sense of reality, and especially constructive imaginativeness, in which reality constraints are integrated into the play (Tower, 1980) that are of great value. Imagery should be used to facilitate understanding and exploration of reality and not to escape from it. We do well to follow Christopher Robin's lead:

> ONE OF THE CHAIRS IS SOUTH AMERICA,
> ONE OF THE CHAIRS IS A SHIP AT SEA,
> ONE IS A CAGE FOR A GREAT BIG LION,
> AND ONE IS A CHAIR FOR ME.

> The First Chair.
>   When I go up the Amazon,
>   I stop at night and fire a gun
>   To call my faithful band.
>   And Indians in two and threes,
>   Come silently between the trees,
>   And wait for me to land.
>   And if I do not want to play
>   With any Indians today,
>   I simply wave my hand.

And then they turn and go away—
They always understand.

The Second Chair.
I'm a great big lion in my cage,
And I often frighten Nanny with a roar.
Then I hold her very tight, and
Tell her not to be so frightened—
And she doesn't be so frightened any more.

The Third Chair.
When I am in my ship, I see
The other ships go sailing by.
A sailor leans and calls to me
As his ship goes sailing by.
Across the sea he leans to me,
Above the winds I hear him cry:
"Is this the way to Round-the-World?"
He calls as he goes by.

The Fourth Chair.
Whenever I sit in a high chair
For breakfast or dinner or tea,
I try to pretend that it's *my* chair,
And that I am a baby of three.
SHALL I GO OFF TO SOUTH AMERICA?
SHALL I PUT OUT IN MY SHIP TO SEA?
OR GET IN MY CAGE AND BE LIONS AND TIGERS?
OR—SHALL I BE ONLY ME?

A. A. Milne, "Nursery Chairs,"
When We Were Very Young, 1924.

REFERENCES

Ainsworth, M. D. S. Infant–mother attachment. *American* Psychologist, 1979, **34,** 932–937.

Ambron, S., & Irwin, D. Role taking and moral judgment in five and seven-year olds. *Developmental Psychology*, 1975, **11,** 102.

Bankart, C. & Anderson, C. Short-term effects of prosocial television viewing on play of preschool boys and girls. *Psychological Reports*, 1979, **44,** 935–941.

Bateson, G. A theory of play and fantasy. *Psychiatric Research Reports*, 1955 (2), 39–51.

Berlyne, D. *Structure and direction in thinking*. New York: Wiley, 1965.

Biblow, E. Imaginative play and the control of aggression. In J. L. Singer (Ed.), *Child's world of make-believe*. New York: Academic Press, 1973.

Bishop, D. W., Chace, C. A. Parental conceptual systems, home play environment, and potential creativity in children. *Journal of Experimental Child Psychology,* 1971, **12**, 318–338.

Blatt, S. J. & Wild, C. *Schizophrenia: A developmental analysis.* New York: Academic Press, 1976.

Block, J., & Block, J. H. Ego development and the provence of thought: A longitudinal study of ego and cognitive development in young children. Unpublished progress report for the National Institute of Mental Health, 1973.

Block, J., & Block, J. H. Ego development and the provence of thought: A longitudinal study of ego and cognitive development in young children, Number 2. Unpublished progress report for the National Institute of Mental Health, 1976.

Burstein, S. & Meichenbaum, D. The work of worrying in children undergoing surgery. *Journal of Abnormal Child Psychology,* 1979, **7**, 121–132.

Carpenter, C., & Huston-Stein, A. Activity structure and sex-typed behavior in preschool children. *Child Development,* 1980, **51**, 862–872.

Cautela, J., & McCullough, L. Covert conditioning: A learning-theory perspective on imagery. In J. L. Singer & K. S. Pope (Eds.), *The power of human imagination.* New York: Plenum, 1978.

Chaille, C. The child's conceptions of play, pretending and toys: Sequences and structural parallels. *Human Development,* 1978, **21**, 201–210.

Chandler, M. Egocentrism and antisocial behavior: The assessment and training of social perspective-taking skills. *Developmental Psychology, 1973,* **9**, 326–332.

Csikszentmihalyi, M. *Beyond boredom and anxiety.* San Francisco: Jossey-Bass, 1975.

Dansky, J. Make-believe: A mediator of the relationship between play and associative fluency. *Child Development,* 1980, **51**, 576–579.

Dansky, J. L., & Silverman, I. W. Effects of play on associative fluency in preschool-aged children. *Developmental Psychology, 1973,* **9**, 38–43.

Dansky, J. L., & Silverman, I. W. Play: A general facilitator of associative fluency. *Developmental Psychology,* 1975, **11**, 104.

Denzin, N. Play, games and interaction: The contents of childhood socialization. *Sociological Quarterly, 1975,* **16**, 458–478.

Ekman, P., Friesen, W., & Ellsworth, P. *Emotions in the human face: Guidelines for research and a review of findings.* New York: Pergamon, 1972.

Emmerich, W., Cocking, R., & Sigel, I. Relationships between cognitive and social functioning in preschool children. *Developmental Psychology, 1978,* **15**, 495–504.

Erikson, E. H. Studies in the interpretation of play. *Genetic Psychology Monographs,* 1940, **22**, 557–671.

Erikson, E. *Childhood and society.* New York: Norton, 1963.

Farran, D., & Haskins, R. Reciprocal influence in the social interactions of mothers and three-year old children from different socioeconomic backgrounds. *Child Development,* 1980, **51**, 780–791.

Fein, G. The effect of chronological age and model reward on imitative behavior. *Developmental Psychology, 1973,* **9**, 283–289.

Fein, G. A transformational analysis of pretending. *Developmental Psychology,* 1975, **11**, 291–296.

Fein, G., & Apfel, N. The development of play: Style, structure and situations. *Genetic Psychology Monographs*. 1979, **99**, 231–250.

Feitelson, D., & Ross, G. The neglected factor: Play. *Human Development*, 1973, **16**, 202–223.

Feshbach, S. The role of fantasy in response to television. *Journal of Social Issues*, 1976, **32**, 71–85.

Field, T. W. Preschool play: Effects of teacher/child ratios and organization of classroom space. *Child Study Journal*, 1980, **10**, 191–205.

Forisha, B., & Liikanen, P. The effects of age and developmental level on imitation in children. *Child Development*, 1975, **46**, 555–558.

Freyberg, J. Increasing the imaginative play of urban disadvantaged kindergarten children through systematic training. In J. L. Singer, (Ed.), *Child's world of make-believe*. New York: Academic Press, 1973.

Furlong, W. The fun in fun: The flow experience. *Psychology Today*, 1976, **10**, 35–38, 1980.

Gardner, R. *Therapeutic communication with children: The mutual story-telling technique*. New York: Science House, 1971.

Garvey, C. Some properties of social play. *Merrill-Palmer Quarterly*, 1974, **20**, 163–180.

Ghiaci, G., & Richardson, J. The effects of dramatic play upon cognitive structure and development. *Journal of Genetic Psychology*, 1980, **136**, 77–83.

Giambra, L. A factor analytic study of daydreaming, imaginal process, and temperament: A replication of an adult male life-span sample. *Journal of Gerontology*, 1977, **32**, 675–680.

Gilbert, D., & Finell, L. Young child's awareness of self. *Psychological Reports*, 1978, **43**, 911–914.

Golumb, C. Symbolic play: The role of substitutions in pretence and puzzle games. *British Journal of Educational Psychology*, 1977, **47**, 175–186.

Golumb, C., & Cornelius, C. Symbolic play and its cognitive significance, *Developmental Psychology*, 1977, **13**, 246–252.

Gottlieb, S. Modeling effects upon fantasy. In J. L. Singer, (Ed.), *Child's world of make-believe*. New York: Academic Press, 1973.

Gould, R. *Child studies through fantasy*. New York: Quadrangle Books, 1972.

Griffing, P. The relationship between socioeconomic status and sociodramatic play among Black kindergarten children. *Genetic Psychology Monographs*, 1980, **101**, 3–34.

Gunner-vonGrechten, M. Changing a frightening toy into a pleasant toy by allowing an infant to control its action. *Developmental Psychology*, 1978, **14**, 157–162.

Harrington, D. M., Block, J. H., & Block, J. Intolerance of ambiguity in preschool children: Psychometric considerations, behavioral manifestations, and parental correlates. *Developmental Psychology*, 1978, **14**, 242–256.

Hebb, D. O. *The organization of behavior*. New York: Wiley, 1949.

Herron, R. E., & Sutton-Smith, B., *Child's play*. New York: Wiley, 1971.

Horowitz, M. J. *Image formation and cognition*. New York: Appleton, 1970.

Huba, G. Daydreaming. In R. H. Woody (Ed.), *The encyclopedia of clinical assessment*. San Francisco: Jossey-Bass, 1979.

Hughes, M., & Hutt, C. Heart-rate correlates of childhood activities: Play, exploration, problem-solving and daydreaming. *Biological Psychology*, 1979, 253–263.

Hurlock, E. In R. E. Herron & Sutton-Smith, *Child's play*, New York: Wiley, 1971.

Huston-Stein, A., Friedrich-Cofer, L., & Susman, E. The relation of classroom structure to social behavior, imaginative play, and self-regulation of economically disadvantaged children. *Child Development*, 1977, **48,** 908–916.

Izard, C. *Human emotions*. New York: Plenum, 1977.

Johnson, J. Mother–child interaction and imaginative behavior of preschool children. *Journal of Psychology*, 1978, **100,** 123–129.

Johnson, J., Ershler, J., & Bell, C. Play behavior in a discovery-based and a formal-education preschool program. *Child Development*, 1980, **51,** 271–274.

Jurkovic, G. Relation of psycholinguistic development to imaginative play of disadvantaged preschool children. *Psychology in the Schools*, 1978, **15,** 560–564.

Kazdin, A. E. Covert modeling: The therapeutic application of imagined rehearsal. In J. L. Singer & K. S. Pope (Eds.), *The power of human imagination: New methods in psychotherapy*. New York: Plenum, 1978.

Klinger, E. *Structure and functions of fantasy*. New York: Wiley, 1971.

Kosslyn, S. *Image and mind*. Cambridge, Mass.: Harvard *University Press*, 1980.

Kulhavy, R. W., & Swenson, I. Imagery instructions and the comprehension of text. *British Journal of Educational Psychology*, 1975, **45,** 47–51.

Lamb, M. E. (Ed.). *The role of the father in child development*. New York: Wiley, 1976.

Lamb, M. E. The father's role in the infant's social world. In J. H. Stevens & M. Mathews (Eds.), *Mother/child, father/child relationships*. Washington, D.C.: National Association for the Education of Young Children, 1978.

Lang, P. Language, image and emotion. In K. Pline, K. R. Blankstein, & I. M. Speigel (Eds.), *Advances in the study of emotion and affect, Vol. 5: Perceptions of emotion in self and others*. New York: Plenum, 1978.

Lazarus, A. A. *Behavior therapy and beyond*. New York: McGraw-Hill, 1971.

Levin, J. R., & Divine-Hawkins, P. Visual imagery as a prose-learning process. *Journal of Reading Behavior*, 1974, **6,** 23–30.

Levin, J., & Pressley, M. A test of the developmental imagery hypothesis in children's associative learning. *Journal of Educational Psychology*, 1978, **70,** 691–694.

Li, A. Effects of play on novel responses in kindergarten children. *Alberta Journal of Educational Research*, 1978, **24,** 31–36.

Lieberman, J. N. Playfulness and divergent thinking: An investigation of their relationship at the kindergarten level. *Journal of Genetic Psychology*, 1965, **107,** 219–224.

Lovinger, S. Socio-dramatic play and language development in preschool disadvantaged children. *Psychology in the Schools*, 1974, **11,** 313–320.

Manosevitz, M., Prentice, N., & Wilson, F. Individual and family correlates of imaginary companions in preschool children. *Developmental Psychology,* 1973, **8,** 72–79.

Marshall, H., & Hahn, S. Experimental modification of dramatic play. *Journal of Personality and Social Psychology,* 1967, **5,** 119–132.

Maslow, A. *Motivation and personality.* New York: Harper, 1969.

Matthews, W. Modes of transformation in the initiation of fantasy play. *Developmental Psychology,* 1977, **13,** 212–216.

Millar, S. Effects of instructions to visualize stimuli during delay on visual recognition by preschool children. *Child Development,* 1972, **43,** 1073–1075.

Milne, A. A. Nursery chairs. In *When we were very young.* New York: Dutton, 1924.

Morison, P. & Gardner, H. Dragons and dinosaurs: The child's capacity to differentiate fantasy from reality. *Child Development,* 1978, **49,** 642–648.

Moore, B., Clyburn, A., & Underwood, B. The role of affect in delay of gratification. *Child Development,* 1976, **47,** 273–276.

Mowbray, C., & Luria, Z. Effects of labeling on children's visual imagery. *Developmental Psychology,* 1973, **9,** 1–8.

Nahme-Huang, L., Singer, D. G., Singer, J. L., & Wheaton, A. Imaginative play and perceptual-motor intervention methods with emotionally-disturbed, hospitalized children: An evaluation study. *American Journal of Orthopsychiatry,* 1977, **47,** 238–249.

Nicholich, L. Beyond sensorimotor intelligence: Assessment of symbolic maturity through analysis of pretend play. *Merrill-Palmer Quarterly,* 1977, **23,** 89–99.

Paivio, A. *Imagery and verbal processes.* New York: Holt, 1971.

Peller, L. W. Models of children's play. In R. E. Herron and B. Sutton-Smith, (Eds.), *Child's play. New York: Wiley, 1971. (reprinted from Mental Hygiene,* 1952, **36,** 66–83).

Perlmutter, M. & Myers, N. Young children's coding and storage of visual and verbal material. *Child Development,* 1975, **46,** 215–219.

Piaget, J. *The origins of intelligence in children.* New York: International University Press, 1952.

Piaget, J. *Play, dreams and imitation in childhood.* New York: Norton, 1962.

Piaget, J. *Intelligence and affectivity: Their relationship during child development.* Palo Alto, Ca.: Annual Reviews, 1981.

Piaget, J., & Inhelder, B. *The Psychology of the child.* New York: Basic Books, 1969.

Piaget, J., & Inhelder, B. *Mental imagery in the child.* New York: Basic Books, 1971.

Pope, K., & Singer, J. L. *The stream of consciousness.* New York: Plenum, 1978.

Prentice, N., Manosevitz, M., & Hubbs, L. Imaginary figures of early childhood: Santa Claus, Easter Bunny, and the Tooth Fairy. *American Journal of Orthopsychiatry,* 1978, **48,** 618–628.

Pulaski, M. Toys and imaginative play. In J. L. Singer (Ed.), *Child's world of make-believe.* New York: Academic Press, 1973.

Pylyshyn, Z. What the mind's eye tells the mind's brain: A critique of mental imagery. *Psychological Bulletin,* 1973, **80,** 1–24.

Qualls, P., & Sheehan, P. Imaginative, make-believe experiences and their role in child development. Unpublished paper, University of Queensland; Queensland, Australia, 1980.

Reese, H. W. Verbal effects in children's visual recognition memory. *Child Development,* 1975, **46,** 400–407.

Rohwer, W. D. Jr. Images and pictures in children's learning: Research results and educational implications. *Psychological Bulletin,* 1970, **73,** 393–403.

Rose, S. *The conscious brain.* New York: Vintage Books, 1976.

Rose, S., Blank, M., & Spalter, I. Situational specificity of behavior in young children. *Child Development,* 1975, **46,** 464–469.

Rubin, K. Relation between social participation and role-taking skill in preschool children. *Psychological Reports,* 1976, **39,** 823–826.

Rubin, K., & Maioni, T. Play preference and its relationship to preschoolers. *Merrill-Palmer Quarterly,* 1975, **21,** 171–179.

Rubin, K., Maioni, T., & Hornung, M. Free play in middle and lower-class preschoolers: Parten and Piaget revisted. *Child Development,* 1976, **47,** 414–419.

Rubin, K., Watson, K., & Jambon, T. Free-play behaviors in preschool and kindergarten children. *Child Development,* 1978, **49,** 534–536.

Saltz, E., & Johnson, J. Training for thematic-fantasy play in culturally disadvantaged children: Preliminary results. *Journal of Educational Psychology,* 1974, **66,** 623–630.

Saltz, E., Dixon, D., & Johnson, J. Training disadvantaged preschoolers on various fantasy activities: Effects on cognitive functioning and impulse control. *Child Development,* 1977, **48,** 367–380.

Sarlin, M., & Altshuler, K. On the inter-relationship of cognition and affect: Fantasies of deaf children. *Child Psychiatry and Human Development,* 1978, **9,** 95–103.

Sheehan, P. (Ed.) *The function and nature of imagery.* New York: Academic Press, 1972.

Sheikh, A., & Shaffer, J. (Eds.). *The potential of fantasy and imagination.* New York: Brandon House, 1979.

Shepard, R. The mental image. *American Psychologist,* 1978, **33,** 125–137.

Shorr, J., Sobel, G., Robin, P., & Cautela, J. *Imagery: Its many dimensions and applications.* New York: Plenum, 1980.

Silver, R. The question of imagination, originality and abstract thinking by deaf children. *American Annals of the Deaf,* 1977, **122,** 349–354.

Singer, D. G., & Lenahan, M. Imagination content in dreams of deaf children. *American Annals of the Deaf,* 1976, **121,** 44–48.

Singer, J. L. Imagination and waiting ability in young children. *Journal of Personality,* 1961, **29,** 396–413.

Singer, J. L. (Ed.). *The control of aggression and violence.* New York: Academic Press, 1971.

Singer, J. L. *The child's world of make-believe.* New York: Academic Press, 1973.

Singer, J. L. *Imagery and daydream methods in psychotherapy and behavior modification*. New York: Academic Press, 1974.

Singer, J. L. *The inner world of daydreaming*. New York: Harper, 1975.

Singer, J. L., & Antrobus, J. S. A factor analytic study of daydreaming and conceptually-related cognitive and personality variables. *Perceptual and Motor Skills,* 1963, **17,** 187–209.

Singer, J. L., & Antrobus, J. S. Daydreaming, imaginal processes, and personality: A normative study. In P. W. Sheehan (Ed.), *The function and nature of imagery*. New York: Academic Press, 1972, pp. 175–202.

Singer, J. L., & Singer, D. G. Fostering imaginative play in preschool children: Television and live model effects. *Journal of Communication,* 1976, **26,** 74–80.

Singer, J. L., & Singer, D. G. Television viewing and imaginative play in preschoolers. National Science Foundation Grant Progress Report. New Haven, Conn., 1977.

Smilansky, S. *The effects of sociodramatic play on disadvantaged preschool children*. New York: Wiley, 1968.

Smith, P., & Dodsworth, C. Social class differences in the fantasy play of preschool children. *Journal of Genetic Psychology,* 1978, **133,** 183–190.

Smith, P., & Syddall, S. Play and non-play tutoring in preschool children: Is it play or tutoring that matters? *British Journal of Educational Psychology,* 1978, **48,** 315–325.

Sroufe, L. A. Attachment and the roots of competence. *Human Nature,* 1978, **1,** 50–59.

Sroufe, L. A. The coherence of individual development: Early care, attachment and subsequent development. *American Psychologist,* 1979, **34,** 834–841.

Sroufe, L., & Waters, E. The ontogenesis of smiling and laughter: A perspective on the organization of development in infancy. *Psychological Review,* 1976, **83,** 173–189.

Sroufe, L. A., & Waters, E. Attachment as an organizational construct. *Child Development,* 1977, **48,** 1184–1199.

Stone, G. P. The play of little children. In R. E. Herron and B. Sutton-Smith (Eds.), *Child's play*. New York: Wiley, 1971 (reprinted from *Quest,* 1965, **4,** 23–31).

Sutton-Smith, B. Boundaries. In R. E. Herron and B. Sutton-Smith (Eds.), *Child's play*. New York: Wiley, 1971.

Sutton-Smith, B. The useless made useful: Play as variability training. *School Review,* 1975, **83,** 197–214.

Sutton-Smith, B., Abrams, D., Botvin, G., Caring, M., Gildesgame, D., & Stevens, T. The importance of the story-taker: An investigation of imaginative life. *Urban Review,* 1975, **8,** 82–95.

Tizard, B., & Philips, J. Play in preschool centres: II. Effects on play of the child's social class and of the educational orientation of the centre. *Journal of Child Psychology and Psychiatry and Allied Disciplines,* 1976, **17,** 265–274.

Tomkins, S. *Affect, imagery, consciousness,* Vols. 1 and 2. New York: Springer, 1962, 1963.

Tower, R. B. The influence of parents' values on preschool children's behaviors. Unpublished doctoral dissertation. New Haven, Conn.: Yale University, 1980.

Tower, R. B., & Singer, J. L. Imagination, interest and joy in early childhood. In P. E. McGhee & A. J. Chapman (Eds.), *Children's Humour*. London: Wiley, 1980.

Tower, R. B., & Singer, J. L. The measurement of imagery: How can it be clinically useful? In P. C. Kendall & S. Hollon (Eds.), *Assessment strategies for cognitive–behavioral interventions*. New York: Academic Press, 1981.

Tower, R. B., Singer, D. G., Singer, J. L., & Biggs, A. Differential effects of television programming on preschoolers' cognition, imagination, and social play. *American Journal of Orthopsychiatry*, 1979, **49**, 265–281.

Tucker, J. The role of fantasy in cognitive–affective functioning: Does reality make a difference? Unpublished doctoral dissertation, Columbia University, 1975.

Tversky, B. Pictorial and verbal encoding in preschool children. *Developmental Psychology*, 1973, **8**, 149–153.

Underwood, B., Moore, B., Rosenhan, D. Affect and self-gratification. *Developmental Psychology*, 1973, **8**, 209–214.

Vandenberg, B. Play and development from an ethological perspective. *American Psychologist*, 1978, **33**, 724–738.

Wehman, P., & Marchant, J. Improving play skills of severely retarded children. *American Journal of Occupational Therapy*, 1978, **32**, 100–104.

Weiner, A. Visual information-processing speed in reflective and impulsive children. *Child Development*, 1975, **46**, 998–1000.

Weisler, A., & McCall, R. Exploration and play: Resumé and redirection. *American Psychologist*, 1976, **31**, 492–508.

White, R. W. Motivation reconsidered: The concept of competence. *Psychological Review, 1959*, **66**, 297–333.

Wilgosh, L. Effects of labels on memory for pictures in four-year-old children. *Journal of Educational Psychology*, 1975, **67**, 375–379.

Wolfgang, C. An exploration of the relationship between the cognitive area of reading and selected developmental aspects of children's play. *Psychology in the Schools*, 1974, **11**, 338–343.

CHAPTER 9

Cerebral Laterality and Imagery

ROBERT G. LEY

INTRODUCTION

It has generally been assumed that the right cerebral hemisphere mediates cognitive activities that involve imagery. This assumption is longstanding. In fact, the eminent English neurologist J. Hughlings Jackson noted an association between the right hemisphere and imagery more than 100 years ago. In 1874 he wrote "The posterior lobe on the right side (of the brain) . . . is the chief seat of the revival of images." Although the acuity of Jackson's clinical observation should have provided some impetus for further study of right-hemisphere functions, such was not the case.

Throughout the late nineteenth and early twentieth centuries, right-hemisphere regions and activities were something of a netherworld and stimulated scant research zest. Jackson's interest in right-brain perceptual processes and Wigan's earlier (1844) dual brain model, which also emphasized right hemispheric properties, were theoretical and empirical backwaters: the left hemisphere was in the scientific limelight.

This rather benign neglect of the right hemisphere was due largely to the predominant interest in cognitive activities of the left hemisphere—a focus that was embodied in the neurological concept of cerebral dominance. Since Paul Broca's discovery in 1861 that some forms of aphasia were related to specific lesions of the left hemisphere, the construct of cerebral dominance had implied that the left hemisphere was major, superior, or dominant, because of its importance for language functions. One outcome of this differential emphasis was a disproportionate scientific scrutiny of left- as opposed to right-hemisphere regions and processes. In fact, although the paradigm of cerebral dominance began to shift around the time of World War II, it really has been only within the last decade that controlled investigations of cerebral laterality and imagery have been undertaken, thereby providing more direct tests of Jackson's century-old hypothesis.

The recent swell of lay and scientific enthusiasm for cerebral laterality represents a renaissance of inquiry into the right hemisphere. In many ways, the historical ebb and flow of interest in the right hemisphere has paralleled that which existed for imagery. Holt's (1964) clarion call for the return of imagery from the ostracized was equally applicable to the study of the right hemisphere. Although the recent popularity of imagery research has helped to define certain characteristics of imagery and imagers (Sheehan, 1972), a clear understanding of the hemispheric mechanisms underlying imagery processes has not been forthcoming.

The present chapter shall be devoted to the relationship between imagery and the cerebral hemispheres. Data derived from clinical observations of brain-injured and psychiatric patients, as well as data from experimentation with normal individuals will be reviewed. A provisional model describing hemispheric functions for imagery will be proposed.

An initial difficulty encountered in reviewing the literature on imagery and brain laterality lies in restricting one's purview. Because imagery may accompany a variety of cognitive events, as varied as language, memory, or hypnosis, and because hemispheric activity necessarily mediates these processes, the course of the following review is a peripatetic one: the line of evidence wanders into domains surveyed throughout this book. However, the studies examined in this chapter, which have been discussed elsewhere in this book, are considered here in light of their pertinence to imagery and cerebral activities.

An advantage in reviewing research on imagery and cerebral functions is that as a "reviewer" one does not struggle unduly to arrive at *the* definition of imagery. Other authors in this book have assumed that Herculean task. The definitions that have underpinned research on hemispheric differences for imagery are generally accepted here as well. Seldom have these definitions been made explicit. Most often research on imagery and brain laterality has implied that mental imagery is an experience of a sensory kind that is not based on actual sensory input. This is something of a consensual definition that emerges from the experiments to be reviewed. Laterality studies have been concerned almost exclusively with imagery in the visual modality. Likewise, this is the modality considered in this chapter. If I am required to define imagery, I prefer retreating to a position like that of William James (1890, p. 225), who said on discussing "consciousness," "Its meaning we know so long as no one asks us to define it, but to give an adequate account of it is the most difficult of philosophic tasks."

Before proceeding to a specific examination of hemispheric differences for imagery, it is important that the reader understand the concept of cerebral laterality and be familiar with hemispheric asymmetries for cognitive and emotional processes in general. Such an understanding will provide both a theoretical and experimental context for research on imagery and laterality.

The Concept of Cerebral Laterality

As mentioned above, the work of nineteenth-century clinicians, such as Broca, Wernicke, and Jackson, foreshadowed the concept of the cortical representation of intellectual skills (Head, 1926). The possible differential organization of the two hemispheres and their asymmetrical function had been explicitly described by Jackson (1874). He identified respective left and right hemispheric faculties for "expression and perception" and also introduced the notion of a "leading" hemisphere. Kleist (1934), a German neurologist, speculated in a study of amusia, that a hemisphere dominant for one function might not be dominant for other functions. However, these rudimentary formulations of asymmetric cerebral function were veiled by polar theoretical positions, such as rigid localization theories (Nielsen, 1946) or global concepts of brain function (Goldstein, 1939). The vigorous activity of the "localizers" in discovering isomorphic brain–behavior correspondences was something like the cortical, map-making activities of Gall, Spurzheim, and other phrenologists of a century earlier. The "holists," who believed in the equipotentiality of the brain, were inspired by Lashley's (1929) studies of maze learning in rats. Lashley's work showed that impaired maze performance was determined by the size, rather than by the locus of the ablation—a finding antithetical to localization theories. Throughout the war years, however, the steady accumulation of studies on the behavioral deficits produced by unilateral brain damage gradually modified the extreme positions of the localizers and the holists. Thus, primarily as a result of clinical evidence, it became apparent that the cerebral hemispheres were asymmetrically organized and that the left hemisphere should not be considered to be dominating an equally active right hemisphere. As Teuber (1962) said, "It appears more and more obvious why we should not retain the term 'dominance' to describe the difference in the role of the two hemispheres."

Research with normal subjects has supported the concept of cerebral asymmetry. Experimental techniques, such as dichotic listening and tachistoscopic viewing, EEG alpha suppression, and evoked potential measurements, have confirmed that the two cerebral hemispheres are specialized for different cognitive functions. It is also known that each hemisphere controls movement in the opposite half of the body. This means that sounds coming to the left ear, images in the left visual field, and sensations in the left hand will be almost exclusively projected to the right hemisphere (there are some same-side, or ipsilateral auditory pathways). Conversely, experiences and percepts in the right half of the body or space are projected to the left hemisphere. One dramatic example of this contralateral ennervation or "crosswiring" is the occurrence of a left-side paralysis of the arm, leg, trunk, or facial musculature following right hemispheric injury.

Typically, in right-handed people, language and verbal processes are primarily dependent on the left hemisphere. The situation is considerably more complex for those who are left-handed. Intuitively, one would expect left-handers to have the opposite cerebral dominance to right-handers. However, such a mirror image is more the exception than the rule. For example, although approximately 95% of right-handers are left-hemisphere dominant for language, it has been estimated that perhaps only 15–35% of left-handers are right-hemisphere dominant for language (Satz, 1980). Although the specific nature of hemispheric speech lateralization is under current debate, it is generally presumed that most "lefties" are also left-hemisphere dominant for language (like right-handers). A smaller percentage of left-handers (15–40%) show "mixed" or bilateral dominance: language functions may be located in both the left and right hemispheres. In the research and theory described below, it is right-handed subjects and a right-hander's brain organization that is the reference point.

By employing many of the above experimental procedures, studies of normal, right-handed, adult subjects have shown lateral asymmetries for an immense diversity of tasks. Dichotic listening and "t-scope" techniques have shown a right-ear (RE) or right visual-field (RVF) (thus left-hemisphere) superiority for perceptual tasks that involve verbal stimuli, such as words, letters, or nonsense syllables (Springer, 1979), and for tasks that involve fine temporal discriminations.

On the other hand or hemisphere, a left-ear (LE) or left visual-field (LVF) (thus right-hemisphere) superiority is found for perceptual tasks that can be broadly construed as visual–spatial in nature (Ornstein et al., 1980). Such right hemispheric functions include activities as varied as face recognition (Geffen et al., 1971), mental rotation (Shepard & Metzler, 1971), and detection of tactile patterns (Dodds, 1978). However, no right hemispheric cognitive ability is as robustly established as the left hemispheric predominance for language; also, one would not suggest the same degree of specialization for nonverbal functions in the right hemisphere as that which exists for language in the left hemisphere.

It should be noted that what best distinguishes each hemisphere is the way in which it works, rather than with what it works: differences in hemispheric functioning relate more to the kind of information processing, rather than to the information that is processed. It is not so much that each hemisphere is specialized to work with different material—the left with words, the right with spatial relationships—but that each is organized to provide a different cognitive style. The styles are more or less efficient in the processing of different types of information. For example, the left hemisphere has been described as a logical, analytic, and sequential processor for which words are most appropriate. The right hemisphere has been characterized as a holistic, gestalt, and diffuse processor for which spatial forms or patterns are most suited (Bogen, 1969).

Lateralization of Emotional Processes

Although some controversy exists as to the relative contribution of each hemisphere to the perception of emotion (Tucker et al., 1981), the majority of experimental studies of normal subjects have found overall right hemispheric superiorities for processing a diversity of emotional stimuli, including speech, music, and facial expressions (Ley & Bryden, 1981). Dichotic listening procedures have shown left-ear advantages (LEA) for recognizing nonverbal, human sounds with affective components such as laughing, crying, and shrieking (Carmon & Nachson, 1973). Left-ear advantages also exist for identifying the affective tone of spoken passages (Ley & Bryden, 1982; Safer & Leventhal, 1977). The fact that music arouses emotions is indisputable, and evidence now supports the likelihood of a right hemispheric superiority for such information processing. Tonal sequences, evoking both positive and negative moods, are rated more accurately and judged more emotional when heard by the left ear (Bryden et al., 1982; Zatorre, 1979). Experiments employing lateral tachistoscopic presentations of human faces also have confirmed a specialized right hemispheric involvement in the perception of emotional stimuli. Photographs and drawings of faces expressing different emotions seem to be more quickly and accurately identified when they are presented in the LVF (Ley & Bryden, 1979; Safer, 1981). In these experiments separate LVF superiorities for judging both the emotional expressions and identities of the stimulus characters yield support for the notion that the emotion recognition effect is independent of the more general right hemispheric superiority for processing faces.

The dichotic and tachistoscopic studies mentioned here largely have investigated the lateralization of emotion *perception*. Evidence also exists that the right hemisphere may be disproportionately involved in emotion *expression*. A number of experiments have found that emotions are expressed more intensely on the left side of the face (Borod & Caron, 1980; Sackheim et al., 1978). Some clinical evidence also points to the special role of the right hemisphere in emotional expression. Studies of hysterical–conversion symptoms (Galin et al., 1977; Ley, 1980) and of anosognosia (Weinstein & Kahn, 1955) have found sidedness differences in symptom manifestation and emotional displays that implicate the right hemisphere.

In contrast, some other clinicians have identified an asymmetry of emotional response that typifies injury to the left or right hemisphere. Research on patients with unilateral brain damage (Gainotti, 1969) and on patients receiving sodium amytal injections (Rossi & Rosadini, 1967) or electroconvulsive shock treatments (Robertson & Inglis, 1977) has found that depressive moods follow left-hemisphere intervention and euphoric or indifferent moods follow right-hemisphere disturbance.

More recently, a few experiments with normal subjects have produced results similar to those of the clinical domain: they suggest that each hemisphere uniquely participates in processing emotions of differing valence (Ahearn

& Schwartz, 1979; Harman & Ray, 1977). Although the results of these studies are somewhat equivocal, the most commonly identified pattern of activity is that the left hemisphere is involved with positive emotional material and the right hemisphere is concerned with the negative. The existence and interpretation of unilateral as opposed to bilateral hemispheric effects for emotional experience is a current controversy in laterality research circles. In summarizing these effects, the majority of experimental evidence shows definite right hemispheric involvement for emotional stimuli, whereas some contrary hemispheric asymmetries have been shown for normal and neurological cases as well as for positive and negative emotions.

Visual–Spatial Abilities, Imagery, and the Right Hemisphere

Paradoxically, an association between the right hemisphere and imagery largely preceded the accumulation of formal evidence testing of this hypothesis. The presumed relationship between the right hemisphere and imagery was perhaps inferred from studies linking visual–spatial tasks to the right hemisphere.

The importance of the right hemisphere to visual–spatial abilities is well documented. Construction apraxia, a difficulty in drawing, copying, or building models and designs, is the disability most commonly associated with right hemispheric damage (Hecaen, 1962). Other clinical studies have repeatedly identified the role of the right hemisphere in spatial perception (McFie et al., 1950), and in recalling and recognizing visual patterns that are not readily encoded in words (Milner & Teuber, 1968). In short, performance on various nonverbal spatial tests, such as drawing, object assembly, block design, rod and frame alignment, and form boards and mazes, is often impaired following right-hemisphere lesions (Newcombe, 1969; Weisenburg & McBride, 1935). However, spatial–perception abilities are not necessarily imagery abilities, although imagery is most likely integral to such skills. In the most extreme case, this distinction is embodied in the difference between building a block design and *imagining* the building of that same design.

In a recent review of factor analytic studies of human spatial abilities, McGee (1979) identified two distinct spatial abilities: visualization and orientation. According to McGee, spatial visualization involves the ability to mentally rotate and manipulate two- and three-dimensional objects. Spatial orientation involves the comprehension of the relationship between elements in a stimulus pattern, the capacity to be unconfused by spatial configurations presented in various orientations, and the determination of spatial orientation in relation to one's own body position. Spatial orientation factors are involved in tests of field dependence–independence, in sense of direction, in mazes, and in various Piagetian cognitive tasks. It is apparent in McGee's definitions of the visualization and orientation factors that imagery processes would be fundamental to both spatial abilities. However, although we can assume that imagery is integral, the exact role played by visual imagery in tests of spatial visualization or orientation is unclear. As McGee notes, no studies have directly examined the relationships between such imagery factors as control or vividness and performance on spatial-ability tasks. Nonetheless, despite minimal empirical confirmation, an association between imagery and visual–spatial abilities has formed. As argued above, an association between imagery and the right hemisphere perhaps occurred as a result of an overgeneralization from the relationship between spatial abilities and the right hemisphere. The "logic" underlying this associational process is best conveyed by the following syllogism:

> The right hemisphere subserves spatial perception.
> Imagery is integral to spatial-perceptual abilities.
> Thus, the right hemisphere subserves imagery processes.

Although the syllogistic reasoning is specious, the final premise may not be. The clinical and experimental literature that follows is evaluated with respect to the ways it validates, invalidates, or otherwise modifies an association between the right hemisphere and imagery. This chapter can be conceptualized as providing an empirical "bootstrapping," so that the existing data pertaining to imagery and laterality can "catch up" with the commonly accepted hypothesis that imagery is largely a right hemispheric function.

STUDIES OF IMAGERY IN CLINICAL GROUPS

Unilateral Brain Damage, Imagery, and the Right Hemisphere

As early as 1883, clinical reports noted disruptions in visual imagery following cerebral accidents. Charcot (1893) described the case of a famous linguist who experienced a complete loss of "visual memory" following a right-sided vascular disturbance. Prior to the stroke, the scholar had been a proficient, probably an eidetic, visualizer. Posttraumatically, however, he was unable to form an image of his wife or children or of his childhood home. Around this same time, Jackson (1876) identified the right posterior lobe as the substrate for visual ideation. Sporadic references to imagery occurred in clinical material throughout the early 1900s. European neurologists, who were examining the right hemisphere's role in visual–spatial functions, were also gently alluding to a right hemispheric involvement in visual and constructional imagery (Lange, 1936). In fact, Lange (1936, p. 848) hyperbolically speculated that perhaps "the right hemisphere provides the ground or foundation of the world image."

The remarks of Charcot, Jackson, Lange, and others about imagery and the right hemisphere were suggestive but not conclusive. The technology of the times did not permit exact statements about the diffuseness, specificity, or severity of the brain disturbance. Some of the cases considered probably had multiple as well as bilateral cerebral damage. In addition, damage was frequently ascertained at autopsy, which further weakened associations between the brain site and the observed behavior. Nevertheless, despite some crudeness of technique and lack of methodological rigor, many of the conclusions derived from these early case reports have withstood the test of time.

Humphrey and Zangwill (1951), for example, describe the cases of three military officers who had sustained mortar wounds to the right posterior parietal region. All three patients experienced a subjective loss in visual memory and had a marked impairment on tests requiring visualization. The experiential reports of these disturbances are revealing. One officer stated that "he had formerly been a good visualizer but at present his visual images were 'very dim' and 'hard to evoke' " (Humphrey & Zangwill, 1951, p. 322). Humphrey and Zangwill (1951, p. 323) quote another patient: "If someone says 'Can you visualize what your home is like?' Well, I can do that, but I can't visualize a lot of things, such as faces, or places I have been to and tried to recall." Humphrey and Zangwill concluded that in all three cases, visual thinking was significantly disturbed by the posterior parietal damage.

Another study of patients with posterior parietal damage of the left or right hemisphere found them to be impaired in a number of tasks, which required the rotation of objects in imagery or thought (Butters & Barton, 1970). Although only four of 35 brain-damaged patients had right-side lesions, they were much poorer at reversing operations in space. The right-hemisphere-injured group had difficulty in taking multiple perspectives in viewing a three-dimensional scene. Presumably this impairment reflects the inability of the patients to represent the scene in their "mind's eye" and to subsequently "view it" from different vantage points. Although the left and right-damaged parietal groups did not differ significantly on two spatial-rotation tasks, it is possible that each group used a different cognitive strategy to solve the problem (i.e., verbal as opposed to visual). Such differential cognitive strategies can confound hemisphere effects, for research indicates that laterality effects can be functionally related to subjects' use of imagery or verbal encoding strategies (Seamon & Gazzaniga, 1973).

Observations similar to those by Humphrey and Zangwill have been made by Newcombe (1969). She conducted a follow-up study of 119 World War II veterans with unilateral left- and right-hemisphere lesions that had resulted from missile injuries to the brain. Newcombe's cases are exceedingly well documented. It is noteworthy that a subgroup of six patients reported difficulty in recognizing faces (prosopagnosia) and also described difficulties in visualization much like those of Humphrey and Zangwill's patients. For instance, one of Newcombe's patients "remarked on a difficulty in visualizing familiar objects and places. Although he often visits the National Gallery to see paintings that he particularly admires, he is unable to visualize them" (Newcombe, 1969, p. 87). Although this subgroup of Newcombe's patients had temperoparietal lesions somewhat anterior to those of Humphrey and Zangwill's posterior parietal-damaged patients, both groups experienced significant difficulties in revisualizing familiar but complex images, such as faces and paintings.

Further clinical evidence of the right hemisphere's role in imagery comes from studies of visual imagery as an aid in recall for brain-damaged individuals. In a series of well-designed studies, Marilyn Jones-Gotman and Brenda Milner (1978) identified the importance of the right temporal lobe for processes involving visual memory. In a preliminary study, they examined the performance of patients with right temporal-lobe lesions on a traditional paired–associate learning task. Just as some of us were taught to remember a shopping list, these patients were instructed to use visual imagery as a mnemonic aid in learning pairs of words. For example, they were encouraged to make weird or funny images showing a relationship between a word pair such as "nail–salad." Jones-Gotman and Milner found that the right temporal–lobectomy group was impaired when compared to normals in recalling image-linked pairs. With some confidence, this deficit could be attributed to the imagery component of the task, because the right temporal group showed normal recall for abstract words linked by sentences (i.e., a condition in which they employed a verbal, "left hemispheric," mnemonic).

A subsequent study (Jones-Gotman, 1979) confirmed and extended these findings. Patients with left and right temporal lobectomies were compared for incidental learning of high- and low-imagery words. Because subjects were not forewarned that word "recall" would be required (i.e., an incidental-learning paradigm), the likelihood was increased that they indeed used the imagery mnemonic as instructed rather than a more habitual, less visual, and likely more verbal strategy. It is interesting that the right temporal group was impaired in recalling visualized words for delayed but not immediate recall. This finding suggests that these patients could form word images but that the images degraded quickly over a 2-hour delay. This outcome points to the importance of the right temporal lobe for visual memory. Likewise, in a study of right temporal lobectomies, Jaccarino (1975) showed recall decrements for pictorial stimuli at a 24-hour delay but not at immediate posttesting. Another study implying a right-hemispheric role for image-mediated memory is that of Cohen et al. (1973), who found that ECT to the right hemisphere produced memory decrements in a nonverbal recall task involving visual imagery.

A putative association between the right hemisphere and visual memory also has keyed a strategy for rehabilitating individuals who experience profound memory defects. Working with a small sample of patients with left hemispheric lesions and accompanying verbal-memory deficits, Patten (1972) was able to facilitate their mnemonic skills. He did this by teaching left-hemisphere-damaged patients to create vivid and ridiculous images that incorporated items of the to-be-recalled information. Using a similar instructional technique, Jones (1974) was also able to improve the performance in paired–associate learning for patients with left temporal-lobe lesions. Consequently, both Jones's and Patten's results indicate that verbal memory defects due to left-hemisphere damage can be overcome by encoding items of information in the preserved imagery modality of the right hemisphere.

In viewing clinical observations and studies of unilaterally brain-injured patients, the importance of the right hemisphere for various imagery processes is apparent. The bulk of evidence indicates that the temporal, parietal, and occipital regions of the right hemisphere are integral for visual memory, visualization, and rotation of objects in imagery. These intrapersonal visualization and imagery processes seem qualitatively different from the visual–spatial skills necessary for extrapersonal performance; however, this question awaits empirical test.

Another motif embedded in many of the above reports of disturbances in waking imagery was the corollary observation of disturbances in dream imagery. Nightly dreams are highly visual experiences, and some research suggests a tripartite relationship between dreams, imagery, and the right hemisphere.

Dreams, Imagery, and the Right Hemisphere

For most people, dreams are richly visual, surreal experiences that often include bizarre spatial and temporal juxtapositions of images. These characteristics are exemplified in the following excerpt from a subject's dream report following a rapid-eye-movement (REM) awakening [cited in Horowitz (1978, p. 14]:

> I was riding with a guy on the back of a motorcycle. I was in my new blue dress, he was dressed all in black. Then suddenly we were sitting in my backyard eating a lot of stuff spread out on a blanket. In the next scene there were a bunch of letters on a sign or something but I could not see them well enough to know what it said.

Such a dream experience typifies the mentation that characterizes the right hemisphere (Ornstein, 1972). Psychoanalytic theorists have often described dreaming cognition as primary-process thinking. "Such thinking is carried out more through pictorial, concrete images . . . it is relatively unorganized, primitive magical, undifferentiated, archaic . . . (and) typified by emotional fantasy" (Fenichel, 1945, p. 47). These descriptions are equally applicable to a right hemispheric cognitive style. Both Galin (1974) and Stone (1977) have employed the metaphor of left- and right-hemispheric differences in function to examine psychoanalytic theory (e.g., unconscious processes, defense mechanisms) and technique (e.g., free association, dream interpretation). Galin (1974) postulated parallels between right-hemispheric cognition and primary-process thinking, dreaming, and repression. He further suggested that the right hemisphere might be an anatomic repository for unconscious-thought contents. Thus, although a variety of theorists suggest that the dream is the "royal road to the unconscious," the question remains as to whether this route traverses the right hemisphere, so to speak. However, although direct evidence of a relationship between dream imagery and the right hemisphere is lacking, some evidence converges on this proposition.

In many of the cases of unilateral right-brain damage described above, disturbances in dreams or dream imagery accompanied disruptions of waking-state imagery. Charcot's (1893) patient, a linguistics scholar, experienced a subjective loss of visual dreaming, and Humphrey and Zangwill's (1951) patients with right posterior parietal lesions also reported cessation of dreaming after the injuries. One patient said that he had "lost the habit of dreaming," while another stated that although he "used to dream fairly often, he had not had a single dream in the last six years" (Humphrey & Zangwill, 1951, p. 323) (i.e., since the shrapnel wound in his right parietal region).

Klaus Hoppe (1977, 1978), a psychoanalyst, made similar observations after analyzing the dreams and fantasy productions of patients who had undergone right-hemisphere surgical excision in an attempt to control epileptic seizures. After the operation, patients generally could not recollect dreams. For those who had some dreams or fantasy experiences, the material tended to be somewhat impoverished in that it was less visual or fantastic, as well as more thoughtlike and reality based than the material of "normal" dreams. Psychological testing confirmed Hoppe's impression: Rorschach responses and TAT stories tended to be short, blunt, descriptive, and lacking in imagination or originality. Removal of the right hemisphere seemed to simultaneously negate the capacity for primary-process thinking in both sleeping and waking states.

Although some reports of disruptions in dreaming, following left-hemisphere lesions, have been recorded (Adler, 1950), these reports have been infrequent and inconsistent (Greenwood et al., 1977).

Experimental studies of normal individuals have provided some confirmation of the right hemisphere's role in dreaming and, by inference, in imagery. For example, Goldstein et al. (1972) offer electrophysiological evidence of right hemispheric mediation of visual dreams. They showed increased right-hemisphere activity accompanying REM periods. Because REM periods are further associated with subjective dream reports, a basis exists for supposing right hemispheric dominance in dreaming. Somewhat similarly, Cohen (1977) noted that the verbal content of a dream was more prominent at the end of the normal night's sleep period, whereas "music, salient spatial features and emotion" predominated throughout the night. Cohen proposed that this difference indicates that the left hemisphere exerts more control over the dream process as the night wears on, whereas the right hemisphere is involved throughout.

Paul Bakan (1976, 1978) has integrated much of the circumstantial evidence on dreaming and right hemispheric functioning and presents a persuasive case for accepting such a relationship. Bakan reviews evidence from studies of EEG, brain injury, epilepsy, schizophrenia, and of sleep and dreaming to buttress his thesis. The following is a summary of the findings that Bakan collates to support the dominance of the right hemisphere for dreaming:

1. Right hemispheric thinking is similar to the visual, surreal, and emotional aspects of the dream (Galin, 1974).
2. The right hemisphere seems most active during REM sleep, the period in which most visual dreaming occurs (Goldstein et al., 1972).
3. Right hemispheric injury tends to disrupt dreaming (Humphrey & Zangwill, 1951).
4. Seizures in the right temporal lobe tend to produce dreamlike experiences (Arseni & Petrovici, 1971).
5. Differential hemispheric involvement in REM and non-REM periods may parallel hemispheric differences for physiological rhythms (a basic rest–activity cycle) during waking periods as well (Kripke & Sonnenshein, 1973).
6. Schizophrenics show disturbances in REM sleep and interhemispheric communication that might explain the "spill-over" of dreamlike experiences into their waking states (Rosenthal & Bigelow, 1972).
7. A decrease in muscle tonus during REM sleep may be accompanied by increased right-hemisphere functioning (Hartmann, 1967).

In short, Bakan does a yeoman job of relating a number of previously disparate findings to the proposition of a right-hemisphere involvement in REM periods and consequently, in visual dreaming. Although some of the research he deploys has been considered above and is also examined below, Bakan's position papers are highly recommended to interested travellers of the "royal road."

Epilepsy, "Dreamy States," and the Right Hemisphere

Visual experiences similar to those occurring in night dreaming or other hallucinatory states are prominent in epileptic conditions and have been observed since the tenth century. Abulquasim, an Arabian physician, recorded examples of epileptic's hallucinations. One of his patients described seeing "a black woman coming towards him (and) having over herself a small leather garment" [cited in Penfield & Perot (1963, p. 599)].

Epilepsy is a state of impaired brain function that may result in recurrent, paroxysmal disturbances of sensation, movement, affects, and consciousness. Although the exact mechanism causing epileptic seizures is not clear, it is known that certain cortical scars, tumors, or inflammations can produce a hypersynchronous neuronal discharge that leads to a generalized seizure. Prior to seizure onset, the epileptic may experience an aura, which could include alterations in perceptual, visual, cognitive, and affective domains.

Jackson (1880) described auras or "dreamy states" that consisted of images, scenes from the individual's past, or unrelated visual hallucinations. While experiencing an aura, one of Jackson's patients "seemed to actually see large buildings . . . a church . . . and certain alms houses" (Jackson, 1880, p. 600). Jackson also noted that his patients' auras were often accompanied by eye and head turning to the left side of space, as well as by spasms, tics, or other convulsive movements on the left side of the body. Such left-sided symptoms suggest right hemispheric activation. Therefore, Jackson was able to attribute "dreamy state" auras to right hemispheric seizure activity. The associations between abnormal hemispheric neuronal activity and the highly visual nature of epileptic auras provides further evidence for right-hemisphere-based imagery productions.

Similar psychical states have also been produced by electrical stimulation of the cortex. In the course of surgical operations for treating epilepsy, Wilder Penfield, a Canadian neurosurgeon, reproduced "dreamy states" comparable to those described by Jackson (Penfield & Perot, 1963). Because patients received local anesthetics during surgery, they were conscious and able to verbally recount the experiences prompted by Penfield's electrodes. For example, a 12-year-old boy (case #3—R. W.) gave the following experiential response when Penfield stimulated his right temporal lobe: "Oh, gee, gosh, robbers are coming at me with guns. . . . There they are, my brother is there. He is aiming a rifle at me" (Penfield & Perot, 1963, p. 615). Another patient, a 25-year-old woman (case #21–A. H.) gave the following report after receiving stimulation of the right anterior parietal region: "Just a minute. Like a figure, on the left side, seems like a man or a woman. I think it was a woman. She seemed to have nothing on. She seemed to be pulling or running after a wagon" (Penfield & Perot, 1963, p. 634). After examining over 1200 patients, Penfield concluded that visual illusions and experiential hallucinations of flashbacks were predominantly associated with the nondominant (right) temporal lobe. Subsequent EEG research has corroborated the impression that temporal-lobe abnormality is the most common point of focal seizures and that auras involving imagery are a corollary symptom of such discharge sites (Arseni & Petrovici, 1971; Ervin, 1975).

Another prominent aspect of psychic seizures are disturbances in self-awareness and body imagery. Feelings of depersonalization and derealization, like those of the schizophrenic, may accompany temporal lobe foci. The epileptic may feel as if he or she is outside of his/her body and is watching it perform some action. Changes in body image also commonly occur. The individual may sense or see his or her body, or some part of it, growing smaller or larger, thinner or fatter, prettier or uglier. Right-hemisphere seizure activity has been shown to predominate in disturbances of body image or body boundaries (Arseni & Petrovici, 1971).

To briefly summarize, the correspondence between imagery-laden experiences and stimulation of the right temporal lobe supports the hypothesis relating imagery to right-hemisphere functioning. The similarity among the experiential reports of Penfield's electrically stimulated patients, the "dreamy-state auras" of Jackson's patients, and the dream reports of normal individuals awakened from REM periods are apparent. The available evidence indicates that each of these imagery processes is mediated by the right hemisphere.

"Split-Brains," Imagery, and the Right Hemisphere

Another radical surgical procedure developed by Bogen, et al. (1969) to control intractable epilepsy provides further information on the role of the right hemisphere in imagery functions. "Split-brain" surgery is the apt designation for this technique. This operation severs the corpus callosum and other nerve fibers (commissures) connecting the two halves of the brain. The commissurotomy is intended to confine seizure activity to one hemisphere and thereby control the intensity of the behavioral response. The operations were largely successful, eliminating almost all attacks, including unilateral ones. In addition to relieving the patient of severe seizures, the operation also provided a "natural" experiment and an opportunity to investigate the separate and unique contributions of each hemisphere to thought and behavior.

The most dramatic consequence of brain bisection was that intrahemispheric functions were absolutely preserved, whereas interhemispheric functions were totally disrupted. As a result, visual, tactual, auditory, and all other sensory information presented to one hemisphere could be processed within that hemisphere, but this information remained outside the "awareness" of the other hemisphere. For example, a picture projected to the largely "mute" right hemisphere could not be described because the sensory perception could not be transferred to the "verbal" left hemisphere for articulation.

The differentiation of the functional capacities of each hemisphere in split-brain patients has been primarily carried out by Michael Gazzaniga and his research team (Gazzaniga & LeDoux, 1978). More recently, this group has attempted to elucidate the brain mechanisms involved in imagery by isolating various imagery tasks and processes in their split-brain patients. Gazzaniga and LeDoux sought to answer two questions: First, is the visual image really visual, and second, does visual imagery utilize the same neural circuitry and cortical areas as visual perception?

The "image-as-picture" question has vexed imagery theorists since the time of the British empiricists, such as David Hume, who treated all mental events as residuals of sensory experience. However, Gazzaniga's experiments with split-brain patient, J. Kn., contradict the philosophical notion that images can be simply construed as faint sensations. Although J. Kn. was tactually split, his anterior commissure, which could transfer visual sensations, was intact: the question remained as to whether these intact nerve fibers could also conduct visual images. The test was as follows: an object, a spoon, for instance, was placed in J. Kn.'s *right* hand, and he was told to *make a picture* of the spoon in his mind (i.e., the left hemisphere). After forming the image, he was repeatedly unable to retrieve the same object with his *left* hand from a hidden display. However, when a picture of a spoon was projected to the left hemisphere, J. Kn. could find the object with his left hand. Therefore, it seemed that the image of the spoon did not transfer from the left hemisphere to the right hemisphere, whereas the picture did. Thus Gazzinaga and LeDoux concluded that the neural mechanisms for visual imagery are likely different from those utilized for visual sensory perception.

Gazzaniga and LeDoux's observations of another split-brain patient, D. S., substantiate the likelihood that visual experience and visual imagery involve distinct patterns of neural circuitry. The experimental results must be understood in the context of D. S.'s unique neurological history. At the age of 4 years his left prefrontal cortex was removed, and at the age of 24 his frontal callosal connection was severed. Prior to the callosal sectioning, D. S. could recall 8 of 10 word pairs on a memory task employing a standard imagery mnemonic (i.e., imagine an "apple" on the "chair"). However postoperatively, he could recall only 2 of 10 word pairs under similar instructions. One implication of this performance decrement is that the normal preoperative performance was likely mediated by the right frontal lobe and its commissural connections, to intact verbal areas of the left hemisphere. This suggests the possibility that the right frontal cortex is also critically involved in imagery experience. Gazzaniga and LeDoux (1978, p. 123) advance the interesting query whether "the flattened affect and the inability to plan ahead typically noted in patients with frontal lobe disease might be related to a loss of capacity to fantasize and imagine what is going to happen next."

In conclusion, studies of split-brain patients suggest that the neural circuitry for mental processes and external perception is distinct. This presents a formidable challenge to "image-as-picture" theories. Indeed, as Gazzaniga and LeDoux state, it is not surprising that the perceptual motor mechanisms that have developed for transactions with the external world are not the same as those used for conducting our mental life.

STUDIES OF IMAGERY IN NORMAL SUBJECTS

To this point, the research that has been reviewed has indicated a predominant involvement of the right hemisphere in various imagery processes. Although the research supporting this proposition is relatively consistent, it is based primarily on patients' behavior and their subjective reports following brain damage or radical brain surgery. Caution is always appropriate when making assertions about normal brain functions following observation of clinical populations, which may exhibit multiple pathology of disparate etiology. Therefore, it is important to assess hemispheric effects for imagery in individuals with intact brains and nervous systems. Three "acronymed," experimental techniques, EEG, GSR, and CLEM (electroencephalogram, galvanic skin response, and conjugate lateral eye movement, respectively) recordings primarily have been used to study imagery processes in the normal brain.

Electrophysiological (EEG and GSR) Studies of Imagery

The electroencephalographic (EEG) recording of brain wave patterns is a useful way to identify the activation of different hemispheric regions. Generally, the interrelationship of two types of electrical activity of the brain is observed: alpha and beta waves. Alpha rhythms, which exhibit a regular wave pattern of 8–13 Hz, are associated with relaxed, resting states (hence the vogue of "alpha training" as a stress reducer). Virtually any stimulus, even one as benign as opening one's eyes, will disrupt the alpha wave form and cause it to be replaced by beta waves, which have faster rhythms (> 13 Hz). This "alpha suppression" or "alpha-blocking" response to perceptual stimuli or cognition provides an index of hemispheric information processing (Adrian & Matthews, 1934; Galin & Ornstein, 1972). Although critics of EEG techniques contend that discerning the nature of hemispheric processing from an EEG recording is something akin to determining a factory's product by observing the smoke emitted from its chimneys, there is a consensus that EEG patterns do indicate when a hemispheric region is engaged. Thus the adage "where there is smoke, there is fire" is applicable to EEG techniques, as well as to factories.

Quite early on, an association between alpha activity and visual imagery was found in studies investigating the EEG characteristics of different types of mental imagery (Short, 1953). With decidedly mixed success, efforts were made to identify the specific alpha rhythm accompanying visual, auditory, or kinesthetic modes of imagery. Reference to the differential hemispheric substrates of these imagery modalities is noticeably absent from EEG research in the 1950s and 1960s. In fact, in Zikmund's (1972) authoritative review of the physiological correlates of visual imagery, no mention is made of hemispheric asymmetries for imagery. More recent physiological experiments have examined specific hemispheric functions for imagery.

A few studies employing EEG recordings have found a connection between the right hemisphere and imagery. Although Morgan et al. (1971) intended to investigate the relationship between alpha activity, hypnotic ability, and various cognitive tasks, their study showed significant hemispheric differences for an imagery task as well. While their EEG was being monitored, subjects were requested to "picture scenes" in their mind, but not to think about them. These scenes included, "picturing a child swinging in a swing," "imagining that you are watching a ballet," and "imagining sitting at a beach and watching the waves come in." Although these tasks were called the "spatial" condition in contrast to an "analytic" condition, it is most likely that the instructions encouraged imaging the scenes. Morgan et al. found an EEG alpha suppression over the right hemisphere during the spatial condition and over the left hemisphere during the analytic condition. Therefore, it seems that the right hemisphere was engaged in imaging the various scenes, while the left hemisphere was involved for arithmetic calculations (e.g., "What is 4 to the third power?") and verbal responses (e.g., "What is the opposite of magnanimous?").

A more direct test of interhemispheric alpha asymmetry and imagery was undertaken by Robbins and McAdam (1974). They requested subjects to covertly image pictorial material (picture postcards) in terms of the shapes and colors of the stimuli (i.e., "form a picture in their minds") or in terms of words (i.e., "subvocally describe the scene"). Like Morgan et al., Robbins and McAdam found alpha blocking and, hence, activation to be greater over the right hemisphere when subjects were imaging the shapes and colors of the postcards. They also noted left hemispheric involvement for "imagery in linguistic terms," but such a designation is rather misleading. It seems inaccurate to consider a subvocal description of a postcard to be a case of imaging in verbal terms. It is perhaps more reasonable to interpret the left-hemisphere effects shown by Robbins and McAdam as consistent with that hemisphere's proclivity for verbal, linguistic processing, rather than for imagery per se.

Another experiment showing sidedness differences in electrophysiological activity for imagery is that conducted by Myslobodsky and Rattok (1977). These researchers recorded differences in the GSR of the left and right hands during imagery and verbal tasks. Galvanic skin response, or EDA (electrodermal activity), as it is now more commonly called, is generally considered to be a nonspecific measure of arousal or emotional reactivity. Most simply, it records the electrical conductivity of the skin. Lateral asymmetries in EDA already have been discovered in certain psychiatric groups, such as schizophrenics (Gruzelier & Venables, 1974), but the research on asymmetries in normals is equivocal. Because of the crossing of the sensory motor system, a heightened GSR of the left hand (or left side of the body) is presumed to represent the increased activation of the right hemisphere. In fact, such a finding was made by Myslobodsky and Rattok when they requested subjects to "hold an image" in their mind of previously presented pictures of artwork, landscapes, and sexual scenes. Greater left-hand skin conductivity was found during the "visual" condition, whereas greater right-hand skin conductivity was found for the "verbal" task, which involved word identification and calculations. Consequently, Myslobodsky and Rattok's data support a hypothesized link between the right hemisphere and visual imagery.

A review of the laterality literature yields the few electrophysiological studies described above, which provide a direct examination of EEG or EDA activity and visual imagery. A number of other EEG studies, however, offer incidental evidence pertinent to imagery and hemispheric functions

(Davidson, 1978; Tucker et al., 1981). The data are considered somewhat circumstantial, because the primary purpose of these studies was to investigate hemispheric differences for emotional experiences.

As mentioned in the introduction to this chapter, most experimental studies of normal subjects have found overall right hemispheric superiorities for processing emotional stimuli. However, more recently a handful of studies have implied that each hemisphere is specialized to mediate either positive or negative emotional information (Tucker et al., 1981). The subgroup of studies fueling this argument also yield indirect information about imagery and the cerebral hemispheres.

One of the first experiments in this domain varied both the mode of imagery and the affective demands on the subjects (Davidson & Schwartz, 1976). Davidson and Schwartz monitored EEG activity while subjects self-induced covert emotional and nonemotional states, using either verbal or imagery-based induction procedures. In the visual-imagery–emotional conditions, subjects were asked to "relive the intense feelings" of angry and relaxing scenes from their past. The verbal–emotional condition required imaging the writing of a letter to a friend describing the angry or relaxing scenes (i.e., visualizing the words being written). The nonemotional condition involved imaging the activities of a particular day. Davidson and Schwartz found that the self-generation of affective imagery was associated with relatively greater right hemispheric activation than was the self-generation of nonaffective imagery. Besides pointing to an enhanced right-hemisphere involvement for emotional imagery, Davidson and Schwartz's study hints at the inextricability of affect and imagery. They note that 70% of their subjects spontaneously mentioned that it was extremely difficult to perform the verbal imagery—emotional trials without evoking visual imagery. The enmeshment of imagery and emotional functions renders problematic any experimental attempts to isolate right hemispheric effects for one or the other process. In fact, many electrophysiological experiments have studied subjects' performance of imagery tasks during different mood states, and thereby they do not provide a pristine examination of hemispheric effects for imagery alone. This is the case in most of the following EEG studies of imagery and emotion.

In general, EEG, GSR, and neuropsychological experiments have suggested an impairment of the information-processing capacity of the right hemisphere in depression (D'Elia & Perris, 1974; Tucker et al., 1981). Of interest here is that individuals who subjectively report greater depression also show decrements in visual imagery as assessed by the Betts Vividness of Mental Imagery Questionnaire [cited in Tucker et al. (1981)]. By inference, such a correlation further links imagery functions with the right hemisphere. In two follow-up studies, Tucker and his research team (1981) were able to establish more directly an interrelationship between depression, deactivation of the right hemisphere, and impairment both in the ease of establishing an image and in its vividness (Tucker et al., 1981). In their first experiment,

Tucker et al. asked the subjects to image such things as an alarm clock or a "young woman pulling weeds in her garden," while they (simultaneously) experienced a hypnotically induced depression. Performance on an auditory-attention task provided an index for hemispheric activity and implied a right-hemispheric deactivation that was accompanied by impoverished imagery production.

In a second experiment, subjects' EEG was recorded while they held a visual image of a butterfly or of a fireworks display during positive or negative moods: an alpha suppression in the right hemisphere was found during the imagery tasks. Somewhat paradoxically, in this second study, Tucker et al. found activation of the right frontal lobe during depression, an effect contrary to those found in the bulk of EEG studies on depression (D'Elia & Perris, 1974). However, Tucker et al. interpreted this right frontal activation as possibly representing an inhibitory action that suppressed more general right hemispheric information processing. By regarding right frontal activation as an indication of inhibitory mechanisms, Tucker et al. were able to align their findings with other data showing the involvement of the anterior portions of the right hemisphere in depression. In such depressive states, parallel decrements in visual imagery seem to accompany "depressed" right hemispheric functioning.

The results of Tucker et al. and their interpretation also are congruent with studies by Davidson (1978), which show a right frontal EEG activation when subjects were asked to generate thoughts, feelings, and *images* about past or present, personally relevant emotional experiences. Although right hemispheric effects for imagery and negative emotions were inextricably confounded in the Davidson studies and partially confounded in the Tucker et al. studies, the data do in part substantiate an association between the right hemisphere and imagery. However, as Tucker et al. note, the observed EEG activity in the right hemisphere for depressed moods, both in their and in Davidson's experiments, occurred anteriorly to the regions of the right hemisphere generally believed to subserve visual imagery processes.

As should be apparent, a central difficulty in the interpretation of behavioral or perceptual asymmetries, whether the observed behavior is a heightened EDA or a left-hand paralysis, lies in relating it to an underlying hemispheric asymmetry (Bryden, 1980). In most cases this is an act of inference, rather than a direct association. In Tucker et al.'s (1981) study, for example, a right-ear attentional bias can be variously interpreted as indicating deactivation of the right hemisphere, activation of the left hemisphere, or activation of the right frontal lobe, which more generally inhibits right hemispheric processing. One could find justification for each position.

A few years ago, a simple, inexpensive, reliable, and seemingly valid index of hemispheric activation was devised. This technique was the observation of conjugate lateral eye movements (CLEMs). This methodological "knight in shining armor" seemed to minimize the experimental and interpretive problems of behavioral or electrophysiological correlates of asymmetrical hemispheric performance. However, recent critical reviews of the CLEM concept (Ehrlichman & Weinberger, 1978; Richardson, 1978), and some failures to replicate the original findings on which the concept was based (Spanos et al., 1980) have somewhat tarnished the CLEMs' armor. Despite these current theoretical shortcomings, much of the CLEM research has directly addressed the hypothesis of hemispheric differences for imagery functions.

CLEMs, Imagery, and the Right Hemisphere

Teitelbaum (1954) was the first to note that people typically break eye contact when they are verbally presented with a question to answer. In his psychotherapy practice, Day (1964) also had observed that his patients momentarily tended to avert their gaze when questioned and that most people habitually looked to either the left or right side of space when engaged in reflective thought. Day (1967) had previously suggested that different directions in eye shift were related to particular personality types. This proposition was supported by Bakan (1969), who found greater hypnotic susceptibility for individuals who looked to the left rather than the right. Because of a consistent preference to look left or right, people have been classified as left or right lookers (Bakan, 1969), movers (Duke, 1968), or breakers (Richardson, 1978). Bakan (1969) also related directionality of eye gaze to contralateral hemispheric activation. Accordingly, it has been presumed that left CLEMs indicate right hemispheric activation and right CLEMs, left hemispheric activation.

Numerous studies have examined the relationship between CLEMs and imagery. In his original experiment Bakan (1969) found that left lookers were slightly more likely than right lookers to use imagery and that they rated their visual imagery as clearer. Likewise, Harnad (1972) showed that left-looking mathematicians tended to utilize imagery to a greater degree than did right lookers in solving problems. Consistent with Day's (1967) initial hypothesis that left lookers were more attuned to internal experience, Meskin and Singer (1974) reported that left CLEMs were positively correlated with "inner attentiveness" and more vivid imagery. Rodin and Singer (1976) found that obese subjects were less likely to make left CLEMs and also reported fewer visual daydreams. Strong preferences for visual as opposed to verbal thinking were disclosed by left movers in two cognitive-style experiments (Richardson, 1977). Left movers were more likely than right movers to endorse statements such as "My thinking consists of mental pictures and images" or "My dreams are extremely vivid." However, a follow-up study by Richardson (1977), with university rather than high-school students, showed a reversal of the previous pattern of results. Although evidence on left CLEMs and imagery is not conclusive, it is consistent with the hypothesis of a right hemispheric mediation of visual-imagery processes.

Paradoxical or nonreplicable effects, such as Richardson's (1977), have plagued research on CLEMs and imagery. Ehrlichman and Weinberger (1978) describe these as "discouraging" efforts to establish consistent individual differences in CLEM patterns for visual imagery. For instance, left and right lookers also have been shown to not differ on tests commonly used to assess preferences for and vividness of imagery, such as the Betts Vividness of Mental Imagery Questionnaire (Spanos et al., 1980; Wolf-Dorlester, 1976) or the Paivio Individual Differences Questionnaire (Hiscock, 1977). A host of moderator variables, including the sex, handedness and cognitive style of the subjects; the position of the examiner and the subject; the symmetry of the room; and the number and type of questions asked, all have been found to attenuate and, in many cases, negate the relationship between left-moving and performance measures of visual imagery (Richardson, 1978).

The equivocal nature of CLEM research has given cause to seriously question the main premises of this literature. Currently, little direct evidence exists supporting the assumption that left–right differences in lateral gaze are a consequence of asymmetrical hemispheric activation. As others have concluded, there is probably insufficient evidence to warrant the use of CLEMs as a method for studying hemispheric function (Ehrlichman & Weinberger, 1978). Because of the conjectural theoretical grounding for the CLEM concept, it is perhaps most prudent to consider the support for the association between visual imagery and the right hemisphere offered by CLEM studies as provisional.

Imageable Language and the Right Hemisphere

A considerable amount of clinical and experimental evidence has been marshalled here to support the hypothesis of a functional relationship between the right hemisphere and processes involving imagery. The case can be further strengthened by one final bit of support; a right hemispheric advantage for imagery might be extended to include the processing of imageable language as well. Some research suggests that concrete, or high-imagery words, are mediated by the right hemisphere (Ley & Bryden, 1983).

Once again, initial support for the proposition comes from the clinical domain. Several studies of dyslexics with localized left-hemisphere lesions have shown that three patients' remembered concrete or imageable nouns despite the loss of grammatical and functional speech and abstract, nonimageable nouns (Patterson & Marcel, 1977). Other studies of dyslexic (left-hemisphere-damaged) patients have implied that they can accomplish some rudimentary "reading" perhaps because printed words generate images, which can then be identified and comprehended (Richardson, 1976). Such image-based "reading" may be the province of the right hemisphere.

This clinical finding has not been consistently verified by recognition studies of laterally presented abstract–concrete or low-/high-imagery words with normal subjects. Ellis and Shepherd (1974) found a greater left-right difference for abstract than for concrete nouns; the latter were better identified than the former when presented in the LVF. The LVF advantage for high-imagery word recognition suggests a right hemisphere superiority for processing these same items. Ellis and Shepherd speculated that a right hemispheric direct lexical access for concrete nouns might occur and would most likely be mediated by an evoked image. Conversely, the left hemisphere might process abstract words by a less direct, phonological route. Likewise, Marcel and Patterson (1978) replicated their findings from phonemic dyslexics with normal subjects: they found that word imageability affected LVF but not RVF word presentations. A number of studies have found similar LVF effects for concrete or high-imagery words (Day, 1977); however, other related or replicatory studies have failed to do so (McFarland & Ashton, 1978). In a recent review of right-hemisphere language, Bradshaw (1980, p. 82) concluded that "a number of clinical and neurological findings support the concept of direct lexical access being possible, via the right hemisphere for high-frequency, concrete or imageable items; the left hemisphere's phonological mechanisms would be more adapted for the analysis and interpretation of low-frequency, abstract or nonimageable material." Although Bradshaw recommends cautious interpretation of this data base, it can safely be said that some evidence exists for right hemispheric word processing and, furthermore, that such "reading" may be mediated by imagery. Similarly, limited language functions for imageable (or emotional) speech have been ascribed to the right hemispheres of certain split-brain patients [see the description of patient P. S. in Gazzaniga & LeDoux (1978)].

Two recent experiments by Ley and Bryden (1983) support the contention that processes involving imageable words engage the right hemisphere. In these studies, subjects initially were tested on a lateralized perceptual task. In one experiment, tachistoscopic face recognition was used as the lateralization task, and in the other experiment, dichotic stop consonant–vowel (CV) pairs were used. Numerous laterality studies have shown that face recognition yields a left visual-field advantage (Ley & Bryden, 1979) and CV identification (e.g., /ba,ga,ka,da,ta/) yields a reliable and robust right-ear advantage (Studdert-Kennedy & Shankweiler, 1970). Thus each experiment employed a traditional, laterality paradigm and task: one that produces a right hemispheric superiority and one which produces a left hemispheric superiority. The tasks were chosen to provide indices of lateralization for the comparison of pretest and posttest recognition performance.

After subjects completed the pretest recognition trials, they were asked to memorize a list of words; the two groups of subjects were given either high- or low-imagery word lists to study. Following the 5-minute word study period, subjects were retested on the initial lateralization task and then required to recall as many words from their word list as possible.

The data of interest are the changes in performance on the lateralized task from the pretest to the posttest while the word list was being held in memory. The major findings in the two experiments were the same: imagery influenced the relative lateralization of the test material. Subjects who were given high-imagery word lists to remember (e.g., ink, elephant, pencil), as opposed to low-imagery ones (e.g., shy, bland, evident), showed a shift to the left side (right hemisphere) in performance. Thus, with the face recognition task, the left visual-field superiority was enhanced by memorizing high-imagery word lists, and the same word lists reduced the dichotic right-ear advantage and improved left-ear performance in the dichotic listening task. These results indicate that the processes involved in remembering a list of high-imagery words serve to activate the right hemisphere and subsequently improve recognition performance for stimuli directed to that hemisphere.

The Ley and Bryden studies also provide a substrate for Paivio's (1978) dual-coding hypothesis. On the basis of a large body of evidence, Paivio has theorized that words are encoded both verbally and pictorially. Although it is most reasonable to assume that *all* words have a left hemispheric lexical representation, it is also possible that the pictorial component suggested by Paivio has its basis in a right hemispheric lexical representation for high-imagery words. Thus the presentation of a high-imagery word might activate both left and right hemispheric components in the lexical representation. Consequently, one would expect to find that the RVF advantage for word recognition would be decreased for high-imagery words. In fact, Day (1977) has shown a reduced RVF superiority for high-imagery words in a lexical decision paradigm.

The proposition of left and right hemispheric lexical representation for high-imagery words also does not necessarily imply that word recognition must occur at a conscious level for the right hemisphere to be engaged. Zajonc (1980), for one, has persuasively argued that the emotional saliency of a stimulus can be registered in the absence of cognitive awareness of the stimulus. Such an interpretative line potentially explains why Day (1977) found a reduced RVF effect for high-imagery words in a lexical decision task, where it was not necessary for one to be consciously aware of the stimulus word, whereas Schmuller and Goodman (1979) failed to show an imagery effect in a word recognition paradigm, where the particular word had to be identified.

In short, the Ley and Bryden imagery word studies indicate that thinking about different kinds of words has different hemispheric effects. Furthermore, it seems that the right hemisphere has a greater responsibility than the left for storing and mediating imageable stimuli; this conclusion is consistent with other findings of enhanced LVF recognition accuracies for high-imagery, concrete words.

Possible Right- and Left-Hemisphere Effects for Imagery

Strong support exists for the proposition that imagery is largely a right hemispheric function. Research on unilaterally brain-injured, epileptic, and split-brain patients, as well as the results of EEG, GSR, CLEM, and visual-recognition studies of normal individuals have indicated that the right hemisphere predominantly subserves imagery processes. However, it should be kept in mind that hemispheric "dominance" for a cognitive activity is a relative, rather than exclusive, information-processing superiority. Naturally this consideration also holds for the hemispheric asymmetry underlying imagery. Therefore, although I have constructed a case for right hemispheric mediation of imagery, I would like to examine challenges to this assertion, namely, those data implying the role of the *left* hemisphere in imagery.

Henry Head (1926), a noted, as well as aptly named, neurologist was of the opinion that left-hemisphere damage seldom interfered with imagery productions. After studying a great number of aphasic patients with left-hemisphere damage, he stated, "It is remarkable how rarely (visual imagery) is affected . . . (and) spontaneous recall of visual images . . . (and) mental pictures remain (after left-hemisphere language disturbances)" (Head, 1926, pp. 370, 373, 392). Other clinicians' observations are largely consistent with Head's, although one of Humphrey and Zangwill's (1951) patients who reported imagery disruptions did have both left and right parietal-occipital damage. However, in that case it is impossible to estimate what proportion of imagery decrement should be ascribed to the left-side damage. Conversely, Adler (1950) provided a more precisely documented case of cessation of visual dreaming following EEG ascertained left parieto-occipital injury. Occasionally, Penfield's epileptic patients did produce visual illusions and visual hallucinatory reports following left temporal stimulations but these experiences seemed less rich visually and quantitatively, and much less frequent than right-side imagery productions. These clinical reports are few, however, and the correspondence between left-hemispheric regions and imagery functions is vague.

Experimental demonstrations of left-hemispheric imagery productions or disturbances are also rare in normal subjects. One research team (Ingvar & Philipson, 1977) did report increases in regional blood flow of the left hemisphere accompanying "motor ideation" (i.e., subjects imagined themselves clenching and unclenching their hands). However, this finding does not present a formidable challenge to a right-hemisphere–imagery association, as, left- and right-hemispheric activity for motor ideation were not compared. Furthermore, the nature of the subjects' imaging was not ascertained. In fact, the authors speculated "whether motor ideation implies that the subject reminds himself by inner verbal commands about the movement he is thinking of" (Ingvar & Philipson, 1977, p. 235). Such verbal cognitions would likely engage left-hemisphere processes and could account for the observed left-side blood flow increases.

Another piece of evidence for a possible left-hemisphere advantage in imagery tasks comes from CLEM research. Bakan (1980) found positive correlations between people who tended to make right CLEMs and performance on imagery-based spatial–visualization tests, such as block and card rotations. In addition, the right movers also had more vivid images as assessed by the Betts questionnaire. Bakan interprets his findings as indicating that some important aspects of imagery, including vividness and spatial visualization, are dependent on left-hemisphere functions. He further suggests dichotomizing imagery functions as primary (i.e., "fuzzy," surreal, passive)- and secondary-process imagery (i.e., vivid, realistic, directed) and considering these types to be mediated by the right and left hemispheres, respectively.

Although Bakan's point, that imagery is not a unitary function, is a cogent one, other interpretations of his data can be made. For example, Richardson (1978) suggests that complex interactions between the emotional state and cognitive style of both the tester and the subject can account for reversals of expected CLEM directions. Such factors could be operating in Bakan's study. Because CLEM studies now have shown that the preferential use of imagery and its vividness correlate with left CLEMs (Bakan, 1969), right CLEMs (Bakan, 1980) and neither left nor right CLEMs (Spanos et al., 1980), it is perhaps wisest to be circumspect in accepting CLEM evidence for an association between the left hemisphere and heightened performance on imagery tasks. This association further remains in question because, to date, little direct evidence exists that gaze shifts are in fact a consequence of differential activation of the contralateral hemisphere. Therefore, a comprehensive understanding of the link between left CLEMs and imagery awaits further experimentation, and for the time being this link is most appropriately viewed in the context of the equivocal CLEM research on imagery.

In summary, the great majority of experimental work on cerebral laterality and imagery indicates the primary role of the right hemisphere in various imagery processes. Sufficient data have not yet accumulated to warrant serious consideration of left-hemispheric mediation of such imagery functions as visualization, orientation, or rotation (Bakan, 1980). At best, such data are suggestive and may inspire researchers in the area of laterality and imagery to attempt to differentiate the roles of the left and right hemisphere for particular imagery types or tasks. Some similar developments are beginning to occur in our understanding of hemispheric asymmetries for language and emotions. In each case an original belief in unilateral "dominance" for linguistic or affective processes is now being modified to recognize and incorporate the subtle or compensatory contributions of the "nondominant" hemisphere to that activity.

A POTPOURRI: CONCLUSIONS, CONJECTURES, AND RECOMMENDATIONS FOR FUTURE RESEARCH

In summary, the right hemisphere is very important for imagery processes, much more so than the left. The evidence sustaining this proposition has been wide ranging, yet largely consistent in its implications. A review of the clinical observations and experimental studies of hemispheric differences for imagery functions permits the following conclusions. First, removal of, or damage to various parts of the right hemisphere frequently leads to loss or disturbance of visualization, visual memory, visual dreaming, and the vividness of imagery. Such right-side damage also impairs imagery-based learning, or performance on spatial tasks with imageable components. Conversely, compensation for verbal memory deficits due to left-hemisphere injury can be achieved by teaching patients to use imagery mnemonics that are mediated by the intact right hemisphere. Second, electrical stimulation of the right temporal lobe generally produces reports of rich images and other visual hallucinatory impressions similar to those occurring in night dreams and epileptic auras. Right hemispheric involvement in visual dreaming and epileptic "dreamy states" also has been postulated. Third, EEG and GSR studies of normal subjects have found that increased activation of the right hemisphere accompanies subjects' imagery experiences. Fourth, CLEM research, although often yielding paradoxical effects, has found left CLEMs and, theoretically, a presumed right hemispheric activation, to correlate with the preferred use and clarity of images, as well as with heightened performance on imagery tasks. Fifth, visual-recognition studies of laterally presented abstract and concrete words have indicated a right hemispheric capacity to "read," store, or otherwise mediate the processing of high-imagery words. Antithetically, reports of left hemispheric participation in imagery processes are infrequent, especially when compared to the vast majority identifying the role of the right hemisphere in imagery. The aggregate of this research on imagery and cerebral laterality provides long-awaited support for the commonly accepted hypothesis that imagery is primarily a right hemispheric function. The hypothesis is further strengthened by the fact that evidence converges on the same conclusion from so many directions.

The immediate question raised by these results is deceptively simple to pose: "Why should a right hemispheric superiority for imagery functions exist?" An answer to this question is considerably more complex and cannot be absolutely determined on the basis of our extant knowledge of brain mcchanisms *or* imagery functions. However, some notions can be ventured that can perhaps serve as rudimentary components in an ultimate model of hemispheric asymmetries for imagery.

It is perhaps most fitting to construe the human brain as a binary system, with two functionally distinct information-processing subsystems (Dimond, 1972). It has been demonstrated that independent parallel processing can occur in each hemisphere for the preferred components of a composite stimulus (Ley & Bryden, 1982). Therefore, if the right and left hemispheres can simultaneously mediate the affective and semantic aspects of a highly emotional command, for instance, it follows that different attributes of a stimulus might be stored at multiple sites in the brain. Gazzaniga and LeDoux (1978) have advanced such a dynamic view of information storage, theorizing that experiences and the neural mechanisms by which they are registered and encoded are multidimensional. Consequently, a verbal linguistic encoding system is only one type of information-processing system. In addition to a verbal-representation system, analogous encoding systems featuring imagery, affect, or kinaesthetic mechanisms might also exist. In principle, all these systems could be working on the same complex experience. Such systems, the stimuli they encode, and the resulting engrams may be subserved by different hemispheres or hemispheric regions. Being mindful of the global and simultaneous cognitive style of the right hemisphere, it seems most reasonable to consign most nonverbal information processing to the right hemisphere, especially that dealing with imageable and affective stimulus attributes.

Other characteristics of the right hemisphere might uniquely bias it for processing imagery. Semmes (1968) has described the right hemisphere as having a diffuse functional organization. Such an organization would lead to a proficiency in integrating diverse units of information and a resultant specialization for "behaviors requiring multimodal coordination, such as the various spatial abilities" (Semmes, 1968, p. 11). The neuropsychological organization of the right hemisphere seems tailored for synthesizing "data" from perceptual, visceral, and motor sensory domains, across space and time into a superordinate whole. Similar processes are likely entailed in imagery functions and consequently may be managed by the right hemisphere.

A right-hemisphere superiority for imagery processes is consistent with many dual-processing models of hemispheric function (Bower, 1970; Dimond, 1972; Paivio, 1978). In all these formulations, each processing channel has been identified with a different hemisphere. Although different theorists have chosen to emphasize slightly different attributes of each hemisphere's functioning, most have related nonverbal, pictorial, or imagery activity with the right hemisphere.

Paivio (1978), for instance, has described a word and picture processor and identified these systems with the left and right hemisphere, respectively. He believes this to be accurate because verbal information tends to be discrete and sequential, whereas pictorial information tends to be organized in a simultaneous and spatially parallel form. Each hemisphere is specialized to handle each type of information. Somewhat similarly, Bower (1970) has defined two contrasting modes of thought and information storage. One is an imagistic, associational memory system, and the other is a verbal, linguistic, propositional memory system. The imagistic system is most conducive to processing concrete information, whereas the verbal system is most appropriate for abstract thought. It is readily apparent how these cognitive modes fit the informational processing styles of the left and right hemispheres.

A suitable model of hemispheric functioning for imagery processes probably would need to incorporate a dual-processing scheme, consider the unique neuropsychological organization and cognitive style of each hemisphere, and recognize the multidimensional encoding of multifaceted experiences by the right and left hemispheres.

Although these conjectures violate proper theory or model-building in a Popperian sense (Popper, 1959), they may provide a first step towards an ultimately comprehensive understanding of hemispheric functions for imagery. Obviously, much experimentation is necessary to broaden the observational data base on which a theory can be founded. Given the present state of our knowledge and the lacunae manifest in the preceding literature review, particular issues in the cerebral laterality and imagery domain should be vigorously pursued: To paraphrase George Orwell, although all research directions are equal, some are more equal than others. These "more equal" research directions are the following:

1. The role played by imagery in tests of spatial visualization needs to be discerned. Because right hemispheric effects for visual–spatial abilities are better defined, we could augment our understanding of right hemispheric effects for imagery by clarifying the relationship between such factors as imagery control or vividness and performance tests of visual–spatial ability.

2. *Intra-* as well as *inter*hemispheric activity underlying imagery processes should be focused on. Clearly, different cortical regions within a hemisphere are involved with different imagery functions. For example, damage to the right posterioparietal lobe impairs reversible operations in space, whereas damage to the right temporo-parietal area affects visualizing familiar things. However, different cortical regions also have been shown to subserve *similar* imagery tasks: imagery mnemonics seemingly are mediated by both right frontal (Gazzaniga & LeDoux, 1978) and right temporal regions (Jones-Gotman & Milner, 1978). The correspondence between specific hemispheric tracts and particular imagery tasks needs further and finer articulation.

3. Hemispheric effects for imagery and emotional experiences need to be experimentally extricated one from the other, just as imagery and visual–spatial factors need to be teased apart. This situation is necessarily complex because these functions are primarily right-hemispheric and a simultaneous dissociation of effects, possible in studying left- and right-hemispheric properties (Ley & Bryden, 1982), cannot be shown. However, experimental designs in which factorial levels of imagery and emotion are represented in the stimuli or task instructions (Ley & Bryden, 1983) as well as appropriate statistical procedures are potential means to disambiguate these effects.

4. A primary consideration for research on hemispheric differences for cognitive activities in general, is to ensure that behavioral indices of laterality measure cerebral–laterality effects and not cognitive–strategy effects. Bryden (1980) has identified some of the ways in which behavioral–laterality effects are profoundly affected by the strategies that subjects employ in carrying out the task set to them. This concern is most acute in laterality and imagery studies because of the manifold

pictorial or verbal ways in which subjects can perform an experimental task. Therefore, experimental procedures should attempt to eliminate subjective strategy effects, hold them constant, or relate behavioral asymmetries to known hemispheric asymmetries, such as those existing for handedness and speech lateralization (Bryden, 1980).

These experimental efforts as well as other research activities are facilitated by related theoretical and technical developments in cerebral-laterality research. For instance, intriguing theoretical relationships between left- and right-hemisphere motor control and approach–avoidance tendencies (Davidson, 1978) offer a potential framework for interpreting hemispheric differences between directed, spontaneous, or passive imagery. On the technological front, sophisticated innovations, such as the PETT scan, can more precisely relate brain action to behavior. The PETT scan, or as it is less affectionately known, *positron emission transaxial tomography,* provides a photograph of hemispheric activation by tracking radioactively tagged glucose utilization in the brain. The radioactive substance "lights up" in response to virtually anything that stimulates brain activity and thereby provides an isomorphic correspondence between a stimulus and a cortical response. Unfortunately, there are less than twenty PETT scanners in the world; thus most researchers will have to be content with less grand refinements such as "t-scopes" and electroencephalographs. However, these instruments are far from primitive and already have provided the good data that support our current knowledge of cerebral laterality.

In closing, an affirmative answer has been provided for the question as to whether the right hemisphere primarily mediates imagery processes. The penultimate question in this research domain concerns which hemispheric regions mediate which imagery functions in what kind of people doing what sorts of things. Neither a quick nor simple response can be expected. One reasonable approach to this issue has been unwittingly implied by Robert Benchley, the humorist. He wryly observed that there are two types of people: those who divide people and things into two groups and those who do not. Although such dichotomizing often has reached faddish dimensions in laterality research, the above question lends itself to bifurcation: a strategy that makes a largely unmanageable problem experimentally tenable.

REFERENCES

Adler A. Course and outcome of visual agnosia. *Journal of Nervous and Mental Disease,* 1950, **111**, 41–51.

Adrian, E. D., & Matthews, B. H. C. The Berger rhythm: Potential changes from the occipital lobes in man. *Brain,* 1934, **57**, 355–384.

Ahearn, G. L., & Schwartz, G. E. Differential lateralization for positive *vs* negative emotion. *Neuropsychologia,* 1979, **17**, 693–698.

Arseni, C., and Petrovici, I. N. Epilepsy in temporal lobe tumors. *European Neurology*, 1971, **5**, 201–214.

Bakan, P. Hypnotizability, laterality of eye movements and functional brain asymmetry. *Perceptual and Motor Skills*, 1969, **28**, 927–932.

Bakan, P. The eyes have it. *Psychology Today*, 1971, **4**, 64–69.

Bakan, P. The right brain is the dreamer. *Psychology Today*, 1976, **11**, 66–68.

Bakan, P. Dreaming, REM sleep, and the right hemisphere: A theoretical integration. *Journal of Altered States of Consciousness*, 1978, **3**, 285–307.

Bakan, P. Imagery raw and cooked: A hemispheric recipe. In J. E.Shorr, G. E. Sobel, P. Robin, and J. A. Connella (Eds.), *Imagery: Its many dimensions and applications*. New York: Plenum, 1980.

Bogen, J. E. The other side of the brain II: An oppositional mind. *Bulletin of the Los Angeles Neurological Societies*, 1969, **34**, 135–162.

Bogen, J. Sperry, R., & Vogel, P. Commissural section and propagation of seizures. In H. H. Jasper, A. A. Ward, A. Pope (Eds.), *Basic mechanisms of the epilepsies*. Boston: Little, Brown, 1969.

Borod, J. C., & Caron, H. F. Facedness and emotion related to lateral dominance, sex, and expression type. *Neuropsychologia*, 1980, **18**, 237–241.

Borod, J. C., & Goodglass, H. Lateralization of linguistic and melodic processing with age. *Neuropsychologia*, 1980, **18**, 79–83.

Bower, G. H. Analysis of mnemonic device. *American Scientist*, 1970, **58**, 496–510.

Bradshaw, J. L. Right hemisphere language: Familial and nonfamilial sinistrals, cognitive deficits and writing hand position in sinistrals, and concrete-abstract, imageable–nonimageable dimensions in word recognition. A review of interrelated issues. *Brain and Language*, 1980, **10**, 172–188.

Bryden, M. P. Splitting the normal brain: Some facts and fallacies. Fellow's address to Division 6 of the American Psychological Association, Montreal, 1980.

Butters, N., & Barton, M. Effect of parietal lobe damage on the performance of reversible operations in space. *Neuropsychologia*, 1970, **8**, 205–214.

Bryden, M. P. Ley, R. G., & Sugarman, J. H. A left-ear advantage for identifying the emotional quality of tonal sequences. *Neuropsychologia*, 1982, **20**, 1, 83-87.

Carmon, A., & Nachson, I. Ear asymmetry in perception of emotional non-verbal stimuli. *Acta Psychologica*, 1973, **37**, 351–357.

Charcot, J. M. La foi qui guerit. *Archives de Neurologie*, 1893, **25**, 72–87.

Cohen, B. D., Berent, S., & Silverman, A. J. Field dependence and lateralization of function in the human brain. *Archives of General Psychiatry*, 1973, **28**, 165–167.

Cohen, D. B. Changes in REM dream content during the night: Implications for hypotheses about changes in cerebral dominance across REM periods. *Perceptual and Motor Skills*, 1977, **44**, 1267–1277.

Davidson, R., & Schwartz, G. Patterns of cerebral lateralization during cardiac biofeedback versus the self-regulation of emotion: Sex differences. *Psychophysiology* 1976, **13**, 62–74.

Davidson, R. J. Hemispheric specialization for affective processes in normals: Behavioral and electrophysiological studies. Paper presented at the meeting of the Society for Biological Psychiatry, Atlanta, 1978.

Day, J. H. Right hemisphere language processing in normal right handers. *Journal of Experimental Psychology: Human Perception and Performance*, 1977, **3**, 518–528.

Day, M. E. An eye-movement phenomenon related to attention, thought and anxiety. *Perceptual and Motor Skills*, 1964, **19**, 443–446.

Day, M. E. Attention, anxiety and psychotherapy. *Psychotherapy: Theory, Research and Practice*, 1967, **5**, 146–149.

D'Elia, G., & Perris, C. Cerebral functional dominance and memory function: An analysis of EEG integrated amplitude in depressive psychotics. *Acta Psychiatrica Scandinavica*, 1974, **244**, 143–157.

Dimond, S. J. *The double brain*. Baltimore: William & Wilkins, 1972.

Dodds, A. G. Hemispheric differences in tactuo-spatial processing. *Neuropsychologia*, 1978, **16**, 247–254.

Duke, J. Lateral eye movement behavior. *Journal of General Psychology*, 1968, **78**, 189–195.

Ehrlichman, H., & Weinberger, A. Lateral eye movements and hemispheric asymmetry: A critical review. *Psychological Bulletin*, 1978, **85**, 1080–1101.

Ellis, H. D., & Shepherd, J. W. Recognition of abstract and concrete words presented in left and right visual fields. *Journal of Experimental Psychology*, 1974, **103**, 1035–1036.

Ervin, F. R., Organic brain syndromes associated with epilepsy. In A. M. Freedman, H. I. Kaplan, & B. J. Sadock (Eds.), *Comprehensive textbook of psychiatry/II*, Baltimore: Williams & Wilkins, 1975.

Fenichel, O. *The psychoanalytic theory of neurosis*. New York: Norton, 1945.

Gainotti, G., Reactions "catastrophiques" et manifestations l'indifference au cours des atteintes cerebrales. *Neuropsychologia*, 1969, **7**, 195–204.

Galin, D. Implications for psychiatry of left and right cerebral specialization. *Archives of General Psychiatry*, 1974, **31**, 572–583.

Galin, D., & Ornstein, R. Lateral specialization of cognitive mode: An EEG study. *Psychophysiology*, 1972, **9**, 412–418.

Galin, D., Diamond, R., & Braff, D. Lateralization of conversion symptoms: More frequent on the left. *American Journal of Psychiatry*, 1977, **134**, 578–580.

Gazzaniga, M. D., & LeDoux, J. E. *The integrated mind*. New York: Plenum, 1978.

Geffen, G., Bradshaw, J., & Wallace, G. Interhemispheric effects on reaction time to verbal and nonverbal stimuli. *Journal of Experimental Psychology*, 1971, **87**, 415–422.

Goldstein, K. *The organism: A holistic approach to biology derived from pathological data in man*. New York: American Books, 1939.

Goldstein, L., Stoltzfus, N., & Gardocki, J. Changes in interhemispheric amplitude relationships in the EEG during sleep. *Physiology and Behavior*, 1972, **8**, 811–815.

Greenwood, P., Wilson, D. H., & Gazzaniga, M. S. Dream report following commissurotomy. *Cortex*, 1977, **13**, 311–316.

Gruzelier, J., & Venables, P. Bimodality and lateral asymmetry of skin conductance orienting activity in schizophrenics: Replication and evidence of lateral asymmetry in patients with depression and disorders of personality. *Biological Psychiatry,* 1974, **8,** 55–73.

Harman, D. W. & Ray, W. J. Hemispheric activity during affective verbal stimuli: An EEG study. *Neuropsychologia,* 1977, **15,** 457–460.

Harnad, S. R. Creativity, lateral saccades and the nondominant hemisphere. *Perceptual and Motor Skills,* 1972, **34,** 653–654.

Hartmann, E. *The biology of dreaming.* Springfield, Il.: Thomas, 1967.

Head, H. *Aphasia and kindred disorders of speech.* Cambridge: Cambridge University Press, 1926.

Hecaen, H. Clinical symptomatology in right and left hemispheric lesions. In V. B. Mountcastle (Ed.), *Interhemispheric relations and cerebral dominance.* Baltimore: Johns Hopkins Press, 1962.

Hines, D. Recognition of verbs, abstract nouns and concrete nouns from the left and right visual half-fields. *Neuropsychologia,* 1976, **14,** 211–216.

Hines, D. Differences in tachistoscopic recognition between abstract and concrete words as a function of visual half-field and frequency. *Cortex,* 1977, **13,** 66–73.

Hiscock, M. Eye movement asymmetry and hemispheric function: An examination of individual differences. *Journal of Psychology,* 1977, **97,** 49–52.

Holt, R. R. Imagery: The return of the ostracized. *American Psychologist,* 1964, **19,** 254–264.

Hoppe, K. D. Split-brains and psychoanalysis. *The Psychoanalytic Quarterly,* 1977, **46,** 220–244.

Hoppe, K. D. Split-brain—psychoanalytic findings and hypotheses. *Journal of the American Academy of Psychoanalysis,* 1978, **6,** 193–213.

Horowitz, M. J. *Image formation and cognition,* 2nd ed. New York: Appleton, 1978.

Humphrey, M. D., & Zangwill, O. L. Cessation of dreaming after brain injury. *Journal of Neurology, Neurosurgery, and Psychiatry,* 1951, **14,** 322–325.

Ingvar, D. H., & Philipson, L. Distribution of cerebral blood flow in the dominant hemisphere during motor ideation and motor performance. *Annals of Neurology,* 1977, **2,** 230–237.

Jaccarino, G. Dual coding in memory: Evidence from temporal lobe lesions in man. Unpublished master's thesis, McGill University, 1975.

Jackson, J. H. On the nature of the duality of the brain. *Medical Press,* 1874, 1, 19 [reprinted in J. Taylor (Ed.), *Selected writings of John Hughlings Jackson.* New York: Basic Books, 1958].

Jackson, J. H. Case of large cerebral tumor without optic neuritis and with left hemiplegia and imperception. *Royal London Ophthamological Hospital Reports,* 1876, **8,** 434 [reprinted in J. Taylor (Ed.), *Selected writings of John Hughlings Jackson.* New York: Basic Books, 1958].

Jackson, J. H. On right-or left-sided spasm at the onset of epileptic paroxysms, and on crude sensation warnings and elaborate mental states. *Brain,* 1880, **3,** 192–206.

James, W. *The principles of psychology.* New York: Holt, 1890. Reprinted New York: Dover, 1950.

Jones, M. Imagery as a mnemonic after left temporal lobectomy: Contrast between material-specific and generalized memory disorders. *Neuropsychologia*, 1974, **12**, 21–30.

Jones-Gotman, M. Incidental learning of image-mediated or pronounced words after right temporal lobectomy. *Cortex*, 1979, **15**, 187–197.

Jones-Gotman, M., & Milner, B. Right temporal lobe contribution to image-mediated verbal learning. *Neuropsychologia*, 1978, **16**, 61–71.

Kleist, K. *Gehern-Pathologie vornehmlich auf Grund der Kriegserfahrungen.* Leipzig: Barth, 1934.

Kripke, D. F., & Sonnenschein, D. A 90-minute daydream cycle. Paper presented at the annual meeting of Association for the Psychophysiological Study of Sleep, San Diego, 1973.

Lange, J. Agnosien und Apraxien. In O. Bumke & O. Fouster (Eds.) *Handbuch der Neurologie*, Berlin: Springer, 1936.

Lashley, R. S. Brain mechanisms and intelligence. Chicago: Chicago University Press, 1929.

Ley, R. G. Cerebral asymmetries, emotional experience, and imagery: Implications for psychotherapy. In A. A. Sheikh & J. T. Shaffer (Eds.), *The potential of fantasy and imagination*. New York: Brandon House, 1979.

Ley, R. G. An archival examination of an asymmetry of hysterical conversion symptoms. *Journal of Clinical Neuropsychology*, 1980, **2**, 1, 1–9.

Ley, R. G., & Bryden, M. P. Hemispheric differences in recognizing faces and emotions. *Brain and Language*, 1979, **1**, 127–138.

Ley, R. G., & Bryden, M. P. Consciousness, emotion, and the right hemisphere. In R. Stevens & G. Underwood (Eds.), *Aspects of consciousness*, II. New York: Academic Press, 1981.

Ley, R. G., & Bryden, M. P. A dissociation of right and left hemispheric effects for recognizing emotional tone and verbal content. *Brian and Cognition*, 1982, **1**, 3-9.

Ley, R. G., & Bryden, M. P. Right hemispheric involvement in imagery and affect. In E. Perecman & J. Brown (Eds.), *Cognitive processing in the right hemisphere,* in press (1983).

Marcel, A. J., & Patterson, K. Word recognition and production: Reciprocity in clinical and normal studies. In J. Requin (Ed.), *Attention and performance VII*, Hillsdale, N.J.: Lawrence Erlbaum Associates, 1978.

McFarland, K., & Ashton, R. The influence of brain lateralization of function on a manual skill. *Cortex*, 1978, **14**, 102–111.

McFie, J., Piercy, M. F., & Zangwill, O. L. Visual–spatial agnosia associated with lesions of the right cerebral hemisphere. *Brain*, 1950, **73**, 167–190.

McGee, M. G. Human spatial abilities: Psychometric studies & environmental, genetic, hormonal, & neurological influences. *Psychological Bulletin*, 1979, **86**, 5, 889–918.

Meskin, B., & Singer, J. L. Daydreaming, reflective thought, and laterality of eye movements. *Journal of Personality and Social Psychology*, 1974, **30**, 64–71.

Milner, B., & Teuber, H.-L. Alterations of perception and memory in man: Reflections on methods. In L. Weiskrantz (Ed.), *Analysis of behavioral change*, New York: Harper, 1968.

Morgan, A. H., McDonald, P. J., & Macdonald, H. Difference in bilateral alpha activity as a function of experimental task with a note on lateral eye movements and hypnotizability. *Neuropsychologia*, 1971, **9**, 459–469.

Myslobodsky, M. S., & Rattok, J. Bilateral electrodermal activity in working man. *Acta Psychologica*, 1977, **41**, 273–282.

Newcombe, F. *Missile wounds of the brain*. London: Oxford University Press, 1969.

Nielsen, J. M. *Agnosia, apraxia, aphasia: Their value in cerebral localization*. New York: Hoeber, 1946.

Ornstein, R. E. *The psychology of consciousness*. San Francisco: Freeman, 1972.

Ornstein, R., Johnstone, J., Herron, J., & Swencionis, C. Differential right hemisphere engagement in visuospatial tasks. *Neuropsychologia*, 1980, **18**, 1, 49–64.

Paivio, A. Dual coding: Theoretical issues and empirical evidence. In J. M. Scandura & C. J. Brainerd (Eds.), *Structural/process models of complex human behavior*. Leiden, The Netherlands: Nordhoff, 1978.

Patten, B. M. The ancient art of memory. *Archives of Neurology*, 1972, **26**, 25–31.

Patterson, K. E., & Marcel, A. J. Aphasia, dyslexia and the phonological coding of written words. *Quarterly Journal of Experimental Psychology*, 1977, **29**, 307–318.

Penfield, W., & Perot, P. The brain's record of auditory and visual experience: A final summary and discussion. *Brain*, 1963, **86**, 595–696.

Popper, K. *The logic of scientific discovery*. New York: Basic Books, 1959.

Richardson, A. Verbalizer–visualizer: A cognitive style dimension. *Journal of Mental Imagery*, 1977, **1**, 109–126.

Richardson, A. Subject, task, and tester variables associated with initial eye movement responses. *Journal of Mental Imagery*, 1978, **2**, 85–100.

Richardson, J. T. F. The effects of stimulus attributes upon latency of word recognition. *British Journal of Psychology*, 1976, **67**, 315–325.

Robbins, K., & McAdams, D. Interhemispheric alpha asymmetry and imagery mode. *Brain and Language*, 1974, **1**, 189–193.

Robertson, A. D., & Inglis, J. The effect of electroconvulsive therapy on human learning and memory. Canadian Psychological Review, 1977, **18**, 285–307.

Rodin, J., & Singer, J. L. Eye shift, thought and obesity. *Journal of Personality*, 1976, **44**, 594–610.

Rosenthal, R., & Bigelow, L. B. Quantitative brain measurements in chronic schizophrenics. *British Journal of Psychiatry*, 1972, **121**, 259–264.

Rossi, G. F. & Rosadini, G. Experimental analysis of cerebral dominance in man. In C. H. Millikan & F. L. Darley (Eds.), *Brain mechanisms underlying speech and language*. New York: Grune and Stratton, 1967.

Sackheim, H. A., Gur, R. C. & Saucy, M. C. Emotions are expressed more intensely on the left side of the face. *Science*, 1978, 434–436.

Safer, M. Sex and hemisphere differences in access to codes for processing emotional expressions and faces. *Journal of Experimental Psychology: General*, 1981, **110**, 86–100.

Safer, M., & Leventhal, H. Ear differences in evaluating emotional tones of voice and verbal content. *Journal of Experimental Psychology: Human Perception and Performance,* 1977, **3,** 1, 75–82.

Satz, P. Incidence of aphasia in left-handers: A test of some hypothetical models of cerebral speech organization. In J. Herron (Ed.), *Neuropsychology of left-handedness.* New York: Academic Press, 1980.

Seamon, J. G., & Gazzaniga, M. S., Coding strategies and cerebral laterality effects. *Cognitive Psychology,* 1973, **5,** 249–259.

Semmes, J. Hemispheric specialization: A possible clue to mechanism. *Neuropsychologia,* 1968, **6,** 11–26.

Sheehan, P. W. *The function and nature of imagery.* New York: Academic Press, 1972.

Shepard, R. N. & Metzler, J. Mental rotation of three-dimensional objects. *Science,* 1971, **171,** 701–703.

Short, P. L. The objective study of mental imagery. *British Journal of Psychology,* 1953, **44,** 38–51.

Spanos, N. P., Pawlak, A. E., Mah, C. D., & D'eon, J. L. Lateral eye movements, hypnotic susceptibility and imaginal ability in right-handers. *Perceptual and Motor Skills,* 1980, **50,** 287–294.

Springer, S. Speech perception and the biology of language. In M. Gazzaniga (Ed.), *Handbook of behavioral neurobiology.* New York: Plenum, 1979.

Stone, M. H. Dreams, free association, and the non-dominant hemisphere: An integration of psychoanalytical, neurophysiological, and historical data. *Journal of the American Academy of Psychoanalysis,* 1977, **5,** 255–284.

Studdert-Kennedy, M., & Shankweiler, D. Hemispheric specialization for speech perception. *Journal of the Acoustical Society of America,* 1970, **48,** 579–594.

Teitelbaum, H. A. Spontaneous rhythmic ocular movements: Their possible relationship to mental activity. *Neurology,* 1954, **4,** 350–354.

Teuber, H.-L. Effects of brain wounds implicating right and left hemisphere in man. In V. B. Mountcastle (Ed.), *Interhemispheric relations and cerebral dominance.* Baltimore: Johns Hopkins Press, 1962.

Tucker, D. M., Stenslie, C. E., Roth, R. S. & Shearer, S. L. Right frontal lobe activation and right hemisphere performance decrement during a depressed mood. *Archives of General Psychiatry,* 1981, **38,** 169–174.

Weinstein, E. A. & Kahn, R. L. Denial of illness: Symbolic and physiological aspects. Springfield, Ill.: Thomas, 1955.

Weisenburg, T. H., & McBride, K. E. Aphasia: A clinical and psychological study. New York: Commonwealth Fund, 1935.

Wigan, A. L. *The duality of the mind.* London: Longman, 1844.

Wolf-Dorlester, B. Creativity, adaptive regression, reflective eye movements, and the Holzman movement response. *Dissertation Abstracts International,* 1976, **36,** 6458–6459B.

Zajonc, R. B. Feeling and thinking: Preferences need no inferences. *American Psychologist,* 1980, **35,** 151–175.

Zatorre, R. J. Recognition of dichotic melodies by musicians and nonmusicians. *Neuropsychologia,* 1979, **17,** 607–617.

Zikmund, V. Physiological correlates of visual imagery. In P. Sheehan (Ed.), *The function and nature of imagery.* New York: Academic Press, 1972.

CHAPTER 10

Imagery and Language

IAN BEGG

Human language is a pervasive phenomenon that has been the subject of a vast quantity of research and theorization. Likewise, research and theory concerning mental imagery encompass an enormous domain of questions and answers. In the main, these two giants, language and imagery, have trundled on oblivious of each other. However, there is a nontrivial intersection between them consisting of research concerning the relationship between imagery and language. The purpose of this chapter is to review that intersection in an attempt to pull some isolated findings together in a sensible context. It should be understood that the relationship between imagery and language is not queried by the majority of linguistic researchers. Accordingly, the research reviewed here is not representative of language research as a whole. It is, however, an important piece of the pie, perhaps much more so than we realize. To establish an interpretive context, let us begin by briefly considering some conceptions of the nature and purpose of imagery.

Historically, the most common and familiar conception of imagery stresses that an image is a record of sensory experience. According to the traditional conception, the world of physical reality is a world of energy, energy that impinges on and stimulates the receiving organism. Environmental stimuli produce activity in the receiving system and, in so doing, change that system, leaving traces, images, or general residue from the activity. In such fashion, psychological reality comes to reflect physical reality. Accordingly, the psychological world consists of images that are ghosts of stimuli past, in a mental storehouse of such fractional sensings. According to Aristole's copy theory, such images are the common possessions of all humanity, thus bestowing on them a central role in language. By the theory, words are simply spoken signs associated with images. A given word is an expression of an image for the speaker. Additionally, the word arouses that image or a succession of images in the hearer. In this view, comprehension is equated with the arousal of those images.

It is not a difficult exercise to find fault with the copy theory. Few theorists today accept the conception of the human cognizer as a passive recorder of experience, and even fewer would equate meaning with a static image or restrict comprehension to the arousal of an image. However, the theory does direct our attention to some important concerns. For instance, Aristotle recognized that even concrete words bear no resemblance in physical form to their referents, whereas images do. He also knew that the meaning of a linguistic signal does not reside in its physical properties, but rather in the cognitive system of the language user. And finally, his conception makes it clear that communication by language is possible only if there is some substantial similarity in the cognitive systems of the communicants. That similarity is effected in the theory by giving each person an identical set of imaginal copies of real-world objects.

It is generally agreed today that the cognitive system is much more complex than Aristotle ceded. Cognizers interact with reality, rather than passively recording it, and psychological reality consists not only of the record of prior interactions, but also of the procedures and capacities that govern those interactions. It is also generally agreed that mental structures and procedures interact among themselves in complex ways. In the face of such nested complexities, however, some parts of the system have been singled out for study. One part of the cognitive system that has received much attention is knowledge of the world; another is knowledge of language. The distinction between the two sorts of knowledge is illustrated by Benjamin Franklin's famous insult: "He was so learned that he could name a horse in nine languages; so ignorant that he bought a cow to ride on." However, we should not let the obvious differences between knowledge of the world and knowledge of language blind us to the fact that they are interdependent as well. After all, we acquire knowledge of language by using language, and the most obvious thing to talk about is something other than language. Consequently, the form of our knowledge of language is influenced by the nature of our knowledge of the world. By the same token, knowledge of the world is not merely a passive record of stimulation; the structure of linguistic knowledge affects at least the classifications and types we impose on the continuous stream of stimulation, and perhaps the units as well.

The intent of this chapter is to discuss the relationship between imagery and language. The stance I shall adopt is that imagery is an important process in the acquisition and use of knowledge of the world, and that images are important representational structures within that knowledge system. Consequently, the focus is to understand the role of imagery in the knowledge system and to understand the relationship between knowledge of the world and knowledge of the language. A useful metaphor for conceptualizing that relation was offered by Ferdinand de Saussure (1915), who compared the language system to a currency system. The value of a dollar can be defined in two different ways. On the one hand, the dollar has a value within its own system of currency, a value that regulates exchanges of currency. Thus a dollar bill is exchangeable for any combination of coins whose total value is 100 cents. On the other hand, the dollar has a value in terms of the range of nonfinancial goods and series for which it can be exchanged. In similar fashion, a linguistic unit has *formal value* by virtue of its relationship to other linguistic units and *reference* by virtue of the range of nonlinguistic circumstances to which it can legally refer. Dictionary entries, linguistic features, and syntactic privileges of occurrence are examples of the formal value of linguistic units; it is of such values that the competence system, knowledge of language, consists. Images, ideas, and intentions are examples of the referential value of the same units; it is of such units that knowledge of the world is comprised. Within such a metaphoric conception, we would be no more tempted to equate the meaning of a word with a particular image in a particular case than to equate the value of a dollar with the cigar it was used to purchase. Rather, the referential meaning of a term is the entire range of circumstances to which it can refer, with any single member of the infinite number of partitionings of that range representing one instance of the use of the term. The same term, of course, has a formal linguistic meaning as well.

The currency metaphor is more useful than the copy theory in directing our attention toward important aspects of language use in relation to imagery. It is clear that a particular image can indeed serve as a mental referent for a particular linguistic term, given that the domain of reference for the term encompasses the domain captured by the image. However, such direct mappings do not exhaust the reference for the term, nor do they exhaust the set of terms that could express the image. For example, the word "dog" may arouse an image of a particular dog, say a pet cocker spaniel. However, the same word could equally well arouse many other images, whereas many other terms could arouse the same image. Although the relationship between a term and an image is not unique, it is by no means random, either. Consequently, some important aspect of imagery's contribution to language use is discriminative rather than constructive. In other words, it is a mistake to seek exhaustive meaning by equating a term to an image. Rather, the existence of a relationship between a term and an image restricts both the set of other possible terms that could have been used and the set of other images that could have been aroused. Imagery thus narrows and focuses a linguistic message, rather than providing *the* meaning in any fundamental way.

The conception of meaning in terms of what is left after much has been removed is not, unfortunately, the majority view at present, although there have been some adherents. Saussure, for example, emphasized that meaning is more aptly described in negative and contrastive terms than in positive and constructive terms. In his view, comprehension is a matter of narrowing down an interpretation from the vague to the specific, rather than of constructing a meaning from features or elements. The interpretation of a message, rather than being an absolute or fixed entity that is merely aroused, is reached by the process of discrimination and consequently is relative to the alternatives that were discarded *en route*. This account grants a considerable degree of context sensitivity to the interpretive process and to the meaning resulting therefrom, regardless of whether that meaning is imaginal in form.

Consequently, we are left with a notion of meaning as a variable, context-relative instantiation carved from a potentially infinite set with fuzzy boundaries, a notion that readily admits imaginal processes in interpretation and that allows particular images to serve as particular instances derived through interpretation.

Simply stated, human language is a tool used by a speaker to direct the interpretive processes of a listener to rule out inappropriate foci within the listener's knowledge of the world. If the tool is skillfully wielded, the listener will derive an instance from within the set intended by the speaker. Imagery, as a system, is one major aspect of knowledge of the world. The imagery system serves both to represent the world in its absence, with static images that preserve experienced perceptual relationships, and to interpret interactions between the cognizer and the world, with procedures for transforming, combining, and decomposing images, generating images that need bear no resemblance to past or potential experiences. In short, an image is simply a perching in the continuous flight of the imagination, and imagination is a key process in the discrimination of linguistic messages.

In the following sections, the contemporary research concerning the interface between imagery and language is selectively and illustratively reviewed. It will become apparent that imagery and language are intimately and interdependently related at many levels of analysis, whether we focus on structure or function, competence or performance, or semantic or episodic memory. It will also be clear that the relation pertains more to the substance of what is said, rather than to the form in which it is said. Let us begin by considering research concerning imagery and the meaning of language.

IMAGERY AND THE MEANING OF LANGUAGE

Most psychological research addresses questions of how meaning is used in comprehension, memory, and communication, rather than what meaning is. As a result, fewer experiments are considered in the present section than in later sections; rather, an attempt is made to frame the issues about which those sections are concerned. Meaning is such a complex concept that there is no single conception that has achieved wide acceptance. However, many useful distinctions have appeared, a few of which are considered here.

David Olson (1970), in an important article, cogently argued for a distinction between the sense and reference of a term. The sense is the linguistic or formal meaning, and the reference is extralinguistic meaning, much as in the distinction made earlier by Saussure (1915). However, Olson went farther than Saussure, arguing that it is the reference of a term that is most important in language use and that reference varies depending on the real or imagined alternatives from which a target is to be distinguished. Although Olson's experiments more clearly fit in a discussion of communication, they illustrate the importance of the distinction he offered and thus are described at this point.

Olson's procedure required that a child describe an object under which a star was located so that another child could use the description to locate the star. Suppose the star was placed under a small white square. If the table included the appropriate square, as well as a number of black squares of various sizes, the child said, "It's under the white one." If the alternatives were all white but larger than the target, the child said, "It's under the small one." The general result was that the description offered was sufficient to identify the intended referent, but that the description of that same referent varied depending on what other alternatives were present. Although the research shows that the same nominal referent is open to various descriptions, an equally important corollary is that the same description could equally apply to many referents. Thus, to the extent that the referent of a statement is a meaning, an expression's meaning will depend on the communicative context and will accordingly vary considerably from utterance to utterance.

Olson (1970), in forcefully drawing our attention to the importance of reference in the meaning of linguistic signals, presents a context in which imagery has a natural place, since the discriminative context is not always physically available to the speaker and hearer. Even when the context is perceptually available, the imagery system is implicated by the fact that the speaker need recognize the objects in the array in the act of describing one relative to the others. Thus, from Olson's work, we can distinguish between the linguistic meaning of language and the referential meaning of the same language, recognizing the primary importance of imagery in reference.

The relationship between imagery and meaning is rendered explicitly in Allan Paivio's theorizing [e.g., in his book on imagery and verbal processes (1971)]. In his dual-coding theory, Paivio makes a broad distinction between two symbolic cognitive systems, one specialized for dealing with language, and the other for dealing with nonlinguistic information. It is important in understanding Paivio's approach to make a clear distinction between the symbolic systems and sensory modalities. For example, linguistic information may be visual (e.g., reading), auditory (e.g., listening to speech), tactile, (e.g., braille), and so on. Likewise, nonlinguistic information can arrive through numerous sensory channels, all requiring the nonverbal system for cognitive processing. The concern here is exclusively with the symbolic systems, not with sensory modalities. Paivio has distinguished between the linguistic and nonlinguistic systems in numerous ways relevant to our discussion of imagery and meaning. Let us consider some of those distinctions.

A fundamental difference between the imagery and verbal systems refers to the properties of the units within those systems, especially as those units relate to external reality. Although the units can be analyzed in various terms, the units in the language system are similar to Morton's (1969) *logogens*, whereas the units in the imagery system are, analogously, *imagens* (Paivio & Begg, 1981). In each case the unit is a cognitive mental unit activated by certain types of information, and capable of generating a mental

word or image in response to that information. The generated word or image
may be relatively specific to the stimulating event, or it can be more general
and prototypic than that event. Thus the word "chair," whether read or
heard, is usually sufficient to activate a logogen capable of generating the
word "chair" as a cognitive response. Likewise, an object chair is usually
sufficient to activate an imagen capable of generating an image of some chair.
This initial level of meaning is *representational* meaning, characterized by
a nonarbitrary relation between the stimulating event and the mental correlate. Because the relationship is nonarbitrary, different language users will
possess more or less equivalent sets of logogens, depending, of course, on
the words that have been read and heard, and they will possess similar sets
of imagens, depending on the events that have been experienced.

Paivio's second level of meaning is *referential*, with emphasis on the
relationships between logogens and imagens. Thus the logogen related to
the linguistic entity "dog" is capable of activating a family of imagens, each
capable of generating an image of a dog. Equivalently, a given imagen is
capable of activating a family of logogens, including the logogen capable of
generating the word "dog" (in the example). In this way the theory gives
the cognizer the capacity to generate particular images from particular verbal
descriptions, and, equivalently, to generate verbal descriptions to express
given images.

The third level of meaning is *associative*, with emphasis on relationships
within each system; logogens activate other logogens, and imagens activate
other imagens. The word "dog" is associated with other words with which
it has often occurred, with categorical relatives, and with both more and
less inclusive terms, to name a few examples. Likewise, an image of a dog
may arouse other images, whether specific or prototypical. Thus, whereas
referential meaning establishes some fairly direct connections between the
two systems, associative meaning allows activation to spread within each
system separately.

The dual-coding theory, therefore, is a coherent account of meaning that
defines imagery rather precisely. An incoming event is classified by the
system as being either a linguistic or nonlinguistic event depending on whether
a logogen or an imagen is activated. Given either type of activation, further
processing may be initiated in the alternate system or within the parent
system. Within this framework it is patent that either system can be active
on its own or that either system can initiate activity in the other. However,
it is also the case that any verbal activity in response to things must be
imaginally mediated, and any nonverbal activity in response to linguistic
events must be verbally mediated. In short, there are important constraints
on processing.

The dual-coding theory has been the stimulus for a truly enormous quantity of research, some pro and some con. At this point some of the research
aimed specifically at the conception of meaning embodied in the theory is
illustrated. One line of research concerns the perceptual identification of

words. For example, a word might be exposed briefly by a tachistoscope with the subject required to respond with the word he or she thought was present on a given trial. By dual-coding theory, a verbal identification of this sort requires only representational meaning. That is, the word activates its logogen, which makes the verbal response cognitively available. The major word attribute relevant to the activation is familiarity or frequency. Other attributes of the word, such as its image-arousing capacity or the number of other words with which it is associated, refer to events that normally occur after the activation of the logogen. Consequently, recognition should be more rapid with more frequently encountered words, but the speed of recognition should not be systematically faster for more imageable or more highly associated words. Paivio and O'Neill (1970) found the expected pattern of results for both visual and auditory recognition; word frequency was highly effective, but there was no systematic advantage for words that are more or less imageable or that have many or few verbal associates.

However, most of the work on word recognition today does not refer to dual-coding theory. For example, the extensive series of experiments of Meyer and his associates (Meyer et al., 1975) has directly addressed the question of word identification. A common finding in their experiments shows associative facilitation of word recognition. Thus the word "nurse" is identified more rapidly as a word if it is preceded by "doctor" rather than by a neutral word, such as "river." The usual account of such effects is that the priming word (doctor) initiates processing that spreads throughout the cognitive system (Collins & Loftus, 1975), making "nurse" more available. Although the work has not specifically addressed dual-coding theory, the results certainly are not at odds with that account. Morton's (1969) logogen, and hence Paivio's logogen (Paivio & Begg, 1981), can be biased by associative information, thus allowing associative effects in recognition. Note that it is not the fact that the words are associates that enhances the identification of the primed word, but rather that the primed word is in a state of readiness at the time of its presentation.

A potentially fruitful marriage of the identification research and the dual-coding conception immediately offers itself. Most of the identification research has dealt with associations within the verbal system, both the semantic associations mentioned above, and episodic connections produced by sentence contexts (McKoon & Ratcliff, 1980). It should also be the case that referential connections will prime word identification; that is, pictures should effectively prime words and vice versa. However, there seems to be little or no published research in this area. Another possibility is that pairs of words that are not associates but do share imaginal reference might prime each other. For example, Katz (1978) has studied the effects of a shared sense impression on concept discovery. Words such as "pearl" and "orange" both share the sense impression "round." It would be interesting to determine whether words that share a dominant sense impression but that are not verbal associates would effectively prime each other. Similarly, would words that refer to normally contiguous sectors of an image, such as "eyebrow" and "forehead," prime each other?

A second type of research explores referential connections quite directly. In a seminal experiment, Robert Moyer (1973) presented pairs of animal names to subjects, asking them to choose the name of the larger animal. The choice was faster if the difference was large (ant–cow) than if it was smaller (dog–fox). In fact, the relationship between reaction time and the ratio of rated size between pair members was quite similar to the relationship between choice time for deciding between objects varying on a physical dimension. Thus choice depends not only on physical distance, but also on the psychological symbolic distance between objects on the dimension along which the choice is made. The inverse relationship between comparison time and symbolic distance has also been found for comparisons along a variety of other dimensions. Some of those dimensions, such as size, shape, brightness, and hue obviously pertain to physical characteristics of the objects whose names are being compared (Paivio 1978a,b). Others, such as pleasantness, dollar value (Paivio 1978b), animal intelligence (Banks & Flora, 1977), and ferocity (Kerst & Howard, 1977), are related more inferentially to the referent.

The fact that comparison times depend on symbolic distances in the same way they depend on "actual" distances suggests that the cognitive system contains information that is nonarbitrarily related to object information and further, that such referential information is accessible from verbal information. However, more evidence is needed for any conclusion that the imagery system is the locus of that referential information. Such evidence does exist. For example, with pairs of pictures of equal depicted size, comparisons are faster than with pairs of words, which should be the case because pictures have direct access to relevant imagens, whereas words require the mediating stage of logogen activation (Paivio, 1975). Even more telling, however, is that while changing the size of printed words to make size incongruent with symbolic size (e.g., the word "ant" bigger than the word "cow") does not slow the comparison, changing picture size (e.g., a large picture of an ant with a small picture of a cow) markedly interferes with the comparison. Clearly, the modality specificity of the interference argues for the involvement of some form of imagery. However, the issue is still in debate (Banks 1977; Moyer & Dumais, 1978; Paivio, 1978a,b), so let us leave this interesting area of research.

The final line of research to be illustrated in this section addresses both referential and associative meaning. Specifically, how are synonyms related to each other? Obviously, synonymous words must be distinct at the representational level; "boy" and "lad," "mistake" and "error," for example, are synonyms but are different words. Equally obvious, the paired synonyms are associatively related or they would not be synonyms. However, dual-coding theory offers a further distinction among synonyms, based on the availability of imaginal referents. Thus concrete synonyms (boy–lad) should share not only verbal associative connections, but also imaginal connections, whereas abstract synonyms (mistake–error) should share only the verbal associative relationship. Clark (1978) reasoned that the concrete synonyms should accordingly have more shared associates than the abstract ones, and this is precisely what he found. Thus abstract synonyms are primarily related associatively, whereas concrete synonyms have, in addition to shared associative meaning in the verbal system, shared reference within the imagery system, affording a second system within which the associative meaning may be shared.

This section has concerned the relationship between imagery and meaning. The research evidence reviewed suggests that the imagery system containing cognitive information nonarbitrarily related to the perceptual characteristics of objects is an important part of the general cognitive meaning system. To retain balance, however, let me point out that research directed at the relationship between imagery and meaning is not representative of the entire range of studies of meaning. Imagery research, of course, is primarily directed at referential meaning. Reference is indeed important, but the concept of meaning is much broader than merely reference. There is a large and important literature concerned with meaning within the linguistic system, exclusive of knowledge of the world, and hence exclusive of imagery (although there is the possibility that the linguistic knowledge develops in interaction with the imagery system). Likewise, there is much concern with formal features, relationships, and procedures and with social aspects of language. Such research is not antithetical to dual-coding theory since the verbal system in that theory is sufficiently sparsely detailed to allow extensive propositional, formal networks or procedures as its structure. Nonetheless, the interface between the language system, however formalized, and a nonlinguistic cognitive system preserving nonlinguistic information about the nonlinguistic world will have an important place in any complete account of people's use of language to communicate with each other.

Imagery's role is elucidated here by studies of function more than structure, performance rather than competence, content rather than form, and reference rather than linguistic definition. Accordingly, let us turn now to studies of language *use*—comprehension and production, memory, and communication.

IMAGERY IN COMPREHENSION AND PRODUCTION

Comprehension is the process by which the receiver interprets linguistic signals. Since interpretation depends on meaning, the model of comprehension one adopts will be in large measure determined by the analysis of meaning one assumes. At a general level, there are two broad choices, depending on whether we focus on linguistic meaning or reference. Linguistic meaning is usually defined in terms of features, nodes, or relationships of a discrete nature. Hence comprehension within such a system is a process in which the discrete mental correlates of the linguistic units are activated and combined. The general stress is on a constructive comprehension process in which cognitive units reached by analysis and abstraction of the signal are combined to yield some overall meaning of the utterance. Such accounts, since they stress linguistic relations exclusively, are only tangentially related to our main interests here.

To consider the role of imagery in comprehension, let us focus on investigations of comprehension that stress reference rather than linguistic meaning. As we have seen, the reference for a given message is potentially comprised of an infinite set of possible instances. Consequently, a referential interpretation of a message requires a broad discrimination for isolation of the appropriate set and a finer-grained discrimination for isolation of an instance from within that set. Such a conception requires that there be referential connections between units of the linguistic system and nonlinguistic information or knowledge of the world. Much of our knowledge of the world is imaginal since the imagery system consists of procedures for interpreting reality in terms of images that preserve perceptual relations characteristic of the events being interpreted. In the following paragraphs I present evidence consistent with the view that comprehension is a process of progressive focusing and that such focusing can occur within the imagery system.

It should be noted that, since comprehension is a private event, studies of comprehension in fact concern overt responses that depend on comprehension, rather than comprehension per se. The simplest procedure that is used widely is to ask subjects whether a particular statement is true or false with reference to some other statement or picture. More rapid decisions can be taken to indicate more rapid comprehension. An experiment by Olson and Filby (1972) illustrates the procedure and presents results suggestive of imaginal involvement in comprehension. Their verification task required that the research participant classify a sentence as true or false with respect to a picture. For example, the picture might show a car hitting a truck, with sentences such as "The car hit the truck" and "The truck was hit by the car" as "true" statements; conversely, "The truck hit the car" and "the car was hit by the truck" are "false" in the given context. The interesting feature of the experiment was that prior to the presentation of the sentence and picture for verification, the subjects had been shown a focus picture of either the car or the truck. Verification was faster with active sentences if the focus was on the logical actor and grammatical subject (car), but for passive sentences, verification was faster if the prior focus was on the logical recipient but grammatical subject of those sentences (truck). Thus information present in the context, presented pictorially, can bias or prime processing of verbal material. Comprehension is most rapid if the topic of the original focus occurs early in the sentence being processed.

The role of imagery in verification was directly explored by Skehan (1970). Sentences were not verified with reference to pictures, but rather with regard to referent sentences that varied in image-arousing capacity. Highly image-able sentences, relative to low-imagery sentences, allow ready access to the referential information of the imagery system. Because of the wealth of information available to these sentences, verification should be relatively rapid. Skehan (1970) found that high-imagery sentences were indeed verified more rapidly than were low-imagery sentences. However, the outcome does not tell us whether the advantage occurs because the high-imagery sentences are more rapidly understood or because the imagery system allows particularly rapid search and comparison, relative to the linguistic system.

Is there evidence that search and comparison processes are particularly rapid within the imagery system? The answer is "yes." For example, once a first stimulus has been encoded, establishing a mental referent, verification of a second stimulus relative to the first is especially rapid if the second stimulus is pictorial (Rosenfeld, 1967; Seymour, 1973a,b). The question was explored in detail by Paivio and Begg (1974), using a matching task with pictures and words as material. Subjects were given either a word or a picture and were asked to locate the appropriate word or picture in a square matrix of 25 pictures or words. The task was most quickly accomplished if the search matrix consisted of pictures. Although the search was faster with picture stimuli than words for which a pictorial match was sought, even the words were matched promptly. Search was slower through matrices of words, and it mattered little whether the target was presented as a picture or a word. It thus appears that comparison, matching, and verification are relatively fast if the context provides or allows access with the imagery system.

However, the advantage in verification of high-imagery material could also reflect more rapid comprehension of such material, as well as the more efficient comparisons within the imagery system. There is evidence that speed of comprehension is related to imagery. Paivio and Begg (1971) found very high correlations between comprehension latencies and image-arousal latencies across sentences of several types and, further, that the correlations were higher in concrete than abstract sentences. That is, it is quite clear that access to the imagery system as indexed by latency measures and prior ratings is related to ease of comprehension.

The evidence reviewed above tells us that imagery has suitable properties for aiding comprehension and mental comparisons. It does not, however, tell us that imagery is actually used in the tasks. As was the case for symbolic distance effects discussed in the previous section, the case for imaginal involvement in comprehension would be strengthened considerably by evidence of modality-specific interference. Brooks (1967, 1968) established that imagery is disrupted by ongoing visual activity, with verbal processing more disrupted by auditory–verbal activity. Reciprocally, Segal and Fusella (1970) showed that visual and acoustic imagery interfere selectively with the perception of visual and acoustic stimuli. Klee and Eysenck (1973) made use of these findings in a study of comprehension. They read sentences to subjects under either visual or auditory–verbal interference conditions. The sentences were either concrete or abstract and were either meaningful or anomalous. The time to decide whether the sentences were meaningful was recorded. The result was that concrete sentences were slowed down more with visual as opposed to verbal interference, with the opposite pattern for abstract sentences. Glass et al. (1980) also found that concrete sentences are verified more rapidly than abstract sentences. They did not find a specific interference in verification of concrete sentences by a visual pattern, but they did find that verification interfered with pattern retention for those concrete sentences. Consequently, the exact nature of imaginal contribution to comprehension is unknown, but that contribution is nonetheless important to any complete account of comprehension.

Another line of evidence pertinent to the question of whether imagery is a factor in comprehension comes from studies reported by Marschark (1978, 1979). Sentences were presented to subjects auditorily one word at a time by use of a procedure that enabled the subjects to control presentation rate. High- and low-imagery paragraphs, carefully matched on comprehensibility and physical characteristics, were compared. The result was that subjects spent relatively more processing time on semantic than syntactic aspects of the high-imagery passages, with the syntactic aspects receiving more time than the semantic aspects for low-imagery passages, and that the high-imagery passages were processed faster than the low-imagery passages. Aaronson and Scarborough (1976), with visual presentation, have found that subjects instructed to understand sentences processed them relatively quickly and with more time spent on semantic than syntactic factors, compared with subjects instructed to remember the statements verbatim. In other words, the processing of high-imagery sentences resembles processing for comprehension, whereas low-imagery sentences are more similar in pattern to processing with an aim of verbatim retention. Marschark compared the two instructions for each type of passage and found that low-imagery sentences were processed with more attention to syntax than semantics under both instructional sets, whereas high-imagery sentences were processed with more attention to semantic than syntactic information with a set to comprehend, but with a reversal of emphasis under a memory set. Subjects also indicated that they employed imagery in comprehending the high-imagery passages.

The final line of research into comprehension to be considered here centers around the concept of the schema. As in imagery research, the general notion is that interpretation of linguistic signals entails information, or knowledge of the world, beyond the semantic content of the individual linguistic units. The comprehender has a general idea or schema in terms of which the message is interpreted in some particular form. For example, Anderson (1978) presented descriptions of a home to subjects instructed to take the perspective of either a home buyer or a burglar. Under the different sets, subjects rated idea units as to importance. Differences in rated importance were predictive of retention by other subjects. For example, a leaky roof is more relevant to a home buyer than a burglar, and the fact of a leaky roof was better retained by the "home buyers" than the "burglars." Similarly, Black et al. (1979) presented compound sentences and measured the time taken to read the second phrase. If the vantage point of the reader changed, reading time was slowed relative to conditions in which the vantage point remained the same. For instance, "Terry finished working in the yard and *went* into the house" is written from the vantage point of an observer in the yard, whereas "Terry finished working in the yard and *came* into the house" requires that the observer change location from the yard to the house. Such a change required time, implicating imagery or some relative in the comprehension process.

As the preceding examples illustrate, there is quite a bit of evidence that is consistent with the involvement of the imagery system in the comprehension of linguistic material, especially if that material is amenable to image arousal. However, as in the section on meaning, let us keep in mind that imagery is neither necessary nor sufficient for comprehension. Rather, imagery is a useful process for particularizing or instantiating a perceptual referent for some type of material processed for some end.

Let us now turn our attention, somewhat briefly, to the question of whether imagery is implicated in the production of speech. The major finding of relevance here is that speech about concrete events, and speech using concrete words, is more rapid and fluent than speech using abstract words or speech about abstract events (Goldman-Eisler, 1961; Lay & Paivio, 1969; Reynolds & Paivio, 1968). Additionally, Osgood and Bock (1975) found that subjects preferred compound sentences in which more vivid constituents preceded rather than those that followed less vivid ones. Again, while sparse, such results cause no discomfiture to conceptions of the imagery system.

One advantage of the imagery conception is that it emphasizes the separation between comprehension and production. Although it is tempting to think of the two processes as just different directions along the same path, the imaginal conception, in regard to referential meaning of concrete signals, stresses comprehension as discrimination among images activated by linguistic units, with production requiring discrimination among linguistic units activated by given images. In short, verbal expression of an image is conceptually independent from evoking an image by a verbal signal. Begg (1976) experimentally investigated the relationship between comprehension and production. In the experiment, nonsense syllables were learned in a meaningful way. Some subjects learned to produce images for the syllables; that is, they learned to *understand* the syllables. Other subjects learned to produce the syllables as responses for given pictures; that is, they learned to *produce* the syllables. Once initial learning had reached a criterion, the subjects were transferred to a new task in which the syllables were either cues for words or responses to word cues. The finding was that transfer performance was highly specific to initial learning. That is, "understandable" syllables were very good cues but were themselves poorly recalled; "producible" syllables, conversely, were well recalled but were poor cues. Thus learning to understand does not mean that what is understood can be readily expressed, and learning to express does not mean that what is expressed will be understood.

IMAGERY AND MEMORY

Perhaps nowhere is imagery's contribution to cognitive processing so apparent as in studies of memory. There is a vast literature documenting the effects of imagery in memory that is entirely relevant to the role of imagery in memory for language. Let us simply consider a few illustrative cases. In overview, there are two common definitions of imagery in memory tasks. On the one hand, the type of material used contrasts concrete, high-imagery words, phrases, sentences, or passages with abstract, low-imagery words, phrases, sentences, or passages in a variety of memory tasks. Presumably, if the materials are closely matched for other characteristics, the differences in retention reflect the consequences of differential imagery. On the other hand, different instructions to subjects are contrasted, with subjects told to image items in various ways or to process the materials in some other way. Presumably, different instructions are effective in altering subjects' encoding, and this differential encoding results in the items being differentially accessible in later retrieval attempts.

Let us first consider the effects of item concreteness in memory tasks. With reference to lists of words, there is simply no variable that rivals image-evoking capacity as a predictor of recall in a host of tasks (Paivio, 1968, 1969, 1971). However, concrete items are not simply better than abstract items in every task. Rather, the advantage for concrete items is sensibly restricted, as it is greater in tasks and in measures that are theoretically related to imagery as a process. For instance, item imagery is seldom associated with enhanced performance in sequential memory tasks, such as memory span (Paivio & Csapo, 1969; Snodgrass et al. 1978). The point is that while an image may be an efficient memory trace for relating several pieces of information, it is a poor trace for representing the order in which those pieces of information arrived.

A second point concerns the effectiveness of concrete and abstract items in associative memory tasks. Performance in such tasks is usually analyzed as requiring recognition of the cue, associative strength between the cue and its response, and response production. Response production requires only the verbal system, although, in theory, both cue recognition and the association between items may benefit from the involvement of the imagery system in the memory process. Consistent with the analysis, concreteness effects are particularly pronounced on measures of cue recognition and interitem association, with smaller effects on measures of response production (Anderson et al., 1977; Lambert & Paivio, 1956; Paivio, 1963).

The final point with regard to concreteness effects in item memory concerns reference. The major difference between concrete and abstract items is theoretically at the level of referential meaning since concrete items are assumed to have connections with the imagery system. Consequently, memory differences between concrete and abstract items should occur only if the initial processing task requires use of the imagery system or referential meaning. Begg and Clark (1975) tested this assumption, using ambiguous words such as "record" and "miss." "Record" is rated as being a concrete word but does have an abstract sense (set a record) in addition to the concrete sense (play a record). "Miss" is normally an abstract word (as in "hit and miss") but does have a concrete sense as well ("pretty young miss"). Presented out of context, such words show the usual effect of concreteness in memory. However, if the words are presented in sentence contexts, it is the concreteness of the context that is most important.

In word lists, then, concrete items usually show better memory than do abstract items. The advantage, however, requires meaningful, referential processing of the items and measures of memory that reflect interitem association and item discrimination, rather than measures of memory for order, or the simple likelihood of producing an item following the retrieval of an appropriate memory trace.

The picture of imagery's contribution to memory for language is substantially the same with more complex material. For example, concrete phrases, such as "white horse," are better recalled than are abstract phrases, such as "basic theory," and the difference is especially great in associative recall and in measures of the organization of recall (Begg, 1972). With sentences as the material, the advantage for concrete information is greater on measures of memory for the meaning or substance of the sentences than in measures of memory for the words used or the form in which the meaning was expressed (Begg & Paivio, 1969; Kuiper & Paivio, 1977; Pezdek & Royer, 1974). Likewise, with longer passages, concrete passages are remembered better than abstract ones, but the advantage is restricted to thematic rather than random passages, and to memory for content words rather than function words in the thematic passages (Philipchalk, 1972; Yuille & Paivio, 1969). Again, the role of imagery in memory for language is firmly tied to the meaning of language.

It should be kept in mind when evaluating the effects of item concreteness that items rarely differ only in concreteness. As a result, a long list of alternative explanations for concreteness effects has appeared and will probably become even longer in the future. However, in experiments in which concreteness and some grammatical variable are pitted against one another, the typical outcome is that concreteness is the more salient variable or that the grammatical variable has different effects in concrete and abstract materials. For example, Danks and Sorce (1973) found that full passives were remembered better than agent-deleted passives only if the sentences were low in imagery. For instance, an abstract full passive such as "The game was played by substitutes," was recalled better than the agent-deleted partner, "The game was played by permission." However, with concrete sentences, such as "The grades were issued by professors" as opposed to "The grades were issued by letter," recall differences were slight. As another example, Rosenberg (1977) found larger effects of the degree of semantic integration among sentence words in concrete sentences than in abstract ones. In addition, several studies have found concreteness effects in materials carefully rate for comprehensibility (Kuiper & Paivio, 1977; Marschark & Paivio, 1977; O'Neill & Paivio, 1978). Nonetheless, the question of whether concreteness effects reflect imaginal processes or the confounding influence of some other variable is not settled, nor will it ever be. Despite the inherent ambiguity of the outcomes, however, it still must be acknowledged that concreteness is a powerful correlate of many memory effects.

One way to avoid many of the problems that arise because of the correlational nature of research using concrete and abstract material is to keep material constant over conditions and vary the instructions given to the subjects. Studies in which imagery instructions are used typically yield results that converge with the studies contrasting concrete and abstract material. For example, if items such as "railroad" and "mother" are imaged together rather than separately, the joint imagery conditions show large advantages in associative recall (Begg, 1973, 1978; Begg & Anderson, 1976; Bower, 1970). However, the instructional studies are not identical in outcome with the concreteness studies. For example, joint imagery does not yield an overall advantage in free recall over separate imagery, because, although subjects recall larger chunks, they recall fewer of them (Begg, 1978). Nor are the items from joint images better recognized than the items from separate images (Begg, 1978; Bower, 1970; Dempster & Rohwer, 1974). Indeed, if joint imaging of items changes the encoding of those items, later recognition may suffer (Begg, 1979); perhaps "mother" imaged with "railroad" is less identifiably a mother than "mother" imaged alone. McGee (1980) has found that separate imagery exceeds joint imagery in tests of item recognition but that joint imagery exceeds separation imagery if the later task requires discrimination between intact pairs and re-paired items. Thus, as was the case above, the particular advantage of imagery is in connecting ideas.

Another similarity between studies of concreteness and studies of imagery instructions is that instructions can often negate or override the effects of linguistic variables. For example, Rohwer (1973) reported that children show better recall if nouns are linked by verbs ("the giant hears the boat") rather than by conjunctions ("the giant and the boat"). However, the difference is not an automatic consequence of the linguistic differences between verbs and conjunctions. Begg and Young (1977) found that the verb–conjunction difference in recall disappeared with both joint and separate imagery instructions. Thus joint imagery *raised* conjunctions to the level of verbs, whereas separate imagery *reduced* verbs to the level of conjunctions.

In all, then, there is little doubt that imagery's role in meaning and comprehension spills over into memory. If the initial study task in which material is understood calls the imagery system into play, the resultant image can serve as a memory trace in which a substantial amount of information is preserved and in which the various components are meaningfully tied together. Of course, such representation is of benefit for associative memory. However, the benefit is not without cost. In particular, the input order of the information may be lost, and there may be loss of item identity as well. That is, an item's unique identity as a word is defined by representational meaning. Consequently, the item's exact identity could be lost if the item's referent merges into a greater whole. Another source of the loss of item information comes from the act of recall itself. Since the image, by definition, contains no words, recall of words requires backtracking the referential connections to the verbal system. This raises the possibility that words other than those presented will be falsely intruded in recall if they are consistent with the retained image. It also raises the possibility of omissions if there are simply too many connections to allow a good choice. Additionally, it should be borne in mind that recall can also be correct. Obviously, referential connections are strong in some cases, and equally obviously, subjects may not have forgotten which representation was aroused during study.

IMAGERY IN COMMUNICATION

The final section in this chapter addresses, rather briefly, a recent focus for imagery research, namely, verbal communication. As pointed out earlier, effective communication requires that the speaker's message provide information to guide the listener's discrimination among plausible alternative interpretations. Most theoretical approaches to imagery would expect imagery to contribute to successful communication. That is, since the imagery system is the residence for knowledge of the nonlinguistic world, and since the information in that system preserves characteristics of the perceptual world nonarbitrarily, the imagery system provides the basis for cognitive commonality across language users. In short, messages that provide access to the imagery system should be especially effective.

The implications of the imagery system for successful communication were recently explored by Begg et al. (1978). Several of their findings point to imaginal facilitation in communication. For example, concrete words are interpreted more similarly from person to person than are abstract words, and, at the same time, the interpretations of concrete words differ more from word to word than do the interpretations of abstract words. Accordingly, concrete words should be particularly useful tokens in actual communication. Begg et al. used a variant of the television game "Password" to assess the effectiveness of communication. Thus one subject, the sender, provided clues to the identity of a given target word. A second subject, the receiver, attempted to guess the target word from the clues. In a variety of contexts, concrete words were guessed in fewer attempts than were abstract words. As was the case with memory, the differential communicative success of the words depended on their being interpreted by the sender in concrete or abstract senses. That is, it is not merely that concrete words are better communicated than abstract words; rather, the active involvement of the imagery system in the sender who is framing a message makes that message more effective.

Although interpersonal communication is a new area in which the role of imagery is being investigated, it is already clear that imagery will have an important function. Olson's (1970) research on reference has provided a useful conception of the meaning that messages are intended to communicate. By adding to that conception the advances in imagery theory in meaning, comprehension, production, and memory, the lines for research in communication are clearly delineated (Begg et al., 1978; Harris et al., 1980). Hopefully, future work will further clarify the function of the imagery system in framing comprehensible messages and in interpreting those messages.

CONCLUDING REMARKS

The present chapter has attempted to demonstrate the usefulness of a particular conception of imagery's place in language use. In that conception, a major aspect of knowledge of the world resides in an imagery system. That system consists of procedures for interpreting world events as images that preserve, in nonarbitrary fashion, perceptual features and information about the nonlinguistic world. The referential meaning of a message is the result of any knowledge made available by connections between the verbal and imaginal systems and further connections within the two systems. In actual use, comprehension is much more than an intralinguistic process. Comprehension occurs when enough referential information is made available to perform any discriminations required by the comprehender. As a result, processing within the imagery system aids comprehension and, almost incidentally, yields highly informative memory traces. Of course, that information is relevant to referential meaning, rather than order information or representational meaning. In addition, again almost incidentally, such cognitive reference is of particular value in the communication process.

The same conception and the results of the studies reviewed could also direct us to consider other areas of research. For example, in their recent book, Paivio and Begg (1981) reviewed the role of imagery in metaphor, bilingualism, brain function, reading, and language acquisition. In each area the notions made salient within imagery theory have currency in directing research and in interpreting the results of that research.

Perhaps the most sensible conclusion to offer is simply to say that there are many advantages to the researcher or theorist who, in addition to other interests, includes a place for imagery in his or her theories, and includes imagery-related variables in his or her experiments. As knowledge of general linguistic theory advances, so will our conceptions of imagery and, equally important, vice versa.

REFERENCES

Aaronson, D. & Scarborough, H. S. Performance theories for sentences coding: Some quantitative evidence. *Journal of Experimental Psychology: Human Perception and Performance*, 1976, **2**, 56–70.

Anderson, R. C. Schema-directed processes in language comprehension. In A. Lesgold, J. Pellegrino, S. Fokkima, & R. Glaser (Eds.), *Cognitive psychology and instruction*. New York: Plenum, 1978.

Anderson, R. C., Goetz, E. T., Pichert, J. W., & Halff H. M. Two faces of the conceptual peg hypothesis. *Journal of Experimental Psychology: Human Learning and Memory*, 1977, **3**, 142–149.

Banks, W. P. Encoding and processing of symbolic information in comparative judgments. In G. H. Bower (Ed.), *Psychology of learning and motivation*, Vol. 11. New York: Academic Press, 1977.

Banks, W. P., & Flora, J. Semantic and perceptual processes in symbolic comparisons. *Journal of Experimental Psychology: Human Perception and Performance*, 1977, **3**, 278–290.

Begg, I. Recall of meaningful phrases. *Journal of Verbal Learning and Verbal Behavior*, 1972, **11**, 431–439.

Begg, I. Imagery and integration in the recall of words. *Canadian Journal of Psychology*, 1973, **27**, 159–167.

Begg, I. Acquisition and transfer of meaningful function by meaningless sounds. *Canadian Journal of Psychology*, 1976, **30**, 178–186.

Begg, I. Imagery and organization in memory: Instructional effects. *Memory and Cognition*, 1978, **6**, 174–183.

Begg, I. Trace loss and the recognition failure of unrecalled words. *Memory and Cognition*, 1979, **7**, 113–123.

Begg, I., & Anderson, M. C. Imagery and associative memory in children. *Journal of Experimental Child Psychology*, 1976, **21**, 480–489.

Begg, I., & Clark, J. M. Contextual imagery in meaning and memory. *Memory and Cognition*, 1975, **3**, 117–122.

Begg, I., & Paivio, A. Concreteness and imagery in sentence meaning. *Journal of Verbal Learning and Verbal Behavior*, 1969, **8**, 821–827.

Begg, I., Upfold, D., & Wilton, T. D. Imagery in verbal communication. *Journal of Mental Imagery*, 1978, **2**, 165–186.

Begg, I., & Young, B. J. An organizational analysis of the form-class effect. *Journal of Experimental Child Psychology*, 1977, **22**, 503–519.

Black, J. B., Turner, T. J., & Bower, G. H. Point of view in narrative comprehension, memory and production. *Journal of Verbal Learning and Verbal Behavior*, 1979, **18**, 187–198.

Bower, G. H. Imagery as a relational organizer in associative learning. *Journal of Verbal Learning and Verbal Behavior*, 1970, **9**, 529–533.

Brooks, L. R. The suppression of visualization in reading. *Quarterly Journal of Experimental Psychology*, 1967, **19**, 289–299.

Brooks, L. R. Spatial and verbal components in the act of recall. *Canadian Journal of Psychology*, 1968, **22**, 349–368.

Clark, J. M. Synonymity and concreteness effects on free recall and free association: Implications for a theory of semantic memory. Unpublished doctoral dissertation, University of Western Ontario, 1978.

Collins, A. M., & Loftus, E. F. A spreading-activation theory of semantic processing. *Psychological Review*, 1975, **82**, 407–428.

Danks, J. H., & Sorce, P. A. Imagery and deep structure in the prompted recall of passive sentences. *Journal of Verbal Learning and Verbal Behavior*, 1973, **12**, 114–117.

Dempster, R. N., & Rohwer, D. W. Component analysis of the elaborative encoding effect in children's learning. *Journal of Experimental Psychology*, 1974, **103**, 400–408.

Glass, A. L., Eddy, J. K., & Schwanenflugel, P. J. The verification of high and low imagery sentences. *Journal of Experimental Psychology: Human Learning and Memory*, 1980, **6**, 692–704.

Goldman-Eisler, F. Hesitation and information in speech. In C. Cherry (Ed.), *Information theory*. London: Butterworths, 1961.

Harris, G., Begg, I., & Upfold, D. On the role of the speaker's expectations in interpersonal communication. *Journal of Verbal Learning and Verbal Behavior*, 1980, **19**, 597–607.

Katz, A. N. Differences in the saliency of sensory features elicited by words. *Canadian Journal of Psychology*, 1978, **32**, 156–179.

Kerst, S. M., & Howard, J. H., Jr. Mental comparisons for ordered information on abstract and concrete dimensions. *Memory and Cognition*, 1977, **5**, 227–234.

Klee, H., & Eysenck, M. W. Comprehension of abstract and concrete sentences. *Journal of Verbal Learning and Verbal Behavior*, 1973, **12**, 522–529.

Kuiper, N. A., & Paivio, A. Incidential recognition memory for concrete and abstract sentences equated for comprehensibility. *Bulletin of the Psychonomic Society*, 1977, **9**, 247–249.

Lambert, W. E., & Paivio, A. The influence of noun–adjective order on learning. *Canadian Journal of Psychology*, 1956, **72**, 77–82.

Lay, C. H., & Paivio, A. The effects of task difficulty and anxiety on hesitations in speech. *Canadian Journal of Behavioral Science*, 1969, **1**, 25–37.

Marschark, M. Prose processing: A chronometric study of the effects of imagability. Unpublished doctoral dissertation, Department of Psychology, University of Western Ontario, 1978.

Marschark, M. The syntax and semantics of comprehension. In G. Prideaux (Ed.), *Perspectives in experimental linguistics*. Amsterdam: Benjamins, 1979.

Marschark, M., & Paivio, A. Integrative processing of concrete and abstract sentences. *Journal of Verbal Learning and Verbal Behavior*, 1977, **16**, 217–231.

McGee, R. Imagery and recognition memory: The effects of relational organization. *Memory and Cognition*, 1980, **8**, 394–399.

McKoon, G., & Ratcliff, R. Priming in item recognition: The organization of propositions in memory for text. *Journal of Verbal Learning and Verbal Behavior*, 1980, **19**, 369–386.

Meyer, D. E., Schvaneveldt, R. W., & Ruddy, M. G. Loci of contextual effects on visual word recognition. In P. M. A. Rabbit and S. Dornic (Eds.), *Attention and performance V.* London: Academic Press, 1975.

Morton, J. Interaction of information in word recognition. *Psychological Review,* 1969, **76**, 165–178.

Moyer, R. S. Comparing objects in memory: Evidence suggesting an internal psychophysics. *Perception and Psychophysics,* 1973, **13**, 180–184.

Moyer, R. S., & Dumais, S. T. Mental comparison. In G. H. Bower (Ed.), *The psychology of learning and motivation* (Vol. 12). New York: Academic Press, 1978.

Olson, D. R. Language and thought: Aspects of a cognitive theory of semantics. *Psychological Review,* 1970, **77**, 257–273.

Olson, D. R., & Filby, N. On comprehension of active and passive sentences. *Cognitive Psychology,* 1972, **3**, 361–381.

O'Neill, B. J., & Paivio, A. Semantic constraints in encoding judgements and free recall of concrete and abstract sentences. *Canadian Journal of Psychology,* 1978, **32**, 3–18.

Osgood C. E., & Bock, J. K. Salience and sentencing: Some production principles. In S. Rosenberg (Ed.), *Sentence production: Development in research and theory.* Hillsdale, N.J.: Lawrence Erlbaum Associates, 1975.

Paivio, A. Learning of adjective–noun paired–associates as a function of adjective–noun word order and noun abstractness. *Canadian Journal of Psychology,* 1963, **17**, 370–379.

Paivio, A. A factor-analytic study of word attributes and verbal learning. *Journal of Verbal Learning and Verbal Behavior,* 1968, **7**, 41–49.

Paivio, A. Mental imagery in associative learning and memory. *Psychological Review,* 1969, **76**, 241–263.

Paivio, A. *Imagery and verbal processes.* New York: Holt, 1971.

Paivio, A. Perceptual comparisons through the mind's eye. *Memory and Cognition,* 1975, **3**, 635–647.

Paivio, A. Mental comparisons involving abstract attributes. *Memory and Cognition,* 1978a, **6**, 199–208.

Paivio, A. On exploring visual knowledge. In B. S. Randhawa and W. E. Coffman (Eds.), *Visual learning, thinking, and communication.* New York: Academic Press, 1978b.

Paivio, A., & Begg, I. Imagery and comprehension latencies as a function of sentence concreteness and structure. *Perception and Psychophysics,* 1971, **10**, 408–412.

Paivio, A., & Begg, I. Pictures and words in visual search. *Memory and Cognition,* 1974, **2**, 515–521.

Paivio, A., & Begg, I. *The psychology of language.* Englewood Cliffs, N.J.: Prentice-Hall, 1981.

Paivio, A., & Csapo, K. Concrete-image and verbal memory codes. *Journal of Experimental Psychology,* 1969, **80**, 279–285.

Paivio, A. & O'Neill, B. J. Visual recognition thresholds and dimensions of word meaning. *Perception and Psychophysics,* 1970, **8**, 273–275.

Pezdek, K., & Royer, J. M. The role of comprehension in learning concrete and abstract sentences. *Journal of Verbal Learning and Verbal Behavior*, 1974, **13**, 551–558.

Philipchalk, R. P. Thematicity, abstractness, and the long-term recall of connected discourse. *Psychonomic Science*, 1972, **27**, 361–362.

Reynolds, A., & Paivio, A. Cognitive and emotional determinants of speech. *Canadian Journal of Psychology*, 1968, **22**, 164–175.

Rohwer, W. D., Jr. Elaboration and learning in childhood and adolescence. In H. W. Reese (Ed.), *Advances in child development and behavior*, Vol. 8. New York: Academic Press, 1973.

Rosenberg, S. Semantics and imagery in sentence recall. Paper presented at the Psychonomic Society, Washington, DC, 1977.

Rosenfeld, J. B. Information processing: Encoding and decoding. Unpublished doctoral dissertation, Indiana University, 1967.

Saussure, F. de. *Course in general linguistics*, W. Baskin (Transl.), C. Bally, and A. Sechehaye (Eds.). Glasgow: Fontana, 1974 (originally published in 1915).

Segal, S. J., & Fusella, V. Influence of imaged pictures and sounds on detection of visual and auditory signals. *Journal of Experimental Psychology*, 1970, **83**, 458–464.

Seymour, P. H. Rule identity classification of name and shape stimuli. *Acta Psychologica*, 1973a, **37**, 131–138.

Seymour, P. H. A model for reading, naming and comparison. *British Journal of Psychology*, 1973b, **64**, 35–49.

Skehan, P. The relation of visual imagery to true–false judgment of simple sentences. Unpublished master's thesis, University of Western Ontario, 1970.

Snodgrass, J. G., Burns, P. M., & Pirone, G. V. Pictures and words in space and time: In search of the elusive interaction. *Journal of Experimental Psychology: General*, 1978, **2**, 206–230.

Yuille, J. C., & Paivio, A. Abstractness and recall of connected discourse. *Journal of Experimental Psychology*, 1969, **82**, 467–471.

CHAPTER 11

Relationship Between Creativity and Mental Imagery: A Question of Cognitive Styles?

BARBARA L. FORISHA

In the last several years I have been investigating the relationship between creativity and mental imagery, with the hope of clarifying the complex and contradictory relationship between the two. Early studies (Forisha, 1978a) revealed that creativity and imagery sometimes did show a strong relationship to each other in male college students—and sometimes did not. In female college students the relationship remained weak but positive. A review of research (Forisha, 1978b) led to the hypothesis that the relationship between creativity and imagery might vary with sex and level of materity. A two year study (Forisha 1981a) of 320 undergraduate and graduate students explored this possibility. It was found that sex and chronological age did affect the relationship between creativity and imagery, but maturity was not consistently related to either variable. In addition, academic disciplines showed distinctly different patterns associated with creativity and imagery.

Other researchers (Kolb & Plovnik, 1977) have suggested that academic major may be strongly related to an individual's approach to learning or, in other words, cognitive style. Since academic major is important in untangling the relationships of creativity and imagery, it is likely that cognitive style may also be significant. Consequently, in a current study we are investigating the relationship between creativity, imagery, and cognitive style in 60 undergraduates drawn from specific disciplines. Preliminary analyses of data from this sample have just been completed and are suggestive of some new relationships between creativity and imagery in individuals of different disciplines. The results suggest that the relationship of creativity and imagery may vary according to the cognitive style of groups of individuals, differentiated by discipline.

Research assistance of Randy Kovach, Jeffrey Pilkington, Helen Linkey, and Ann Handrinos is gratefully acknowledged.

In the recent literature on creativity, imagery, and cognitive styles, however, there is one other recurring theme. The literature on all three subjects is periodically punctuated by descriptions of the functions of the left and right hemispheres of the brain. Creativity is the process by which something new is brought into being. Experts on creativity, moreover, assert that the creative process requires the use of both hemispheres. Mental imagery is defined as the act of schematically representing things internally or the process of transforming these schematic representations. Imagery is then often associated with the right side of the brain. The construct of cognitive styles refers to an array of particular orientations encompassing traits from the cognitive and affective domains that guide an individual's thinking processes. Yet researchers in the area of cognitive styles sometimes associate particular styles or orientations with a reliance on one hemisphere or the other.

In reviewing the literature, therefore, we begin with hemispheric functioning and proceed to creativity, imagery, and cognitive styles. From the research review we shall draw a theoretical framework within which to interpret our current research findings.

LEFT AND RIGHT-HEMISPHERIC FUNCTIONS

There has been considerable evidence that the functioning of the two cerebral hemispheres does differ (Bogen, 1969; Levy et al., 1972; Nebes, 1971). The left hemisphere has been termed *analytical* and the right, *global*. The left has a facility with words and numbers and the right, with images. Processing in the left hemisphere is sequential, and in the right it is parallel. It seems reasonable that the left hemisphere is also the source of the reality oriented secondary process first described by Freud (1949); the right hemisphere would then be associated with the metaphorical, emotion-laden, sometimes primitive, primary process. The left hemisphere governs everyday verbal interactions with others; the right hemisphere is the origin of fantasies and dreams. It has been concluded, further, that people who tend to be verbal and analytic are left-hemisphere dominant, whereas subjects who favor holistic approaches are right-hemisphere dominant (Bakan, 1971; Mintzberg, 1976; Restak, 1976).

In considering males and females separately, numerous theorists (Buffery & Gray, 1972; Burstein et al., 1980; Lake & Bryden, 1976) have suggested that the functions of the two hemispheres may not be specialized in quite the same way. For example, spatial ability is generally attributed to the right hemisphere and verbal ability to the left. Women, however, are generally less skilled than men in spatial tasks (Maccoby & Jacklin, 1974), which might be explained by a bilateral representation of verbal functions in women that could interfere with spatial processing. This may account for the finding that men tend to prefer a visuospatial type of processing in cases where women use a verbal strategy (Bagnara et al., 1980; Hannay, 1977). This preference for a visuospatial strategy may be even stronger in the case of men who are left-handed (Kashihara, 1979; McGee, 1978; Peterson & Lansky, 1980). Hemispheric functioning is, therefore, likely to differ in women and men, and may differ even more in left-handed men.

Many connections have been drawn between hemispheric functioning, creativity, imagery, and cognitive styles. In general, it is hypothesized that creativity draws on the processes of both hemispheres, although there is some controversy over whether the processes alternate with each other (Galin & Ornstein, 1974) or operate in an integrative fashion (Sperry, 1974). Because most individuals in our culture tend to be predominantly left-brained, strong evidence of right-brain activity suggests the possibility of creativity since the right-hemisphere processes are then available to work together with those of the left.

In turning to imagery, there is evidence to associate imagery with the right hemisphere. For example, Galin and Ornstein (1974) found that subjects involved in imagery tasks have higher alpha amplitude in the left hemisphere than in the right. Alpha amplitude indicates a relative idling of processing, so this finding is suggestive of a right-hemisphere specialization in imagery. Also, Richardson (1978) reported that male subjects who were classified as visualizers, in contrast to verbalizers, had more left-eye movements when responding to a series of 20 questions than did verbalizers. Left-eye movements are also indicative of right-hemisphere activity (Kimura, 1973; Nebes, 1974). In men, therefore, imagery is associated with greater activity in the right hemisphere. In women, on the other hand, the evidence is less clear-cut.

The research on hemispheric specialization also has implications for cognitive styles. Descriptions of cognitive styles range widely, drawing on many different personality characteristics and mental processes. Yet many of these characteristics may be paired with differential hemispheric functions. Some cognitive styles clearly draw on one hemisphere or the other, whereas others, it may be inferred, draw on both. We may speculate that cognitive styles that emphasize the imposition of external structure, whether in abstract and/ or task-oriented ways, are more left-brained. In contrast, those styles that emphasize fluidity of perception and a resistance to the imposition of external structures are more right-brained in orientation.

We turn now from hemispheric functioning to a brief review of recent literature on creativity, mental imagery, and cognitive styles. The focus is predominantly on current thinking in each area since other reviews of past literature are available (Forisha, 1978b).

RESEARCH ON CREATIVITY

Research on the general topic of creativity often emphasizes the union of polarities or the assembling of the hitherto unconnected. When the focus is on the process of creativity, research often revolves around the interplay of two forms of thought. When the focus is on the creative personality, there is frequent mention of polarities, dualities, and the capacity to live in two different worlds. The emphasis on two different ways of thought and two different modes of being is reflective of the dualism that is also prevalent in analyses of the two hemispheres of the brain. The connection is still theoretical, however, for research has yet to tie the varied thought processes and personality styles definitively into hemispheric function. In what follows, we examine the recent research on the creative process and the creative personality with some reference to earlier works in this field.

The Creative Process

Some descriptions of the creative process outline stages through which an individual moves in a linear fashion when creating a new idea or product. Other descriptions emphasize the "layering" of creative thought or the two parallel processes that are interwoven in the creative endeavor.

The earliest description of stages was proposed by Wallas (1926), who described four phases of the creative process: preparation, incubation, illumination, and verification. The stage of preparation, of immersion in the material, gives rise to an original insight that matures through a period of incubation and comes to full consciousness in the illumination phase. The idea must then be tested in the real world, refined, examined, and finally made whole in the stage of verification. In later work MacKinnon (1962) described the stages of creativity in a slightly different way. He saw three components in creativity that generally followed one another in a linear fashion: (1) the originality or novelty of an individual response (the idea is conceived); (2) adaptation to reality (the idea is modified to fit the boundaries of the known world); and (3) the realization or the sustaining of the original insight in developing it to the fullest (a product is brought into being).

Wallas's stages and MacKinnon's components of creativity both emphasize the importance of originality and relevance. A creative act is original in that it emanates from a novel response and is relevant in that it is meaningful in terms of known reality. Likewise, originality and relevance are important in "layered" descriptions of creativity. In these descriptions, however, the novelty of response and the ability to shape it into a form that fits our reality are often seen as springing from two different layers of the psyche or personality.

There are many examples in the theoretical literature of the "layered" view of creativity. May (1975) sees the creative process as a dialectic interaction between the free play of imagination and the logical structure of form. Barron (1963a) discusses the alternating experiences of diffusion and integration. Bowers and Bowers (1972) describe the oscillation between imaginal and realistic modes of functioning. Finally, in a recent review, Suler

(1980) examines the creative experience in terms of the Freudian concepts of primary and secondary process.

Primary process thinking is defined as unconscious and primitive, motivated by the pleasure principle and aiming at the discharge of tension. The organization of primary process thinking is centered on the self, revolving around the emotional meanings attached to symbols and images. Primary process thinking is thus neither logical nor categorical. As Suler (1980, p. 144) stated, "primary process thinking is essentially metaphoric, since it ignores distinctions and equates anything with anything else, even when only a rudimentary similiarity exists."

In contrast, secondary process thinking is attuned to the reality principle. An object stands for itself and is not easily represented by another. Ideas are organized according to the relationship one object bears to another, instead of how they relate to the self. Since secondary process thinking is concerned with how external objects relate to each other, it requires continual interaction with the environment.

Primary and secondary process thinking may be used to conceptualize the two layers involved in creative thought. From the time of Freud (1953), psychologists have argued that both primary and secondary process thinking are involved in creativity. Beginning with Freud, however, primary process thinking was regarded as more primitive than secondary process thinking, and a return to primary process thinking was termed a "regression" and later a "regression in the service of the ego." Even later work (Bush, 1969; Hartmann, 1956) has suggested that primary and secondary process thinking may be more interwoven than Freud had suggested and that use of either primary or secondary process thinking was not to be termed a regression but simply defined as *access* to one or the other mode of thinking.

In the earlier interpretation in which primary process thinking was regarded as regressive, inner psychic conflict also played a theoretical role. Conflict was seen as the motivational force that prompted individuals into regressive thinking. In the more recent interpretation, conflict plays a lesser role in the theory of creativity, and access to either primary or secondary process thinking is viewed as more under the control of the individual person. Suler (1980) suggests that the role of conflict, and accompanying emphasis on regression, may be differently interpreted in terms of various creative personality styles. For example, artists may rely more than scientists on inner conflict and early traumas as motivational forces. The balance of primary and secondary process thinking required for creative production may also be different in artistic and scientific spheres, with a stronger emphasis on primary process thinking in artistic creation.

Suler (1980) clearly states, however, that a balance must be maintained. Those individuals who defend against primary process thinking (neurotics) and those who surrender completely to it (psychotics) are not good candidates for the creative personality. Neither the absence of primary nor secondary process thinking can engender creative production. Rather, a balance is required, with perhaps more emphasis on primary process thinking for artistic production, and more emphasis on secondary process thinking for scientific production.

Research has given some support for the differing balance of primary and secondary processes in creative thinking. Often this is reflected in studies showing that the *control* of primary process is important in creativity. Many have found stronger evidence of primary process thinking in artists than other persons (Cohen, 1974; Dudek, 1968; Hersch, 1962). Yet control of primary process thinking, which, one may infer, requires an interaction of primary and secondary processes, is also vital for creative individuals (Pine, 1959; Pine & Holt, 1960; Rogolsky, 1968). Having access to primary process and being able to control the flow of primary process thinking may be the necessary requirements for the creative process. As Suler (1980, p. 159) stated: "Being openly receptive to unusual ideas and experiences and being able to control the cognitive complexities they impose are the cornerstones of creativity."

The Creative Individual

The theme of balance is also important in the descriptions of the creative individual. This makes sense if the creative person is one who has access to both hemispheres and to the two types of thinking associated with each hemisphere. Some time ago Schachtel (1959) noted that creative individuals transcend polarities rather than being limited by an either/or view of the world. Other researchers in the field have noted that creative individuals encompass both a high level of sensitivity and a high level of ego strength (Barron, 1963b; MacKinnon, 1961, 1962, 1976). They appear to have a high level of both right- and left-hemisphere activity; their access to primary thinking is balanced by their ability to control their imagination and maintain a firm grip on reality.

In terms of characteristics, creative individuals have been found to be more independent, autonomous, introverted, unconventional, and asocial than less creative persons. They also demonstrate a relative lack of defensiveness and repression; are intuitive; have strong, intrinsic motivation; and are risk takers with a need for order (Barron, 1963b; Gough, 1961; MacKinnon, 1961). In addition, creative individuals are flexible and seek out cognitive complexity and tolerate ambiguity (Barron, 1963a; Suler, 1980).

Some sex differences emerge, however, in discussing creative individuals. The descriptions above have been drawn primarily from male samples. Bachtold and Werner (1970, 1972, 1973), however, find that creative women are not much different from men in personality. They write that women authors and artists are similar to women psychologists in that both groups are aloof, bright, aggressive, adventuresome, imaginative, radical, and self-sufficient. In contrast, Helson (1967) has described creative women mathematicians as more inward and more passive than their male peers. It is likely that women are both like and unlike their male peers in the qualities that move them toward creativity. The differences may be related to differential hemispheric functioning between the sexes.

Creative persons also tend to have a greater receptivity to information, both internal and external. Martindale (1971, 1972) suggests that creative people possess an above-average ability for shifting between states of low arousal associated with primary process thinking and higher states of arousal characterized by secondary process thinking. Furthermore, creative individuals may have a lower basal level of arousal, which accounts for the broadening of attention and higher sensitivity to stimuli (Martindale, 1971, 1972). Some psychologists, however, suggest that the same increased receptivity to stimuli is due to lower sensory thresholds but higher cortical arousal. Others see the increased sensitivity resulting from greater perceptual instability (Bergum & Bergum, 1979a, b). Although different in particulars, the conclusion of all these psychologists is the same: the creative person is more receptive to external and internal stimuli.

Psychologically, moreover, the greater receptivity of creative persons may stem from personal conflict [Adler in Ansbacher (1956); Galton (1874)]. The issue of conflict as a prelude to creativity was emphasized in a comprehensive review article by MacKinnon (1976) when he cited again an early opinion that led to his future work in creativity. He stated that after World War II he and others were suprised by the evidence gathered during the war showing that ''large numbers of highly effective persons were intensively studied by psychologists and psychiatrists who, to their surprise, discovered again and again that persons of the most extraordinary effectiveness had had life histories marked by severe frustrations, deprivations and traumatic experiences'' (MacKinnon, 1976, p. 62). The early experiences of trauma may be viewed as prompting the individual to gather information and ask questions that are seldom asked by the less creative. Conflict may be the cause for opening the wells of the self deeper than usual and increasing receptivity to internal as well as external stimuli.

The greater receptivity to stimuli of creative persons may also lead to a higher degree of emotionality. As these individuals are more open to both their inner and outer environments, they may also be receptive to greater doses of dissonant information. Subject to greater amounts of information, creative persons may experience a need to impose order on this world. The need to achieve order, moreover, is likely to carry emotional overtones of some urgency. Galton (1874), for example, remarked that creative persons are ''driven'' to create. MacKinnon also is well aware of the affective component. He wrote (MacKinnon, 1976, p. 74):

> In the arts, the great productions appear to be exquisite attempts to resolve an internal turbulence. In the sciences, the important theoretical efforts seem to be personal cosmologies as much as anything else. . . . The validity of the

creative product thus is almost (but not quite) incidental to the forces driving its expression. And the forces are largely affective.

Hence creativity involves emotion as well as thought.

Emotionally, creative individuals may feel compelled to bring harmony into their world. However, to bring order out of disorder, as Bachtold (1980) remarks, a high degree of intelligence and a high level of energy are required. Whereas other individuals may sometimes be psychologically paralyzed by the experience of disorder, creative individuals respond with a high level of activity. They work hard, show a high degree of curiosity and persistence (Roe, 1974) and are assertive and adventuresome (Bachtold & Werner, 1970, 1972, 1973). The search for a new order thus involves both affective and cognitive components and requires that creative persons look beyond the facts as others know them.

Several recent research studies support the contention that creative individuals are not content with given data but want to go beyond the facts to discover what they symbolize and represent. In doing so, they generate new ways of seeking information. In one study (Glover, 1979), creative students were more likely to ask questions that concerned application, synthesis, and evaluation of an essay rather than questions dealing with factual matters. The researcher suggests that "creative behavior appears to be more than the generation of ideas; it also appears to be the generation of ways of obtaining more complex information." In another study it was concluded that "information processing strategies of creatives appear to be richer and they have access to more sources of information to broaden the base of their productions" than do less creative persons (Glover et al., 1980).

MacKinnon (1962, p. 490) summarized many of the characteristics of the creative person as follows:

> Creative persons are relatively uninterested in small details or in facts for their own sake, and more concerned with their meanings and implications, possessed of considerable cognitive flexibility, verbally skillful, interested in communicating with others and accurate in so doing, intellectually curious, and relatively disinterested in policing either their own impulses and images or those of others.

In short, creative individuals draw from complexity and bring a new order to give meaning to this complexity. Creativity results from receptivity to diverse input that is then used to shape a new and meaningful integrative form. It is likely that, in the process, imagery plays an important part.

RESEARCH ON IMAGERY

The nature and function of mental imagery have been the focus of considerable research since Holt (1964) first heralded the resurrection of mental imagery as a topic of psychological study. The nature of mental imagery, however, is no longer such a controversial area as its function. The nature of imagery is understood in a generally accepted definition: Imagery is a representation of schematic sensory impressions which operates across all sense modalities. Yet the function that such schematic representations may play in cognitive processes is still fiercely debated.

The Function of Imagery

Although the existence of imagery appears now to be taken for granted, psychologists disagree about the centrality of imagery in thought. The chief proponents of two opposing points of view on this issue are Kosslyn (1975, 1981; Kosslyn & Pomerantz, 1977; Kosslyn & Schwartz, 1977) and Pylyshyn (1973, 1979, 1981). Kosslyn argues that imagery is centrally involved in directing thought processes, whereas Pylyshyn counters that imagery is a by-product of thought that is directed by underlying knowledge and belief systems. Kosslyn further sees imagery processing as different in kind from language processing and argues that imagery itself places constraints on thought. Pylyshyn, on the other hand, argues that images do not constrain cognitive processes but that cognitive processes, including imagery, are constrained by tacit knowledge, or that reservoir of information that individuals bring to a situation. This debate not only underlies the importance of imagery in current psychological research, but suggests that individuals may use different thought processes that rely to a greater or lesser extent on the use of imagery.

One researcher (Zenhausern, 1978) has suggested that both Kosslyn's and Pylyshyn's models may be correct—for different individuals. Zenhausern argues that individuals may be differentiated along the dimensions of inductive versus deductive thought. Inductive thinkers may use both words and images, but verbal sequential processes will be central to thought in the manner described by Pylyshyn. These individuals may rely more on the left hemisphere than the right. Deductive thinkers, in contrast, will also use both words and images, but imaginal holistic processes will be central to their thinking. Such individuals might be more constrained by their imagery in the manner suggested by Kosslyn. They would also be more dependent on right-hemisphere functioning. Thus it may be possible that for some individuals, imagery serves a central function and for others, a peripheral one. Thus Zenhausern (1978) implies that the uses of imagery will differ according to one's style of thought—or one's cognitive style.

Although the degree to which imagery constrains the thought processes or merely accompanies them is still at issue, it is clear that some individuals appear to have more imagery than others, or more of a tendency to use a right-hemisphere mode of thought. Are there differences in personality between those who image and those who do not? Can we assume that right-hemisphere dominance may incline toward a different style of personality than left-hemisphere dominance?

Imagery and Personality

Some studies have reported correlates between imagery and personality, including Gordon's (1972) observation that uncontrolled imagery was related to neuroticism. This relationship has been documented elsewhere (Costello, 1956, 1957; Euse & Haney, 1975). Furthermore, the clarity of imagery in one study was also inversely related to neuroticism and introversion (Euse & Haney, 1975). This suggests that the ability to image, both clearly and controllably, may contribute to psychological health.

Other relationships between imagery and personality can be drawn from the work of Singer and Antrobus (1972), who state that the existence of imagery per se has little relationship to mental health. Imagery may appear in less healthy personalities in an intrusive and obsessive form. Imagery also appears in healthy individuals who have vivid auditory and visual imagery that is interwoven with other thought processes and that is neither rigid nor uncontrollable. Flexible and controlled imagery does appear, once again, to be a contributing factor to healthy personalities.

Finally, in the work of McClelland (1975) there are some clues as to the role of imagery in the personalities of men and women at different levels of maturity. In lower levels of maturity McClelland suggests that imagery plays a strong role in the thought processes of both men and women, without being clearly differentiated from reality. Moreover, McClelland implies that imagery recedes in importance in men as they become more differentiated and also more powerful, whereas in women imagery continues to play an important role throughout development. One may infer, however, from McClelland's work that at the highest levels of development imagery may once again be a significant part of cognitive processes in both men and women. In regard to personality, McClelland sees imagery as more important in the processes of men when aggression and conquest are not primary themes in their lives. When men are most in touch with "the feminine principle," that of openness and receptivity, they are more likely to be aware of their own imagery. In contrast, women are aware of imagery even when they are at their most assertive and individualistic. The continuous appearance of imagery in the lives of women is in contrast to the periodic appearance of imagery in the lives of men.

If we turn to the two-hemisphere hypothesis, these findings can be interpreted in accord with the work of Singer and Antrobus (1972). If imagery is indicative of right-brain functioning, it is available to most people most of the time. Recognition of imagery would occur at times when the right hemisphere's activity is not overwhelmed by that of the left. This would occur in both early and late (or low and high) developmental stages for men and possibly throughout the developmental cycle of women. The psychological health of the individual would be determined, however, by the balance of the two hemispheres. Uncontrollable imagery without a left hemisphere counterpoint would lead to various forms of psychological distress. On the other hand, repressive left-hemisphere functioning may lead to the occasional and intrusive eruption of unwelcome imagery—again, not a prognosis for health. Hence, just as the right hemisphere represents only half of our capacities, so the presence or absence of imagery cannot tell the whole story in regard to psychological health. As Singer and Antrobus stated(1972, p. 201), "imagery and fantasy are perhaps best regarded as fundamental human capacities or cognitive skills that can reflect serious pathology or distress but that can also be employed as valuable tools for self-gratification, planning, or creative activity, 'experimental action,' as Freud put it, but in a most adaptive way." Yet the various uses of imagery could be described in terms of an individual's orientation to the world, or what psychologists have come to call *cognitive styles*.

RESEARCH ON COGNITIVE STYLES

The studies that relate imagery to personality variables overlap with the research on cognitive style. The concept of cognitive style unites both cognitive and personality variables in one framework. As researchers in imagery begin to talk about *how* people think and the personality factors associated with doing so, they are describing the same processes of concern to cognitive style theorists. Thus we turn now to recent research in this area.

There are various definitions of cognitive styles. Broverman (1960a,b, 1964) speaks of cognitive styles as a cluster of different variables or the relationships between abilities within individuals. Guilford (1980) points out that we must include functions as well as traits in our definition of cognitive styles. Cognitive styles are also referred to as a "configuration of problem solving strategies adopted by an individual construing reality" (Faschingbauer et al., 1978) or "a hypothetical construct that has been developed to explain the process of mediation between stimuli and responses" (Goldstein & Blackman, 1978, p. 2).

Cognitive styles have also been conceptualized as integrators of personality that link cognitive and affective traits, influencing an individual's self-image, world view, and life-style. Styles, as numerous theorists have pointed out, indicate "how" we approach a problem or the world in general, not what it is we see or how well we manipulate data. Theorists differentiate style from ability and describe style as the typical or preferred means by which one approaches the task rather than the level or degree of performance (Kurtz, 1969).

Various cognitive styles have been identified according to a multiplicity of variables. These styles are not coherently related to each other, and research attempting to draw interrelationships between different definitions of styles has had meager results (Faschingbauer et al., 1978). The most well-known definitions of cognitive styles are those of Witkin and his colleagues (Witkin et al., 1962) who defined the polar clusters of field dependence and field independence. Other work has drawn on the concepts of "origence" and "intellectence" developed by Welsh (1975) and the Jungian polarities of intuiting–sensing, thinking–feeling, and perceiving–judging as measured by Myers (1962).

Each of these three typologies is briefly described below since they are central to our own research. In addition, each of these descriptions of cognitive style have been explicitly or implicitly related to creativity and imagery, as well as hemispheric functioning.

Field Dependence and Field Independence

The initial theory of field dependence and field independence as developed by Witkin and his colleagues (Witkin et al., 1962) distinguished between global and articulative tendencies in cognitive processes. The articulative tendencies were defined first as the more general tendency to restructure stimuli. Articulation was seen as encompassing both analysis and synthesis; yet as research progressed, emphasis fell almost solely on the analytic mode. The global style was then defined as the absence of articulation, particularly analysis. Finally, the global and analytic styles came to be identified with field dependence and field independence.

In recent work, Witkin and Goodenough (1977) have emphasized the importance of each style. They state that field-dependent individuals are more interpersonal; they attend selectively to social cues, are more socially outgoing, and get along with people better. In contrast, field-independent individuals have a more impersonal orientation, prefer solitary situations, are often cold, and are concerned with ideas and principles. Although field independence has generally been considered of great value, Witkin (1979, p. 362) argues that both styles have their particular arena of importance:

> Relatively field-dependent and field-independent people thus make their main developmental investments in different psychological domains, with the result that their growth proceeds along different pathways. Implicit in this perspective is the view that cognitive styles, which are process variables, influence the development of skills and interpersonal competencies in an inverse relation— and so may be regarded as expressing themselves in ability patterns.

Witkin here not only defends the value of each style but associates styles with ability patterns, thus asserting that field dependents would have greater ability in interpersonal tasks and field independents, in cognitive tasks. Field dependents also appear to be both global and subjective in their approach to the world. Field independents, on the other hand, are both analytic and objective. It is likely that a loose connection can be drawn between these two styles and right- and left-brain dominance, respectively. The same connection can be made with the concepts of origence and intellectence, to be described below.

Origence and Intellectence

The dimensions of origence and intellectence were developed by Welsh (1975, 1980) in his studies of creativity and intelligence to define two dimensions of thought. In multitudinous research studies, personality characteristics and vocational aptitudes have also come to be identified with various scores on origence and intellectence. Welsh defines origence as the degree to which subjects prefer "an implicit and open universe which they can structure and order in their own subjective way" (Welsh, 1980, p. 26). In contrast, a high score on intellectence represents "an abstract attitude . . . that leads to concern with figurative or symbolic expression and generalized principles of comprehension" (Welsh, 1980, p. 26). Intellectence also indicates a preference for structure and order in the world.

If subjects score high on both dimensions, they are termed *intuitive* and have a tendency toward the arts and humanities. If they are high on origence and low on intellectence, they are typed as *imaginative* and often found in sales and business. A high score on intellectence and a low score on origence leads to a grouping called *intellective* and refers to those found in the sciences and professions. Finally, those who are low on both dimensions are termed *industrious* and often are found in commercial and service occupations.

More clearly than many other typologies, Welsh's origence and intellectence are aligned with descriptions of processes associated with the right and left hemispheres. The descriptions of intuitive and imaginative types are typical of right-brained thinkers. On the other hand, both the intuitive and the intellective are typical of left-brained thinkers. The intuitive represents high levels of both right- and left-brained thought and the industrious type, high levels of neither. The intuitive and intellective styles find their counterpart in another, older typology.

An Eight-Part Typology

Jung (1923) developed an eight-part typology of personality types, which has been referred to as descriptive of cognitive styles (Viernstein et al., 1977). Jung's types arise from crossing extroversion and introversion with four other categories. Each pair, including extroversion and introversion, is inversely related to each other. Individuals may thus be relatively intuitive or sensing in their approach to the world (but an individual will not be strong in both approaches); that is, individuals may rely on global assessments of others or on assessments based on particular facts. Individuals may also be either thinking or feeling. If one is primarily a "thinker," that person relies on logical processes to come to a point of view; if one is a "feeler," sentiments and emotions shape the path to assessing value and orientation. With any of these four orientations, an individual may be either extroverted or introverted.

In 1962 Myers developed a measure to assess Jung's types, called the Myers–Briggs Personality Inventory. In this inventory one receives a score for the four basic types (intuiting, sensing, thinking, and feeling); for introversion and extroversion; and for two more general cognitive orientations, perceiving and judging. The high scores are indicative of one's orientation to the world or one's cognitive style. Again, one might anticipate that the intuitive person, for example, has more access to right-hemisphere processing and the sensing person to the left hemisphere, and so forth.

Other Descriptions of Cognitive Styles

Other researchers have drawn other models of cognitive styles. Considerable work has sprung from Kagan's dimensions of reflectivity and impulsivity (Kagan et al., 1963, 1964) and Barron's (1953) dimensions of complexity and simplicity. Others have utilized the Piagetian (Piaget, 1955; Piaget & Inhelder, 1969) categories of formal and operational thought as a basis for their work in this area. Recently, Hogan (Hogan, 1980; Viernstein et al., 1977) has developed a model of logical and intuitive personalities based on the amount of difference between students' scores on verbal and mathematical aptitude tests. A spate of other research studies has also appeared recently that have either used these categories or created new ones (Giannini et al., 1978; Goebal & Harris, 1980; Harren et al., 1978). Few of these studies, however, define any cognitive style that reflects a balance of both hemispheres of the brain.

CREATIVITY, IMAGERY, AND COGNITIVE STYLES

Having reviewed, in summary fashion, the literature on creativity, imagery, and cognitive styles, we turn to the research that seeks to establish interconnections between these three constructs. The research testifying to the relationship between creativity and imagery has grown during the past decade, whereas that relating either of the above to cognitive styles is still in the beginning stages.

The connections between creativity and imagery are sometimes made directly (Austin, 1971; Forisha, 1978a,b, 1981a; Schmeidler, 1965) and sometimes indirectly. In the latter category, creativity and imagery have both been associated with a third variable, thus suggesting that the relationship may also exist between creativity and imagery. Creativity has been related to primary process (Pine & Holt, 1960; Suler, 1980), to dream recall (Austin, 1971; Cohen, 1974; Schechter et al., 1965), and hypnotic susceptability (Bowers, 1979). Since imagery has also been associated with primary process

(Reyher and Smeltzer, 1968), with dream recall (Cohen, 1974; Hiscock & Cohen, 1973; Orlinsky, 1966), and with hypnotic susceptibility (Bowers, 1979), the possibility of a consistent relationship between creativity and imagery is further strengthened.

In the relationship of creativity and imagery, however, the control of imagery appears as important (if not more so) than the vividness of imagery. In Forisha's (1981a) work the control of imagery was related to creativity more frequently than vividness of imagery. This was true only in the case of males when the sexes were considered separately. These findings are similar to those of Pine and Holt (1960), who found that control of primary process thinking was more highly correlated with creativity than the amount of primary process thinking. These findings were true only for males and not for females.

One series of experiments has been designed particularly to elucidate the relationship between creativity and imagery. Work by Sobel and Rothenberg (Rothenberg & Sobel, 1980; Rothenberg, 1976, 1979; Sobel & Rothenberg, 1980) has focused on homospatial thinking in which two images and/or representations from any sensory modality are brought into the same spatial location. The resulting mental conception is hypothesized to further the development of new forms, structures, and integrations. In effect, homospatial thinking (related to imagery) is expected to facilitate creativity.

To investigate this expectation, Sobel and Rothenberg showed one group of students two superimposed slides and another group, the same two slides shown side by side. Subjects were then asked to draw sketches that were rated for creativity. There was partial evidence to support the connection between homospatial thinking and creativity (Sobel & Rothenberg, 1980). In another experiment (Rothenberg & Sobel, 1980), when subjects were asked to write brief verbal metaphors, the creativity of those who had seen the superimposed slides surpassed the control group. Both experiments provided evidence for the relationship between imagery, particularly imagery that juxtaposes hitherto unconnected percepts, and creativity.

Many psychologists have also associated creativity with certain cognitive styles. When divergent thinking is termed a *cognitive style* (although it is often used as a measure of creative thought), there is a clear and direct connection between creativity and cognitive styles. In one other instance, the definitions of creativity and cognitive style overlap. Welsh's (1975) inventory, which yields cognitive styles, was also developed as a measure of creativity, and recently Gough (1979) has developed a Creative Personality Scale that correlates with Welsh's description of cognitive styles. In both cases the relationship between creativity and cognitive style arises from overlapping definitions of the two constructs.

There have also been attempts to find a connection between creativity and cognitive styles when their definitions do not overlap. Witkin's field-independent subjects have often been regarded as more creative than the field-dependent subjects. Studies indicate that although all subjects who score high on field independence are not necessarily creative, those scoring high on creativity tend to score higher on field independence (Bloomberg, 1971, 1976; Noppe & Gallagher, 1977; Spotts & Mackler, 1967). Also, students majoring in concentrations termed "more creative" have been found to be more field independent than students in other majors. For example, Bergum (Bergum, 1977; Morris & Bergum, 1978) found that students of architecture regard themselves as more creative than business students and are also more field independent than business students.

Another study (Walker et al., 1979) has investigated the relationship between field independence and imagery. These researchers suggested that mental imagery would be more often utilized by field-independent individuals since they are dependent on internal as opposed to external referents and differentiate (one would suppose) internal as well as external fields from each other. Since incidental memory is generally better in individuals who use more imagery (Paivio, 1971), it was hypothesized that field-independent individuals would have better incidental memory than field-dependent individuals. This was confirmed by the results of the study and the relationship between imagery and field independence was verified.

To summarize, the initial findings on the interrelationships of creativity, imagery, and cognitive style can be interpreted in terms of the functioning of the two hemispheres of the brain. Creativity may be seen as the interaction of two hemispheres of thought, one associated with holistic thinking or primary process and the other with analytic thinking or secondary process. Creativity then requires the interaction of both primary and secondary processes, or the holistic and analytic thought represented by the two halves of the brain. Imagery, on the other hand, is one of the main processes of the right half of the brain and thus bears a relationship to primary process and to other variables connected with primary process, such as dream recall and hypnotic susceptibility. Imagery is then at least potentially an integral part of the creative process. Yet the degree to which one utilizes imagery in creative tasks may be reflective of a complex of personality and cognitive variables, linked together under the construct of cognitive style.

CREATIVITY AND IMAGERY AS POSSIBLE FUNCTIONS OF STYLE

The connecting theoretical thread between creativity, imagery, and cognitive style in the recent literature lies in their relationship to hemispheric functioning. In our current research we did not set out to investigate this specific relationship. Rather, we intended to establish *what* theoretical framework might make the most sense of our empirical data on creativity, imagery, and cognitive styles. Consequently, we used a shotgun approach, pelting our subjects with a multitude of instruments that assess cognitive style, two that assess creativity and imagery, and three instruments of our own making designed to assess personality styles. Our results are suggestive of a theoretical framework that is not incompatible with the relationships of hemispheric dominance, creativity, and imagery suggested by other theorists.

Our subjects were selected from four disciplines, in line with earlier suggestions (Forisha, 1981a; Kolb and Plovnick, 1977) that cognitive approaches differed by academic discipline. Fifteen subjects were selected from each of the following disciplines: engineering, business, education, and psychology. All were undergraduates, ranging in age from 18 to 21 years, with a mean age of 19.1. The final sample held slightly more women than men. Although an attempt was made to equalize the number of each sex in each discipline, the paucity of men in education led to a subsample of significantly more women than men in this field.

Subjects were administered Torrance's Unusual Uses Subtest from Thinking Creatively with Words (Torrance, 1966) and Gordon's Control of Imagery Questionnaire (Gordon, 1949). Cognitive styles were assessed by the Group Embedded Figures Test (Oltman et al., 1971), which yields a score for field independence; the Welsh Art Preference Inventory (Welsh, 1975, 1980), which was scored for origence and intellectence; and the Myers–Briggs Personality Inventory (Myers, 1962), which results in scores for each of the Jungian types. Subjects also wrote four stories in response to Thematic Apperception Test (TAT) cards that were scored according to McClelland's (1975) and Winter's (1973) descriptions of the need for power.

In addition, subjects were administered two other instruments that we developed to assess individuals' expectations of themselves and others. In previous studies (Forisha, 1981b) these instruments have yielded scores that correlate with creativity, locus of control, personality flexibility, and various socioeconomic and life experience factors. In our own work we have used them as measures of personality orientation. In this study we wanted to determine their relationship to measures of cognitive styles.

The first of these instruments is the Personal Expectations Inventory (PXI) (Forisha & Morris, 1980). Scores from this instrument are classified under six headings: Openness to People, Openness to Ideas, Analysis, Synthesis, Decision Making, and Performance. In addition, scores from the six factors were averaged to find a mean PXI score. The second instrument is the Organizational Expectations Inventory (OXI) (Forisha et al., 1980). Although designed to measure expectations of organizational systems, three overall scores were important in our findings: Effectiveness, which indicates a perception of desired balance between external and internal structures; Power—0, which shows a preference for external structures; and Affiliation—0, which reveals a preference for a people-oriented environment.

In addition, all subjects were videotaped in a 2-minute segment in which they talked about themselves and their future plans. The videotape presentations were scaled by two trained scorers on the dimensions of power and affiliation. Power is defined as a sense of competence and confidence in self. Affiliation is defined as responsiveness and awareness of others. Previous work with the Power-Affiliation Diagnostic Inventory (PADI) (Forisha et al., 1980) has shown that this instrument's scaling of power and affiliation is related to a subject's ability to influence his or her environment.

Initially, the data from this array of instruments were subjected to correlational, regression, and principle component analyses. Numerous relationships between creativity, imagery, and cognitive style were apparent. However, it was difficult to clearly distinguish the relationship patterns from each other because of the multiplicity of variables. Consequently, two salient dimensions were selected on which to plot the variables. The first dimension was *extroversion–introversion*. The second dimension was more difficult to define. However, we termed this dimension *objectivity–subjectivity*. Objectivity was taken to encompass a preference for focusing on a task and other external referents. Subjectivity, on the other hand, encompasses a perference for people-oriented factors with some resistance to the imposition of external structure. It would seem that this dimension is also related to the descriptions of left and right hemispheric functioning. The left hemisphere would be associated with objectivity and the right hemisphere, with subjectivity. Zenhausern's (1978) work would also suggest that left-hemisphere objectivity would lead to an inductive cognitive style and right-hemisphere subjectivity, to one that is more deductive.

In accord with both descriptions and our empirical results, all variables but creativity and imagery were plotted on the two-dimensional graph. The variables studied and their relationship to the two dimensions are shown in Figure 11.1. For the total sample, and for each subgrouping, the relationships of creativity and imagery to the other variables were indicated on the graphs by oval areas that encompass the variables to which they were related. (Relationships were indicated when correlations were found with a significance of $p<.05$). In this way creativity and imagery both appear in specific quadrants of the graph. The quadrants are used to define the dimensions of cognitive style. Furthermore, the relationship of creativity and imagery for each subgroup is visually apparent. The two oval areas overlap only when a relationship is present. The relationships for creativity and imagery for the total sample and for each subgroup are shown in Figures 11.2 and 11.3, and specific results are described below.

Research Findings: Creativity

Analyses of variance showed that there were no significant differences between the sexes or among disciplines on creativity. Cross-comparison between subgroups, however, revealed strikingly different relational patterns between creativity and the other variables.

In the total sample, correlational analyses show that creativity is related to Synthesis (PXI), and the need for power and feeling and is opposed to Power—0. In the sample of men, creativity is related to imagery. In contrast,

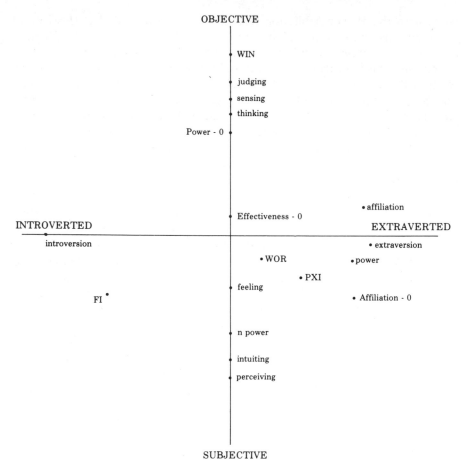

Figure 11.1. Dimensions of Cognitive Style: introversion–extroversion and objectivity–subjectivity.

in the sample of women, creativity is related to the need for power, intuition, and perceiving and is opposed to Power—0.

In the engineering sample, creativity had a very different pattern of relationships: it was opposed to Openness to Ideas (PXI) and intuition and was related to Power—0. Other disciplines revealed a more expected pattern: in business majors, creativity was related to Decision Making (PXI) and the need for power and was opposed to Power—0. Education students were similar. In psychology students, creativity was related to Openness to Ideas (PXI), in contrast to the engineering students. Regression analyses for the total sample showed that creativity was predicted by Synthesis (PXI), control of imagery, and need for power and was opposed to Power—0.

In the principal component analysis, creativity appeared on all primary factors and was related to Synthesis (PXI) throughout. For engineers, however, creativity did not appear until the third factor and could thus be assumed to be a less central component in their thought patterns.

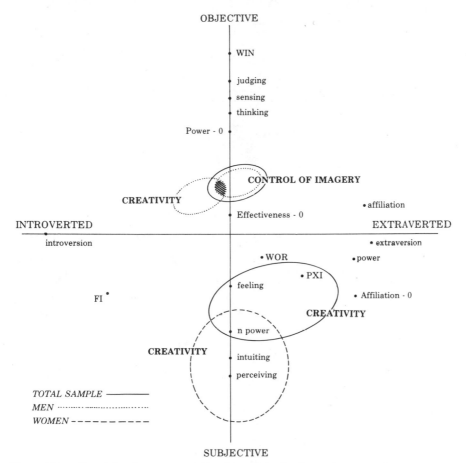

Figure 11.2. Creativity, Imagery, and Cognitive Style: total sample, men and women.

In summary, creativity is related to Synthesis (PXI) or the preference for seeing the "big picture" and uniting unconnected parts. It is not related to outgoingness or responsiveness and is aligned more with introversion than extroversion. Specific subsamples, however, differed. For engineering students, creativity falls within the sector defined as objectivity or preference for external structure. For all other students, it is aligned with a preference for internal structuring of material. For engineering students, again, creativity is more closely aligned with introversion than for other groupings, where it is associated with extroversion.

Research Findings: Control of Imagery

In previous research (Forisha, 1978a; 1981a,c), control of imagery had been a more salient variable than vividness of imagery (Betts, 1909). Consequently, this was the only aspect of imagery measured in this study. Analyses

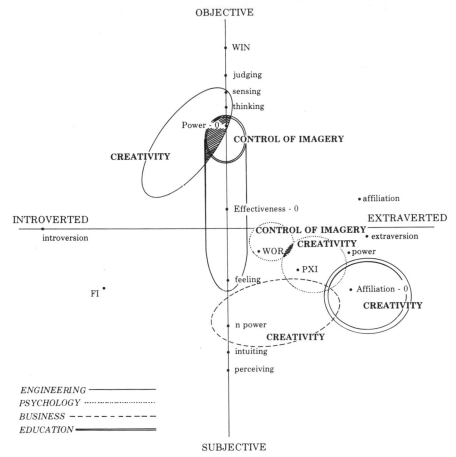

Figure 11.3. Creativity, Imagery, and Cognitive Style: engineering, business, education, and psychology majors.

of variance showed that there were no significant differences in control of imagery between the sexes or among the disciplines. The patterns of relationship with other variables were different, however, for the various subgroupings.

Control of imagery was related to creativity in the sample of men but not in women. In the sample of engineering students, imagery was related to feeling and to Power—0 and Effectiveness. Furthermore, control of imagery was negatively related to the need for power, which was positively related to creativity in both the total sample and the sample of men. Regression analyses bore out these findings, showing that control of imagery was predictive of creativity in the total sample.

Finally, in the principal component analysis for the total sample, control of imagery appears on the primary factors in company with creativity and in opposition to power, affiliation, extroversion, and need for power. In the sample of men, control of imagery appeared as an important variable on three of the first four factors, accompanied by creativity and opposed by power, affiliation, and extroversion. For women, control of imagery did not appear until the third factor when it was in company with Effectiveness and Power—0 and opposed by need for power.

In the disciplines the patterns were slightly different. For engineers, Control of Imagery appeared on the second factor along with feeling and Effectiveness. For business students, the imagery variable was related to Effectiveness but opposed to extroversion, intuition, feeling, and the need for power. In education majors, imagery did not appear until the fourth factor, and here it was accompanied by Affiliation—0. In psychology students, control of imagery was associated with creativity and opposed to Power—0.

In summary, control of imagery is more often related to objectivity than subjectivity, which would imply that the control dimension is more salient than the imaginal one. Control of imagery is also related more often to introversion than extroversion though the relationship is not consistently present. In general, then, control of imagery is an indication of an objective, slightly introverted, cognitive style. This is confirmed when creativity for the specific group falls in the same quadrant as control of imagery. When it does not, conclusions remain tentative, but creativity is taken as the predominant indication of style.

Research Findings: Creativity and Imagery

The relationships of creativity and imagery with each of the other variables define their position on the two-dimensional plot. The position held by each in a specific quadrant indicates the prevalent cognitive style for that group. When creativity and imagery fall in divergent quadrants, the quadrant that holds creativity is taken as the predominant indicator of cognitive style.

In general, creativity and imagery are closely interwoven with other personality variables. In the principal component analyses, for example, neither creativity nor imagery dominated one specific factor. Rather, they appeared in conjunction with other personality variables on a variety of factors. Further, the variables to which they were most strongly related varied by subgroup, indicating that they are shaped by and serve different functions for different cognitive styles.

In some cases imagery did not show any specific relationship to other variables. In these cases imagery is not plotted on the graphs for the subgroups, and conclusions for those subgroups must remain tentative. However, when creativity is plotted on the graph, although imagery for that group is not, creativity is taken as an indication of cognitive style.

Finally, the areas in which the oval outlines of creativity and control of imagery overlap indicate the degree of relationship between the two variables. Creativity and imagery clearly overlap for men, but not for women. They also overlap for engineering and psychology students. Yet the nature of both creativity and imagery appears to be very different for these two groups. For psychology students, both are associated with extroversion and subjectivity. For engineering students, in contrast, both creativity and imagery are more marked by a preference for introversion and objectivity. Thus the fact that imagery and creativity may be interrelated does not by itself indicate how those processes might operate for certain individuals.

Conclusions and Implications

These findings suggest that the relationship between creativity and imagery is central for some individuals and not for others, and that even for those for whom the relationship is operative, it may vary in terms of the total personality. The variability may be defined in terms of the dimensions of extroversion–introversion and objectivity–subjectivity. In this light, the engineering students, and men in general, prefer a more structured universe than do the women in this sample. They are also, at least at this age, less extroverted than other groups. In contrast, the women lean more to the intuitive, nonstructured approach and are more extroverted in their orientation; however, control of imagery is not a salient factor in their style. The cognitive styles of all other subgroups except engineering may be defined within the extroverted–subjective quadrant, with education students being the most extroverted.

In short, we have defined four quadrants as a framework for studying cognitive styles: subjective–introverted; subjective–extroverted; objective–extroverted; and objective–introverted. The extroverted–introverted dimension is clearly related to one's willingness to express oneself to others—about personal as well as nonpersonal matters—and one's receptivity to the experience of others. The subjective–objective dimension is very likely related to hemispheric functioning. A number of polarities studied by others may be listed as related to our dimensions of subjectivity and objectivity:

Subjectivity	Objectivity
Right hemisphere	Left hemisphere
Global orientation	Analytic orientation
People-oriented	Task-oriented
Resistance to structure	Preference for structure
Intuitive	Logical
Deductive	Inductive

Many of these connections are subject to debate and further empirical work. Clearly, there will not be a one-to-one correspondence between many of these polarities. Yet the parallels are suggested by both theoretical and empirical relationships. Parallels may also be drawn with McClelland's maturity scale (McClelland, 1975; Stewart, 1977). McClelland suggested that men have more imagery at the lowest level of maturity; here they are more subjective, intuitive, and fluid in their thought. He has placed his "creative scientists" in this category. In many ways this level of his scale suggests a style that might be located in the subjective–extroverted quadrant with the psychology, education, and business students. In his middle levels for men, in which control becomes a more important factor, and processes are less fluid, it is likely that the cognitive styles would fall in the two quadrants at the objective end of the spectrum, particularly the objective–introverted quadrant. Here we find the engineering students. It would be unlikely that any of these students, at the age of about 19 years, would show the integration that McClelland implies might occur at other levels. Yet such an integration might result in areas of creativity and imagery closer to the central point, where they may be both objective and subjective, extroverted and introverted.

Our model is still tentative and subject to further empirical work. However, it strongly suggests that creativity and imagery are both closely intertwined with other personality factors. Furthermore, the functions they serve in the total personality may differ for individuals of different specialties and different cognitive styles. At higher levels of maturity, we may speculate that highly creative individuals from different disciplines may find themselves closer to the center, reflecting a balance of extroversion–introversion and subjectivity–objectivity. Thus at higher levels of integration, creativity and imagery may reflect a balance between originality and relevance, imagination and logic, and an ability to utilize both internal and external referents. Such a balance at the moment remains only a theoretical possibility—a vision and not an empirical reality.

REFERENCE NOTES

1. Supported in part by a grant from the Spencer Foundation, 1980–1981.

REFERENCES

Ansbacher, H. L. & Ansbacher, R. R (Eds.), *The individual psychology of Alfred Adler*. New York: Basic Books, 1956.

Austin, M. D. Dream recall and the bias of intellectual ability. *Nature*, 1971, **231**, 59–61.

Bachtold, L. J. Speculation on a theory of creativity: A physiological basis. *Perceptual and Motor Skills*, 1980, **40**, 699–702.

Bachtold, L. M., & Werner, E. E. Personality profiles of gifted women psychologists. *American Psychologist,* 1970, **25,** 234–243.

Bachtold, L. M. & Werner, E. E. Personality characteristics of women scientists. *Psychological Reports,* 1972, **36,** 391–396.

Bachtold, L. M., & Werner, E. E. Personality characteristics of creative women. *Perceptual and Motor Skills,* 1973, **36,** 311–319.

Bagnara, S., Roncato, S., Simion, F., & Umilta, C. Sex-related differences in hemispheric asymmetries in processing simple geometric figures. *Perceptual and Motor Skills,* 1980, **51,** 223–229.

Bakan, P. The eyes have it. *Psychology Today,* April 1971, 64–67, 90.

Barron, F. Complexity–simplicity as a personality variable. *Journal of Abnormal and Social Psychology,* 1953, **48,** 163–172.

Barron, F. Diffusion, integration and enduring attention in the creative process. In R. White (Ed.), *The study of lives.* Englewood Cliffs, N.J.: Prentice-Hall, 1963a.

Barron, F. *Creativity and psychological health.* New York: D. Van Nostrand, 1963b.

Bergum, B. O. Undergraduate self-perceptions of creativity and independence. *Perceptual and Motor Skills,* 1977, **44,** 187–190.

Bergum, B. O., & Bergum, J. E. Creativity, perceptual stability and self-perception. *Bulletin of the Psychonomic Society,* 1979a, **14,** 61–63.

Bergum, J. E.& Bergum, B. O. Self-perceived creativity and ambiguous figure rever rates. *Bulletin of the Psychonomic Society.* 1979b, **14,** 373–374.

Betts, G. H. The distribution of functions of mental imagery. *Teachers College, Columbia University, Contributions to Education.* 1909, **26,** 1–99.

Bloomberg, M. Creativity as related to field independence and mobility. *The Journal of Genetic Psychology,* 1971, **118,** 3–12.

Bloomberg, M. An inquiry into the relationship between field-independence–dependence and creativity. *The Journal of Psychology,* 1976, **67,** 127–140.

Bogen, J. E. The other side of the brain: An appositional mind. *Bulletin of the Los Angeles Neurological Society,* 1969, **34,** 135–162.

Bowers, K. S., & Bowers, P. G. Hypnosis and creativity: A theoretical and empirical rapprochement. In E. Fromm & R. Shor (Eds.) *Hypnosis.* Chicago: Aldine–Atherton, 1972.

Bowers, P. G. Hypnosis and creativity: The search for the missing link. *Journal of Abnormal Psychology,* 1979, **88,** 547–555.

Broverman, D. M. Cognitive style and intra-individual variation in abilities. *Journal of Personality,* 1960a, **28,** 240–256. (a).

Broverman, D. M. Dimensions of cognitive style. *Journal of Personality,* 1960b, **28,** 167–185.

Broverman, D. M. Generality and behavioral correlates of cognitive styles. *Journal of Consulting Psychology,* 1964, **28,** 487–500.

Buffery, A. W. H., & Gray, J. H. Sex differences in the development of spatial and linguistic skills. In C. Ounstead & D. C. Taylor (Eds.), *Gender differences: Their ontogeny and significance.* London: Churchill, 1972.

Burstein, B., Bank, L., & Jarvik, L. F. Sex differences in cognitive functioning: Evidence, determinants, implications. *Human Development,* 1980, **23,** 289–313.

Bush, M. Psychoanalysis and scientific creativity. *Journal of the American Psychoanalytic Association,* 1979, **17,** 136–191.

Cohen, D. B. Toward a theory of dream recall. *Psychological Bulletin,* 1974, **81,** 138–154.

Costello, C. G. The effects of prefrontal leucotomy upon visual imagery and ability to perform complex operations. *Journal of Mental Science,* 1956, **102,** 507–516.

Costello, C. G. The control of visual imagery in mental disorder. *Journal of Mental Science,* 1957, **102,** 840–849.

Dudek, S. Z. Regression and creativity: A comparison of the Rorschach records of successful versus unsuccessful painters and writers. *Journal of Nervous and Mental Disease,* 1968, **147,** 535–546.

Euse, F. J., & Haney, J. N. Clarity, controlability, and emotional intensity of image: Correlations with introversion, neuroticism, and subjective anxiety. *Perceptual and Motor Skills,* 1975, **40,** 443–447.

Faschingbauer, T. R., Moore, C. D., & Stone, L. Cognitive style, dogmatism, and creativity: Some implications regarding cognitive development. *Psychological Reports,* 1978, **42,** 795–804.

Forisha, B. L. Creativity and imagery in men and women. *Perceptual and Motor Skills,* 1978a, **47,** 1255–1264.

Forisha, B. L. Mental imagery and creativity; Review and speculations. *Journal of Mental Imagery,* 1978b, **2,** 209–238.

Forisha, B. L. Patterns of mental imagery and creativity in men and women. *Journal of Mental Imagery* (in press, 1981a).

Forisha, B. Personal expectations and organizational synchrony: A new model for individual behavior in organizations (unpublished manuscript, 1981b).

Forisha, B. Imagery and creativity: Assessing cognitive styles. *Journal of Educational Technology* (in press, 1981c).

Forisha, B., & Morris, G. *Personal expectations Inventory.* Ann Arbor, Mich.: Human Systems Analysis, 1980.

Forisha, B., Morris, G., & Binford, M. Organizational expectations inventory. Ann Arbor, Mich.: Human Systems Analysis, 1980.

Forisha, B., Wolfe, C., & Tajer, R. *Power–affiliation diagnostic inventory.* Ann Arbor, Mich.: Human Systems Analysis, 1980.

Freud, S. The unconscious. *Collected papers,* Vol. 4. London: Hogarth, 1949.

Freud, S. *A general introduction to psychoanalysis.* (J. Riviere, transl.) New York: Pocket Books, 1953 (originally published in 1920).

Galin, D., & Ornstein, R. Individual differences in cognitive style. I. Reflective eye movements. *Neuropsychologia,* 1974, **12,** 367–390.

Galton, F. *English men of science, their nature and nurture.* London: Macmillan, 1874.

Giannini, A. J., Daood, J., Giannini, M. C., Boniface, R., & Rhodes, G. Intellect vs. intuition: A dichotomy in the reception of nonverbal communication. *Journal of General Psychology,* 1978, **99,** 19–24.

Glover, J. A. Levels of questions asked in interview and reading sessions by creative and relatively noncreative students. *Journal of Genetic Psychology,* 1979, **135,** 103–108.

Glover, J. A., Zimmer, J. W., & Bruning, R. H. Information processing approaches among creative students. *Journal of Psychology,* 1980, **105,** 93–97.

Goebel, B. L., & Harris, E. L. Cognitive strategy and personality across age levels. *Perceptual and Motor Skills,* 1980, **40,** 803–811.

Goldstein, K. M., & Blackman, S. Assessment of cognitive style. In P. McReynolds (Ed.), *Advances in psychological assessment,* Vol. 4. San Francisco: Jossey-Bass, 1978.

Gordon, R. An investigation into some of the factors that favour the formation of stereotyped images. *British Journal of Psychology,* 1949, **39,** 156–167.

Gordon, R. A very private world. In P. Sheehan (Ed.), *The function and nature of mental imagery.* New York: Academic Press, 1972.

Gotz, K. O., & Gotz, K. Personality characteristics of professional artists. *Perceptual and Motor Skills,* 1979, **49,** 327–334.

Gough, H. Techniques for identifying the creative research scientist. In *Conferences on the creative person.* Berkeley: University of California. Institute of Personality Assessment and Research, 1961, Chapter 3.

Gough, H. G. A creative personality scale for the adjective check list. *Journal of Personality and Social Psychology,* 1979, **38,** 1398–1405.

Guilford, J. P. Cognitive styles: What are they? *Educational and Psychological Measurement,* 1980, **40,** 715–735.

Hannay, H. J. Real or imagined incomplete lateralization of functions in females? *Perception and Psychophysics,* 1977, **19,** 349–352.

Harren, V. A., Kass, R. A., Tinsley, H. E. A., & Moreland, J. R. Influence of sex role attitudes and cognitive styles on career decision making. *Journal of Counseling Psychology,* 1978, **25,** 390–398.

Hartmann, H. Ego psychology and the problems of adaptation. In D. Rapaport (Ed.), *Organization and pathology of thought.* New York: Columbia University Press, 1956.

Helson, R. Sex differences in creative style. *Journal of Personality,* 1967, **35,** 214–233.

Hersch, C. The cognitive functioning of the creative person: A developmental analysis. *Journal of Projective Techniques,* 1962, **26,** 195–200.

Hiscock, M., & Cohen, D. B. Visual imagery and dream recall. *Journal of Research on Personality,* 1973, **7,** 179–188.

Hogan, R. The gifted adolescent. In J. Adelson (Ed.), *Handbook of adolescent psychology.* New York: Wiley, 1980.

Holt, R. R. Imagery: The return of the ostracised. *American Psychologist,* 1964, **19,** 254–264.

Jung, C. G. *Psychological types.* New York: Harcourt, 1923.

Kagan, J., Moss, M. A., & Siegel, I. E. Psychological significance of styles of conceptualization. *Monographs of the Society for Research in Child Development,* 1963, **28,** 73–112.

Kagan, J., Rosman, B., Day, D., Albert, J., & Phillips, W. Information processing in the child: Significance of analytic and reflective attitudes. *Psychological Monographs,* 1964, **78** (1, Whole No. 578).

Kashihara, E. Lateral preference and style of cognition. *Perceptual and Motor Skills,* 1979, **48,** 1167–1172.

Kimura, D. The asymmetry of the human brain. *Scientific American,* 1973, **288,** 70–78.

Kolb, D., & Plovnick, M. The *experiential* learning theory of career development. In J. Van Maanen (Ed.), *Organizational Careers: Some new perspectives.* New York: Wiley, 1977.

Kosslyn, S. M. Information representation in visual images. *Cognitive Psychology,* 1975, **7,** 341–370.

Kosslyn, S. M. The medium and the message in mental imagery. *Psychological Review,* 1981, **88,** 46–66.

Kosslyn, S. M., & Pomerantz, J. R. Imagery, propositions, and the form of internal representations. *Cognitive Psychology,* 1977, **9,** 52–76.

Kosslyn, S. M., & Shwartz, S. P. A simulation of visual imagery. *Cognitive Science,* 1977, **1,** 265–295.

Kurtz, R. A. A conceptual investigation of Witkin's notion of perceptual style. *Mind,* 1969, **78,** 522–533.

Lake, D. A. & Bryden, M. P. Handedness and sex differences in hemispheric asymmetry. *Brain and Language,* 1976, **3,** 266–282.

Levy, J., Trevarthen, C., & Sperry, R. W. Perceptions of bilateral chimeric figures following hemispheric deconnection. *Brain,* 1972, **94,** 61–78.

Maccoby, E. E., & Jacklin, C. N. *The psychology of sex differences.* Stanford, Cal.: Stanford University Press, 1974.

MacKinnon, D. W. The study of creativity and creativity in architects. In *Conference on the creative person.* Berkeley: University of California, Institute of Personality Assessment and Research, 1961.

MacKinnon, D. W. The nature and nurture of creative talent. *American Psychologist, 1962,* **17,** 484–495.

MacKinnon, D. W. IPAR's contribution to the conceptualization and study of creativity. In I. A. Taylor, & J. W. Getzels (Eds.), *Perspectives in creativity.* Chicago: Aldine, 1976.

Martindale, C. Degeneration, disinhibition and genius. *Journal of the History of the Behavioral Sciences,* 1971, **7,** 177–182.

Martindale, C. Anxiety, intelligence and access to primitive modes of thought in high and low scorers on the Remote Associates Test. *Perceptual and Motor Skills,* 1972, **35,** 275–281.

May, R. *The courage to create.* New York: Norton, 1975.

McClelland, D. *Power: The inner experience.* New York: Halstead, 1975.

McGee, M. G. Handedness and mental rotation. *Perceptual and Motor Skills,* 1978, **47,** 641–642.

Mintzberg, H. Planning on the left side and managing on the right. *Harvard Business Review.* 1976, **54,** 49–56.

Morris, T. L., & Bergum, B. O. A note on the relationship between field-independence and creativity. *Perceptual and Motor Skills,* 1978, **46,** 1114.

Myers, I. B. 1962. *The Myers–Briggs type indicator manual.* Princeton: Educational Testing Service, 1962.

Nebes, R. Superiority of the minor hemisphere in commissurotomized man for perception of part–whole relations. *Cortex,* 1971, **7,** 333–349.

Nebes, R. Hemispheric specialization in commissurotomized man. *Psychological Bulletin,* 1974, **81,** 1–14.

Noppe, L. D., & Gallagher, J. M. A cognitive style approach to creative thought. *Journal of Personality Assessment,* 1977, **41,** 85–90.

Oltman, P. K., Raskin, E., & Witkin, H. A. *Group Embedded Figures Test.* Palo Alto, Cal.: Consulting Psychologists' Press, 1971.

Orlinsky, D. E. Rorschach test correlates of dreaming and dream recall. *Journal of Projective Techniques and Personality Assessment,* 1966, **30,** 250–253.

Paivio, A. *Imagery and verbal processes.* New York: Holt, 1971.

Peterson, J. M., & Lansky, L. M. Success in architecture: Handedness and/or visual thinking. *Perceptual and Motor Skills,* 1980, **50,** 1139–1143.

Piaget, J. The growth of logical reasoning. New York: Basic Books, 1955.

Piaget, J., & Inhelder, B. *The psychology of the child.* New York: Basic Books, 1969.

Pine, F. Thematic drive content and creativity. *Journal of Personality,* 1959, **27,** 136–151.

Pine, F. & Holt, R. Creativity and primary process: A study of adaptive regression. *Journal of Abnormal and Social Psychology,* 1960, **61,** 370–379.

Pylyshyn, Z. W. What the mind's eye tells the mind's brain: A critique of mental imagery. *Psychological Bulletin,* 1973, **80,** 1–24.

Pylyshyn, Z. W. The rate of "mental rotation" of images: A test of a holistic analogue hypothesis. *Memory and Cognition.* 1979, **7,** 19–28.

Pylyshyn, Z. W. The imagery debate: Analogue media versus tacit knowledge. *Psychological Review,* 1981, **87,** 16–45.

Restak, R. M. The hemispheres of the brain have minds of their own. *New York Times,* January 25, 1976, Section 4, p. 8.

Reyher, J., & Smeltzer, W. The uncovering process of visual imagery and verbal associations: A comparative study. *Journal of Abnormal Psychology,* 1968, **73,** 218–222.

Richardson, A. Subject, task, and tester variables associated with initial eye movements. *Journal of Mental Imagery,* 1978, **2,** 85–100.

Roe, A. Painters and painting. In I. A. Taylor, J. W. Getzels (Eds.), *Perspectives in creativity.* Chicago: Aldine, 1974.

Rogolsky, M. M. Artistic creativity and adaptive regression in third grade children. *Journal of Projective Techniques and Personality Assessment,* 1968, **32,** 53–62.

Rothenberg, A. Homospatial thinking in creativity. *Archives of General Psychiatry,* 1976, **33,** 17–26.

Rothenberg, A. *The emerging goddess: The creative process in art, science and other fields.* Chicago: University of Chicago Press, 1979.

Rothenberg, A., & Sobel, R. S. Creation of literary metaphors as stimulated by superimposed versus separated visual images. *Journal of Mental Imagery,* 1980, **4,** 77–91.

Schachtel, E. G. *Metamorphosis: On the development of affect, perception, attention and memory.* New York: Basic Books, 1959.

Schechter, N., Schmeidler, G. & Staal, M. Dream reports and creative tendencies in students of the arts, sciences, and engineering. *Journal of Consulting Psychology,* 1965, **29,** 415–421.

Schmeidler, G. R. Visual imagery correlated to a measure of creativity. *Journal of Consulting Psychology,* 1965, **29,** 78–80.

Singer, J., & Antrobus, J. S. Daydreaming, imaginal processes, and personality: A normative study. In P. Sheehan (Ed.), *The function and nature of mental imagery.* New York: Academic Press, 1972.

Sobel, R. S., & Rothenberg, A. Artistic creation as stimulated by superimposed versus separated visual images. *Journal of Personality and Social Psychology,* 1980, **39,** 953–961.

Sperry, R. W. Messages from the laboratory. *Engineering and Science.* January 1974.

Spotts, J. V. & Mackler, B. Relationships of field-dependent and field-independent cognitive styles to creative test performance. *Perceptual and Motor Skills,* 1967, **24,** 239–268, Monograph Supplement 2-24.

Stewart, A. *Scoring manual for stages of psychological adaptation to the environment.* Cambridge, Mass.: Boston University, 1977.

Suler, J. R. Primary process thinking and creativity. *Psychological Bulletin.* 1980, **88,** 144–165.

Torrance, E. P. *Torrance tests of creative thinking.* Lexington, Mass.: Personnel Press/Gimand Company, 1966.

Viernstein, M. C., Hogan, R., & McGinn, P. V. Personality correlates of differential verbal and mathematical ability in talented adolescents. *Journal of Youth and Adolescence,* 1977, **6,** 169–178.

Walker, M. R., O'Leary, M. R., Chaney, E. F., & Fauria, T. M. Influence of cognitive style on an incidental memory task. *Perceptual and Motor Skills.* 1979, **48,** 195–198.

Wallas, G. *The art of thought.* New York: Harcourt, 1926.

Welsh, G. *Creativity and intelligence: A personality approach.* Chapel Hill, N.C.: Institute for Research in Social Science, 1975.

Welsh, G. *Manual: Welsh figure preference test.* Palo Alto, Cal.: Consulting Psychologists' Press, 1980.

Winter, D. G. *The power motive.* New York: Free Press, 1973.

Witkin, H. A. Socialization, culture, and ecology in the development of group and sex differences in cognitive style. *Human Development,* 1979, **22,** 358–372.

Witkin, H. A., Dyk, R. B., Faterson, H. F., Goodenough, D. R., & Karp, S. A. *Psychological differentiation.* New York: Wiley, 1962.

Witkin, H. A., & Goodenough, D. R. Field dependence and interpersonal behavior. *Psychological Bulletin,* 1977, **84,** 661–689.

Zenhausern, R. Imagery, cerebral dominance, and style of thinking: A unified field model. *Bulletin of the Psychonomic Society,* 1978, **12,** 381–384.

CHAPTER 12

The Fantasy-Prone Personality: Implications for Understanding Imagery, Hypnosis, and Parapsychological Phenomena

SHERYL C. WILSON AND THEODORE X. BARBER

During recent years we interviewed in depth 27 women whom we had rated as excellent hypnotic subjects and a comparison group of 25 women whom we had rated as nonexcellent (poor, medium, and medium good) hypnotic subjects. These interviews focused on childhood and adult memories, fantasies, and psychic experiences. We discovered that, with one exception, the excellent hypnotic subjects had a profound fantasy life, their fantasies were often "as real as real" (hallucinatory), and their involvement in fantasy played an important role in producing their superb hypnotic performance. Although this study provided a broader understanding of the kinds of life experiences that may underlie the ability to be an excellent hypnotic subject, it also led to a serendipitous finding that has wide implications for all of psychology—it has shown that there exists a small group of individuals (possibly 4% of the population) who fantasize a large part of the time, who typically "see," "hear," "smell," "touch," and fully experience what they fantasize; and who can be labeled *fantasy-prone personalities*. Their extensive and deep involvement in fantasy seems to be their basic characteristic and their other major talents—their ability to hallucinate voluntarily, their superb hypnotic performances, their vivid memories of their life experiences, and their talents as psychics or sensitives—seem to derive from or to grow out of their profound fantasy life. In this chapter we refer to these subjects as *fantasy-prone subjects* or *fantasizers* since this seems to be their most

This research was supported by a grant from Proseminar Institute. We are indebted to Susan Myers and Susan King Cimbrelo for assistance in carrying out this study and to Dr. Steven Jay Lynn and Michael R. Nash for carrying out the supplementary study described in note 3.

fundamental characteristic that serves as the matrix from which their other talents arise.

METHOD

Subjects

To date we have administered our battery of tests and interviews to 52 women subjects, of whom 27 were excellent hypnotic subjects and the remaining 25 were spread more or less evenly throughout the low, medium, and medium high range of hypnotic responsiveness. With two exceptions, these women have attended college or are college graduates. One has an M.D. degree (psychiatrist), one has a Ph.D. degree (psychologist), four are Ph.D. candidates in psychology, 10 have bachelor's or master's degrees in psychology or counseling, 9 have a bachelor's or master's degree in other areas, and 25 are college students. Their ages range from 19 to 63, with a mean of 28.

Procedure

Although there were some variations in the order of test administration, we typically first evaluated the subjects for a type of imagining ability and a type of hypnotic responsiveness by administering the Creative Imagination Scale (Barber & Wilson, 1978–1979; Wilson & Barber, 1978). The Creative Imagination Scale is a standardized instrument that measures equally well (1) responsiveness to guided imagining and (2) responsiveness to hypnotic suggestions of the type that emphasize the imagining–hallucinatory aspects of hypnosis. The scale includes 10 items that ask the subjects to imagine, for example, that: a strong stream of water from a garden hose is pushing against the palm of the outstretched hand (pushing the hand up); novocaine has been injected into the side of the hand (making two fingers numb); they are "hearing" music; they are feeling the sun shining on the right hand (making it hot); they are reexperiencing themselves as children in elementary school; and so on.

After the subjects had been evaluated on the Creative Imagination Scale, they were typically tested on the Barber Suggestibility Scale (Barber, 1969; Barber & Wilson, 1978–1979), which assesses responsiveness to eight suggestions of the type commonly used in hypnosis experiments (hand lock, verbal inhibition, body immobility, posthypnotic response, selective amnesia, etc.).

Typically, subjects who responded in a profound way and passed all or virtually all of the items on the Creative Imagination Scale and the Barber Suggestibility Scale were tested further by administering one or more traditional or nontraditional hypnotic induction procedures (Barber, 1978b, 1979a,b; Barber & Wilson, 1978); a series of suggestions of the type included in the Stanford Hypnotic Susceptibility Scales (Weitzenhoffer & Hilgard, 1959, 1962); and several additional suggestions, for example, to experience extreme happiness, a superconscious state, a mystical state, and a past life. Subjects who did not respond profoundly and pass virtually all of the items on the Creative Imagination Scale and the Barber Suggestibility Scale were considered as nonexcellent hypnotic subjects and were not tested further for hypnotic responsiveness, but they were interviewed as described below.

Our criterion for designating a subject as an excellent hypnotic subject was that she responded profoundly to and passed all or virtually all of the items on the Creative Imagination Scale and the Barber Suggestibility Scale and also responded profoundly to and passed all or virtually all of the suggestions she was given after the hypnotic induction procedure. The excellent hypnotic subjects had thus responded easily, quickly, and fully to a large variety of suggestions, including the classical hypnotic suggestions for anesthesia, rigidity, positive and negative hallucinations, age regression, post-hypnotic behavior, and amnesia.

Interview

After being evaluated on the Creative Imagination Scale and the other hypnosis tests in the manner described above, each subject was interviewed individually on the Memory, Imagining, and Creativity Interview Schedule. This interview, which we constructed for this investigation, was derived in the following way.

First, we became very well acquainted with two women who were in individual short-term psychotherapy with us (one with T. X. B. and the other with S. C. W.) for a phobia and for being overweight, respectively. During the course of the therapy sessions, each of these two subjects had been evaluated on the Creative Imagination Scale and on a variety of hypnotic induction procedures and hypnotic suggestions; they passed all the items on the Creative Imagination Scale and, in addition, responded as superb hypnotic subjects. We also obtained in-depth data pertaining to their early memories, childhood experiences, past and present involvement in daydreaming, imagining and fantasizing, psychic experiences, and many other aspects of their lives. As we became well acquainted with both subjects, we realized that, although they differed markedly in many respects, they had a number of unusual characteristics in common. For instance, they had a profound involvement in fantasy, spent much of their life fantasizing, and typically experienced their fantasies "as real as real" (at hallucinatory intensities). (An operational definition of *fantasy*, in the sense used here, is that the subjects set the theme, and then an imaginative scenario unfolds that has some of the characteristics of a dream and some of a motion picture.[1]) In addition, both subjects had vivid memories of their life experiences, and both had many ostensibly psychic or paranormal experiences.

Next, we conjectured that perhaps other women who score at the top of the Creative Imagination Scale and, in addition, are excellent hypnotic subjects may also have the same characteristics that were shared by the two original subjects we described above. To test this conjecture, we first constructed an interview schedule with 88 questions, of which 73 pertained to those characteristics shared by our two original subjects. These 73 questions covered areas such as early childhood memories, childhood and adult fantasies, empathy and role playing as a child and as an adult, feelings about self, sleep behaviors, hypnagogic imagery, hallucinatory imagery, psychosomatic illnesses, psychic experiences, and out-of-the-body experiences. We also included in our interview 15 additional questions that Josephine R. Hilgard (1970) had found to be correlated with hypnotic susceptibility. These questions pertained to the subject's degree of involvement in such areas as reading, dramatic arts, religion, and sensory experiences and to identification with parents, severity of childhood punishment, and motivation to experience hypnosis. As we continued interviewing additional subjects, we occasionally added new questions to amplify the original questions and, as a result, the Memory, Imagining, and Creativity Interview Schedule now contains 100 items.

The length of time required to interview each subject varied drastically, depending primarily on the extensiveness of her memories and fantasy life. Interviews of subjects who were deeply involved in fantasy required a minimum of 4 hours and, with the two most verbal subjects, as much as 32 hours. The subjects who were low on fantasy could be interviewed in much less time, often in about 2 hours, since they simply answered "no" to many of the questions and thus their responses could not be probed for details.

Origin of Subjects

The 52 subjects who have as of now been evaluated for hypnotic responsiveness (27 excellent and 25 nonexcellent hypnotic subjects) and interviewed in depth on the Memory, Imagining, and Creativity Interview Schedule were recruited as follows:

1.   As stated above, the two original subjects were being treated by us for overweight and a phobia, and both were excellent hypnotic subjects.

2.   We solicited volunteers from the women students of a nearby college for a study in which they were told they would be paid $10, tested for imaginative ability, and interviewed for several hours on memories, imagination, and creativity. One of the 25 women who volunteered for this study passed all the items on the Creative Imagination Scale and was also a superb hypnotic subject who quickly, easily, and profoundly experienced all the classical hypnotic phenomena. This subject was thus considered as part of our excellent hypnotic subject group, and the remaining 24 subjects were part of our comparison group of nonexcellent hypnotic subjects. (It can be noted paranthetically that 1 of the 25 (4%) of the college women whom we

tested was an excellent hypnotic subject, which is in line with other estimates of the percentage of excellent hypnotic subjects in the population.)

3.   Five additional subjects were paraprofessional therapists who were working at Cushing Hospital. When we tested these women, we were very surprised to find that four of the five passed and responded profoundly to all or virtually all of the items on the Creative Imagination Scale, the Barber Suggestibility Scale, the Stanford Hypnotic Susceptibility Scale, and so on. Since the percentage of excellent hypnotic subjects in this group far exceeds the percentage in the general population, we should describe them in more detail. These paraprofessional women were recent college graduates who wanted to help people and were willing to work, with relatively little monetary compensation, at a very difficult job assisting geriatric patients in a state hospital. Some of the geriatric patients (average age 81, with a range of 68–103) were dying; most were medically ill; and the great majority were also suffering from senile dementia, schizophrenia, or mental retardation. The paraprofessional therapists' approach to these patients consisted of various combinations of talking with them; giving positive suggestions and encouragement; transmitting friendship, caring, and empathy; and performing "therapeutic touch" (Krieger, 1979) or "laying-on-of-hands" (Kastenbaum et al. 1981; Wilson et al., 1982). As mentioned above, four of the women in this group were included among our excellent hypnotic subjects, and the one remaining good but not excellent hypnotic subject was included in our comparison group.

4.   Five additional excellent hypnotic subjects came from our list of individuals who had participated in earlier studies conducted by us or our associates and who were still available to be interviewed in this study. In the previous studies they had performed at the top of the Creative Imagination Scale and had also responded as superb hypnotic subjects on a variety of hypnosis measures.

5.   Fifteen excellent hypnotic subjects were obtained from the women participants in the hypnosis workshops that we conducted during recent years. During the workshops, we carefully observed the responses of the women participants to the items of the Creative Imagination Scale and to the large variety of hypnotic suggestions administered. Judging from their observable responses and also from their subsequent testimony, these 15 women clearly responded profoundly to the Creative Imagination Scale and to the classical hypnotic suggestions and thus were rated as excellent hypnotic subjects.

RESULTS

The findings supported our conjecture that other women who score extremely high on the Creative Imagination Scale and who, in addition, are excellent hypnotic subjects might also share the unusual characteristics that we observed in our original two subjects. Although our 27 excellent hypnotic subjects differed markedly in personality—for example, some were extraverted and others introverted, some were high and others low on self-esteem—26 of the 27 shared a series of interrelated characteristics, a syndrome or personality type that we are labeling as the *fantasy-prone personality*.

Before we describe the many facets of this syndrome, we should emphasize that of the 27 excellent hypnotic subjects, 26 could be accurately characterized as fantasy-prone personalities or fantasizers. One of the excellent hypnotic subjects and all 25 of the nonexcellent hypnotic subjects differed from the fantasizers in their answers to the interview questions on fantasy (and also to the other questions regarding memories, psychic experiences, etc.) and thus could not be labeled as fantasy-prone personalities. We do not attempt to analyze in this limited space why one of the excellent hypnotic subjects differed from the others in that she was not especially involved in fantasy. This anomalous subject is important, however, in leading to a *qualified* conclusion, namely, that a very large percentage of, *but not all,* women excellent hypnotic subjects appear to be fantasy-prone personalities.

We defer for a more lengthy publication discussion of the one anomalous subject and present here the data for the 26 excellent hypnotic subjects who were also very high on fantasy (and related characteristics) and the data for the 25 subjects in the comparison group who were neither excellent hypnotic subjects nor especially high on fantasy.

Shared Characteristics During Childhood

Fantasy

As children, the 26 fantasy-prone subjects lived in a make-believe world much or most of the time. All who played with dolls and toy animals (80%) believed that these objects were alive, had feelings, and had unique personalities. Consequently, they consistently treated their dolls and stuffed animals with respect and consideration. For instance, a number of the fantasizers informed us that they slept each night with a different doll or stuffed animal so that none would have hurt feelings. Also, when they were not playing with them, they would leave them in a comfortable position such as lying in bed or sitting in a chair so that they could look out the window. If they were at all careless with or inadvertently "hurt" a doll or stuffed animal, they would apologize. They also felt sorry for their dolls and toy animals when they left them home alone because they thought they would feel lonely.

The extent to which dolls and stuffed animals seemed to be alive and to have their own personalities is illustrated by the following statement made by one of our fantasizers: "It [playing with dolls] would be its own world. They'd have their own problems, and things would come up that I was not aware of. They'd have their own things to say and their own feelings."

A small number of the fantasizers did not play with dolls for specific reasons: one was cruelly teased by an older brother if she played with dolls, two had real babies to look after, one came from a very poor family that simply could not afford any toys, and one had several brothers with whom she played and never considered owning a doll. All of the remaining fantasizers played with dolls and believed them to be alive. In fact, some suffered a severe trauma when a worn-out doll or stuffed animal that, to them, was a dear old friend and fully alive, was discarded in the trash or left behind when the family moved.

Many of the 25 subjects in the comparison group also *pretended* their dolls or stuffed animals were alive; however, with three exceptions, they did so only when they were playing with them. Although they made believe that the dolls and toy animals had personalities and said and did specific things, the make-believe play was always confined to a specific period and the toys did not seem to have an independent life.

When they were children, almost all of the fantasizers believed in fairies, leprechauns, elves, guardian angels, and other such beings. The strength of these beliefs is illustrated by one subject's statement that, when she was finally convinced that Santa Claus was a fabrication, she could not understand why adults had tried to "make up" such a person when there were so many real beings around such as tree spirits and fairies. The strength of the fantasy-prone subjects' beliefs in such beings probably originates in their conviction that they have seen, heard, or even played with them. Many saw no more than "little legs disappearing around corners." However, for some, encounters with such beings were vivid and "as real as real"; for instance, one told us how as a child she would spend hours watching in fascination the little people who lived in her grandmother's cactus garden that adults kept insisting were not there. With few exceptions, their belief in elves, leprechauns, fairies, guardian angels, tree spirits, and other such creatures did not terminate during childhood; as adults, they either still believe in them or are not absolutely sure that they really do not exist.

More than half of the fantasizers (58%), as compared to 8% in the comparison group, spent a large part of their childhood playing and interacting with imaginary companions (fantasized people or animals); they report having clearly seen, heard, and felt them in the same way that they perceived living people and animals. Those who, as children, were most isolated from other children and most lonely tended to have not just one, but rather a whole world of imaginary companions. For instance, one subject had a score of imaginary animals and another had two dozen imaginary children with whom she played continually.

Sometimes imaginary companions served the same functions as dolls or stuffed animals. For instance, during early childhood one subject was frequently tied to a tree without any toys. She remembers building mud houses and then populating them with (imaginary) little people who seemed alive with feelings and unique personalities. She saw, heard, experienced, and played with them the way other children played with actual dolls.

Another subject had a stuffed rabbit who she says "told me many wise things and taught me a lot." She reports that he also introduced her to a whole world of imaginary animals. However, when her stuffed rabbit was left behind in a hotel room, her world of imaginary animals also vanished.

The fantasizers typically reported that when they were children (and also as adults) they would become one of the characters in a book they were reading; they would see, hear, feel, and experience the character's life. Sometimes characters from these books became imaginary companions. One subject, for example, told us that while reading *Peter Pan* she totally identified herself with Wendy and "lived" all the adventures with Peter and the other children. After completing the book, she continued having exciting adventures daily (as Wendy) with Peter and the other children; they became her imaginary companions and, she says, they were as real as real children.

A small number of the fantasizers had either God or Jesus as an imaginary companion. Since these subjects were from broken homes or were abused children, their personal relationship with God or Jesus can be viewed as serving important needs. They had created an ideal companion who gave them unconditional love, approval, support, and advice in a world that otherwise was unstable, unsupportive, critical, and cruel.

With only two exceptions, the fantasy-prone subjects would pretend during childhood that they were someone else such as an orphan, a princess, an animal, a bird, or a fairytale character such as Cinderella or Snow White. They became so absorbed in these roles that they felt they actually became the character they were pretending to be. Their pretending often extended well beyond any delimited play period and continued into their daily life. For instance, one subject felt, not that she was pretending to be a bird, but that she was a bird pretending to be a girl. Similarly, another subject who continually pretended to be a princess told us that she actually felt that *she was a princess pretending to be an ordinary child* doing things ordinary children do, such as going to school, riding a bike, and so on. She saw her house as a castle complete with a real moat and drawbridge, and she told the children at her school that she was a princess and that she lived in a castle with a moat.

Subjects in our comparison group also at times pretended to be various characters. However, their pretending was confined to a limited period. It usually occurred in the context of a group play situation with other children in which each child pretended to be someone else. All our comparison subjects retained awareness of their true identity when they were pretending; none indicated that they became totally absorbed in the part.

Coping with Fantasy

Although their very realistic childhood pretending and fantasizing caused problems for the fantasy-prone subjects, they all developed methods for coping. For instance, one told us how she began as a 7- or 8-year-old child to differentiate her fantasy from what was "out there" in the real world by asking people whether they also were perceiving what she was perceiving. All the fantasizers learned, during early or late childhood or early adolescence, to be very secretive about their pretending and their fantasies. The following is an example of how they learned to be secretive. The "princess" whom we mentioned earlier was accused of lying by her school friends when she brought them to see her fantasied castle (actually her middle-class home). She was shocked that they could not see the castle since it was real to her. Her secretiveness derives from that moment; henceforth, she never tried to share her fantasies and pretending with friends. However, she does share this "secret" aspect of her life with strangers who cannot check the validity of what she says. In fact, when talking to strangers, she becomes so involved in her pretending and fantasies that she believes what she is saying, and the strangers never seem to doubt the validity of what she tells them.

The more the subjects become immersed in fantasy, the less they are aware of their surroundings. The following example illustrates the potential dangers involved in becoming "lost" in fantasy and how the fantasizers learn to maintain a safe level of awareness. One of the fantasy-prone subjects described for us a time when she was 11 years old and was "lost" in a fantasy in which she was walking with her imaginary pet lamb through an imaginary meadow. As she was concentrating on stepping with deliberately high steps through the tall grass, she was startled out of her fantasy by the sounds of automobile horns. She was shocked to find herself surrounded by heavy traffic in the middle of a busy city street. She recalls how she instantly decided always to maintain some awareness of her surroundings whenever she was in any potentially dangerous situation. From that moment on she says she has exerted effort to follow that policy and has not found herself in such a dangerous situation again.

Factors Leading to Fantasy Proneness

Most, if not all, children in our culture at some time in their lives play make-believe games and are exposed to fantasy stories and fairytales. However, it seems that, for most children, involvement in fantasy is limited in time and place and becomes minimal or nonexistent as they progress through adolescence and become adults. The subjects in the fantasy-prone group, but not in the comparison group, seem to have become extremely involved in fantasy from a very early age, and they have continued this intense involvement into their adult life. This raises the question: How did they become, and why did they remain, so involved in fantasy?

From careful study of their early lives, four patterns seemed to emerge: (1) most were encouraged to fantasize by significant adults; (2) some fantasized because they were isolated and lonely; (3) some fantasized in order to escape from a bad environment; and (4) a few had a special life situation that led to an extensive involvement in fantasy. Most of the fantasy-prone subjects had two or more of these patterns in their lives. Let us look more closely at each pattern in turn.

1.   At least 70% of the fantasizers recall being encouraged to fantasize by a significant adult. This adult was either a parent, a grandparent, an aunt, an uncle, a friend's mother, a neighbor, a librarian, or a teacher. The adult directly encouraged the child to fantasize by one or more of the following means: (a) the adult read to the child or told the child fairytales or fantasy stories; (b) the adult praised the child for her make-believe and her fantasies; and (c) the adult treated the child's dolls and stuffed animals as if they were alive, thus encouraging the child to believe they were alive. For example, the adult might pick up the child's doll Mary and begin conversing with the doll in the following manner, "How are you feeling today, Mary? (Pause.) That's too bad. Maybe Janie (the child) can help you feel happier."

2.   Sixteen of the fantasizers, in contrast to only one subject in the comparison group, perceived themselves as having been very lonely and isolated as children. These fantasizers felt they became deeply involved in fantasy to overcome their isolation and saw it as providing companionship and entertainment. In fact, 9 of these 16 "overcame" their isolation by creating imaginary companions.

3.   Nine of the fantasizers (and none of the subjects in the comparison group) reported that they had had a difficult or stressful early life. Their reports include: (a) serious physical abuse from a parent, a foster parent, or an older sibling (at times necessitating medical treatment), (b) a mother who had severe emotional problems, (c) a mother who deserted the family, (d) unstable living conditions such as living with various relatives and at several foster homes, and (e) various combinations or all of the above. All nine of the subjects in this group told us that they used fantasy to escape from their surroundings. Surprisingly, most of these had a secret hiding place (e.g., in a nearby meadow or behind the sofa) where they would habitually "hide" in order to be undisturbed while they lived an entirely different life in fantasy.

4.   At least nine fantasy-prone subjects had a special life situation that contributed to an extreme involvement in fantasy. By the time they were 2, 3, or 4 years of age, all nine subjects had begun intensive studies in piano, ballet, dramatic acting, or art; and six of the nine had begun studying two or more of these areas intensively. They utilized fantasy when carrying out these activities that they typically continued for 12 or more years. (Although several other fantasizers and several subjects in the comparison group also studied piano, ballet, dramatics, or art, they did *not* begin their studies at such an early, and thus highly impressionable, age.) Examples of how early practice in these areas apparently contributed to fantasy development are as follows. One subject who began serious piano lessons when she was 4

years old recalls practicing about 3 hours each day. She states that, while she was practicing, she would be "lost" in fantasy so that, for example, she was no longer sitting in a hot city apartment but was out running on the beach with other children. Another subject who began ballet at 2½ years (and piano and dramatics at 4 years) told us that when practicing ballet at home she would fantasize hearing the music that was played during her ballet classes and would time her dance steps to the (hallucinated) music.

Shared Characteristics as Adults

Extensive and Vivid Fantasy

Now that they are adults, the extensiveness and vividness of their fantasy has not significantly decreased. From a very young age and continuing into the present, they typically spend a large part of their time fantasizing. They view imagining or fantasizing as central to their lives. In fact, they say they practically live their lives in fantasy.

Each subject has a secret fantasy life that she has typically revealed to no one. It can be said that somewhere in the transition from childhood to adulthood they became "closet fantasizers." Their extensive, vivid fantasizing has become their carefully guarded secret—typically even their husbands, children, and closest friends are unaware of it!

When asked to estimate what percent of their waking day they spend fantasizing, 92% of the fantasy-prone subjects (and none of the subjects in the comparison group) estimated more than 50% of the time. Some stated that they are fantasizing throughout the day since they usually continue fantasizing without interruption while they are engaged in other activities or interacting with others. These subjects often found it easier to estimate the amount of time they did *not* fantasize. One subject, for example, said she does not allow herself to fantasize while driving or when carrying out other tasks requiring concentration but otherwise she fantasizes practically all the time.

The contents of their fantasies as adults are varied and creative. The following are brief examples of some of the kinds of fantasies they experience in specific situations:

1.   During a social conversation, while they are speaking or listening to another speak, they typically "see," "hear," "smell," and "feel" what is being described. When they become bored at a social gathering, they might escape from the boring situation by imagining that the people are clowns or by fantasizing themselves alone with a lover on an exotic tropical island.

2.   Specific stimuli set off correlated fantasies. When they hear the word "Egypt," they might imagine in detail their life as the wife of a pharaoh. When they are taking a shower, the shower might become a waterfall in the Caribbean. When they are watching a bird or looking at a tree, they may suddenly lose the sense of their body and feel they are the bird or the tree.

3.   While performing routine tasks at home or at work, they tend to fantasize that they are doing something else, or are somewhere else. For instance, while washing dishes a fantasizer might imagine that she is living an entirely different life in another country or on another planet, or while dressing for work she might fantasize an involved love affair with her boss.

4.   When they have free time, they may sit down or lie down and fantasize for 15 minutes, or $\frac{1}{2}$ hour, or 1 or 2 hours. Even though they fantasize throughout much of the day, they may also set aside a special time and place solely for fantasizing. Also, when they are alone for a weekend, they might spend the entire weekend in fantasy.

5.   Before falling asleep at night, they are apt to fantasize a complete scenario that they describe as better than most television shows or motion pictures. Almost every night, two of our subjects fantasize a new and complete fairy-tale-like story involving animated animals, trees, flowers, etc. and other objects that talk, interact, and have adventures.

6.   If they are doing something unpleasant, they may reward themselves with a sexual fantasy. In fact, almost all of the fantasy-prone subjects have vivid sexual fantasies that they experience "as real as real" with all the sights, sounds, smells, emotions, feelings, and physical sensations. The sexual fantasies are so realistic that 75% of the fantasizers report that they have had orgasms produced *solely* by sexual fantasies. (This surprising occurrence was also reported by one subject in the comparison group.) Since a fantasized lover can be far more ideal than most living men, the fantasizers often obtain greater satisfaction and enjoyment from these fantasized sexual relationships than from actual sexual relationships. (The comparison subjects also report sexual fantasies, but with the exception of one subject, they are much more limited and not as "real as real.")

These subjects view imagining or fantasizing as a necessary and integral part of their lives. It is as necessary to them as sleeping and eating. We asked what it would be like for them if they were never able to imagine or fantasize again (even though they still would be able to think, dream, and plan for the future). All found this question extremely distressing; they just could not imagine life without fantasizing. The typical initial reaction to this question was an expression of disbelief that they were being asked to consider such a dreadful prospect. This usually was followed by an expression of doubt as to whether they could continue living more than a few hours without fantasizing. Many compared the loss of fantasy to the loss of one or more of the senses, especially vision—it would be like going blind. All indicated that if they did continue living without imagining or fantasizing, they would not be the same person; they would be basically different. Typical replies were: "I would have no purpose, I wouldn't be me—like not being able to see"; "I'd be dead or a robot"; "Forget it! Take away my food or clothes. Fantasizing is far more important to me than any of these. Without fantasy, I'd be someone I don't even like"; and "I don't know if I could survive.

It's a part of me, I've learned to rely on it so much." When asked what imagining or fantasy means to her, our most verbal subject blurted out, "It's being anything you can be, could be, or are. It's possibilities made possible. It's soaring, thrilling, living. Why's to say what's happening right now is reality? Fantasy is your own private world. You set the stage. You make it. It's being godlike. Anything you believe, if you believe it, it's true."

In sharp contrast to the fantasizers' emotional replies to the question were the calm reactions of subjects in the comparison group. They were not at all shocked when they were asked what it would be like for them if they were never able to imagine or fantasize again. They typically responded either that it would not matter or that it might be somewhat boring but it would probably be a good thing since they would waste less time and get more done.

Hallucinatory Intensities of Fantasies

All the fantasy-prone subjects spend much time fantasizing and consider fantasy very important in their lives. Sixty-five percent of the fantasizers typically experience their fantasies "as real as real" (as hallucinatory) *in all sense modalities*. They see imagined sights equally well with their eyes opened or closed. Also, imagined aromas are sensed, imagined sounds are heard, and imagined tactile sensations are felt as convincingly as those produced by actual stimuli. Other imagined sensations are equally "real" and often accompany the visual, olfactory, auditory, and tactile (hallucinated) sensations. Their memories, which we describe later in this chapter, are also hallucinatory. When they recall an event, they are able to see, hear, and feel it again in much the same way as they did originally; thus they are able to reexperience it and relive it again. In addition, their fantasies and memories typically seem to be located outside in the environment. For example, when we ask them either to remember or imagine a dog, they typically see it run into the room, feel it lick their face, and so on. Furthermore, they react to their memories and fantasies with feelings and emotions that would be appropriate if what they were remembering and fantasizing were actually occurring in the present space and time.

The fantasies of these subjects, which commonly attain hallucinatory intensities whether their eyes are open or closed, can perhaps best be understood by comparing them to an engrossing motion picture. In fact, some of these subjects describe their fantasies as being like a really good movie, except better because they are *in* the movie. In the same way as a good movie, the fantasy can be fun and exciting and can be experienced as vividly and realistically as any other aspect of life. They can experience anything in fantasy—people can be seen and heard to speak; food can be smelled and tasted; sensations such as touch, heat, and cold can be felt; and emotions such as fright and joy can be experienced—and, *when immersed in fantasy,* they do not ask whether their experiences are real.

Sixty-five percent of the fantasy-prone subjects fit the above description—

with their eyes open, they commonly experience fantasies of hallucinatory intensity in all sense modalities. When their eyes are open, the other 35% of the fantasy-prone subjects also commonly experience fantasies of hallucinatory intensity in all senses except vision—they hear imagined sounds, smell imagined aromas, taste imagined food, and so forth—but the visual component of the fantasy is located either in the "mind's eye," where it can be "vivid," or in the external environment, where it is more vague and "ghostlike" and not "as real as real." To experience their fantasies at hallucinatory intensities ("as real as real") in all sense modalities, including visually, these subjects must fantasize with their eyes closed. The fantasies of these subjects can perhaps best be understood by comparing them to other people's most vivid dreams. In the same way as others are totally involved in and participating in their vivid dreams, so are these fantasizers involved and participating in their fantasies. While they are fantasizing, they experience imagined people and events as "real" in somewhat the same way as sleeping individuals accept the events in their vivid dreams as "real."

It should be noted that fantasy becomes hallucinatory *in all sense modalities* (for about 35% of the subjects with their eyes closed and for the other 65% with their eyes closed or open) when they are absorbed and involved in their fantasy to such an extent that they are not concerned about anything else and they lose either partial or complete awareness of time and place. With the possible exception of some sexual fantasies, subjects in the comparison group did *not* have these hallucinatory experiences because they were too involved in reality to become immersed in fantasy to this degree.

For all the fantasy-prone subjects, it can be said that they live another life when they fantasize because they create for themselves another world that is at least as real to them as the ordinary world. Several told us spontaneously that, compared with their fantasy, reality becomes a pale copy. They sometimes feel that their fantasy world is real and that the actual world is a fantasy. In fact, their fantasies are typically so realistic that 85% of the fantasizers (as contrasted to 24% of the subjects in the comparison group) stated that they tend to confuse their *memories* of their fantasies with their *memories* of actual events. For instance, when one subject fantasizes interactions with her boyfriend while he is away, her fantasies are so realistic that later she has difficulty determining which of her remembered interactions with him actually occurred and which were fantasy.

Many of our fantasy-prone subjects use fantasy as a coping device. Thus they never need to be bored, feel miserable, or feel stuck in an unbearable life situation because they can always escape into fantasy. In fantasy they can be free, spontaneous, and creative since fantasy does not have the same rules as the nonfantasy world. In fantasy they can do anything—experience a previous lifetime, experience their own birth, go off into the future, go off into space, and so on.

All the fantasy-prone subjects (and none of the comparison subjects) state that their fantasies have an involuntary, automatic, or self-propelling quality.

It appears that their fantasies are produced automatically in response to their conscious and unconscious thoughts and feelings. As they describe it, they "set the stage," that is, they begin with certain characters, settings, or themes, and then sit back and watch the drama unfold.

Although the self-propelling quality of their fantasies can be very useful and entertaining for the fantasizers (e.g., they never need to be bored), the same involuntary quality can present problems. For instance, 70% of the fantasizers (especially those whose fantasies are associated with visual hallucinatory imagery when their eyes are open) have difficulty when driving. They might imagine or "see" in front of them on the road whatever they may be expecting. For example, if any of these subjects happens to think to herself while driving, "I better be careful because a child or animal might dart into the street," then she is very apt to see an imaginary child or animal run into the street. To block their fantasies while driving, they typically force themselves to concentrate on the mechanics of driving and to carry on a continuous verbal monologue such as "I'm now approaching an intersection, there's a lot of traffic, slow down, be ready to stop, and so on." Some of the fantasizers also reported other strategies that they feel help to make their driving safer; for instance, three subjects picture a protective white light around the car and another imagines four small angels, one on each corner of her car, that help her to focus on driving.

Pretending to Be Someone Else

A characteristic shared by 64% of the fantasy-prone subjects (and by 16% in the comparison group) is that as adults they still occasionally pretend to be someone else just as they did when they were children. While they are pretending, they become totally absorbed in the character and tend to lose awareness of their real identity.

Most are as secretive about their pretending to be someone else as they are about other aspects of their fantasy proneness. However, some do share their pretend selves with select others. One shares her pretending with her husband, who she says finds his life more interesting since he never knows who he is coming home to—Lady Godiva, a gypsy, a professional business woman, a teenager, or other. Six of the fantasy-prone subjects enjoy pretending they are someone else when they are with strangers. For instance, while riding on a bus just the day before the interview, one of our subjects who has lived in New York all her life introduced herself as an Eskimo to the person sitting next to her and then proceeded to tell the intrigued stranger all about her (fantasized) life in Alaska.

Vivid Sensory Experiences Since Childhood

An impressive shared characteristic of the fantasy-prone subjects is an intense, profound involvement in sensory experiences *since early childhood*. Twenty-one of the 22 fantasizers who were asked, in sharp contrast to only one of the 11 comparison subjects asked, say that, since a very young age, they have been acutely aware of and have focused on sensory experiences because they found them then and still find them now innately pleasurable and enjoyable.

Typical responses by the 21 fantasizers and one comparison subject who stated that they were highly aware of sensory experiences during childhood (as well as now) are as follows:

> I loved touch best and smell next best—the feel of my grandmother's skin, soft but wrinkled, the smell of grandpa's pipe and the perfume on a woman who was a friend of mother's, the smell of Sunday morning's roast in the oven, outside after the rain, the woods in autumn, smelling the crushed leaves and hearing them too, my soft velvet dress when I was 6, running in the rain, cold drops, shivering. . . .

> [On the family farm] I loved running grain through my fingers . . . the smell of the earth . . . the fresh cut grass . . . touching ducks and feeling their smoothness. . . .

Some of the fantasy-prone subjects spontaneously reported special events during their childhood that appeared to have led to a heightened awareness of sensory stimuli. A characteristic report was from a subject who said that, during early childhood, she was given a huge book containing many pieces of fabrics that she never tried of paging through, looking at the colors, and feeling each piece of material. Another fantasizer told us she clearly recalls a time before she began kindergarten when she was outside on a warm summer day "enjoying the warmth of the sun, the smell and feel of the grass and flowers . . . the beauty of it all." She reports that she suddenly realized that "the reason we have bodies is so we can enjoy feeling, smelling, hearing, and so on." From that moment on she says she purposely tried to experience as much as possible and she also tried to focus on her experiences so that she could always remember what they felt like. She also described for us how, as a child, she created her own "games" that aimed to sharpen her senses; for example, she would spend many hours walking around her house and yard with her eyes closed in order to perfect her visual memory, and she would focus on the unique way each object felt when she touched it so that later, when her eyes were closed, she could identify objects solely by touch.

Another fantasy-prone subject told us how by the age of 4 years she had become acutely sensitive to sensory stimuli, especially visual. When she was 4, she recalls how surprised her parents were when they saw her drawing of ice skaters. She had included, from memory, numerous details such as scratch marks on the ice and the skaters' scarves flying in the wind. Now as an adult she paints realistic portraits by memory—her subjects do not have to "sit" for her.

As we discuss in the next section of this chapter, the fantasy-prone subjects have especially vivid memories of their childhood; consequently, it is possible that they report more acute sensory experiences in their early life not because they had more of these kinds of experiences, but simply because they remember them better. Although we are sensitive to this possibility, we do not accept it at the present time because (1) the subjects who told us that they began focusing on sensory experiences in early childhood still clearly focus on such experiences as adults and (2) those who denied childhood involvement in sensory experiences did so in a firm way that gave every indication that they simply did not have then (and they do not have now) any special involvement in such experiences.

Vivid Personal Memories

Our data show that there is a very close relationship (and possibly an identity when the "noise" in the data is removed) between the ability to fantasize at hallucinatory intensities and the ability to relive vividly personal experiences while recalling them, that is, to recall in a hallucinatory way. A striking characteristic shared by 96% of the fantasy-prone subjects (in contrast to 4% in the comparison group) is their unusually vivid personal memories. Their memories appear to be reinstatements of original experiences; when they are asked to recall a past experience, they do not merely remember it, they also seem to reexperience and relive it. In other words, their personal memories appear to be hallucinatory in that they seem again to see, hear, taste, smell, and feel the events that they are recalling and to reexperience the emotions that they felt in the original situation. Thus, when they are recalling a past experience, they typically bring it into the present space and time. In contrast, when subjects in the comparison group are recalling a previous experience, they are remembering back and the experience is still where it was—in the past, not in the present.

A surprising aspect of their vivid personal memories is that they seem to have little childhood amnesia. Of the 26 fantasizers, 24 (and only 3 subjects in the comparison group) report many vivid memories of events that occurred prior to their third birthday. Of these, 8 report clear memories of events that occurred on or before their first birthday.

When they try to remember their very early life, they appear to reexperience the thoughts, emotions, and feelings, including the feeling of being in their baby body, in the same way they did originally. For example, when one of our subjects was describing her memory of her first birthday, she vividly reexperienced her father singing "Happy Birthday," her mother standing behind her encouraging her to try to blow out the candle, and her sister sitting next to her. She could feel herself sitting in her high chair and could feel herself in her body as it was at that time ("with my big, fat tummy"). Immediately following this vivid recall, she cried out to us, "Life was wonderful back them.'"[2]

In addition to developing vivid memories for personal experiences, two of the fantasizers, apparently as a result of unusual circumstances in their early lives, also developed very superior auditory memories for spoken material. By age 4 one of the fantasy-prone subjects appeared to read all her children's books perfectly out loud from cover to cover. However, she could not read at all. She would look at each page of the book and rehear word for word the voice of the adult who originally read it to her. She retained this exceptional auditory eidetic imagery throughout her life and found it very useful. For instance, in her art history courses, she took no notes and did not study at all, yet she obtained perfect examination scores. The examinations consisted of presentations of art slides while the students wrote down everything they knew about each slide. When she saw a slide, she would "hear" again the professor in class presenting the information about it; all she had to do was write down what she "heard" word for word.

Along similar lines, another subject stated that she replays entire conversations and lectures in her mind and hears both what she heard originally and also the words and sentences to which she did not originally attend. She perfected this talent, which she calls her "echo box," because her mother, who had emotional problems, was always "hollering" at her. She would become very upset when her mother was yelling at her, so she learned to remain completely detached at that time by not really attending to what her mother was saying. Later, she would "rerun" everything that had been said through her private "echo box" and deal with it in fantasy by imaginatively transforming it into a more acceptable encounter.

In apparent contradiction to their otherwise vivid personal memories, a small number of the fantasizers have amnesia for certain times and events in their lives. They recognize that these amnesiac periods are related to painful, traumatic happenings. In the same way as other individuals who have pockets of amnesia in their personal memories, there is a conscious or unconscious motivation not to remember the material; however, with the fantasy-prone subjects the motivation not to recall unpleasant events can become exceptionally strong. As stated above, when they recall a previous experience, they tend to relive the experience and to feel the associated emotions as if they are occurring in the present. Consequently, when they begin to recall a painful or traumatic experience, they begin to reinstate the pain or trauma at its original intensity and there is thus an exceedingly strong motivation to avoid further pain or trauma by avoiding further recall.

Physical Effects Associated with Vivid Fantasies and Memories

A striking characteristic shared by all but two of the fantasy-prone subjects is that their vivid fantasies and memories are at times associated with physical concomitants. For instance, as we described earlier in this chapter, their realistic sexual fantasies can give rise to an orgasm. Also, 15 spontaneously reported that they become ill whenever they see violence on television or in the movies. They cannot let themselves fantasize anything with violence because they are certain that they will become sick. Although we did not directly ask this in the interview, 17 told us that imagined heat and cold affect them in the same way as actual heat and cold. A typical report was given by the subject who described how she was freezing as she sat bundled up in a blanket in a warm living room while she was watching Dr. Zhivago in Siberia on television. [Hilgard (1979) reported similar reactions to those "Dr. Zhivago" by good hypnotic subjects who were presumably fantasizers.]

Nineteen of the fantasizers, in sharp contrast to only two subjects from the comparison group, reported having illnesses or physical symptoms that seemed to have been directly related to their thoughts, fantasies, or memories. For instance, most said they had experienced quite frequently throughout their lives something such as the following: becoming physically ill when they thought (incorrectly) that they had eaten spoiled food or developing an uncomfortable and continuous itch when they (incorrectly) believed that they had been contaminated with lice. An illustrative report was given by a subject who told us about the time she recaptured a neighboring child's pet frog that had escaped, remembered that she had been told that frogs cause warts, and then developed a wart on her hand that was highly resistant to treatment. Another fantasy-prone subject told how she literally fainted or "passed out" when she was forced to make an "impossible" decision since whatever she decided would arouse the wrath of one or the other of her divorced parents. Another who has always had perfect teeth told us how she developed severe and increasing pain in her teeth and gums during the six months between teeth cleaning appointments with a dentist who told her, "You have the mouth of a 7- or 8-year old. That's when teeth begin to decay." Thus she believed that her teeth were decaying, and she was in pain until her next dental appointment, when she was told her teeth again were in perfect condition. The pain vanished when she received the good news. A fourth subject related how she initially was unable to breast-feed her second child. She nursed her firstborn, a daughter, with no difficulty and planned to nurse the second also. However, her second child, a boy, looked so much like his father, from whom she had a conflictual separation, that she produced no milk until a wise physician told her, "You know he is not his father. He is a separate individual." From that moment on she was able to breast-feed the baby.

A very surprising number of fantasizers—13 of 22 (60%) of those asked—reported that they have had a false pregnancy (pseudocyesis) at least once. They believed that they were pregnant, and they had many of the symptoms. In addition to amenorrhea (stoppage of menstruation), they typically experienced at least four of the following: breast changes, abdominal enlargement, morning sickness, cravings, and "fetal" movements. Two of the subjects went for abortions, following which they were told that no fetus had been found. All of the other false pregnancies terminated quickly when negative results were received from pregnancy tests. (In the comparison group, 4 of the 25 subjects (16%) had failed to menstruate and believed they were pregnant; 3 of these stated that they experienced only one of the symptoms mentioned above, namely, nausea or morning sickness. The fourth comparison subject, however, gave a more dramatic report, which more closely resembled those given by the 13 fantasizers, stating that she had experienced nausea, breast changes, fatigue, and lower-back pain.)

Independently from our study, five subjects from the fantasy-prone group were involved in clinical or experimental biofeedback. All five stated that those who were to administer the biofeedback to them were consistently impressed by their talent, manifested *prior* to the biofeedback training, for controlling psychophysiological processes, such as speeding up and slowing down heart rate, raising and lowering blood pressure, or increasing and decreasing skin temperature.

Telepathy, Precognition, and Other Psychic Experiences

Ninety-two percent of the fantasy-prone subjects see themselves as psychic or sensitive and report numerous telepathic and precognitive experiences. (Sixteen percent of the subjects in the comparison group also reported some experiences of this type.)

The fantasizers typically state that (by some kind of extrasensory perception) they often know what is happening at a specific moment in the life of a friend or a person they are close to. Similarly, they claim that they often know what a friend is thinking or feeling when he or she is many miles away. They also claim that they very often feel (in an extrasensory way) that a certain person is about to call them on the telephone, and the feeling is confirmed within a minute or two. Although the contents of their premonitions vary widely, all but two of the fantasizers claim precognitive experiences. For example, several are certain that they correctly predicted serious illnesses and deaths of family members, close friends, or relatives (often living a long distance away); two assert that they always know beforehand exactly where they will find a parking place in large, crowded parking lots; and one seriously claims to have consistently predicted all the Kentucky Derby winners for the past 10 years (but has not made money on her precognitions because that is an inappropriate way to use her "gift"). The same fantasy-prone subjects also report precognitive dreams. In a typical report of this type a subject reported dreaming that a Christlike person told her that she would soon be kidnapped and explained to her what to do during the kidnapping so that she would not be harmed. She soon afterward was kidnapped (actually abducted for sexual purposes), literally followed the instructions from the dream, and was released without molestation or harm.

Almost all of the fantasizers report other kinds of psychic experiences or psychic talents that differ from subject to subject. For instance, each of the following is reported by one or two subjects: conducting impressive psychic readings, past life readings or readings by psychometry; entering a mediumistic trance; seeing auras around people; feeling each day the presence of spirits; "seeing" people's thoughts in images above their heads; believing that they have a powerful influence on electrical appliances (fuses blow, television sets "go crazy," etc.); and feeling a dowsing rod being pulled down strongly (whenever there is hidden underground water beneath them) regardless of how hard they try to hold it up.

Out-of-the-Body Experiences

The overwhelming majority of subjects (88%) in the fantasy-prone group, as contrasted to few (8%) in the comparison group, report realistic out-of-the-body experiences. Many of the fantasizers report having out-of-the-body experiences while they are "meditating." One subject claims that she has had realistic out-of-the-body experiences almost every day *as far back as she can remember,* usually during the time she sets aside for fantasy. When we asked her to tell us what these experiences are like for her, she unhesitatingly described them as "a weightless, floating sensation. But it's not exactly floating because there's nothing holding me up. It's like a mixing with the air. I have the feeling I could go any speed because there's no holding back of matter. I'm part of space, not a foreign object in space." She reports that, at the beginning of the out-of-the-body experience, she can look back and see her body if she wants to, but she usually doesn't pay attention to it. She usually goes off into space and feels as if she "becomes" space. She was surprised when she saw the motion picture on space travel, *2001,* because what she sees during her out-of-the-body or "astral travel" experiences resembles the movie. She knows that people study, train, or practice to have out-of-the-body experiences, but she doubts that they can attain it in that way. She strongly believes that such experiences must occur naturally. (Another fantasizer also claims to have had "as real as real" out-of-the-body experiences *since early childhood.)*

Although a substantial proportion of out-of-the-body experiences occur during periods of fantasy or "meditation," others occur during dreams or dreamlike states. For instance, three of the fantasy-prone subjects are convinced that they have out-of-the-body or astral travel experiences very often during their dreams; that is, they travel to other places or other times while their physical body lies sleeping. One says that she sometimes awakens and finds herself half in and half out of her body. She states that during her astral travels she typically goes to sick individuals and heals them. She feels she has received external validation for this since people have told her, for instance, that they awoke in the middle of the night and felt a hand on their shoulder on the very night that she believed that she traveled to heal them. The second subject states that, beginning during her childhood and continuing into the present, she astrally travels almost every night through hospitals helping and healing sick children. A third claims that while astrally traveling at night she goes to the dying and helps them through the transition to the next life. Each of these three subjects told us they worried that if people knew about them, they might think they were "crazy" or "witches." This fear seems justified since Wilson (1978, p. 50) and other writers have presented cases of women reputed to astrally travel at night who were definitely viewed as witches by their neighbors.

The fantasy-prone subjects also reported out-of-the-body experiences under other special circumstances. One subject had one of her out-of-the-body experiences when she took LSD, and another had one of her experiences while she was in a sensory isolation tank. Another subject had her most memorable out-of-the-body experience during a severe illness when she was 4 years old. She recalls feeling sick, miserable, and bored while she lay in bed day after day. Consequently, she states, she left her body lying on the bed and was enjoying "sitting" on top of her bedroom door looking over her room from her new perspective. Then she looked down and saw her father walk in. She was surprised to see a little bald spot on the top and back part of his head that she had never seen before. He went over to her body and seemed alarmed when he could not arouse her. She tried to attract his attention, but since he apparently was unable to see her, she decided she should get back into her body so as not to worry him. She then felt herself "fall backwards and land" in her body. She opened her eyes and began excitedly telling her father of her experience. He tried to calm her, telling her that she was very sick with a high temperature but would be well soon. (We asked her parents, and they recalled that these events did occur when she was 4 years of age. They had assumed she was delirious from her high fever.)

Two of the fantasizers have had out-of-the-body experiences during "near-death experiences." For instance, one subject was thrown from the car during an automobile accident in England and landed face down on the cobblestone street. She reports that she found herself standing on the sidewalk, in the midst of a gathering crowd, looking at her own body lying face down on the street. An ambulance arrived and she watched as they placed her body on a stretcher and carried it into the ambulance. She decided to accompany them, so she "walked" over and "climbed" into the ambulance. Then she heard an attendant say that she was dead and nothing more could be done. She recalls thinking, "I'm not ready to die yet." She then got back into her body and tried to move to let them know she was alive. However, she was unable to move. Then she thought that if she put all her effort into it, she might be able to move her eyelids. She reports that the attendant saw her move her eyelids, realized that she was alive, "worked on her," and saved her. (She also states that a friend who escaped serious injury in the accident later verified that the attendant had truly pronounced her dead.)

Automatic Writing

Fifty percent of the fantasy-prone subjects (as contrasted with 8% in the comparison group) have had the feeling that someone was using them to write a poem, song, or message. Those who experienced this kind of automatic writing believed that the writing did not originate from them but came from a spirit or a higher intelligence which was guiding them. For instance, one who wrote "automatically" a poem entitled "Coming Home" is certain that it was written by a recently deceased young man because it was written from the perspective of the young man attempting to comfort his mourning family and friends.

Another subject who has at times sung formally at funerals initially declined a request to sing at the funeral of a man whom she did not know. Then on hanging up the phone, she quickly and "automatically" wrote down the words and music of a song, following which she returned the call and accepted the request, with a deep conviction that it was very important for her to sing that song at the funeral. She felt certain that the deceased man was the composer since it was written from the perspective of a recently deceased father talking to his bereaved daughter. After the funeral, the widow expressed her gratitude for the song, saying that her daughter had been unable to accept and mourn her father's death until the song was sung. (Prior to the funeral the subject did not know the deceased or his family.)

In addition to writing poems and songs automatically, six of the fantasy-prone subjects and none of the comparison group have experienced frequent automatic writing, which they interpret as messages for them. Sometimes such "messages" are mundane instructions about what they should do at work or at school; at other times the "messages" contain encouragement, praise, or philosophical ideas.

Religious Visions

Six subjects in the fantasy-prone group and none in the comparison group have had religious visions that were the most impactful and memorable experiences of their lives. They describe these experiences as overwhelming, awesome, deeply moving, both wonderful and frightening, and as having totally changed their lives. These intense religious experiences are reported by three subjects as occurring when they were children, by two when they were adolescents, and by one when she was an adult.

One reports that she saw a striking vision of the Virgin Mary when she was 8 years old. Another reports having seen God when she was 8; following the vision of God, she says that "Peace ascended on me. It invaded my body. Like an anointing." From then on she felt she had a unique destiny.

Another subject reports that, at 9 years of age, while she was sitting in a meadow and was "deep into nature" (e.g., touching blades of grass), she felt lonely and isolated. She was also questioning why she had been born at this time and at this place. Suddenly, she heard a voice, which she strongly felt was the voice of God, saying, "My child. My child. I am. I am." At the same time, she felt as if she were being hugged, and she experienced a deep sense of security because she now felt that she belonged to God. From that moment on she, too, has believed that she has a special destiny. She also reports that she trembled at the awesomeness of the experience and "I knew, instinctively, I could share this with no one." (Apparently she did not reveal it to anyone until she participated in our interviews.)

As a young teenager at a church service, the fourth subject heard God tell her the purpose of her life while "everything else stood still." When she was about 19, the fifth subject had a vision of Christ on the cross. She reports, "It was a really powerful experience where I just dropped to my knees. One side of him was the whole universe suffering and the other side was the whole universe in joy. . . . . After that I saw the whole world had a golden light—for a good day after. And I thought, 'Oh, I can't tell anybody'. . . . it was hard because I couldn't feel my feet on the ground. I'd keep looking to be sure they were on the ground, but I couldn't feel them."

When she was 24 years old, the sixth subject was lying down meditating with a Buddha pin over her "third eye." She says that suddenly she "saw the full face of Buddha and heard, 'I am the voice of god.'" She states that during this striking experience she felt an overpowering and overwhelming feeling that was either Kundalini or a very powerful orgasm.

Healing

More than two-thirds of the fantasy-prone subjects (and none of the comparison controls) feel that they have the ability to heal; that is, they feel a natural tendency to move toward injured or sick individuals while empathizing with them and touching them. During this close interaction they feel that they transmit energy and health to the sick or injured. Most of these subjects have participated in nondramatic "healings"; for instance, they have felt healing energy flowing from them to their sick child while holding him or her in their arms. However, nine of the fantasizers are more profoundly involved in "healing," such as attending classes, lectures, and workshops on healing or therapeutic touch; participating in healing groups; or performing overt or covert "healings" whenever they are with a sick or injured individual.

In general, the fantasy-prone subjects who saw themselves as "healers" also stated that they personally had been healed of an illness or injury by a healer at least once in their lives. Although some of these "healings" were undramatic (e.g., the "healing" of a headache), others were reported to us in a very dramatic way (e.g., sudden "healing" of severe arthritis). In brief, our data suggest that fantasy-prone individuals are heavily overrepresented among both "healers" and "healees." Further studies in this area could prove very useful in explaining the phenomena of "healing" (Barber, 1981).

Experiences with Apparitions

Seventy-three percent of the fantasizers (as contrasted with 16% of the comparison subjects) reported impressive experiences of encounters with apparitions (spirits or ghosts). Some have seen apparitions of deceased people whom they have known. For instance, one subject, who was feeling guilty for not trying to stop her family from cremating her dead grandmother, saw a striking apparition of her grandmother (a figure radiating a brilliant light) who communicated telepathically that she was happy, safe, and not angry. Another subject also saw her deceased grandmother, who told her correctly where her missing Will could be found.

Others have encountered ghosts who seem to be haunting their new residence. Some were told by neighbors about the ghost who haunted their newly purchased home prior to their seeing it; others saw a ghost and concluded on their own that their new residence was "haunted."

As a very young child one subject frequently awoke to see "an elderly white-haired man with sad blue eyes" standing by her bedside who never spoke. She regrets that she never spoke to him either since she now feels certain that he was one of her spirit guides. Another subject told us that she often wonders if her childhood imaginery companions who were to her as real as real, might *really* have been *real*, that is, might have been apparitions of children who had actually lived but now were deceased.

Hypnagogic Imagery

Some individuals experience vivid visual imagery while their eyes are open when they are about to fall asleep or immediately on waking. This imagery, which is associated with the state between waking and sleep (the hypnagogic state), is frequently of hallucinatory vividness, and the images seem to individuals experiencing them to come from another world, not from their own mind (McKellar, 1979b). These hypnagogic images may last from a few seconds to many minutes and may be either static (resembling a colorful bright slide projected on the wall) or in motion (resembling the moving images on a television screen). They typically include faces, landscapes, and familiar and unfamiliar objects, persons, or scenes, such as a wharf, the head of a bird, an old building, or marine shells (McKellar, 1979a, p. 190).

In our study 16 of the 25 fantasizers who were asked (64%) and 2 of the 25 comparison subjects (8%) reported that they *frequently* experienced vivid visual images just before falling asleep or immediately on wakening. (An additional comparison subject stated that she had experienced such imagery once, when deprived of sleep, and three other comparison subjects reported occasional "shadowy" or vague imagery.)

Although one fantasizer reported frequently seeing "colors, patterns, and moving lights," the other 15 fantasizers and the 2 comparison subjects reported classical hypnagogic imagery, that is, said that they *frequently* saw in a close-to-sleep situation unknown faces that were sometimes ordinary but often bizarre or grotesque, demon-type beings, goblins, gargoyles, mosters that seemed to be from outer space, scenes of mountains, lakes, buildings, oddly decorated rooms, an airplane wreck, a train crash, and so on.

Six of the fantasizers, who told us during the interview how they had been frequently experiencing visual hallucinations in the dark with their eyes open since early childhood, were very relieved and grateful when we explained that these (hypnagogic hallucinations) were normally experienced by some people when they were in a state between sleep and waking. They were especially grateful to learn that the "monsters" they saw nightly when they were young children could be discussed in terms of "what the mind does when it is nearly, but not quite, asleep."

All 15 fantasy-prone subjects who reported classical hypnagogic imagery are also able to hallucinate with their eyes open when they are fantasizing or reliving memories. However, they feel that their hypnagogic hallucinations are clearly different from the hallucinations they experience when they are fantasizing or reliving a memory because the hypnagogic hallucinations seem totally and impressively external in origin. During such hypnagogic experiences most feel as if they are seeing something that really exists out there or that they are looking into another dimension.

When asked if she has ever seen a spirit, ghost, or apparition, one fantasy-prone subject first described the ghost of a judge (in a black robe) who haunted her new residence and then described the "goblins, doglike creatures with short squat legs and forked tails" that she frequently sees and watches before she falls asleep at night. These goblins are clearly classical hypnagogic hallucinations (and we classified them as such) even though they were described by the subject when she was asked about seeing a spirit, ghost, or apparition. It also appears likely to us that other reported apparitions are actually hypnagogic hallucinations. For instance, the subject who, as a child, often saw an elderly man (her "spirit guide") standing by her bedside, at other times experiences classical hypnagogic hallucinations. The elderly man she saw at night could easily have been a hypnagogic hallucination.

Related to the above was the important finding that all fantasizers who had clearly seen impressive, solid apparitions also reported classical, visual hypnagogic imagery. However, some of the subjects who reported frequently experiencing (hypnagogic) images when they were in a close-to-sleep situation did not report seeing ghosts or apparitions at other times. We would suggest, however, that these individuals who commonly experience hypnagogic images are much more likely than other individuals to someday see a ghost or apparition. Out data suggest that there may be a close relationship between fantasy proneness; ability to fantasize with hallucinatory vividness equally well with eyes open or closed; frequently experiencing vivid hypnagogic images; and perceiving spirits, ghosts, or apparitions. We believe that research that probes much more intensively into the relationships among these variables will go far toward explaining what kinds of individuals report perceiving ghosts or apparitions and what conditions are most conducive to such experiences.

Social Awareness and Secret Fantasy Life

An additional shared characteristic that we cannot overemphasize is that all 26 fantasy-prone subjects *are socially aware* and work and function much like any other group of educated American women. With two exceptions, they are all either married, have a regular boyfriend, or are dating more than one man. They range in emotional stability or mental health across the entire range of the normal curve. We would categorize five of the fantasizers as self-actualizing individuals (Maslow, 1954) in that they are happy, popular, competent, loving, and have high self-esteem. On the other hand, four have had difficulties in adjustment; at times they become depressed, and one of these subjects was hospitalized for a brief period with what she called a "nervous breakdown." The remaining 17 fantasy-prone subjects appear to us and to others who know them to be more or less as adjusted as the average educated American woman.

Because they are sensitive to social norms, they have told virtually no one about the extent or depth of their fantasy life or the hallucinatory qualities of their fantasies and memories. For instance, three have been married for over 20 years, and their husbands, who see them as normal, competent wives and mothers, have no knowledge of their fantasy lives. Each wife's fantasy life has been her own well-guarded secret.

During our interviews with these women, they told us secrets they had never told anyone. They revealed their secrets to us for the following reasons: (1) we asked them questions that were meaningful to them but that no one had ever asked them before (about their childhood, memories, daydreams, fantasies, night dreams, psychic experiences, etc.; they were typically surprised by the questions, and a few were startled by them, because, they told us, they felt as if we were "reading" their minds); (2) we were accepting and understanding of everything they told us; (3) we clearly communicated to them our belief that fantasy can be creative and valuable; and (4) they saw our investigation as very important because they all believe that fantasy is useful, "wonderful," and essential in their own lives.

Most of those we saw again later told us that our interviews had made a significant difference in their lives. They typically stated that they had gained greater understanding of themselves and felt less alone—previously they had assumed that no one else was like them. Following participation in our project, some of the fantasizers felt ready to share their "secret" with important people in their lives. One told her husband of 20 years and gave him a copy of our preliminary report of the study (Wilson & Barber, 1981) so that he could see her as she really was. Another gave a copy of our preliminary paper to her counselor so that he could understand her. Also, two fantasizers who had been close friends for many years had never suspected how important fantasizing was to the other until each realized that the other had participated in our project!

DISCUSSION

This study has delineated a fact that is very important for understanding the range of human psychology: a relatively small group of more or less satisfactorily adjusted individuals who live, work, and play like the rest of us differ from the majority of their fellows in that they live much of the time in a world of their own making—in a world of imagery, imagination, and fantasy. They fantasize much of the time when they are not busy; they also fantasize much of the time when they are engaged in relatively nondemanding tasks; and their fantasies tend to become hallucinatory—they are often "as real as real" and, at times, "more real than real."

Extreme Abilities on the Normal Curve

If we keep in mind that human traits, including the trait of fantasy-proneness, can be expected to fall on a normal curve of distribution, we would not be too surprised that these individuals exist. It appears to us, from the interviews we conducted with the fantasizers and the comparison group, that both the amount of time devoted to fantasy and the hallucinatory intensity of the fantasies is distributed on a normal curve, with the fantasy-prone subjects simply falling at the extreme end of the curve. (Our data also indicate that these two variables—amount of time fantasizing and hallucinatory intensity—are highly correlated and thus in the present study, which just begins to dig into the complexities of the topic, they are considered as two aspects of the same phenomenon that we term *fantasy proneness*.)

Individuals who are very high on fantasy proneness thus fall at the extreme end of a normal curve of distribution, and their fantasy becomes more and more "real as real" (hallucinatory) as we move further and further out on the curve. Of course, many other human abilities are also strikingly different and difficult to believe when they lie at the extreme end of the normal curve. To take examples from musical ability, "Blind Tom," who was a poor, blind, black slave youngster in the South, found his way to his master's piano when 4 years of age and was then and thereafter able to play perfectly by ear each of the many compositions he had previously heard (Brawley, 1937; Goldenson, 1973).

"Blind Tom's" phenomenal auditory memory for music is matched by another kind of extreme musical talent that was displayed by Mozart, who began to compose beautiful violin sonatas and symphonies when he was about 7 years of age (Landon, 1977). In the same way we find individuals who are on the extreme end of the normal curve on calculating ability who can, for example, in a few seconds derive mentally the cube root of 413,993,348,677 and other such numbers (Barlow, 1952, p. 26).

Earlier Reports of Hallucinatory Ability

To the best of our knowledge, the syndrome that we have uncovered, which includes involvement in fantasy, hallucinatory ability, vivid memories, hypnotizability, and psychic abilities, has not been delineated previously as a unitary entity. However, each separate facet of the syndrome has been studied separately, and, at times, two or more facets have been interrelated.

The hallucinatory ability (especially the visual hallucinatory ability) shown by our subjects has been noted previously under a variety of names. It was noted about 100 years ago by Galton (1883, p. 12) when he found in "sane and healthy" persons that there is "continuity between all the forms of visualization, beginning with an almost total absence of it, and ending with a complete hallucination.'' Galton noted that individuals who had the ability to hallucinate at will were found in all walks of life—one was a lawyer, another a judge, and so on. Parish (1897) later reported similar findings and appropriately labeled the phenomenon ''the waking hallucinations of healthy persons.'' During the early part of the present century the phenomenon of visual hallucinatory ability in normal individuals was also noted by investigators such as Jaensch (1930), who labeled the subjects as eidetikers or individuals with eidetic imagery.

Let us briefly consider representative journal articles and books that have been written on individuals of the type we have described in this chapter. The writers of these articles and books were amazed that such an individual could exist. (Although we, too, were surprised when we began to interview subjects, it soon became clear that fantasy-prone individuals who have developed the ability to hallucinate may comprise as much as 4% of the population but are well hidden because they are aware that it is socially taboo to inform others of their extensive and vivid fantasy life.)

Vogt & Sultan (1977, pp. 215–216) discuss with astonishment the famous inventor, Nikola Tesla, who was able to hallucinate whatever he was thinking or imagining. This ability caused him much ''mental anguish'' during his childhood; for example, he had difficulty in differentiating between a visualized apple and a real apple. As he got older, however, he learned to discriminate more clearly between his visualizations and reality and used his ability to great advantage in visually constructing his inventions such as the alternating current generator, the induction coil, fluorescent lighting, and neon bulbs.

Along similar lines, Purdy (1936, p. 441) presented a detailed case study of a 21-year-old college woman who had ''strong eidetic imagery in the visual, auditory, olfactory, and tactual fields.'' When asked to visualize absent objects, she insisted that she could see them ''out there'' in literally the same way as objects that were present. When asked to imagine the sun, she reported seeing a glaring bright sun, her eyes watered and smarted, and her discomfort did not disappear for several minutes. When she imagined the roar of the sea, the imagined sounds were so intense as to weaken actual sounds in her environment. When she imagined a rose, she both saw it and smelled it vividly. When she imagined herself running, she experienced a strong pounding of the heart. She could abolish the perception of a person standing before her and, in his place, ''see'' an absent person. Also, she could see a person without his head, place green leaves on barren winter trees, and see a beard on a beardless man. Occasionally she mistook imagined objects for actual objects. When traveling in an automobile, for example, she at times would warn the driver about objects in the road that she soon discovered to be figments of her imagination.

One of the world's foremost psychologists, A. R. Luria of the Soviet Union, wrote an entire book on one man who had the typical characteristics of our fantasizers and, in addition, had specialized in learning and practicing mnemonic methods for remembering long lists of words, numbers, and events. Luria's (1968) book about this man, entitled *The Mind of a Mnemonist,* has been widely read and has become a classic in psychology. Luria states that his subject "could actually see what other people think or only imagine to themselves; vivid images would appear to him that were so palpable as to verge on being real" (Luria, 1968, p. 96). After studying this subject intensively, Luria concluded that "Indeed, one would be hard put to say which was more real for him: the world of imagination in which he lived, or the world of reality in which he was a temporary guest" (Luria, 1968, p. 159). Like some of the fantasy-prone individuals described in this chapter, Luria's subject had a vivid memory, could clearly recall early childhood events, could accelerate his heart rate by imagining running, could make his hand hot or cold by imagining placing it on a hot stove or in ice water, and could block the experience of pain when in the dentist's chair by hallucinating himself sitting in another part of the room observing the ongoing dentistry.

Although Luria's subject is interesting, he is not as unusual or exceptional as was originally assumed when the book was first published in the United States in 1968. It is now clear that he belongs to a group of fantasy-prone individuals who are able to hallucinate at will. In fact, it appears that he differs from the individuals discussed in this chapter in only one significant way: he is able to remember for long periods of time lengthy lists of words or numbers that he has learned. In learning and then recalling the long lists, he uses his imagery, his exceptional memory, and *mnemonic techniques* (principles of memory) that he previously mastered after intensive practice. His "talent" for remembering long lists becomes much more understandable when we realize that mnemonic techniques can be learned by any intelligent person who is willing to make the effort (Yates, 1966).

Recently, another individual who has the abilities that characterize our fantasy-prone subjects was immortalized in a best-selling book entitled *The Story of Ruth* (Schatzman, 1980). An important aspect of Ruth's difficulties, which she revealed early in psychiatric therapy, was that she became nervous and agitated whenever she saw (an apparition of) her father in her house. (Her father was alive at that time!) Ruth stated that [the apparition of] her father would sit in a chair in her house and would watch her. Sometimes "he" would laugh or smile. At other times, she could hear "him" coming and going and could smell the smoke from his pipe—in fact, the "smoke" made her house smelly. It appeared from Ruth's statements that the apparition of her father had the same characteristics and was practically indistinguishable from her real father.

After a series of sessions, the psychiatrist, Dr. Schatzman, asked Ruth, "Why don't you try to produce the apparition?" Ruth finally agreed, stared at an empty space in the corner of the room and then announced, "I'm seeing him now. He's wearing a white shirt that's well pressed. . . ." As Ruth described the details of the apparition vividly, Dr. Schatzman asked her to make it go away. She concentrated for about 10 seconds and then announced, "He's gone now." What she had done previously unconsciously—creating the apparition—now became conscious: she realized that she could make "him" come and she could make "him" go; that "he" was under her control; and that she had been creating "him" all along but had not realized that she was doing it. Furthermore, after further discussions between Ruth and Dr. Schatzman, she realized that there were other "people" in her life whom she thought were real but may have been hallucinated.

As might be expected, Ruth possesses all the striking characteristics that are found in our fantasy-prone subjects. She can make her hand very hot or very cold by fantasizing a hot or cold situation. When she is simply asked to recall events during her childhood, she naturally age regresses—she experiences herself as a child, her handwriting is clearly childlike, and she responds in the way expected of a child on tests such as the Rorschach. Also, as might be expected, when she was a child, she perceived her dolls as literally alive and had (imaginary) children as playmates and companions.

After working many months with Ruth, Dr. Schatzman concluded that her basic talent was her ability for "suppressing or discounting her knowledge of what was real so as to experience something else" (Schatzman, 1980, p. 288). To the present writers, this is another way of saying that Ruth's basic talent is the same as that of our fantasy-prone subjects; namely, an ability to hallucinate—to become so absorbed and involved in an imagined or fantasized event that it becomes real and consensus reality is not perceived.

The authors of the three reports discussed above—Purdy (1936), Luria (1968), and Schatzman (1980)—do not say very much about the "psychic" experiences of their subjects. From our data with individuals who have similar characteristics, we would surmise that this is due to failure on the part of the investigators to probe into their subjects' "psychic" experiences rather than to the alternative possibility that the subjects simply did not have such experiences.

Another recent article on a woman who has the abilities that characterize our fantasy-prone subjects emphasizes her "psychic" experiences more than her other attributes. This article (Nietzke, 1979) describes a well-functioning and successful individual, Rosalyn Bruyere, who "sees" and reads auras, "sees" inside a person's body, performs psychic healings, talks to dead people, has out-of-the-body experiences, and is in touch with spirit guides. Ms. Bruyere's talents are not especially surprising to us. Some of our fantasy-prone subjects claim that they see auras, some perform psychic healings, many have out-of-the-body experiences, and so on. In fact, our data lead to the prediction that when Ms. Bruyere and others who show similar psychic talents are interviewed in depth, they will be found to possess the characteristics of fantasy-prone individuals—the ability to become deeply involved in fantasies that reach hallucinatory intensities; the ability to revive earlier memories so vividly that they bring back the sights, sounds, and smells that existed at a former time; the ability to be excellent hypnotic subjects; and so forth.

Mediums, Psychics, and Religious Visionaries

Our data also suggest that individuals manifesting the fantasy-prone syndrome may have been overrepresented among famous mediums, psychics, and religious visionaries of the past. To test the validity of this conjecture, we have begun to look at the biographies of individuals in these categories. For instance, we looked at a recent biography of Madame Blavatsky, who, in addition to founding modern theosophy, was also reputed to be a "sensitive" and to have psychic powers. She is described by her biographer (Meade, 1980) as thoroughly believing in ghosts, monsters, and various other magical creatures as a young child and thinking that they obeyed her commands and as having many hallucinatory and psychic experiences during later childhood, adolescence, and adulthood. The best short description of her, which was provided by the poet William Butler Yeats after he became well acquainted with her is, "She dreams while awake." These and other indications of a profound fantasy life reaching hallucinatory intensities leads us to conclude that Madame Blavatsky had characteristics very similar to those of the fantasy-prone subjects we interviewed in this project.

Famous mediums such as Mrs. Leonard and Eileen Garrett also had similar attributes. As children, both lived a great part of the time in a make-believe world, had imaginary playmates who looked and felt like ordinary children, had "visitations" from dead relatives, and had difficulty distinguishing fantasized from nonfantasized events and persons (Garrett, 1968; Roll, 1981). As adults they were excellent hypnotic subjects who became trance mediums, continued to spend much time fantasizing at hallucinatory intensities, and had many psychic experiences.

When we look further back in history, we find that famous psychics and mediums of the past also had the characteristics we have found in fantasy-prone subjects. For instance, Wilson (1971, pp. 270–271) writes that Jerome Cardan, a noted psychic or occultist of the sixteenth century

> was a "witch" in the precise sense of the word: that is, he possessed a high degree of second sight and other occult faculties. There seems to be no reason to suspect Cardan of lying when he declares (in his memoirs) that he could project his spirit outside his body. He also makes the interesting assertion that he could, from childhood on, "see" imaginary things with a sense of total reality. As a child, he says, he could not control this faculty, but later he learned how to select things he wanted to "see". . . . He believed himself to be accompanied by a familiar spirit. . . . He certainly qualifies as one of the most remarkable psychological curiosities of all time.

Individuals who are characterized by the fantasy-prone syndrome also seem to be overrepresented among religious visionaries. Since we develop this topic in detail in a more lengthy publication, we list only a few brief examples here.

By age 13, Joan of Arc had seen and heard "as real as real" God, St. Michele, St. Catherine, and St. Marguerite. She believed so thoroughly in her visions that she convinced her listeners of their reality; her converts then followed her to lift the seige of Orleans and to change the fate of France. Along similar lines, St. Bernadette believed so sincerely that she had many times seen and spoken with the Virgin Mary that she convinced her listeners; Mary Baker Eddy also was convinced that she talked with spirits; Joseph Smith saw visions of God, Jesus, and a messenger from heaven who showed him the records that later became the book of Mormon; and Paramhansa Yogananda, founder of the Self-Realization Fellowship, firmly convinced himself and also convinced at least some of his readers that he could transport himself in a flash to distant locations, could see and talk with his (deceased) guru, and so on. We believe that the data presented in this chapter pertaining to the ability to fantasize with hallucinatory vividness should be taken into consideration in further attempts to formulate the factors that gave rise to these visions.

Out-of-the-Body and Near-Death Experiences

In our sample, almost all individuals who had many realistic out-of-the-body experiences and all who had the prototypic "near-death experience" came from the fantasy-prone group. Along the same lines other recent investigations, reviewed by Blackmore (1978) and Siegel (1980), indicate that such experiences may be expected much more often among fantasy-prone individuals than among the remainder of the population. Let us glance briefly at their relevant reviews.

Blackmore (1978) reviewed the evidence that indicates that out-of-the-body experiences have the following characteristics that can be expected of hallucinatory fantasies: (1) imaginary perceptions; (2) errors in perception; (3) perceptual distortions (such as seeing through things); (4) instantaneous traveling to distant locations; and (5) fantasylike perceptions of self such as not having a body, having a replica of one's body, and perceiving oneself as a point or a ball of light. She concluded from the data that out-of-the-body experiences should be viewed as hallucinatory fantasies.

The prototypical "near-death experience," which is reported by a small number of individuals who come close to dying, typically includes such characteristics as the following: the individuals may hear themselves pronounced dead; experience themselves as out of the body; look down on their inert body; and see spirits of relatives and friends who have died. A number of investigators have argued that these prototypical "near-death experiences" are *not* hallucinations because of such reasons as the following: they have more similarities in content than would be expected among independently experienced hallucinations; the dying patients were not confused or delirious and could not be expected to be hallucinating; and the "near-death experiences" were "as real as real" or "more real than real" (Crookall, 1961; Moody, 1975; Osis & Haraldsson, 1977; Ring, 1980). In a penetrating review of the data, Siegel (1980) demonstrated that these (and other) arguments are invalid—for instance, the similarities in content are just what one would expect from a thorough knowledge of hallucinations, a person need not be confused or delirious to experience hallucinations, and hallucinations are typically "as real as real" and, at times, "more real than real." In addition, Siegel analyzed representative reports of prototypical "near-death experiences" and provided cogent internal evidence from their contents that they should be categorized as hallucinatory fantasies.

Fantasy Proneness, Hallucinatory Ability, and Hypnosis

In addition to casting a new light on a variety of psychological and parapsychological phenomena, the data from this study also clarify the topic of hypnosis. The data show that hypnotic phenomena are natural for some individuals; fantasy-prone personalities have had many experiences throughout their lives that are similar to the classical hypnosis experiences, and they find the suggestions of the hypnotist very harmonious with their own ongoing experiential life. Let us look at the clarification of hypnosis provided by the data we have presented.

It has been clear for many years that the hypnotic situation can be viewed as a social interaction in which one person communicates ideas and suggestions and another person accepts and acts on the communications according to his or her understandings, attitudes, expectations, and motivations in the situation and his or her relationship with the person proffering the communications (Barber, 1969, 1970; Barber, et al., 1974; Sarbin & Coe, 1972). Although much about hypnosis can be understood by viewing it as a social interaction that is affected by a large number of social psychological variables, there still remains something very important that needs to be explained: When other important factors are apparently held constant (e.g., subjects' attitudes, expectancies, and motivations, the relationship between subject and hypnotist, and the wording and tone of the suggestions), why does one subject respond quickly, easily, and profoundly to a wide variety of suggestions whereas other subjects respond perfunctorily to only a few suggestions? The striking aspect of hypnosis that has made it such an important topic is that there are individuals who can be given any of the classical hypnotic suggestions—such as suggestions for hand anesthesia, age regression, visual hallucinations, auditory hallucinations, deep relaxation, or "trance"—and they quickly and easily give every indication of experiencing hand numbness, regression to childhood, hallucinations, and so forth. The present study helps to clarify hypnosis by showing that there are individuals who have a life-time history of intense fantasy, who have developed hallucinatory abilities, and who—as a result of these talents—are able to quickly, easily, and profoundly experience the classical hypnotic phenomena.

In the 1950s, 1960s, and 1970s intensive research was conducted to ascertain the personality characteristics that were related to hypnotic responsiveness. These studies, reviewed by Barber (1964) and Hilgard (1965), failed to confirm many hypothesized relationships between personality traits and responsiveness in a hypnotic situation. In general, the research showed that hypnotic responsiveness was not related to such hypothesized correlates as submissiveness, extroversion, neuroticism, sociability, ego strength, outer-directedness, or other traits.

Although a large number of hypothesized personality traits failed to correlate consistently with hypnotic responsiveness, the large number of studies carried out in the 1950s, 1960s, and 1970s yielded two very important findings: hypnotic responsiveness was shown to be related to (1) motivational and attitudinal variables that lead to willingness to cooperate in fulfilling the aims of the suggestions and (2) variables that produce involvement in activities that are related to imagining (Spanos & Barber, 1974).

With regard to the first set of variables, investigators found that positive attitudes and motivations toward hypnosis are correlated with hypnotic responsiveness (Andersen, 1963; Barber & Calverley, 1966; Coe, 1964; Coe & Sarbin, 1966; Diamond et al., 1972; Hilgard, 1970; London et al., 1962; Melei & Hilgard, 1964; Shor et al., 1966). Also, studies that experimentally manipulated subjects' attitudes and motives found that inculcation of positive attitudes and motives toward the hypnotic or suggestive situation raised responsiveness to hypnotic suggestions, whereas the inculcation of negative or critical attitudes and motivations reduced responsiveness (Barber & Calverley, 1964a,b; Cronin et al., 1971; Diamond, 1972; Kinney, 1969; Spanos & McPeake, 1975b).

With regard to the second set of variables, a series of studies indicated that hypnotic responsiveness is related to propensity to become engrossed in activities that involve imagining. Although several lines of research seemed to converge on this conclusion (Spanos & Barber, 1974), the critical set of studies correlated subjects' hypnotic responsiveness with the degree to which they became involved in imaginative activities outside the hypnotic situation. Three sets of strategies were used to assess the degree of involvement in imaginative activities: (1) use of scales that assessed the extent to which the subjects reported becoming involved in imagination-related activities such as daydreaming and becoming absorbed in a novel (As, 1962; Barber & Glass, 1962; Shor et al., 1962); (2) interviews that assessed subjects' degree of involvement in activities that seem to pivot around imagining such as dramatic acting, reading novels, and having imaginary companions (Hilgard, 1970); and (3) measures of performance in skills that involve imagining such as dramatic acting (Coe & Sarbin, 1966). These studies generally found positive correlations between responsiveness in a hypnotic situation and the degree to which subjects became involved in imagination-related activities

(Andersen, 1963; As, 1962; As et al., 1962; Atkinson, 1971; Barber & Glass, 1962; Barber & Wilson, 1979; Coe, 1964; Coe & Sarbin, 1966; Hilgard, 1970; Lee-Teng, 1965; Sarbin & Lim, 1963; Shor et al., 1962; Spanos & McPeake, 1975a; Tellegen & Atkinson, 1974).[3]

Another set of studies have a degree of overlap with those cited above in that they assessed the subjects' imagery reports. These studies, which have been reviewed by Sheehan (1979), generally found positive correlations between subjects' responsiveness to hypnotic suggestions and their scores on the Betts test of mental imagery and the Gordon test for control of imagery (Hilgard, 1970; Perry, 1973; Shor et al., 1966; Spanos et al., 1973; Sutcliffe, 1958; Sutcliffe et al., 1970).

The data we have presented in this chapter are harmonious with the data summarized above. Furthermore, our data extend the earlier studies by showing that there exists a group of individuals who are not only involved in imagination-related activities but, in addition, are heavily involved in fantasy per se, have developed an ability to hallucinate at will in most or all sense modalities, and, as a result of their highly developed skills in fantasying and hallucinating, have the ability to respond easily and profoundly to the classical hypnotic suggestions.

In fact, as our data accumulated, we realized that the major reason why some individuals are excellent hypnotic subjects is that they live in a fantasy world of their own creation that is very much like the world the hypnotist asks them to "go into." For the 26 fantasizers, there is a reduction or fading of the generalized reality orientation to self, time, and place (Shor, 1959) whenever they become involved in either their own fantasies and memories or in the experiences that are typically suggested by a hypnotist. Furthermore, there are many close parallels between classical hypnotic phenomena and the experiences of fantasizers in their everyday life. Let us consider some of these parallels.

The hypnotic phenomenon of age regression would not be difficult for the subject described earlier who, when simply asked about her early memories during the interview, recalled and vividly reexperienced her first birthday with all the associated sights, sounds, feelings, and emotions. In fact, age regression (reliving previous experiences) is something virtually all the fantasizers do naturally in their daily lives since (1) when they recall the past, they relive it to a surprisingly vivid extent, and (2) they have vivid memories of their experiences extending back to their very early life.

Another classical hypnotic phenomenon has been labeled as *visual and auditory hallucinations*. The majority of the fantasy-prone subjects do not find it especially difficult to respond to hypnotic suggestions to hallucinate visually, acoustically, or in any other sensory modality. These subjects typically fantasize at least half their waking day and commonly experience the people and objects in their fantasies "as real as real" (hallucinatory). Their superb memory of personal experiences also plays an important role in their ability to respond to suggestions to hallucinate. For instance, if a hypnotist tells a fantasy-prone subject that he or she is presenting her with a rose while presenting her with ammonia, her vivid (hallucinatory) memory of the odor of a rose (to which she is attending) can conceal the odor of the ammonia (to which she is not attending).

The classical hypnotic phenomenon labeled as *negative hallucination* (not seeing or hearing a person or object in the room) is also not too difficult for most fantasy-prone subjects. When they are given such a suggestion, they can "block out" the person or object from their perceptual field by fantasizing (hallucinating) something else in the place of the person or object they are not to perceive.

The classical hypnotic situation also includes suggestions that a limb or part of the body feels heavy, rigid, light, hot, cold, numb, and so on. These suggestions are not especially difficult for subjects who have vivid (hallucinatory) memories and are able to remember vividly and reexperience a time when a limb or part of the body felt heavy, light, hot, numb, or the like.

Other classical hypnotic suggestions associated with observable bodily changes, such as increasing the blood flow to a limb, raising or lowering the heart rate, or removing warts or producing blisters (Barber, 1970, 1976, 1978a), appear to be within the potential of fantasy-prone individuals whose sexual fantasies can produce orgasms, whose fantasies of pregnancy can produce pseudocyesis, whose fantasies of eating spoiled food can produce illness, and so on.

In brief, individuals whom we have labeled as *fantasy-prone personalities* have many experiences, as part of their ongoing lives, that are similar to those that have been associated with hypnosis. We would conjecture that these are the people who are the subjects when we hear dramatic accounts of hypnotic phenomena. We would also conjecture that throughout the history of hypnotism, when these individuals were the subjects, most hypnotists and observers believed (incorrectly) that they manifested limb rigidity, positive hallucinations, negative hallucinations, anesthesia, age regression, automatic writing, and so on, *because* they had been hypnotized. Apparently most hypnotists did not realize that these excelent hypnotic subjects (or "somnambules") were able to experience the classical hypnotic phenomena primarily *because* they had had practice in experiencing similar phenomena during their daily lives. Our data indicate that the hypnosis setting provides a situation in which those with a secret fantasy life can publicly demonstrate their special abilities or talents. In the hypnosis situation, their ability to fantasize with hallucinatory intensity is not only socially permissible; it is also rewarded.

In brief, the fantasy-prone subjects who participated in this project experience a reduction in orientation to time, place, and person that is characteristic of hypnosis or trance during their daily lives whenever they are deeply involved in a fantasy; have experiences during their ongoing lives which resemble the classical hypnotic phenomena; and can be said to have the classical hypnotic behaviors as part of their behavioral repertoire. Perhaps this has been an important "secret" of hypnosis. The experiences and behaviors that have been traditionally labeled as *hypnotic phenomena* are in the repertoire of fantasy-prone individuals prior to their having any formal experiences in a hypnosis situation. Hence when we give them "hypnotic suggestions," such as, suggestions for visual and auditory hallucinations, negative hallucinations, age regression, limb rigidity, anesthesia, and sensory hallucinations, we are asking them to do for us the kind of thing they can do independently of us in their daily lives. However, as we described previously, they have learned to be highly secretive and private about their fantasy life. The hypnosis situation provides them with a social situation in which they are encouraged to do, and rewarded for doing, what they usually do only secretly and privately in their fantasy life. In fact their responding to the classical hypnotic suggestions that involve an ability to hallucinate differs from their daily fantasizing at hallucinatory intensities primarily in that someone else (the hypnotist) rather than themselves is guiding their fantasy and structuring its content. Since the specific content suggested by the hypnotist usually differs from the specific content of their daily fantasies, both the subject and the hypnotist can miss the close similarities in the *processes* involved.

There are three important considerations that need to be underscored in order to fully clarify the relationship between fantasy-proneness and responsiveness in a hypnotic situation:

1. Because of their highly practiced abilities or talents, fantasizers are "naturals" at experiencing classical hypnotic phenomena, but they do not *have to* experience any hypnotic phenomena. If they have unfavorable or negative attitudes toward the hypnotist or the specific suggestions, they simply do not cooperate or they resist the suggestions (Barber, 1961; Erickson, 1939). For instance, one of our fantasy-prone excellent hypnotic subjects did not cooperate with a hypnotist she saw for weight reduction (and he rated her as a poor hypnotic subject) because, she said, he overemphasized sexual matters during the pre-hypnosis interview and she "wasn't about to trust that turkey." Similarly, another fantasy-prone excellent hypnotic subject, who was also overweight, did not cooperate with a stage hypnotist because she felt he was very insensitive when he told a subject earlier in the performance, "Laugh at the fat lady in the circus." In our own hypnotic sessions with the excellent hypnotic subjects, if they had a reason for not accepting a suggestion, they did not do so and usually told us why later; for instance, one subject stated that she did not let herself experience the suggestion that her left hand was becoming hot (even though she deeply experienced all of the other suggestions) because she had severely burned the same hand as a child and could not let herself revive that memory.

2. Although fantasy-prone subjects have the ability to experience profoundly the *classical* hypnotic effects such as age regression and negative

and positive hallucinations, they may or may not accept other suggestions—
for instance, suggestions that simply require compliance, other suggestions
that do not require an ability to imagine or fantasize, and also suggestions
that are intended to have a therapeutic effect. In fact, whether an individual
is an excellent hypnotic subject in that he or she responds profoundly to
classical hypnotic suggestions is not correlated with his or her responsiveness to *therapeutic* suggestions to lose weight, stop smoking, become relieved of back pain, and other ailments (Barber, 1982; Perry, et al., 1979).
Response to therapeutic suggestions is much more closely related to the
subject's own strength of motivation for stopping smoking, losing weight,
and so on, to the strength of secondary gains that are associated with the
habit or "symptom" that is to be removed, and to many other variables
(e.g., the nature of the relationship or transference between the patient and
the hypnotist–therapist).

   3.   Although fantasy-prone individuals have the ability to respond profoundly to the classical hypnotic suggestions, other individuals who are not
especially high in fantasy proneness are also at times rated as excellent
hypnotic subjects. (The reader will recall that we found one subject of the
latter type in this project.) Although fantasy proneness appears to account
for an important aspect of hypnotic performance, much more research is
needed to ascertain all the relevant characteristics of individuals who are
rated as excellent hypnotic subjects in different types of hypnotic situations
(involving different kinds of hypnotists, different types of suggestions, etc.).[4]

Before closing this discussion on hypnosis, we should mention that the data
presented in this chapter also cast a new light on two important unexplained
historical facts about hypnosis. During the early part of the nineteenth century, the phenomena thought to be associated with hypnosis included hallucinations, delusions, catalepsy, anesthesia, amnesia, and *telepathy, clair-
voyance, and precognition* (Dingwall, 1968). It was apparently assumed at
that time that the latter three phenomena were explained by the postulate
that hypnosis gave rise to psychic sensitiveness. Our data, however, suggest
an alternative interpretation: although deep hypnosis may encourage an individual to manifest his or her psychic abilities, it does not produce them;
instead, sensitivity to telepathic, clairvoyant, and precognitive impressions
and ability to reduce orientation to time, place, and person (enter deep
hypnosis) tend to be found in the same kind of person who has a history of
profound involvement in fantasy.

   Our data also provide an explanation for the assertion made by Charcot
and Janet during the nineteenth century that excellent hypnotic subjects are
hysterics and for its modern reformulation that patients diagnosed as hysterics tend to be better hypnotic subjects than do patients who receive other
diagnoses (such as schizophrenia, manic–depressive, depressed, chronic brain
syndrome, or obsessive–compulsive).[5] It appears that many of the individuals diagnosed as hysterics by Charcot and Janet at the Salpetriere Hospital

in Paris were fantasy-prone personalities. Janet (1901) points out many times that individuals diagnosed as hysterics dream while they are awake (Janet, 1901, pp. 201, 343, 460–462), and one of their most important characteristics is a "tendency to ceaseless reverie. Hystericals are not content to dream constantly at night; they dream all day long. Whether they walk, or work, or sew, their minds are not wholly occupied with what they are doing. They carry on in their heads an interminable story which unrolls before them . . ." (Janet, 1901, p. 201).

In brief, it appears that a substantial number of Charcot and Janet's hysterics were fantasy-prone personalities. However, as we discuss next, the overwhelming majority of fantasy-prone individuals seem to fall within the broad range of normal functioning, and it is thus inappropriate to apply a psychiatric diagnosis to them.

Fantasy, Normality, and Psychopathology

It needs to be strongly emphasized that our subjects with a propensity for hallucinatory fantasy are as well adjusted as our comparison group or as the average person. It appears that the life experiences and skill developments that underlie the ability for hallucinatory fantasy are more or less independent of the kinds of life experience that lead to psychopathology. Five of the fantasy-prone subjects are happy, popular, competent, and loving and have high self-esteem; four have had difficulties in adjustment; and the remainder work, love, and socialize within the broad average range of adjustment.

Although our fantasizers are "normal" people who function as well as our comparison group or as well as the average person, it may be that some individuals with psychopathology are also fantasizers. As stated above, it appears that, during the days of Charcot and Janet, a substantial proportion of those diagnosed as hysterics were fantasizers.

It also may be that some of the present-day hospitalized individuals who are diagnosed as schizophrenic may also be fantasy-prone personalities. However, our own experience with hospitalized individuals diagnosed as schizophrenic leads us to hypothesize that, although they have peculiar cognitive distortions, they differ widely in their fantasy proneness—some have a poverty of fantasy, some fall within the average range on involvement in fantasy, and some (Green, 1964) have a very rich fantasy life that attains hallucinatory intensity. It should be noted here that although a significant number of diagnosed schizophrenics "hear voices," it does not follow that they have a profound fantasy life; when "hearing voices," these patients may be simply hearing their own verbal accusations or criticisms of themselves.

Vividness of Sensory Experiences, Memories, and Fantasies

We have noted that our fantasy-prone subjects tend to have vivid sensory experiences; they experience touch, sights, sounds, and smells more vividly than do comparison subjects. Hilgard (1970, 1979) had previously found that vivid sensory experiences also characterize good hypnotic subjects whom we would expect to be high in fantasy proneness.

We have also noted that our fantasy-prone subjects also seem to have vivid personal memories; when they recall earlier events in their lives, they tend to reexperience them—to see, hear, smell, and feel, what they had experienced previously. Earlier investigators had similarly noted that an excellent memory was found in individuals who we would expect to be high in fantasy. Spiegel (1974) noted that his best hypnotic subjects in a clinical situation were characterized by an excellent memory (plus empathy, trust in people, and absorption in the present). Along similar lines, Roll (1966) summarized evidence indicating that individuals with psychic abilities also have exceptional memories. He refers, for example, to Osty, Bekhterev, Abramowski, William James, Sir Oliver Lodge, Tenhaeff, and other investigators who found that the best subjects in ESP experiments and also well-known psychics who have been studied intensively, such as Mrs. Piper and Mrs. Leonard, manifested a remarkably vivid memory.

We would hypothesize that vivid sensory experiences, vivid memories, and vivid fantasies are causally interrelated as follows: individuals who focus on and vividly feel their sensory experiences, have relatively vivid memories of their experiences; and individuals with vivid memories of their experiences are able to have relatively vivid fantasies because they can use their vivid memories as raw material from which they can creatively construct their fantasies.

Although the above hypotheses appear difficult to test, the relationships we have noted between sensory experiences, memories, and fantasies leads to predictions that are easily testable. For instance, we should be able to predict the vividness of individuals' fantasies by assessing the vividness of their sensory experiences or by asking them to recall specific personal events, for instance, their first day in school, the first time they smoked a cigarette, or the first time they became inebriated. The degree to which they have vivid sensory experiences and the degree to which they recall and reexperience earlier personal events vividly in all sense modalities should predict the vividness (hallucinatory qualities) of their fantasies (and correlated variables such as hypnotizability and psychic abilities).

Childhood Make-Believe Play and the Development of Fantasy Proneness

Our data indicate that fantasy-prone personalities became involved in fantasy during early childhood and then continued their fantasy involvement (secretly) into adulthood. Both our data and Hilgard's (1970, 1979) indicate that early childhood involvement in fantasy can be elicited in several ways, for instance, when a child is isolated, is restricted, or is encouraged by others to play make-believe games. The relationship between make-believe play during childhood and the development of a profound fantasy life has been noted previously. Singer (1977), for instance, reviewed a series of studies that indicate that make-believe play in early life is associated with imagery, imagination, and fantasy skills. Also, a series of studies (Dennis, 1976; Fein, 1975; Freyberg, 1973; Griffing, 1974; Litt, 1973; Pavenstedt, 1967) indicate that (1) there are marked individual differences in the extent of make-believe play in early childhood and (2) its extent is affected by particular parent–child interaction patterns and by its acceptance and encouragement by ' significant adults. Paranthetically, we should note Sarbin's (1976, 1978) important point that profound involvement in pretend play during early childhood closely resembles profound involvement in hypnotic suggestions. For instance, when excellent hypnotic subjects are responding to suggestions that they are riding on a horse, their experiences are at times very similar to children who, while making believe that a stick is a horse, lose awareness of the stick and feel and believe that they are on a horse.

Of course, much further research is needed to determine how fantasy and hallucinatory ability develop in both males and females in our culture and in other cultures; how these abilities are lost, maintained, or strengthened during the life span; and how they are related to hypnotizability, psychic experiences, and other normal and abnormal psychological phenomena.

REFERENCE NOTES

1. We prefer to use the terms "fantasy" and "fantasize" to refer to the phenomena we are describing in this paper, even though others (including many of our subjects) use the terms "imagining" or "daydreaming" to refer to the same phenomena. We chose not to use the term "imagining" primarily because it becomes too easily confused with the euphemistic term "imaginative" (which can refer to being creative without necessarily fantasizing). We chose not to use the term "daydreaming" primarily because it has unwanted connotations of laziness, aimlessness, and uselessness.

2. We are aware of the possibility that these very early memories may be fantasies instead of realities. We shall keep this question open as we continue the research.

3. J.R. Hilgard's (1970, 1979) earlier research had also unearthed specific findings, such as the following, which we confirmed in this project: hypnotic susceptibility is correlated with (a) having had imaginary playmates during childhood, (b) being able to "become" the character in a novel, and (c) having experienced special life situations that led to an extensive involvement in imagining.

4. In a recent study, we tested again, in a different way, the hypothesis that individuals who are very fantasy-prone are excellent hypnotic subjects. First, we constructed a brief paper-and-pencil test that asked for simple "yes" or "no" answers to 46 shortened but representative items from our original 100-item Memory, Imagining, and Creativity Interview Schedule. This paper-and-pencil test was then administered by Dr. Steven Jay Lynn and Michael R. Nash at Ohio University to 23 excellent and 15 poor male and female hypnotic subjects whom they had preselected (for another experiment they were conducting) on the basis of their very high or very low scores on the Harvard Group Scale of Hypnotic Susceptibility and the Stanford Hypnotic Susceptibility Scale (Form

C). The results strikingly confirmed the hypothesis that individuals who are very high on the fantasy-prone syndrome are excellent hypnotic subjects. Of the 38 subjects participating in the study, 6 obtained very high scores on the simplified and shortened Memory, Imagining, and Creativity Interview Schedule; that is, they answered the items in the way that characterizes high fantasy-prone subjects. All six of these high fantasy-prone subjects had been previously rated by Dr. Lynn and Michael R. Nash as excellent hypnotic subjects. Although the data from Ohio University again showed that individuals similar to those we have described in this chapter (who clearly show the fantasy-prone syndrome) make excellent hypnotic subjects, they also showed that there exists another type of excellent hypnotic subject who is not fantasy prone—of those rated as excellent hypnotic subjects at Ohio University, 34% were below the overall mean for fantasy proneness as indicated by our paper-and-pencil test.

5.   Although patients diagnosed as hysterics tend to be better hypnotic subjects than other patients, some patients with a diagnosis of hysteria are poor hypnotic subjects, and the great majority of excellent hypnotic subjects are not hysterics but instead fall within the broad range of normal functioning (Gill & Brenman, 1959).

REFERENCES

Andersen, M. L. Correlates of hypnotic performance: An historical and role-theoretical analysis. Unpublished doctoral dissertation, University of California, Berkeley, 1963.

As, A. Non-hypnotic experiences related to hypnotizability in male and female college students. *Scandinavian Journal of Psychology,* 1962, **3,** 112–121.

As, A., O'Hara, J. W., & Munger, M. P. The measurement of subjective experiences presumably related to hypnotic susceptibility. *Scandinavian Journal of Psychology,* 1962, **3,** 47–64.

Atkinson, G. A. Personality and hypnotic cognition. Unpublished doctoral dissertation, University of Minnesota, 1971.

Barber, T. X. Antisocial and criminal acts induced by "hypnosis": A review of clinical and experimental findings. *Archives of General Psychiatry,* 1961, **5,** 301–312.

Barber, T. X. Hypnotizability, suggestibility, and personality: V. A critical review of research findings. *Psychological Reports,* 1964, **14,** 299–320.

Barber, T. X. *Hypnosis: A scientific approach.* New York: Van Nostrand, 1969.

Barber, T. X. *LSD, marihuana, yoga, and hypnosis.* Hawthorne, N.Y.: Aldine, 1970.

Barber, T. X. Self-control: Temperature biofeedback, hypnosis, yoga, and relaxation. In T. X. Barber, L. V. DiCara, J. Kamiya, N. E. Miller, D. Shapiro, and J. Stoyva (Eds.), *Biofeedback and self-control, 1975/76.* Hawthorne, N.Y.: Aldine, 1976.

Barber, T. X. Hypnosis, suggestions, and psychosomatic phenomena: A new look from the standpoint of recent experimental studies. *American Journal of Clinical Hypnosis,* 1978a, **21,** 13–27.

Barber, T. X. *Positive suggestions for effective living and philosophical hypnosis* (cassette tape). Medfield, Mass.: Medfield Foundation, 1978b.

Barber, T. X. *Hypnotic suggestions for weight control and smoking cessation* (cassette tape). Medfield, Mass.: Medfield Foundation, 1979a.

Barber, T. X. *Hypnotic and self-hypnotic suggestions for study-concentration, relaxation, pain control, and mystical experiences* (cassette tape). Medfield, Mass.: Medfield Foundation, 1979b.

Barber, T. X. Medicine, suggestive therapy, and healing. In R. J. Kastenbaum, T. X. Barber, S. C. Wilson, B. L. Ryder, and L. B. Hathaway, *Old, sick, and helpless: Where therapy begins.* Cambridge, Mass.: Ballinger, 1981.

Barber, T. X. Hypnosuggestive procedures in the treatment of clinical pain: Implications for theories of hypnosis and suggestive therapy. In T. Millon, C. J. Green, and R. B. Meagher, Jr. (Eds), *Handbook of clinical health psychology.* New York: Plenum, 1982.

Barber, T. X., & Calverley, D. S. Definition of the situation as a variable affecting "hypnotic-like" suggestibility. *Journal of Clinical Psychology,* 1964a, **20,** 438–440.

Barber, T. X., and Calverley, D. S. Empirical evidence for a theory of "hypnotic" behavior: Effects of pretest instructions on response to primary suggestions. *Psychological Record,* 1964b, **14,** 457–467.

Barber, T. X., & Calverley, D. S. Toward a theory of hypnotic behavior: Experimental evaluation of Hull's postulate that hypnotic susceptibility is a habit phenomenon. *Journal of Personality,* 1966, **34,** 416–433.

Barber, T. X., & Glass, L. B. Significant factors in hypnotic behavior. *Journal of Abnormal and Social Psychology,* 1962, **64,** 222–228.

Barber, T. X., Spanos, N. P., Chaves, J. F. *Hypnosis, imagination, and human potentialities.* Elmsford, New York: Pergamon, 1974.

Barber, T. X., & Wilson, S. C. *Hypnotic inductions, mental relaxation, and permissive suggestions* (cassette tape). Medfield, Mass.: Medfield Foundation, 1978.

Barber, T. X., & Wilson, S. C. The Barber Suggestibility Scale and the Creative Imagination Scale: Experimental and clinical applications. *American Journal of Clinical Hypnosis,* 1978–1979, **21,** 84–108.

Barber, T. X., & Wilson, S. C. Guided imagining and hypnosis: Theoretical and empirical overlap and convergence in a new Creative Imagination Scale. In A. A. Sheikh and J. T. Shaffer (Eds.) *The potential of fantasy and imagination.* New York: Brandon House, 1979.

Barlow, F. *Mental prodigies.* London: Hutchinson's Scientific and Technical Publications, 1952.

Blackmore, S. *Parapsychology and out-of-the-body experiences.* Hove, East Sussex, England: Transpersonal Books, 1978.

Brawley, B. G. *The Negro genius.* New York: Dodd, Mead, 1937.

Coe, W. C. The heuristic value of role theory and hypnosis. Unpublished doctoral dissertation, University of California, Berkeley, 1964.

Coe, W. C., & Sarbin, T. R. An experimental demonstration of hypnosis as role enactment. *Journal of Abnormal Psychology,* 1966, **71,** 400–405.

Cronin, D. M., Spanos, N. P., & Barber, T. X. Augmenting hypnotic suggestibility by providing favorable information about hypnosis. *American Journal of Clinical Hypnosis,* 1971, **13,** 259–264.

Crookall, R. *The supreme adventure: Analyses of psychic communications.* London: James Clarke, 1961.

Dennis, L. G. Individual and family correlates of children's fantasy play. Unpublished doctoral dissertation, University of Florida, 1976.

Diamond, M. J. The use of observationally presented information to modify hypnotic susceptibility. *Journal of Abnormal Psychology,* 1972, **79,** 174–180.

Diamond, M. J. Gregory, J., Lenney, E., Steadman, C., & Talone, J. Personality and hypnosis: The role of hypnosis-specific mediational attitudes in predicting hypnotic responsivity. *Proceedings of the 80th Annual Convention of the American Psychological Association,* 1972, **7,** 865–866.

Dingwall, E. J. (Ed.) *Abnormal hypnotic phenomena: A survey of nineteenth-century cases,* Vols. 1–4. New York: Barnes & Noble, 1968.

Erickson, M. H. An experimental investigation of the possible antisocial use of hypnosis. *Psychiatry,* 1939, **2,** 391–414.

Fein, G. A transformational analysis of pretending. *Developmental Psychology,* 1975, **11,** 291–296.

Freyberg, J. Increasing the imaginative play of urban disadvantaged kindergarten children through systematic training. In J. L. Singer, *The child's world of make-believe.* New York: Academic Press, 1973.

Galton, F. *Inquiries into human faculty and its development.* London: Dent, 1883.

Garrett, E. J. *Many voices: The autobiography of a medium.* New York: Putnam, 1968.

Gill, M. M., & Brenman, M. *Hypnosis and related states: Psychoanalytic studies in regression.* New York: International Universities Press, 1959.

Goldenson, R. M. *Mysteries of the mind: The drama of human behavior.* Garden City, N.Y.: Doubleday, 1973.

Green, H. *I never promised you a rose garden.* New York: Holt, 1964.

Griffing, P. Sociodramatic play among young black children. *Theory and Practice,* 1974, **13,** 257–264.

Hilgard, E. R. *Hypnotic susceptibility.* New York: Harcourt, 1965.

Hilgard, J. R. *Personality and hypnosis: A study of imaginative involvement,* Chicago: University of Chicago Press, 1970.

Hilgard, J. R. Imaginative and sensory-affective involvements: in everyday life and in hypnosis. In E. Fromm and R. E. Shor (Eds.), *Hypnosis: Developments in research and new perspectives* (new and revised 2nd ed.). Hawthorne, N.Y.: Aldine, 1979.

Jaensch, E. R. *Eidetic imagery and typological methods of investigation.* London: Kegan Paul, Trench, Trubner, 1930.

Janet, P. *The mental state of hystericals.* New York: Putnam, 1901.

Kastenbaum, R. J., Barber, T. X., Wilson, S. C., Ryder, B. L., & Hathaway, L. B. *Old, sick, and helpless: Where therapy begins.* Cambridge, Mass.: Ballinger, 1981.

Kinney, J. C. M. Modification of hypnotic susceptibility. Unpublished doctoral dissertation, Stanford University, 1969.

Krieger, D. *The therapeutic touch.* Englewood Cliffs, N.J.: Prentice-Hall, 1979.

Landon, H. C. R. Mozart, Wolfgang Amadeus. In *Encyclopaedia Britannica: Macropaedia.* Vol. 12. Chicago: Encyclopaedia Britannica, 1977, pp. 600–604.

Lee-Teng, E. Trance-susceptibility, induction susceptibility, and acquiescence as factors in hypnotic performance. *Journal of Abnormal Psychology,* 1965, **70,** 383–389.

Litt, H. Imagery in children's thinking. Unpublished doctoral dissertation, Liverpool University, 1973.

London, P., Cooper, L. M., & Johnson, M. J. Subject characteristics in hypnosis research: II. Attitudes toward hypnosis, volunteer status, and personality measures. III. Some correlates of hypnotic susceptibility. *International Journal of Clinical and Experimental Hypnosis,* 1962, **10,** 13–21.

Luria, A. R. *The mind of a mnemonist.* New York: Basic Books, 1968.

Maslow, A. H. *Motivation and personality.* New York: Harper, 1954.

McKellar, P. Between wakefulness and sleep: Hypnagogic fantasy. In A. A. Sheikh and J. T. Shaffer (Eds.), *The potential of fantasy and imagination.* New York: Brandon House, 1979a.

McKellar, P. *Mindsplit: The psychology of multiple personality and the dissociated self.* London: Dent, 1979b.

Meade, M. *Madame Blavatsky: The woman behind the myth.* New York: Putnam, 1980.

Melei, J. P., & Hilgard, E. R. Attitudes toward hypnosis, self-predictions, and hypnotic susceptibility. *International Journal of Clinical and Experimental Hypnosis,* 1964, **12,** 99–108.

Moody, R. A. *Life after death.* New York: Bantam/Mockingbird, 1975.

Nietzke, A. Portrait of an aura reader. *Human Behavior,* February 1979, 28–35.

Osis, K., & Haraldsson, E. *At the hour of death.* New York: Avon Books, 1977.

Parish, E. *Hallucinations and illusions, a study of the fallacies of perception.* London: Scott, 1897.

Pavenstedt, E. (Ed.). *The drifters.* Boston: Little, Brown, 1967.

Perry, C. Imagery, fantasy and hypnotic susceptibility: A multidimensional approach. *Journal of Personality and Social Psychology,* 1973, **26,** 217–221.

Perry, C., Gelfand, R., & Marcovitch, P. The relevance of hypnotic susceptibility in the clinical context. *Journal of Abnormal Psychology,* 1979, **88,** 592–603.

Purdy, D. M. Eidetic imagery and plasticity of perception. *Journal of General Psychology,* 1936, **15,** 437–454.

Ring, K. *Life at death: A scientific investigation of the near death experience.* New York: Coward-McCann & Geoghegan, 1980.

Roll, W. G. ESP and memory. *International Journal of Neuropsychiatry,* 1966, **2,** 505–521.

Roll, W. G. *The Changing Perspective on Life After Death.* Chapel Hill, N.C.: Psychical Research Foundation, 1981.

Sarbin, T. R. The quixotic principle: Believed-in imaginings. Santa Cruz: Calif. Department of Psychology, Stevenson College, University of California, 1976.

Sarbin, T. R. Metaphorical encounters of the fourth kind. Paper presented at annual meeting of the American Psychological Association, Toronto, August 28, 1978.

Sarbin, T. R., & Coe, W. C. *Hypnosis: A Social Psychological Analysis of Influence Communication*. New York: Holt, 1972.

Sarbin, T. R., & Lim, D. T. Some evidence in support of the role-taking hypothesis in hypnosis. *International Journal of Clinical and Experimental Hypnosis*, 1963, **11**, 98–103.

Schatzman, M. *The Story of Ruth*. New York: Putnam, 1980.

Sheehan, P. W. Hypnosis and the process of imagination. In E. Fromm and R. E. Shor (Eds.), *Hypnosis: Developments in research and new perspectives*. Hawthorne, N.Y.: Aldine, 1979.

Shor, R. E. Hypnosis and the concept of the gneralized reality-orientation. *American Journal of Psychotherapy*, 1959, **13**, 582–602.

Shor, R. E., Orne, M. T., & O'Connell, D. N. Validation and cross-validation of a scale of self-reported personal experiences which predicts hypnotizability. *Journal of Psychology*, 1962, **53**, 55–75.

Shor, R.E., Orne, M. T., & O'Connell, D. N. Psychological correlates of plateau hypnotizability in a special volunteer sample. *Journal of Personality and Social Psychology*, 1966, **3**, 80–95.

Siegel, R. K. The psychology of life after death. *American Psychologist*, 1980, **35**, 911–931.

Singer, J. L. Imagination and make-believe play in early childhood: Some educational implications. *Journal of Mental Imagery*, 1977, **1**, 127–144.

Spanos, N. P., & Barber, T. X. Toward a convergence in hypnosis research. *American Psychologist*, 1974, **29**, 500–511.

Spanos, N. P., & McPeake, J. D. The effects of involvement in everyday imaginative activities and attitudes toward hypnosis on hypnotic susceptibility. *Journal of Personality and Social Psychology*, 1975a, **31**, 594–598.

Spanos, N. P., & McPeake, J. D. The interaction of attitudes toward hypnosis and involvement in everyday imaginative activities on hypnotic susceptibility. *American Journal of Clinical Hypnosis*, 1975b, **17**, 247–252.

Spanos, N. P., Valois, R., Ham, M. W., & Ham, M. L. Suggestibility, and vividness and control of imagery. *International Journal of Clinical and Experimental Hypnosis*, 1973, **21**, 305–311.

Spiegel, H. The grade 5 syndrome: The highly hypnotizable person. *International Journal of Clinical and Experimental Hypnosis*. 1974, **22**, 303–319.

Sutcliffe, J. P. Hypnotic-behaviour: Fantasy or simulation? Unpublished doctoral dissertation, University of Sydney, Australia, 1958.

Sutcliffe, J. P., Perry, C. W., & Sheehan, P. W. The relation of some aspects of imagery and fantasy to hypnotizability. *Journal of Abnormal Psychology*, 1970, **76**, 279–287.

Tellegen, A., and Atkinson, G. Openness to absorbing and self-altering experiences ("absorption"), a trait related to hypnotic susceptibility. *Journal of Abnormal Psychology*, 1974, **83**, 268–277.

Vogt, D., & Sultan, G. *Reality revealed: The theory of multidimensional reality*. San Jose, Cal.: Vector Associates, 1977.

Weitzenhoffer, A. M., & Hilgard, E. R. *Stanford hypnotic susceptibility scale, Forms A and B*. Palo Alto, Cal.: Consulting Psychologists Press, 1959.

Weitzenhoffer, A. M., & Hilgard, E. R. *Stanford hypnotic susceptibility scale, Form C.* Palo Alto, Cal.: Consulting Psychologists Press, 1962.

Wilson, C. *The Occult.* New York: Random House, 1971.

Wilson, C. *Mysteries.* New York: Putnam, 1978.

Wilson, S. C., & Barber, T. X. The Creative Imagination Scale as a measure of hypnotic responsiveness: Applications to experimental and clinical hypnosis. *American Journal of Clinical Hypnosis,* 1978, **20,** 235–249.

Wilson, S. C., & Barber, T. X. Vivid fantasy and hallucinatory abilities in the life histories of excellent hypnotic subjects ("somnambules"): Preliminary report with female subjects. In E. Klinger (Ed.), *Imagery: Concepts, results, and applications.* New York: Plenum, 1981, pp. 133–149.

Wilson, S. C., Ryder, B. L., Doran, J. M., & Enos, L. M. Supportive therapy: A new approach to hospitalized geriatric patients. In L. E. Abt and I. R. Stuart (Eds.), *The newer therapies: A workbook.* New York: Van Nostrand, 1982.

Yates, F. A. *The art of memory.* Chicago: University of Chicago Press, 1966.

PART THREE

Application

CHAPTER 13

Clinical Uses of Mental Imagery

ANEES A. SHEIKH AND CHARLES S. JORDAN

Horowitz (1978) has distinguished three main modalities of cognition and expression and termed them the *enactive*, *image*, and *lexical* modalities. The enactive system involves the motoric aspects of our existence and is presumed to be associated with the cortical motor regions and the limbic system. The image modality apparently is largely dependent on the right hemisphere of the brain, permits continued information processing following perception, and lends a sensory character to ideas and feelings. The lexical or linguistic mode is predominantly coordinated through the left hemisphere and is particularly effective in integrating extremely diverse phenomena into one language label that permits very rapid subsequent retrieval (Singer & Pope, 1978).

Although many clinicians have recognized that the three modalities in their intricate interrelationships are equally important, language traditionally has been the main medium of therapeutic intervention.

Verbal processes have been credited with enhancing our ability to communicate, with providing ways for consensual validation of our beliefs, and with giving logical direction to our flow of thinking (Forisha, 1979; Paivio, 1975). Although language is probably the most common and precise means of interpsychic communication, numerous writers have pointed out limitations in this medium that are of extreme relevance to the clinical field.

Bowers and Bowers (1972, p. 265) indicate that the linguistic mode is limiting because it subtly forces us "to exclude from consideration and even from consciousness those aspects of our subjectivity that evade easy articulation." Schachtel (1959, p. 243) argues that "unseeingness" is frequently due to "the encroachment of an already labeled word upon our spontaneous

---

A few paragraphs in this chapter are slightly modified versions of parts of previously published papers (Jordan, 1979; Sheikh & Panagiotou, 1975; Sheikh et al., 1979a,b). They are included here with permission of the publishers of those papers. The senior author of this chapter expresses his sincere appreciation to Nancy Much for her valuable assistance in the preparation of the manuscript. The contributions of the second author are limited to the sections on European approaches and group applications of imagery.

sensory and intellectual capacities.'' Singer and Pope (1978, p. 9) contend that ''as events are encoded into language . . . they become abstracted and lose their immediate impact on our experience; as such they become less emotional events, make less cogent demands, tend not to present the vivid here-and-now challenge for processing stimulation, which Tomkins (1962, 1963) argues is the basis for affects.'' Bruner (1968, p. 407) notices that ''once language becomes a medium for the translation of experience, there is a progressive release from immediacy.'' Forisha (1979, p. 3) warns that ''verbal processes alone fragment experience by dividing it up into preconceived categories, which separate us from our immediate experience.'' Hall (1977, p. 153) states that ''much of the truly integrative behavior . . . is under the control of those parts of the brain that are not concerned with speech.'' Sheikh (1978) speculates that perhaps, after having been severed from visions, warped by words, and stifled by semantics for a long time, we are ready to restore our wholeness by returning to the nonverbal springs of our existence.

Both Hall (1977) and Sheikh (1978) are undoubtedly referring to the significance of mental images in the growth process. After having been banned from the ''portals of legitimacy'' (Forisha, 1979, p. 2) for decades, mental images, the ''ostracized'' ghosts (Holt, 1964) from ''psychology's dead past'' (Watson, 1913) have made a robust return in both experimental and clinical psychology. Arguments in favor of the efficacy of imagery in the clinic are presented in the first section of this chapter. The second part consists of a classification and discussion of a multitude of image approaches to therapy from around the world. The third segment deals with the significance of images to psychodiagnosis and presents a brief review of various attempts. In the concluding section a few overall integrative remarks are presented, and the ultimate interaction that should exist between the clinicians and the researchers is stressed.

BASES FOR THE EFFICACY OF IMAGERY IN THE CLINIC

Although imagery has been an instrument of therapeutic intervention throughout the recorded history of medicine, recently interest in widely varied imagery techniques has greatly expanded and intensified. (Horowitz, 1978; Sheikh, 1977; Sheikh & Panagiotou, 1975). The importance of the use of mental imagery in psychotherapy is being realized, and the possibility of the supremacy of images over words is being examined (Ahsen, 1977; Sheikh & Shaffer, 1979; Singer, 1974; Singer & Pope, 1978). Several writers have indicated numerous characteristics of the imagery mode that make it an eminently suitable vehicle for clinical work. A number of these are listed in the paragraphs that follow:

1.   Klinger (1980, p. 5) states: ''It seems quite likely that imagery rep-

resents the functioning of important parts of the same psychological apparatus that we exercise in all our activities. That is, imagery represents the central core of perceptual, retrieval, and response mechanisms." Thus "experiencing something in imagery can be considered to be in many essential ways psychologically equivalent to experiencing the thing in actuality." This view is shared by other authors (Kosslyn, 1980; Neisser, 976; Sheikh & Shaffer, 1979). A number of studies, including those by Perky (1910), Leuba (1940), John (1967), and Segal and Fusella (1970), indicate that imagery and perception are experientially and neurophysiologically comparable processes and cannot be distinguished from each other by any intrinsic qualities (Richardson, 1969). Hebb's and Pribram's views tend to support this assertion (Singer, 1974). Penfield (1963) demonstrated that the locus of image excitation corresponded to localization of sensory functions in the brain.

2. Aristotle asserted that images act as the sources of activation and guide behavior by representing the goal object (McMahon, 1973, p. 465). Several contemporary psychologists similarly contend that images are capable of representing situations or objects and, consequently, act as motivators for future behavior (Miller et al., 1960; Mowrer, 1977; Sarbin & Coe, 1972; Sheikh et al., 1979a). Shepard (1978) and Tower and Singer (1981) indicate that individuals seem to act more on the basis of imaginal consequences than according to actual probabilities.

3. It appears that meaning is largely dependent on images; words arouse images that have accompanying emotional responses, and these responses are the source of the meaning of words (Bugelski, 1970; Forisha, 1979). Arieti (1976) offers support to this conclusion by indicating that images make it possible for us to preserve an emotional attitude toward absent objects.

4. Mental images provide a unique opportunity to examine "the integration of perception, motivation, subjective meaning, and realistic abstract thought" [Shorr (1980, p. 99); see also Escalona (1973)].

5. Schachtel (1959) laments that as individuals are socialized, they tend to rely more and more on empty verbal clichés or abstractions, thereby losing the direct contact with experience. Singer and Pope (1978, p. 10) assert that this contact is implicit in the "concrete modality-specific imagery system" and is a source of extensive details about specific occurrences in the past (Singer, 1979).

6. Imagery may be the main access to important preverbal memories or to memories encoded at developmental stages at which language, while present, was not yet predominant (Kepecs, 1954; Sheikh & Panagiotou, 1975).

7. Klinger believes that the imaginal stream observed in image therapies tends to overrepresent the client's problem area or "current concerns . . . . Unlike polite social discourse, imaginal techniques invite material that is likely to move selectively into the troubled areas of the client's life" [Klinger(1980, p. 12); see also Breger et al., (1971)].

8. Klinger (1980) also points out that images are accompanied by emo-

tional responses to internal and external cues present in the situation. Singer (1979, p. 36) concurs by stating that "the imagery system increases the likelihood that we will experience more fully a range of emotions." Many others have noted that when focused on, images may uncover very intense affective changes or generate emotional reactions (Horowitz, 1970; Reyher & Smeltzer, 1968; Shapiro, 1970; Sheehan, 1968; Sheikh & Panagiotou, 1975). It appears that "images may have a greater capacity than the linguistic mode for the attraction and focusing of emotionally loaded associations in concentrated forms: Verbal logic is linear; whereas the image is a simultaneous representation. The quality of simultaneity gives imagery greater isomorphism with the qualities of perception, and therefore greater capacity for descriptive accuracy" (Sheikh & Panagiotou, 1975, p. 557).

9.   Numerous studies have demonstrated the power of imagery to produce a wide variety of physiological changes. For example, Barber et al. (1964) observed that the instruction to imagine that tap water was sour resulted in increased salivation. Simpson and Paivio (1966) noted changes in pupillary size during imagery. May and Johnson (1973) observed increased heart rate due to arousing images. Yaremko and Butler (1975) found that imagining a tone or shock and real presentation of these stimuli produced comparable habituation. Changes in electromyograms due to images also have been observed by several investigators (Craig, 1969; Jacobsen, 1929; McGuigan, 1971). Also, Barber (1961, 1969, 1978) reported that images were capable of producing blood glucose increases, inhibition of gastrointestinal activity, increases in gastric-acid secretion, blister formation, and alterations in skin temperature [see also Jordan & Lenington (1979), Paivio (1973), and Sheikh et al. (1979a)]. Several studies of meditation and of biofeedback that undoubtedly often involved imagery have indicated reduction in blood pressure, oxygen consumption, and heart rate, as well as changes in gastrointestinal activity and body temperature (Sheikh et al., 1979a). Neal Miller (1972) has remarked that imagery might be the only practical way to develop some control over autonomic processes.

10.   It has been observed that spontaneous images occur in some individuals at times of verbal blockage; the images fill in with perceptual, usually pictorial representation when the individual is unable to continue to formulate experiences verbally (Pangiotou & Sheikh, 1977). Also, imagery frequently opens up new avenues of exploration when therapy seems to come to a halt (Singer, 1974). Davé (1976) reports that during an impasse on some problem the visualization of elements in the problem is of greater benefit than the utilization of a rational cognitive approach.

11.   It has been demonstrated that "free imagery," an analogue of free association, is extremely effective in circumventing even very stubborn defenses and uncovering repressed material (Klinger, 1980; Panagiotou & Sheikh, 1977; Reyher, 1963). "The resort to imagery may catch the patient by surprise and outwit his defenses" (Singer, 1974, p. 251).

12.   Horowitz (1970, 1974) states that the image mode is the medium

most sympathetic with unconscious organization. It permits the spanning of the conscious–unconscious continuum more readily than does overt or covert language; elements from the unconscious more easily "slip into" imagoic cognition, and image forms more readily act as symbols (Panagiotou & Sheikh, 1977). "Images are less likely to be filtered through the conscious critical apparatus than is linguistic expression. In most cases, words and phrases must be consciously understood before they are spoken; for in order to assume a grammatical order they must first pass through a rational censorship. Imagery, perhaps, is not subject to this filtering process, and therefore may have the opportunity to be a more direct expression of the unconscious" (Sheikh & Panagiotou, 1975, p. 556). In the same vein, Jellinek (1949) explains that imagery, because of its primordial forms, has a special function as the "direct voice of the unconscious."

13.   Jellinek (1949) notes the intrapsychic prophetic function of imagoic cognition: Ideas and responses often occur in imagery and appear only later in verbal cognition and behavior.

14.   Guided-daydream images in many cases are likely to produce therapeutic consequences in the absence of any interpretation by the guide or intellectual insight by the client (Desoille, 1961; Frétigny & Virel, 1968; Klinger, 1980; Leuner, 1977).

15.   Solutions rehearsed at the imaginal level during therapy appear to generalize outside of the therapy situation (Klinger, 1980; Richardson, 1969).

The foregoing paragraphs make it abundantly evident why an increasing number of clinicians are showing interest in including imagery in their therapeutic armamentarium. A variety of image-based therapies are discussed in the next section.

IMAGERY-BASED THERAPEUTIC METHODS

Numerous widely varied imagery-based therapies have emerged over the years abroad and in this country. Because of limited space, it is impossible to discuss the details of all these procedures. Interested readers are referred to other sources for more comprehensive discussions (Sheikh & Panagiotou, 1975; Sheikh & Shaffer, 1979; Singer, 1974; Singer & Pope, 1978). A brief discussion of only the major European and American approaches is presented in this section.

It is noteworthy that the issue of whether images represent a direct encoding of perceptual experiences (Paivio, 1973), an artifact of propositional structuring of reality (Pylyshyn, 1973), or a constructive and reconstructive process (Kosslyn, 1980) has not been of any real concern to the majority of clinicians. They assume that everyone experiences mental representations of objects and events, and these representations constitute their subject matter. A definition of imagery, such as the one provided by Richardson

9), is implicit in most of these approaches: "Mental imagery refers to all those quasi-sensory or quasi-perceptual experiences of which we are self-consciously aware, and which exist for us in the absence of those stimulus conditions that are known to produce their genuine sensory or perceptual counterparts" (Richardson, 1969, p. 2).

European Approaches

European psychologists, particularly clinicians, in contrast to their American colleagues, for a long time have demonstrated a deep sensitivity to and involvement in the realm of imagination. This attitude was relatively unperturbed by the growing emphasis on behavioristic psychology in America. The antecedents of this largely subjective approach to imagery are many; some are as follows: (1) many of the experimentalists fled Europe during World Wars I and II; (2) the phenomenology of German and French origin permeated the philosophical roots of European clinical and scientific systems; (3) Jung's subjective approaches to the exploration of symbols in fantasies, dreams, and myths profoundly affected many European practitioners; and (4) Europe had been subtly seeded by a profound legacy of subjective Eastern psychology (Jordan 1979).

Early Contributions

Pierre Janet (1898) was probably the first European to employ imagery in therapeutic work. He discovered that substituting one image for another was helpful in overcoming the "idées fixes" of hysterical patients. This substitution technique is still being used by various therapists interested in imagery (Crampton, 1974). Alfred Binet (1922), although primarily interested in studying the relationship of intelligence to various mental faculties, made contributions in the clinical field as well. He encouraged his patients to converse with the visual images in an introspective state that he called "provoked introspection." He labeled this technique the "dialogue method." Both Janet and Binet believed that pictures emerging during this introspection revealed the client's diverse unconscious subpersonalities.

The first therapeutic approach based largely on images was used by Carl Happich (1932) in Germany. He expanded Binet's work by inducing "emergent images" through encouraging the patients to employ muscular relaxation, passive respiration, and meditation. He speculated that between the conscious and the unconscious lies a penumbric region or the "meditative zone" in which productions that have matured in the unconscious become visible to the mind's eye. To stimulate imagery, Happich used a number of predetermined scenes, such as a chapel, a meadow, or a mountain. The symbolic significance of such scenes was later investigated by Kretschmer (1969) and incorporated into his meditative technique in psychotherapy.

In France, Eugéne Caslant (1921) was using a technique for psychic development in which he encouraged his subjects to ascend or descend in imaginal space. He noted that, during these movements, subjects experienced different emotions and varying degrees of vividness of images. Through these ascending and descending images, Caslant had tried to free his subjects and thus enable them to generate a creative form of imagery that could lead to extrasensory experience (Singer, 1974).

A few other researchers arrived at similar uses of images by way of a biophysical approach to consciousness. Oskar Vogt, a brain physiologist who carried out his research on sleep and hypnosis at the Berlin Institute during 1890–1900, noted that intelligent patients who had undergone a number of hypnotic sessions were able to put themselves into a state that seemed to be similar to a hypnotic state. His patients reported that such "autohypnotic" experiences had a remarkable recuperative influence and enhanced their general efficiency (Jordan, 1979). Stimulated by Vogt's work, Schultz started to investigate, in 1905, whether hypnotherapy could be employed without cultivating in the patient a form of passivity and a detrimental dependence on the therapist. Schultz observed that during hypnosis his subjects experienced a feeling of relaxation, warmth, and heaviness in the extremities. Subsequently, without inducing a hypnotic state, he encouraged his patients to imagine that they were having the same physiological feelings. This method was later developed by Schultz in collaboration with Luthe (Schultz & Luthe, 1959) and is currently known as *autogenic training*.

Ludwig Frank (1910) discovered the significance of deep relaxation for the spontaneous occurrence of hypnagogic images, which he believed to be cathartic in nature. Marc Guillerey, in Switzerland, began his experiments with *rêverie dirigée* (directed revery) as early as 1925. His theoretical orientation stemmed partly from the psychosomatic conceptions of Roger Vittoz (Vittoz, 1907). Guillerey stressed the neuromuscular correlates of images and believed that the resolution of conflicts at the level of imagery produced psychophysiological harmonization (Guillerey, 1945).

The methods of Schultz, Frank, and Guillerey represent a significant milestone in the history of the clinical uses of imagery. Particularly Schultz's autogenic training may be seen as the forerunner of various modern methods of deep-muscle relaxation and the many uses of imagery in behavior modification. The autogenic method also can be regarded as a self-generated and self-regulated biofeedback technique and may have inspired the recent technological approach to biofeedback. Furthermore, autogenic training has influenced many European and American clinicians and has become a standard therapy in various fields of medicine in recent years.

A few psychoanalysts also are among the early contributors to the clinical use of imagery. It was perhaps Silberer, in 1909, who first recognized the-symbolic nature of hypnagogic images and their value in the exploration of unconscious and preconscious processes (Kosbab, 1974). Pierce Clark (1925) employed visual imagery ("phantasms") to gain access to childhood memories. He was probably the first to use free association of imagery, a method that has recently been revived by Reyher (1978). Anna Freud , used both free and directed imagery with children(Crampton , 1974). The contributions of Sigmund Freud and Jung are explored in greater detail in the following segments.

Freud, Psychoanalysis, and Imagery

It appears that Freud was well aware, as early as the 1890s, of spontaneous images experienced by his patients (Kosbab, 1974). He talked about the "plastic form and natural colors" of the imagined scenes that the patients perceived "with all the vividness of reality" (Breuer & Freud, 1955, p. 53). Appprently, Freud's use of imagery was extensive prior to 1900. In fact, he abandoned the use of hypnosis in favor of an imagery procedure that was more under the patient's conscious control. Freud started using a technique in which he would press on the patient's head and instruct him or her to observe the images which appeared as he relaxed the pressure. Freud reported that the patients started to see, in rapid succession, various scenes related to the central conflict. These scenes surfaced spontaneously in chronological order. During the use of this procedure, Freud discovered the nature of resistance perhaps for the first time (Jordan, 1979; Singer, 1974). Apparently around 1900, Freud decided against explicitly using imagery for analytic purposes. He remarked, "My therapy consists in wiping away these pictures"(Kosbab, 1974, p. 284). Thereafter, he gravitated toward verbal methods including free association and dream interpretation. He came to regard imagery as a kind of resistance that stood in the way of free association and defended the client against unacceptable impulses. Thus Freud's influence, particularly among psychoanalysts, resulted in emphasis on the secondary process or the verbal content of the client's productions. Imagery was termed a more primitive, primary-process functioning associated with regressive features and was "downplayed in favor of directed, logical thought" [Singer & Pope (1978, p. 5); see also Jordan (1979)]. Ernest Kris (1952), a psychoanalyst who moved away from this extremely rational perspective, suggested that creative thinking perhaps can benefit from "regression in the service of the ego." However, his use of the term "regression" reveals that even he was biased in favor of rational thought. "How sad it is that we categorize the poet who illuminates our private experiences through vivid images, creative word combinations, and a sensitive ear for the tone of a phrase as relying on a 'regressed' human capacity" (Singer & Pope, 1978, p. 6).

It is intriguing to note that even though Freud and most of his followers tended to shy away from the explicit use of imagery in therapy, numerous characteristics of the psychoanalytic situation appear to encourage the elicitation of images. These include reclining in a restful attitude, mild sensory deprivation that is produced by looking at the blank ceiling, emphasis on dreams and transference fantasies, use of free association, and emphasis on early memories (Pope, 1977; Singer & Pope, 1978).

Jung and Active Imagination

Unlike Freud, Jung regarded mental imagery as a creative process of the psyche to be employed for attaining greater individual, interpersonal, and spiritual integration (Jordan, 1979). He stated, "The psyche consists essentially of images. It is a series of images in the truest sense, not an accidental juxtaposition or sequence but a structure that is throughout full of meaning and purpose; it is a 'picturing' of vital activities. And just as the material of the body that is ready for life has a need of the psyche in order to be capable of life, so the psyche presupposes the living body in order that its images may live" (Jung, 1960, pp. 325–326). Through this recognition of the reciprocity of psyche and body, Jung expressed the belief in mind–body unity as a life process and suggested that imagery is a means of perceiving and experiencing this life process.

Jung's utilization of imagery in therapy is best represented by the method he called "active imagination," which could grow out of a dream, hypnagogic image, or fantasy. Apparently, Jung developed the method of active imagination during his extended and open-minded descent into the unconscious from 1912 to 1917. He discovered that the unconscious was in a sense constantly dreaming. However, since the individual's attention is focused on the external, he or she is unaware of the mythic dream being developed and becomes conscious of the imaginal world within only if he or she specifically focuses on it. Jung was careful to discriminate between imagination and fantasy. He stated, "A fantasy is more or less your own invention, and remains on the surface of personal things and conscious expectations. But active imagination, as the term denotes, means that the images have a life of their own and that the symbolic events develop according to their own logic—that is, of course, if your conscious reason does not interfere"(Jung, 1976, p. 171). Jung also remarked, "When you concentrate on a mental picture, it begins to stir, the image becomes enriched by details. It moves and develops . . . and so when we concentrate on inner pictures and when we are careful not to interrupt the natural flow of events, our unconscious will produce a series of images which makes a complete story" (Jung, 1976, p 172). Jung commented further that this active imagination process was superior to dreams in "defeating" the unconscious and quickening maturation in analysis. He cautioned, however, that many people are not ready for this direct confrontation with their natural flow of images until later in analysis or even after the completion of analysis.

It appears that Jungian analysis does not always involve active imagination. Watkins (1976, p. 49) lists six reasons that Jung gave for employing active imagination in therapy; he recommended its use in the following instances:

1. When it is obvious that the unconscious is overflowing with fantasies
2. To reduce the number of dreams when there are too many

3. When not enough dreams are being remembered
4. When someone feels or seems to be under indefinable influences under a sort of spell
5. When adaptation to life has been injured
6. When someone falls into the same hole again and again

It is said that, through active imagination and through subsequent relating of the emerging material to his or her own life, the patient receives the "inestimable advantage of assisting the analyst with his own resources and of breaking a dependence which is often felt as humiliating. It is a way of attaining liberation by one's own efforts and of finding courage to be oneself" (Jung   1960, p. 91).

It should be noted that only a few references to the procedure of active imagination as such occur in Jung's works, and little technical information has been added by his followers. Consequently, there has been some confusion concerning what he actually meant by it. However, there is little doubt that Jung's method played a significant role in the imagery movement in psychotherapy.

The Oneirotherapies

Jung regarded active imagination as a procedure to be employed largely indepently by the patient and generally toward the end of analysis or after it; however, several French and German clinicians investigated the potential of fantasy for use as a primary method of conducting psychotherapy (Watkins, 1976). The best known of these approaches include Desoille's (19761, 1965) *directed daydream*, Frétigny and Virel's (1968) *oneirodrama*, and Leuner's (1977, 1978) *guided affective imagery*. The term "oneirotherapy" (from the Greek "oneiros" meaning "dream," hence also known as "dream therapy" or "waking-dream therapy") is used here to describe all three therapies.

There is little doubt that the primary impetus to the development of oneirotherapies in Europe came from the investigations of Desoille (Crampton, 1974; Singer, 1974). Desoille called his technique "le rêve éveillé dirigé," a name he borrowed from Léon Daudet. His main "source for the method though never officially acknowledged, was the occultist, Eugène Caslant, who taught a technique in which subjects visualized themselves as rising or descending in imaginal space as a means of psychic development . . . . From his occultist origins Desoille went through a period in which he was influenced by Freudian thought, then by Jung, and finally by Pavlov . . . though it seems that the latter may have been more related to his political leanings than to his basic psychological affinities" (Crampton, 1974, p. 3). André Virel spent 2 years with Desoille and the influence of Desoille's ideas on Frétigny and Virel's "oneirodrama" is evident. In fact, Virel and Frétigny were keenly aware of the varied imagery techniques and have provided an expert synthesis of the history of the imagery approaches in Europe (Frétigny

& Virel, 1968; Virel, 1968). Leuner traces his technique to Freud's early use of imagery, but similarities with Desoille's technique are striking. However, Leuner's approach is much more systematized. Also, among the oneirotherapists, Leuner has taken the greatest initiative in conducting research dealing with therapy outcome.

For a detailed description of each of these three oneirotherapies, the reader is referred to the original works. This presentation is largely limited to a discussion of the numerous elements shared by all three approaches.

All the oneirotherapeutic methods used *extended* visual fantasies in *narrative* form to obtain information about the motivational system of the individual, including elements of conflict, perceptual distortion, self-perception, and early memories. The individual is usually prepared for using his or her visual imagination by conditions that help him or her to relax; if necessary, preliminary training in muscular relaxation may be given. The reverie itself is typically accompanied by a hypnoidal state of consciousness in which the participant focuses attention on his or her fantasy experience rather than on his or her social environmental and bodily conditions. Leuner does not necessarily take measures to prepare the participant with relaxation training; often, if the participant is able to become involved in fantasy productions, the relaxation of bodily tensions is concomitant.

The oneirotherapists use the products of visual imagination in conjunction with associations, discussion, and interpretation. The participant's verbal contribution plays an important part in discovering the meaning of his or her imagery. Affective accompaniments of the imaginary experience are discussed along with associated ideas and memories; these are interpreted in the light of a detailed anamnesis. If a participant has difficulty experiencing vivid images, repetitive practice often helps, unless his or her inability is rooted in some deep-seated resistances. The oneirotherapists may assume more or less directivity and may choose to introduce into the narrative elements that do not occur spontaneously. Desoille's technique is the most directive and structured of the three.

Usually, in any form of oneirotherapy, certain standard symbolic scenes, that presumably reflect common areas of conflict, are presented to the participant as starting images. The response to any starting image tends to be quite lengthy, and the diagnostic technique blends into other aspects of therapy—abreaction and insight.

The oneirotherapeutic method is generally a psychodynamic approach with respect to its assumptions and interpretations. The primary assumption is that the symbolism inherent in visual imagery constitutes an affective language that can express unconscious motives without causing them to fully impose themselves on conscious recognition. Consequently, it is hypothesized that the participant will have less resistance to the expression of the underlying motives. The "language of the unconscious" hypothesis implies that some kind of symbolism is at work in the imagery. Most oneirotherapists take into account Freudian dream symbolism and Jungian mythological–

literary symbolism, as well as idiosyncratic symbols derived from the individual's associations and anamnesis.

In general, oneirotherapists claim that their methods are effective in discovering the structural details of the patient's personality, in revealing the nature of the affective traumatism, and in alleviating the symptoms rapidly. Frétigny and Virel (1968) claim certain other advantages for their use of imagery, and these may be considered to apply to all three oneirotherapies discussed here. They state: (1) mental imagery can be practiced with people who are incapable of systematic reflection because of their low level of sophistication; (2) through the use of imagery, the snares of rational thinking are avoided; (3) by this approach the pitfalls of encouraging individuals predisposed to sterile rumination are evaded; and (4) mental imagery is oriented directly toward the individual's affective experience.

In short, by the use of imagery in oneirotherapy the problems typically encountered with verbal expression in psychotherapy are eliminated. However, each of these points deserves a modicum of individual attention.

It is quite reasonable to suppose that less educated or simply less verbally reflective individuals have trouble comprehending and fulfilling the requirements of analytically oriented verbal therapy. The American behavior therapists (many of whom also rely on imagery) have used a similar argument in support of their methods—it is much easier for the "average" individual to accept what he or she can readily understand and to understand what is conceptually most concrete. This may be one of the most compelling reasons for conducting psychotherapy through images instead of through words. But does giving the "average"individual only what he or she can readily accept not deprive him or her of an opportunity for enrichment through the discovery of dimensions of life of which he or she was unaware? In other words, should psychotherapy not teach the individual something he or she does not know? Perhaps the psychodynamic image techniques, such as the oneirotherapies, offer a good middle ground. The second point refers to the issue of the requirement that verbal thought "make sense" and the difficulty of representing certain complex perceptions within the confines of verbal syntax. The third point is self-explanatory but not self-evident. Is it not possible that individuals could engage in the very same kind of rumination using imagoic thinking? It may be that persons who are predisposed to verbal rumination are not disposed to or not able to maintain this habit through imagoic thinking. That, however, is a question to be answered through observation. There are no logical grounds for supposing that the defense style involved should be inoperative in imagoic thinking. Concerning the fourth point, Frétigny and Virel assert that oneirotherapy is oriented directly toward affective experience. As indicated earlier in this chapter, this is the central claim of most therapists who prefer to use induced images at some point during therapy. This claim is best substantiated by the testimony of a considerable variety of clinicians.

Psychosynthesis

This therapeutic system was originated and developed by Roberto Assagioli, an Italian psychiatrist (Assagioli, 1965). Compared to the methods of Freud, Jung, Desoille, Leuner, Frétigny, Virel, and others, psychosynthesis is more holistic and eclectic. One of its aims is to develop human personal and spiritual capacities, and to this end the analytical, behavioral, and humanistic methods of the West, as well as meditative techniques from the East are utilized. Assagioli and his followers view human personality as having a number of layers of experience or awareness. "The goal of psychosynthesis is not only the explication of these various levels of awareness and the relief of personal difficulties. Rather, its goal is a thorough reconstruction of the total personality, exploration of the various levels of personality, and eventually the shift of personality to a new center through exploration of its fundamental core" (Singer, 1974, p. 109).

Mental imagery is only one among a number of different procedures used in psychosynthesis. Assagioli draws on numerous imagery methods that reflect the principles of Jung (1954), Desoille (1965), and Leuner (1977) as well as the conditioning and cognitive restructuring approaches (to be discussed later). The practitioners of psychosynthesis are thoroughly acquainted with techniques such as symbolic visualization, initiated symbol projection, guided daydreaming, spontaneous imagery, active imagination, meditation on positive symbols, and a number of other "transcendence techniques" (Gerard, 1964). For example, in Assagioli's "dissolution of the body" exercise the patient imagines that his or her body is consumed in flames; subsequently he or she is expected to experience a great sense of freedom and release and an awareness that the existence of one's spiritual essence is independent of the body. In the "temple of silence" exercise, the subject imagines himself or herself climbing a mountain that has a temple of silence on its peak. In that temple the subject allows all the body cells to be filled with silence. Subsequently, he or she brings this silence down the mountain with him or her and radiates it to the world around.

In psychosynthesis the therapist often simply asks the patient to "picture" what he or she is trying to describe. In the beginning, if images do not readily come to the subject, the therapist may urge him or her to focus on one of his or her dreams or drawings. The images are interpreted on the basis of accompanying verbal association and other available data (Crampton, 1969).

An important assumption underlying the analytic interpretation is that every element of the image represents, at one level or another, a characteristic of the personality, albeit projected, distorted, or displaced. Thus the image not only reflects interpersonal responses, but also reveals dynamic relationships between elements of the personality or psyche. Figures in imagery representing actual persons and expressing the quality of the individual's relationship with them still are considered to ultimately characterize projections of the individual's own needs and motives. Identification with all elements of the image drama is regarded as a way of assimilating repressed elements, in socialized form, and expanding the boundaries of the self.

If the significance of an image is not readily evident, a technique based on directed association from the images often is used. If the symbolic material is difficult to decipher, a more academic approach to interpretation also may be employed.

It is interesting that, although Assagioli's influence on the imagery school in Europe remained somewhat limited, in the United States and in Canada, because of the efforts of Robert Gerard (1964), Martha Crampton (1969), and others, he has had considerable impact. His acceptance in North America is most probably due to the current humanistic movement that embraces holistic and spiritual approaches.

It should be noted that the techniques discussed in this section represent only the major European approaches. Several others have been advanced (Donnars, 1970; Rigo, 1968; Rigo-Uberto, 1968). However, in our opinion, they do not represent any significant departures from the ones already presented here.

European clinicians deserve the credit for keeping alive the use of images in psychotherapy in the wake of behaviorism in the early 1900s. Although they have contributed relatively little to the systematic scientific investigation of imaginal processes, they have provided a rich heritage of therapeutic methods on which American psychologists interested in dynamic, behavioral, and humanistic approaches could draw. Philosophically, Europeans have kept us in contact with the unavoidable phenomenological nature of perception and have constructed a bridge between Eastern and Western approaches to the comprehension of the nature of human consciousness (Jordan, 1979). Currently, as a result of the strenghtening of the "third force" in American psychology, the ideas of the European image therapists are beginning to find their way more readily into American clinical psychology.

Imagery Approaches in America

As Klinger (1971) notes, from 1920 to 1960, with the emergence of behaviorism, there was a "moratorium" in North American psychology on inner experience, including imagery, and not a single book on this topic was published. As Holt (1964) and Watkins (1976) observe, the return of interest in imagery was brought about chiefly by developments in areas outside of mainstream psychology, such as engineering psychology (Holt, 1964; Paloszi-Horvath, 1959), sensory or perceptual deprivation studies (Hebb, 1960; Holt, 1964), biochemical and neuropsychological research (Penfield & Jaspers, 1954; Short, 1953), and studies of sleep and inactivity (Kleitman, 1963). Gradually, however, psychologists began to realize that they could bring the research techniques developed by the behaviorist to bear on the topics that had been discarded but were necessary to the understanding of human beings (Hebb, 1960; Sheehan, 1972; Watkins, 1976). Both experimental and clinical psychologists responded enthusiastically to Holt's (1964) plea, "Come on in—the water's fine." The appearance of the "third force," the humanistic trend in psychology, gave the study and use of imagery further respectability. However, it is really ironic that it was the behavior therapists who were the first to play a significant role in indirectly compelling the clinicians to reexamine the relevance of imagery (Tower & Singer, 1981).

Imagery in Behavior and Cognitive-Behavior Therapy

A number of behavioristic procedures based primarily on the Pavlovian or the Skinnerian models have been developed. They demonstrate the surface relationships between images and emotional reactions as well as the power of images to act as potent stimuli. It should be noted that in these approaches the "image is not used for its own intrinsic sake, but for its pragmatic use in symptom control. Its power is recognized but not its purpose" (Watkins, 1976, p. 82). These methods consist of several variations of counterconditioning and emotional flooding. Besides the usual stress on associative factors, cogent explanations in cognitive terms also have been advanced.

Systematic desensitization, a prototype of counterconditioning, has been one of the most widely used varieties of behavioral treatment. Although Wolpe (1958, 1969) commonly has been given the credit for the development of this method, references to this technique go as far back as 1922. Kretschmer (1922) called it "systematic habituation therapy," Williams (1923) referred to it as "reconditioning," and Howard and Patry (1935) named it "corrective habit training." Salter (1949) was perhaps the first clinician to use this procedure with primary emphasis on the patient's imagery rather than on the real feared stimuli. One of his clients called this technique the "anticlaustrophobic vaccination."

The procedure of systematic desensitization consists essentially of the following steps: (1) preparation of a hierarchy of anxiety-producing stimuli; (2) training in progressive relaxation; (3) visualizing the least anxiety-arousing response while relaxed until relaxation replaces anxiety; and (4) moving on to the next scene of the hierarchy. The anxiety response to an anxiety-producing stimulus is blocked by the compatible relaxation response to the same stimulus. Images are generally used in place of actual stimulus situations because the latter are often extremely impractical. It should be pointed out that in desensitization there is no element of symbolism in the prescribed images. However, it is not known what the subject is actually imagining; idiosyncratic distortions probably do enter into the imagery.

A number of clinicians have suggested variations in the procedure, which they think enhance its effectiveness. With children, Lazarus and Abramovitz (1962) recommend the use of emotive imagery instead of relaxation for counterconditioning anxiety, for they feel that children may not readily learn deep relaxation. Wolpin (1969) prefers to use a continuous image depicting the complete series of responses in which the subject likes to engage rather than the piecemeal hierarchical presentation. Also, he does not interrupt the imagined scene if the patient begins to become anxious, nor does he suggest excessively anxiety-arousing, unrealistic scenes. The patient is simply to behave in imagination as he or she would like to act in real life. Brown (1969) emphasizes that the efficiency of Wople's method would be enhanced if "it is modified to take into account the possibility that a patient's fear of a particular object or situation might be related to the idiosyncratic way he conceptualizes the phobic object" (Brown, 1969, p. 120).

Although there are a number of clinical and laboratory investigations that substantiate the efficacy of systematic desensitization in alleviating fear and anxiety (Sheikh & Panagiotou, 1975; Singer, 1974; Singer & Pope, 1978), there is a good deal of disagreement concerning the mechanism of change. Several alternative explanations in terms of learning and cognitive theory have been suggested (Davison & Wilson, 1972; Lang, 1969, 1970). According to Singer's (1974) review, the crucial element in treatment is not really the hierarchy or the use of progressive relaxation. It is essentially the familiarity with the phobic situation, created through a series of images. The critical factors in the effectiveness of this method also could be "a change in the private anticipations, in the images, self-communication, and daydreams that the patient holds with respect to the critical situations for which treatment has been sought" (Singer & Pope, 1978, p. 23).

In contrast to systematic desensitization, in *implosion* (Stampfl & Levis, 1967) or in *flooding* (Rachman, 1968) the client is repeatedly exposed in imagery to very intense fear stimuli expected to arouse maximal anxiety. This exposure, without the aversive consequences experienced in real life, is presumed to gradually result in extinction of the fear response. Forerunners of this method appear to be two other extinction-based therapies: Dunlap's (1932) "negative practice" and Malleson's (1959) "reactive inhibition therapy."

The results of this method, which have been reported so far, are equivocal (Sheikh & Panagiotou, 1975). Furthermore, "the crucial theoretical underpinnings are still in doubt. Various investigators have suggested explanatory constructs dealing with extinction, adaptation level, fatigue, modeling, habituation, cognitive rehearsal, and discrimination" (Smith et al., 1973, p.358). However, it is fascinating to speculate about this procedure, since the image in it is distorted in the direction of the subject's distortion and elaborated with his or her morbid details. "The imagined scene is extended far beyond what the client in all likelihood will ever meet in reality, for the imagery represents his wildest dreams. The possibility of the symbolic content of this kind of image must be admitted, and mechanisms other than that of extinction must be considered: Abreaction, or other nonconscious transformations or even defenses may be relevant" (Sheikh & Panagiotou, 1975, pp. 563–564).

Joseph Cautela (1977) has developed a series of *covert conditioning tech-*

niques that are the covert analogues of a number of operant and social-learning procedures. These techniques include covert positive reinforcement, covert negative reinforcement, covert sensitization, covert extinction, covert response cost, and covert modeling. These methods are different from their operant conditioning and social-learning counterparts in the sense that both the responses and their consequences take place at the imaginal level. Cautela bases his techniques on what he terms the *homogeneity assumption* (covert and overt events obey the same laws) and the *interaction assumption* (covert and overt events influence each other through interaction). Mahoney (1974) points out a third underlying assumption in covert conditioning that he calls the *automaticity assumption* (conditioning takes place automatically when two events take place in temporal contiguity).

Although Cautela's procedures have received modest empirical support, the conditioning basis of these techniques as well as the underlying assumptions have been questioned, and different mechanisms of change have been suggested (Kazdin, 1977, 1978; Little & Curran, 1978; Singer, 1974).

Meichenbaum (1977, 1978) has provided a model that describes how cognitive mediating events account for behavior change. His cognitive theory postulates a three-phase process that can describe behavior change. These three phases represent a flexible sequence in which covert and evironmental events interact to produce change. The first phase in this change process involves increasing self-awareness by encouraging the patient to become an observer of his or her own behavior, thoughts, feelings, physiological reactions, and/or interpersonal behaviors. In the second phase the patient learns new adaptive thoughts and responses that interfere with maladaptive ones. In the third phase the patient is urged to practice these new adaptive thoughts and behaviors in real life. It is worthy of mention that Meichenbaum stresses the role of self-talk, or private monologues, in producing, maintaining, and dealing with anxiety. His use of imagery is distinguished by the deliberate inclusion of this self-talk in the imaginal behavior. Meichenbaum has developed a number of procedures, including *coping imagery* and *stress innoculation*; for details, the reader is referred to his book (Meichenbaum, 1977).

In addition to the approaches discussed in this segment, numerous other variations of these methods have been advanced. These include thought stopping (Wolpe & Lazarus, 1966), induced anxiety (Sipprelle, 1967), self-control desensitization (Goldfriend, 1971), systematic rational restructuring (Goldfriend et al., 1974), and many others (Anderson, 1980; Strosahl & Ascough, 1981).

In concluding this section, it is worthy of mention that a number of clinicians, without feeling the need to posit a relationship between images and unconscious structures, have noted the potency of images as vehicles of learning. They have treated mental images very much like real events, and they have noted that, on occasion, the images may be subjectively indistinguishable from the corresponding events. These approaches, however, have been criticized for neglecting the symbolic and inordinately emphasizing the spatial and temporal associations (Sheikh & Panagiotou, 1975).

Cognitive–Affective Restructuring

A number of clinicians hold that images very effectively provide the client with a clear understanding of his or her perceptual and affective distortions. Unlike the cognitive behavior therapists, they do not subscribe to the conditioning principles.

Beck (1970), for example, attempts to explain the conditioning effects of repetitive fantasy in cognitivie terms. He maintains that the repetition of images provides valuable information and clarifies the cognitive and affective distortions for the individual.

Gendlin and his colleagues (Gendlin, 1978; Gendlin & Olsen, 1970) use *experiential focusing* to bring about a clear recognition of all aspects of the feelings. They maintain that emergence of an image often moves the individual from a "global sense of feeling to a specific crux feeling." This image, "typically becomes quite stable as the feel of it is focused on and even refuses to change until one comes to know what the feeling it gives one is. Then one feels not only the characteristic release, but the image then changes . . . both the feeling and the image, refuse to change or shift until its felt meaning has opened up" (Glendlin & Olsen, 1970, p. 221).

Morrison (1979, 1980) emphasizes "the value of retracing early developmental experiences in order to apply the adult's more adequate construct system" to better comprehend those experiences (Morrison, 1980, p. 313). In his *emotive–reconstructive therapy*, images are used as the primary therapeutic agents. As the term indicates, the procedure consists of two phases. During "the emotive phase the focus is on the eliciting of strong feelings about some person with whom the client has reported some problems . . . In the *reconstructive* phase . . . the client attempts to integrate what he or she has learned" (Morrison, 1980, pp. 314–315). Morrison indicates that the theoretical roots of his approach lie in the cognitive theories of Kelley (1955), Piaget (1972), and Fiske and Maddi (1961).

Image Therapies with Psychoanalytic Orientation

A number of psychotherapists in America, who are basically committed to various aspects of psychoanalytic theorizing about the development of the normal and pathological personality, have been employing imagery in their clinical work. Joseph Reyher and Joseph Shorr stand out in this respect. Reyher has continued the classical free-association method with emphasis on images rather than words. One cannot help but wonder how psychoanalysis would have evolved if Freud had continued to stress image association instead of shifting to the verbal procedures (Singer & Pope, 1978). Extended free imagery eventually tends to be accompanied by anxiety and/or resistance. "This is puzzling to clients when these pathogenic images or scenes appear to be innocent. Their curiosity thus piqued, they are invited to revisualize these images. Anxiety and resistance is intensified and symptoms are exacerbated as the underlying strivings become depicted with increasing clarity" (Reyher, 1977, p. 253). This procedure has been called *emergent uncovering* (Reyher, 1977, p. 253). Reyher believes that valuable insight is gained by the patient through ongoing imagery even in the absence of any interpretation by the therapist. Reyher is one of the few image therapists who also has contributed significantly to the experimental investigation of imaginal processes.

Unlike Reyher, Shorr (1972, 1978) employs much more active intervention and direction in his approach, called *psycho-imagination therapy*. Shorr believes that his orientation is primarily existential and phenomenological in nature. However, a perusal of his works persuades one to concur with Singer (1974) that his technique basically represents Sullivan's interpersonal school of psychoanalysis. In the therapeutic interaction he stresses identifying oneself and distinguishing one's own view of oneself from the self attributed to one by the significant others of one's childhood. To Shorr, imagination lies at the center of consciousness, and he has very ingeniously devised numerous imaginative situations to be employed during therapy. For a discussion of these situations, the reader is referred to Shorr's books and articles. Some further discussion of Shorr's ideas are presented in a section on the use of imagery in group psychotherapy.

Mardi Horowitz (1968, 1970, 1978), another psychoanalytically oriented clinician, has made distinguished contributions to the investigation of the role of imagery in cognitive psychology. Although his name is not associated with any particular image psychotherapy, any serious clinician interested in comprehending the function of "internal pictures" will find Horowitz's work extremely enlightening.

In concluding this segment, we would like to draw attention to the numerous insights invaluable to image therapists found in the works of the neo-Freudians, Harry Stack Sullivan (1956) and Eric Fromm (1951) and their followers, Tauber and Green (1959).

Eidetic Psychotherapy

This approach does not fit into any of the categories discussed in this section on American approaches. It was born in Pakistan (Ahsen, 1968, 1972, 1977; Dolan & Sheikh, 1976; Panagiotou & Sheikh, 1974; Sheikh, 1978; Sheikh & Jordan, 1981). Consequently, it consists of a rare blend of Eastern and Western ideas, and the complexity of this blend at times becomes somewhat bewildering to the Western rational mind. In eidetic psychotherapy, the healing of the psyche is placed back into the "magical" model, where the emphasis is on transformation through "irrational" procedures as opposed to rational or reflex therapies. In this respect it is very similar to the Jungian active imaginative and European oneirotherapies. However, it is also quite unlike the latter; the image responses do not consist of extended narrations or imagery trips. Eidetic psychotherapy is more direct, and the emphasis is on a repetitious piecemeal projection of images. Furthermore, the underlying personality theory is distinct from that of other approaches in its emphasis on the multiplicity of the states that comprise the personality rather than on the unity of the ego that makes them adhere.

Eidetic therapy relies on the elicitation and manipulation of eidetic images. Eidetic psychotherapists, in contrast to most experimental researchers, view the eidetic as a semipermanent representation that has been figuratively impressed on the memory in response to the formative events in the past. Every significant event in one's developmental course is purported to implant an eidetic in the system. The visual part, the *image*, is considered to be always accompanied by a *somatic pattern*—a set of bodily feelings and tensions, including somatic correlates of emotion—and a cognitive or experiential *meaning*. This tridimensional unity, the eidetic, displays certain lawful tendencies toward change and has specific meaningful relations to psychological processes. This observation is very much in line with Jung's conception of the image as an integrated unity with a life and purpose of its own (Panagiotou & Sheikh, 1977).

Eidetics are observed to be bipolarly configurated and involve ego-positive and ego-negative elements of the experience. It is believed that, among other factors, a quasi-separation of the visual part from other components, a fixation on the negative pole, or repression of a significant experience can lead to a variety of problems. Eidetic therapists largely aim at reviving the tridimensional unity, shifting attention to the negative pole, and uncovering appropriate healthful experiences through eidetic progression. Eidetic therapy includes a number of procedures designed to elicit the relevant eidetics. Some of these are discussed later in a section on imagery and diagnosis.

Varying degrees of success with a wide variety of patients have been reported. Controlled studies of therapeutic outcome, however, are yet lacking. Questions have been raised concerning the use of the term "eidetic," for the meaning it has in this context differs widely from the meaning it has in the experimental literature. It is an issue that needs close examination and is being addressed elsewhere (Sheikh, 1983a).

Imagery and Hypnosis

As Barber and Wilson (1979, p. 67) point out, hypnosis generally refers to the effects brought about by a variety of procedures that lead the client (1) to enter an altered state of consciousness, (2) to expect that certain effects are occurring or will occur, and (3) to imagine a specific target effect. It seems that there is a significant degree of overlap between hypnosis and several imagery procedures (e.g., directed fantasy, guided imagery). Barber and Wilson (1979) specify several overlapping features, which are discussed below.

The commission appointed by the King of France to investigate Mesmer's claims concluded that his cures were due primarily to the excitement of the imagination of the patient. This view of hypnosis has recently reemerged, and there is increasing evidence that hypnosis and imagery are closely related (Barber, 1978). It has been noted that suggestions used in the hypnotic setting generally direct the subject to imagine various situations (Honiotes, 1977; Weitzenhoffer & Hilgard, 1962). Hypnotic responsiveness and the ability to be absorbed in activities involving imagination and fantasy have been found to be positively correlated (Barber & Glass, 1962; Hilgard, 1970; Sheehan, 1979). Sarbin (1976) compares the responsive hypnotic subject to the child engaged in imaginative play. Furthermore, several investigators, on the basis of their research, have concluded that hypnosis essentially intensifies the subject's imaginative process (Barber et al., 1974; Hilgard, 1965; Sarbin & Coe, 1972). In the light of the above evidence, it seems safe to hypothesize that the wide variety of effects produced through hypnosis is due largely to the imagery involved. For a detailed review of literature concerning the relationship between imagery and hypnosis, the reader is referred to Sheehan(1979).

Humanistic–Transpersonal Approaches

With the advent of the "third force" in psychology, there has been increasing emphasis on greater access to experience, on various states of consciousness, and on expansion of the uses of one's potentials. This change in the general zeitgeist has encouraged the emergence of a number of novel imagery techniques that are aimed at accomplishing the above goals. Many of these techniques represent a more or less direct importation of European oneirotherapies, psychosynthesis procedures, autogenic training, Jungian active imagination, and Eastern meditative practices (Cramptom, 1969; Gerard, 1964; Hammer, 1967; Johnsgard, 1969; Lewis & Steitfeld, 1971; Masters & Houston, 1972; Scheidler, 1972). Thanks to the group versions of these therapies, the ideas at the basis of these uses of fantasy have become accessible to a much greater segment of the population.

Fritz Perls and other gestalt therapists have played a major role in popularizing a number of such techniques (Perls, 1970, 1972; Perls, et al., 1951; Singer, 1974). They often use fantasy in a quasipsychodramatic fashion: The client is expected to act the role of various segments and characters in the dreams, fantasies, memories, and life situations. Thus the client discovers that they are really parts of himself or herself and "that their energy, formerly often inhibiting growth, can be reintegrated into the conscious personality" (Watkins, 1976, p. 96). Also relevant is the emphasis that these therapists place on body-oriented imagery; they assume that various body attitudes stand for encapsulated memories or fantasies (Singer, 1974).

Ira Progoff (1963, 1970), utilizing what he calls an "intensive journal," has also popularized a number of techniques based particularly on imaginary dialoguing with internal parts of oneself.

Numerous clinicians (Jaffe & Bresler, 1980; Oyle, 1976; Rossman, 1980; Samuels & Bennett, 1973; Sheikh, 1983b) have utilized a technique in which the client creates and interacts with an *inner advisor* in his or her imagery to gain significant knowledge from the subconscious and to be able to feel at ease with various parts of himself or herself that previously had been beyond the reach of the conscious mind. For example, the inner advisor has been used to provide advice on how to reduce pain and stress, to give support and protection, to discern the message behind symptoms, and to provide symptom relief (Jaffe & Bresler, 1980).

Sheikh et al., (1979b) have developed a "death imagery" technique: essentially all the client has to do is to relax, confront his or her death in imagination, let go to the natural flow, and be willing to accept responsibility for whatever arises. The technique is based on the premise that purposeful life is possible only through an unflinching acceptance of death as an integral constituent of life: confronting death draws one to the threshold of life. The death imagery procedures, paradoxically, often lead to "life-giving" experiences, and they have yielded these promising results with a wide variety of clients. The precursors of this approach include the Buddhist meditation on death (Long, 1975), Sufi contemplation on death (Ajmal, 1979), Plato's practicing death [see *Collected Dialogues of Plato*, edited by Hamilton & Cairns, (1973) and the ideas concerning "living toward death" presented in *The Tibetan Book of the Dead* (Evans-Wentz, 1960)].

A host of other techniques that fall within the general rubric "humanistic–transpersonal" have been developed. They range from taking an imaginary inventory of the body; visualizing communication between the two hemispheres of the brain; crawling into the heart, brain, eye, and other organs of the body for observatory and reparatory purposes; exorcising the parents from various parts of the body; to regressing into the "previous life" (Huxley, 1963; Shaffer, 1979; Shorr, 1978; Shorr et al., 1980; Stevens, 1971; Watkins, 1976). Singer (1974) terms many of these the "parlor game imagery methods." The increasing proliferation of the clinical uses of fantasy and imagery, justifies Singer's (1979, p. 29) comments that "imagery can come to be regarded by psychotherapists as an almost magical symbol, a new panacea, in this most faddish of the areas of applied psychology." On the other hand, the danger exists that, disgusted by the faddish nature of this movement, scientifically oriented investigators may throw out the baby with the bath water. After all, it is quite possible that some seemingly silly procedures may have invaluable potential for promoting health and growth.

Group Applications of Imagery

Since the late 1960s group therapists of diverse persuasions have been employing imagery techniques to augment individual growth and to improve interpersonal relationships. The rationale behind the utilization of imagery in group situations is no different from the one given for employing it in individual therapy. Furthermore, almost all the imagery techniques used in individual therapy have found their way into group therapy. Gestalt therapists and other humanistically and transpersonally oriented clinicians probably have played the most significant role in popularizing the uses of imagery in group therapy (Perls, 1970; Schutz, 1967; Stevens, 1971). However, group applications of imagery by therapists with other orientations are not uncommon.

The most extensive source book of structured exercises and imagery methods within psychoanalytic group psychotherapy is Saretsky's (1977) *Active Techniques and Group Psychotherapy*; in which he presents many useful techniques in detail and provides suggestions concerning the correct timing and the appropriateness of the techniques. Shorr's (1978) neoanalytically based psycho-imagination therapy involves a much more extensive use of waking imagery in group situations than other psychoanalytically based approaches. His procedure may involve everyone in the group imaging about a particular member and the latter's reaction and imagery to the others' imagery, one individual imaging about every other group member in rotation and their imagery about this individual in return—reaction, and everyone in the group imaging about the therapist and the therapist's images of each member of the group.

Eidetic therapy also includes a "positive group method" that relies on eidetic images as the vehicle for empathy and change. While one group member describes his or her eidetic image, the others are expected to experience an empathy image. The empathy images are then shared by the group members; the group discussion revolves around the assimilation of the richness of the possible meanings, feelings, and actions. The resolution of problems often evolves spontaneously following empathy and discussion (Ahsen, 1977; Ahsen & Sheikh, 1977; Jordan et al., 1980).

Behavioral and cognitive—behavioral approaches to the use of imagery in group therapy have received the most attention from researchers. The efficacy of group desensitization in the treatment of a number of problems has been documented. These include test anxiety (Cohen, 1969; McManus, 1971; Paul & Shannon, 1966), speech anxiety (Meichenbaum et al. 1971), snake phobia (Litvak, 1969), and opposite-sex phobia (Dua, 1972). Meichenbaum's stress innoculation has been successfully applied to group treatment of problems relating to anger, anxiety, and lack of assertiveness (Lange & Jakubowski, 1976). The group method of Sipprelle's induced affect has been proven effective for obtaining weight loss (Bornstein & Sipprelle, 1973). Kroger and Fezler (1976) discuss the use of group hypnosis relying heavily on imagery to treat the problems of alcoholism, drug addiction, and obesity. Generally, images are evoked to induce relaxation; then positive images of avoiding abuse of substances are rehearsed. If these positive images fail, negative images involving aversive consequences associated with substance use are employed to facilitate avoidance learning. Many of these techniques incorporate cognitive—behavioral strategies into the context of hypnosis.

The preceding survey of imagery-based therapies is by no means intended to convey that exclusive dependence on images is the royal road to therapeutic success. Whereas behavior therapists have emphasized the enactive mode, psychoanalysts have preferred the lexical mode, and image therapists have chosen the imagery mode, it is our feeling that any really meaningful therapeutic venture must take into account all three modes in their complex interrelationships.

Also, in this chapter the emphasis has been on the imagery of the patient. Singer and Pope (1978) argue in favor of the therapist's attempts to produce images that concretize the patient's descriptions of his or her experiences. Singer and Pope seem to be aware of the danger that, since the therapist draws on a different set of past experiences to conjure up images, he or she may "fail to capture the patient's experience." Nevertheless, they concur with Tauber and Green (1959) in asserting that "the private images of the therapist may clarify the experiences going on between patient and therapist" (Singer & Pope, 1978, p. 18). It is certainly an issue that deserves further inquiry.

Also, it is noteworthy that the use of imagery may free not only the patient but also the therapist from verbal logic. The patient's communication through images may lead the therapist to be more creative in his or her interpretation and quicker to establish empathy. As Sheikh and Panagiotou indicate, the images may appeal to the therapist's own primary-process thinking and help him or her to "regress in the service of the ego" (Kris, 1952), or the therapist who prefers dealing with the concrete may feel more comfortable with imagery. Also, a shift to the imagery mode may make the therapeutic interchange more interesting for the therapist for various reasons. It is obvious that, whatever positive impact the images have on the therapist, it will eventually "feedback into the therapeutic relationship" (Singer, 1974, p. 235).

IMAGERY AND DIAGNOSIS

A therapist's instructions to a client to try to visualize a particular thing, person, or event can be regarded as a type of projective stimulus. In principle, these instructions resemble the presentation of a Rorschach card with the request to "see" something in it, or the presentation of a TAT card with the request to "imagine" a story. The projective methods present to the individual stimuli with ambiguous demands to which he or she must respond with his or her idiosyncratic structuring. Because of the ambiguity of the stimuli, the individual must structure his or her responses according to his or her private mode of organization; he or she must partially define the stimuli themselves through his or her own way of seeing things. Therefore, it is said that the individual "projects" on the stimuli idiosyncratic perceptions that reflect his or her way of viewing life, his or her meanings, significances, patterns, and particularly feelings.

However vague the stimulus may be in Rorschach, TAT, or other projective tests, it still places some limitations on the response possibilities. Imagery tests may be considered even more projective than the conventional projective techniques because they rely on internal rather than external images. Although some minimal restrictions often are placed on the nature of the image through verbal instructions, the client still is free to conjure up one of a limitless variety of images.

Also, in most of the conventional projective tests, the subject is expected to "see" or "imagine," but not enough emphasis is placed on this visual aspect, and measures are not taken to ensure that the subject remains at the image level. The subject has the freedom to become enmeshed mainly in verbal associations. Recently, Yanovski and Fogel (1978) have made attempts to study the effects of visual-imagery instructions on Rorschach responses. In the imagery condition the subject looks at each card for a brief period and then visualizes the image of the plate with eyes closed. He or she is then asked "to produce and report any imagery sequences which developed from the initial image spontaneously without intervention from the experimenter" (Yanovski & Fogel, 1978, p. 301). The analysis of the responses includes all conventional scoring categories. A great deal of new information, which is not available through the conventional administration, is believed to surface.

Evidence is accumulating that spontaneous and induced visual images are a rich and readily accessible source of diagnostic information. The use of these images for diagnosis is based on a number of assumptions. First, it is assumed that some meaning is inherent in the images and that it has reference to the individual's motivational system. Second, if images are regarded as useful information sources, there is implication of at least some admission that there are things in the subject's perception and motivation of which he or she is unaware. Third, if the information carried by visual fantasy is to be accessible and intelligible to the therapist-observer, he or she must have a set of algorithms for interpretation. These might derive from (1) theory, (2) collected clinical experience, or (3) empirical or actuarial norms. Only the first two sources have been widely used thus far. Also, it should be noted that, while discussing the diagnostic value of images, most clinicians discuss uncovering rather than diagnostic categorizing.

Jellinek (1949), a psychoanalyst, considered image productions a form of nonrational thinking through which it is possible to initiate a dialogue with the unconscious, approaching it "on its own terms," that is, on a nonrational basis. The assumption is that imagery is the mode of expression indigenous to the unconscious and that unconscious thought cannot be adequately expressed in words.

Kanzer (1958), who worked within the psychoanalytic tradition, has studied the spontaneous images that often arise during free association. He shows how these may be used for uncovering purposes and for following the patient's motivational state through the analytic session. Most of these images are found to have transference content. According to Kanzer, the images, like dreams, represent an attempt to simultaneously give expression to disturbing impulses and conceal them from awareness. Another psychoanalyst, Kepecs (1954), discusses the so-called screen or barrier images that sometimes arise during free association. These are considered to be a form of resistance whose function is to block the flow of associations. Kepecs finds, however, that asking the patient to describe the elements of the image and to associate to them often leads to the very memory or impulse that was the object of resistance. The image is a compromise between expression and concealment, and although it may incorporate many elements of camouflage, the impulse source must still be represented.

Goldberger (1957) describes a method he has devised for obtaining simple dreamlike images in the waking state. His technique is quite simple: The patient is instructed to visualize a particular verbal thought, usually one that he or she has found difficult to elaborate verbally in the psychotherapeutic session. The thoughts chosen for visualization are those that represent bodily aches and pains, strong affect, or motor action. The resulting image is used as a source of interpretive material and verbal associations. Goldberger has found the images useful in clarifying relationships, particularly between somatic sensations (e.g., muscular tension, aches, and pains) and affect-arousing life circumstances.

Reyher and Smeltzer (1968) compared the uncovering power of "free imagery" with that of "free association." Specifically, they tested the following four hypothesis: (1) visual imagery is accompanied by more anxiety than is verbal association; (2) visual imagery shows more signs of primary-process regulation than does verbal association; (3) the expression of drives (e.g., sex and aggression) is more direct in visual imagery than in free association; and (4) mechanisms of defense are less effective during visual imagery than during verbal association. The results upheld all four hypotheses, and the authors concluded that visual imagery was superior to verbal associations in uncovering properties.

Horowitz (1967) believes that the use of the imagoic mode and the context in which it occurs may identify the individual's style of cognitive control or defense. According to Horowitz, patients in all diagnostic categories report images, but imagoic thought is more frequent in some categories than in others. In addition to noting the content of the image, Horowitz believes that it is quite valuable to observe the timing and context of shifts to imagoic thinking. To date, there are few published observations dealing with this question.

The ideas covered so far in this section have been derived from the works of investigators with psychoanalytic orientations. But clinicians with different orientations also have contributed significantly to this topic. Hypnotists often use imagery diagnostically through techniques involving age regression and reconstruction of traumatic and developmental events (Fromm & Shor, 1979). Clinicians working within the general confines of psychosynthesis (Crampton, 1969) and cognitive–affective restructuring approaches (Beck, 1970; Gendlin, 1978; Morrison, 1979) have provided evidence that mental images are valuable in helping the subject and the therapist to clarify with greater precision the nature of feelings and experiences. Beck observes that when free association and direct discussion fail to reveal the relevant cognitions underlying a problem, visualization often will bring these into sharp focus. He further states that specific themes appearing frequently in visual fantasies are correlated with each of the nosologic categories. For example, according to Beck, themes of personal deprivation, failure, and personal danger are associated with anxiety reaction or phobias; self-debasement is linked to depression; fantasies of grandiose achievement accompany hypomaniac or manic conditions; and themes of unjust abuse or persecution are tied to paranoid conditions. The associations Beck finds among these fantasy themes and corresponding syndromes are not novel to clinicians. However, Beck's point is that pictorial fantasies are consistent with the respective syndromes and thus provide another source of evidence.

The European oneirotherapists have been firm believers in the diagnostic value of the imaginal responses. They believe that their methods allow them to disclose the conflictual material present in the individual's fantasy themes and to discover the so-called structural details of the individual's personality (the term "structural" refers primarily to any repetitious patterns of reaction, overt or covert, and especially to defense style). Their methods do not, however, yield a typological or nosologic report. Frétighy and Virel (1968) regard this as an advantage: the technique bypasses typing and connects directly with the ontogenetic roots of the symptomatic feelings and behavior. Through mental imagery, the difficulty is localized and attached to specific fantasies or events. For example, Frétigny and Virel (1968) claim that where psychiatry may be able to do little beyond the mere diagnosis of a state of shock, mental imagery can retrace and identify the nature of the emotional trauma, date it, and reveal its context. They refer to this as "localization diagnosis."

In oneirotherapies, as in most of the other imagery procedures, the diagnostic and therapeutic procedures are virtually inseparably intertwined. For example, the response to any particular starting image tends to be quite lengthy, and the diagnostic technique tends to blend into other aspects of therapy: abreaction and insight. Leuner (1978) advocates separation of the diagnostic and therapeutic phases by moving the participant quickly through the series of stimuli during the initial diagnostic phase, thus avoiding the full-blown affective reaction. Since oneirotherapies involve sequences of images in response to common starting images, future researchers could contemplate applying "the same types of normative and reliable judging or rating procedures . . . that have been employed in studies with projective techniques . . . or in scoring dreams or fantasy material"(Singer, 1974, p. 89).

In addition to the rather informal uses of imagery for uncovering purposes, a few clinicians have developed standard imagery tests: the Age Projection Test, the Eidetic Parents Test, the Imaginary Collage, and the Shorr Imagery Test. The remainder of this section is largely devoted to a brief discussion of each of these tests.

Age Projection Test

This test was developed by Ahsen (1965) and has been employed by a number of clinicans in its original or modified form. In this procedure the therapist obtains from the patient his or her first, middle, and last names, nicknames, and any other names by which he or she has been called since childhood, for these names are assumed to refer to an individual's various identities. Subsequently, the patient is asked to pay relaxed attention to what the therapist says. He or she is told that when the therapist repeats certain words over and over again, he or she will see an image of himself or herself somewhere in his or her past. Dolan and Sheikh (1977, p. 599) write:

> The salient features of the symptom discovered during symptom composition are now reiterated to the patient in his own words in a repetitious manner. In the course of this repetition, the patient is addressed by his various names alternately. This repetition artificially activates the symptom to an almost unbearable acuteness. As this point five seconds of total silence are allowed to elapse. Suddenly the therapist starts talking about the time when the patient was healthy and happy. As the therapist talks about health in those areas where the symptom now exists, the patient spontaneously forms a self-image subliminally. The patient is now suddenly asked to project a self-image and describe the following: (a) the self-image itself; (b) the clothing on the self-image; (c) the place where it appears; (d) the events occurring during the age projected in the self-image; (e) the events occurring during the year prior to the age projected in the image.

This procedure usually uncovers an event that precipitated the symptom or that began a series of events that eventually led to symptom formation. Once the self-image related to this event is formed, the patient is asked to project it repeatedly until it becomes clear and then is interrogated further about the critical period. Often the meaning and origin of the symptom, particularly of the somatic or quasi-somatic symptom, are purported to become evident. On the basis of information revealed by the test, a therapeutic image is then constructed, and the patient is asked to project it repeatedly.

A number of therapists have reported success with the procedure. However, controlled and systematic exploration of the crucial elements of the test is lacking. It may turn out that many of the procedural details of the test are superfluous. Perhaps a simple procedure, similar to the one employed by Freud, which consists of telling the patient that at a certain moment an image of an important causal event related to the problem will emerge, will be equally effective. This question can be answered only through systematic research.

Eidetic Parents Test

In eidetic psychotherapy, special significance is attached to the patterns of interaction between the patient's parents and the patient's perception of polarities that existed in their relationship. The Eidetic Parents Test (EPT) was designed specifically to uncover eidetics in these areas (Ahsen, 1972). These eidetics have been shown to reveal, to a significant extent, the quality of the familial relationships and their predominant pathological themes. The test provides not only the means for identifying areas of conflict but also the format for therapeutic procedure.

The entire EPT consists of 30 situation images in which various aspects of the parents and the parental relationships are visualized. Each image is repeatedly projected until its essential elements are sharpened and separated from its vague or changing aspects.

An individual's ability to produce a sufficiently rich eidetic response is interpreted as a sign of the openness to his or her internal life. A "structural defect" in the imagery signifies a particularly problematic area (Ahsen, 1972). Two major forms of imagery defects have been identified: meager responses and mutilated responses. Meager responses may occur only in limited areas of eidetic imagery and may reflect the individual's particular problems in relating to those areas. However, insufficient responses also may be a general pattern and may point to habitual suppression of emotional experiences. But both the individual who gives meager responses in a restricted area and the one who does so generally often learn to respond adequately if they are repeatedly encouraged. There are three sources that are considered likely to be the root of extremely persistent imagery repression: (1) a perseverative fantasy theme, such as a phobia, which competes with the imagery; (2) religious or moral aversion to eidetic images; and (3) strong tendencies to acting out. To deal with the first source the use of the Age Projection Test is suggested: It will bring the dynamics of the perseverative theme to the surface. The second source is interpreted as a resistance of a disturbed patient to the experience, and evidently it is best counteracted by instilling in the patient an informed conviction that knowledge about his or her parents is absolutely essential to his or her well-being. The third source, the acting-out tendencies, is likely to be based on an identification with the negative aspects of one or the other parent. It follows that, for the individual to realize an internalized image of the parent, he or she must be able to differentiate himself or herself from that parental image (Sheikh, 1978). The aforementioned three sources quite possibly do not exhaust all the causes of the inability to produce adequate imagery responses, and this inadequacy continues to be a nightmare for clinicians interested in using imagery as the main tool for diagnosis and treatment (Sheikh & Moleski, 1983).

In contrast to meager responses, preponderant multilated figures presumably indicate widespread trauma in the history of the individual. Common mutilations are undersized, oversized, or entirely absent parent figures. Each of these is regarded to refer to a specific theme: undersized parents generally signify the individual's need to maintain a distance between himself or herself and his or her parents; oversized parents commonly reveal that the parents are perceived as incorporative; and absent parents, in most cases, mean that the parents made themselves unavailable and the child wished them away or dead. Partially mutilated images, such as those with vague eyes or limbs, faint voices, and so on, usually represent related defects in parental behavior. However, grossly mutilated parental images, such as disembodied heads, limbs, or eyes, ghostly bodies, and the like, may indicate "terrorizing themes" (Ahsen, 1972; Sheikh & Jordan, 1981).

A number of inadequate and mutilated responses to the EPT should be expected. When these are elicited by only some EPT items and do not seem to represent a pervasive tendency, they are supposed to point to the areas of experience to which the participant relates with most difficulty and that, therefore, are most in need of attention.

The interpretations suggested for the EPT items may appear surprising to some. A number of items are assigned meanings that many investigators would readily accept, independent of theory-specific symbolism; these items include, for example, the image of the parents in the home, standing separate or side by side, looking happy or otherwise. Other items, however, such as those dealing with anatomic details, have less logical appeal and may seem to be strange choices unless one follows unflinchingly Ahsen's conception of the importance of psychosomatic symbolism. Need for further research is obviously indicated. Also, it is important to recognize that the EPT and, in fact, the whole eidetic method is a parent-centered approach. Not all clinicians would agree to the central importance of examining the familial interactions in such great detail.

Imaginary Collage

This technique, developed by Stanley Lipkin (1970), most clearly resembles the established projective methods. Lipkin proposes its use at points in therapy when the client's involvement and interest begin to dwindle or where blocking occurs. Lipkin recognizes that, apart from any advantage imagery might have for reaching the client's "unconscious," it also is regarded as novel and interesting by many people and thereby stimulates conscious involvement in the task at hand. The imaginary collage is quite simple; the participant is asked to assemble in his or her imagination a collage composed of anything he or she wishes. As the individual works at the task, he or she describes its progress to the therapist. The therapist questions the client about the placement of particular items and invites him or her to elaborate on their possible significance. When the individual feels that the collage is finished, he or she is asked to discuss his or her general reaction to it. Lipkin regards the imaginary collage as an application of McLuhan's concept of nonlinearity to communication within the therapeutic process. The linearity of the verbal statement by nature prohibits the simultaneous expression of several perceptions, but several perceptions may, in fact, occur in simultaneous relation to one another. The imaginary collage was developed to be an expressive medium that would not be bound by linearity.

The imaginary collage is different in one sense from every other image technique reviewed in this chapter; in this procedure the individual is required to exert intellectual or critical control over the resulting image. The individual is not explicitly told to apply control, but the production of an artistic composition (even an imaginary one) implies conscious manipulation, trial and error, and planned inclusion and exclusion. The individual is asked to place in the collage whatever he or she "likes," whatever he or she thinks belongs there, and to offer a rationale for the presence of any item among the others. This approach is in direct contrast to most other image procedures, which take advantage of the unexpected quality of the image response and often use measures such as deep relaxation to reduce the critical function and to foster hypnoidal states.

The Shorr Imagery Test

Joseph Shorr claims that this imagery test is a vehicle for bypassing the defenses and to uncover the individual's self-image, areas of conflict, and coping strategies. To achieve these goals, the subject is asked to imagine 15 different situations, such as "Imagine being seated on a gold throne (pause) and tell me what you see, what you do, and what you feel" (Shorr, 1974, p. 5). Occasionally the subject is expected to give adjectives descriptive of the image or to imagine a dialogue with the image or between certain images. Very little normative or other psychometric data have been offered by Shorr, and many of his interpretations are open to question. However, Shorr (1978) has adapted this test for use with groups; and, for the group version, he does present some evidence of validity and interscorer and test–retest reliability. Perhaps this is the only diagnostic imagery test for which a preliminary attempt to obtain such data has been made. Although many clinicians attest to the clinical usefulness of the instrument, need for further research to test these claims is evident.

Possible Diagnostic Uses of Nondiagnostic Imagery Tests

There are numerous measures of mental imagery available that were not developed with an eye toward diagnosis. These include the Betts Questionnaire upon Mental Imagery (Betts, 1909; Sheehan, 1967), the Gordon Test of Visual Imagery Control (Gordon, 1949), the Vividness of Visual Imagery Questionnaire (Marks, 1973), the Brower Self-Report Test (Brower, 1947); the Imagery Survey Questionnaire (Cautela, 1977); the Imagery Research Questionnaire (Lane, 1977); the Survey of Mental Imagery (Switras, 1979); the Individual Differences Questionnaire (Paivio, 1971); the Verbalizer–Visualizer Questionnaire (Richardson, 1977); the Imaginal Process Inventory (Singer & Antrobus, 1972); the Creative Imagination Scale (Wilson & Barber, 1976); and the Experiential Analysis Technique (Sheehan, 1979). Many of these tests have potential diagnostic uses and should be examined closely from that point of view. For example, high scores on Gordon's Test of Imagery Control indicate a tendency toward stereotyping (Gordon, 1949); high imagers on Paivio's Individual Differences Questionnaire tend to have introceptive values (Pavio, 1971); anxious–distractible and guilty–dysphoric styles of daydreaming, according to Singer and Antrobus's Imaginal Process Inventory, indicate a propensity for emotional disturbance (Singer & Antrobus, 1972); visualizers, on Richardson's Verbalizer–Visualizer Questionnaire, give more emotional, imaginative, and integrated responses to Rorschach inkblots than do verbalizers (Richardson, 1969); and high scores on the Creative Imagination Scale are predictive of success in eliminating pain perception and curing rare skin diseases (Barber, 1978). For detailed discussions of many of these tests, the reader is referred to other sources (Tower & Singer, 1981; White et al., 1977).

Some General Comments about Imagery and Diagnosis

The literature on the clinical uses of imagery is replete with clinicians' testimonies concerning the diagnostic efficacy of mental images. These extensive claims cannot easily be ignored. However, to date, aside from the development of a number of informal tests, not much systematic work has been done that provides clear guidelines for a confident and meaningful use of images in this area. The existing diagnostic tests need extensive refinements to be of real value to clinicians and researchers. Studies of reliability and validity are sadly lacking. Besides further work on the existing tests and the development of new tests, a number of aspects of the imaging process need to be examined from the diagnostic point of view. For instance, do spontaneous and induced images operate differently, and are they of different value for diagnosis? Is the examination of variety, style, range, intensity, frequency, context, and active control of images relevant to the diagnostician? Is a relationship between actual perceptions and their image representations of diagnostic value? Should a distinction be made between conscious and unconscious imagery? Which measures are more suitable for which type? Is the ease with which spontaneous and induced images are produced diagnostically significant? Are considerations of individual differences in imaginal style, such as the verbalizer–visualizer dimension, of any relevance?

CONCLUDING REMARKS

A rapidly growing body of evidence indicates the effectiveness of mental imagery in the treatment of a whole spectrum of problems. These include depression (Schultz, 1978), insomnia (Sheikh, 1976), obesity (Bornstein & Sipprelle, 1973), sexual malfunctioning (Singer & Switzer, 1980), chronic pain (Jaffe & Bresler, 1980), a variety of phobias and anxieties (Meichenbaum, 1977; Singer, 1974), and a host of other neurotic and psychosomatic problems (Ahsen, 1968; Sheikh, 1983; Sheikh et al., 1979a). Imagery is purported to produce especially good results with psychosomatic symptoms, a category of illness that often has not benefited from traditional verbal and behavioral therapies (Sheikh & Kunzendorf, in press).

The proponents of all image approaches claim significant successes and cite numerous supporting case histories. Unfortunately, at the present time, there is no way of clearly determining whether some methods work better than others and whether some characteristics of the client (e.g., sex, age, cognitive style) make him or her a more suitable candidate for image-based therapies.

Numerous mechanisms that presumably underlie the effectiveness of imagery in the clinic have been suggested; they almost equal the number of methods available. Singer (1974) and Meichenbaum (1978) have attempted to extract the elements common to all approaches. Singer tends to believe that the efficacy of imagery may essentially depend on the following factors: (1) clear discrimination by the client of his or her own ongoing fantasy processes; (2) clues provided by the therapist concerning alternative ways of approaching various situations; (3) awareness of generally avoided situations; (4) encouragement by the therapist to engage in covert rehearsal of alternatives; and (5) consequent decrease in fear of making overt approaches to the avoided situations. To these, Singer adds the factor of general increase in positive affect that, according to him, results essentially from the novelty of the imagery experience, from the translation of symbolic material into "current interpersonal dilemmas," and from the feeling of mastery over the difficult situation in imagery.

Meichenbaum (1978) attempts to simplify matters even further. He proposes that the following three psychological processes explain the effectiveness of all imagery-based therapies: (1) the feeling of control which the client gains as a result of the monitoring and rehearsing of various images; (2) the modified meaning or changed internal dialogue that precedes, attends, and succeeds examples of maladaptive behavior; and (3) the mental rehearsal of alternative responses that lead to the enhancement of coping skills.

The foregoing constitute significant attempts at "cutting through" varied imagery approaches and developing conceptual frameworks that explain why image therapies lead to change. However, in striving for parsimony, one may frequently ignore some crucial points. It is our feeling that the nonconscious, the symbolic, and the magical factors, equally emphasized by Jung, by the oneirotherapists, by eidetic therapists, and by many others cannot be ignored if one aims to fully comprehend the nature and function of therapeutic imagery. The final answer, of course, will have to come from carefully conceived research.

It is unfortunate that, although there has been a burst of interest in the clinical application of imagery, very scant experimental work has been devoted to the verification of the pivotal process assumptions that underlie these procedures. Behavior therapists, in contrast, have done a great deal of research, but they have neglected developing sufficiently broad theoretical foundations to support the research data on the effects of imagistic experience. To expedite research, they have placed mental imagery "outside the individual by equating the principles governing covert behavior with those known to influence overt behavior" (Strosahl & Ascough, 1981, p. 423).

An impressive volume of experimental and theoretical literature concerning imagery has accumulated in the last decade, and much of it has important implications for therapeutic and diagnostic situations (Kosslyn, 1975, 1980). Unfortunately, it has been largely ignored by the clinical psychologists interested in imagery. Experimental psychologists, on the other hand, regretably have ignored some fascinating hypotheses that have emerged from image therapies.

During the last few years, largely as a result of the efforts of a handful of psychologists interested in both experimental work and clinical application (Anderson, 1980; Barber & Wilson, 1979; Cautela, 1977; Klinger, 1980; Meichenbaum, 1977, 1978; Singer, 1974, 1979), some cross-fertilization has occurred. For example, Paivio's (1971) well-known "dual-coding hypothesis" that went unnoticed by clinicians for almost a decade finally has been shown to have therapeutic implications: Imagery rehearsal may result in better memory for the newly learned responses; descriptions of a scene in concrete terms may enhance the likelihood of experiencing imagery; concrete descriptions may enhance imagery experience in the client reporting lack of vivid imagery; and the concreteness of a client's description of imagery may be regarded as an indication of the quality of his or her imagery (Anderson 1980). Anderson also has expertly drawn out the therapeutic implications of a number of other theoretical positions, and his paper deserves close scrutiny by clinicians interested in imagery. Strosahl and Ascough (1981), too, have made a significant attempt to review some of experimental literature on imagery and to show its relevance to the clinical situation. Also, they raised a number of important and clinically relevant questions that urgently invite scientific investigation.

In conclusion, once again, we would like to strike a note of caution amid the rapidly growing enthusiasm for therapeutic imagery. It is true that creativity can be suffocated by a compulsion for rigid scientific methodology. On the other hand, however, roaming, unbridled fancy is unproductive. Overly enthusiastic image therapists perhaps should keep in mind that there was a time in history when the clinical significance of imagery was widely accepted, but that this period regrettably did not last. It is imperative that the creative surge be accompanied by sobering scrutiny, lest the future of imagery in the clinic be written in its past.

REFERENCES

Ahsen, A. *Eidetic psychotherapy: A short introduction.* Lahore, Pakistan: Nai Matbooat, 1965.

Ahsen, A. *Basic concepts in eidetic psychotherapy.* New York: Brandon House, 1968.

Ahsen, A. *Eidetic parents test and analysis.* New York: Brandon House, 1972.

Ahsen, A. *Psycheye: Self-analytic consciousness.* New York: Brandon House, 1977.

Ahsen, A., & Sheikh, A. A. Group psychotherapy through eidetic imagery. Paper presented at the International Group Psychotherapy Congress, Philadelphia, 1977.

Ajmal, M. Sufi contemplation upon death. Unpublished paper. National Institute of Psychology, Islamabad, Pakistan, 1979.

Anderson, M. P. Imaginal processes: Therapeutic application and theoretical models. In M. J. Mahoney (Ed.), *Psychotherapy process: Current issues and future trends.* New York: Plenum, 1980.

Arieti, S. *Creativity: The magic synthesis.* New York: Basic Books, 1976.

Assagioli, R. *Psychosynthesis: A collection of basic writings.* New York: Viking, 1965.

Barber, T. X. Physiological aspects of hypnosis. *Psychological Bulletin,* 1961, **58,** 390–419.

Barber, T. X. *Hypnosis: A scientific approach.* New York: Van Nostrand, 1969.

Barber, T. X. Hypnosis, suggestions and psychosomatic phenomena: A new look from the standpoint of recent experimental studies. *The American Journal of Clinical Hypnosis,* 1978, **21,** 13–27.

Barber, T. X., Chauncey, H. M., & Winer, R. A. The effect of hypnotic and non-hypnotic suggestions on parotid gland response to gustatory stimuli. *Psychosomatic Medicine,* 1964, **26,** 374–380.

Barber, T. X., & Glass, L. B. Significant factors in hypnotic behavior. *Journal of Abnormal and Social Psychology,* 1962, **64,** 222–228.

Barber, T. X., Spanos, N. P., & Chaves, J. F. *Hypnosis, imagination and human potentialities.* Elmsford, N.Y.: Pergamon, 1974.

Barber, T. X., & Wilson, S. C. Guided imagining and hypnosis: Theoretical and empirical overlap and convergence in a new creative imagination scale. In A. A. Sheikh & J. T. Shaffer (Eds.), *The potential of fantasy and imagination.* New York: Brandon House, 1979.

Beck, A. T. Role of fantasies in psychotherapy and psychopathology. *Journal of Nervous and Mental Diseases,* 1970, **150,** 3–17.

Betts, G. H. The distribution and functions of mental imagery. *Teachers' College Columbia University Contributions to Education,* 1909 (26), 1–99.

Binet, A. *L'étude expérimentale de l' intelligence.* Paris: Costes, 1922.

Bornstein, P. H., & Sipprelle, C. N. Clinical applications of induced anxiety in the treatment of obesity. Paper presented at the Southeastern Psychological Association meeting, April 6, 1973.

Bowers, S., & Bowers, P. G. Hypnosis and creativity: A theoretical and empirical reapproachment. In E. Fromm, & R. Shorr (Eds.), *Hypnosis.* Chicago: Aldine-Atherton, 1972.

Breger, L., Hunter, I., & Lane, R. W. *The effect of stress dreams.* New York: International Universities Press, 1971.

Breuer, J., & Freud, S. Studies in hysteria. *In J. Strachey (Ed.), The standard edition of the complete psychological works of Sigmund Freud.* London: Hogarth Press, 1955.

Brower, D. The experimental study of imagery: 1. The relation of imagery to intelligence. *Journal of Genetic Psychology,* 1947, **37,** 229–231.

Brown, B. M. The use of induced imagery in psychotherapy. *Psychotherapy: Theory, Research, and Practice,* 1969, **6,** 120–121.

Bruner, J. S. The course of cognitive growth. In P. C. Wason & P. N. Johnson-Laird (Eds.), *Thinking and reasoning.* Baltimore: Penguin, 1968.

Bugelski, B. R. Words and things and images. *American Psychologist,* 1970, **25,** 1002–1012.

Caslant, E. *Méthodede développement des facultés supranormales.* Paris: Edition Rhea, 1921.

Cautela, J. R. Covert conditioning: Assumptions and procedures. *Journal of Mental Imagery,* 1977, **1,** 53–64.

Clark, P. The phantasy method of analyzing narcissistic neurosis. *Psychoanalytic Review,* 1925, **13,** 225–232.

Cohen, R. The effects of group interaction and progressive hierarchy presentation on desensitization of test anxiety. *Behavior Research and Therapy,* 1969, **7,** 15–25.

Craig, K. D. Physiological arousal as a function of imagined, vicarious, and direct stress experiences. *Journal of Abnormal Psychology,* 1969, **73,** 513–520.

Crampton, M. The use of mental imagery in psychosynthesis. *Journal of Humanistic Psychology,* 1969, **9,** 139–153.

Crampton, M. *An historical survey of mental imagery techniques in psychotherapy and description of the dialogic imaginal intergration method.* Montreal: Quebec Center for Psychosynthesis, 1974.

Davé, R. P. The effect of hypnotically induced dreams on creative problem solving. Unpublished master's thesis, Michigan State University, 1976.

Davison, G. C., & Wilson, G. T. Critique of "desensitization" social and cognitive factors underlying the effectiveness of Wolpe's procedure. *Psychological Bulletin,* 1972, **78,** 28–31.

Desoille, R. *Théorie et pratique du rve éveillé dirigé.* Geneva: Mont Blanc, 1961.

Desoille, R. *The directed daydream.* New York: Psychosynthesis Research Foundation, 1965.

Dolan, A. T., & Sheikh, A. A. Eidetics: A visual approach to psychotherapy. *Psychologia,* 1976, **19,** 210–219.

Dolan, A. T., & Sheikh, A. A. Short-term treatment of phobias through eidetic imagery. *American Journal of Psychotherapy,* 1977, **31,** 595–604.

Donnars, J. Troubles la sphère ano-génito-urinaire révélés par l'imagerie mentale. Proceedings of 3rd International Congress of Le Société Internationale des Techniques d'Imagerie Mentale, Cortina, Italy, 1970.

Dua, P. S. Group desensitization of a phobia with three massing procedures. *Journal of Counseling Psychology,* 1972, **19,** 125–129.

Dunlap, K. *Habits: Their making and unmaking.* New York: Livewright, 1932.

Escalona, S. K. Book review of *Mental imagery in children* by Jean Piaget and Barbel Inhelder (New York: Basic Books, 1969). *Journal of Nervous and Mental Diseases,* 1973, **156,** 70–77.

Evans-Wentz, W. Y. *The Tibetan book of the dead*. New York: Oxford University Press, 1960.

Fiske, D., & Maddi, S. *Functions of varied experience*. Homewood, Ill.: Dorsey Press, 1961.

Forisha, B. L. The outside and the inside: Compartmentalization or integration. In A. A. Sheikh & J. T. Shaffer (Eds.), *The potential of fantasy and imagination*. New York: Brandon House, 1979.

Frank, L. *Die Psychoanalyse*. Munich: E. Reinhardt, 1910.

Frétigny, R., & Virel, A. *L'imagerie mentale*. Geneva: Mont-Blanc, 1968.

Fromm, E. *The forgotten language*. New York: Rinehart, 1951.

Fromm, E., & Shor, R. Hypnosis: Developments in research and new perspectives. New York: Aldine, 1979.

Gendlin, E. T. *Focusing*. New York: Everest House, 1978.

Gendlin, E. T., & Olsen, L. The use of imagery in experiential focusing. *Psychotherapy: Theory, Research and Practice*, 1970, **7**, 221–223.

Gerard, R. *Psychosynthesis: A psychotherapy for the whole man*. New York: Psychosynthesis Research Foundation, 1964.

Goldberger, E. Simple method of producing dreamlike visual images in the waking state. *Psychosomatic Medicine*, 1957, **19**, 127–33.

Goldfriend, M. Systematic desensitization as training in self-control. *Journal of Consulting and Clinical Psychology*, 1971, **37**, 288–234.

Goldfriend, M., Decentecio, E., & Weisberg, L. Systematic rational restructuring as a self-control technique. *Behavior Therapy*, 1974, **5**, 247–254.

Gordon, R. An investigation into some of the factors that favor the formation of stereotyped images. *British Journal of Psychology*, 1949, **39**, 156–167.

Guillerey, M. Medecine psychologique. In *Médecine officielle et médecine hérétique*. Paris: Plon, 1945.

Hall, E. T. *Beyond culture*. Garden City, N.Y.: Anchor Press/Doubleday, 1977.

Hamilton, E., & Cairns, H. (Eds.). *Collected dialogues of Plato*. Princeton: Princeton University Press, 1973.

Hammer, M. The directed daydream technique. *Psychotherapy: Theory, Research, and Practice*, 1967, **4**, 173–181.

Happich, C. Das Bildbewusstsein als Ansatzstelle psychischer Behandling. *Zbl. Psychotherap.*, 1932, **5**, 663–667.

Hebb, D. O. The American revolution. *American Psychologist*, 1960, **15**, 735–745.

Hilgard, E. R. *Hypnotic susceptibility*. New York: Harcourt, 1965.

Hilgard, J. R. *Personality and hypnosis*. Chicago: University of Chicago Press, 1970.

Holt, R. R. Imagery: The return of the ostracized. *American Psychologist*, 1964, **19**, 254–264.

Honiotes, G. J. Hypnosis and breast enlargement: A pilot study. *Journal of the International Society for Professional Hypnosis*, 1977, **6**, 8–12.

Horowitz, M. J. Visual imagery and cognitive organization. *American Journal of Psychiatry*, 1967, **123**, 938–946.

Horowitz, M. J. Visual thought images in psychotherapy. *American Journal of Psychotherapy*, 1968, **22**, 55–75.

Horowitz, M. J. *Image formation and cognition*. New York: Appleton, 1970.

Horowitz, M. J. Image techniques in psychotherapy. New York: Behavioral Science Tape Library, 1974.

Horowitz, M. J. Controls of visual imagery and therapeutic intervention. In J. L. Singer & K. S. Pope (Eds.), *The power of human imagination*. New York: Plenum, 1978.

Howard, F. E., & Patry, F. L. *Mental health*. New York: Harper, 1935.

Huxley, L. *You are not the target*. Hollywood, Cal.: Wilshuri, 1963.

Jacobsen, E. Electrical measurements of neuromuscular states during mental activities: 1. Imagination of movement involving skeletal muscles. *American Journal of Physiology*, 1929, **91**, 567–608.

Jaffe, D. T., & Bresler, D. E. Guided imagery: Healing through the mind's eye. In J. E. Shorr Sobel, G. E. Robin P., & Connella, J. A. (Eds.), *Imagery: Its many dimensions and applications*. New York: Plenum, 1980.

Janet, P. *Nervoses et idées fixes*. Paris: Alcan, 1898.

Jellinek, A. Spontaneous imagery: A new psychotherapeutic approach. *American Journal of Psychotherapy*, 1949, **3**, 372–391.

John, E. R. *Mechanisms of memory*. New York: Academic Press, 1967.

Johnsgard, K. W. Symbol confrontation in a recurrent nightmare. *Psychotherapy: Theory, Research, & Practice*, 1969, **6**, 177–187.

Jordan, C. S. Mental imagery and psychotherapy: European approaches. In A. A. Sheikh & J. T. Shaffer (Eds.), *The potential of fantasy and imagination*. New York: Brandon House, 1979.

Jordan, C. S., Davis, M., Kahn, P., & Sinnott, R. H. Eidetic imagery group methods of assertion training. *Journal of Mental Imagery*, 1980, **4**, 41–48.

Jordan, C. S., & Lenington, K. T. Physiological correlates of eidetic imagery and induced anxiety. *Journal of Mental Imagery*, 1979, **3**, 31–42.

Jung, C. G. *The development of personality*. Collected Works, Vol. 17. Princeton: Princeton University Press, 1954.

Jung, C. G. *The structure and dynamics of the psyche* (R. F. C. Hull, transl.) Collected works, Vol. 8, Princeton:Princeton University Press, 1960. (originally published in 1926).

Jung, C. G. *The symbolic life* (R. F. C. Hull, transl.). Collected works, Vol. 18. Princeton: Princeton University Press, 1976 (originally published in 1935).

Kanzer, M. Image formation during free association. *Psychoanalytic Quarterly*, 1958, **27**, 465–484.

Kazdin, A. E. Research issues in covert conditioning. *Cognitive Therapy and Research*, 1977, **1**, 45–49.

Kazdin, A. E. Covert conditioning: The therapeutic application of imagined rehearsal. In J. L. Singer & K. S. Pope (Eds.), *The power of human imagination*. New York: Plenum, 1978.

Kelley, G. *The psychology of personal constructs*, Vol. 2. New York: Norton, 1955.

Kepecs, J. G. Observations on screens and barriers in the mind. *Psychoanalytic Quarterly,* 1954, **23,** 62–77.

Kleitman, N. *Sleep and wakefulness.* Chicago: University of Chicago Press, 1963.

Klinger, E. *The structure and function of fantasy.* New York: Wiley, 1971.

Klinger, E. Therapy and the flow of thought. In J. E. Shorr, G. E. Sobel, P. Robin, & J. A. Connella (Eds.), *Imagery: Its many dimensions and applications.* New York: Plenum, 1980.

Kosbab, F. P. Imagery techniques in psychiatry. *Archives of General Psychiatry,* 1974, **31,** 283–290.

Kosslyn, S. Information representation in visual images. *Cognitive Psychology,* 1975, **43,** 601–607.

Kosslyn, S. *Image and mind.* Cambridge, Mass.: Harvard University Press, 1980.

Kretschmer, E. *Kretschmer's textbook of medical psychology.* London: Oxford University Press, 1922.

Kretschmer, W. Meditative techniques in psychotherapy. In C. Tart (Ed.), *Altered states of consciousness.* New York: Wiley, 1969.

Kris, E. *Psychological explorations in art.* New York: International University Press, 1952.

Kroger, W. S. & Fezler, W. D. *Hypnosis and behavior modification: Imagery conditioning.* Philadelphia: Lippincott, 1976.

Lane, J. B. Problems of assessment of vividness and control of imagery. *Perceptual and Motor Skills,* 1977, **45,** 363–368.

Lang, P. J. The mechanics of desensitization and the laboratory study of human fear. In C. M. Franks (Ed.), *Assessment and status of the behavior therapies.* New York: McGraw-Hill, 1969.

Lang, P. J. Stimulus control, response control and the desentization of fear. In D. J. Levis (Ed.), *Learning approaches to therapeutic behavior.* Chicago: Aldine, 1970.

Lange, A. J., & Jakubowski, P. *Responsible assertive behavior.* Champagne, Ill.: Research Press, 1976.

Lazarus, A. A., & Abramovitz, A. The use of "emotive imagery" in the treatment of children's phobias. *Journal of Mental Science, 1962,* **108,** 191–195.

Leuba, C. Images as conditioned sensations. *Journal of Experimental Psychology,* 1940, **26,** 345–351.

Leuner, H. Guided affective imagery: An account of its development. *Journal of Mental Imagery,* 1977, **1,** 73–92.

Leuner, H. Basic principles and therapeutic efficacy of guided affective imagery. In J. L. Singer & K. S. Pope (Eds.), *The power of human imagination.* New York: Plenum, 1978.

Lewis, H. R., & Streitfeld, S. *Growth games.* New York: Harcourt, 1971.

Lipkin, S. The imaginary collage and its use in psychotherapy. *Psychotherapy: Theory Research and Practice,* 1970, **7,** 238–242.

Little, L. M., & Curran, P. J. Covert sensitization: A clinical procedure in need of some explanations. *Psychological Bulletin,* 1978, **85,** 513–531.

Litvak, S. B. A comparison of two brief group behavior therapy techniques in the reduction of avoidance behavior. *Psychological Record,* 1969, **19**, 329–331.

Long, J. B. The death that ends death in Hinduism and Buddhism. In E. Kübler-Ross (Ed.), *Death: The final stage of growth.* Englewood Cliffs, N.J.: Prentice-Hall, 1975.

Mahoney, M. J. *Cognition and behavior modification.* Cambridge, Mass.: Ballinger, 1974.

Malleson, N. Panic & phobias: Possible method of treatment. *Lancet,* 1959, **1**, 225–227

Marks, D. F. Visual imagery differences in the recall of pictures. *British Journal of Psychology,* 1973, **64**, 17–24.

Masters, R., & Houston, J. *Mind games.* New York: Viking Press, 1972.

May, J., & Johnson, H. Physiological activity to internally-elicited arousal and inhibitory thoughts. *Journal of Abnormal Psychology,* 1973, **82**, 239–245.

McGuigan, F. J. Covert linguistic behavior in deaf subjects during thinking. *Journal of Comparative and Physiological Psychology,* 1971, **75**, 417–420.

McMahon, C. E. Images as motives and motivators: A historical perspective. *American Journal of Psychology,* 1973, **86**, 465–490.

McManus, M. Group desensitization of test anxiety. *Behavior Research & Therapy,* 1971, **9**, 51–56.

Meichenbaum, D. *Cognitive-behavior modification: An integrative approach.* New York: Plenum, 1977.

Meichenbaum, D. Why does using imagery in psychotherapy lead to change? In J. L. Singer & K. S. Pope (Eds.), *The power of human imagination.* New York: Plenum, 1978.

Meichenbaum, D. H., Gilmore, J. B., & Fedoravicius, A. Group insight versus group desensitization in treating speech anxiety. *Journal of Consulting and Clinical Psychology,* 1971, **36**, 410–421.

Miller, G. A., Galanter, E., & Pribram, K. H. *Plans and the structure of behavior.* New York: Holt, 1960.

Miller, N. E. Interactions between learned and physical factors in mental illness. In D. Shapiro et al. (Eds.), *Biofeedback and self-control.* Chicago: Aldine, 1972.

Morrison, J. K. Emotive–reconstructive psychotherapy: Changing constructs by means of mental imagery. In A. A. Sheikh & J. T. Shaffer (Eds.), *The potential of fantasy and imagination.* New York: Brandon House, 1979.

Morrison, J. K. Emotive–reconstructive therapy: A short-term psychotherapeutic use of mental imagery. In J. E. Shorr Sobel, G. E., Robin, P., & Connela, J. A. (Eds.), *Imagery: Its many dimensions and applications.* New York: Plenum, 1980.

Mowrer, O. H. Mental imagery: An indispensable psychological concept. *Journal of Mental Imagery,* 1977, **1**, 303–326.

Neisser, U. *Cognition and reality.* San Francisco: Freeman, 1976.

Oyle, I. *Time, space, and the mind.* Millbrae, Cal.: Celestial Arts, 1976.

Paivio, A. *Imagery and verbal processes.* New York: Holt, 1971.

Paivio, A. Psychophysiological correlates of imagery. In F. J. McGuigan & R. A. Schoonover (Eds.), *The psychophysiology of thinking.* New York: Academic Press, 1973.

Paivio, A. Imagery and synchronic thinking. *Canadian Psychological Review.* 1975, **16,** 147–163.

Paloszi-Horvath, G. *The undefeated.* Boston: Little, Brown, 1959.

Panagiotou, N., & Sheikh, A. A. Eidetic psychotherapy: Introduction and evaluation. *International Journal of Social Psychiatry,* 1974, **20,** 231–241.

Panagiotou, N., & Sheikh, A. A. The image and the unconscious. *International Journal of Social Psychiatry,* 1977, **23,** 169–186.

Paul, G. L., & Shannon, D. T. Treatment of anxiety through systematic desensitization in therapy groups. *Journal of Abnormal Psychology,* 1966, **73,** 119–130.

Penfield, W. The brains record of auditory and visual experience—final summary. *Brain,* 1963, **86,** 595–696.

Penfield, W., & Jaspers, H. *Epilepsy and the functional anatonomy of the human brain.* Boston: Little, Brown, 1954.

Perky, C. W. An experiemental study of imagination. *American Journal of Psychology,* 1910, **21,** 422–452.

Perls, F. *Gestalt therapy verbatim.* New York: Bantam, 1970.

Perls, F. *In and out of the garbage pail.* New York: Bantam, 1972.

Perls, F., Goodman, P., & Hefferline, R. *Gestalt therapy.* New York: Dell, 1951.

Piaget, J. *Judgement and reasoning in the child.* Totowa, N.J.: Littlefield, Adams, 1972.

Pope, K. S. The flow of consciousness. Unpublished doctoral dissertation, Yale University, 1977.

Progoff, I. *The symbolic and the real.* New York: Julian Press, 1963.

Progoff, I. Waking dream and living myth. In J. Campbell (Ed.), *Myths, dreams and religion.* New York: Dutton, 1970.

Pylyshyn, Z. W. What the mind's eye tells the mind's brain: A critique of mental imagery. *Psychological Bulletin,* 1973, **80,** 1–24.

Rachman, S. *Phobias: Their nature and control.* Springfield, Ill.: Thomas, 1968.

Reyher, J. Free imagery, an uncovering procedure. *Journal of Clinical Psychology,* 1963, **19,** 454–459.

Reyher, J. Spontaneous visual imagery: Implications for psychoanalysis, psychopathology, and psychotherapy. *Journal of Mental Imagery,* 1977, **2,** 253–274.

Reyher, J. Emergent uncovering psychotherapy: The use of imagoic and linguistic vehicles in objectifying psychodynamic processes. In J. L. Singer & K. S. Pope (Eds.), *The power of human imagination.* New York: Plenum, 1978.

Reyher, J., & Smeltzer, W. Uncovering properties of visual imagery and verbal association: A comparative study. *Journal of Abnormal Psychology,* 1968, **73,** 218–222.

Richardson, A. *Mental imagery.* New York: Springer, 1969.

Richardson, A. Verbalizer–visualizer: A cognitive style dimension. *Journal of Mental Imagery,* 1977, **1,** 109–126.

Rigo, L. The imagination technique of analysis and restructuration of the profound. Unpublished paper presented at the meeting of the International Society for Mental Imagery Techniques, Geneva, Switzerland, 1968.

Rigo-Uberto, S. Imagery techniques with play in child psychotherapy. Unpublished paper presented at the meeting of the International Society for Mental Imagery Techniques, Geneva, Switzerland, 1968.

Rossman, M. *Meeting your inner advisor*. Mill Valley, Cal.: Insight Publications Tape, 1980.

Salter, A. *Conditioned reflex therapy*. New York: Farrar, Strauss, 1949.

Samuels, M., & Bennett, H. *The well body book*. New York: Random House, 1973.

Sarbin, T. R. The quixotic principle: Believed-in imaginings. Santa Cruz: Cal.: Deptartment of Psychology, University of California, 1976.

Sarbin, T. R., & Coe, W. C. *Hypnosis: A social psychological analysis of influence communication*. New York: Holt, 1972.

Saretsky ,T. *Active techniques and group psychotherapy*. New York: Jason Aronson, 1977.

Schachtel, E. G. *Metamorphosis: On the development of affect, perception, attention, and memory*. New York: Basic Books, 1959.

Scheidler, T. Use of fantasy as a therapeutic agent in latency age groups. *Psychotherapy: Theory, Research, & Practice,* 1972, **9,** 299–303.

Schultz, D. Imagery and the control of depression. In J. L. Singer & K. S. Pope (Eds.), *The power of human imagination*. New York: Plenum, 1978.

Schultz, J. H., & Luthe, W. *Autogenic training: A physiological approach to psychotherapy*. New York: Grune & Stratton, 1959.

Schutz, W. C. *Joy: Expanding human awareness*. New York: Grove Press, 1967

Segal, S. J., & Fusella, Y. Influence of imaged pictures and sounds on detection of visual and auditory signals. *Journal of Experimental Psychology,* 1970, **83,** 458–464.

Shaffer, J. T. The experience of the holistic mind. In A. A. Sheikh & J. T. Shaffer (Eds.), *The potential of fantasy and imagination*. New York: Brandon House, 1979.

Shapiro, D. L. The significance of the visual image in psychotherapy. *Psychotherapy: Theory, Research, and Practice,* 1970, **7,** 209–212.

Sheehan, P. W. A shortened form of Betts' questionnaire upon mental imagery *Journal of Clinical Psychology,* 1967, **23,** 386–389.

Sheehan, P. W. Some comment on the nature of visual imagery: A problem of affect. Paper presented at the meeting of the International Society for Mental Imagery Techniques, Geneva, Switzerland, 1968.

Sheehan, P. W. (Ed.). *The function and nature of imagery*. New York: Academic Press, 1972.

Sheehan, P. W. Hypnosis and processes of imagination. In E. Fromm & R. E. Shor (Eds.), *Hypnosis: Developments in research and new perspectives*. New York: Aldine, 1979.

Sheikh, A. A. Treatment of insomnia through eidetic imagery: A new technique. *Perceptual and Motor Skills,* 1976, **43,** 994.

Sheikh, A. A. Mental images: Ghosts of sensations? *Journal of Mental Imagery,* 1977, **1,** 1–4.

Sheikh, A. A. Eidetic psychotherapy. In J. L. Singer & K. S. Pope (Eds.), *The power of human imagination.* New York: Plenum, 1978.

Sheikh, A. A. Eidetic imagery revisited. Paper in preparation, Marquette University, 1983a.

Sheikh, A. A. (Ed.), *Imagination and healing.* New York: Baywood, 1983b.

Sheikh, A. A., & Jordan, C. S. Eidetic Psychotherapy. In R. J. Corsini (Ed.), *Handbook of innovative psychotherapies.* New York: Wiley, 1981.

Sheikh, A. A. & Kunzendorf, R. Imagery, physiology and psychosomatic illness. *International Review of Mental Imagery,* in press.

Sheikh, A. A., & Moleski, L. M. Enhancement of mental imagery: A review. Manuscript in preparation, 1983.

Sheikh, A. A., & Panagiotou, N. C. Use of mental imagery in psychotherapy: A critical review. *Perceptual and Motor Skills,* 1975, **41,** 555–585.

Sheikh, A. A., & Shaffer, J. T. (Eds.). *The potential of fantasy and imagination.* New York: Brandon House, 1979.

Sheikh, A. A., Twente, G. E., & Turner, D. Death imagery: Therapeutic uses. In A. A. Sheikh & J. T. Shaffer (Eds.), *The potential of fantasy and imagination.* New York: Brandon House, 1979b.

Sheikh, A. A., Richardson, P., & , Moleski, L. M. Psychosomatics and mental imagery: A brief review. In A. A. Sheikh & J. T. Shaffer (Eds.), *The potential of fantasy and imagination.* New York: Brandon House, 1979a.

Shepard, R. N. The mental image. *American Psychologist,* 1978, **33,** 125–137.

Shorr, J. E. *Psycho-imagination therapy: The integration of phenomenology and imagination.* New York: Intercontinental Medical Book Corporation, 1972.

Shorr, J. E. *Shorr Imagery Test.* Los Angeles: Institute for Psycho-Imagination Therapy, 1974.

Shorr, J. E. Clinical use of categories of therapeutic imagery. In J. L. Singer & K. S. Pope (Eds.), *The power of human imagination.* New York: Plenum, 1978.

Shorr, J. E. Discoveries about the mind's ability to organize and find meaning in imagery. In Shorr, E., Sobel, G. E., Robin, P., & Connella, J.A. (Eds.), *Imagery: Its many dimensions and applications.* New York: Plenum, 1980.

Shorr, J. E., Sobel, G. E., Robin, P., & Connella, J. A. (Eds.). *Imagery: Its many dimensions and applications.* New York: Plenum, 1980.

Short, P. L. The objective study of psychology. *British Journal of Psychology,* 1953, **44,** 38–51.

Simpson, H. M., & Paivio, A. Changes in pupil size during an imagery task without motor involvement. *Psychonomic Science,* 1966, **5,** 405–406.

Singer, J. L. *Imagery and daydream methods in psychotherapy and behavior modification.* New York: Academic Press, 1974.

Singer, J. L. Imagery and affect psychotherapy: Elaborating private scripts and generating contexts. In A.A. Sheikh & J. T. Shaffer (Eds.), *The potential of fantasy and imagination.* New York: Brandon House, 1979.

Singer, J. L., & Antrobus, J. S. Daydreaming, imaginal processes, and personality:

A normative study. In P. W. Sheehan (Ed.), *The function and nature of imagery.* New York: Academic, 1972.

Singer, J. L. & Pope, K. S. The use of imagery and fantasy techniques in psychotherapy. In J. L. Singer & K. S. Pope (Eds.), *The power of human imagination.* New York: Plenum, 1978.

Singer, J. L., & Switzer, E. *Mind play: The creative uses of imagery.* Englewood Cliffs, N.J.: Prentice-Hall, 1980.

Sipprelle, C. N. Induced anxiety. *Psychotherapy: Theory, Research, and Practice,* 1967, **4,** 36–40.

Smith, E. D., Dickson, A. L., & Sheppard, L. Review of flooding procedures (implosion) in animals and man. *Perceptual and Motor Skills,* 1973, **37,** 351–374.

Stampfl, T., & Levis, D. Essentials of therapy: A learning theory-based psychodynamic behavioral therapy. *Journal of Abnormal Psychology,* 1967, **72,** 496–503.

Stevens, J. O. *Awareness: Exploring, experimenting and experiencing.* Lafayette, Cal.: Real People Press, 1971

Strosahl, K. D., & Ascough, J. C. Clinical uses of mental imagery: Experiemental foundations, theoretical misconceptions, and research issues. *Psychological Bulletin,* 1981, **89,** 422–438.

Sullivan, H. S. *Clinical studies in psychiatry.* New York: Norton, 1956.

Switras, J. E. *Survey of mental imagery test manual.* Unpublished manuscript, 1979.

Tauber, E. S., & Green, M. G. *Prelogical experience.* New York: Basic Books, 1959.

Tomkins, S. *Affect, imagery, and consciousness,* Vols. 1 and 11. New York: Springer, 1962, 1963.

Tower, R. B., & Singer, J. L. The measurement of imagery: How can it be clinically useful? In P. C. Kendall & S. Holland (Eds.), *Cognitive–behavioral interventions: Assessment methods.* New York: Academic Press, 1981.

Virel, A. *Histoire de notre image.* Geneva: Mont Blanc, 1968.

Vittoz, R. *Traitement des psychonervoses par la reeducation du controle cerebral.* Paris: Bailliere, 1907.

Watkins, M. J. *Waking dreams.* New York: Harper, 1976.

Watson, J. B. Psychology as the behaviorist views it. *Psychological Review,* 1913, **20,** 158–177.

Weitzenhoffer, A. M., & Hilgard, E. R. *Stanford hypnotic susceptibility scale, Form C.* Palo Alto, Cal.: Consulting Psychologist Press, 1962.

White, K. D., Sheehan, P. W., & Ashton, R. Imagery assessment: A survey of self-report measures. *Journal of Mental Imagery,* 1977, **1,** 145–170.

Williams, T. A. *Dreads and besetting fears.* Boston: Little, Brown, 1923.

Wilson, S. C., & Barber, T. X. The *Creative imagination scale: Applications to clinical and experimental hypnosis.* Medfield, Mass.: Medfield Foundation, 1976.

Wolpe, J. *Psychotherapy by reciprocol inhibition.* Stanford: Stanford University Press, 1958.

Wolpe, J. *The practice of behavior therapy.* New York: Pergamon, 1969.

Wolpe, J., & Lazarus, A. *Behavior therapy techniques*. New York: Pergamon, 1966.

Wolpin, M. Guided imagining to reduce avoidance behavior. *Psychotherapy: Theory, Research and Practice,* 1969, **6,** 122–124.

Yanovski, A., & Fogel, M. L. Some diagnostic and therapeutic implications of visual imagery reactivity. *Journal of Mental Imagery,* 1978, **2,** 301–302.

Yaremko, R. M., & Butler, M. C. Imaginal experience and attenuation of the galvanic skin response to shock. *Bulletin of the Psychonomic Society,* 1975, **5,** 317–318.

CHAPTER 14

The Role of Imagery
in Sexual Behavior

D. P. J. PRZYBYLA, DONN BYRNE, AND KATHRYN KELLEY

The capacity to create and process sexual imagery adds depth and complexity
to human behavior. For most individuals, cognitive processes, such as imaginative fantasizing, supersede hormonal processes in initiating and directing sexual arousal. Fantasies influence the motivational–emotional responses of the individual, provide behavioral guidelines, and eventually affect
sexual interactions with others.

   Unlike most mammals, humans become aroused primarily in response to
visual images rather than to olfactory cues, such as species-specific sexual
pheromones (Money, 1973). Internally and externally generated sexual imagery is sufficiently potent and prevalent that sexual behavior seems to be
rooted more firmly in cultural influences than in genetic constitution. Even
with respect to individual patterns of learning, development is shaped by
particular social influences. In modern society we are bombarded by magazines, movies, television programs, songs, commercials, and other imaginal
productions whose sexual messages constitute an integral part of our concept
of reality. In the present chapter both individual sexual images and those
shared within a culture are examined with respect to their development,
interaction, and influence on behavior.

THE UBIQUITY OF SEXUAL IMAGERY

Internal Sources

One of the more fascinating aspects of a person's inner life is the way each
of us weaves stories and pictures into a series of private scenarios. It is
possible to classify and distinguish among these events that take place "in
the mind's eye" (Byrne & Kelley, 1981). First, there are the involuntary
images that occur during sleep. Dream content ranges from replays of events
in the individual's waking life to wish fulfillment to problem solving. Second,
there is the type of waking reverie that involves the imaginative reenactment

436

of past events in one's life. Such memories may be accurate or can involve major or minor distortions of what occurred. Third, there is the purposeful generation of scenes in which roles are assumed and events acted out in imaginative play. Finally, there are anticipatory fantasies about future pleasures to be sought and future discomforts to be avoided. Whether one's hopes and fears are realistic provides one index of psychological adjustment.

Dreams

Sexual expression, both overt and in disguised form, is a major component of dream content. As Money (1973, p. 412) put it, "Nature is her own pornographer." At puberty the individual usually begins regularly to focus on the sexual images that appear unbidden in dreams. This nocturnal confrontation with one's own sexuality helps to make it increasingly salient. The onset of a dream-induced orgasm during sleep is often the first intense sexual pleasure that a young male or female experiences.

Erotic dreams and their physiological concomitants can also be used diagnostically. Medical therapists currently employ the criterion of nocturnal penile tumescence to distinguish organic from psychogenic erectile dysfunction (Marshall et al., 1981). This approach assumes that organically based impotence would prohibit an erection during sleep, whereas psychogenic factors would interfere primarily when the patient was awake. Dream imagery is also considered relevant to sexual dysfunctions. Levay and Weissberg (1979) have proposed that dreams can be useful in providing clues to the unconscious factors underlying dysfunction, in interpreting these factors to the client, and in working through the necessary changes. Both the content and the client's affective response to the content are hypothesized to be highly specific to the individual's conflicts involving sexuality. These therapists also hypothesize that frankly sexual dreams frequently suggest the preferred modes of arousal as well as areas of inhibition. In addition, some investigators believe that dreams reflect the emotionally arousing current concerns of the dreamer, such as unconsumated behavior sequences (Klinger, 1971). In a relevant experiment by Brown et al. (1976), male subjects were shown a variety of slides dealing with explicit heterosexual activity. Compared to the previous week, subjects reported an increase in masturbation in the 24 hours following the slide presentation and a decrease in "wet dreams." During the subsequent week, the number of wet dreams increased while the incidence of masturbation decreased. It is suggested that among the short-term effects of erotica is the creation of a "current concern" about orgasm. If a sexual act does not occur in waking life, the concern remains and the behavior sequence is completed while the individual sleeps.

Past Events

Anecdotal evidence plus a great deal of autobiographical literature suggests strongly that certain landmark sexual experiences are remembered with great clarity and are interwoven with strong emotional content. An example is the first sexual encounter of a teenage boy in *The Summer of '42* (Raucher, 1971). Although the imagery-eliciting capacity of such affect-laden sexual interactions has not been investigated systematically, research has demonstrated that reliving aspects of previous sexual relationships does play an important role in the individual's private imagery catalog (Kelley, 1979).

An interesting aspect of such memories is that they act as special sources of sexual arousal that can activate and guide subsequent sexual acts (Kelley & Byrne, 1978). For example, Sue (1979) reported that about 40% of both males and females in his sample fantasized about former lovers during intercourse. Crepault and Couture (1980) found that about 80% of their male subjects fantasized about previous sexual encounters during masturbation and during heterosexual interactions. Although such reminiscences are characteristic of both genders, McCauley and Swann (1978, 1980) found that thinking of past experiences is relatively more popular among males than among females, who prefer fictional fantasies.

Imaginative Play

The term "sexual fantasy" is most often applied to purposeful erotic imagery in which roles are assumed and idiosyncratically arousing scenes are created and guided to their climactic conclusions. Such fantasies allow the individual to remove any barrier to excitement that may exist in the real world (Byrne, 1977b). In imagination, there are no limits in terms of stamina, attractiveness, legalities, or moral codes. Creativity is all that is required to give birth to a fantasy and to nourish it over time. Depending on the fantasizer's predilections, it is possible to bring about an instantaneous change of mood, partners, or activities. Erotic fantasies seem to be generated by both males and females during sexual acts as well as at other, random times (Crepault & Couture, 1980; Hariton & Singer, 1974). Masters and Johnson (1979) have described the development of favorite fantasies into what they call "old friends"—sure-fire instigators of arousal that the person can use, modify, and rely on when needed.

When subjects are asked to report their personal sexual fantasies, sex differences are usually obtained, although not with absolute consistency across studies. Several investigations indicate that males are slightly more likely to initiate such fantasies than are females. For example, both Wagman (1967) and Hessellund (1976) found that males exceeded females in the proportion of daydreams devoted to sexual themes. Such gender differences appear to be especially true in the 17–29-year-old age group (Giambra, in press). Barclay (1973), using a college sample, found that male fantasies contained much visual imagery and anatomic detail, whereas female sexual fantasies emphasized emotions, plot, and dialogue.

Other sex differences also have been found (Hunt, 1974). Males' masturbation fantasies are more likely than females' to include intercourse with a stranger, group sex, and forcing someone to have sex. Females are more likely to fantasize acts in which they would never actually engage and being forced to have sex. The female image of being sexually dominated is a recurrent theme in the literature (Barclay, 1973; Hariton, 1972; Maslow, 1942). It should be noted that Hunt (1974) reported one major similarity between the sexes—fantasies of intercourse with the one they love.

More recently, Przybyla et al. (1981) asked college student volunteers anonymously to write descriptions of their most exciting sexual fantasies. Both genders produced stories that would more aptly be characterized as sexual rather than romantic, but there were still sex differences. Male fantasies contained more explicit sex, whereas interpersonal affection was more common in female fantasies. In addition, males were more likely to report details of the partner's attractiveness and bodily proportions, to specify multiple partners, and to describe scenes of oral sex. The latter topic provides an interesting example of the egocentrism of one's fantasy world. Oral sex was included by 45% of the male respondents; *all* wrote of being fellated, whereas only a handful mentioned cunnilingus. Analogously, among the females who mentioned oral sex (3%), *all* the fantasies involved cunnilingus and none involved fellatio. In an individual's own imaginative creations, it is clearly more blessed to receive than to give.

Some studies have dealt with other types of individual differences in fantasy content. For example, female subjects high in sex guilt report shorter and less explicit fantasies than do those low in guilt (Moreault & Follingstad, 1978). Only recently have there been any attempts to compare heterosexual and homosexual fantasies. Masters and Johnson (1979) found more active and more diverse patterns of fantasy activity among their homosexual subjects than among heterosexuals. The lesbian sample recorded the highest fantasy incidence of any group. Interestingly, their fantasies most frequently involved forcing or being forced to have sex. Male homosexual fantasies centered on imagery of specific parts of the anatomy (primarily penis and buttocks) and on physical abuse.

Anticipatory Fantasies

Imagery that anticipates future sexual events is perhaps the least studied of the self-generated imaginative processes. As yet there has been no systematic attempt to examine imagery-expectations preceding the initiation of dating, the first intercourse experience, and so forth, nor to relate such imagery to the subsequent reality. Only with respect to love has it been shown that those who think most about the phenomenon are more likely to experience it (Tesser & Paulhus, 1976).

Another potentially fruitful area of research is the possible relationship between anticipatory sexual anxieties and performance problems, such as erectile difficulties or anorgasmia. It seems reasonable to expect that the individual who dwells on possible performance "failures" and on the negative consequences of sexual interactions would be especially prone to undergo sexual dysfunctions. If the imagery were focused on the pleasures of sex or possibly on ways to deal with any problems that occur, it may well be that dysfunctional behavior would be diminished.

External Sources

It is obvious that sexual images are not confined to internal processes. Throughout recorded history members of our species have sought to concretize their intangible mental images. For thousands of years, human beings have represented and communicated erotic images with whatever artistic and technological skills they possessed. Erotic creations have included Latin American clay figures, African phallic statues, Indian temple sculptures, the underground literature of Victorian England, the "French postcards" of the early 1900s, and today's movies and video recordings (Byrne, 1977a). Although written material has been, and continues to be, an extremely important aspect of external imagery, we concentrate here on pictorial imagery.

Members of each generation harbor the suspicion that they invented sexual pleasure, whereas their parents and others who preceded them were confined to infrequent, duty-bound, procreational acts (Pocs & Godow, 1977). When undergraduates are exposed to ancient erotica for the first time, many seem surprised to find, for example, Greek and Roman depictions of cunnilingus, fellatio, anal intercourse, group sex, and every position of copulation depicted in today's pornographic books and movies. What differs most over the centuries is not the sex itself but certain aspects of style and content. In his history of erotic art, Bradley Smith (1974) relates that in eighteenth-century Europe the emphasis was on heterosexual acts between members of the nobility. Total nudity was rare. Instead, the vogue was to depict sex being conducted in a state of partial undress with elegant clothing slightly disheveled. Sadism and masochism were represented by scenes in which women birched men's bare bottoms and, less frequently, men birched the bottoms of women.

Similarly, during this same period, according to Smith, Chinese erotic art was produced primarily for royalty, and this class also was the one depicted. Costume was as important in Asia as in Europe. Bedchambers were elaborately decorated in erotic art with intricate designs. Even in the most intimate scenes, there was a languid atmosphere with no visible signs of exertion by the male or the female. Both the Chinese and Japanese erotic artists routinely exaggerated the size of the genitals, but Indian art during the same period maintained realism with respect to the lingam (penis) and yoni (female genitalia). In India, such art was of religious significance.

By the nineteenth century, the Western world had come to accept greater realism in its erotic art. Ordinary men and women were shown engaging in sexual acts, and many widely recognized artists produced some examples of this genre. Despite cyclic repression of sexual freedom during the nineteenth century, there was a gradual movement toward more open attitudes about sexual expression. In many respects, erotica simply mirrors aspects of the society that produces it. For example, Moyle (1975) examined sexual elements in eighteenth-century Samoan art forms and found that references to sexuality, whether humorous, instructive, or moralistic in nature, tended to reflect traditional guidelines for sexual behavior found in that society.

The invention of photography in the latter half of the 1800s opened new vistas for erotica. Sexual paintings and drawings were supplanted by sexual photographs and eventually by movies, videotapes, and videodisks. Among the unusual aspects of photographic erotica is that *real* people are depicted in a state of *genuine* arousal engaging in *actual* sex acts. Thus viewers are titillated not only by the fictional depiction, but also by the real-life activity of the actors and actresses. Such parallels do not hold for other emotional depictions in which those being photographed only pretend to be happy, sad, and so forth.

Advances in technology and changes in societal tolerance have thus made it possible for individuals to stimulate themselves as frequently as they wish with a wide variety of realistic sexual imagery. In theaters, adult bookstores, and in the home, even the least imaginative person can saturate himself or herself with a vast panoply of erotic fantasies. As even this brief overview suggests, external sexual imagery is a ubiquitous and timeless phenomenon.

THE CONTENT OF AMERICAN SEXUAL IMAGERY

It is proposed that external imagery plays a major role in shaping internal imagery and that internal imagery mediates and sometimes initiates overt behavior (Byrne, 1977b). It follows, then, that the specific content of external imagery is of potentially crucial importance in shaping behavior.

"Acceptable" Imagery

The arbitors of acceptable sexual imagery were identified by the U.S. Supreme Court in 1957 as one's fellow citizens who set "local community standards." Thirty years later, research described the attitudes of residents of one community toward pornography as a relatively simple relationship between measures of conservatism and acceptance–rejection of explicit sexual pictures (Brown et al., 1978). It seems that societal changes in values bring about corresponding changes in judgments of acceptability—older residents express less positive reactions to erotica than do younger ones (Merritt et al., 1975). Even the censorship of movies passes with time, since the otherwise fairly traditional Roman Catholic Church has discontinued its system of publishing lists of objectionable works on the basis of erotic content (Ostling et al., 1980). A new wave of censorship has surfaced in the 1980s, however, with the "moral majority" movement. Their pressure led a major sponsor (Proctor & Gamble) to dissociate itself from dozens of television programs on the basis of unacceptable content.

Perhaps the most ambitious examination of American sexual imagery was undertaken by Ellis in 1950 and again in 1960. Selecting the first day of each of these years, he conducted content analyses of the mass media, analyzing a number of periodicals available to the public that day plus popular books, plays, and movies. His stated purpose was to determine what American mass media were preaching on such topics as masturbation, contraception, fornication, illegitimacy, homosexuality, and "any and all other aspects of sexual behavior." He concluded that there was an increase in sexual references between 1950 and 1960 and that a permissive shift occurred. By 1960, there was a general endorsement of almost all forms of sexual behavior. Following Ellis, other investigators have attempted to document sexual expression in various aspects of the media.

Magazines

Scott and Franklin (1972) examined the seven highest-circulation periodicals in the United States in 1970 and compared their content then with that in 1950 and 1960. The publications were *Readers' Digest, McCall's, Life, Look, Saturday Evening Post, Time,* and *Newsweek.* It was found that the number of sex references increased by 82% from 1950 to 1960 and by 111% from 1950 to 1970. Thus the greatest change took place in the 1950s.

With respect to specific sexual activities, views about fornication, adultery, prostitution, promiscuity, and venereal disease became increasingly liberal. There was actually a decrease in references to kissing, petting, and masturbation. By 1970, the topics most likely to be discussed were nudity, obscenity, the genitals, and sexual preferences.

Literature

Studies of the sexual imagery present in novels have dealt less with content than with the underlying meaning—the imagery behind the imagery. Some content data *are* available, however. On the basis of a survey of established literature, Atkins (1970) suggests the following sexual content schema. There are accounts of sensual pleasure (e.g., Henry Miller), attempts to create sexual stimulation in the reader (e.g., Cleland), philosophical presentations (e.g., de Sade), dramatic works emphasizing characters and situations (e.g., Boccacio), bawdiness (e.g., Rabelais), surrealistic sexual works (e.g., Promlo), instructional manuals (e.g., *The Kama Sutra*), and reports of scientific inquiry (e.g., Kinsey). To date, there have been no attempts to utilize these classifications to plot trends.

An examination of the best-selling novels of 1959, 1969, and 1979 in the United States was conducted by Abramson and Mechanic (in press). Over those three decades there was a progressive increase in the sexual content of these books. The trends within the sexual depictions included a decrease in the time that characters were acquainted prior to intercourse and a decrease in the depiction of romantic love. Like the inhabitants of the hard-core fantasy world, most of the men and women in these novels were "ready, willing, and able" to engage in sex when the opportunity arose.

Television

The concern with violence has overshadowed most investigations of television content. Some of this research, coupled with public pressure, has brought about a slight decrease in the amount of violence in network programming (Dienstbier, 1977). It has been suggested that television violence is being replaced with sex, and there are many references to the popularity of "T and A" (tits and ass) programs and "jiggle" shows. It seems clear from many years of research that exposure to aggressive imagery results in an increase in aggressive behavior (Bandura et al., 1963; Bryan & Schwartz, 1971; Eron, 1963; Eron et al., 1972; Liebert & Baron, 1972). Does the same sort of relationship hold true for sexual imagery?

Several investigators have been interested in documenting the specific kinds of sexual interactions and references that occur during prime time. Data are available for the 1975 broadcasting season (Franzblau et al., 1977), the 1976 season (Fernandez-Collado et al., 1978), and the 1977 season (Silverman et al., 1979). The major finding in the 1975 study was that physical intimacy appeared less than one might expect from public outcries about what is shown. Sexual activities were confined primarily to suggestive actions or comments, innuendos, and affectionate displays such as kissing and embracing. Physically intimate acts such as intercourse were not shown. By 1976, there were many more portrayals of or references to intercourse, homosexuality, and illegal sexual behavior.

In the 1977 study, 64 prime-time programs on the three networks were analyzed during a 1-week period. Once again, it was found that there were no overt portrayals of coitus. Nevertheless, the context made it clear that this act had occurred or was about to occur a total of 15 times during the sampled week. Suggestive behavior (e.g., physical flirtation) was shown 3.26 times per hour. Verbal flirtations took place 7.38 times per hour. These frequencies represent an increase since 1975 when, for example, there were *no* contextual implications of intercourse. Furthermore, in 1975 there was less than one seductive act per hour of programming, whereas in 1977 there were more than three per hour.

The *type* of program is found to be a major predictor of sexual content. For example, situation comedies contain the greatest amount of kissing, embracing, nonaggressive touching, and innuendos. Franzblau et al. (1977) suggest that this is consistent with the contention that sex is a disturbing topic in our culture and is best handled humorously. Dramas tended to be much more conservative about sexuality.

It should be noted that most of the negative reactions to sex on television are based on the assumption that children should be protected from the effects of exposure. Interestingly, there is no available research indicating how children interpret sexual references on television or how their present or future attitudes and behavior might be affected.

Advertising

Among the variables identified as effective in gaining the consumer's attention and in inducing favorable product evaluation is sex. Sex in advertising tends to be implicit rather than explicit, wholesome rather than illicit. Within these constraints, there is a steady increase in the sexual content of advertising. Acceptable content includes partial nudity, romance, and suggestiveness (Wilson & Moore, 1979). Such content is most likely to be used with products that must compete intensely for the attention of consumers (Danielenko, 1974).

The sexual stimulus of choice is a woman, and this has contributed substantially to the perception that women are viewed as sex objects in advertisements (Kerin et al., 1979). Venkatesan and Losco (1975) reported that about 65% of the ads during 1969–1971 in best-selling magazines portrayed women as sexual objects, whereas 13% portrayed them as "sexy." Similar results were reported by Belkaoui and Belkaoui (1976) in an analysis of magazines in 1972. They reported that 95% of the ads showing females in a nonworking context used them simply as decoration.

Surprisingly little empirical evidence deals with the use of more obvious sexual imagery. Casual observation reveals such ads as those for tight-fitting jeans worn by partially nude models, including the chic version of kiddie porn with Brooke Shields saying that "nothin' comes between me and my Calvin Kleins." A husky-voiced female on television urges a male shaving his face to "Take it off; take it all off." The presence of these ads suggests that a systematic study of content and trends would be of considerable interest.

Johnson and Satow (1978) asked a female sample to give examples of commercials that portray "too much sex." Some of the most frequently mentioned were Bic Razor ("Use Bic and get stroked every morning"), Underalls ("Feels like you have on nothing at all"), Aviance ("It's going to be an Aviance night"), and Muriel Cigars (sexy woman lights man's cigar and sits on his lap). In general, older women were more favorable to the male-fantasy commercials than were younger ones. Female-fantasy ads such as Aviance were acceptable to young white-collar females, but not to those in blue-collar jobs.

Movies

Abramson and Mechanic (in press) analyzed the content of the top five money-making films of 1959, 1969, and 1979. In the 15 films there were only 12 sexually relevant themes. Such scenes showed a small increase from 1959 to 1979. As in novels, sex tended to occur between people only recently acquainted and not as part of a long-term relationship. None of these financially successful films contained a high degree of eroticism, and topics such as masturbation, incest, and homosexuality were totally absent.

Underground Imagery: From Pornography to Graffiti

Although the sexual presentations of television programs and commercials may be mild, nonexplicit, and at times wholesome, there is a specialized body of sexual stimuli that is quite the opposite. While no longer illegal, the hard-core market of books, movies, and videotapes most often exists in a somewhat shady world of tawdry adult bookstores, run-down theaters, and plain brown wrappers. As a rough guide, there is a dividing line between soft-core, simulated sex such as appears in *Playboy* and similar publications sold at the supermarket, and hard-core, genuine sex such as appears in *SCREW, Puritan, At Home,* and a multitude of underground publications. Hard-core pornography depicts full erections, penetration of a bodily orifice, and/or visible ejaculate.

According to Gagnon and Simon (1973), pornography is sought out not simply because it deals with explicit sex, but because it deals with illicit sex. They propose a general rule: if the activity is conventional, the context is not; if the context is conventional, the activity is not.

Paperbacks

A peculiar omission in the controversies regarding pornography and its effects is the absence of comprehensive investigations of its content. In the report of the ground-breaking Commission on Obscenity and Pornography, the major content study was the Sonneschein et al. (1971) analysis of romance and confession magazines. We have learned much more about who buys actual pornography and its subsequent behavioral effects than about what is in it.

One investigation has attempted an analysis of "adults only" (as opposed to mass market) paperback books (Smith, 1976). Among books published between 1968 and 1974, the major characteristic is a series of sexual episodes held together by a limited number of pages describing nonsexual activity. Little inducement is needed for either the male or female characters to engage in frequent sexual encounters of extended duration. In fact, 60% of the erotic episodes are characterized by sex for the sake of physical gratification with no emotional attachment between or among the participants. The theme of machismo dominates these stories. The traditional male stereotypes of virility and strength are magnified. Males are the dominant characters regardless of who is doing what to whom in whatever setting. Interestingly, fellatio and anal intercourse are treated as the ultimate acts of female humiliation. These interactions are either forced on the female, or she volunteers her orifices as an ultimate act of submission, homage, and tribute. Cunnilingus, in contrast, is a device used by the male to ensure that the aloof, unattainable beauty will be transformed into a companion who is wanton, lustful, and insatiable. Over the years of the study, the plots were unaffected by world events, women's liberation, or political concerns. Smith (1976, p. 25) noted, "There is virtually no change in the sex roles portrayed, the nature of sex, or the relationship of the sexes to each other. Almost defiantly it remains a male's world."

8-mm Movies

Unlike the erotic art of earlier centuries, the hard-core movies of twentieth-century America and western Europe no longer depict the erotic acts of the nobility. Instead, other common characteristics are revealed by an informal and nonsystematic survey of explicit 8-mm film ads. Several occupations, for example, are frequently represented in explicit erotica—stewardess, nurse, repairman, gardener, doctor, delivery boy, housewife, and secretary. Once the identifying outer clothing has been removed, however, the sexual acts tend to be those that have been depicted for many centuries.

According to a survey of *SCREW* readers, the most popular stories involve heterosexual couples engaging in intercourse and oral sex. Interracial sex is fairly common: the most usual pairings are a white female with a black male or a white male with an Oriental female. Group sex is frequently shown, with three or more interacting participants. Only a small and highly specialized segment of the market is interested in such subject matter as rape, bestiality, kiddie porn, scatology, or "special" partners (e.g., male dwarfs, obese females, amputees, elderly performers, lactating mothers).

It should also be mentioned that total nudity is often avoided. Through the 1930s, male erotic actors tended to wear black socks and sometimes a Lone Ranger sort of mask, while the females wore stockings and a hat. Since that time, the males are more likely to be either nude or clad only in their shirts while a female is likely to have a garter belt, high heeled shoes, and a bright scarf around her neck. There is, by the way, a separate erotic marketplace for male homosexuals, but not for female homosexuals.

Pornographic Comics

During the 1930s, the marketing of eight-page pornocomics (also known as "Tijuana bibles") developed into a multi-million-dollar business (Gilmore, 1971). These comic strips were usually based on popular characters in the funnies; such as Popeye, Moon Mullins, and Joe Palooka. They were typified by oversized sexual organs and constant sexual activity.

Palmer (1979) documented the content of these publications. He found that the females were shown to be as sexually motivated and aggressive as the males, and sometimes more so. Although the drawings were blatant and explicit (intercourse and oral and anal sex), they tended to be confined to adult monogomous heterosexual behavior.

Sex and Violence

A subtopic of considerable research interest is the degree to which aggressive behavior is sometimes combined with sexuality. Most of the research has dealt with the effects of this combination rather than with its detailed content or frequency of occurrence. One exception is a longitudinal content analysis of sexual violence in *Playboy* and *Penthouse*. Malamuth and Spinner (1980) found that from January 1973 through December 1977 the amount of sexual violence in these magazines increased significantly. Nevertheless, by 1977 only about 5% of the pictorial content was rated as sexually violent. It seems likely that the aggression was primarily initiated by males against females, but that was not specifically stated. In the Abramson and Mechanic (in press) study of the most popular books and movies of the last 20 years, sexual interactions were usually shown to be a matter of mutual consent. There was an almost total absence of sexual aggression.

There is a popular trend in movies made for general release and not usually sexually explicit, in which young, attractive women attempt to behave in an independent fashion and are then victimized. Gene Siskell and Roger Ebert, formerly of *Sneak Previews* on PBS television, identified a number of films that fall into that classification: *Don't Answer the Phone, When a Stranger Calls, Terror Train,* and *Silent Scream* are examples. Typically, advertisements for such fare present an attractive woman screaming in shrill terror or cowering in a corner. Thus women are portrayed as helpless, isolated victims. Siskell and Ebert note that most of the terror scenes are photographed from the killer's viewpoint rather than that of the victim. It seems that the audience is being asked to identify with the attacker. These films can be conceptualized as a primitive warning to women to "get back into their place," to abandon the independent life-style and become dependent on men once again.

Graffiti

A final way in which external imagery is communicated is by means of what is written and drawn on walls, usually in public rest rooms. Why are these messages created? Possibly, the goal is to make a statement, elicit laughter, and/or relieve boredom, but the content generally centers around sex.

Consistent with the general pattern of sex differences they reported, Kinsey et al. (1953) found that men wrote more graffiti with more sexual content than did women. More recent examinations of this phenomenon reveal dramatic changes. Farr and Gordon (1975) found that college women wrote more in their rest rooms than did college men. In addition, there were proportionally five times as many sexual references in the female productions as in those of males.

In another study, Wales and Brewer (1976) found 88% of public high school graffiti in female rest rooms. There was a great deal of romantic content and, interestingly, the proportion of erotic content increased as the socioeconomic level of the school district increased.

Bates and Martin (1980) also found more female than male sexual graffiti. In addition, more than half of the material written by women expressed sexual conflict such as emotional difficulties concerning sex and uncertainties about personal behavior. Only about 12% of the male writings expressed such conflicts.

INFLUENCE OF SEXUAL IMAGES ON BEHAVIOR

Much of the interest in sexual imagery is based on assumptions about its effect on overt behavior. Thus laws about pornography, concern about dream content, the movie rating system, protests about television programming content, and opposition to sex education all rest on the belief that imagery affects behavior. Does it?

Assumed Effects

In the realm of movies, the 1934 Production Code governed the content of American films for a quarter of a century. The code prohibited such things as excessive and lustful kissing, lustful embraces, suggestive postures and gestures, miscegenation, sexual hygiene, venereal disease, and illicit sex. The rationale for these and other restrictions was clear (Moley, 1945, p. 108):

> Illicit sex is contrary to divine law and in a number of cases contrary to human law; (and) because of the natural and spontaneous reaction of normal human beings to sexual stimuli, the portrayal of definite manifestations of sex is harmful to individual morality, subversive to the interests of society and a peril to the human race.

In educational contexts, the expectation often is expressed by traditionally oriented individuals that exposure of the young to sexual information of any kind will increase premarital sex activity and interfere with later marital adjustment (Mahoney, 1979). Actually, research has shown that even a sexual experience as impressive as the witnessing of a primal scene does not increase the incidence of dysfunction or sexual dissatisfaction (Hoyt, 1979). In addition, formal sex education, rather than acting as an impetus to sexual wantonness, is generally found to increase tolerance for the behavior of others, shift attitudes in the liberal and permissive direction, and widen the student's factual knowledge. There are, however, very few studies on the precollege population and only limited data dealing with the extent of behavioral influences (Kilmann et al., 1981).

As the Commission on Obscenity and Pornography discovered to its surprise, data on the behavioral effects of erotic images of any kind were simply nonexistent prior to 1970. We summarize what has been found during the past decade. There are limitations to this research that must be noted. One problem with gathering relevant evidence is the possible importance of the context within which the imagery is experienced (Gagnon & Simon, 1973).

For example, the effect of viewing an explicit sexual film in a university research room as one of several volunteer subjects may differ from the effect of viewing an equally explicit film in a drive-in movie with a date while smoking marijuana. It is also possible that reactions to an explicit movie in a sex education class are different from reactions to memories of that movie that recur in a later social setting. In any event, what is known about the effects of sexual imagery?

Physiological Arousal

The most obvious effect of internal or external sexual imagery is physiological arousal in both males and females (Byrne, 1977a). Both genders are sexually aroused by thoughts, stories, photographs, and movies as indicated by both self-report and physiological measures (Byrne & Lamberth, 1971; Fisher & Byrne, 1978a,b; Griffitt, 1973).

Sex differences in arousal generally are found only with respect to specific content variations. For example, sexual exploitation of a female by a male is more arousing to men than to women (Herrell, 1975). In response to a movie of group rape of a female victim, Schmidt (1975) found that both males and females were highly aroused. In addition, though, females expressed feelings of helplessness while males felt guilty. Rape depictions are often quite unrealistic, by the way, with the female experiencing excitement and orgasm once the act is forced on her. Malamuth and Check (1980) found that male subjects are much more excited by that kind of theme than by scenes where the victim dislikes being assaulted.

Sexual Behavior

There has been very little research attempting to link television sexual content with subsequent behavior. The available data suggest little or no behavioral impact. For example, Rubens (1978) reported a 3-year NBC study of television exposure in relation to the behavior of children and teenagers. One question was whether teenage boys who frequently watch sexually oriented television were more likely to "neck," "go all the way," or express more liberal sexual attitudes than were those who watch infrequently. The data indicated no measurable effect of TV habits on these aspects of sexuality.

With hard-core pornography, the fear that seeing leads to doing also lacks empirical support. The research conducted under the auspices of the Commission on Obscenity and Pornography as well as that conducted subsequently show only limited behavioral effects. Generally it is found that those who are exposed to erotica report a slight increase in the probability (during the next few hours) of engaging in a sexual act already in their repertoire. Among unmarried students, the probability of masturbation increases (Amoroso et al., 1971; Brown et al., 1976), whereas the probability of intercourse increases for married couples (Cattell et al., 1972). Even these mild effects tend to decline over time with repeated exposure to erotica (Mann et al., 1974), but arousal can be reactivated by novel erotica (Howard et al., 1971; Kelley, 1982). It has also been found that increases in sexual activity are most likely to occur among those individuals who have the least experience with and most negative reactions to explicit sexual imagery (Fisher & Byrne, 1978b).

It should be noted that these findings do not fit the expectancies of either those favoring repressive censorship nor of social learning theorists (Bandura, 1977). Research on modeling has shown that exposure to filmed activity leads to imitative behavior ranging from aggression (Bandura et al., 1963) to interactions with dogs (Bandura & Menlove, 1968) and snakes (Bandura et al., 1969). With sexual stimuli, the only hint of a modeling effect has been in the therapeutic use of explicit films to reduce anxiety among inorgasmic female patients to enable them to engage more freely in a variety of sexual activities (Nemetz et al., 1978). Remember, of course, that not only is the context of laboratory erotica a very special one, but no one has yet studied the effects of long-term exposure.

Interpersonal Behavior

Erotica-induced sexual arousal has been shown to elicit changes in interpersonal behavior involving a member of the opposite sex. For example, sexually aroused males tend to perceive females as more physically attractive and as more sexually responsive than do unaroused males (Stephan et al., 1971). Following arousal by erotic slides, college students who reacted positively to them sat closer to an opposite-sex stranger than did unaroused students or those who reacted negatively to erotica (Griffitt et al., 1974).

Arousal also seems to heighten an individual's positive and negative evaluations of relevant cues. When males or females are sexually aroused by erotic stimuli, they find an attractive member of the opposite sex more attractive and more desirable as a date than when not aroused. When the opposite-sex stimulus person is unattractive, however, sexual arousal leads to more negative perceptions compared to an unaroused state (Istvan & Griffitt, 1978; Weidner, et al., 1979). It has also been shown that a male expresses more love in relation to a female partner following sexual arousal than in an unaroused state (Dermer & Pyszczynski., 1978). It seems that one effect of erotica is to intensify responses to members of the opposite sex.

Sex Crimes

A special belief about the consequences of unrestricted pornography is that the viewer will lose sexual self-control and be motivated to commit sexual crimes ranging from exhibitionism to child molestation and rape. Although it is easy to find fault with the data that are now available on this topic, the data are consistent in refuting the dire expectations. In fact, there are repeated indications that the *opposite* may be true—that unfamiliarity with erotica is more common in the socialization of sex criminals than of normals. For one thing, the patrons of adult movie theaters and bookstores are largely white male adults who are members of the middle or upper middle class. The typical consumer of pornography, then, is more likely to be a relatively affluent businessman exposing himself to erotica during his lunch hour than an emotionally disturbed deviant who leaves the bookstore to lurk in a dark alley and await his victim (Byrne & Byrne, 1977). It is possible, of course, that an otherwise sexually normal individual could be adversely affected by explicit erotica. Two types of disconfirming evidence are relevant.

First, convicted sex criminals have been compared with other types of criminal and with noncriminals with respect to their pornographic experience. Sex offenders actually are found to have had less contact with erotica during adolescence than nonoffenders (Goldstein et al., 1974). Sex offenders tend to report a history of fairly restrictive and repressive sexual upbringing. By the time they reach adulthood, they have heard less, seen less, and read less about sex than comparable individuals who do not commit sex crimes. Although the average male has seen a picture of a couple having intercourse by the time he reaches 14, the average sex offender is 18 before seeing such a picture (Eysenck, 1972). It must be pointed out that these data involve the self-reports of convicted criminals and may conceivably reflect socially desirable responses rather than accurate reconstructions of the past.

If restricted access to erotica can indeed foster the development of sexual problems as the previous findings suggest, unrestricted access in a community could be a factor in lowering the incidence of antisocial acts. Denmark in 1965 passed legislation allowing all forms of explicit sexual material to be produced and sold. The result was an immediate decrease in the frequency of sex crimes committed in that country—a downward trend that continued over succeeding years. There was a dramatic drop, for example, in rape, child molestation, homosexual offenses, and voyeurism (Kutchinsky, 1973).

Why might pornography have a positive effect on an individual or a society? It has been proposed that those with deviant desires are enabled by erotica to act out their desires on the fantasy level and achieve satisfaction by means of masturbation. Without the availability of external fantasy stimuli, the same individuals would be more likely to express their needs overtly with real rather than imaginary victims.

Aggressive Behavior

A link between sex and aggression has been proposed by a variety of otherwise diverse theorists. For example, Freud (1933) contended that the wish to hurt or be hurt by one's lover is a normal component of a sexual relationship. More recently, psychological experiments have sought to identify the conditions under which sexual arousal affects the probability of an aggressive response (Donnerstein & Hallam, 1978; Zillmann et al., 1981).

The usual experimental procedure is to expose subjects to some type of erotic stimulus and then to provide them with the opportunity to aggress against another person (ordinarily a confederate who has provoked the subject in some way). The results of the first of such experiments were quite inconsistent. Exposure to erotic imagery was found, in some experiments, to increase aggressive behavior (Zillman, 1971) and in others to decrease its incidence (Baron, 1974). In further research it was found that the likelihood of aggression depended on whether the sexual material was mild or strong (Baron & Bell, 1977). With stimuli as mild as *Playboy* cheesecake photos, aggression decreased; with explicit sexual interactions, aggression increased. It was also found that exposure to cues of sexual violence reduces male inhibitions against harming females (Donnerstein, 1980; Donnerstein & Hallam, 1978).

A more comprehensive explanation of the varying effects is based on the type of affective response elicited by the erotica. If the stimulus material (e.g., deviant practices) elicits negative affect, aggression is enhanced. If the stimulus (e.g., heterosexual petting) elicits positive affect, this response is incompatible with aggression (Baron, 1977). In a similar way, dispositional variables, such as sex guilt, can induce different individuals to respond with differential affect to the same erotic stimulus. Some research has lent support to this affective theory (White, 1979), but the final word on the relationship between sexual arousal and aggression awaits additional experimentation (Baron & Byrne, 1981; Sapolsky & Zillman, 1980).

ALTERATION OF SEXUAL FANTASIES

Since many private fantasies have their origins in external sources and since such sources are subject to manipulation, it follows that the content of an individual's fantasies may be altered. Sachs and Duffy (1976) demonstrated that a verbal description of a couple's purely sexual encounter subsequently led to greater sexual imagery by both males and females than did a story about a casual date, suggesting that modeling effects can promote specific types of sexual fantasizing. Deliberate efforts to bring about such changes were first employed in the context of therapy (Kelley & Byrne, 1978). It is generally agreed that sexual imagery has at least a mediating effect on overt behavior (Byrne, 1977a,b). For that reason, therapy designed to produce behavioral change often focuses on the client's sexual imagery as the initial target in both normal (Heiman et al., 1976; Kaplan, 1974) and deviant (Abel & Blanchard, 1974) populations.

Processing Erotic Stimuli

There does not seem to be an automatic sexual response to external symbols such as the words and pictures that portray erotic activity. Instead, such material initiates thought processes (fantasy), and it is this cognitive functioning that brings about arousal. It is proposed that a person will become sexually aroused to the extent that he or she can find a correspondence between self and the characters or the actions of the erotica.

Arousal also requires that one attend to the stimulus material and actively process it. The interfering effects of distraction on arousal (usually encountered clinically in the form of competing thoughts) have been shown experimentally by Geer and Fuhr (1976). Through the use of a dichotic listening paradigm, the investigators found that with the imposition of increasingly difficult cognitive tasks, subjects became less aroused by erotic audio tapes. Briefly, male subjects were exposed to a taped account of a heterosexual encounter directed into one ear via a set of headphones and simultaneously to a series of single digits directed into the other ear. Subjects were asked to perform one of a series of tasks ranging in complexity from simple attending to the digits to adding and classifying adjacent numbers. The more complex the processing required, the less the physiological arousal as indicated by penile tumescence.

Przybyla and Byrne (1981) found that *both* males and females report less subjective arousal to auditory tapes as distraction increases. With visual erotica and auditory distraction, however, a gender difference emerged. Among males, increased task complexity did not lead to decreased arousal, but among females, arousal was decreased by task complexity. This latter finding of sex differences in response to visual erotica resulted despite the fact that males and females did not differ in their recall of visual erotic content.

These various findings suggest that cognitive processing plays an essential mediating role between an erotic stimulus and both physiological and subjective arousal. Further, it is suggested that auditory stimulation is more subject to interference than visual stimulation, possibly because it involves a two-step process in which the words and sentences are transformed into pictorial form in the recipient's imagination. Finally, the sex differences in response to the visual stimuli may be based on affective differences—females express more negative and less positive affect than males.Thus, to the females, auditory distraction may provide a welcome alternative to processing the unacceptable visual cues.

Imagery Training

In many instances of sexual dysfunction, therapists encourage their clients to use fantasy to enhance sexual arousal. Flowers and Booraem (1975) have noted that a failure to fantasize about sex often occurs in conjunction with sexual problems, such as orgasmic dysfunction, and that failure fantasies may generate anxiety and such attendant problems as impotence and vaginismus. Individuals with such fantasy "defects" may have been taught that thinking about sex is morally wrong. To alter this pattern of behavior, training sessions can be instituted in which the therapist encourages positive sex fantasies and relabels them as normal, healthful experiences. Imagination training usually involves a series of gradual, concrete steps. External stimuli can be used to facilitate or suggest sexual fantasies. The visualization training begins with nonsexual objects and situations and then moves toward the inclusion of gradually more explicit, tailor-made detailed erotic scenes.

Whereas overt sexual stimuli are useful in this regard, covert stimuli are more commonly used in desensitization and reconditioning therapy. In general, the client is instructed to evoke specific sexual imagery in a context that facilitates the association of that imagery with a positive affective state. In one such technique, *desensitization*, the client is encouraged to begin with the least threatening scenes and to move gradually toward more and more anxiety-evoking material. Since positive feelings and labels are associated with the fantasy at each level of threat, there is counterconditioning in that sexual thoughts come to elicit arousal and good feelings rather than anxiety, fear, and guilt.

In addition to the therapist's reassurance and calm acceptance of the client's imagery, other positive reinforcement may be utilized during the fantasizing. Guided masturbation is a procedure through which specific sexual imagery can become associated with the rewarding experience of masturbation and orgasm. Denholtz (1974), for example, reported a case in which a nonorgasmic female was instructed to imagine being raped as she masturbated. Her particular fantasy involved no physical harm, but the rape scenario made sexual excitement acceptable in that she was not responsible for what was done to her. Her orgasmic difficulties were eventually resolved through a series of such fantasy–masturbation pairings.

Imagery Reconditioning

A frequent complaint among dysfunctional couples is the inability of one or both partners to become sexually aroused in response to the other. A masturbatory training program for enhancing sexual-arousal levels in such couples is used by Lobitz and LoPiccolo (1972). The program is based on a classical conditioning procedure known as *orgasmic reconditioning* (Marquis, 1970). Masturbatory fantasies are a common starting point for a change in sexual response. For example, when sexual guilt and negative attitudes interfere with sexual enjoyment, the positive aspects of masturbation and the accompanying thoughts can reduce the guilt and negativity (Abramson & Mosher, 1979).

In therapy, a client is instructed to focus on any erotic stimulus (heterosexual, homosexual, sadistic, or whatever) that he or she finds arousing during masturbation. Just prior to orgasm, however, the individual is told to switch the content to a sexual interaction with his or her partner. On subsequent occasions, the client is instructed to switch to fantasies of the partner earlier in the masturbatory sequence. Thus the conditioned stimulus (the sexual partner) comes to elicit the excitement and pleasure previously associated only with some other erotic stimulus (the unconditioned stimulus). For clients who have difficulty in producing fantasies of the partner, the therapist supplies a Polaroid camera with instructions to photograph the partner engaging in erotic activity. The photograph is then used in place of or as an adjunct to fantasy.

This same conditioning procedure is subsequently applied to sexual interactions with the partner. That is, the client first fantasizes erotic scenes that he or she finds arousing, focuses on that fantasy during intercourse, and as orgasm approaches switches attention to thoughts of the present reality (LoPiccolo et al., 1972).

Sexual Deviations

Fantasy manipulations also plays a role in the treatment of sexual deviations, ranging from those that are largely personal in nature (e.g., fetishism) to those that may intrude on the affective states of others (e.g., cross-dressing) to those that involve physical and psychological damage to others (e.g., rape). Although an exhaustive review is not possible here, some examples of such application are described.

It should be pointed out that the conceptualization of fantasy in therapy has changed over the years. In reviewing the parallel views of the role of sexual fantasies in the treatment of sexual deviations by psychoanalytic and behavioral therapists, Abel and Blanchard (1974) report that in both orientations deviant fantasies were historically conceptualized as an index to gauge how treatment was progressing—in other words, as a dependent variable. Next, fantasy was considered as an intervening variable, partly responsible for the generation of deviant behavior. More recently, behaviorists have given sexual fantasy the position of an independent variable to be altered directly as a major element of the treatment process. Both approaches seem to be moving closer to a view of fantasy as a process that is a central antecedent of deviant behavior.

Personal Behavior

Barlow et al. (1973) defined, measured, and modified each individual component of the female-role behavior of a 17-year-old male. Most of the patient's overt social behavior and vocal characteristics became clearly masculine, but gender identity problems remained, as manifested by the presence of transsexual ideation. At that point, a direct attempt to modify his thoughts and fantasies was made. In the patient's strongest and most frequent fantasy, he imagined having a female body and engaging in intercourse with a man. The therapists attempted to develop competing gender-appropriate fantasies in which the patient, as a man, had intercourse with a woman. The procedure involved the patient's choosing several pictures of a female sex object who was least unattractive to him and then imagining sexual involvement with her. When the fantasy image was clear, the patient gave a signal and received lavish praise. Periodically, the therapist would suggest pertinent behaviors with which to enrich the fantasy, such as explicit details of foreplay. At the end of this phase of the treatment, the patient behaved, felt, and thought like a man but was still sexually aroused by male stimuli. In other words, he was now diagnostically a homosexual rather than a transexual. This case illustrates the importance of fantasies in initiating, guiding, and defining one's sexual behavior. The patient retained the female role until his fantasies were changed, despite the earlier changes in his overt behavioral style.

Annon (1974) suggests that any sexual act can be viewed as a succession of classical conditioning trials in which fantasies are associated with a series of positive sensations as the act progresses. Thus orgasm is not the only available reinforcing stimulus. It follows that, for example, by changing a patient's fantasies throughout masturbation rather than just prior to orgasm, the fantasy–pleasure association can be made multiple times during the act rather than just once. In Annon's treatment program, a patient is encouraged to change his or her deviant fantasies gradually. For example, he reports the case of a young female who was most aroused by masochistic fantasies of sexual assaults on her by a group of men. Leaving aside the question of whether such a fantasy *should* be altered, we note that treatment consisted of the successive use of masturbation paired with a progressive array of different fantasies. First there were images of a large group of sexually assaultive men, then of a small group of such men, then of one man assaulting her—the final step was a fantasy of nonassaultive sex with one man. Thus the masturbatory fantasy underwent a radical change of content. The next phase involved an alteration in the context in which the fantasy was used: a progression from masturbation to intercourse.

Interpersonal Behavior: Rapists and Their Fantasies

The relationship between arousal by certain types of sexual imagery and corresponding overt behaviors has been dramatically documented by Abel et al. (1977). With explicit descriptions of rape and nonrape sexual interactions as stimuli, rapists were discriminated from nonrapists on the basis of erectile responses. Nonrapists were aroused only by scenes of mutually enjoyable intercourse whereas rapists were excited both by such scenes and by rape imagery.

On the basis of the rapists' histories of sexual assault, they could be placed along a continuum of increasingly aggressive sexual behavior. Along this dimension were also plotted their erectile responses in terms of relative arousal in response to mutually enjoyable intercourse, sexual aggressiveness, and purely aggressive stimuli. On one end of this continuum is the nonrapist. He reports aversion to the thought of forcing himself on an unwilling partner. His erotic response to sexual stimuli indicates the importance of mutuality in the interaction (mean erectile response = 61%). When elements of force or rape are added to the image, the nonrapist becomes much less aroused (mean erectile response = 16%). These men show no excitement in response to scenes of aggression devoid of intercourse. Further along the continuum is the rapist with a history of forcing himself aggressively on his victims. These men deny, by the way, a preference for using force and indicate their desire for a compliant partner. These men are also aroused by images of mutually enjoyable intercourse (60%), but the addition of force and rape does not lead to a significant decrease in excitement (55%). Aggressive cues devoid of sex produce some arousal for the individual (20%). At the extreme end of the continuum are the sadistic rapists. They do not find ordinary intercourse very arousing (17%), but the erectile response becomes evident when force is present (61%). With purely aggressive cues, there is the greatest amount of arousal (79%).

At the very least, such findings indicate the parallels between physiological responses to specific fantasy content and related overt behavior. They raise the possibility that changes in the fantasy–arousal associations could lead to changes in overt behavior. One aspect of treatment has been the attempt to increase the rapist's arousal in response to normal heterosexual stimuli through such techniques as masturbatory conditioning. That is, the client is taught to substitute nonaggressive sexual fantasies for those involving force (Abel & Blanchard, 1974). The other goal is to decrease the arousal response to rape stimuli. Covert sensitization has been used effectively for this purpose. The rapist is asked to imagine situations conducive to rape, including the events preceding the act, the surroundings, and the victim's appearance and behavior. Once such a scene is established in the rapist's imagination, aversive elements are added. The client is asked to intersperse scenes of being chased and shot by the police or being confronted with his tearful wife or girlfriend. These new scenes elicit responses that are incompatible with sexual excitement. The goal is to induce the individual to summon up such scenes whenever there is an urge to respond to images of rape in fantasy or in overt behavior.

Other Manipulations of Fantasy Content

Although entertainment, advertising, and propaganda all employ procedures designed to alter our fantasies, there has been only a limited amount of research dealing with the process by which external images come to affect internal images or with individual differences in responding to fantasy manipulation. We briefly examine one such line of research.

Contraception and Fantasy

Literature, paintings, and photography have depicted seemingly all aspects of sexuality, but there is very rarely a reference to contraception (Abramson & Mechanic, in press). In popular books and movies, the occasional reference to contraception is not really associated with eroticism but usually functions as an antierotic intrusion. For example, contraception is portrayed as the cause of parental discovery of sexual activity (*Goodbye, Columbus!*), ridicule and embarrassment (*Summer of '42*), or mockery (*Looking for Mr. Goodbar*). In *Saturday Night Fever*, when a female is quizzed just prior to intercourse and found not to be prepared contraceptively, the John Travolta character refuses to continue the sexual interaction—an intelligent though nonerotic response to contraceptive cues. Only in condom ads in men's magazines in recent years have contraceptives been linked to sexual pleasure and eroticism.

The importance of these observations lies in the fact that a great many individuals, especially adolescents, are engaging in sexual intercourse totally or inadequately unprotected by contraception (Fisher et al., 1979). The resulting 1,000,000 teenage pregnancies in the United States each year might possibly decline if more people associated sexual excitement with contraceptive cues. In other words, this is another realm in which the alteration of sexual imagery could be expected to alter overt behavior.

Byrne and Przybyla (1981) attempted to manipulate erotic fantasy by combining contraceptive cues with erotic sexual stimuli. Male and female subjects were shown one of three versions of an explicit film, *Methods and Positions of Coitus* (EDCOA Productions, Inc.). One version depicted an attractive couple engaging in intercourse in several different positions. The other two versions were identical except that the sexual interaction was preceded by a brief scene in which either the female inserted a diaphragm or the male inserted it in his partner. A comparison of sexual fantasies written by subjects in response to TAT slides immediately after the movie revealed a number of differences, depending on the version seen. Interestingly, there was no obvious modeling of the film with fantasies of diaphragm insertion. Instead, the male and female insertion conditions (compared to the noncontraceptive control condition) elicited fantasies that differed markedly in terms of the quality of the relationship between the characters. It seems that viewing an erotic movie in which a birth control device is used promotes fantasies containing affection and interpersonal concern, fantasies in which overt positive feelings are likely to be expressed.

Although such research is in its initial stages, the findings offer promise of finding the way in which external fantasies bring about changes in internal ones. Furthermore, the suggestion of a more equal and positive relationship in the postcontraception fantasies is at least consistent with more open communication about contraception. If one brief exposure to purposeful, nonhumorous contraception can have a measurable effect on subsequent responses, the impact of repeated samples of such sexual interaction in the mass media could potentially bring about remarkable changes in attitudes and behaviors through changes in internal fantasies.

Gender Differences in Response to Erotic Fantasy

In the recent past it was believed, on the basis of survey studies, that males liked and were excited by erotica whereas females were indifferent to such stimuli (Kinsey et al., 1948; 1953). It was suggested that males were genetically more responsive to visual cues involving hard-core, explicit sex, whereas females were somehow built to respond sexually to romantic verbal cues. In the 1970s, the laboratory research of the Hamburg group and of various investigators in the United States revealed that males and females were equally aroused by explicit pictorial and verbal stimuli. The earlier survey results apparently reflected culturally imposed gender differences in experience with pornography and in the social acceptability of admitting consequent arousal. When romantic themes are compared with simple lustful ones, there are still no gender differences (Fisher & Byrne, 1978a,; Schmidt, 1975). Most of these studies used erotic films as stimuli. When undergraduates were exposed to color *slides* of explicit heterosexual or masturbatory activity, females reported less resultant sexual arousal than did males (Kelley, 1981a). Perhaps the difference is related to the fact that the genders differ in response to erotic stories versus discrete erotic images (Miller et al., 1980), or perhaps the difference lies in the mode of stimulus presentation. In any event, there is a need for parametric studies in this area.

Consistently found, however, are gender differences in affective responses. Despite equal levels of arousal, males are more likely to respond to erotic stimuli with positive feelings, whereas negative feelings are more common for females.

Until recently, another aspect of responsivity had been ignored—the effects of erotica on subsequent fantasy responses. A recent investigation of such effects reveals some unexpected gender differences (Byrne et al., 1981). Male and female subjects were shown an explicit heterosexual film prefaced with one of two instructional sets or without any preliminary information. An affectional, romantic set was established by identifying the filmed couple as lovers in a committed relationship. A nonaffectional, unromantic set was created by indicating that the film was of a prostitute and her client. All three experimental groups viewed the identical movie. Marked gender differences in TAT fantasy responses were found. Females created positive fantasies containing affection and mutual concern after viewing the film prefaced with the affectional set and created negative fantasies containing verbal and physical aggression following exposure to the nonaffectional theme. Males, in contrast, responded with negative fantasies after the romantic movie and with positive fantasies after the nonaffectional film. Aggression and mutual intimidation were common in male fantasies created after viewing an explicit film of a loving, committed couple but not in those created after a prostitute–client interaction. It appears that the external imagery of romance versus lust, while both conducive to sexual arousal, elicits different affective states in males and females and different internal imagery.

Certain erotic themes set the stage for subsequent sexual fantasies. In a study by Kelley (1981b) that compared the effects of exposure to mildly titillating erotica in conjunction with explicit heterosexual acts, males and females again differed in the extent to which they used aggressiveness and affection in their resultant verbal fantasies. After viewing the "beefcake" slides, males developed more aggressive imagery, while females had more affection oriented imagery. For males, the homophobic effects of same-sex stimuli were apparent, but not for females viewing the "cheesecake" slides. Females in a variety of studies express more tolerance for homosexual stimuli, whereas males give evidence of being threatened by such cues.

CONCLUSIONS

The purposeful creation of sexual imagery has been a central human enterprise throughout history, and the creation of internal and external images represents a reciprocal process. An individual's fantasies are shaped from the content of external images and are probably heavily influenced by the social experience of these images. Imagery from the various media is combined with individual creativity and emotional responses to form private fantasies. The result may be a close approximation of the original image, or it may be a highly individualized depiction only distantly related to the original stimulus. On the other hand, the sexual images of a culture are physical representations of the mental images of individuals. These, too, may closely approximate the original fantasies, or they may be a highly edited version of internal visions. As these internal and external images interact and reinforce one another, they slowly change over time and across cultures.

Although research has indicated that external imagery affects subsequent fantasy, its effects on behavior remain to be clearly understood. The study of sexual imagery has dealt primarily with explicit sexual stimuli and not with the mild erotica and innuendoes to which all individuals in our culture are repeatedly exposed. Modeling of explicit sexual behavior occurs infrequently, if ever, for most individuals, whereas modeling of implicit sex is probably a regular occurrence. The effects of the latter fantasies obviously should be investigated. Although studies of sexual imagery have suggested little effect on behavior, almost all have been single-exposure investigations. Logically, a precise estimation of the consequences of prolonged exposure to explicit stimuli requires longitudinal research. As noted previously, the social context must be taken into account. The identical stimuli viewed in a university research laboratory and at a party lead to quite different effects (Clark, 1952; Clark & Sensibar, 1955).

We are only beginning to examine sexual imagery, discover what fantasies are created by individuals, and estimate the sexual content of our culture's imagery. Imagery, sexual or otherwise, internal or external, is in itself neither positive nor negative, but basic to human experience. It is not too much to hope, however, that research will show us how to maximize its creative and positive potential.

REFERENCES

Abel, G. G., & Blanchard, E. B. The role of fantasy in the treatment of sexual deviation. *Archives of General Psychiatry*, 1974, **30**, 467–475.

Abel, G. G., Barlow, D. H., Blanchard, E. G., & Guild, D. The components of rapists' sexual arousal. *Archives of General Psychiatry*, 1977, **34**, 895–906.

Abramson, P. R., & Mechanic, M. B. *Sex and the media: Three decades of best selling books and major motion pictures. Archives of Sexual Behavior,* in press.

Abramson, P. R., & Mosher, D. L. An empirical investigation of experimentally induced masturbatory fantasies. *Archives of Sexual Behavior*, 1979, **8**, 27–39.

Amoroso, D. M., Brown, M., Pruesse, M., Ware, E. E., & Pilkey, D. W. An investigation of behavioral, psychological, and physiological reactions to pornographic stimuli. In *Technical report of the Commission on Obscenity and Pornography*, Vol. 8. Washington, D.C.: U.S. Government Printing Office, 1971.

Annon, J. S. *The behavioral treatment of sexual problems: Brief therapy*. Honolulu, Hawaii: Enabling Systems, 1974.

Atkins, J. *Sex in literature*. London: Calder, 1970.

Bandura, A. *Social learning theory*. Englewood Cliffs, N.J.: Prentice-Hall, 1977.

Bandura, A., & Menlove, F. L. Factors determining vicarious extinction of avoidance behavior through symbolic modeling. *Journal of Personality and Social Psychology*, 1968, **8**, 99–108.

Bandura, A., Ross, D., & Ross, S. A. Imitation of film-mediated aggressive models. *Journal of Abnormal and Social Psychology*, 1963, **66**, 3–11.

Bandura, A., Blanchard, E. B., & Ritter, B. Relative efficacy of desensitization and modeling approaches for inducing behavioral, affective, and attitudinal changes. *Journal of Personality and Social Psychology*, 1969, **13**, 173–199.

Barclay, A. M. Sexual fantasies in men and women. *Medical Aspects of Human Sexuality*, 1973, **7**, 205–216.

Barlow, D. H., Reynolds, E. J., & Agras, W. S. Gender identity change in a transsexual. *Archives of General Psychiatry*, 1973, **28**, 569–576.

Baron, R. A. The aggression-inhibiting influence of heightened sexual arousal. *Journal of Personality and Social Psychology*, 1974, **30**, 318–322.

Baron, R. A. *Human aggression*. New York: Plenum, 1977.

Baron, R. A., & Bell, P. A. Sexual arousal and aggression by males. Effects of type of erotic stimuli and prior provocation. *Journal of Personality and Social Psychology*, 1977, **35**, 79–87.

Baron, R. A., & Byrne, D. *Social psychology: Understanding human interaction.* Boston: Allyn and Bacon, 1981.

Bates, J. A., & Martin, M. The thematic content of graffiti as a nonreactive indicator of male and female attitudes. *The Journal of Sex Research*, 1980, **16**, 300–315.

Belkaoui, A., & Belkaoui, J. A comparative analysis of the roles portrayed by women in print advertisements. 1958, 1970, 1972. *Journal of Marketing Research*, 1976, **13**, 168–172.

Brown, C., Anderson, J., Burggraf, L., & Thompson, N. Community standards, conservatism, and judgments of pornography. *Journal of Sex Research*, 1978, **14**, 81–95.

Brown, M. Amoroso, D. M., & Ware, E. E. Behavioral effects of viewing pornography. *Journal of Social Psychology*, 1976, **98**, 235–248.

Bryan, J. H., & Schwartz, T. Effects of film material upon children's behavior. *Psychological Bulletin*, 1971, **75**, 50–59.

Byrne, D. The imagery of sex. In J. Money and H. Musaph (Eds.), *Handbook of sexology*. Amsterdam: Excerpta Medica, 1977a.

Byrne, D. Social psychology and the study of sexual behavior. *Personality and Social Psychology Bulletin*, 1977b, **3**, 3–30.

Byrne, D., & Byrne, L. *Exploring human sexuality*. New York: Harper, 1977.

Byrne, D., & Kelley, K. *An introduction to personality*. 3rd Edition. Englewood Cliffs, N.J.: Prentice-Hall, 1981.

Byrne, D., & Lamberth, J. The effect of erotic stimuli on sex arousal, evaluative responses, and subsequent behavior. In *Technical report of the Commission on Obscentity and Pornography*, Vol. 8. Washington, D. C.: U.S. Government Printing Office, 1971.

Byrne, D., & Przybyla, D. P. J. *The effect of contraceptive imagery in erotica on subsequent fantasy content, behavioral expectancies, and evaluations of erotica.* Unpublished manuscript, SUNY—Albany, 1981.

Byrne, D., Przybyla, D. P. J., & Fisher, W. A. Sex differences in the influence-ability of imaginative responses to erotica. Paper presented at the meeting of the Society for the Scientific Study of Sex, Philadelphia, April 1981.

Cattell, R. B., Kawash, G. F., & DeYoung, G. E. Validation of objective measures of ergic tension: Response of the sex erg to visual stimulation. *Journal of Experimental Research in Personality*, 1972, **6**, 76–83.

Clark, R. A. The projective measurement of experimentally induced levels of sexual motivation. *Journal of Experimental Psychology*, 1952, **44**, 391–399.

Crepault, C., & Couture, M. Men's erotic fantasies. *Archives of Sexual Behavior*, 1980, **9**, 565–582.

Danielenko, R., Do sexy ads sell products? *Product Management*, 1974, **40**, 21–26.

Denholtz, M. Behavior therapy in sexual disorders. Paper presented at the Institute for Sex Research, Bloomington, Indiana, 1974.

Dermer, M., & Pyszczynski, T. A. Effects of erotica upon men's loving and liking responses for women they love. *Journal of Personality and Social Psychology*, 1978, **36,** 1302-1309.

Dienstbier, R. A. Sex and violence: Can research have it both ways? *Journal of Communication*, 1977, **27**, 176–188.

Donnerstein, E. Aggressive erotica and violence against women. *Journal of Personality and Social Psychology*, 1980, **39**, 269–277.

Donnerstein, E., & Hallam, J. Facilitating effects of erotica on aggression against women. *Journal of Personality and Social Psychology*, 1978, **36**, 1270–1277.

Eron, L. D. Relationship of TV viewing habits and aggressive behavior in children. *Journal of Abnormal and Social Psychology*, 1963, **67**, 193–196.

Eron, L. D., Lefkowitz, M. M., Huesmann, L. R., & Walder, L. O. Does television violence cause aggression? *American Psychologist*, 1972, **27**, 253–263.

Eysenck, H. J. Obscenity—officially speaking. *Penthouse*, 1972, **3**, 95–102.

Farr, J. H., & Gordon, C. A partial replication of Kinsey's graffiti study. *The Journal of Sex Research*, 1975, **11**, 158–162.

Fernandez-Collado, C., Greenberg, B. S., Korzenny, F., & Atkin, C. K. Sexual intimacy and drug use in TV series. *Journal of Communication*, 1978, **28**, 30–37.

Fisher, W. A., & Byrne, D. Sex differences in response to erotica? Love versus lust. *Journal of Personality and Social Psychology*, 1978a, **36**, 119–125.

Fisher, W. A., & Byrne, D. Individual differences in affective, evaluative, and behavioral responses to an erotic film. *Journal of Applied Social Psychology*, 1978b, **8**, 355–365.

Fisher, W. A., Byrne, D., Edmunds, M., Miller, C. T., Kelley, K., & White, L. A.Psychological and situation-specific correlates of contraceptive behavior among university women. *Journal of Sex Research*, 1979, **15**, 38–55.

Flowers, J. V., & Booraem, C. D. Imagination training in the treatment of sexual dysfunction. *The Counseling Psychologist*, 1975, **5**, 50–51.

Franzblau, S., Spratkin, N., & Rubinstein, E. A. Sex on TV: A content analysis. *Journal of Communication*, 1977, **27**, 164–170.

Freud, S. *New introductory lectures on psychoanalysis*. New York: Norton, 1933.

Gagnon, S., & Simon, W. *Sexual conduct*. Chicago: Aldine, 1973.

Geer, J. H., & Fuhr, R. Cognitive factors in sexual arousal: The role of distraction. *Journal of Consulting and Clinical Psychology*, 1976, **44**, 238–243.

Giambra, L. M. Sex differences in daydreams and related mental activity from the late teens to the early nineties. *International Journal of Aging and Human Development*, in press.

Gilmore, D. H. *Sex in comics: A history of the eight pagers* (4 vols.). San Diego: Greenleaf Classics, 1971.

Goldstein, M. J., Kant, H. S., & Hartman, J. J. *Pornography and sexual deviance*. Berkeley: University of California Press, 1974.

Griffitt, W. Response to erotica and the projection of response to erotica in the opposite sex. *Journal of Experimental Research in Personality*, 1973, **6**, 330–338.

Griffitt, W., May, J., & Veitch, R. Sexual stimulation and interpersonal behavior: Heterosexual evaluative responses, visual behavior, and physical proximity. *Journal of Personality and Social Psychology*, 1974, **30**, 367–377.

Hariton, B. E. Women's fantasies during sexual intercourse with their husbands: A normative study with tests of personality and theoretical models. Unpublished doctoral dissertation, City University of New York, 1972.

Hariton, B. E., & Singer, J. L. Women's fantasies during sexual intercourse: Normative and theoretical implications. *Journal of Consulting and Clinical Psychology*, 1974, **42**, 313–322.

Heiman, J., Lo Piccolo, L., & Lo Piccolo, J. *Becoming orgasmic: A sexual growth program for women*. Englewood Cliffs, N.J.: Prentice-Hall, 1976.

Herrell, J. M. Sex differences in emotional responses to "erotic literature." *Journal of Consulting and Clinical Psychology*, 1975, **43**, 921.

Hessellund, H. Masturbation and sexual fantasies in married couples. *Archives of Sexual Behavior*, 1976, **5**, 133–147.

Howard, J. L., Reifler, C. B., & Liptzin, M. B. Effects of exposure to pornography. In *Technical report of the Commission on Obscenity and Pornography*, Vol. 8. Washington, D.C.: U.S. Government Printing Office, 1971.

Hoyt, M. G. Primal-scene experiences: Qualitative assessment of an interview study. *Archives of Sexual Behavior*, 1979, **8**, 225–245.

Hunt, M. *Sexual behavior in the 1970's*. Chicago: Playboy Press, 1974.

Istvan, J., & Griffitt, W. *Emotional arousal and sexual attraction*. Unpublished manuscript, Kansas State University, 1978.

Johnson, D. K., & Satow, K. Consumer's reactions to sex in TV commercials. In H. K. Hunt (Ed.), *Advances in consumer research*, Vol. 5. Ann Arbor, Mich.: Association for Consumer Research, 1978.

Kaplan, H. S. *The new sex therapy*. New York: Brunner/Mazel, 1974.

Kelley, K. Socialization factors in contraceptive attitudes: Roles of affective responses, parental attitudes, and sexual experience. *Journal of Sex Research*. 1979, **15**, 6–20.

Kelley, K. *The effects of gender, sex guilt, and authoritarianism on response to heterosexual and masturbatory stimuli*. Unpublished manuscript. State University of New York at Albany, 1981a.

Kelley, K. Sexual fantasy and attitudes in relation to gender variations. Presented at the Society for the Scientific Study of Sex, New York, November, 1981b.

Kelley, K. Variety is the spice of erotica: Repeated exposure, novelty, and sexual attitudes. Presented at the meeting of the Eastern Psychological Association, Baltimore, April 1982.

Kelley, K., & Byrne, D. The function of imaginative fantasy in sexual behavior. *Journal of Mental Imagery*, 1978, **2**, 139–146.

Kerin, R. A., Lundstrom, W. J. & Sciglimpaglia, D. Women in advertisements: Retrospect and prospect. *Journal of Advertising*, 1979, **8**, 37–42.

Kilmann, P. R., Wanlass, R. L., Sabalis, R. F., & Sullivan, B. Sex education: A review of its effects. *Archives of Sexual Behavior*, 1981, **10**, 177–205.

Kinsey, A. C., Pomeroy, W. B., & Martin, C. E. *Sexual behavior in the human male*. Philadelphia: Saunders, 1948.

Kinsey, A. C., Pomeroy, W. B., Martin, C. E., & Gebhard, P. H. *Sexual behavior in the human female*. Philadelphia: Saunders, 1953.

Klinger, E. *Structure and functions of fantasy*. New York: Wiley-Interscience, 1971.

Kutchinsky, B. The effect of easy availability of pornography on the incidence of sex crimes: The Danish experience. *Journal of Social Issues*, 1973, **29**, 163–181.

Levay, A. N., & Weissberg, J. The role of dreams in sex therapy. *Journal of Sex and Marital Therapy*, 1979, **5**, 334–339.

Liebert, R. M., & Baron, R. A. Some immediate effects of televised violence on children's behavior. *Developmental Psychology*, 1972, **6**, 469–475.

Lobitz, W. C., & L. Piccolo, J. New methods in the treatment of sexual dysfunction. *Journal of Behavior Therapy and Experimental Psychiatry*, 1972, **3**, 265–271.

Lo Piccolo, J., Stewart, R., & Watkins, B. Treatment of erectile failure and ejaculatory incompetence of homosexual etiology. *Journal of Behavior Therapy and Experimental Psychiatry*, 1972, **3**, 233–236.

Mahoney, E. R. Sex education in the public schools: A discriminant analysis of characteristics of pro and anti individuals. *Journal of Sex Research*, 1979, **15**, 264–265.

Malamuth, N. M., & Check, J. V. P. Penile tumescence and perceptual responses to rape as a function of victims' perceived reactions. Unpublished manuscript, University of Manitoba, 1980.

Malamuth, N. M., & Spinner, B. A longitudinal content analysis of sexual violence in the best-selling erotic magazines. *The Journal of Sex Research*, 1980, **16**, 226–237.

Mann, J., Berkowitz, L., Sidman, J., Starr, S., & West, S. Satiation of the transient stimulating effect of erotic films. *Journal of Personality and Social Psychology*, 1974, **30**, 729–735.

Marquis, J. N. Orgasmic reconditioning: Changing sexual object choice through controlling masturbation fantasies. *Journal of Behavior Therapy and Experimental Psychiatry*, 1970, **1**, 263–271.

Marshall, P., Surridge, D., & Delva, N. The role of nocturnal penile tumescence in differentiating between organic and psychogenic impotence: The first stage of validation. *Archives of Sexual Behavior*, 1981, **10**, 1–10.

Maslow, H. H. Self-esteem (dominance feeling) and sexuality in women. *Journal of Social Psychology*, 1942, **16**, 259–294.

Masters, W. H., & Johnson, V. E. *Homosexuality in perspective*. Boston: Little, Brown, 1979.

McCauley, C., & Swann, C. P. Male–female differences in sexual fantasy. *Journal of Research in Personality*, 1978, **12**, 76–86.

McCauley, C., & Swann, C. P. Sex differences in the frequency and functions of fantasies during sexual activity. *Journal of Research in Personality*, 1980, **14**, 400–411.

Merritt, C. G., Gerstl, J. E., & LoSciuto, L. A. Age and perceived effects of erotica-pornography: A national sample study. *Archives of Sexual Behavior*, 1975, **4**, 605–621.

Miller, C. T., Byrne, D., & Fisher, J. D. Order effects on responses to sexual stimuli by males and females. *Journal of Sex Research*, 1980, **16**, 131–147.

Moley, R. *The Hays office*. New York: Bobbs-Merrill, 1945.

Money, J. Pornography in the home: A topic in medical education. In J. Zubin and

J. Money (Eds.), *Contemporary Sexual Behavior: Central Issues in the 1970's*. Baltimore: Johns Hopkins University Press, 1973.

Moreault, D., & Hollingstead, D. R. Sexual fantasies of females as a function of sex guilt and experimental response cues. *Journal of Consulting and Clinical Psychology*, 1978, **46**, 1385–1393.

Moyle, R. M. Sexuality in Samoan art forms. *Archives of Sexual Behavior*, 1975, **4**, 227–247.

Nemetz, G. H., Craig, K. D., & Reith, G. Treatment of female sexual dysfunction through symbolic modeling. *Journal of Consulting and Clinical Psychology*, 1978, **46**, 62–73.

Ostling, R. N., Coutu, D., & Cronin, M. A scrupulous monitor closes shop. *Time*, October 6, 1980, 70–71.

Palmer, C.E. Pornographic comics: A content analysis. *The Journal of Sex Research*, 1979, **15**, 285–298.

Pocs, O., & Godow, A. G. The shock of recognizing parents as sexual beings. In D. Byrne and L. A. Byrne (Eds.), *Exploring human sexuality*. New York: Harper, 1977.

Przybyla, D. P. J., & Byrne, D. The role of incompatible responses in the experience of cognitive sexual arousal. Paper presented at the meeting of the Eastern Psychological Association, New York, April 1981.

Przybyla, D. P. J., Miller, C. T., & Byrne, D. Fantasy content in relation to gender and erotophobia–erotophilia. Unpublished manuscript, SUNY—Albany, 1981.

Raucher, H. *Summer of '42*. New York: Putnam, 1971.

Rubens, W. S. Sex on television, more or less. In H. K. Hunt (Ed.), *Advances in consumer research*, Vol. 5. Ann Arbor, Mich.: Association for Consumer Research, 1978.

Sachs, D. H., & Duffy, K. G. Effect of modeling on sexual imagery. *Archives of Sexual Behavior*, 1976, **5**, 301–311.

Sapolsky, B. S., & Zillmann, D. The effects of soft-core and hard-core erotica on provoked and unprovoked hostile behavior. *Journal of Applied Social Psychology*, 1980.

Schmidt, G. Male–female differences in sexual arousal and behavior during and after exposure to sexually explicit stimuli. *Archives of Sexual Behavior*, 1975, **4**, 353–363.

Scott, J. E., & Franklin, J. L. The changing nature of sex references in mass circulation magazines. *Population Quarterly*, 1972, **36**, 80–86.

Silverman, L. T. Sprafkin, J. N., & Rubinstein, E. A. Physical contact and sexual behavior on prime-time TV. *Journal of Communication*, 1979, **29**, 33–43.

Smith, B. *Erotic art of the masters*. New York: Gemini-Smith, 1974.

Smith, D. The social content of pornography. *Journal of Communication*, 1976, **4**, 16–24.

Sonneschein, D., Ross, M., Bauman, R. Swartz, L., & Machlachlan, M. A study of mass media erotica. In *Technical reports of the Commission on Obscenity and Pornography*, Vol. 9. Washington, D.C.: U.S. Government Printing Office, 1971.

Stephan, W., Berscheid, E., & Walster, E. Sexual arousal and heterosexual perception. *Journal of Personality and Social Psychology*, 1971, **20**, 93–101.

Sue, D. Erotic fantasies of college students during coitus. *Journal of Sex Research*, 1979, **15**, 299–305.

Tesser, A., & Paulhus, D. L. Toward a causal model of love. *Journal of Personality and Social Psychology*, 1976, **34**, 1095–1105.

Venkatesan, M., & Losco, J. Women in magazine ads: 1959–1971. *Journal of Advertising Research*, 1975, **15**, 49–54.

Wagman, M. Sex differences in types of daydreams. *Journal of Personality and Social Psychology*, 1967, **7**, 329–332.

Wales, E., & Brewer, B. Graffiti in the 1970's. *Journal of Social Psychology*, 1976, **99**, 115–123.

Weidner, G., Istvan, J., & Griffit, W. B. Beauty in the eye of the horny beholder. Paper presented at the Midwestern Psychological Association meeting, Chicago, 1979.

White, L. A. Erotica and aggression: The influence of sexual arousal, positive affect, and negative affect on aggressive behavior. *Journal of Personality and Social Psychology*, 1979, **37**, 591–601.

Wilson, R. D., & Moore, N. K. The role of sexually-oriented stimuli in advertising: Theory and literature review. In W. L. Wilkie (Ed.), *Advances in consumer research*, Vol 6. Ann Arbor, Mich.: Association for Consumer Research, 1979.

Zillmann, D. Excitation transfer in communication-mediated aggression behavior. *Journal of Experimental Social Psychology*, 1971, **7**, 419–439.

Zillmann, D. , Bryant, J., Comisky, P. W., & Medoff, N. J. Excitation and hedonic valence in the effect of erotica on motivated intermale aggression. *European Journal of Social Psychology*, 1981, **11**, 233-252.

CHAPTER 15

Imagery and the Arts

MARTIN S. LINDAUER

To know is nothing at all; to imagine is everything.
ANATOLE FRANCE

To put it most grandly (and succinctly), the arts provide observers with images they otherwise would not have (Munro, 1956; Osborne, 1970; Richards, et al., 1971; Sommer, 1978). (The term "arts" in this chapter is used broadly to include the fine arts, such as painting and music, and the performing arts, such as dance and theater, as well as literature and aesthetic matters in general.) Images to the arts enchant us for the moment; afterward, they enable us to see (or hear or feel) the world in a new way. The artist, in this ideal conception, has the capacity to create extraordinary images and the skill to translate them into a medium (to which we respond with images). An examination of imagery and the arts must therefore consider three major components: the artist, the art object, and the arts observer. These are discussed in detail, from an empirical perspective, in this chapter.

There are nonempirical, much broader, and speculative approaches to imagery and the arts (Albrecht, et al., 1970; Kiell, 1963, 1965; Tatarkiewicz, 1970). For art historians, critics, and aestheticians, the images of art are views of the world and the self that represent a particular time and place and yet have universal appeal. For psychoanalysts and depth psychologists in general, the images of the arts are cathartic, resolve tensions, and fulfill unconscious wishes. For sociologically and anthropologically oriented theorists (Wilson, 1973), the sociocultural mileau provides the inspiration and content of artists' imagery and sets the boundaries for their audience's imagery (Martindale, 1975). These wider perspectives are only briefly mentioned in this chapter.

There are thus views on imagery and the arts other than those in empirical psychology. There are also empirical ways of looking at the arts other than those from the perspective of imagery (Kreitler & Kreitler, 1972). Some psychologists emphasize the emotional and pleasurable consequences of art

(Child, 1978), others look for the correlates between art and personal variables such as extraversion–introversion (Eysenck, 1971), and in the cognitive area some concentrate on the effects of stimulus complexity and novelty on preference (Berlyne, 1971, 1974).

The empirical literature on imagery in general (Paivio, 1971; Sheehan, 1972) has little to say about the arts. There we find extremely active investigations of the sensory representation of input (the icon) and its processing, storage, and retrieval in memory. Very little of this work on the existence of images and the function of imagery includes much about the imagery of artists, the images evoked by the arts in their audiences, or the role of imaging in the aesthetic response. Instead, one finds largely anecdotal or passing mention of imagery (or its absence) in such artistic luminaries as Wordsworth, Coleridge, Poe, Leonardo, and Wagner (McKellar, 1957; Richardson, 1969; Rugg, 1963).

STATUS OF THE PROBLEM

The Scholarly Tradition

In contrast to psychological treatments, scholarly discussions of imagery and the arts are abundant, and the presence and importance of imagery is generally accepted. One of the earliest and still respected treatments of imagery in the arts was Addison's (1961, p. 61): "Homer excelled in imagining what is great; Virgil in imagining what is beautiful; Ovid in imagining what is new. Milton [was best] in all three respects." Addison discussed how various types of art and poetry bring pleasure by means of the images they arouse, and the difference between the relationship of imagery to the arts and to everyday objects; he also suggested that the arts differ from one another in their capacity to evoke imagery. Other extensive critical analyses are found in Hazlett (Sallé, 1964) and Prescott (1959). Philosophical discussions of imagery and the arts are found in Furlong (1961) and Casey (1976); McMahon (1973) traces the concept from Aristotle.

Bronowski (1967), the scientist, poet, humanist, educator, and critic, illustrates the general acceptance of imagery in artistic (and scientific) contexts. He considers imagination to be composed largely (but not exclusively) of picturelike images. "To imagine means to make images and to move them about inside one's head in new arrangements" (Bronowski, 1967, p. 195). Bronowski insists that the scientist and the artist are linked by their dependence on imagination; there "is [not] much to choose . . . between science and the arts; the imagination is not much more free and not much less free, in one than in the other. [Imagination] is the common root from which science and literature both spring and grow and flourish together" (Bronowski, 1967, pp. 199–200). Bronowski approvingly paraphrases Blake: "What is now proved [in science] was once only imagin'd [by art]." The scientist expresses his imagination, continues Bronowski, in an experiment; the artist, on a canvas, or on an instrument, or on paper. "In science, the imaginary experiment is tested by confronting it with physical experience, and in literature, the imaginative conception is tested by confronting it with human experience" (Bronowski, 1967, p. 198).

Although supportive, these literary, critical, and aesthetic commentaries on imagery and the arts are rather imprecise. For example, objective, figurative, literal, sensory, symbolic, rhetorical, metaphorical, and other meanings of imagery are used interchangeably and loosely; and the relationship between imagery and imagination (and between imagination and thinking) are left vague and implicit. Whether people do in fact have images is hardly ever questioned. These scholarly essays also are uninformed about current developments in cognitive psychology (although they are usually quite aware of the psychoanalytic treatment of images in fantasy, dreams and symbols). This ignorance is matched by the indifference of psychology to the treatment of imagery in literary, critical, and aesthetic writings.

Despite these problems, the scholarly tradition offers several working (and testable) assumptions: artists may be especially good at and dependent on imaging; the arts are particularly appropriate vehicles for evoking and sustaining imagery that we would otherwise not have (or for enriching the imagery we already have); and some observers of art are more likely than others to seek out and rely on imagery through artistic pursuits. These views of the arts are also found in popular thought (Sommer, 1978). If these assumptions have any merit at all, then research on imagery would benefit from the inclusion of subjects, materials, and observations related to the arts. These additions would highlight people, phenomena, and processes that are probably more muted and hence less observable in ordinary observers, stimuli, and viewing circumstances.

Yet the strategy of including artists, aesthetic persons, or art in studies of imagery, with few exceptions, has hardly been pursued in contemporary psychology. A case in point is research on creativity.

Imagery and the Study of Creative Artists

Creative people, according to many theorists, researchers, and clinicians, are likely to have a high degree of imagery. This ability stimulates, energizes, propogates, and organizes original ideas (Casey, 1976; Khatena, 1978, p. 36). Studies that attempt to demonstrate this argument use the strategy of selecting participants on the basis of high scores on standardized (and usually verbal) creativity tests (Khatena & Torrance, 1973). But the relationship between creativity and imagery has remained elusive. Only a few correlations have been found, and these are usually low (Ernest, 1977; Forisha, 1978). These disappointing results have not dampened the enthusiasm of those who hypothesize a link between imagery and creativity. But the presumed link rests largely on anecdotal reports (Ghiselin, 1955).

Perhaps the failure to find supporting evidence is due to the type of sample used (Khatena, 1977). The participants, usually college undergraduates, have high test scores. But they have not fulfilled either a performance or consensual criterion of creativity, such as professional activity or reputation in the arts (MacKinnon, 1972; Roe, 1975). In addition to being told to imagize on demand in a relatively sterile laboratory environment, subjects are asked to imagize to rather ordinary stimuli (e.g., isolated words). Given the absence of good imagizers, which people in the arts may be, and the lack of provocative things to imagize to, which art objects might be, the unsatisfactory outcome of studies on imagery and creativity may not be too surprising.

Imagery and Cognitive Psychology

Cognitive psychology's research on imagery is highly specialized, intricate, and technical (Paivio, 1971). Despite the increased sophistication, some find the results disappointing. New theoretical models rapidly come and go, and progress is slow, if not stalled (Cohen, 1977, p. 213). The cognitive movement, so liberating when it first began, has become increasingly removed from what people actually think and say about imagery (i.e., it has lost its ecological validity). When complex imagery phenomena are discussed, like playing chess, self-reports rather than experiments are relied on. It is difficult to imagine the relevance of contemporary cognitive psychology to the arts. [An excellent attempt to apply current cognitive research to media specialists, in the context of audiovisual education, is found in Fleming (1977).] Kosslyn and Pomerantz (1977, p. 52) have warned that since the concept of imagery has periodically disappeared from psychology (although not elsewhere), it may do so again. This likelihood might be reduced if imagery research would increase its contacts with the very real world of art.

Purpose of This Chapter

The purpose of this chapter is to affirm the importance of using artistic people, materials, and settings in the study of imagery. The arts not only provide psychology with dramatic examples, but are a resource for research and a font of testable hypotheses. To demonstrate these points, research on the imagery of the arts audience, the art objects, and the artist are outlined. Much of the work has been reviewed elsewhere (Lindauer, 1974, 1976/1977). Although relatively scant, the research is placed in the context of discursive (but testable) speculations on imagery and the arts. Examples from unpublished research are described in some detail. Before these topics can be presented, certain preliminary but important matters of definition and method must be examined.

DEFINITION AND METHOD

Two questions that bear on the study of imagery in the arts must be faced at the outset, even though they can hardly be resolved here. The first concerns how we are to define an image. There are at least 18 different definitions (Oxford, 1933/1970, pp. 51–53). Second, can we accept self-reports of imagery? Much of the history of psychology revolves about the rejection of the introspective method. Definitional and methodological issues are controversial and have received considerable attention elsewhere (Nisbett & Wilson, 1977; Pylyshyn, 1973). But if we are to move on to the main themes of this chapter, we must take rather oversimplified (but still tentative) positions.

Images as Pictures

Not all psychologists accept the existence of images, and among those who do, images' status as "pictures in the head" or as sensory–perceptual in content is challenged (Kosslyn & Pomerantz, 1977, p. 57). How can we picture something that we have never seen or that does not exist (e.g., a centaur)? The concept of an image as a replica or a reproduction is not even appropriate for perception (the "picture-in-the-eye" analogy) since reality is neither duplicated nor mirrored by the sensory–perceptual system.

These arguments are at least partially echoed by Arnheim (1966b, 1969), who offers an extensive and cogent analysis of images in art, music, and poetry. Arnheim takes the position that images are more likely to be symbolic or abstract than pictorial. The image, whether in art or in the mind, he argues, contains the essential structure and underlying properties of things, events, and persons. A Rembrandt portrait represents a certain kind of human being, that is, a "generic image." Great artists use and great art gives us images that select, organize, and heighten the structure and forces of the objects they represent. The suggestiveness of an impressionistic painting or a Chinese watercolor is not there to be simply "filled in" by the imagination of an observer. Instead, they provide images that guide, illuminate, and elevate our thinking; images reveal something basic about ourselves and the world. The art of amateurs, like too detailed and meticulous an image, says Arnheim, is restrictive, unimpressive, and unexciting. Images are thus emergent and creative products.

But Arnheim also defines the image as a literal representation, at least at the beginning of the thinking process. For many, it is a level of abstraction that is never exceeded. Many others in the arts (Wolf, 1951, p. 346) and literature (Beckson & Ganz, 1960/1969, pp. 85–86) also regard the image as primarily a likeness of the world. Artists and scholars are quite comfortable with images as "pictures." Indeed, many definitions of images in physics, engineering, and technology (e.g., "the image on the screen"), use the term "image" when they mean stimulus or external object. Even in so hardheaded an approach as conditioning, in both theory (King, 1977, 1978) and therapy (Sheikh & Panagiotou, 1975), imagery is defined as an internal representation of an external stimulus. Images may be much more than replicas of reality, but they can be at least that. Images-as-pictures have the advantage of being more concrete than abstract types of image. Hence they are easier to describe and study, at least initially.

There are probably several types (or levels) of imagery. McKellar (1957, 1972), for example, refers to imagination and memory images, voluntary and involuntary images, and other distinctions (based on length of imagery, perseverance, and familiarity). Distinctions are also made between verbal and pictorial imagery.

The theoretical importance of any definition of imagery chosen is apparent. But the practical question is where we should begin. It seems simplest to start with an image that is sensory–perceptual. It has the sort of concreteness that is meant when we refer to visual, auditory, kinesthetic, and other modes of imagery; the term "visualize" implies something tangible. A "picture-in-the-head" (sound or touch) may not be exactly a perception, but it is something like it. It is closer to perceptual experience than it is to abstract conceptualization; it is more like perception (without necessarily being a copy or replica) than it is like memory, an idea, or a thought (Mathews, 1969). In any event, the fuzziness of this definition, falling somewhere between perception and thinking (but closer to the former), should not be the sole basis for deciding on the usefulness of the phenomenon.

Self-Reports of Imagery

To treat imagery as picturelike leads to a related question that must be at least recognized if not resolved. Can self-reports of artists' (and observers of arts') imagery be accepted with confidence? (Self-reports include interviews, questionnaires, checklists, and rating scales.) To see (or hear) an image, after all, is a kind of hallucination (of something that is not present). Are people willing to report so strange a phenomenon, and do they do so accurately?

Historically, psychology has been plagued by an unease if not mistrust over conscious data. The imageless-thought controversy occurred even before Behaviorism. The study of imagery is itself an example of a long-standing battle for the acceptance of mental (cognitive) processes. Even so, there still remains among many theorists a grudging acceptance of imagery, and at the same time, a seemingly paradoxical denial of its function (Neisser, 1967; Nisbett & Wilson, 1977; Pylyshyn, 1973). Imagery for many is considered to be an epiphenomenon: it is there but it does not do anything (like one's shadow). Hence, there is the reluctance to study imagery on a phenomenological (descriptive) level. However, the apparent irrelevance of self-reports may be less a fault of the method than a fault of those who have been asked about their imagery, i.e., how the questions were asked and where they were obtained (Neisser, 1972). Even if the value of self-reports of imagery were minimal, it remains to be explained why they are maintained so vigorously.

The conscious identity of imagery is undeniable and self-evident to most artists and scholars, (Kosslyn & Pomerantz, 1977). In the visual arts, "sketches are tried out in the mind's eye before they emerge onto the [canvas]" (Cohen, 1976, p. 520). Indeed, the enormous variation in imagery reported by individuals—whether artists, scientists, or others—has been of major interest since Galton (1883). There is thus an enormous amount of consensual validation for the existence of imagery.

Psychologists have felt more secure with spatial or manipulative (chronometric) tests of imagery than with self-reports (DiVesta et al., 1971; Ernest, 1977; White et al., 1977). Self-reports of imagery are easily confused with associations and memories and are confounded by response bias and social–desirability pressures. However, results of spatial tests pertain only to visual imagery and to its controllability characteristic. In general, they refer to how imagery works rather than to what it is (on a conscious level). To study imagery, operationally excluding consciousness (i.e., nonconscious imagery!) would be unacceptable to many (Marks, 1972, 1977).

Experimental and correlational approaches to imagery are controversial and disappointing (Allport, 1975; Cohen, 1977). But the descriptive approach has hardly been pursued (McKellar, 1972). A phenomenology of imagery offers information on types of imagery and imager (i.e., the visual and auditory modes, and visualizers and audiles) and on the frequency, originality, autonomy, and changes over time and place of imagery. These are interesting questions that can be empirically investigated by self-reports. Their elucidation may help advance some of the problems faced by the more analytical and molecular approaches to imagery. Some of their assumptions—that imagery exists as a normally distributed trait and that subjects can image on command—might be challenged by phenomenological analysis.

The results and interpretations of so-called chronometric tests of imagery and laboratory-oriented research are introspectively meaningless to artists and scholars; that is, they have no face validity. To those in the art world, impersonal and objective information is "counterintuitive" and only marginally relevant at most. If scientists on imagery are ignored by a community so committed to the concept of imagery, how valid can such information be? To establish credibility, artists and other participants in the arts should be observed and questioned. If we use a descriptive language and a subjective frame of reference familiar to those in the arts, perhaps they may then listen to what psychology has to offer (and perhaps offer us something in return).

Doubts about introspective data are legitimate. There must be checks (e.g., converging operations) on the reliability of personal reflection. But whatever remains ambiguous should be offset by artists' (and especially writers') unquestioned skills in introspecting on and communicating their inner states (Lindauer, 1974). Whatever personal biases exist (i.e., the exaggerations and distortions of "dramatic license") are compensated for by creative persons' powers of revelation, lucidity, and expression.

Self-reports on imagery from those in the arts can be very useful. A phenomenologically oriented research strategy within the arts, one that is minimally committed to existing theoretical conceptions, offers a fresh start, a new look at unexplored possibilities, a hint of unexamined directions, and a source of questions that may have been overlooked.

There are few phenomenological studies in the arts to cite as precedents (Lindauer, 1981a; Sardello, 1978). Casey's (1976) philosophical approach, although apparently based on an N of 1 (and that may be an imaginary example), provides an extensively detailed analysis of the role of imagery in the arts. But phenomenology is not enough.

Ultimately, phenomenological reports must be translated into testable hypotheses and experimental and other standard procedures. But consider too that sophisticated theoretical and methodological efforts eventually have to make phenomenological sense. This is not to deny that there are serious problems with phenomenology. Some artists report little or no imagery and yet have a marvelous artistic capacity (e.g., Leonardo da Vinci). But judgments about the value of phenomenological data should await further developments. Introspective data on imagery in an artistic context have not been given an adequate test.

THE OBSERVER OF THE ARTS

Most of those who enjoy any one or several of the various arts are nonartists. Yet much of the psychological attention, understandably, is on the artist (e.g., on creativity). Although vital, the artist is still only part of the total picture in which there is also the work of art itself, the social context in which the artist produces, and the audience which responds to the artistic product. Of all these components, the observer of art is given relatively minor consideration. We study artists and art—and randomly selected undergraduates' responses to art. Yet it is the art audience, whose sentiments and allegiances are sustained over time, that draws critics' attention to a work and scholars' interest to an artist.

Experts on the arts (Dewey, 1934; Osborne, 1964, 1970) unquestioningly hold that the experience and behavior of observers of the arts are profoundly affected by the arts. The philosopher Berleant (1970, p. 110) maintains that the arts open "our eyes to the sensuous qualities of the world around us," and the critic Osborne (1970, p. 202) believes that through art our "awareness of the world . . . is expanded and made more vivid." These widely held assumptions are expanded on in the following paragraph.

Great art is better at achieving transcendental goals than indifferent art. Exposure to the arts leads to new perceptions, thoughts, and feelings; these, in turn, bring us pleasure, illumination, and motives that can alter our actions. Art therapy (Hammer, 1975; Robbins, 1973) can be effective because art deepens, broadens, and opens up our experience for the moment as well as for future possibilities. The arts allow us to escape from or face afresh the humdrum banality of everyday existence. Unfortunately, not everyone responds so affirmatively to art. Some are confused, indifferent, or hostile. But these negative consequences are probably the fault of art education, which has the responsibility of fostering a positive reaction (although some people may be naturally more or less responsive to the arts than others).

These conjectures about the various effects of art on its observers can be easily fitted, in a similarly speculative way, to some of the possible functions of imagery. Cognitive, emotional, and other consequences of the arts might be mediated by imagery. That is, the images aroused by the arts lead to motivational and personal dispositions; perceptions, ideas, and thinking are "sparked" by images; and goals, impulses, and models of action are set in motion by images. For some, however, images may accompany art without directly initiating these effects. Also, those without imagery may still be moved by art, and those with imagery may be indifferent to art.

Despite all these possibilities, imagery and the aesthetic experience have seldom been discussed. Perhaps the sense of awe and wonder we feel in the presence of art is caused not only by the art itself but also by the images evoked by art. Another possible role of imagery is related to psychic distance (Bullough, 1957), one of the most well-known concepts in aesthetic theory. Psychic distance is a mode of perception (or attention) in which the observer is detached from ordinary perception (or worldly concerns). Instead, the observer "loses himself or herself" in the work of art.

This suspended condition may be akin to what has been called a *hypnagogic state* (Schachter, 1976). It is an altered mode of consciousness that includes feelings related to drowsiness and dreamlike and "dissociative" states. Thus inhibitions are relaxed and imagery can be enhanced; that is, autonomous (spontaneous) imagery may occur (McKellar, 1977). The ease with which images are evoked by art, as well as their frequency, vividness, and controllability, may be related to the achievement of psychic distance, that is, a sense of detachment from the self that releases the flow of images.

This state may be facilitated by the context in which we observe the arts; hence, the darkened theater and the specialized environmental settings created by architects and designers of art museums. Many artists are said to require special conditions in order to work effectively and perhaps to enhance their imagery (Hollingsworth, 1911). Mark Twain is reported to have been able to work only while lying in bed (so as to possibly achieve a dreamlike imagery state more easily). The connection between the art setting and the inducement of imagery, for both the observer and the artist, deserves further exploration. However, these research possibilities lie far in the future, if research on more basic problems, reviewed next, is any indication of progress in the field.

The Research: Past and Prologue

One of the first references to aesthetics and imagery in psychology is Stetson's (1896). He argued that we appreciate poetry, music, and even archi-

tecture when we empathize motoric and tactile images to these artistic stimuli. Despite this early interest, empirical support for the abundance of
speculative claims made for imagery and the arts, outlined above, is almost
totally lacking.

Readers' imagery to literature is probably more frequently studied than
any other type of audience response to art (Lindauer, 1974). Nearly all of
it, however, is quite old (Downey, 1915; Patrick, 1939; Valentine, 1923).
There is some recent work, however. In a dissertation, Dilworth (1975)
reported that readers' imagery to poetry affected their liking, recall, and
interpretation. A promising line of research is Klinger's (1978) on listeners'
selective attention to prose that matches their imagery. Beth Maess asked,
in an informal unpublished poll of 57 college students, if they liked poetry
and whether they heard a voice (either their own or someone else's) while
reading poetry. A simple "yes" or "no" response was obtained for each
question. Of the 35 subjects who said they liked poetry, 32 (91%) said they
heard a voice; and of the 22 who said they did not like poetry, only two
(9%) said they heard a voice. Although the results seem rather clear-cut,
one source of ambiguity is that those who do not like poetry may not read
it. Hence, they have less opportunity than do readers of poetry to "hear
voices." Also unknown is whether visualizers like poetry less than do those
who can "hear voices." This sort of descriptive research, although seemingly
so basic, has not been systematically pursued.

Imagery to music is much less frequently mentioned than imagery to
literature (e.g., Capurso, 1952). In a classical series of experiments on imagery by Betts (1909), only one of 12 studies measured the imagery of music
teachers (to single notes). A brief report by Randolph (1977) indicated that
music led to higher vividness-of-imagery scores than other conditions. Khatena and Torrance (1973) reported that music students' imagery score was
higher than that of some (but not of all) comparison groups. The emotional
characteristics of music apparently hold more interest than its imagery (Farnsworth, 1958; Schoen, 1927/1968; Seashore, 1938).

This brief sketch suggests that research on imagery in the arts observer
is not very extensive. It also reveals how little empirical support there is for
the range of speculations noted earlier. There is quite a large gap between
the broad issues raised by scholars in the arts and the topics investigated
by empirical psychologists. It cannot be argued that the reason for the absence of recent studies is that the existence of imagery in the arts observer
has already been well established by earlier research, for this is not so. It
has not yet been established in current studies of the nonarts observer.
However, there are some relevant findings in the general imagery literature
that are at least encouraging.

The facilitative effect of imagery on perception, learning, memory, and
thinking has been shown in some (but not all) studies that take place outside
the context of art. Perhaps similar kinds of cognitive enhancement occur
when observers image to art. Consider the well-known Perky effect (Segal,

1968, 1972). A faint stimulus is more clearly seen when observers (unaware of the presence of the stimulus) are told to image the stimulus. There are other suggestive examples. Fleming (1977) demonstrated that learning increased when pictures (images?) were used to supplement verbal instructions. The storage of memories and the ease of their recall were facilitated when the material was initially tied to images (Hampson & Morris, 1979; King, 1978). Thinking, too, defined by the ease with which concepts are manipulated and reconstructed, was enhanced when the material was easier to image (Pinker & Kosslyn, 1978). Speidel and Pickens (1979) report a training program for reading based on working with clay. The authors contend that the clay task evoked imagery, and this ability transferred to the cognitive task (although the presence of imagery was not independently established).

Studies of the sort reviewed above could be replicated with arts observers, tasks, and materials. An important methodological decision would have to be made: should subjects be instructed to image, as they are in most studies in the general imagery literature? This demand is not present in the art situation, where imagery is more spontaneous (Richardson, 1972). But there is an alternative to the strategy of replicating psychological research with procedures related to the arts.

The speculative commentary, noted earlier, might be examined to find issues that can be empirically explored. An approach that begins within the broader tradition of the arts may avoid inappropriate or nonfruitful paths of inquiry. Wysong (1979) examined the general imagery findings from a literary perspective and concluded that "Psychological research . . . confirms, extends, or *contradicts* oral interpretation theory of the way readers respond to verbal stimuli and how mental images influence their . . . responses" [Wysong (1979, p. 6398-A), emphasis added].

Two related questions from the speculative tradition deserve immediate empirical inquiry. The first is whether different types of art (say, music and theater, or more narrowly, abstract and representational paintings) differ in their power to evoke images. The second empirical question is whether observers differ in their imagery to the same kind of art. These questions about imagery differences between art, and imagery differences between art observers, were examined in the research which follows in the next section.

A Study: Observers' Imagery After Art and Music

Discussions of the arts and the role played by imagery raise many profound issues. Yet most depend on affirmative answers to several rather basic questions. Do people in fact have images to the arts; do these images differ between the various arts; are the images to art different from those inspired by nonart; and does exposure to art affect subsequent imagery to nonart? These questions do not appear too difficult to test, yet they have nevertheless not been examined.

A study by Bilotta (Bilotta & Lindauer, 1978), reported in detail below, examined the effect of exposure to music and art on subsequent imagery to nonart. It was hypothesized that imagery vividness ratings to everyday visual and auditory examples (e.g., "Your mother's face [or voice]") would be increased following exposure to art or music. It was also assumed that the effects would be specific to the mode of presentation used; that is, music would increase auditory imagery and art would increase visual imagery. Finally, it was hypothesized that exposure to nonart (or no stimuli), compared to art stimuli, would have less or no effect on subsequent imagery.

Method

Two types of artistic material were used. Music was represented by 14 brief (1–2-minute) and well-known themes from the "popular classics" by 14 composers. Art was represented by 58 slides of familiar masterpieces by artists of time periods and nationalities similar to those of the composers; each slide was shown for 20 seconds. (Their familiarity was judged to be high by an art librarian.) Corresponding to the music and art stimuli were two other auditory and visual conditions. In the art information condition, biographical and historical information from standard texts [e.g., Novotny (1952)] on the composers and artists used in the study was presented in a taped lecture (recorded by a professional broadcaster). In the visual information condition, the same information was presented in a typed booklet. In the nonart conditions, either sound effects were played from albums of everyday sounds (e.g., street noises) or color slides of people and everyday scenes were shown (they corresponded as closely as possible to the subject matter of the art). The total time of presentation for each of the six stimulus conditions was 20 minutes. The orders of stimuli in each series were randomly arranged into three different sequences. A control group did nothing for 10 minutes on arriving at the experimental session. They were told to "wait until everyone arrived."

The effects of the seven treatments on the vividness of imagery was measured by items taken from the Modal Imagery Test (Lindauer, 1972, 1977). Subjects used a 7-point scale (1 = low) to rate their vividness of imagery to two auditory referents ("the sound of food frying" and "the ringing of church bells") and to two visual referents ("the Statue of Liberty" and "the face of your watch"). These examples, it had been found in a pilot study ($N = 25$), evoked a modest rather than extreme (high or low) degree of imagery in most subjects. Hence these four items had the potential of being either raised or lowered. Five items from four additional sensory modes (taste, touch, smell, and movement) were used as fillers to disguise the sensory focus of the study. (Three additional items from the visual and auditory modes were also included.) In all, subjects received 30 examples from six sensory modes, although the responses to only four auditory and visual items were of primary interest in the posttest. After the posttest, subjects retrospectively rated their auditory and visual imagery during the earlier exposure to the various stimulus conditions. Subjects had been pre-tested on imagery in their classes several days before the experiment. They received a set of 30 items (not the same as the posttest) from the six modes of the Modal Imagery Test. At that time two measures of the groups' artistic backgrounds were also obtained. Subjects rated (on a 7-point scale) their appreciation of and activities in the arts. The seven groups did not differ from one another in either appreciation or activity ratings (F (6, 85) ≤ 1.62, p > .05). Nor did they differ in pretest imagery scores (F (6, 85) = 1.66, p > .05). The groups were thus equivalent on several relevant measures.

Ninety-two subjects (42 men and 50 women) participated as volunteers (for credit) from several undergraduate introductory psychology classes. Subjects were randomly assigned, prior to their appearance at the experimental sessions, to one of the seven groups. Testing took place in small groups of 4–10. Fourteen additional subjects were excluded from the study because their pretest imagery scores were at or near the extreme ends of the scale. Subjects were told that the experimental treatments would provide them with a relaxed and neutral experience that would put them in the same relative state of mind before the study began. Thus, obtaining the posttest imagery measure, rather than responding to the music and the other stimulus conditions, was the ostensible purpose of the study.

Results

The posttest scores of the vividness of imagery following music were higher than the imagery scores which followed art (M = 5.80 and 4.90, respectively). This effect was unique to music and art compared to the other stimulus conditions (see Fig. 15.1). Auditory stimuli led to higher imagery vividness than visual stimuli only when music was played (i.e., not when lectures or sounds were played), and visual stimuli led to lower imagery vividness than did auditory stimuli only when art was shown (i.e., not when reading material or photographs were presented). In statistical terms, there was a significant difference within the artistic condition [(F 1, 75) = 3.95, p < .05], and this was the sole basis for a statistically significant interaction between the type of stimulus presented and the mode of presentation used [F (2, 76) = 3.52, p < .05]. Furthermore, the difference between music and art was independent of the sensory referent used, whether auditory or visual [F (1 − 2) ≤ 1.76, p > .05]. Music increased the imagery accompanying everyday sounds as well as sights, whereas art led to decreased imagery in both modes.

A similar pattern, favoring music over art, was found on other analyses. Music was superior to art (M = 5.40 and 4.30, respectively) when the filler items from all six modes were included [F (5, 76) = 6.19, p < .01; see Fig. 15.2]. The superiority of music over art (M = 5.40 and 4.20, respectively) was again revealed in the subjects' retrospective recall [F (2, 78), = 7.20, p < .01; see Fig. 15.3].

Despite these encouraging findings (although those for art were unex-

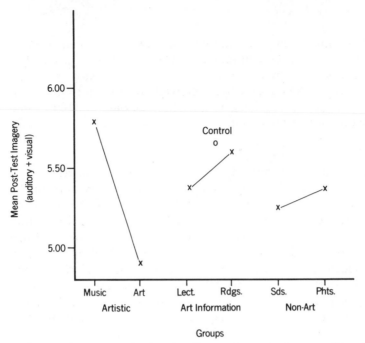

Figure 15.1. Posttest imagery to visual and auditory referents in three conditions by seven groups (Lect.—lectures, Rdgs.—readings, Sds.—sounds, Phts.—photographs).

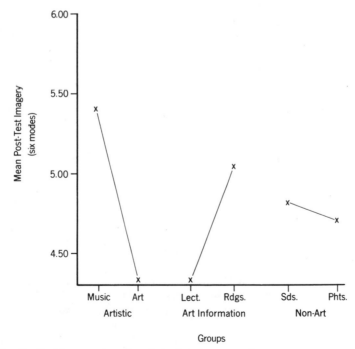

Figure 15.2. Posttest imagery to referents in six sonsory modes.

pected), it must be emphasized that most of the other predictions were either not confirmed or were contradicted. The two artistic groups did not differ from the other four treatment groups or from the control group [F (1, 76) $\leq$ 1.45, $p > .05$]. The imagery that followed art differed from the imagery that followed music, but the imagery of either one did not differ from that which followed nonart or no stimuli.

Discussion

Neither music nor art had any special capacity, compared to nonart or even no stimuli, for increasing the vividness of the imagery of relatively ordinary referents to events and people that followed exposure to artistic stimuli. But imagery succeeding music was more vivid than that which followed art. Furthermore, music facilitated not only the auditory mode of imagery, but also the visual and other modes, whereas the effect of art was the reverse on all modes. It should be kept in mind, though, that these imagery effects were not to art and music directly, but to everyday events. (A more direct imagery response to music and art was obtained in a study reported later.)

The heightened effects on imagery following music, compared to art, could be interpreted in several ways. Music is constantly changing over time. The unfolding nature of music, compared to the more immediately complete impression of art, may have encouraged listeners to "fill in" with images. These provided temporal continuity. Another possibility is that music, com-

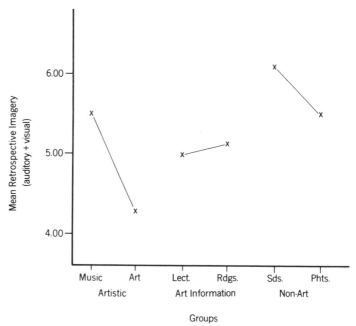

Figure 15.3.   Retrospective visual and auditory imagery.

pared to representative art, is (relatively) more abstract. The lack of any concrete focus encouraged listeners to "turn inward" (i.e., to reflect and introspect). Hence their imagination was encouraged. In contrast, the scenes and people in the paintings directed the observers' attention "outward," that is, to exploring the meaning of the "stories" in the work. If this reasoning is correct, then imagery following concrete music (e.g., lyrical) should be less vivid than the imagery following abstract (nonrepresentational) art. (This is exactly the reverse of the present findings.)

The high imagery of the control and nonart treatments may be explained by a "practice effect." Those who read or heard a lecture on art, listened to a series of unconnected sounds or looked at irrelevant "family type" photos or did nothing were likely to have been bored. They may thus have daydreamed or fantasized during the presentation of these uninteresting stimuli. But this "warm-up" increased their imagery scores.

The consequences of music and art on subsequent imagery deserve further study. Imagery *to* art may be different than imagery *after* art. The generalized effects of music and art across all sensory modes also need additional investigation. Several methodological ambiguities also have to be clarified. For example, the amount of exposure to music and art (20 minutes each) was confounded by the number of works presented (17 and 58, respectively). These two variables have to be controlled, as do the characteristics of the stimuli. (For example, the imagery of the art and music and the degree to which they were appreciated were unknown.)

Individual Differences in Imagery Ability and The Aesthetic Person

Any imagery that might be inspired by the arts may depend on the observers' capacity to image (or to have certain kinds of images). The enjoyment of literature may hinge on visual imagery, whereas that of music or dance may require auditory and kinesthetic imagery, respectively. If we are disappointed in a film based on a book, or if we are unable to read a play but like to see it on a stage, it may be because we have trouble processing the different modes of imagery in each case. Intermodal imagery disparities may also account for different responses to television and radio drama (and to telephone and in-person voices) and may also lie behind the failure of some actors from the silent screen to achieve success in the "talkies." [Gordon (1972) has also discussed the problem of communication between the various arts as a function of differences in preferred modes of imagery.]

That there are great individual differences in imagery ability is one of the few widely accepted facts about imagery (Marks, 1972). Yet experimental studies of imagery usually fail to preselect, pretest, or question their subjects on imagery. It is implicitly assumed that everyone has imagery or that it is normally distributed. Inconsistent findings in the literature may be the result of subjects failing to image as instructed or simply being unable to image. Random selection also will tend to cancel out any imagery effect in the group as a whole, if the sample includes some subjects with high or others with low imagery. In studies of the arts, there would be similar canceling-out or minimizing effects (even if the participants' imagery were high) if subjects' interest, attitudes, and backgrounds in the arts were mixed. Investigations of imagery in the arts, therefore, need to take both the observers' imagery ability and involvement in the arts into account.

There are only a few studies that relate observers' imagery and artistic responses. Leonard and Lindauer (1973) found a modest but significant relationship between degree of involvement in the arts and imagery ability. (Involvement was based on combined self-reported ratings of attendance at theater, music, and art events and the amount of literature read; imagery ability was based on vividness ratings of words in six sensory modes.) But Bilotta and Lindauer (1980) failed to find any relationship between imagery ability and art background. (Majors and professors in theater, dance, and art were compared to comparable groups in psychology.) However, when Bilotta and Lindauer used aesthetic test scores to divide the subjects, imagery scores were higher among aesthetic than nonaesthetic persons irrespective of their arts background. The absence of an imagery difference between arts and nonarts people, a seemingly self-evident expectation, remains puzzling. Perhaps the testing situation, with its demand for forced imagery, inhibited the normally spontaneous imagery of people in the arts.

However, the presence of imagery among aesthetic persons has been shown in a number of studies (Lindauer, 1976/1977, 1977). Aesthetic persons were defined—on the basis of several tests, checklists, self-reports, and inventories of activities—as having strong feelings about and activities in several of the arts. The major distinction between aesthetic and nonaesthetic persons was in their imagery responses. In the aesthetic group, in contrast to the nonaesthetic group, there were significantly more correlations between several imagery measures and between these and other art-related measures (e.g., art aptitude and creativity). No other measure (and over a dozen were used) distinguished the groups as sharply as did imagery. The consistency of the imagery response in the aesthetic group suggests an ability to control its use ("to turn on") during an art event.

There are advantages to using aesthetic rather than artistic or randomly selected subjects in studies of observers' imagery to the arts. The responses of art students are probably overanalytical, and randomly chosen undergraduates' responses are probably too unsophisticated. Aesthetic subjects fall somewhere between these two extremes. Their imagery to the arts is likely to be less muted than ordinary observers' imagery but less specialized than that of art students. But studies of aesthetic persons' imagery to the arts have yet to be done. Nor has imagery been included in tests of art (or music) aptitude and aesthetics. Even in aesthetic theories (Richards et al., 1971; Spranger, 1928/1966) imagery is overlooked. The encouraging results of research on aesthetic persons indicate a major oversight in theory and practice.

IMAGERY TO WORKS OF ART

An observer's ability to image is not the only factor to consider in the response to the arts. There is also the art object's capacity to arouse images. Electronic music or op art may arouse fewer images than (or images different from those in) other kinds of music or art. Also, art and music differ from literature and drama in their immediacy. Art and music are relatively directly channeled into the visual and auditory system and are thus likely to evoke sensory–perceptual images. But the relatively less immediate response to literature and drama, unfolding over time, is more likely to evoke imaginative images. Another possibility is that literature is better at arousing imagery than music, which is primarily tied to emotions. Unfortunately, few studies compare imagery across the arts. The imagery of literature, of all the arts, has probably received the greatest amount of research attention.

The Imagery of Literature

There are scores of essays on the imagery of specific authors and works [e.g., Spockes (1970) on Pope]. In psychology, probably the best known is Spurgeon's (1935/1952) analysis of the textual imagery in Shakespeare's plays. A content analysis approach, the primary empirical investigative tool in literature, is illustrated by an unpublished study of two works of Melville by Nancy Hoag.

The Imagery in Melville's Works and the Method of Content Analysis

Melville's reputation as a writer rests, in part, on his use of many richly descriptive and vivid images (Hillway, 1963, p. 21). The two works chosen for analysis, *Moby Dick* and *Pierre* (Melville, 1929, 1969), were written at two different periods in Melville's life. His early life was full of adventure and outdoor experiences at sea; it is represented by *Moby Dick*. Later in life, Melville was more introspective, and he wrote *Pierre*, his only novel without a maritime background (Arvin, 1950).

Sentences from selected pages of the two novels were coded for their sensory referents. Every twentieth page in *Moby Dick* and every fifteenth page in *Pierre* was chosen. (The difference in sample size was due to the difference in length of the two novels.) Sentences on these sample pages with words that referred to the sense of taste, vision, smell, touch, and sound (Lindauer, 1972) were marked, classified, and counted by two judges. If more than one sense was mentioned, the most emphasized was tallied. Disagreements between the two judges (of which there were only a few) were resolved in all but 4% of the total number of sentences found; these were discarded. Examples of sensory phrases were "The village . . . had no pleasant savor" and "Whales are of ill odor" (*Moby Dick*), and "The letter retarded any answering warmth" and "His generous flame would embrace me" (*Pierre*).

There were 376 sensory referents in the samples from the two novels, 192 in *Moby Dick* and 184 in *Pierre*. Table 15.1 presents the number and type for each of the five senses. It also indicates the number of sensory referents for each half of the novel. This latter measure was a check on the judges' reliability in classifying the material, since the assignment of imagery values in the two halves should be similar if the scoring were consistent. The two measures are also indicative of the similarity of an author's style (or more literally, word usage) in the early and late parts of a work. The number of sensory referents in the two halves of each novel did not differ from one another [x^2 (4) = 3.10, p > .05].

The two novels did differ from one another in their use of different sensory referents [x^2 (4) = 17.82, p < .01]. *Moby Dick* had more visual references than *Pierre* (55% vs. 37%), whereas *Pierre* had more tactile references than *Moby Dick* (44% vs. 23%). The tactile and visual referents differed from the other three senses in each novel [x^2 (4) ≥ 144.11, p < .01].

Moby Dick, with its many references to the sea and its colors, is a more visual novel than *Pierre*—and it has more visual images. In contrast, *Pierre* is a more introspective novel, in which Melville referred most often to the sense of touch (a so-called near sense). However intuitively satisfying these data may appear, intuition fails to account for the equivalence in both novels of sound referents (a distance sense) and smell and taste referents (which are near senses). (The frequencies involved are all rather low.)

Other works of Melville need to be examined to note parallel trends in sensory use and to determine whether the visual and tactile senses have been similarly treated over the whole body of his works. Related questions are whether sight and touch are predominant in other authors, especially in those from the same time period (or style), in those thought to be indebted to Melville, and in other adventure or introspective books.

Frequency tallies of sensory words in a literary work can be a reliable

TABLE 15.1. Sensory Referents in Two Novels of Melville

	Sensory References					
	Olfactory	Tactile	Taste	Sight	Hearing	Overall
Moby Dick						
First half	3	23	0	49	17	92
Second half	6	21	3	56	14	100
Overall (%)	9 (5%)	45 (23%)	3 (1%)	104 (55%)	31 (16%)	192
Pierre						
First half	2	43	2	34	14	95
Second half	1	38	0	35	18	89
Overall (%)	3 (1%)	81 (44%)	2 (1%)	68 (37%)	32 (17%)	184

and quantitative source of information. Content analyses of literary texts have often been used to investigate disputed authorship (Lindauer, 1974). But imagery analysis of textual material is not without ambiguity. For example, had we not known that the two novels were by Melville, the imagery differences between them could have been interpreted as reflecting different authorships! Furthermore, textual analysis does not directly examine the readers' reactions. Unknown is whether the textual imagery in fact aroused readers' imagery. (Literary scholars usually assume that it is so.) Others have raised similar objections to the inherent oversimplifications of frequency counts of words in texts (Hornstein, 1942; Tune, 1942). These include a failure to consider the times in which authors worked and how these might have influenced the images used. Although it is logically possible to consider a literary work separately from the reader (and the author from both), an ideal study should include all components.

The Metaphor and the Image

The study of the metaphor is currently a lively area of inquiry in psychology (Honeck & Hoffman, 1980; Ortony, 1979), although the topic has always attracted considerable attention from literary scholars and philosophers. The metaphor, with its characteristic juxtaposition of apparently unrelated material ("To suffer the slings and arrows of outrageous fortune"), is a vital part of the imaginative response to literature (MacCormac, 1972). Of concern to us is whether the metaphor arouses images in the reader, and if so, whether they are perceptuallike (i.e., surrealistic and bizarre), symbolic, or associative.

There are only a few studies that touch on literary images, and these minimize the place of imagery and the role of imaging. Riechman and Coste (1980) studied proverbs, a form related to the metaphor that they felt would be easier to study. Proverbs that were rated high on imagery and accompanied by instructions to use imagery were not more easily comprehended. Indeed, the authors suggest that imagery may have interfered with the processing of information. Harris (1976) compared Shakespearean and similarly constructed metaphors with nonmetaphoric sentences (with the same meaning as the two kinds of literary metaphors). No special advantage was found for either of the metaphors on several measures (e.g., latency of understanding). Although imagery was not measured, Harris (Harris et al., 1980) elsewhere reported that Shakespearean metaphors did invoke more images and were better recognized than nonmetaphors.

Most of the work on the metaphor is more concerned with its processing (encoding) and its role in memory, language comprehension, and development than with a description of its perceptual (and imaging) nature (Billow, 1977; Ortony et al., 1978). Although much has been accomplished, and in a highly sophisticated way, many of the same questions that plague general imagery research abound in the study of the metaphor, such as whether imagery exists, whether it is perceptual or mnemonic, how early in the sequence of processing it takes place, whether literal meanings are processed before metaphoric meanings, and how one can have imagery of unimaginable material.

Phenomenological analysis, here as elsewhere, would be helpful. What is the predominant content of literary metaphors of high imagery (people or things)? Do high-imagery metaphors enhance or detract from the literary response? Although the presumed role of imagery in metaphors is appealing and research is promising, its presence remains unknown. It would be useful to focus on the reactions and imagery responses to literary metaphors of those who know and enjoy literature.

A Study: The Images of Art and Music

The study of the imagery of one art form, although welcome, would still be limited. It leaves unanswered the question of whether the imagery to music, for example, is different from the imagery to art. The Bilotta study, reported earlier, dealt with the imagery effects of music and art. But it did not examine (except retrospectively) the imagery to art and music themselves. It would also be useful to include reactions to art other than imagery (e.g., its pleasingness). Obtaining an array of different responses to art would provide a perspective from which to weigh the importance of imagery. For example, is the imagery to art greater than the imagery to music, and is the imagery to music less than its emotional meaning? Ratings of music and art on imagery and five other attributes were obtained by David Griffin in an unpublished study reported next.

Method

Nearly all of the art and music examples used by Bilotta in the study reported earlier were rated on six scales. Slides of 57 representational paintings by 14 artists from the eighteenth and nineteenth centuries were used. (Each artist was represented by three to five works.) There were also 17 brief musical extracts by 14 composers of the seventeenth to nineteenth centuries. Both types of artistic stimuli were "classics."

Small groups of men and women, totalling 17 and 15 subjects, rated either the art or the music. Each art slide was shown for 20 seconds and each musical piece was heard for 60–90 seconds, with a few seconds between trials for the ratings. The subjects were untrained in art, randomly assigned to either the art or music group, and were volunteers from undergraduate psychology classes.

Each work was rated on six 7-point scales anchored by adjectival opposites at each end of the scale. The six scales were printed on one sheet of paper and were arranged in three orders of presentation; the directionality of the labels on the scales were also alternated. The scales were labeled imagery–no imagery, emotional–unemotional, familiar–unfamiliar, relaxed–

tense, pleasant–unpleasant, and abstract–concrete. Minimal explanations of the scales and their use were given.

Results

The results are reported for art and music separately and then for both together.

Art

The 57 works of art evoked a twofold range of imagery ratings, $M = 3.20$–6.40. In order to discern any special features of the art that received high and low imagery ratings, the 24 works with extremely high or low ratings (± 1 SD, respectively) were chosen (Table 15.2).

The 13 works of art with the highest imagery were predominantly scenic; there were eight landscapes and one seascape. Only one of the remaining four paintings (the "Courbet with black dog") could be called a people-oriented work. In contrast, 11 of the 12 low-imagery works were people-oriented (i.e., portraits, nudes, and small to large groups of people in allegorical, mythological, and historical settings). The one exception was a portrait, too, but of a horse. In order to weigh these findings, it should be noted that most of the 57 paintings (71%) were people-oriented.

The distinction between the two classes of art, as either high in imagery (and scenic) or low in imagery (and people-oriented) was fairly clear. But the assignment of artists to high- or low-imagery categories, based on where their works fell, was not consistent. Artists with at least one work in the low-imagery group (Ingres, Gericault, Daumier, and Goya) also had one work in the high-imagery group, and the three artists who had several works

TABLE 15.2. High and Low Imagery Art[a]

High	Low
The Cross in the Mountain (Friedrich)	Odalesque with Slave (Ingres)
Chalk Cliffs at Rugen (Friedrich)	Bather of Valpincon (Ingres)
Napolean on His Imperial Throne (Ingres)	Madam Recamier (David)
Courbet with Black Dog (Courbet)	Family of Charles IV (Goya)
Avignon from the West (Corot)	Return from the Market (Daumier)
Forest of Fontunebleau (Corot)	Horse Frightened by Lightning (Gericault)
Saturn Eating His Son (Goya)	Satan Melting Job (Blake)
Haywain (Constable)	The Countess D'Hausson (Ingres)
The Cornfield (Constable)	Third-Class Carriage (Daumier)
Snowstorm (Turner)	Death of Sardanapolis (Delacroix)
Wreck of the Hope (Friedrich)	Rue Transion An (Daumier)
10 O'Clock Rock (Daumier)	
Officer of the Imperial Guard (Gericault)	

[a]High $M \geq 5.82$; low $M \leq 4.44$. The only artists not represented in this table, of the 14 used, are Degas and Runge.

in the high-imagery category (Friedrich, Corot, and Constable) had about half of their remaining works in the intermediate group.

High- and low-imagery art also differed from one another when their ratings on the five other scales were compared. The high-imagery group's ratings were about evenly distributed in the high and low ranges of the other scales (i.e., 46% of the ratings of high-imagery art fell at $M \geq 5.50$ on five scales and 54% fell at $M \leq 4.50$). In contrast, most (72%) of the low-imagery art ratings fell at the low ranges ($M \leq 4.50$) of the five other scales.

Music

The range of imagery ratings for the 17 selections of music was almost as great as that found for art, $M = 3.60–6.90$. The median was used to divide the music into high- and low-imagery groups (Table 15.3). Unlike art, however, it was not possible to distinguish the two groups of music (e.g., by type of music represented). Those pieces in the high-imagery group tended to be "dramatic, powerful, strong, and rhythmic," and those in the low-imagery group tended to be "slow, dreamy, and delicate." However, there were several exceptions to these descriptions. The small number of selections (17, compared to the 57 in art) also makes it difficult to reach any generalization. (Two professional musicologists also were unable to describe the distinguishing features of one set over another.)

It was also difficult, as it was for art, to note any distinctions between the composers in each group. All three of Beethoven's works were in the high-imagery group, but four composers (Strauss, Tchaikovsky, Verdi, and Chopin) had works in both the high- and low-imagery groups.

A striking parallel between music and art emerged when comparisons were made between music's imagery and the other five attributes. Ratings for high-imagery music, like those for high-imagery art, were as likely to fall at the high as at the low ends of the five other scales (50% of the ratings fell either above $M = 5.50$ or below 4.50 on the other scales). But the majority

TABLE 15.3.   High- and Low-Imagery Music[a]

High	Low
Blue Danube (Strauss)	Romeo and Juliet (Tchaikovsky)
Hungarian Dance (Brahms)	Nutcracker (Tchaikovsky)
Clair de Lune (Debussy)	La Traviata (Verdi)
Prelude in A Major (Chopin)	Largo (Handel)
Ode to Joy (Beethoven)	Emperor's Waltz (Strauss)
Symphony No. 5 (Beethoven)	Minute Waltz (Chopin)
Piano Concerto (Tchaikovsky)	William Tell (Rossini)
Anvil Chorus (Verdi)	Marriage of Figaro (Mozart)
Concerto No. 5 (Beethoven)	

[a]High $M \geq 4.70$; low $M \leq 4.10$.

of the low-imagery music (77%), like art, fell at the low ends of the other five scales.

Music and Art Compared

Several similarities between art and music have already been noted. Both show a wide range of imagery ratings; the rating of the imagery of artists and composers, as indicated by the rating given to their works, was inconsistent; and low-, but not high-imagery art and music fell consistently at one end of five descriptive scales. One difference has already been noted: it was fairly easy to describe the distinction between high- and low-imagery art (as scenic or people oriented, respectively), but this was not true for music. Other similarities and differences emerged when the complete set of art was examined (i.e., the high- and low-imagery distinctions within both types of art were ignored).

There was no difference between the imagery ratings of art and music (M = 5.13 and 4.76, respectively; t = 1.25, p > .05). The similarity of their imagery was also indicated by the lack of a difference in the number of art and music works whose ratings fell above or below the overall median [x^2 (1) = 1.91, p > .05]. Where music and art did differ from one another was in relation to the other descriptive scales.

Unexpectedly (on the basis of the stereotypes usually held about music), the emotional response to music was lower than the emotional response to art (M = 4.60 and 5.15, respectively; t = 2.52, p < .05). Perhaps also unexpected was the higher pleasantness ratings of music in comparison to those for art (M = 5.01 and 4.25, respectively; t = 2.78, p < .05). (The differences between art and music on the remaining three scales were insignificant; t < 1.00.) Imagery was involved in other differences between music and art when the responses were correlated with one another. For art, only imagery and emotion were correlated (r = .35, p < .05; r ≤ .17, p > .05, for the other sets; one-tailed tests were used here and throughout). But for music, imagery was correlated with all but one of the other scales (r ≥ .54, p < .05); the exception was tenseness (r = .19, p > .05). These differences between art and music were also noted when the magnitudes of the responses on the various scales were compared. The imagery ratings for art were higher than all other attributes but one (t ≥ 4.43, p < .05); the exception was emotion (t = 0.03, p > .05). The imagery ratings for music, on the other hand, did not differ from three of the scales (t ≤ 1.87, p > .05); imagery ratings were higher than tenseness and concreteness ratings (t ≥ 2.21, p < .05).

These correlational and magnitude data suggest that imagery to art, unlike imagery to music, is more unique. In art, only imagery and emotion were closely related, whereas in music, imagery was closely tied to emotion, pleasantness, and familiarity, and to some degree, to concreteness as well.

Imagery to music is closely related to other characteristics of music, whereas imagery to art stands by itself.

Discussion

It was argued earlier, in the discussion of the Bilotta results, that music may have established a contemplative set that encouraged observers' imagery. If this is valid, observers may feel relatively more open and unrestricted in their thoughts and feelings. Consequently, not only imagery, but other responses (e.g., feelings of pleasantness) are more likely to occur at the same time. Hence closer associations between the responses to music than to art can occur. A contemplative and uninhibited state also probably was present for scenic art; hence it evoked high imagery. But the portrayal of human character in people-oriented art prompted a more analytical set; hence it elicited low imagery. Thus a key element in understanding the imagery distinctions within (and between) the arts lies in their inducement of a relatively relaxed orientation in an observer.

Space limitations prevent a fuller discussion of this point and of other provocative findings. Worth mentioning are the wide imagery differences between works of art and music. Just as there are individual differences between observers' imagery, so too are there differences between works of art. A work of art is not necessarily high on imagery just because it is a work of art, or because it is music rather than a painting. Similarly, the mere fact that a work of art is high in imagery does not mean that the work is more pleasant or emotional (although low-imagery works are, for unknown reasons, more predictable).

The study also raises some questions about the consistency of artists' imagery. This was indirectly shown by the relatively unpredictable placement of an artist's works in either the high- or low-imagery category. In the next section on the artist, the third and last component relating the arts to imagery, the imagery of artists is both directly and indirectly examined.

THE IMAGERY OF ARTISTS

Whatever the extent of imagery in observers of the arts may be, or in types of art, most scholars (and artists) strongly feel that imagery among artists exists and is highly useful (Ernest, 1977; Forisha, 1978; Ghiselin, 1955; Khatena, 1978; Lindauer, 1974, 1977). Indeed, a uniquely defining attribute of artists just may be their capacity to have and manipulate original images for creative purposes (McMahan, 1973; Richardson, 1969; Walkup, 1965). Images may be a source of inspiration (Wallas, 1926), as well as the "canvas and notebook" on which creative ideas are tried out and modified before they are put down (Mandelbrojt, 1970). Artists are also adept at selecting images that give us new insights and knowing how to translate their own images effectively into a medium. "Surely, much of the craft of the creative writer consists in his ability to transfer to the mind of his reader the images he has constructed within his own mind" (Cohen, 1976, p. 517). In short, the artist is talented at forming, controlling, choosing, and presenting images to the delight and edification of an audience. "Poetic vision," and the ability "to see the old in new ways" (or to "see the new in old ways") may very well depend on imagery.

The status of artists' imagery in scholarly and critical writings is thus not an issue, although a few (Richards, 1925) have raised some questions regarding its function. For the most part, though, inquiry is not focused on the existence of imagery, but on its distinctive use by a particular artist (or period of art) compared to other artists (or periods), or on changes in the imagery of an artist over time. Analysis is also concerned with the most useful definition of imagery among the many that exist (Friedman, 1953; Lindauer, 1972, 1974). Scholars seem confident in their belief that a good place to study imagery in the arts is among artists.

Approach of Psychology to Artists' Imagery as Illustrative

In contrast to scholars' acceptance of imagery in artists, psychologists are much more cautious. Artists on imagery, whether expressed indirectly through their work or stated directly in commentaries on their own or others' work, receive a peripheral place in psychology. For example, scientific treatments of imagery are often introduced by artists' quotes on imagery, or relevant biographical passages are strategically placed within the more technical content of the text (McKellar, 1957; Swartz, 1978). Readers interested in further accounts are directed to collections of artists' autobiographies (Ghiselin, 1955). Artists on imagery are thus minor grace notes in psychological analysis, and the molecular details of the laboratory are preferred. Appeals are sometimes made for more systematic study of artists' imagery (Paivio, 1971, p. 532; Richardson, 1969, p. 126). Artists and their imagery nevertheless receive a rather circumscribed place in psychology, one of illustration; they serve as a kind of dramatic decoration for the more serious study of imagery pursued elsewhere.

There are some very good illustrative uses of artists' imagery. Marks's (1978) book on synesthesia (i.e., cross-modal sensory references, e.g., the colors of music), a phenomenon closely related to imagery, has two concluding chapters on poets' works and analyses. "Sweet sound [is married to] the grace of form" (Keats). But the literary material serves mainly to illustrate what has already been established earlier with much simpler materials in a more analytical manner (i.e., psychophysical studies of ratings of vowels). Sommer (1978) is another psychologist who effectively uses illustrative materials on artists' imagery in his popular presentation on imagery. But in typical fashion, artists' contributions are placed within a context predetermined by psychology's perspective. Consequently, we discover that some of psychology's findings are supported by what some artists have said about their own imagery. But there are no systematic investigations of what artists have said about imagery in their own terms, from their perspective, unencumbered by the historical and methodological preoccupations of psychology. The problem with a selective sampling of artists on imagery, chosen according to how they fit into psychology, is that we lose sight of their unique contribution. A phenomenologically oriented study of artists' imagery could offer psychology some fresh viewpoints and new directions. The use of artists' quotes mainly for illustrative purposes does not significantly further psychology's understanding of imagery, especially when it is under attack.

The characteristics of imagery in artists should be examined carefully, especially since its existence in creative persons has not been established, nor shown to be greater in artists than in nonartists (Bilotta & Lindauer, 1980). The presumed superiority of artists' imagery is based on informal, anecdotal, and hearsay evidence, or on personal experience (Gordon, 1972; Walkup, 1965). Despite the claims of many, both in or out of psychology, that artists are supreme in their expression and use of imagery, there is little evidence. Some unpublished studies on this issue are presented below.

Studies of Artists' Imagery

Reported next are three studies that approach the question of what artists say about their own imagery. Several methods were used in these exploratory and preliminary efforts, including content analyses of two kinds of historical records, quotations and autobiographies, and interviews with a small set of artists.

Artists' Quotes on Imagery

A library shelf of general and specialized books of quotations were examined for statements by artists, and others involved in the arts, on images and imagery and related phenomena (e.g., inspiration and imagination). The indices of these collections were searched; and, where these were nonexistent, sections on the arts were scanned directly. Some examples of those found follow: "When the real world is shut out, [imagination] can create a world for itself . . . can conjure up glorious shapes and forms, and brilliant visions" (Irving); "I live in my imagination . . . making a perceptual pageant" (Woolf); "You have to pay dearly for being an imaginative person. You see a great deal . . . but there is ugliness to see . . . as well as beauty" (Anderson); "There are many things in music which must be imagined without being heard" (C. Bach); "Music scatters the sparks of images" (Nietzsche).

In general, though, there was relatively little on imagery. Among the quotations on imagery, images as pictures were mentioned less often than were images as associations, memories, or metaphors. Consider these examples: "Mind, like water, receives and reflects images" (H. Adams); "Time is the image of eternity" (various); "His imagination resembled the wings of an ostrich. It enabled him to run, though not to soar" (Macaulay). Imagination is mentioned much more than imagery, although images are implied. For example: "Imagination is as good as many voyages—and how much cheaper" (Curtis); "Imagination is a wide-open eye" (Fry); "Man consists of body, mind, and imagination . . . but his imagination has made him remarkable" (Masefield); "Only in men's imagination does every truth find an effective and undeniable existence" (Conrad); "What the imagination seizes as beauty must be truth" (Keats). Generally, the quotations tell us that images are used, rather than how they are used or what they are about.

The paucity of quotations on imagery is shown by a detailed examination of the collection by Murphy (1978), which has an extensive number of quotations on the arts. It contains 27 pages of quotations on writing and writers, dance, music, art and artists, architecture, and photography (about 400 in all). But only 17 quotations on imagination were listed in the index (imagery was not mentioned), and of these, only one or two clearly could be categorized as referring to imagery. "The artist does not draw what he sees, but what he must make others see" (Degas). "[The music] felt like velvet to one's inner being" (Amriel). A similar result was found in a specialized book of quotations on music (Lewis, 1963). A random sample selected from over 200 selections revealed only 2% on images. Even fewer were estimated to be in another specialized book of about 500 quotations by authors on writing (Charlton, 1980).

The scarcity of quotations on imagery may be due to a number of factors: it is difficult for artists and others to say (or for editors to find) quotable things about imagery; other quotable matters are easier to talk about (and find), such as the origins or consequences of creativity; artists feel no need to talk about what to them is obvious; and good indices are rare. Most quotations by artists were about an assortment of matters quite unrelated to imagery: the amount of work involved (and one's way of working); the pain of creativity; the lack of recognition; one's feelings when a work is done; and money matters.

Another factor to consider is that brief quotations out of context do not do justice to statements about imagery. These are more appropriately found in longer autobiographical works. This possibility, at least in one instance, was not borne out. An autobiographical essay by Sherwood Anderson on imagination [in Centeno (1941/1970)] looked like a good source. He discusses the origins of his imagination in everyday experiences and how reality can be changed in imagination. But in only one paragraph (p. 50) does Anderson actually refer to images: he discusses dreams in which characters for some of his books were found.

Despite the dearth of references to imagery in one autobiographical account, the possibility still exists that more success would be found in a systematic search of many autobiographies. This possibility was pursued by

Ann Henderson in an unpublished study, reported next (Henderson & Lindauer, 1976). She surveyed the autobiographical works of three kinds of artists over three centuries for statements on creativity. Part of her findings bear on artists on imagery.

Artists' Autobiographical Statements on Imagery

Henderson sampled a library's collection of 115 autobiographical works (essays, collections, and books) by 72 painters, 30 musicians, and 13 writers from the eighteenth to the twentieth centuries. She found 501 statements on various aspects of creativity. She and another judge classified these statements into 80 categories that were then further classified into 16 categories that had 10 or more related statements. (These accounted for only 51% of the total number of statements found. Artists have a diversity of things to say about creativity, but it is difficult to categorize them.)

The largest number of classifiable statements by artists was on emotion (34), and the second largest number was on ideas (27). Imagery was mentioned 17 times (as was the unconscious). Other frequently mentioned categories were nature (13) and inspiration (10). The imagery category was expanded to include related categories (imagination, hallucinations, dreams, fantasy, perception, the senses, flashes, memories, and sounds). The new imagery-related category now had 97 statements (or 19% of the total). Most were made by painters (46%), with musicians and writers tied at 27% each; and most were from the twentieth century (61%), with the nineteenth and eighteenth centuries accounting for 12 and 27%, respectively. (The sample included more painters than other artists, and more twentieth-century artists than artists of other periods.)

When imagery was broadly defined, it was mentioned a modest amount in artists' self-reports on creativity. Its frequency thus was greater than the quotation data suggested. However, its incidence was not overwhelming, and less than that of other categories (e.g., the stages of creativity). Nevertheless, the results encourage further inquiry.

Autobiographical material is an indirect and ambiguous indication of what artists think and feel about imagery. What one finds depends on editorial choice and the happenstance of artists spontaneously saying something recordable about imagery. In short, neither collections of quotes nor autobiographies are written for scientific purposes. For this, we need more direct and structured measures. In the next study reported, artists were directly interviewed about their imagery.

Interviews with Artists

Nine artists (six men and three women) were randomly chosen from the art, music, English, theater, and dance departments of a college. (Two people were interviewed in each field, except in dance, which was represented by one person.) Nearly all were primarily professionals, that is, working artists rather than historians, aestheticians, or educators; and most had national reputations.

The artists were asked a series of open-ended questions, mainly by telephone, in interviews that lasted for $\frac{1}{2}$–1 hour. The first question was asked to establish the presence of sensory–perceptual ("picturelike") images in their everyday (nonworking) life. "Can you picture (or hear) your spouse's (or child's) face (or voice)?" All said that they were easily able to do this. (Since the term "image" is used in so many different ways, it was important to emphasize that I was interested in this literal meaning. It seemed to be a good place to start.) The artists were told that I was interested in the sensory–perceptual imagery that occurred while they worked, that is, if it existed. As respondents drifted away from this literal definition of imagery (their responses tended to be rather wide ranging), they were reminded of the concrete example of imagery with which the interview began.

The intent of the study was to establish the existence, use, and importance of imagery in these artists' work (an "existential" question that is so contentious an issue among psychologists). Questions were also asked about the frequency, mode, clarity, vividness, control, locus, importance, and variability over time of their work-related imagery. Respondents were also asked about their everyday and their colleague's imagery.

The primary concern of the study was posed this way: "In your work as artist [poet, composer, director, dancer], do you have and use imagery of the sort we've just described [in everyday life]?" All but one respondent answered affirmatively. A theater director (who was also an actor and poet) indignantly replied, "It's insulting to ask. Of course I do. It's like asking a physicist if electrons exist!" A poet patiently explained, "All great poetry is imagery, there is no poetry without imagery" and then ruefully added "I'd rather write images than talk about them." (Respondents generally seemed amused to hear, when it was later pointed out at the debriefing, that many psychologists held serious reservations about the presence and importance of imagery.)

The one respondent who reported no imagery while working as a painter (his works are highly abstract), said that he had images in everyday life, especially in his fantasies and dreams. He also insisted that other artists had no images while they worked. Exactly the opposite view, given just as adamantly, was expressed by the other artist interviewed (whose paintings, incidentally, are more representative in content). As subsequent questions indicated, opposing views on imagery are not likely to be contradicted, since artists do not seem to talk to one another about how they work (Gordon, 1972).

Replies to questions about the vividness and clarity of the artists' images were not startling. All respondents indicated a high degree of both. The poet said, "Images are as clear and vivid to me as if they were there (although I know I'm imagining them)." Similarly unrevealing were indications that imagery was both voluntary and spontaneous, although several respondents said that they preferred the latter type. The artists also generally believed that imagery could be improved with practice. More surprising, perhaps, was the nearly unanimous belief that their imagery today was different from that of the past. In all but one instance, this change was thought to be an improvement: it is more "heightened, spontaneous, conscious, frequent, or important" now. Reports of the frequency of imagery indicated that it was at least modest ("50% of the time" and "often"). The group was about evenly split on whether imagery occurred around the beginning of their work or throughout. With respect to the importance of imagery in their work, replies were emphatically affirmative. A poet said, "I can't imagine what I'd do without it; I couldn't write anything except perhaps abstract work." This sentiment was echoed by the musician. "It would be a tremendous loss." The artist reported that he played background music while he worked to help increase his imagery. But in contrast, the dancer concluded, "I'd find something else [if I lost my imagery], perhaps relying more on my emotions." The mode of imagery most often mentioned was vision. Although no artist used it exclusively, several said it was primary. Nearly all other sensory modes were represented; several respondents listed at least three. A musician "saw" as well as "heard" and "felt" notes. Seashore (1938, p. 161) states: "Perhaps the most outstanding mark of the musician's mind is auditory imagery." His data, however, were based on comparisons between musicians and nonmusicians. The question of whether different artists use different images (Sommer, 1978) remains an intriguing one (Bilotta & Lindauer, 1980; Parsons & Lindauer, 1980). The artists in this sample tentatively believed that artists in general differ from one another in their imagery. A larger sample of different groups of artists is needed to answer this question.

It was puzzling to learn that the majority of the artists did not discuss their imagery with colleagues. As the painter put it, "let the work speak for itself." A musician explained that his reluctance was due to embarrassment. To talk about one's work would be "like showing off, and it's also too personal to put one's 'craziness' on display." A few artists did say that imagery was discussed as a standard technique in theory and practice (especially in the theater while directing).

Also rather unexpected was the general feeling, reported at the end of the interview, that imagery in art and in everyday life were not that different from one another. Differences existed, but only in degree or subject matter. Only one person (the dancer) reported that her everyday imagery, unlike her work-related imagery, lacked visual imagery.

These interviews indicated that information about artists' imagery can be fairly easily obtained. Artists had no problems understanding what was meant by sensory–perceptual images. They reported that they had such images, both in real life and in their work, and that they relied on them a great deal. In fact, with eight of the first nine participants emphatically affirming the existence, use, and importance of imagery, it was quickly realized that the interviews' focus and schedule of questions were superfluous.

The next step is to build on and go beyond this elementary but necessary first step. A larger sample is needed, representing different areas of the arts, to determine whether there are different ways of using imagery in each area of art. Furthermore, questions on nonimagery also have to be included (e.g., on the role of emotions, the unconscious, and the stages of creativity). These would place the role of imagery into some perspective. Here, as in the study of the art object and the art observer, much remains to be done from an empirical point of view.

EPILOGUE

Since so little research on imagery and the arts has been done and some promising leads are just beginning to be pursued, it would be presumptuous to end this chapter with so final a term as "Conclusion." One conclusion that can be offered with some certainty, although it is applicable mainly to artists and scholars in the arts, is that there is a rich storehouse of personal, scholarly, and clinical commentary on the importance of imagery. Biographical reports, critical essays, and case studies point out the power of imagery by the way a work of art moves us, by the soaring of an artist's imaginative talents, and by the enrichment of the experiences of those who are exposed to the arts. Empirical psychology cannot match these claims or be so emphatic in its interpretations of the place of imagery. We have much to learn about imagery from the arts, more than those in the arts can learn about imagery from psychology.

A ringing affirmation of faith in the existence of imagery is valuable, but psychology needs more. The analytical detail required by empirical psychology cannot be met by the broad generalities provided by the arts. Most of the "who, what, where, how, and how much" of imagery in the arts still remains to be sketched in by research. Yet any beginning is thwarted by the many research psychologists who question the very existence of imagery. Even imagery's function, despite highly sophisticated measuring techniques and elaborate information-processing conceptualizations, is theoretically insecure. So fundamental a matter as the locus of imagery, whether primarily in perception or memory, remains in doubt.

There could be a fruitful synthesis of the generalities of the arts, with their insistence on the place of imagery, and the methodological rigor of empirical psychology, with its uncertainties over the status of imagery. A joining of faith on the one hand, and method on the other hand, might move each discipline away from its present impasse and mutual neglect. Some suggestions are offered below.

Psychological studies have traditionally depended on rather restricted procedures. Materials relatively low in imagery have been used (e.g., isolated concrete nouns or outline drawings), and subjects have been selected (through randomization) whose imagery ability is low, mixed, or unknown. But the study of imagery enriched by an arts perspective encourages the use of highly imageable material (perhaps music) and the selection of subjects with high imagery (e.g., aesthetic persons).

Replications and extensions of earlier studies but with new stimulus and subject variables drawn from the arts would be interesting. But these additions are not enough. To simply transfer the old paradigms of research from the neutral psychology laboratory to an enriched arts context still would be shortsighted. There are some serious reservations about our present understanding of imagery. Reliance on previously formulated preconceptions could bias new research directions into making the mistakes of the past or in taking the same blind alleys. Research on imagery must be more open to the new opportunities offered by the arts.

The phenomenological approach, relying on interviews, content '(qualitative) analysis, self-reports of artists, and aesthetic persons' responses to artistic stimuli, is a way of exploring what the arts have to offer psychology. It minimizes the bias developed from nonaesthetic research strategies. The arts suggest hypotheses about such issues as differences in imagery between types of art and artists, whether painters are primarily visual whereas musicians are auditory in their imagery modes, and whether the imagery of artists, compared to nonartists, is more spontaneous. These questions bear on more general issues, such as the distribution of imagery and imagery types in the population, the primacy of the visual mode, the perceptual or abstract nature of images, and individual differences in imagery. No doubt other important matters about imagery in general can be amplified by examining the perspective provided by the arts.

Since there is so little research on imagery and the arts, initial efforts should be exploratory and descriptive rather than primarily hypothesis testing or theory building. It is thus difficult to predict the outcome of research on imagery using an arts framework or its consequence on psychological (or aesthetic) theory. The arts offer the psychology of imagery an opportunity to expand its research borders. That challenge, hardly recognized, has yet to be grasped.

REFERENCES

Addison, J. The pleasures of the imagination. In S. Elledge (Ed.), *Eighteenth-century critical essays*, Vol. 1. Ithaca, New York: Cornell University Press, 1961.

Albrecht, M. C., Barnett, J. H., & Griff, M. (Eds.). *The sociology of art and literature: A reader*. New York: Praeger, 1970.

Allport, D. A. The state of cognitive psychology. *Quarterly Journal of Experimental Psychology*, 1975, **27**, 141–152.

Arnheim, R. *Art and visual perception*. Berkeley: University of California Press, 1966a.

Arnheim, R. Images and thought. In G. Kepes (Ed.), *Sign, images, symbol.* New York: Braziller, 1966b.

Arnheim, R. *Visual thinking.* Berkeley: University of California Press, 1969.

Arvin, N. *Herman Melville.* New York: Sloane, 1950.

Beckson, K., & Ganz, A. *A reader's guide to literary terms: A dictionary.* New York: Farrar, 1960/1969.

Berleant, A. *The aesthetic field: A phenomenology of aesthetic experience.* Springfield, Ill.:C Thomas, 1970.

Berlyne, D. E. *Psychobiology and aesthetic* . New York: Appleton, 1971.

Berlyne, D. E. *Studies in the new experimental aesthetics.* New York: Wiley, 1974.

Betts, G. H. *The distribution and function of mental imagery.* New York: Teachers College, Columbia University, 1909.

Billow, R. M. Metaphor: A review of the psychological literature. *Psychological Bulletin,* 1977, **84**, 81–92.

Bilotta, J., & Lindauer, M. S. Imagery arousel as a function of exposure to artistic stimuli. Paper presented at the 5th Annual Convention, Genesee Valley Psychological Association, Rochester, N.Y. 1978.

Bilotta, J., & Lindauer, M. S. Artistic and nonartistic backgrounds as determinants of the cognitive response to the arts. *Bulletin of the Psychonomic Society,* 1980, **15**, 354–356.

Bronowski, J. The reach of imagination. *American Scholar,* 1967, **36**, 193–201.

Bullough, E. *Aesthetics: Lectures and essays.* Stanford, Cal.: Stanford University Press, 1957.

Capurso, A. A. *Music and your emotions.* New York: Liveright, 1952.

Casey, E. S. *Imagining: A phenomenological study.* Bloomington: Indiana University Press, 1976.

Centeno, A. (Ed.). *The intent of the artist.* New York: Russell & Russell, 1941/1970.

Charlton, J. (Ed.). *The writer's quotation book: A literary companion.* Yonkers, New York: Pushcart, 1980.

Child, I. L. Aesthetic theories. In E. C. Carterette & M. P. Friedman (Eds.), *Handbook of perception,* Vol. X. New York: Academic Press, 1978.

Cohen, G. Visual imagery in thought. *New Literary History,* 1976, **7**, 513–523.

Cohen, G. *The psychology of cognition.* New York: Academic Press, 1977.

Dewey, J. *Art as experience.* New York: Putnam, 1934.

Dilworth, C. B., Jr. Visualization and the experience of poetry: A study of selected variables in reader response. *Dissertation Abstracts International,* 1975, **8**, 4978-A.

DiVesta, F. J., Ingersoll, G., & Sunshine, P. A factor analysis of imagery tests. *Journal of Verbal Learning & Verbal Behavior,* 1971, **10**, 471–479.

Downey, J. E. Emotional poetry and preference judgment. *Psychological Review,* 1915, **22**, 259–278.

Ernest, C. H. Imagery ability and cognition: A critical review. *Journal of Mental Imagery,* 1977, **2**, 181–216.

Eysenck, H. J. Factors determining aesthetic preference for geometrical designs and devices. *British Journal of Aesthetics,* 1971, **11**, 154–166.

Farnsworth, P. R. *The social psychology of music*. New York: Rinehart & Winston, 1958.

Fleming, M. L. The picture in your mind. *AV Communication Review*, 1977, **25**, 43–62.

Forisha, B. L. Mental Imagery and creativity: Review and speculation. *Journal of Mental Imagery*, 1978, **2**, 209–238.

Friedman, N. Imagery: From sensation to symbol. *Journal of Aesthetics and Art Criticism*, 1953, **12**, 25–37.

Furlong, E. J. *Imagination*. New York: Macmillan, 1961.

Galton, F. *Inquiries into human faculty and its development*. London: Dent, 1883.

Ghiselin, B. (Ed.). *The creative process*. New York: Mentor, 1955.

Gordon, R. A very private world. In P. W. Sheehan (Ed.), *The function and nature of imagery*. New York: Academic Press, 1972.

Hammer, E. F. Imagery: The artistic style in the therapist's communications. *Art Psychotherapy*, 1975, **2**, 225–231.

Hampson, P. J., & Morris, P. E. Cyclical processing: A framework for imagery research. *Journal of Mental Imagery*, 1979, **3**, 11–22.

Harris, R. J. Comprehension of metaphors: A test of the two-stage processing model. *Bulletin of the Psychonomic Society*, 1976, **8**, 312–314.

Harris, R. J., Lahey, M. A., & Marsalek, F. Metaphors and images: Ratings, reporting, and remembering. In R. P. Honeck & R. R. Hoffman (Eds.), *Cognition and figurative language*. Hillsdale, N.J.: Lawrence Erlbaum Associates, 1980.

Henderson, A., & Lindauer, M. S. Autobiographical statements on creativity by artists, musicians, and writers. In M. S. Lindauer (Ed.), *Research in psychological aesthetics and the arts: A personal collection*. Brockport, N.Y., 1976.

Hillway, T. *Herman Melville*. New York: Twayne, 1963.

Hollingsworth, H. L. The psychology of drowsiness: An introspective and analytical study. *American Journal of Psychology*, 1911, **22**, 99–111.

Honeck, R. P., & Hoffman, R. R. (Eds.). *Cognition and figurative language*. Hillsdale, N.J.: Lawrence Erlbaum Associates, 1980.

Hornstein, L. H. Analysis of imagery: A critique of literary method. *Publications of the Modern Language Association*, 1942, **57**, 638–653.

Khatena, J. Major directions in creativity research. *Gifted Child Quarterly*, 1976, **20**, 336–349.

Khatena, J. Advances in research on creative imagination imagery. *Gifted Child Quarterly*, 1977, **21**, 433–439.

Khatena, J. Frontiers of creative imaginative imagery. *Journal of Mental Imagery*, 1978, **2**, 33–46.

Khatena, J. & Torrance, E. P. *Thinking creatively with sounds and words*. Lexington, Mass.: Ginn, 1973.

Kiell, N. (Ed.). *Psychoanalysis, psychology and literature: A bibliography*. Madison: University of Wisconsin Press, 1963.

Kiell, N. (Ed.). *Psychiatry and psychology in the visual arts and aesthetics. A bibliography*. Madison: University of Wisconsin Press, 1965.

King, D. L. *Conditioning: An image approach*. New York: Halstead-Wiley, 1977.

King, D. L. Image theory of conditioning, memory, forgetting, functional similarity, fusion, and dominance. *Journal of Mental Imagery*, 1978, **2**, 47–62.

Klinger, E. The flow of thought and its implications for literary communication. *Poetics*, 1978, **7**, 191–205.

Kosslyn, S. M., & Pomerantz, J. R. Imagery, propositions, and the form of internal representations. *Cognitive Psychology*, 1977, **9**, 52–76.

Kreitler, H., & Kreitler, S. *Psychology and the arts*. Durham, N.C.: Duke University Press, 1972.

Leonard, G., & Lindauer, M. S. Aesthetic participation and imagery arousal. *Perceptual and Motor Skills*, 1973, **36**, 977–978.

Lewis, R. (Ed.). *In praise of music*. New York: Orion, 1973.

Lindauer, M. S. The sensory attributes and functions of imagery and imagery evoking stimule. In P. W. Sheehan (Ed.), *The function and nature of imagery*. New York: Academic Press, 1972.

Lindauer, M. S. *The psychological study of literature*. Chicago: Nelson-Hall, 1974.

Lindauer, M. S. In search of the aesthetic person. Paper presented at the 6th Colloquium of Empirical Aesthetics, Paris, France, 1976. Also in *Bulletin De Psychologie*, 1976/77, **30**, 628–636.

Lindauer, M. S. Imagery from the point of view of psychological aesthetics, the arts, and creativity. *Journal of Mental Imagery*, 1977, **1**, 343–362.

Lindauer, M. S. Aesthetic experience: A neglected topic in the psychology of the arts. In D. C. O'Hare (Ed.), *Psychology and the arts*. Sussex, England: Lancaster Press, 1981.

Lindauer, M. S. Psychology and literature: An empirical perspective. In M. H. Bornstein (Ed.), *Psychology in relation to allied disciplines*, Vol. 1. Hillsdale, N.J.: Lawrence Erlbaum Associates, in press.

MacCormac, E. R. Metaphor and literature. *Journal of Aesthetic Education*, 1972, **6**, 57–70.

MacKinnon, D. The nature and nurture of creative talent. *American Psychologist*, 1962, **17**, 484–495.

Mandelbrojt, J. On mental images and their pictorial representation. *Leonardo*, 1970, **3**, 19–26.

Marks, D. F. Individual differences in the vividness of visual imagery and their effect on function. In P. W. Sheehan (Ed.), *The function and nature of imagery*. New York: Academic Press, 1972.

Marks, D. F. Imagery and consciousness: A theoretical review from an individual differences perspective. *Journal of Mental Imagery*, 1977, **2**, 275–290.

Marks, L. E. *The unity of the senses: Interrelations of the senses*. New York: Academic Press, 1978.

Martindale, C. *Romantic progression*. New York: Halsted-Wiley, 1975.

Mathews, G. B. Mental copies. *Philosophical Review*, 1969, **78**, 53–73.

McKellar, P. *Imagination and thinking*. New York: Basic Books, 1957.

McKellar, P. Imagery from the standpoint of introspection. In P. W. Sheehan (Ed.), *The function and nature of imagery*. New York: Academic Press, 1972.

McKellar, P. Autonomy, imagery, and dissociation. *Journal of Mental Imagery,* 1977, **1**, 93–108.

McKellar, P. Between wakefulness and sleep: Hypnagogic fantasy. In A. A. Sheikh & J. T. Shaffer (Eds.), *The potential of fantasy and imagination.* New York: Brandon House, 1979.

McMahon, C. E. Images as motives and motivators: A historical perspective. *American Journal of Psychology,* 1973, **86**, 465–490.

Melville, H. *Pierre of the ambiguities.* New York: Dutton, 1929.

Melville, H. *Moby Dick or the whale.* New York: Dell, 1969.

Munro, T. *Toward science in aesthetics.* New York: Liberal Arts, 1956.

Murphy, E. F. J. *The Crown treasury of relevant quotations.* New York: Crown, 1978.

Neisser, U. *Cognitive psychology.* New York: Appleton, 1967.

Neisser, U. A paradigm shift in psychology. *Science,* 1972, **176**, 628–630.

Nisbett, R. E., & Wilson, T. De C. Telling more than we can know: Verbal reports on mental processes. *Psychological Review,* 1977, **84**, 231–259.

Novotny, E. *Art and architecture of 18th century Europe.* New York: Penguin, 1952.

Ortony, A. (Ed.), *Metaphor and thought.* Cambridge: Cambridge University Press, 1979.

Ortony, A., Reynolds, R. E., & Arter, J. A. Metaphor: Theoretical and empirical research. *Psychological Bulletin,* 1978, **85**, 919–943.

Osborne, H. The elucidation of aesthetic experience. *Journal of Aesthetics and Art Criticism,* 1964, **23**, 145–151.

Osborne, H. *The art of appreciation.* London: Oxford, 1970.

The Oxford English dictionary, Vol. V. Oxford: University/Clarendon Press, 1933/1970.

Paivio, A. V. *Imagery and verbal processes.* New York: Holt, 1971.

Parsons, C., & Lindauer, M. S. Dance and theater: Their psychological importance and the aesthetic characteristics of their participants. *JSAS Catalog of Selected Documents in Psychology,* 1980, **10**, MS #2143.

Patrick, C. How responses to good and bad poetry differ. *Journal of Psychology,* 1939, **8,** 253–283.

Pinker, S., & Kosslyn, S. M. The representation and manipulation of three dimensional space in mental images. *Journal of Mental Imagery,* 1978, **2**, 69–84.

Prescott, F. C. *The poetic mind.* Ithaca, N.Y.: Cornell University Press, 1922/1959.

Pylyshyn, Z. What the mind's eye tells the mind's brain: A critique of mental imagery. *Psychological Bulletin,* 1973, **80**, 1–24.

Randolph, S. Verbal and musical facilitation of vividness of mental imagery: A comparative study. *Dissertation Abstracts International,* 1977, **38**, 345B.

Reichmann, P. F., & Coste, E. L. Mental imagery and the comprehension of figurative language: Is there a relationship? In R. P. Honeck & R. R. Hoffman (Eds.), *Cognition and figurative language.* Hillsdale, N.J.: Lawrence Erlbaum Associates, 1980.

Richards, I. A. *Principles of literary criticism.* New York: Harcourt, 1925.

Richards, I. A., Ogden, C. K., & Wood, J. *The foundations of aesthetics.* New York: Haskell House, 1971.

Richardson, A. *Mental imagery*. New York: Springer, 1969.

Richardson, A. Voluntary control of the memory image. In P. W. Sheehan (Ed.), *The function and nature of imagery*. New York: Academic Press, 1972.

Robbins, A. The art therapist's imagery as a response to a therapeutic dialogue. *Art Psychotherapy, 1973,* **1**, 181–184.

Roe, A. Painters and painting. In J. A. Taylor & J. W. Getzels (Eds.), *Perspectives in creativity*. Chicago: Aldine, 1975.

Rugg, H. *Imagination*. New York: Harper, 1963.

Sallé, J. C. Hazlett the associationist. *Review of English Studies*, 1964, **15**, 38–51.

Sardello, R. An empirical–phenomenological study of fantasy, with a note on J. R. R. Tolkien and C. S. Lewis. *Psychocultural Review*, 1978, **2**, 195–220.

Schachter, D. L. The hypnagogic state: A critical review of the literature. *Psychological Bulletin*, 1976, **83**, 452–481.

Schoen, M. *The effects of music*. Freeport, N.Y.: Books for Libraries Press, 1927/1968.

Seashore, C. E. *The psychology of music*. New York: McGraw-Hill, 1938.

Segal, S. J. The Perky effect: Changes in reality judgment with changing methods of inquiry. *Psychonomic Science*, 1968, **12**, 393–394.

Segal, S. J. Assimilation of a stimulus in the construction of an image: The Perky effect revisited. In P. W. Sheehan (Ed.), *The function and nature of imagery*. New York: Academic Press, 1972.

Sheehan, P. W. *The function and nature of imagery*. New York: Academic Press, 1972.

Sheikh, A. A., & Panagiotou, N. C. Use of mental imagery in psychotherapy: A critical review. *Perceptual and Motor Skills*, 1975, **41**, 555–585.

Sommer, R. *The mind's eye: Imagery in everyday life*. New York: Delacorte, 1978.

Speidel, G. E., & Pickens, A. L. Art, mental imagery, and cognition. In A. A. Sheikh & J. T. Shaffer (Eds.), *The potential of fantasy and imagination*. New York: Brandon House, 1979.

Spockes, P. M. Imagery and method in the Essay on Criticism. *Publication of the Modern Language Association*, 1970, **85**, 97–106.

Spranger, E. *Types of men* (P. W. Pigors, transl.). Haale (Saale): Max Neimeyer Verlag, 1928/1966.

Spurgeon, C. F. E. *Shakespeare's imagery and what it tells us*. London: Cambridge, 1935/1952.

Stetson, R. H. Types of imagination. *Psychological Review*, 1896, **3**, 398–411.

Swartz, P. Marcel Proust and the problem of time and place. *Psychological Reports*, 1978, **34**, 291–299.

Tatarkiewicz, W. *History of aesthetics*. The Hague: Mouton, 1970.

Tune, R. Imagery and logic: Ramus and metaphysical poets. *Journal of the History of Ideas*, 1942, **3/4**, 365–400.

Valentine, C. W. The function of images in the appreciation of poetry. *British Journal of Psychology*, 1923, **14**, 164–191.

Walkup, L. E. Creativity in science through visualization. *Perceptual and Motor Skills*, 1965, **21**, 35–41.

Wallas, R. *The art of thought*. New York: Harcourt, 1926.

White, K., Sheehan, P. W., & Ashton, R. Imagery assessment: A survey of self-report measures. *Journal of Mental Imagery*, 1977, **1**, 145–170.

Wilson, R. N. *The sociology and psychology of art*. Morristown, N.J.: General Learning Press, 1973.

Wolf, M. L. *Dictionary of the arts*. New York: Philosophical Library, 1951.

Wysong, P. A. A. An appraisal of oral interpretation theory in light of recent psychological research on mental imagery. *Dissertation Abstracts International*, 1979, **39**, 6398.

CHAPTER 16

Imagery and Sports

RICHARD M. SUINN

Psychological training in competitive athletics is gradually assuming new meaning. At one time, psychological training to the lay person had the connotations of "psyching up" or "psyching out." Psyching up an athlete conveys the notion of self-initiated or coach-initiated increase in motivational or activation level. A weightlifter might stare at the weights, building a feeling of intense hate or a sense of domination, until self-activation built to a peak level. A coach might employ a range of strategies to develop intensity in his or her team, sometimes depending on the old reliable Knute Rockne "win this one for the Gipper" ploy and, at other times, quietly posting derogatory quotations attributed to opponents. Whereas psyching up seems to be a precompetition exercise, psyching out may be employed during competition. It means that the athlete seeks to rely on knowledge of human psychology to put the opponent at an immediate psychological disadvantage. The boxer Ali who predicts the knockout round or the Olympic ski racer Klammer who casually lets rumors circulate that he has a specially engineered ski that is unbeatable is practicing psyching-out techniques. More recently, however, sports psychology has shifted from motivation, personality studies, and work on emotional states to a broader interest in psychological training that derives from modern psychological theory of behavior change. Two papers on sports performance theory illustrate this current outlook. Suinn (1980) begins with athletic performance itself and builds a conceptual model that links performance to psychological training goals (see Fig. 16.1). Performance is said to be the product of aptitude and skill acquisition. Skill acquisition is analyzed into three components: strengthening the correct responses; extinguishing or controlling incorrect responses; and transferring correct responses to game conditions. This model applies to skill acquisition in novices, and in persons at the recreational level, as well as to skill enhancement and development in experts or in athletes at the competitive level. The three components are in turn divided into subgoals; for example, correct responses may be the simple motor response of hitting the ball for a novice, or the moves of a new routine for a gymnast, diver, or figure skater. Some of the subgoals are strictly motor, some are ideomotor, and others are mainly

507

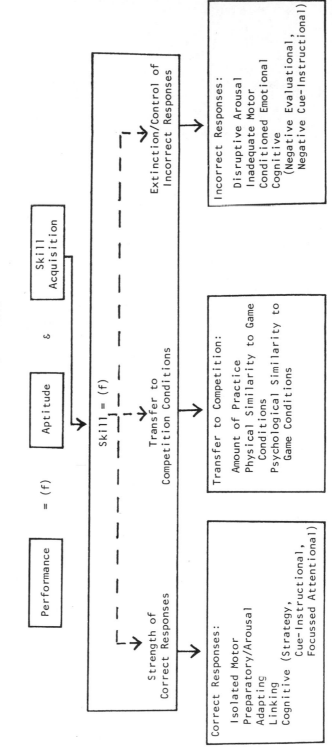

Figure 16.1. Factors affecting sports performance.

mental. The advantage of the model lies in determining from the goals or subgoals the appropriate training programs to introduce. For the subgoal of increasing preparatory–arousal responses, autogenic training or biofeedback might be used. For control of conditioned emotionality, applied relaxation methods or stress management procedures are appropriate. Imagery rehearsal techniques, the topic of this chapter, are particularly useful for goals of increasing transfer to competition and for enhancing certain correct responses.

Another theory of sports psychology is that due to Mahoney (1977). From a cognitive framework, he emphasizes the role of cognitive skills in athletic performance. From his own experiences and the work of others, he identifies four categories of cognitive skills: self-efficacy; arousal regulation; attentional focus; and imagery. Mahoney does not intend to provide a complete coverage of the psychological dimensions in performance but to highlight what he feels to be a much overlooked set of parameters. Similar to Suinn, he gives imagery a significant role as one of these parameters.

It is the purpose of this chapter to review what is known about imagery in sports performance. The next two major sections provide some information on mental rehearsal and a detailed review on imagery rehearsal. For the sake of clarity in this chapter, mental rehearsal and imagery rehearsal are separated, since the literature has not always been careful about this distinction. *Mental rehearsal* or *mental practice* has been defined in a way mainly to distinguish it from physical practice. Hence Corbin (1972, p. 94) defines mental practice as the "repetition of a task, without observable movement, with the specific intent of learning." This definition broadly encompasses any form of covert practice or symbolic rehearsal, including simply thinking through a motor action. *Imagery rehearsal*, on the other hand, is a more narrow term used here to mean covert practice where imagery is the dominant experience to achieve the rehearsal. With these two definitions in mind, we now proceed with information on the contributions of mental rehearsal and of imagery rehearsal to performance.

MENTAL REHEARSAL

Since there are already available systematic reviews on mental practice (Corbin, 1972; Oxendine, 1968; Richardson, 1967a, b), we briefly summarize conclusions from these reviews. In 1967 Richardson published a two-part series covering 25 studies on mental practice over a 30-year time span. By 1972, Corbin discovered and carefully evaluated over 50 studies of mental practice. These two reviewers, along with Oxendine, summarized the results of their analyses of research on imaginary practice, symbolic rehearsal, implicit practice, ideational functioning, introspective rehearsal, and conceptualization practice. Several conclusions have been drawn about the value of mental practice in influencing physical performance:

> Mental practice can lead to gains in motor performance, although it may not always do so. Richardson found 18 studies showing positive but three studies with negative results for mental practice; Corbin found that 26 of 50 studies showed mental practice gains, but he also found four where gains did not occur.

> Mental practice may result in below-threshold muscular responses associated with the overt performance of the skill being rehearsed. Both Oxendine and Corbin found such evidence in the research literature; this evidence was provided by significant electromyographic (EMG) tracings during mental rehearsal.

> Mental practice seems best used in combination with physical practice. The reviewers say that there is no firm evidence that exclusive use of mental practice would be superior to the exclusive use of physical practice. However, there is a trend for mental practice effects to be better when mental practice is alternated with physical practice.

Beyond the demonstration that mental practice can influence performance, there is also an emerging pattern of the variables that affect mental practice itself. These are based on studies that have investigated the role of the subjects' backgrounds, the nature of the task being rehearsed, and the type of mental practice program used. Some tentative conclusions are:

> Persons with experience in the task may profit more than novices. Beginners seem to profit more from physical practice, whereas varsity athletes are better able to use mental practice effectively.

> Simple motor tasks may be more readily enhanced through mental practice than complex tasks; but if the subject is experienced or trained in the complex task, mental practice can contribute further improvements in performance.

> There is some evidence that distributing rather than massing mental practice sessions increases their value. This is often achieved through alternating mental practice with physical practice sessions.

Overall, reviews of mental practice studies have led to optimistic conclusions; however, caution must be used. There is general agreement that mental practice can have a positive influence in the acquisition or the performance of a skill. On the other hand, research designs have been such that conclusive or consistent results have not always been possible. Most of the conclusions we have reported are trends across research studies. A major difficulty lies in the diverse methodologies used in the various studies. Tasks have ranged from card sorting to mirror drawing to dart throwing to basketball free throws. Studies have sometimes measured skill acquisition (new learning) and sometimes skill performance. Mental practice has sometimes involved thinking about the movements, sometimes attempting to experience the feelings associated with the movements ("kinesthetic imagery"), and sometimes simply attending to the total "gestalt" of the skill. The contribution of much of the already published research is that it points out the variables that will refine future research. The aims of researchers should be to:

Develop more replicated studies that control important variables, such as experience level of the subjects, the performance task being assessed, the exact instructions for setting up mental practice (and hence the content of the mental practice exercise), the time devoted to practice, the focus of the mental practice. (Does one concentrate on being relaxed, or on isolated movement, or on a sequence of coordinated movements, or on the end product such as accuracy?)

Develop a better framework for understanding the principles or theory of mental practice prior to the design of a study. Is it theorized that mental practice will have value because such practice strengthens the ideomotor–psychomotor associations? If so, tasks that require cognitive–muscular coordination should show greater gains. On the other hand, if mental practice is viewed as another way of "programming" kinesthetic muscle memory, such practice should prove as effective for simple motor tasks as for overlearned complex tasks.

Does the learning that derives from mental practice follow the usual laws of learning? If so, mental practice should involve a setting where the cues and required responses are as similar as possible to the criterion setting. This would argue for the use of imagery since imagery enables capturing more closely the conditions of performance.

Does the mental practice itself represent a skill? If imagery is important to mental practice, a person with poor control over imagery would also show poorer gains from mental practice using imagery. There is some evidence for this (Clark, 1960; Start & Richardson, 1964). The value of mental practice is thus influenced by the subject's level of skill in the mental practice process itself.

Is it possible that there is a right and a wrong type of mental practice content? We know that a person who physically "practices" an error will soon develop a habitual mistake or "bad habit" that may be very resistant to extinction and an obstacle to improvement. Perhaps novices may not do well on complex or unfamiliar tasks because they are actually rehearsing incorrect actions during their mental practice.

IMAGERY REHEARSAL

At this point it would be helpful to define the term "imagery" as used in this chapter. Imagery or *imagery rehearsal*, or what I have elsewhere called *visuomotor behavioral rehearsal* (VMBR) (Suinn, 1976), is a covert activity whereby a person experiences sensory–motor sensations that reintegrate reality experiences. Although the activity is usually, but not always,[1] performed with the eyes closed, there is evidence of motor, emotional, and physiological involvement during the imagery. For the sake of clarity, this chapter considers imagery as the covert experience and imagery rehearsal or VMBR as the technique of applying imagery to repetition of an activity, usually with the intent of improving the skill with which it is performed. Thus imagery is involved when an athlete reports having a flashback memory of a game-saving catch. Dreams, drug-induced hallucinatory experiences, or sensory memories reproduced by direct stimulation of the brain may be considered as forms of imagery. Imagery rehearsal refers to training in the use of imagery and is a skill whereby the individual gains control over the experience. In contrast to dreams, imagery rehearsal or VMBR activity is not random but subject to control in terms of what images are produced and what actions occur. The term "covert rehearsal" is sometimes used synonymously in certain behavior modification programs, for instance, in certain stages of covert sensitization, covert reinforcement, desensitization, implosion, or anxiety management training (Cautela, 1967, 1970; Stampfl & Levis, 1967; Suinn, 1977; Wolpe, 1958). In descriptions of these imagery rehearsal activities, the distinguishing feature seems to be the total reintegration of the experience. According to Suinn (1976, p. 41):

> The imagery of visuo-motor behavior rehearsal apparently is more than sheer imagination. It is a well-controlled copy of experience, a sort of body-thinking similar to the powerful illusion of certain dreams at night. Perhaps the major difference between such dreams and VMBR is that the imagery rehearsal is subject to conscious control.

Whereas mental rehearsal studies have included activities during which subjects closed their eyes, the instruction may have been, "Think about making that move" (e.g., throwing the dart). Imagery rehearsal goes beyond the isolated, one-dimensional thinking process; it is a more total retrieval of experience that is holistic and fully dimensional in sensations (Suinn, 1976, pp. 40–41):

> This imagery is more than visual. It is also tactile, auditory, emotional, and muscular. One swimmer reported that the scene in her mind changed from black and white to color as soon as she dove mentally into a pool, and she could feel the coldness of the water. A skier who qualified for the former U.S.

Alpine ski team experienced the same "irritability" that she felt during actual races, when she mentally practiced being in the starting gate. Without fail, athletes feel their muscles in action as they rehearse their sport. One professional racer who took the training actually moved his boots when skiing a slalom course in his mind.

The distinction between "thinking about" an action and using imagery to rehearse that action, is shown in electromyographic recordings obtained from a ski racer. As Figure 16.2 illustrates, no gastrocnemius muscle activity occurred when the subject was instructed to "think about skiing through those gates." However, when the instruction involved rehearsal, not only were there bursts of activity, but the activity matched that expected on the particular course being visualized (Suinn & Dickinson, 1978). Except for the element of control, the experience of imagery is akin to experiences during direct electrical stimulation of the human brain as reported by Penfield (1965): complex memories flood the person as sensory–motor–emotional experiences rather than as intellectual recall. In intellective recall, or remembering, a person may be able to reconstruct the situation, events, and emotional responses. However, the individual can easily be inaccurate in this reconstruction. During imagery rehearsal, the participant actually lives the situation anew and thus can actually be asked to observe and notice events. In working with a ski racer who had been disqualified on one run because he fell on the seventh gate, I asked for his explanation. In recalling the event, he firmly remembered that he fell because the condition of the snow differed in the area approaching the gate from the condition at the turn. However, when VMBR was used to retrieve the experience and he was asked to take notice of what was happening on that turn, the skier *observed*, "I have my weight on the wrong ski." The fact that thinking about or recalling a prior incident is different from experiencing the incident is demonstrated by some recent work on eidetic imagery in children. Haber (1980) presented children with eidetic imagery talents with two sketches, and after their removal, asked them to describe what they had observed by mentally putting them together.

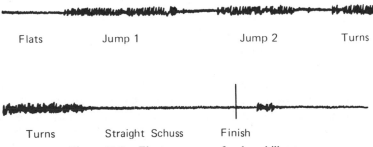

Figure 16.2.   Electromyogram for downhill racer.

Those with eidetic imagery were able to describe a face, whereas those without had to rely upon memory and could not reconstruct the end product.

In the sections to follow, we review what is known about imagery in sports performance. Discussion is limited to the literature that relates the use of imagery to enhance performance and is divided into a section on case studies and a section on group or experimental studies.

CASE REPORTS

Reports of this type tend to be variable in rigor, ranging from self-reports by well-known athletes to observational reports from consultants on changes following imagery rehearsal. They offer a kind of "grass roots," "folk medicine," and self-discovery background to the value of imagery rehearsal. Their validity is really a post hoc validity, a validity by association, rather than by controlled study. If an athlete uses imagery in training and if that athlete has achieved a level of success in his or her sport, some of the success must be due to imagery. Testimonials of this type actually do not add much to scientific support since too many problems surface when the information is examined more carefully. For example, is it possible that the athlete also was engaging in other training activities concurrent with mental training? Might a new weight training program or a change of technique or even equipment not be the more crucial factor? It is possible that the success is actually the final culmination of several years of effort with the one regime and that the addition of imagery rehearsal this year was coincidental to the success; for example, it takes several years for a professional quarterback to learn to read defenses, and the payoff of the cumulative learning happens to occur in the same year that he tries out imagery rehearsal. It is conceivable that just believing in the value of psychological training, along with the expectation of success, has a form of placebo effect and indirectly alters performance (Mahoney, 1977). And finally, how does one explain performances that are below par even while imagery rehearsal is being used? Clearly, the anecdotal reports or even reasonably detailed and careful case studies do not provide the answers. However, they do provide an encouraging preliminary introduction that might stimulate needed controlled research and study.

The literature uncovers a number of world-famous competitive athletes who attribute their success to imagery rehearsal. The gold medalist in three events, Alpine skier Jean Claude Killy, reports that the only preparation he had for one race was to mentally ski the course because an injury prevented on-snow practice. He believes that this race turned out to be one of his best performances. Jack Nicklaus, the omnipresent golf champion, writes about an imagery rehearsal method that he uses (Nicklaus, 1974). He first visualizes the ball landing on the green and actually seeing the bounce, then he visualizes the arc of the ball in flight, and then his swing and the ball leaving the ground. His final step is to link these together in proper sequence: visualizing the swing; the ball's trajectory; and its landing and bouncing on the green. The Olympic high jumper Dwight Stones is identified by his prejump preparation, during which his head can be seen bobbing in rhythm with his mental image of himself approaching and clearing the bar. Tennis player Chris Evert Lloyd, known for her consistent high-quality tournament strokes, revealed in a radio interview that she painstakingly rehearses the forthcoming match. She centers on anticipating her opponent's strategy and style and visualizes herself countering with her own attack (Lazarus, 1977). Bill Glass, a defensive end for the Cleveland Browns professional football team in the 1960s, attributes his achievement of becoming an "all-pro" in part to imagery. He learned to rehearse the quick-step across the line, throwing off the offensive tackle, and charging the retreating quarterback, as if it were in a "motion picture" (Furlong, 1979). Although some athletes, such as Glass, received training in imagery rehearsal from a consultant, many seem to have evolved the approach on their own or after hearing of the preparation from others. Following a demonstration to members of the U.S. Olympic Cross-Country team, one world class competitor challenged, "Visualizing is not new to me, I have done this before every race for years on my own . . . my problem is turning the scenes off."

According to a number of reports, imagery rehearsal has been systematically prescribed by sports consultants. These case reports differ from the testimonials previously reviewed in that the imagery rehearsal tended to be an intervention aimed at altering poor performance. In two cases some baseline data were available that permit comparisons between preintervention and postintervention performance. Titley (1976) was called in as a consultant to a university football team by its coach. Prior to VMBR training, the team's field goal kicker had missed three field goals from within 35 yards, and all of these had been very crucial to the outcome of the game. Visuomotor behavior rehearsal was initiated for stress management and to ingrain a standardized kicking motion (skill development). In the games following VMBR, this athlete began to improve his consistency and accuracy from greater distances. He became the leader in the conference in scoring, established 14 school records, and completed an NCAA field goal distance record of 63 yards.

Winning Associates (1978) provides a program including relaxation training, desensitization, mental coping, and imagery rehearsal. Among the individuals this group helped are: a bowler who averaged 185 before training and 215 after; a tennis player who won less than 20% of her matches prior to training and lost only one during the remainder of the season, and a college basketball player who improved from shooting 38% from the floor to 50% and 61% from the free-throw line to 90%.

GROUP OR EXPERIMENTAL STUDIES

On the whole, carefully controlled studies of imagery rehearsal effects have been difficult to find. Whereas mental rehearsal studies have leaned toward analogue studies subject to laboratory control, studies on imagery rehearsal (mainly VMBR) have been with competitive athletes less subject to laboratory control. A number of practical limitations are involved in studies of competitors. As is described later, one problem is obtaining a control group. If athletes are matched on skill level and if the coaching staff members are not uninformed or "blind" to the study, comparable data may be lacking. For example, if the outcome data are end-of-season rankings from meets, but if some athletes were entered while others were not, group comparisons may be impossible. Even if the coaches are uninformed about which athletes are being trained and which are "controls," some problems may develop. If the trained, or for that matter the control, athletes start to show improved performances, it will be the rare coach who still stays with the original agreement to enter all competitors in every meet in order to have an equivalent number of subjects in the experimental and in the control groups and thus to satisfy the researcher's needs. The coach needs to field the best team or best athletes; for, after all, the goal of the varsity team is to win games or meets, and the provision of research data under controlled conditions is only a secondary aim. Nevertheless, there have been some reasonably controlled group studies, and some general trends have emerged from less rigorous studies.

Imagery Rehearsal to Strengthen Correct Responses

Kolonay (1977) designed a master's thesis, using VMBR with 72 male basketball players from eight college basketball teams. The basketball teams were randomly assigned to four groups: group A received VMBR training (relaxation followed by imagery rehearsal); group B received relaxation training alone; group C received imagery rehearsal but without relaxation; and group D received no training. Training was provided through audiotape recordings in order to ensure standardized experiences. These recordings were played prior to each of 15 basketball practices, covering a 6-week period. The target behavior involved was free-throw shooting. The results were straightforward: the VMBR athletes increased their foul-shooting accuracy by 7%, a significant improvement not only statistically but also since, according to the coaches, it made the difference of eight more winning games in the season (Fensterheim, 1980). The relaxation-only and the imagery-rehearsal-only groups showed no change whatsoever. This is possibly the best designed study in print since there were two types of control group, a large sample size, and an avoidance of the problem of confounding since all members of a team were trained or not trained and thus individual coaching decisions of whom to play were avoided. The selection of the two types of control group derived from consultation between Kolonay and myself. It has been my contention that VMBR, which always begins with relaxation and then proceeds to imagery rehearsal, should be more beneficial than imagery rehearsal alone since the latter could be simply a version of the more intellective "thinking about making free throws." The results seem to confirm this hypothesis. It is also consistent with other data that relaxation alone, without training in how to use the relaxation under stress conditions, does not provide a consistent method for achieving stress management (Denney, 1980). If there had been some gains in the relaxation-only athletes, such results might mean that free-throw accuracy was helped by tension reduction rather than by the rehearsal value of VMBR.[2]

Lane (1978, 1980) initiated studies of basketball and baseball players using VMBR. Working with 16 members of a high-school basketball team, Lane divided them into two groups matched on free-throw percentage accuracy. One group was assigned to VMBR training, and the other received relaxation-only training. Unlike the athletes in Kolonay's study, these athletes were trained in six sessions over 3 weeks, prior to the competitive season. Baselines on free-throw accuracy were obtained over 3 days and compared with results obtained during the period of psychological training. Comparison of the VMBR group with the relaxation-only group showed no statistically significant differences, although the author reported a trend "in favor of the VMBR group" (Lane, 1978, p. 9). Unfortunately, no statistical comparisons were computed between baseline and posttreatment, although a figure in the manuscript suggests an improvement over baseline by both groups. This failure to show differential results between the two groups is inconsistent with the findings reported in the Kolonay study. Among the differences between the two studies are the differences in sample size and in age: Kolonay's study involved substantially more subjects and college-age athletes. Either difference could explain the inconsistency in results. It is interesting to note that Lane adds that his subjects did not feel that relaxation itself was of much help in improving their free-throw shooting.

In a follow-up, Lane provided VMBR training to three starters on the basketball team, whereas three other starters refused such training and hence formed a natural control group. Visuomotor behavior rehearsal training continued "at various times during the competitive season" (Lane, 1978, p. 11). Direct comparison between the VMBR and the control group on improvement in free-throw accuracy, from the previous season to the current season, showed a trend favoring the VMBR group, but the results did not reach statistical significance. However, with the use of χ^2 analyses, the VMBR subjects showed significant increase in free-throw accuracy ($p = .05$) when their previous year's performances were compared with the current (VMBR) year's effort; similar analyses for the control group did not reach significance. For the VMBR athletes, there was a 12% increase in free-throws made; whereas the control subjects showed a decrease over the same time period. Further analyses showed that the VMBR players demonstrated a greater increase in accuracy on "away" games than on "home" games, leading Lane to conclude that "under the most extreme conditions of competition . . . (of away games) the advantages of VMBR training become most clearly evident" (Lane, 1978, p. 3, 6).

In some further follow-up work with baseball players, Lane administered the Rotter (1966) I–E scale, which assesses internal versus external locus of control. He found a significant biserial correlation of 0.95 ($p = .02$) between the I–E scores and coach's rating of improvement shown by the athletes over the season. Specifically, the VMBR-trained athletes who improved the most over the season showed low external scores, whereas the VMBR-trained athletes who decreased in athletic performance showed high external scores. Since the sample size was small ($n = 5$), this finding must be viewed with caution, although the implication is interesting. Finally, Lane asked his subjects to personally evaluate the effectiveness of the VMBR training. He then discovered that image clarity and ability to develop imagery of actually performing (as opposed to "watching oneself from afar") were related to self-reports of the effectiveness of the VMBR training.

Noel (1980) recruited male tennis players entered in a tournament ($n = 14$) and formed a VMBR and a control group. To determine their baseline performance levels, all subjects played one set of tennis, during which measures of service accuracy and points played were obtained. Subjects differed in levels of skill and were grouped as "high ability" and "low ability" for later analyses. The VMBR training involved seven sessions of relaxation and visualizing of tennis serves. Instructions and training were provided by audio tapes, lasting approximately 30 minutes per session. The total training process was completed 10 days prior to the first tournament match. In VMBR imagery, the subjects were specifically helped to visualize themselves arriving at the match site, warming up, practicing serves, observing any service errors, and making corrections on the service. The data compared baseline performance against performance during the first set in the tournament for each subject. Analysis of covariance showed that high-ability VMBR subjects improved on service accuracy from baseline, whereas low-ability VMBR subjects worsened. This was consistent with self-report data in which high-ability VMBR subjects rated their serves as better during the tournament match, and control subjects rated their serves as worse during the tournament match. Furthermore, the low-ability VMBR subjects rated themselves lower on their service accuracy than the control subjects. Although the VMBR aimed only at improving service accuracy, data also were obtained on points played. A point was rated as a "winner" if the shot placement was so difficult that the opponent could not position himself or herself for a good return. A point was rated as an "error" if the player was in a position to make a shot but did not. Data were reported in terms of the ratio of winners to errors. They showed that high-ability VMBR subjects tended to have a higher number of winners than errors in comparison to high-ability control subjects; however, low-ability VMBR subjects tended to show a lower ratio in comparison with low-ability control subjects. These data suggest that imagery rehearsal alone does not guarantee improvement, and they are consistent with the earlier mental rehearsal research on the influence of player skill level on performance. As we stated earlier, it is possible that the higher-skill-level athlete uses VMBR to overlearn correct behaviors already in the repertoire. On the other hand, without careful guidance, the lower-ability athlete might actually be rehearsing incorrect behaviors and thus become worse rather than better. Another possibility is that differences in ability to control the imagery might have occurred, so that the subject is unable to visualize the correct behaviors. An early study by Clark (1960) discovered that not all subjects were able to control their imagery in practicing basketball free throws. In fact, one subject reported that his basketball would not bounce but stuck to the floor in his imagery rehearsal. Clark reported that, as subjects reported gains in their ability to visualize and to control their imagery, they experienced gains in self-confidence and in the ability to identify errors in their behaviors.

Nideffer (1971) used VMBR with AAU competitive divers in rehearsing the technical aspects of their dives, including body movement, relationship of body position to the position of the water, and so on. The VMBR procedure was practiced both at home and at the start of pool practice for about 10 minutes. The VMBR practice was continued for one month, during which data were obtained on total numbers of dives executed during practice, on number of new dives attempted, and on self-report of anxiety. Nideffer reports that there were more dives completed in practice following VMBR, even though some of the time was now taken up by VMBR. There were also increases in the total number of new dives attempted and a decrease in reported anxiety. These data could be interpreted to mean that VMBR practice increased the confidence of the divers in their abilities.

Kirchenbaum and Bale (1980) examined the benefits of a broad-based psychological training (BPG) program that included relaxation and imagery rehearsal, self-monitoring, and the use of positive self-instruction. Because of their initial success with one varsity golf team in a prior year, the researchers were given further access to the next year's team as subjects. In fact, the coach had been so impressed by the gains (his golfer went on to win several tournaments) that he used the opportunity for psychological training as inducement during recruitment of new players. The subjects of the study had to meet two criteria: they had to be on the varsity squad in the university; and they had to have no previous experience with psychological training. These criteria limited the research to three subjects since the other three starters on the squad had some experience with the training during the prior year. Because of the small sample size ($n = 3$), a multiple baseline across subjects research design was used. The first competitive round of 18 holes each was used to obtain a baseline on all subjects. Subject 1 was then provided with BPG training; and his later performances were recorded. Subject 2 was required to wait until three more rounds of competition were complete before being offered BPG training; this method provided an extended baseline. Subject 3 was a control subject who did not participate in the training. By this research design, it was expected that Subject 1 would show an improvement in performance starting from the date of exposure to BPG training (called *Period 1*), whereas no changes were expected in Subject 2 or Subject 3 over this same period. During Period 2, the period following the introduction of Subject 2 to psychological training, it was expected that this subject also would show improvements in performance, whereas Subject 3 would still show no gains and Subject 1 would continue to retain his prior gains. The results tended to confirm these predictions. Subject 1 showed an improvement by reducing his golf scores by two strokes; and Subject 2 showed no improvement during Period 1 but then reduced his scores by one stroke in Period 2. Subject 3, contrary to expectation, showed a one-stroke improvement during Period 1 but relapsed to his baseline during Period 2. An evaluation of the relative merits of each part of the BPG training showed that imagery rehearsal and self-monitoring received the highest ratings; relaxation was next; and positive self-instruction was last. It should be noted that the authors observed the level of improvement to fluctuate over the season. This may have been a function of the insufficient training time since the program was limited to one instructional session, followed later by one to three follow-up meetings. This is quite short when compared, for example, to the Kolonay training period. Finally, the authors correctly call attention to the unique problem of assessing improvement in this sport. Is a one- or two-stroke change substantial enough to be considered "improvement"? Kirschenbaum and Bale (1980, p. 338) reply by noting that a "one-stroke differential in mean 18-hole performance separated Jack Nicklaus from a player who earned $100,000 less than Nicklaus in 1976." This issue of outcome evaluation will remain a difficult one for what is essentially field research with competitive athletic performance. Studies outside of the laboratory thus far have used well-trained athletes rather than novices. One reason, of course, is that varsity level competitors have sufficient skill to be able to rehearse the correct responses in imagery rehearsal, instead of inadvertently rehearsing incorrect responses. However, working with athletes of this level means that the baseline performance level is already high and statistically less subject to change. Kolonay's basketball players started at a baseline of 68% free-throw accuracy; had the starting level been 50%, improvements might have been more dramatic. Consider the improvement possible for a person high jumping 6'2" prior to training versus the improvement realistically probable for a person already jumping 7'2". Finally, different sports have different scoring systems, and this will affect research. For example, compare the obvious difference between the spread of outcome measures of a marathon race (the New York Marathon was competied in 2 hours to 7 hours) and that of a single gymnastic or diving event (with scores of 1–10).

Imagery Rehearsal to Eliminate Incorrect Responses

Instead of using imagery rehearsal to practice and strengthen the correct behaviors, imagery might be employed to eliminate incorrect responses. One set of incorrect responses is the conditioned emotional reaction (see Fig. 16.1), namely, anxiety. Although applied relaxation, desensitization, anxiety management training, and stress innoculation are all direct methods for controlling anxiety, Bennett and Stothart (1978) used VMBR with their athletes. Subjects were 44 athletes on teams in four sports: gymnastics, archery, wrestling, and badminton. In addition to relaxation, the treated sample used VMBR to practice cognitive controls over anxiety. The cognitive skills practiced included identifying the presence of anxiety, remembering how to cope, confronting the stress by relaxing, and initiating self-reinforcing statements for progress (Meichenbaum & Cameron, 1974). Control subjects spent an equal time engaged in tasks unrelated to stress control or sports performance, such as card sorting. Anxiety was measured through the Spielberger State–Trait Anxiety Inventory (STAI). Training covered seven sessions. Analysis of variance reached significance for the comparison of pre- to posttest scores, and the results were not significant across groups, but the interaction "just failed to reach the conventional level of significance ($p < .05$)" (Meichenbaum & Cameron, 1974, p. 10). In further analysis, the authors discovered that the VMBR group had a higher pretest level of anxiety than the control group; however, since the authors did not report an analysis of covariance, it is not known whether group differences could have existed. Through inspection, the authors do conclude that the VMBR group showed "a decline in post-treatment state anxiety scores while the control group did not" (Meichenbaum & Cameron, 1974, p. 11). The study also analyzed coaches' ratings of sports performances that had been videotaped before and after treatment. Results were not statistically significant. The authors observe that this lack of marked improvement could have been due to the fact that subjects already were at a skill level sufficiently high that improvements in technique would not be noticeable. They also suggest the possibility that the videotape condition did not represent stress, and hence improvements related to stress reduction could not be ascertained. Two other possibilities also exist. One is that the evidence of gains following stress reduction might be best measured, not in technique in practice, but in outcome measures, such as consistency or reduction in errors under game conditions. Finally, it is possible that the lack of results simply means that the VMBR rehearsal of cognitive anxiety reduction skills either is not useful or that the cognitive skills are not helpful in anxiety reduction.

Gravel et al. (1980) also used VMBR as the mechanism to eliminate incorrect responses. The incorrect responses are the negative evaluational or negative cue–instructional cognitive responses identified by Suinn (1980; see also Fig. 16.1) and include feeling inferior to other racers, thinking about pain, and being preoccupied with race conditions. Visuomotor behavior reversal was used to develop competitive scenes where such ruminations would occur, and subjects were trained to use thought stopping to control these ruminations. Subjects were 12 members of a university cross-country ski team, randomly assigned to the VMBR or the placebo control group. The placebo group watched films of ski racing, and were asked to freely associate on words unrelated to racing and, then to discuss the results. Results indicated that the VMBR group showed a statistically significant decrease in the frequencies of interfering ruminations ($p = < .01$), whereas the placebo group showed no significant changes. Two ancillary findings are important. First, the reported reduction in ruminations occurred mainly between posttest (end of treatment) and follow-up (21 days after treatment ended). The authors suggest that the athletes consolidated their gains during follow-up as a result of *in vivo* competitive experiences. Second, the athletes reported that VMBR aided them in focusing on their body state during a race and that doing so was helpful. This practice is similar to the "associative" running reported by Morgan (1978), which he found to be characteristic of the better elite runners. In associative runners, attention is focused on "reading" feedback from muscle groups, respiration, and other physiological signs in order to adopt an appropriate pace. Hence, although the work with the cross-country racers began with the objective of removing an interfering cognitive response, it also had the result of training the athletes in acquiring an adaptive response.

Desiderato and Miller (1979) used a combination of VMBR and stress innoculation in a single-subject design with a tennis player. The subject was an experienced tournament competitor on a local and regional club level, but he reported persistent anxiety and frequent negative evaluations. Examples of negative cognitions and verbalizations were thoughts or statements such as, "You blew it!" "Damn dummy!" or "Why did you do that?". The VMBR training emphasized playing a crucial point two alternate ways, each ending in winning the point. The one way involved the subject serving and then playing out the winning point. The other way involved the subject receiving the serve and then playing out the point to win. Stress innoculation (Meichenbaum, 1977) involves the preparation and use of positive self-instructional statements ("Stay cool"), constructive self-statements to cope with errors ("O.K., you double faulted, concentrate on the next serve"), and self-reinforcing statements ("That's the way to do it, stay in control!"). Since the subject appeared to do worse in competitive matches than in social playing during baseline, data were collected on both competitive and social games. During three baseline weeks, the percentage of deuce games won actually was higher for noncompetitive games than competitive matches, 49% versus 29%. After 1 week of the intervention program, the subject was winning 55% of noncompetitive games and 60% of competitive games. In addition, the subject reported a disappearance of "feelings of disaster" that previously often had preceded matches, an increase in confidence, and an eagerness for competitive challenges.

Schleser et al. (1980) also used a combination of VMBR and cognitive techniques to help correct performances in two women collegiate basketball players. One was a center who needed help with her free-throw shooting, and the other was a forward who wanted help on her field goal shooting. First the subjects used relaxation training and imagery to practice successful behaviors, that is, accurate free throws or field goals. Then they used imagery rehearsal to visualize an unsuccessful scene, and next they rehearsed stress innoculation and self-instructional statements. Later, the athletes used relaxation, imagery rehearsal, and self-instructional statements just prior to physical practice on the basketball court. Two types of comparative data became available. Since the basketball center wanted help only with free throws and the forward wanted help only on field goals, the imagery rehearsal training for the center was limited to free throws, and for the forward it was limited to field goals. This permitted each person to be her own control: free throws versus field goals could be compared for each subject. The center's free-throw accuracy (the behavior treated) improved from a baseline of 41.3 to 54.8%; in contrast, her field goal accuracy (the untreated behavior) remained relatively constant, changing from 48.9 and 47.8%. The forward's field goal accuracy (the treated behavior) improved from 36.7 to 52.2%; in contrast, her free-throw accuracy (the untreated behavior) changed from 67.9 to 68.0%. Another type of comparison was possible because the center discontinued involvement in the intervention program after 6 weeks but before the season ended. Hence a multiple baseline with a reversal design was possible, involving a 7-game baseline, a 13-game intervention period, and an 11-game reversal after intervention was discontinued. On free-throw accuracy the three-percentage-accuracy figures were 41.3, 54.8, and 28.6%; this shows the expected improvement during intervention and decline during reversal on the treated behavior. For the untreated behavior of field goal accuracy, the figures were 48.9, 47.8, and 54.7%. Although the data did not reach statistical significance, the trends were in the predicted directions and were supported by self-reports from the athletes about the efficacy of the training. Reversal designs generally involve operant reinforcement training, where the reversal comes from the withholding of the reinforcer and where the newly acquired behavior returns to the level prior to training. In this report the reversal really means the discontinuation of practice with VMBR and with cognitive controls, rather than the removal of reward. If these methods helped in increasing the basketball skills they were meant to correct, a reversal would not be expected since the methods do not apply a reinforcement model. Instead, it would appear that the decline represents a motivational change; the skill level remained the same, but the athlete's desire to perform decreased. This is supported by the decline of percentage accuracy to 28.6%, far below the baseline skill level. In addition, it is interesting to note that the center discontinued the program because she became bored with the repetitiousness of the training. Therefore, the authors point out the importance of designing changes in the interventions, perhaps by increasing the fading to self-control of the techniques.

A laboratory study by Suinn et al. (1980) used VMBR to train members of a university cross-country (track) team in "how to run relaxed" during an event. Subjects were initially eight VMBR and eight controls. Training began with relaxation training, followed by VMBR with imagery involving identifying muscle signs of tenseness in running and cues for running more relaxed. Subjects were encouraged to employ the more relaxed style during in vivo training and in between VMBR sessions. Total training in VMBR covered eight sessions. This study is similar to the previous two studies in the use of imagery rehearsal to practice behaviors not usually associated with the techniques of the sport itself but that theoretically could enhance performance. In this case, it was predicted that running more relaxed would lead to greater physiological efficiency since less effort would be employed. Physiological and self-report measures were used. Subjects were tested on a standard treadmill, providing oxygen consumption (Vo_2) and heart rate (HR) data, as well as the anaerobic threshold (AT) of each athlete. The AT served as the baseline for equating the workload at posttesting across athletes; for example, each athlete was later tested at a treadmill workload equal to 75% of his or her AT. This method is equivalent to matching subjects on pretest scores and permits using each subject as his or her own baseline control. The self-report measure was the Borg Perceived Exertion Scale: the athlete assigns a numerical value to his or her estimate of the effort being required on the treadmill. Prior to posttesting, a number of control subjects were unavailable, and hence a trained control group comparison was not possible. However, with the AT design, it was possible to compare each trained athlete against his or her own baseline. Subjects ran for 10 minutes to establish a baseline for each workload level (e.g., 10 minutes at 75% AT) and were then instructed to "run relaxed" for 10 minutes. Results from the first 10 minutes were then compared against results of the second 10 minutes. Results showed that the three women runners showed a significant mean decrease in HR from the first to the second 10 minutes, at the 65% AT workload ($p = .05$). On individual athletes, a trend analysis comparing the slopes of measurements for the first 10 minutes versus the second 10 minutes reached significance for two athletes at the 65% AT, 75% AT, and 85% AT levels of effort, on Vo_2 consumption. The trend was for Vo_2 consumption to decrease during the second 10 minutes. On the Perceived Effort measure, the VMBR trained subjects rated the second 10 minutes as requiring less effort, whereas the two remaining control subjects in the study rated the second 10 minutes as requiring more effort. It should be kept in mind that the treadmill test was kept at the same workload throughout. The results of this study were encouraging especially since they were obtained by a more direct assessment of the possible impact of imagery rehearsal on a performance measure than self-report. The previously reported research on cross-country racers did collect performance data in terms of race results, but the authors did not calculate any statistical analyses because the subjects differed from one another in sex and age level and hence did not run comparable events. The current study on treadmill performance adds some information on performance, even though the performance is not directly associated with running a race. Nevertheless, the change in heart rate and the decrease in oxygen consumption, were in keeping with the hypothesis that running relaxed is more efficient and that VMBR can aid in the acquisition of this style. The data do not answer the question as to whether race results, such as times, also would show improvement; however, anecdotally, one of the female athletes had the best season she ever had experienced. Also not explained is the difference between the individual athlete's results. Not all athletes improved from the training; there was a tendency for the women to show greater gains than the men. It is important to note that the results of relaxation on physiological efficiency are consistent with those produced by the work of Benson et al. (1978). Finally, it is noteworthy that one of the athletes in the current study participated in VMBR with her eyes open. She indicated that she had no problem visualizing with her eyes open and that she preferred to do this because it resembled reality more closely, since she runs a race with her eyes open. Observationally, the VMBR trainer (Suinn) did not perceive any obstruction to VMBR in this athlete because she had her eyes open; in fact, she showed reductions in oxygen consumption and in heart rate on posttesting.

One study illustrates the problems of attempting to do controlled research with varsity athletes during a competitive year. Suinn (1972) matched Alpine ski racers on skill levels prior to the race season and assigned one of each matched pair to the VMBR program and the other to a no-treatment control group. However, although the coach earlier had agreed to race all subjects during the season, in fact, he raced only those who displayed on-snow improvements. It turned out that only one of the control subjects (but all of the VMBR subjects) was entered in the season's meets. What began as a well-controlled study, with race results being the outcome variable from matched samples, ended as a group study with a control comparison. One could consider the coach's decision as data in itself; however, since the coach was not blind to the study, his decision may well have been subject to confounding.

Imagery in Imagery Rehearsal

To conclude the review of research efforts, a look at a number of studies on imagery itself is useful. These studies tended to survey athletes about their use of imagery rehearsal. Mahoney and Avener (1977) administered a questionnaire to the finalists at the Olympic trials in gymnastics in 1976. The questionnaire covered personality, self-concept, psychological strategies, stress, and cognitive activities. Point biserial correlations were calculated between questionnaire results and final standings in the trials (selection for the Olympics versus not qualifying). Although not reaching statistical significance, a correlation of -0.51 between type of imagery and final standing was reported. This result indicated that Olympic qualifiers used more "internal" than "external" perspective in their imagery rehearsals. All the athletes reported using imagery extensively, but the qualifiers were inside their bodies "experiencing those sensations which might be expected in actual situations" (Mahoney & Avener, 1977, p. 137) instead of viewing themselves from the outside as in "home movies."

Meyers et al. (1979) repeated the use of the Mahoney–Avener questionnaire with members of a university racquetball team. The subjects were nine members of the racquetball team who had been national champions during 3 of the last 4 years. Outcome assessment included the coach's rankings of the players at various points in the competitive season and performance measures from the championships. Performance measures included the number of rounds the athlete won and point scores during the championships. Finally, since season performance was associated with divisional ranking, this ranking also was used in the statistical analyses. In other words, skill level was assessed by the coach's rankings, by divisional rankings, and by performance during the state championships. Meyers et al. discovered that the better players were those who had greater clarity of imagery ($r = -.70$, $p = .05$, coach ranking; $r = -.62$, $p = .05$, divisional ranking). Also, the better athletes reported less difficulty in controlling their imagery rehearsal ($r = .51$, divisional ranking). In general, differences in the performance measures did not appear to be associated with differences on many of the questionnaire variables. In fact, there was a suggestion that lesser difficulty in controlling imagery was associated with poorer performance (the manuscript is somewhat unclear on this since details on the computations were not reported). Given the high caliber of the team members (e.g., four members held national titles) and hence the narrow spread of skill levels, it is not surprising that performance measures were not very useful in this study. In fact, it is surprising that Mahoney and Avener and Meyers et al. obtained any differences at all with such highly skilled subjects. There are two possible interpretations of these findings on such subjects. One is that the findings may be nongeneralizable and limited to only the most well-trained competitors, to those who are so skilled in the physical aspects of their sport that the psychological one now becomes a critical distinguishing factor. Indeed, I have often heard coaches of U.S. Olympic teams say exactly this. Another interpretation would be that the role of imagery rehearsal or imagery perspective might turn out to be even more substantial with less proficient performers. This hypothesis is based on the report by Lane (1980) that concentration was listed as a primary contribution of VMBR and the observations by Gravel et al. (1980) that body awareness replaced ruminations about failure. However, these effects of imagery rehearsal often are viewed as obstacles to improved performances by recreational-level athletes. Obviously, these interpretations are speculative. The clear implication is that further research is needed. Are there differences in the frequency of use of imagery rehearsal among skilled versus novice competitors? Are such differences related to the differences in performance? Will performance improve if the athlete is trained to use imagery rehearsal more frequently? What is the best content and perspective for imagery rehearsal? What is the best training format for imagery rehearsal programming?

Doyle and Landers (1980) revised the Mahoney–Avener questionnaire and administered it to 184 rifle and pistol shooters. Two major skill groups were involved: an elite and a subelite. The elite competitors were adults who participated in the U.S. International Shooting Championships in Arizona in 1979; the subelite competitors were state- and junior-level champions who had attended a Junior Olympic Shooting Camp at the Colorado Springs Olympic Training Center in 1979. In examining the discriminant ability of 13 variables in order to separate elite from subelite performers, self-confidence was by far the major factor. However, the greater use of mental imagery in training and in competition turned out to also be one of four other relevant factors. The authors also discovered that elite rifle shooters used predominantly internal imagery, whereas subelite rifle shooters used a mixture of internal and external imagery. Once again, it is surprising that differences can be found among persons of high-caliber level, since even a subelite competitor has clearly reached a high performance level. Doyle and Landers also report an analysis of the 31% of the competitors who were misclassified by the discriminant analysis; they found that 69% of these persons were on the broderlines of their classifications as either elite or subelite. The brief report does not give details on the exact statistical procedures. However, this conclusion is again a surprising support for the hypothesis that variables, such as confidence and imagery rehearsal, relate to performance. The strong evidence for confidence points out some of the issues yet to be resolved in studies of this type of research design. Does the relationship between self-confidence and the elite level mean that confidence is a causative factor in achieving elite performances, or is it a consequence of the high-level achievement? The same issue develops in interpreting the association between mental imagery rehearsal and skill status. We are unable to determine whether there is a true cause–effect relationship.

Epstein (1980) attempted to design a controlled study of the influence of imagery as a result of the Mahoney–Avener finding on the importance of internal imagery. She trained 30 persons in dart throwing with a combination of mental rehearsal and internal imagery and another 30 persons with mental rehearsal and external imagery. When compared against a control group, neither type of mental-rehearsal training seemed to make a difference in performance. In effect, two conclusions may be considered: mental rehearsal is not beneficial in improving performance, and neither internal nor external imagery in mental practice contribute to improving performance. However, on the basis of the training technique involved, this study should be properly classified as a *mental practice* study rather than a study of *imagery rehearsal*. Subjects were simply instructed to "try to relax" and then to "imagine these scenes" (Epstein, 1980, p. 214). The dominant theme of the instructions from the experimenter was encouragement or urging: "Try to see . . . ," "Try to shut out all sounds," "It is important that . . . your imaginary scene . . . is . . . vivid . . . ." In contrast, during imagery rehearsal procedures the person usually is trained in relaxation, and then imagery is initiated and control is practiced across several sessions and feedback is obtained on the clarity of and the control over the imagery. In the Epstein experiment, the entire process took 1 hour; this period probably is too short to enable any subject to convert the mental practice instructions into an imagery rehearsal process. That is, it seems unlikely that a person can learn to relax or to develop controlled imagery during this brief exposure. It is noteworthy that Start and Richardson (1964) discovered that vividness and control of imagery were important in mental practice effects. Among gymnasts, those with vivid and controlled imagery showed the best gains from mental practice. They were followed by those with less vivid controlled imagery, then by those with less vivid uncontrolled imagery, and finally by those with vivid uncontrolled imagery. Again, it appears that imagery rehearsal should be viewed as a skill that needs to be gained before subjects can gain from its use. In addition, it seems important that skill in developing imagery (as measured by vividness) is combined with the right image content (as seen in control); otherwise incorrect responses may be rehearsed.

Suinn and Andrews (1981) also surveyed a group of highly proficient competitors, members of a professional Alpine ski tour. Subjects were members of either the more elite "A" level or the "B" level. The survey was administered by a member of the A circuit, a former president of the skiers association, in the form of a questionnaire. The questionnaire had different goals from the Mahoney–Avener survey, but a few items were similar. Although there was no evidence that the racers differed in frequency of imagery rehearsal, there was a suggestion that the better skiers' imagery was more vivid and clear. Vividness ranged from "experiencing sensations of being once again in the race" to "thinking about being on the course." No trends were found on internal versus external perspective during imagery rehearsal. Significant differences ($p = .05$) were found on negative thoughts.

These studies on the parameters of imagery as they relate to performance and use of imagery rehearsal are only beginning steps rather than sophisticated designs. Thus far, the more common model for the research has been the selection of persons whose group identity (members of a competitive team) suggests the possession of characteristics that may be important for skill acquisition or skill enhancement. By examining these characteristics, hypotheses may be generated for future testing. Each study has compared the elite performers with those of less skill in order to further tease out the

characteristics. However, as pointed out before, the actual differences between the final Olympic team members and the nonqualifiers is clearly much
smaller than between the nonqualifiers and the majority of amateur athletes
who compete on varsity teams but who do not even receive an invitation to
the Olympic trials! On the other hand, even with such a limitation on research
design, the fact that some dimensions of imagery and imagery rehearsal are
being uncovered is promising. Inconsistencies are evident. Mahoney and
Avener identified internal perspective as important; this was not confirmed
by the studies of Meyer et al., Doyle and Landers, Epstein, or Suinn and
Andrews. Meyers et al., and Suinn and Andrews reported that clarity of
imagery was helpful, but Mahoney and Avener did not support this. Meyers
et al. and Start and Richardson found controllability of imagery rehearsal
associated with better standings, but for Meyers et al., this was apparently
associated with lower actual performance in the state championships. Mahoney and Avener conclude that there was little clear correlation between
control of imagery rehearsal and final standing (the actual correlation was
$-.34$). Meyers et al. and Doyle and Landers discovered less skilled competitors to harbor more self-doubts about their abilities, and Suinn and Andrews discovered the lower skilled skiers to have more negative interfering
thoughts; however, Mahoney and Avener's data, obtained from their work
with gymnasts, do not confirm this. It is noteworthy that Gravel's group
used VMBR with apparent success to control negative ruminations in cross-
country racers. The restricted range of the athlete sample (across individual
skill differences) is a possible explanation of such inconsistencies. But there
are other possible research design explanations. First, it is conceivable that
there are across-sport differences. Modern theory about the relationship
between activation–arousal level and performance suggests that very low
arousal may be optimum for golf performance, but that much higher arousal
may be ideal for weight lifting. This theory takes into account across-sport
differences on skill enhancement factors instead of simply personality factors. The discrepancies across studies of imagery may, therefore, relate to
differences in imagery requirements demanded for skill enhancement by each
sport. Second, the inconsistencies may reflect a more basic measurement
problem. Questionnaires may be viewed either as a source of information
in a hypothesis-forming way or as an actual assessment-measuring device.
In other words, the questionnaire can survey various characteristics, and
the following statistical comparisons that are computed highlight differences
that may be further evaluated. The approach resembles that used in a census;
namely, that conclusions may be drawn about hypothesized characteristics
of different people, but the strength of such conclusions are determined in
part by the sampling methodology, for example, the sample size, the means
for ensuring representativeness, and so on. However, if a questionnaire is
used as a measuring instrument equivalent to a test, the requirements of
psychometrics must be considered. These include data on reliability or errors
of measurement, validity, and normative information. Thus far the studies

of the elite athletes have not provided any of these data. Hence it is indeed possible that differences in results may be due to differences in the assessment properties of the questionnaires. Specifically, discrepancies may represent reliability differences rather than real differences across the subject populations. There may well be an interaction between reliability of the questionnaires and sampling, that is, the very small sample sizes used in the studies.

CONCLUDING STATEMENTS

To conclude this chapter, a few final statements are in order. Thus far the studies on the potential value of imagery rehearsal in athletics are promising. At the minimum, they have yielded results that are consistent with those of prior reports on the value of mental rehearsal, but the evidence is not conclusive. Controlled studies are rare. Findings tentatively support the *apparent* value of imagery rehearsal in skill enhancement among proficient athletes. It is hoped that more substantial improvements will be documented, and with larger sample sizes. A number of different goals have been targeted by imagery rehearsal, including strengthening correct responses, reducing incorrect responses, and increasing transfer of training from practice to game conditions. The work of Kolonay, Lane, Noel, and Nideffer was directed at improving the correct skills associated with accuracy. Bennett and Stothart aimed at reducing the incorrect responses of conditioned emotionality associated with stress. The studies of Gravel et al., Desiderato and Miller, and Schleser et al. aimed at controlling the incorrect responses that were negative evaluational or negative-cue instructional cognitions; and it is consistent with the findings of Meyers et al. and Suinn and Andrews that negative ruminations are associated with lower performances. The case reports by Winning Associates contain a discussion of the use of imagery rehearsal to enable an athlete who "chokes during competition" to better transfer the skill shown in practice to competitive conditions. Suinn has used VMBR for a variety of specific goals: "to practice technique, to practice strategy, to practice a general approach (e.g., being aggressive), to prepare so well for a difficult part of a course that the right moves are ingrained (overlearning), to build confidence, or just to obtain a sense of being familiar with the course by reason of rehearsing it so often" (Suinn, 1980, p. 35). Also, he has used imagery rehearsal to enable an athlete to identify an error in technique, and given this new information, to correct the error by preparing for the unfamiliar or unexpected and by training in concentration, stress management, and transfer of learning (Suinn, 1976, 1979, in press). Given the variety of goals that may be attained by VMBR, it becomes evident that imagery rehearsal is a tool. Research on whether the tool is useful must take into account the expertise of the user of the tool, the work (goal) to which the tool is applied, and the nature of the job demands. Certainly, imagery rehearsal is available for use to nearly anyone who has access to the literature

and who is willing to conduct imagery rehearsal sessions, either for others
or for himself or herself. Audio tapes and written instructions are available,
and indeed, the primary objective of a program may well be self-directed
training. However, information is needed on whether imagery rehearsal is
enhanced or obstructed by the person providing the experience. Is the technique a skill in itself, so that an athlete must be *trained* in imagery rehearsal?
If so, better-quality training and greater length in training could make a
difference in outcome. Also to be considered is the issue of the work required. Obviously, imagery rehearsal can be applied for skill enhancement
through rehearsal of performance. But what part of the performance should
be practiced? What should an athlete be instructed to rehearse: propriocep-
tive feedback in the movement; one part of the total or the entire move;
focusing on externals or intervals; emphasizing concentration without attention to the body mechanics; or dissociating? The value of the coach lies
in providing advice on the best content when the imagery is applied to
physical technique practice, as opposed to psychological skill training. Indeed, it may well be possible to rehearse incorrect behaviors and errors,
rather than correct responses, and thereby to reduce performance rather
than to enhance it. Finally, the "job demands" in the use of a tool may
mean, in terms of imagery rehearsal, the overall level of demands being
faced by the participant. A highly proficient athlete has the basic physical
and technique skills so overlearned that his or her new learning task may
be limited to the acquisition of psychological skills. On the other hand, a
beginner may be faced with an overwhelming set of demands including
emotional control, lower body technique, upper-body technique, balance,
coordinated motion, concentration, timing, and retrieval of short-term-mem-
ory instructional data. The proper application of imagery rehearsal may be
a much more complex issue: What should the primary target behaviors or
goals be for rehearsal? Conflict exists among instructors today: Some feel
that part-learning is superior to whole-learning; others feel that learning body
awareness should precede learning a technique of control; and others recommend letting the natural instincts of the body do the instruction without
interference by formal rules. Imagery rehearsal may be a dual application
of acquisition enhancement and performance enhancement for the novice,
but performance enhancement may be more crucial for the expert. Another
problem facing the user of imagery who is a novice is whether he or she has
sufficient experience to develop an appropriate image. Can a beginner visualize the sensations of coming smoothly out of a tuck, if he or she has not
yet physically experienced the movement? And finally, in research investigations, the selection of the proper outcome measure may be crucial for
valid assessment of the contributions of the imagery rehearsal. Since a novice's ability to improve on a skill is influenced by a variety of variables, it
may be unrealistic to expect a precise, narrow measure to be an accurate
way of assessing improvement. For example, rating improvement by counting the number of aces a novice serves would be less sensitive to the kind
of improvements expected of a tennis player than by assessing the distance

of each serve from the service block or by counting the number of serves within the service block. In contrast, for the elite athlete, the amount of improvement left may be very limited. If a basketball player, golfer, runner, racer is already performing physically close to his or her limits, large changes in accuracy, scores, or times would not be expected. However, it might be useful to use measure of consistency instead. The study of imagery rehearsal is to some extent a problem of research into a tool, and to some extent, a problem of research into the whole concept of acquisition and performance. As a tool, imagery rehearsal must be investigated from the perspective of the parameters that improve its utilization. As a tool used to implement principles of learning and performance, it is dependent on the successful application of what is known about rules of acquisition, skill building, and skill enhancement. As this chapter demonstrates, imagery rehearsal is not a simple process. The potential and the promise are there and await the researcher, the practitioner, and the performer.

REFERENCE NOTES

1. One athlete insisted that since she competed in real life with her eyes open, she should use mental practice with her eyes open! Although I had some qualms about this, it appeared that her ability to relax and to visualize was not impaired. Generally, VMBR is conducted with eyes closed on the assumption that visual distraction is minimized and concentration improved.

2. Since this writing, Weinberg, et al., confirmed the value of VMBR when he compared its effects on performance against those of relaxation only, imagery only, and an attention placebo.

REFERENCES

Bennett, B. K., & Stothart, C. M. The effects of a relaxation-based cognitive technique on sports performances. Paper presented at the Congress of the Canadian Society for Motor Learning and Sport Psychology, Toronto, Canada, 1978.

Benson, H., Dryer, T., & Hartley, L. H. Decreased V_{O_2} consumption during exercise with elicitation of the relaxation response. *Journal of Human Stress, 1978,* **4,** 38–42.

Cautela, J. Covert sensitization. *Psychological Reports*, 1967, **20**, 459–468.

Cautela, J. Covert reinforcement. *Behavior Therapy*, 1970, **1**, 33–50.

Clark, L. The effect of mental practice on the development of certain motor skills. *Research Quarterly*, 1960, **31**, 560–569.

Corbin, C. Mental practice. In W. Morgan (Ed.), *Ergogenic aids and muscular performance*. New York: Academic Press, 1972.

Denney, D. R. Self-control approaches to the treatment of test anxiety. In I. G. Sarason (Ed.), *Text anxiety: Theory, research and applications*. Hillsdale, N.J.: Lawrence Erlbaum Associates, 1980, pp. 209–243.

Desiderato, O., & Miller, I. B. Improving tennis performance by cognitive behavior modification techniques. *The Behavior Therapist*, 1979, **2**, 19.

Doyle, L. A., & Landers, D. M. *Psychological skills in elite and subelite shooters.* Unpublished manuscript, 1980.

Epstein, M. L. The relationship of mental imagery and mental rehearsal to performance of a motor task. *Journal of Sport Psychology*, 1980, **2**, 211–220.

Fensterheim, H. A behavioral method for improving sport performance. *Psychiatric Annals*, March 1980, **10** (3).

Furlong, W. Coping: The power of imagination. *Quest*, May 1979, 95–96.

Gravel, R., Lemieux, G., & Ladouceur, R. Effectiveness of a cognitive behavioral treatment package for cross-country ski racers. *Cognitive Therapy and Research*, 1980, **4**, 83–90.

Haber, R. N. Eidetic images are not just imaginary. *Psychology Today*, 1980, **14**, 72–82.

Kirchenbaum, D. S., & Bale, R. M. Cognitive–behavioral skills in golf: Brain power golf. In R. Suinn (Ed.), *Psychology in sports: Methods and applications.* Minneapolis: Burgess, 1980, pp. 334–343.

Kolonay, B. J. The effects of visuo-motor behavior rehearsal on athletic performance. Unpublished master's thesis, City University of New York, 1977.

Lane, J. F. Four studies of visuo-motor behavior rehearsal. Unpublished manuscript, 1978.

Lane, J. F. Improving athletic performance through visuo-motor behavior rehearsal. In R. Suinn (Ed.), *Psychology in sports: Methods and applications.* Minneapolis: Burgess, 1980, pp. 316–320.

Lazarus, A. *In the mind's eye.* New York: Lawson, 1977.

Mahoney, M. J. *Cognitive skills and athletics performance.* Paper presented to the 11th Annual Meeting of the Association for Advancement of Behavior Therapy, Atlanta, December 1977.

Mahoney, M. J., & Avener, M. Psychology of the elite athlete: An exploratory study. *Cognitive Therapy and Research*, 1977, **1**, 135–141.

Meichenbaum, D. *Cognitive behavior modification.* New York: Plenum, 1977.

Meichenbaum, D., & Cameron, R. The clinical potential of modifying what clients say to themselves. In M. Mahoney & C. Thoresen (Eds.), *Self-control: Power to the person.* Belmont, Cal.: Brooks/Cole, 1974.

Meyers, A. W., Cooke, C. J., Cullen, J., & Liles, L. Psychological aspects of athletic competitors: A replication across sports. *Cognitive Therapy and Research*, 1979, **3**, 361–366.

Morgan, W. The mind of the marathoner. *Psychology Today*, 1978, **11**, 38–49.

Nicklaus, J. *Golf my way.* New York: Simon & Schuster, 1974.

Nideffer, R. M. Deep muscle relaxation: An aid to diving. *Coach and Athlete*, 1971, **24**, 38.

Noel, R. C. The effect of visuo-motor behavior rehearsal on tennis performance. *Journal of Sport Psychology*, 1980, **2**, 220–226.

Oxendine, J. *Psychology of motor learning.* New York: Meredith, 1968.

Penfield, W. Speech, perception and the uncommitted cortex. *Pontifasiae Academiae Scientarum, Scripta Varia*, 1965, **30**, 319–347.

Richardson, A. Mental practice: A review and discussion. Part I. *Research Quarterly*, 1967a, **38**, 95–107.

Richardson, A. Mental practice: A review and discussion. Part II. *Research Quarterly*, 1967b, **38**, 263–273.

Rotter, J. B. Generalized expectancies for internal versus external control of reinforcement. *Psychological Monographs*, 1966, **80**, 1–28.

Schleser, R., Meyers, A. W., & Montgomery, T. A cognitive behavioral intervention for improving basketball performance. Paper presented at the Association for the Advancement of Behavior Therapy, 18th Annual Convention, New York, November 1980.

Stampfl, T., & Levis, D. Essentials of implosive therapy: A learning-theory-based psychodynamic behavioral therapy. *Journal of Abnormal Psychology*, 1967, **72**, 496–503.

Start, K., & Richardson, A. Imagery and mental practice. *British Journal of Educational Psychology*, 1964, **34**, 280–284.

Suinn, R. M. Behavior rehearsal training for ski racers. *Behavior Therapy*, 1972, **3**, 519.

Suinn, R. M. Visual motor behavior rehearsal for adaptive behavior. In J. Krumboltz & C. Thoresen (Eds.), *Counseling methods*. New York: Holt, 1976.

Suinn, R. M. *Manual: Anxiety management training (AMT)*. Fort Collins, Colo.: Rocky Mountain Behavioral Sciences Institute, 1977.

Suinn, R. M. Behavioral applications of psychology to U.S. world class competitors. In P. Klavora (Ed.), *Coach, athlete and the sport psychologist*. Toronto: University of Toronto Press, 1979.

Suinn, R. M. Psychology and sports performance: Principles and applications. In R. Suinn (Ed.), *Psychology in sports: Methods and applications*. Minneapolis: Burgess, 1980.

Suinn, R. M. Stress management for elite athletes. In Y. Hanin (Ed.), *Stress and anxiety in sport*. Moscow: Physical Culture and Sport Publications, in press.

Suinn, R. M., & Andrews, F. A. *Psychological strategies of professional competitors*. Manuscript in preparation, 1981.

Suinn, R. M., & Dickinson, A. *Imagery rehearsal as a form of motor skill*. Unpublished manuscript, 1978.

Suinn, R., Morton, M., & Brammell, H. *Psychological and mental training to increase efficiency in endurance athletes*. Technical Report to Developmental Subcommittee, U.S. Olympic Women's Athletics, 1980.

Titley, R. W. The loneliness of a long-distance kicker. *The Athletic Journal*, 1976, 74–80.

Weinberg, R., Seabourne, T., & Jackson, A. Effects of visiomotor behavior rehearsal, relaxation, and imagery on karate performance. *Journal of Sports Psychology*, 1981, **3**, 228-238.

Winning Associates. *Athletes' homework manual*. Morgantown, W.V., 1978.

Wolpe, J. *Psychotherapy by reciprocal inhibition*. Stanford, California: Stanford University Press, 1958.

CHAPTER 17

Research on Imagery: Implications for Advertising

KATHRYN LUTZ ALESANDRINI AND ANEES A. SHEIKH

Whether the goal is to improve advertising effectivenss or to assess and understand the impact of advertising messages, an imagery perspective can be valuable to the researcher, practitioner, or evaluator. Bettman (1979) provides a broad perspective for applying psychological principles to advertising and offers some general strategies that may be used to enhance advertising and marketing effectiveness. A number of specific strategies that may aid advertising effectiveness have been identified and discussed; of these, imagery-eliciting strategies are the most promising (Alesandrini, in press). This chapter focuses on several imagery-eliciting memory strategies; the principles emerging from imagery research and the implications of those principles for advertising are discussed. Pictorial strategies are emphasized, since the use of pictures in advertising is probably the most commonly used technique to elicit mental imagery. Subsequently, the impact of specific picture characteristics, such as color, is examined. Research on picture characteristics primarily has dealt with physical attributes of pictures. However, the function that a picture serves relative to the viewer's thoughts and attitudes also may be worthy of consideration when evaluating picture effects. In addition to the pictorial strategies, several other imagery-eliciting strategies are described, and advertising implications are discussed. Then the use of imagery strategies in conjunction with other memory strategies is considered. In conclusion, the implications of imagery research are summarized for advertising decision making in several areas, including advertising design and creativity, media selection and scheduling, and advertising regulation and public policy.

PICTORIAL STRATEGIES

General Principles and Advertising Implications

Picture Relevance

Most researchers investigating picture strategies have used illustrations that are conceptually related in some way to the topic of the communication. A recent reviewer of the literature on picture effects concluded that illustrations should be conceptually related to the topic of the communication since there is evidence that unrelated or inaccurate pictures can adversely affect memory (Alesandrini, 1982). However, irrelevant pictures seem to be used rather frequently in advertising. For example, many ads show sexy models along with the product, although the model has no conceptual relationship to the product whatsoever. Showing a sexy model does not appear to facilitate memory for the product and may even promote negative attitudes toward the product or company (*Marketing News*, 1977; Steadman, 1969). The studies discussed in this chapter used relevant pictures unless otherwise indicated.

Superiority of Picture Memory

Paivio (1971) reviewed a number of studies that compared memory for pictures to memory for words. The studies overwhelmingly indicate that pictures are remembered better than words. More recent studies have confirmed the "pictorial superiority effect" (Paivio & Csapo 1973) and suggest that memory for pictures does not decrease over time as rapidly as does memory for words (Erdelyi & Becker, 1974).

The superiority of memory for pictures in advertising has been demonstrated by Shepard (1967). He showed people 612 illustrations from magazines and found that the viewers later were able to recognize a median of 98.5% of these pictures.

Pictures Facilitate Word Memory

The literature indicates that presentation of a picture along with its verbal counterpart facilitates word learning (Paivio, 1971). In other words, words are later recognized or recalled better if they were originally presented pictorially as well as verbally. It is interesting to note, however, that pictorial recognition may actually suffer if a picture is accompanied by verbal labels. In several studies the addition of verbal labels to a picture adversely affected later recognition and resulted in longer response latencies to recognize the picture (Fleming & Sheikhian, 1972).

The use of pictures to supplement words has been tested in an advertising context with noteworthy results. Logos were selected from the Yellow Pages of a metropolitan phone directory that either portrayed the brand name or the product or service pictorially. Results showed that viewers recalled more company or brand names after seeing a pictorial depiction or elaboration of that name (Lutz & Lutz, 1977). Only logos that included a pictorial depiction or elaboration of the brand name facilitated recall of that name. For example, a logo such as example D in Figure 17.1 for All-State Tree Surgery may be visually interesting or amusing, but it did not help the viewer remember the company name; however, a picture like example C in Figure 17.1 for Western Glass Company did result in better recall of the brand and company name.

Not all companies have the kind of name that readily lends itself to depiction. Some names are more concrete and easily pictured, whereas others are more abstract and difficult to portray. In our study the companies with concrete names used pictorial "equivalents" of the brand or company name, for example, Arrow Pest Control (see example A in Figure 17.1), Bird Carpet Company, Hose King, Rhino Tires, and Rocket Messenger Service. Some of the companies included in the study had more abstract names but also managed to use a picture strategy by showing a pictorial "associate" rather than a pictorial equivalent of the name. For example, the following companies used a picture indicated in parentheses: Gonzales–Murphy Buick (sombrero with clover leaf), Leo Cleaners (lion), Su Wrench Supply (oriental character), Weisz Auctioneers (owl), and Western Glass Supply (cactus cowboy). An interesting question for research is whether pictures that are equivalent to their verbal counterparts facilitate memory for the company name better than do pictures that are only indirectly related to the name.

INTERACTIVE IMAGERY

PICTURE INTERACTION   LETTER ACCENTUATION

A. Arrow Pest Control   B. Cooper Donuts

NON-INTERACTIVE IMAGERY

BRAND OR COMPANY NAME   PRODUCT OR SERVICE

C. Western Glass Co.   D. All State Tree Surgery

Figure 17.1. Types of visual strategy used in advertising. (The logos shown here are used only to illustrate the research described; no endorsement of this book or the research study reported herein is implied).

Interactive Pictures

There are many studies in paired–associated learning that indicate that an interactive picture helps the learner remember the two items to be learned better than repeated viewing of the separate items (Reese, 1965). An interactive picture figurally integrates the two items to be associated in some mutual or reciprocal action. When the picture is not interactive and the items are depicted side by side, paired–associated learning is not facilitated in spite of the pictorial presentation (Neisser & Kerr, 1973).

Interactive pictures facilitate memory for ads, according to the study described above by Lutz and Lutz (1977) that used company–product pairs and their accompanying pictorial logos from ads in the Yellow Pages of a telephone directory. In that study the group that saw the interactive pictures recalled significantly more company names than did those who viewed the noninteractive pictures. The interactive logos integrated the brand and product in one picture, whereas noninteractive logos showed the brand and product separately.

In our study the interactive-picture group actually saw two types of picture: picture interaction logos and letter accentuation logos (see Figure 17.1). In the latter type, some letter or letters in the brand name are made to resemble the product or one of its characteristics. Letter accentuation is used in the logo for Mullin Lumber Company, which depicts the letters of "Mullin" as wood-grained boards arranged as letters. This type of letter accentuation has been termed *inclusion* by other researchers, who found that this pictorial strategy facilitates learning (Lippman & Shanahan, 1973). Another type of letter accentuation strategy involves figural interaction between one letter in the brand name and a picture of the product or service. The logo for Dixon Crane Company uses this type of strategy by showing two cranes crossing at the top to form the "x" in "Dixon." More often, the accentuated letter is the first letter in the brand name. An example is the logo for Cooper Donuts given in Figure 17.1 (example B) in which the "C" in "Cooper" resembles a doughnut with a bite out of it. A letter accentuation strategy may be the only pictorial strategy that can be used by some companies, such as those with abstract or proper names.

An interactive-picture strategy appears to be the most effective strategy according to our study and can be used by companies with portrayable names (although some ingenuity may be required to create a pictorial depiction for some names). Picture interaction logos unite a depiction of the brand with a picture of the product or service on one picture. The logo for Arrow Pest Control is an example of how both the company name and service can be shown pictorially in one integrated image (see example A in Figure 17.1). Another example is the logo for Jack's Camera Shop, which shows a playing-card jack holding a movie camera to his eye. People in the study recalled more company names that had picture interaction logos than did those using letter accentuation logos. Both types of interactive logo—completely pictorial interactions and letter accentuations—facilitated brand-name memory more than did noninteractive pictures and an all-verbal presentation. Thus companies with names that have no pictorial equivalent or associate can still capitalize on interactive imagery benefits by using a letter accentuation logo. Some of the picture logos used in the noninteractive condition were unique and memorable in their own right, such as the depiction of "Western" shown in Figure 17.1. However, the company or brand name was not associated with the product (in this case glass) because the logo did not graphically depict the product and brand interacting.

Communicating Other Concepts Pictorially

Ads can communicate pictorially not only brands and products, but also attributes, characteristics, and concepts. Studies indicate that learning and attitude can be positively enhanced when pictures are used to convey abstract concepts or information (Alesandrini, 1982). However, research suggests that when information is presented only in pictorial form, comprehension may not be facilitated (Levin, 1973); perhaps this is so because the verbal comprehension tests typically used in research studies may not test the kind of knowledge resulting from a pictorial presentation. Several studies indicated that pictorial strategies result in graphic knowledge not assessed by a verbal test but reflected on a visual or spatial test (Dwyer, 1972; Lutz & Rigney, 1977). A study of children's knowledge of breakfast cereal revealed that the children had a great deal of pictorial information that was not assessed by a verbal test but was reflected by assessments sensitive to spatial and visual information (Rossiter, 1976).

Researchers have explored the statement that "a picture is worth a thousand words" (Mandler & Johnson, 1976) and discovered that viewers can learn more quickly and effectively from information presented pictorially rather than verbally (Alesandrini, 1982). Pictures have been used effectively as advance organizers and may be more helpful than verbal advance organizers (Weisberg, 1970). Pictures also can be used to influence consumer behavior by means of modeling. Wright (1979), for example, was able to increase the reading of warning labels by consumers when the behavior was modeled in the advertisement for the product. Finally, research on picture communication indicates that viewers weigh pictorial information more heavily; thus, for example, concrete information is much more influential in decision making than is more abstract information (Nisbett et al., 1976).

Advertising messages can use visuals in a variety of ways to communicate product information or company characteristics. Graphs and pictographs are one way to convey certain types of quantitative information and concepts of equivalence. Pictorial simulation is another way to communicate difficult concepts visually. Symbol substitution is another technique to visually communicate information. This technique involves use of a pictorial symbol in place of verbal material to more effectively and efficiently convey the message. Researchers have applied this technique to advertising and found that using visuals to convey product attributes can affect attitude toward the brand (Mitchell & Olson, 1981).

The Effects of Specific Picture Characteristics

The pictures used in the various studies on pictorial strategies differed considerably on a number of dimensions, including realism, color, motion, size, complexity, labeling, and media vehicle [see Alesandrini (1982) for a more detailed discussion]. For example, some researchers used stylized or abstract drawings, whereas some used realistic drawings or photographs. Some of the pictures were black and white, whereas some materials had one additional color, and some were in full color. Most visuals were static, whereas some were animated. The presentation conditions also varied widely among the studies. Some researchers presented still photographs to the viewers, and others presented films or showed computer-generated graphics. Unfortunately, there is little conclusive information available to date about how these particular variables influence the effects of picture strategies. Also, there is little theory from which to generate a useful taxonomy of picture characteristics that affect learning and memory, although a few taxonomies have been suggested (Clark, 1973; Twyman, 1979). The only areas in which a number of studies have been conducted and relevant findings have been reported are those of color and realism.

The Effects of Colored Pictures

A number of studies have been conducted to determine the effects of color on affective and cognitive outcomes (i.e., attitudes and memory). Investigations of affective responses to color have been rather successful in determining the effects that different colors can have on both physiological and emotional responses. In general, people report that they prefer to view colored pictures rather than black-and-white pictures, and behavioral observations confirm this reported preference by finding that viewers look longer at colored pictures (Chute, 1979; Lamberski, 1980). Some research also indicates that the chromatic colors are more arousing than the nonchromatic colors but that people prefer to view the so-called cooler colors; these colors, ordered from cool to warm, include blue, green, yellow, orange, and red. Research shows, for example, that viewing blue results in less arousal than viewing red or white and that looking at blue is associated with greater relaxation and less anxiety, whereas viewing red elicits more tension and excitement in the viewer.

Color, however, is a complex variable that consists of several component variables, including hue, lightness or brightness, and saturation. Research studies that have investigated these component variables have found that viewers generally prefer cool hues and high saturation (with females preferring the lighter colors) and that viewers show a decreasing preference for high saturation with increasing age.

The effect of color on cognitive outcomes, such as learning and memory, is not understood as well as affective responses to color. Since people prefer colored pictures to black and white, one may assume that viewers would be more attentive to color materials and, therefore, remember more from them. In general, research has not supported this assumption. For example, Vander Meer (1954) found that, although viewers preferred color films to black-and-white films, they did not learn more from the color films. Studies on the use of color to facilitate learning and memory have not yielded consistent findings. The reviewers mentioned above looked at many studies of colored pictures in films, television, textbooks, photographs, slides, and so on, and found that the addition of color did not aid learning. Some studies, however, did find that color promoted memory under certain circumstances. For example, color facilitated learning when it was used to emphasize relevant information rather than simply to provide embellishment. Other studies found that color can promote memory of some information but sometimes at the expense of more relevant information.

Color may be important in advertising. The link between preference for color and improved memory was observed in a study of colored versus black-and-white television commercials conducted by Burke Marketing Research Company (1960). Viewers in their study who saw the commercials in color gave them higher ratings and tended to watch the entire commercial. In addition, the viewers recalled more details from the color commercials. Practitioners know that color can dramatically affect attention and thereby learning and attitude in ads, but research in this area is lagging.

Effects of Realistic Pictures

The other picture attribute receiving much research attention is that of realism versus abstractness. Realistic pictures generally refer to depictions that have clearly represented and easily identifiable objects, whereas non-realistic or abstract pictures are nonobjective. In other words, the more qualities a visual shares with the object or situation depicted, the more realistic it is. Research indicates that viewers prefer realistic to abstract pictures (Travers & Alvarado, 1970).

Some authors have defined realism as the amount of detail in a picture and have referred to the variable as pictorial "complexity." Most research on complexity versus simplicity of visuals indicates that people prefer to view visual displays that are complex and that the preference increases with age (Fleming & Sheikhian, 1972). For example, in one study, 6- and 7-year-old children preferred to view simple line drawings of objects, whereas 11-year-olds preferred sketchy, irregular, complex pictures. Of course, there may be some optimum preferred level of complexity, since extreme complexity may result in a state of chaos.

The effects of realism on learning and memory are unclear. There are several theoretical orientations, called *realism theories*, which predict that realistic pictures are more memorable than abstract ones. The main assertion of realism theories is that learning will be more complete as the number of cues in the learning situation increases. As noted above, realism is often operationally defined as amount of detail or complexity; thus a realistic picture presumably provides more cues to the learner. Several studies involving recognition memory indicate that paintings judged to be realistic were more easily recognized than were paintings judged to be abstract (Fleming & Sheikhian, 1972). Although recognition memory for realistic pictures is great, the effect of realism on recall is unclear. When operationally defined as amount of detail, realism does not facilitate learning and memory.

A Functional Approach to Understanding Picture Effects

In the previous section, the effects of physical attributes of pictures, including color and realism, were discussed. Several theorists have proposed a functional approach to developing taxonomic categories of pictures based on the various functions that the pictures serve rather than on the physical forms of the pictures. In other words, a functional approach is not concerned with how a picture looks but rather focuses on how a picture functions in a particular context. For example, one of the earlier functional approaches to understanding picture effects was suggested by Knowlton (1966), who categorized pictures as either realistic, analogical or logical. A realistic picture directly depicts its referent, an analogical picture presents an analogy (i.e., lumberjacks moving a tree to represent a muscle moving a bone), and a logical picture is a schematic representation.

Learning Functions

One approach to understanding picture effects is to examine and categorize pictures based on their function in the learning context. Duchastel (1980) categorizes pictures on the basis of the role they play during learning: (1) those pictures that interest and motivate the learner play an *attentional* role; (2) those pictures that help explain a point play an *explicative* role; and (3) those pictures that enhance long-term recall play a *retentional* role. A more extensive functional taxonomy proposed by Levin (1979) includes eight hierarchically ordered categories for pictures that progressively facilitate memory and attitude. At the lowest benefit level of Levin's taxonomy are pictures that serve merely a "decorative" function and usually are included in a presentation simply because they enhance attractiveness. Higher up the hierarchy are "motivational" pictures that increase the viewer's interest in the information. The highest levels of the taxonomy include pictures that serve an "interpretation" or "transformation" function by making the information more comprehensible or more memorable.

Studies have not yet been conducted to test the usefulness of a functional taxonomy of pictures in an advertising context. However, it may be that pictures that serve only a decorative function in an advertising message are better omitted (*Marketing News*, 1977; Steadman, 1969).

Attitude Functions

Pictures may also be categorized on the basis of the attitude functions they serve. Lutz (1979) proposed five functions that attitudes serve and identified advertising approaches geared to each: (1) value expressive—the ad reinforces or stimulates the viewer's self-concept or personal values; (2) ego-defensive—the ad allows the viewer to indirectly satisfy an unacceptable motive; (3) social adjustment—the ad plays on the viewer's need to satisfy social conformity motives; (4) knowledge—the ad gives viewers information and allows them to satisfy their quest for knowledge, organization, and so on; and (5) utilitarian—the ad is based on the viewer's needs to maximize rewards and minimize punishments.

Ads designed to appeal to value-expressive needs often use visuals to portray the viewer's ideal self-concept. An example is the campaign for Pepsi that shows product users as part of the "Pepsi Generation" who "think young." Ads that are based on the ego-defense function are designed to bolster the ego. Showing sexy models in ads falls into this category. The social adjustment function deals with a person's needs to socialize and experience identification with significant others. Showing well-known and respected spokespersons in ads is an example of this type of appeal. Ads that serve the knowledge function fulfill the viewer's need to cognitively create order and meaning from a message. Verbal strategies are more often used in these ads, giving specific information about the characteristics of a product, how it works, why it is effective, and so on. Finally, many ads appear to deal with utilitarian functions by stressing product benefits. For example, advertisements portray the good taste of a food product or the high performance of an automobile.

A functional approach may be more useful than a formal approach in categorizing pictures used in ads. More research is needed to develop and test picture taxonomies in advertising.

OTHER IMAGERY-ELICITING STRATEGIES

Concretization

Concretization refers to making information more memorable by making it more concrete. The variable of concreteness or "imagery value" refers to the likelihood that a word will elicit a mental image in the mind of the reader. Imagery values for hundreds of words have been established by asking readers to rate the ease with which a word arouses sensory images. Imagery values are based on mean ratings and are available for nouns (Paivio et al., 1968), for verbs (Lippman, 1974), and for words frequently used by children (Van der Veur, 1975). According to these ratings, words such as "bottle" and "nail" are more concrete with higher imagery values (> 6 on a 7-point scale), whereas words such as "gist" and "concept" are more abstract with lower imagery values (< 2). Research results indicate that words high in imagery value are remembered better than words of low imagery value (Paivio, 1969).

Concrete Words

The implication of research on concreteness for advertising design is that brand names that are concrete should be more memorable than names based on abstract words, proper nouns, or abbreviations. If a new brand name were being selected, concrete nouns would be the best choice and action verbs may be the next best choice. Abstract or proper nouns, stative verbs, and adjectives probably would be the least desirable choice. In the following examples, imagery ratings are shown in parentheses if available in one of the published word lists. Examples of companies with concrete brand names include Arrow (6.57) shirts and Ocean Spray (6.77 & 6.17) juice. It should be noted that viewers may recall abstract brand names quite well because of the ad's use of other memory strategies, such as repetition of the name. Some companies quite successfully use action verbs as brand names; examples include Tickle (6.26) deodorant and Shout (6.05) cleaner. Abstract and proper nouns, although often used as brand names, are not memorable unless they are used in conjunction with other memory strategies; examples include Glory (4.13) rug cleaner and Pride (4.23) furniture polish. Brand names based on stative or abstract verbs also are not the most memorable names. An example is Vanish (4.90) cleaner. The use of adjectives as brand names is one of the least effective approaches according to concretization research. If brands such as Glad (3.70) storage bags and All (3.70) detergent are to be remembered, other, perhaps more expensive, strategies such as repetition are required. However, the adjective may be effective when it is combined with a concrete noun so that the combination is easily pictured, as is Green Giant vegetables. Nevertheless, the use of adjectives as brand names is popular because of the assumption that important characteristics about the product are being communicated by the adjective. Consider, for example, the intended message behind Kool (3.34—cool) cigarettes and Soft 'n Dry (5.13 & 4.00) deodorant. Although research has not specifically compared the memorability of nouns, verbs, and adjectives (holding other factors constant), the implication from the literature is that adjectives are one of the poorer choices for a brand name.

So how can the advertiser communicate some of the desirable product characteristics in the brand name? One approach is to select a concrete noun that has desirable, associated attributes. The automobile industry sets a good example in selecting names that convey desirable attributes. The implications of concrete names such as Audi Fox (6.07) and Volkswagen Rabbit (6.57) are clear in comparison to the associations of a more abstract name such as Chevy Citation (3.57). An added benefit of using concrete brand names is that concrete nouns lend themselves more readily to pictorial ad campaigns based on the characteristics of the concrete noun.

Concrete Connective Words

The use of concrete connectives in advertising messages has not yet been investigated experimentally. However, the preceding evidence suggests that messages that use concrete words to relate brand names and product claims should be very memorable. Furthermore, since a visual inspection of the tabled values indicates that action verbs are more concrete than linking verbs, the more effective ad would tell what the product *does* (its usage benefits) rather than what the product *is* (its attributes). An ad would be more memorable if it used high-imagery verbs (ratings over 6) such as "attack," "break," "climb," "fall," "fly," "itch," "jump," "kick," "laugh," "run," "scream," "shout," "smile," and "tickle" rather than verbs with lower imagery values (ratings > 3) such as "be," "contain," "do," "get," "has," "is," "keep," "set," "try," "use," and "will."

Concrete Stories and Other Concrete Materials

A number of researchers have used sentences, passages, and texts to study various aspects of concreteness. Some of these studies tested response latency and recognition, whereas some investigated recall to determine how people encode, store, and retrieve concrete versus abstract information. Results from this research indicate that concrete information is recognized and verified faster than is abstract information [see review of research on concreteness by Alesandrini (1982)]. The reviewer concludes that studies investigating verbal recall show that concreteness correlates highly with recall. The variable of concreteness was directly manipulated in several studies, and results show that sentences that contain concrete adjectives and modifiers were recalled better by adults than were sentences with equivalent but abstract adjectives and modifiers. In other experiments, concrete versions of prose passages were better remembered than otherwise equivalent, abstracted passages (the passages were constructed by the experimenters). Finally, one study found that concrete passages taken from published texts on a variety of topics were comprehended better by the readers than were passages judged to be more abstract.

The effects of concrete and vivid stories in advertising have not been empirically investigated, but the implication of this research is that vivid, concrete stories and scenarios will be more memorable than abstract decriptions or stories.

After considering the evidence concerning the effectiveness of concreteness, the FTC Task Force on Consumer Information Remedies suggested that abstract warning messages such as "this product could be hazardous to your health" be changed to more concrete warnings such as "consuming this product will increase the user's chance of death by 5%" (FTC, 1979).

Imagery Instructions and Inducements

The results of numerous studies on mental imagery instructions are reviewed and discussed by Paivio (1971). The research indicates that giving learners imagery instructions—telling them to mentally visualize the information to be remembered—facilitates learning, and the effects on memory closely resemble picture effects. The interactive feature of the mental image remains a necessary condition for maximum effectiveness. Learners told to mentally imagine two objects in interaction remember more word pairs than do learners told to mentally picture the objects side by side or on opposite sides of a room.

One advantage of eliciting mental imagery in the viewer as opposed to showing the viewer interactive pictures is that the self-generated mental imagery will probably be more personally meaningful and even more bizarre. Memory experts claim that bizarre, unique, individualized mental images are the most effective (Lorayne & Lucas, 1974); however, this claim has not been supported unequivocally by empirical investigation (Weber & Marshall, 1978). In fact, people may take longer to form bizarre mental images than "common" images with no associated memory benefits (Nappe & Wollen, 1973). Although the bizarreness of a mental image may not affect memory, the "vividness" of the image is related to recall according to a review by Higbee (1979). A vivid image is defined as one that is clear, distinct, and strong. The effectiveness of images elicited through ambiguous pictures, similar to the stimuli in projective tests, is also being examined (Akhter & Sheikh, 1981).

There are no studies on the effects of imagery instructions on remembering brand names and product claims in advertising. However, Mowen (1980) tested an imagery strategy in an advertising context by showing consumers an ad for a hypothetical brand of shampoo that either included instructions to imagine themselves using the product or contained no such instructions. Viewers who were given the imagery instructions later reported no stronger intentions to try the product than viewers who had not seen the imagery instructions. Yogurt directs the listener to "look for the sunny yellow cups," probably eliciting a mental image in the listener that is easy to visualize but is distinctive from images aroused by other advertisers of that type of product. Another way for an ad to elicit mental imagery is by telling listeners to picture themselves in a given situation. The directive in an ad by a life insurance company to "imagine yourself *out* of the picture" is a variant of this approach.

Caution should be used in adopting imagery strategies in print media advertising. Findings suggest that imagery generation is a more successful strategy when applied during listening rather than during reading (Brooks,

1967). The effects of telling an audience to form mental images while hearing or reading an advertising message have not been empirically tested, but the literature on imagery inducement suggests that imagery instructions should generally facilitate memory for an ad and may be especially effective with nonprint media, such as radio and television.

IMAGERY COMBINED WITH OTHER STRATEGIES

Imagery-eliciting strategies are only one general class of learning strategies, and their effectiveness may be enhanced if they are used in conjunction with other types of learning strategy. Alesandrini (in press) has reviewed the advertising implications of another main class of learning strategies called *holistic learning strategies*. These strategies help the learner to see the bigger picture and remember information more easily by putting it "in a nutshell." The following strategies combine holistic and visual strategies to facilitate memory.

VISUAL ANALOGIES

Supplying a learner with analogies or comparisons between new information and something more familiar is a strategy that facilitates learning [see overview by Lutz, (1980)]. Providing the learners with analogies and metaphors helps them to relate new information to familiar information; relating the new to the familiar is a necessary condition for learning, according to cognitive-learning theorists (Wittrock, 1974).

The use of visual analogies in advertising is common, although no studies have tested the effectiveness of this strategy in an advertising context. Products named after an analogous object rather than after attributes are more easily portrayed graphically. One example of an effective visual analogy in ads is the Audi Fox television commercial that visually superimposes a running fox over the automobile to communicate the speed and handling capabilities of the car. The stability of the car is likened to the fox's characteristic of surefootedness. The Ford Mustang ad uses a similar strategy. Print media also can make use of a visual-analogy strategy. For example, a savings and loan institution uses a visual analogy in their newspaper ad for home equity loans. The ad campaign is "tap your assets," and the visual analogy shows a faucet pouring money out of a house. This type of visual analogy is probably a very effective way to communicate a rather abstract concept.

Visual Chunking

People presumably can remember only a limited number of information units or "chunks" in short-term memory at any one time; that number ranges from 5 to 9 bits of information (Miller, 1956). For example, most people can temporarily remember a 7-digit phone number but probably cannot remember several unfamiliar phone numbers simultaneously without using mnemonic strategies (such as writing them down). Although short-term memory limits the number of chunks that can be processed simultaneously, the number of information bits contained in those chunks is not restricted to the 7 $\pm$ 2 limit. Information chunks may range in complexity from a single bit of information to many bits. Memory for information can be increased by chunking the information—combining separate bits of the information into larger patterns or groups. The new groups or chunks are then easier to remember than all the separate items.

A chunking strategy is probably the most important strategy in promoting advertising effectiveness, especially when it is combined with pictorial or concretization strategies. Brand names, slogans, logos, and jingles can all be powerful chunks that communicate a great many bits of information. The brand name can summarize the main product characteristics or the bits of information that the advertiser wishes to communicate. An example of a brand name that chunks various bits of information together is Tide detergent: Tide sums up the notions of clean, refreshing, powerful water in motion. The use of slogans is another approach to chunking information. Ford Motor Company's slogan that "Ford has a better idea" summarizes their campaign and also uses a pictorial strategy (letter accentuation) by replacing the "o" in "Ford" with a light bulb.

A good logo can be the most effective way to visually chunk information and promote memory. The interactive pictures discussed in an earlier section are good examples of effective chunking strategies. For example, the logo for Arrow Pest Control Company shows a bug killed by an arrow. In one chunk of visual information, the logo communicates the brand name (Arrow) as well as the company's service (pest extermination).

Visual Advance Organizers

An advance organizer is an overview that cues the listener or viewer to the topic and main points of the information to be presented, thereby eliciting the proper mental set. A number of experiments concerning the effects of verbal advance organizers on learning and memory have been conducted, and they show that advance organizers often facilitate learning (Faw & Wallter, 1976). Verbal advance organizers in ads may include catchy titles for the ad, such as "Free" or "Win Money."

Several studies indicate that visual advance organizers also are facilitative (Weisberg, 1970). Although visual advance organizers in advertising may facilitate memory, they also may have the negative effect of "turning off" the viewer. Commercials may successfully use this strategy in several ways; ads can show a bad situation that the viewer would like to avoid, or a positive situation that the viewer would like to achieve, or pose a problem that the viewer would like to solve. For example, the ad for heavy-duty trash bags begins by showing how some bags break and spill their contents, a situation that the viewer certainly wants to avoid.

Visual Context

Providing a context for information is another strategy for promoting memory. Jenkins (1974) emphasizes the importance of context in learning and points out that learning and memory are constructive processes in which the information that is remembered depends heavily on the context. Advertisers know this, for they are careful to show cigarette smokers in front of a waterfall or out in the open plains rather than in a hot, stuffy, smoke-filled room. The kind of visual context in which a product is shown can have major effects on what the viewer learns and remembers from the message, according to the research on picture effects. Since no studies have tested the effects of the visual context of an ad, such as a cigarette smoker in a refreshing setting, we do not know how much influence the context has. Perhaps future researchers can provide insight into the effects of visual context.

One technique for embedding information in a context is to use a scenario or story format. Research indicates that people recall stories better than other kinds of information, probably because stories have a familiar and useful structure that aids memory (Gordon et al., 1978). Television ads use a story technique more often than do ads in the other media because a short story or scenario can be developed very quickly by way of pictorial communication. Miller beer ads, for example, often portray a story complete with characters, a plot, setting, purpose, attempt, and outcome—the outcome always is "It's Miller time."

SUMMARY OF IMPLICATIONS FOR ADVERTISING

The results of research on imagery-eliciting strategies discussed in this chapter are relevant to a number of important considerations in advertising. Despite the few studies of imagery-eliciting strategies within the advertising context, the principles and perspective provided by this imagery literature can be helpful in guiding advertising decision making. Suggestions for the use of imagery strategies are made in the areas of (1) advertising design and creativity, (2) media selection and scheduling, and (3) advertising regulation and public policy, for these areas would benefit the most from an imagery perspective.

Advertising Design and Creativity

The use of pictures in ads is certainly not novel, but the principles from imagery research provide a more effective approach to using pictures for communication. Some illustrations are more facilitative than others. For instance, the use of an interactive picture to visually relate the brand name and product should result in better brand name recall. In contrast, a non-interactive picture portraying either the brand or its benefits separately rather than in a single, integrative picture may result in retention of the pictorially depicted word but not of the critical relationship between the brand and the product.

Although the research findings concerning picture attributes are not conclusive, they do allow speculation that colored pictures and realistic pictures may be more effective than abstract and black-and-white graphics. The form of the picture may not be as important as the function it serves. The designer should plan and structure the pictorial display with an awareness of the intended purpose of the graphics. Are the pictorial materials included only as embellishments, or do they serve some motivational or informational purpose? The content and nature of the graphics will depend greatly on their intended function.

Concretization is another strategy that can be applied to advertising decisions. Use of concrete language in an ad will facilitate memory for the advertising message. In choosing brand names, it will be useful to keep in mind that concrete nouns are most memorable; action verbs are fairly memorable; and abstract or proper nouns, stative verbs, and adjectives are among the least memorable. Hence the advertiser would do well to base a brand name on a concrete noun that has the desired associated attributes. Also, it is preferable to use action verbs in the ad to describe what the product does or can do for the user rather than to use stative verbs to tell what the product or service is (its attributes). Finally, when it is not possible to present the picture, as in radio advertising, it is advisable to use concrete words in describing a picture since they are more successful in arousing clear images.

The strategy of mental imagery instructions, although successful in learning contexts, may have limited application to advertising. However, this strategy should not be ignored by the advertiser because of the low cost of imagery inducements compared with visuals and the high potential benefits of mental imagery. Some consumers may not be able to produce an appropriate image without being shown one by the advertiser. The ability to visualize is not equally present in all audience members, and some will be "lost" when told to create a mental image. However, those consumers who do form mental images may produce mental pictures that are more personally relevant, more vivid, and more powerful than images stimulated by the provided illustrations.

Imagery-eliciting strategies may be especially effective when used in conjunction with holistic strategies. Visual analogies are recommended because they aid the viewer to visually relate the new information in the ad to familiar concepts and ideas, thus making the ad more memorable. Visual chunking is another technique that makes use of both imagery and holistic strategies. Some logos make use of this technique to convey not only the brand name, but also a product attribute or slogan in one chunk of visual information. Another combination is to use a visual advance organizer that can catch viewers' attention and prepare them for the ensuing message. Finally, the technique of embedding the desired message in a favorable visual context can cause the viewer to remember aspects of the setting rather than the central message. This technique may be used more frequently with products that have few favorable attributes, such as cigarettes.

Media Selection and Scheduling

Some media vehicles are more suited to certain kinds of imagery application. The various media have different strengths and weaknesses that must be taken into account when planning an ad campaign using imagery strategies. One basic distinction is that between the broadcast media (television and radio) and print media (magazines and newspapers). The former are presumably more "intrusive" but characterized by less audience involvement than the latter (Krugman, 1965), and this is a source of concern to many advertisers. Consideration of imagery principles may help advertisers to overcome and perhaps even benefit from low involvement on the part of consumers (Alesandrini & Sheikh, 1980).

Television

This medium is suited especially to the use of interactive pictures and thus can make full use of the power of illustrations. The use of action in the commercial can focus the viewer's attention on the critical interaction between the brand and product, rendering the message much more memorable. The use of motion in pictures may not be effective if attention is not directed to the ad's important information. An example of motion that may not direct attention to the brand–benefit association is the ad for American Motors that shows a number of interesting pictures appearing next to a moving, flashing line. The flashing line holds the viewer's attention very well, but the viewer may fail to notice what was being advertised.

Viewers are said to be characterized by "low involvement" when viewing TV ads (Krugman, 1965). The use of picture strategies becomes crucial for low-involvement media since less effort seems to be required for attending to and comprehending a picture than for reading and understanding an equivalent amount of verbal information. Therefore, television can overcome some of the disadvantages of being a low-involvement medium by relying heavily on effective picture strategies.

Radio

The use of imagery in radio advertising is restricted by certain limitations of the medium, such as low involvement of the listener and inability to present information pictorially. Nevertheless, creative inducements to use mental imagery could make radio ads as effective as—if not more effective than—ads presented in media that can use pictures. The literature on mental imagery indicates that learner-generated imagery may be more potent than pictures shown by another party. Some claim that bizarre, unique, individualized mental images are the most effective. Instructions to use individual mental imagery not only may result in improved memory for the message, but also may increase involvement by the listener.

Print

Magazines and newspapers are assumed to enjoy higher involvement on the part of the reader, so ads in these media can safely leave more of the communications task to verbal information. The relationship between the verbal and visual information presented in print media may be different than this relationship in media with lower audience involvement. Pictures can supplement the main points made verbally.

Also, as a result of higher reader involvement, mental imagery instructions presented in the print media are more likely to be followed by a larger portion of the audience.

Outdoor Advertising

Outdoor advertising or billboards can benefit greatly from the use of imagery principles. Severely restricted in both space and exposure time, a billboard will be most effective by arousing some mental imagery in the viewer, either through the use of illustrations or brief imagery instructions. Strategies that combine imagery and holistic techniques should be especially useful for this medium because of exposure limitations. Certain types of mechanical billboard even may simulate motion or action to direct attention to the critical information. A visually simple yet compelling billboard ad has been the one for Camel Lights cigarettes, which shows a camel standing in front of a pyramid with beams of light shooting from it.

Media Mix

In selecting the media mix for a complete advertising campaign, integrated use of imagery-eliciting strategies in the various media should be one of the objectives. For instance, the more involving print media might use concrete language and imagery instructions, and the broadcast media might have the function of eliciting a reconstruction of those images. In other words, television advertising might show interactive pictures in motion, and the print media might present static portrayals of the same interactive pictures. Each medium should be utilized to its own particular advantage, and the mix should be shifted to match the type of imagery appeal being used. A campaign emphasizing interactive imagery may use more television and print media initially and later rely more on radio.

Media Scheduling

One advantage of using imagery-eliciting strategies in advertising is the improved efficiency of communication. Ads using such strategies presumably can communicate their messages with fewer exposures than are needed by their verbal counterparts or by ads that do not use pictures effectively. Several researchers argue that "any incident that makes the occurrence of an event easy to *imagine* or recall is likely to enhance its perceived frequency" (Tversky & Kahneman, 1973). Their claim has implications for the issue of ad wearout. If imagery-eliciting strategies are used in an ad, viewers are likely to believe that they have seen the ad more often. Thus the ad may have a shorter "life cycle" before becoming an annoyance to consumers. To counteract this effect, the ad can be scheduled less frequently, and this, of course, means improved cost-effectiveness.

Advertising Regulation and Public Policy

Recent consumer-oriented public policy has heavily emphasized the need for advertising to serve an informational function. The essential thrusts of affirmative disclosure, nutrient labeling, and advertising claims substantiation all rest on the notion that the consumer is essentially a verbal-information processor, but recent research suggests that people may be better visual-information processors. It is quite possible that implied claims have a much larger impact than verbally stated claims on what a viewer thinks about an ad and remembers from it.

Although the FTC is concerned about "implied" product claims, unfortunately, most of the focus has tended to be on verbally presented information rather than on visually presented information. As noted by Eighmey (1979), much of the work being done presently in the area of public policy relies on the use of copy testing that focuses on verbal copy claims rather than on the visual context. Yet imagery-eliciting strategies especially when combined with holistic strategies can be much more effective than verbal approaches. Thus the makers of public policy dealing with advertising should shift greater attention to the pictures and other imagery strategies used in the ad so as to more adequately perform the job of protecting and informing consumers. They must keep in mind that the consumer is not only a verbal-information processor but also a visual-information processor.

This chapter has attempted to summarize briefly the research on pictorial and other imagery-eliciting strategies. Implications of these findings for research and practice in advertising seem to be rather far-ranging. A number of potential issues have been raised for the application of imagery principles to advertising decisions. Further research is needed to determine which areas of advertising can be most affected by an imagery perspective.

REFERENCES

Akhter, H., & Sheikh, A. Apperceptive advertising: A suggestion. *Marketing News*, December 1981.

Alesandrini, K. L. Strategies that influence memory for advertising communications. In R. J. Harris (Ed.), *Information processing research in advertising*. New York: Erlbaum, in press.

Alesandrini, K. L. Imagery-eliciting strategies and meaningful learning. *Journal of Mental Imagery*, 1982,6,125-140b.

Alesandrini, K. L., & Sheikh, A. A. Implications of imagery research for advertising. Paper presented at the Fourth American Imagery Conference, San Francisco, 1980.

Bettman, J. R. Memory factors in consumer choice: A review. *Journal of Marketing*, 1979, **43**, 37–53.

Brooks, L. R. The suppression of visualization by reading. *The Quarterly Journal of Experimental Psychology*, 1967, **19**, 289–299.

Burke Marketing Research, Inc. *Burke color study*. Cleveland: AVCO Broadcasting Corporation, 1960.

Chute, A. G. Analysis of the instructional functions of color and monochrome cuing in media presentations. *Educational Communications and Technology*, 1979, **27**, 251–263.

Clark, R. E. Constructing a taxonomy of media attributes for research purposes. *AV Communications Review*, 1975, **23**, 197–215.

Duchastel, P. C. *Research on illustrations in instructional texts*. (Occasional Paper No. 3.) Bryn Mawr, Pa.: The American College, Learning Systems Division, Winter 1980.

Dwyer, F. M. The effect of overt responses in improving visually programmed science instruction. *Journal of Research in Science Teaching*, 1972, **9**, 47–55.

Eighmey, J. A perspective on advertising copy research and advertising law enforcement. In J. C. Maloney & B. Silverman (Eds.), *Attitude research plays for high stakes*. Chicago: American Marketing Association, 1979.

Erdelyi, M. H., & Becker, J. Hypermnesia for pictures: Incremental memory for pictures but not words in multiples recall trials. *Cognitive Psychology*, 1974, **6**, 158–171.

Faw, H. W., & Waller, T. G. Mathemagnic behaviors and efficiency in learning from prose materials: Review, critique and recommendations. *Review of Educational Research*, 1976, **46**, 691–720. Federal Trade Commission. *Consumer Information Remedies*. Washington, D.C.: U.S. Government Printing Office, 1979.

Fleming, M. L., & Sheikhian, M. Influence of pictorial attributes on recognition memory. *AV Communication Review*, 1972, **20**, 423–441.

FTC, *Consumer information remedies*. U.S. Government Printing Press, 1979.

Gordon, L., Monro, A., Rigney, J. W., & Lutz, K. A. *Summaries and recalls for three types of texts* (Tech. Report No. 85). Los Angeles: University of Southern California, Behavioral Technology Laboratory, May 1978.

Higbee, K. L. Recent research on visual mnemonics: Historical roots and educational fruits. *Review of Educational Research*, 1979, **49**, 611–629.

Jenkins, J. J. Remember that old theory of memory? Well, forget it! *American Psychologist*, 1974, **29**, 785–795.

Knowlton, J. On the definition of "picture." *AV Communication Review*, 1966, **14**, 157–183.

Krugman, H. E. The impact of television advertising: Learning without involvement. *Public Opinion Quarterly*, 1965, **30**, 583–596.

Lamberski, R. J. A comprehensive and critical review of the methodology and findings in color investigations. Paper presented at the meeting of the Association for Educational Communications and Technology, Denver, April 1980.

Levin, J. R. Inducing comprehension in poor readers: A test of a recent model. *Journal of Educational Psychology*, 1973, **65**, 19–24.

Levin, J. R. On functions of pictures in prose (theoretical Paper No. 80). Madison, Wi.: University of Wisconsin, Wisconsin Research and Development Center for Individualized Schooling, December 1979.

Lippman, M. Z. Enactive imagery in paired-associate learning. *Memory and Cognition*, 1974, **2**, 385–390.

Lippman, M. Z., & Shanahan, M. W. Pictorial facilitation of paired–associate learning: Implications for vocabulary training. *Journal of Educational Psychology*, 1973, **64**, 216–222.

Lorayne, H., & Lucas, J. *The memory book*. New York: Stein and Day, 1974.

Lutz, K. A. Learning and instructional strategies related to visual literacy. *Method: Alaskan Perspectives*, 1980, **2**, 9–12.

Lutz, K. A., & Lutz, R. L. The effects of interactive imagery on learning: Application to advertising. *Journal of Applied Psychology*, 1977, **62**, 493–498.

Lutz, K. A., & Rigney, J. W. *The effects of student-generated elaboration during acquisition of concepts in science* (Technical Report No. 82). Los Angeles: University of Southern California, Behavioral Technology Laboratories, September 1977.

Lutz, R. L. A functional theory frameword for designing and pretesting advertising themes. In J. C. Maloney & B. Silverman (Eds.), *Attitude research plays for high stakes*. Chicago: American Marketing Association, 1979.

Mandler, J. M., & Johnson, N. S. Some of the thousand words a picture is worth. *Journal of Experimental Psychology: Human Learning and Memory*, 1976, **2**, 529–540.

Marketing News, "To Sell Products, Model Must Keep Shirts on, Research Indicates," August 12, 1977.

Miller, G. A. The magical number seven, plus or minus two: Some limits on our capacity for processing information. *Psychological Review*, 1956, **63**, 81–97.

Mitchell, A. A. & Olsen, J. C. Are product attribute beliefs the only mediator of advertising effects on brand attitude. *Journal of Marketing Research*, 1981, **18**, 318–332.

Mowen, J. C. The availablity heuristic: The effect of imaging the use of a product on product perceptions. In J. C. Olsen (Ed.), *Advances in Consumer Research* (vol. VII.) Ann Arbor: Association for Consumer Research, 1980.

Nappe, G. W. & Wollen, K. A. Effects of instructions to form common and bizarre mental images on retention. *Journal of Experimental Psychology*, 1973, **100**, 6–9.

Neisser, U., & Kerr, N. Spatial and mnemonic properties of visual images. *Cognitive Psychology*, 1973, **5**, 138–150.

Nisbett, R. E., Borgida, E., Crandall, R., & Reed, H. Popular indiction: Information is not necessarily informative. in J. B. Carrol & J. W. Payne (Eds.), *Cognition and social behavior*. Hillsdale, N.J.: Lawrence Erlbaum Associates, 1976.

Paivio, A. Mental imagery and associative learning and memory. *Psychological Review*, 1969, **76**, 241–263.

Paivio, A. *Imagery and verbal processes*. New York: Holt, 1971.

Paivio, A., & Csapo, K. Picture superiority in free recall: Imagery or dual coding? *Cognitive Psychology*, 1973, **5**, 176–206.

Paivio, A., Yuille, J. C., & Madigan, S. A. Concreteness, imagery, and meaningfulness values for 925 nouns. *Journal of Experimental Psychology*, 1968, **76**, 1–25.

Reese, H. W. Imagery in paired-associate learning in children. *Journal of Experimental Child Psychology*, 1965, **2**, 290–296.

Rigney, J. W., & Lutz, K. A. Effect of graphic analogies of concepts in chemistry on learning and attitude. *Journal of Educational Psychology*, 1976, **68**, 305–311.

Rossiter, J. R. Visual and verbal memory in children's product information utilization. In B. B. Anderson (Ed.), *Advances in consumer research*, Vol. III. Cincinnati: Association for Consumer Research, 1976, pp. 523–527.

Shepard, R. N. Recognition memory for words, sentences and pictures. *Journal of Verbal Learning and Verbal Behavior*, 1967, **6**, 156–163.

Steadman, M. How sexy illustrations affect brand recall. *Journal of Advertising Research*, 1969, **9**, 15–20.

Travers, R. M. W., & Alvarado, V. The design of pictures for teaching children in elementary school. *AV Communication Review*, 1970, **18**, 47–74.

Tversky, A., & Kahneman, D. Availability: A heuristic for judging frequency and probability. *Cognitive Psychology*, 1973, **5**, 207–232.

Twyman, M. A schema for the study of graphic language. In P. Kolers, M. Wrolstad, & H. Bouma (Eds.), *Processing of visible language*. New York: Plenum, 1979, 117–150.

Van der Meer, A. W. Color vs. black and white in instructional films, *AV Communication Review*, 1954, **2**, 121–134.

Van der Veur, B. W. Imagery rating of 1,000 frequently used words. *Journal of Educational Psychology*, 1975, **67**, 44–56.

Weber, S. M., & Marshall, P. H. Bizarreness effects in imagery. *Journal of Mental Imagery*, 1978, **2**, 291–299.

Weisburg, J. S. The use of visual advance organizers for learning in earth science concepts. *Journal of Research in Science Teaching*. 1970, **7**, 161–165.

Wittrock, M. C. Learning as a generative process. *Educational Psychologist*, 1974, **11**, 87–95.

Wright, P. Concrete action plans in TV messages to increase reading of drug warning. *Journal of Consumer Research*, 1979, **6**, 256-269.

Wright, P. Concrete action plans in TV messages to increase reading of drug warning. *Journal of Consumer Research*, 1979, **6**, 256–269.

Author Index

Page numbers in bold type indicate pages with complete references.

Subject Index

Psychology and Psychiatry in Courts and Corrections: Controversy and Change
  by Ellsworth A. Fersch, Jr.
Restricted Environmental Stimulation: Research and Clinical Applications
  by Peter Suedfeld
Personal Construct Psychology: Psychotherapy and Personality
  edited by Alvin W. Landfield and Larry M. Leitner
Mothers, Grandmothers, and Daughters: Personality and Child Care in
Three-Generation Families
  by Bertram J. Cohler and Henry U. Grunebaum
Further Explorations in Personality
  edited by A. I. Rabin, Joel Aronoff, Andrew M. Barclay, and Robert A. Zucker
Hypnosis and Relaxation: Modern Verification of an Old Equation
  by William E. Edmonston, Jr.
Handbook of Clinical Behavior Therapy
  edited by Samuel M. Turner, Karen S. Calhoun, and Henry E. Adams
Handbook of Clinical Neuropsychology
  edited by Susan B. Filskov and Thomas J. Boll
The Course of Alcoholism: Four Years After Treatment
  by J. Michael Polich, David J. Armor, and Harriet B. Braiker
Handbook of Innovative Psychotherapies
  edited by Raymond J. Corsini
The Role of the Father in Child Development (Second Edition)
  edited by Michael E. Lamb
Behavioral Medicine: Clinical Applications
  by Susan S. Pinkerton, Howard Hughes, and W. W. Wenrich
Handbook for the Practice of Pediatric Psychology
  edited by June M. Tuma
Change Through Interaction: Social Psychological Processes of Counseling and
Psychotherapy
  by Stanley R. Strong and Charles D. Claiborn
Drugs and Behavior (Second Edition)
  by Fred Leavitt
Handbook of Research Methods in Clinical Psychology
  edited by Philip C. Kendall and James N. Butcher
A Social Psychology of Developing Adults
  by Thomas O. Blank
Women in the Middle Years: Current Knowledge and Directions for Research and Policy
  edited by Janet Zollinger Giele
Loneliness: A Sourcebook of Current Theory, Research and Therapy
  edited by Letitia Anne Peplau and Daniel Perlman
Hyperactivity: Current Issues, Research, and Theory (Second Edition)
  by Dorothea M. Ross and Sheila A. Ross
Review of Human Development
  *edited by Tiffany M. Field, Aletha Huston, Herbert C. Quay, Lillian Troll,
  and Gordon E. Finley*
Agoraphobia: Multiple Perspectives on Theory and Treatment
  edited by Dianne L. Chambless and Alan J. Goldstein
The Rorschach: A Comprehensive System, Volume III: Assessment of Children and Adolescents
  by John E. Exner, Jr. and Irving B. Weiner
Handbook of Play Therapy
  edited by Charles E. Schaefer and Kevin J. O'Connor
Adolescent Sexuality in a Changing American Society: Social and Psychological Perspectives
for the Human Service Professions (Second Edition)
  by Catherine S. Chilman
Failures in Behavior Therapy
  edited by Edna B. Foa and Paul M.G. Emmelkamp